An Introduction to Programming Using Visual Basic

David I. Schneider
University of Maryland

 Prentice Hall, Englewood Cliffs, New Jersey 07632

Library of Congress Cataloging-in-Publication Data

Schneider, David I.
    An introduction to programming using Visual Basic / David
I. Schneider.
      p.   cm.
    Includes index.
    ISBN 0-13-191263-1
    1. BASIC (Computer program language) 2. Microsoft Visual BASIC.
I. Title.
QA76.73.B3S333   1995
005.265—dc20   94-47127
                                 CIP

Publisher: Alan Apt
Production Editor: Mona Pompili
Copy Editor: Shirley Michaels
Interior Design and Composition: Rebecca Evans & Associates
Photography: John Drooyan
Cover Designer: Bruce Kenselaar
Production Coordinator: Trudy Pisciotti
Editorial Assistant: Shirley McGuire

© 1995 by Prentice-Hall, Inc.
A Simon & Schuster Company
Englewood Cliffs, New Jersey 07632

The author and publisher of this book have used their best efforts in preparing this book. These efforts include the development, research, and testing of the theories and programs to determine their effectiveness. The author and publisher shall not be liable in any event for incidental or consequential damages in connection with, or arising out of, the furnishing, performance, or use of these programs.

TRADEMARK INFORMATION

IBM is a registered trademark of International Business Machines Corporation.
Hercules is a trademark of Hercules Computer Technology.
Microsoft is a registered trademark of Microsoft Corporation.

Printed in the United States of America.

005.265
S358i
1995

10 9 8 7 6 5 4 3 2 1

ISBN   0-13-191263-1

PRENTICE-HALL INTERNATIONAL (UK) LIMITED, *London*
PRENTICE-HALL OF AUSTRALIA PTY. LIMITED, *Sydney*
PRENTICE-HALL CANADA INC., *Toronto*
PRENTICE-HALL HISPANOAMERICACA, S.A., *Mexico*
PRENTICE-HALL OF INDIA PRIVATE LIMITED, *New Delhi*
PRENTICE-HALL OF JAPAN, INC., *Tokyo*
SIMON & SCHUSTER ASIA PTE. LTD., *Singapore*
EDITORA PRENTIC-HALL DO BRASIL, LTDA., *Rio de Janeiro*

Preface

This text provides an introduction to programming using Microsoft® Visual Basic™ on IBM PC and IBM PC compatible computers running Windows. Due to its extraordinary combination of power and ease of use, Visual Basic for Windows has become the tool of choice for developing user-friendly applications in the business world. In addition, Microsoft has made Visual Basic the language used to take full control of its best selling Windows applications such as Microsoft Word or Microsoft Excel. Not only is Visual Basic the state of the art in Basic programming, but Visual Basic is fun! Learning Visual Basic was very exciting to me and most students have similar reactions when they see how easy it is to build powerful visual interfaces using it.

My objectives when writing this text were as follows:

1. To develop focused chapters. Rather than covering many topics superficially, I concentrate on important subjects and cover them thoroughly.

2. To use examples and exercises with which students can relate, appreciate, and feel comfortable. I frequently use real data. Examples do not have so many embellishments that students are distracted from the programming techniques illustrated.

3. To produce compactly written text that students will find both readable and informative. The main points of each topic are discussed first and then the peripheral details are presented as comments.

4. To teach good programming practices that are in step with modern programming methodology. Problem solving techniques and structured programming are discussed early and used throughout the book.

5. To provide insights into the major applications of computers.

Unique and Distinguishing Features

Exercises for Most Sections. Each section that teaches programming has an exercise set. The exercises both reinforce the understanding of the key ideas of the section and challenge the student to explore applications. Most of the exercise sets require the student to trace programs, find errors, and write programs. The answers to all the odd-numbered short answer exercises and most other odd-numbered programming exercises are given at the end of the text.

Practice Problems. Practice problems are carefully selected exercises located at the end of a section, just before the exercise set. Complete solutions are given following the exercise set. The practice problems often focus on points that are potentially confusing or are best appreciated after the student has worked on

iii

them. The reader should seriously attempt the practice problems and study their solutions before moving on to the exercises.

Programming Projects. Beginning with Chapter 3, every chapter contains programming projects. The programming projects not only reflect the variety of ways that computers are used in the business and engineering communities, but also present some games and general interest topics. The large number and range of difficulty of the programming projects provide the flexibility to adapt the course to the interests and abilities of the students. Some programming projects in Chapters 7 through 11 can be assigned as end-of-the- semester projects.

Comments. Extensions and fine points of new topics are reserved for the "Comments" portion at the end of each section so that they will not interfere with the flow of the presentation.

Case Studies. Each of the four case studies focuses on an important programming application. The problems are analyzed and the programs are developed with hierarchy charts and pseudocode. The programs can be found in the EXAMPLES directory of the enclosed diskette.

Chapter Summaries. In Chapters 3 through 11, the key results are stated and the important terms are highlighted.

Procedures. The early introduction of general procedures in Chapter 4 allows structured programming to be used in simple situations before being applied to complex problems. However, the text is written so that the presentation of procedures easily can be postponed until decision and repetition structures have been presented. In Chapters 5 and 6 (and Sections 7.1 and 7.2), all programs using procedures appear at the ends of sections and can be deferred or omitted.

Arrays. Arrays are introduced gently in two sections. The first section presents the basic definitions and avoids procedures. The second section presents the techniques for manipulating arrays and shows how to pass arrays to procedures.

Appendix on Debugging. The placement of the discussion of Visual Basic's sophisticated debugger in an appendix allows the instructor flexibility in deciding when to cover this topic.

Reference Appendices. Appendices serve as a compact reference manual for Visual Basic's environment and statements.

Examples, Case Studies, and Visual Basic Diskette. Each book contains a diskette holding all the case studies, the examples from this text, and a copy of the Primer Edition of Visual Basic 2.0.

Instructors Diskette. A diskette containing every program in the text, the solution to every exercise and programming project, and a test item file for each chapter is available to the instructor.

Acknowledgments

Many talented instructors, students, and programmers provided helpful comments and thoughtful suggestions at each stage in the preparation of this text. I extend my gratitude for their contributions to the quality of the book to Timothy Babbitt, Rochester Institute of Technology; William Burrows, University of Washington; Robert Coil, Cincinnati State Technical and Community College; Gary Cornell, University of Connecticut; Ward Deutschman, Briarcliff; Ralph Duffy, North Seattle Community Collete; Gary Haw, MIPS Software Dev. Inc.; Dan Joseph, Rochester Institute of Technology; David Lakein, University of Maryland; David Leitch, Devry Institute; Kieran Mathieson, Oakland University; Charlie Miri, Delaware Tech; George Nezlek, DePaul University; Arland Richmond, Computer Learning Center; David Rosser, Essex County College; Melinda White, Santa Fe Community College; Ronald Williams, Central Piedmont Community College.

John Drooyan contributed creative photographs and artwork, Rebecca Evans & Associates used state-of-the-art technology to compose the text, and my editor, Alan Apt, ably handled the many details needed to bring the book to production.

Last, but not least, I am grateful to the Microsoft Corporation for their commitment to producing outstanding programming languages and for their permission to include a copy of the Primer Edition of Visual Basic with each book.

Contents

1

An Introduction to Computers and Visual Basic

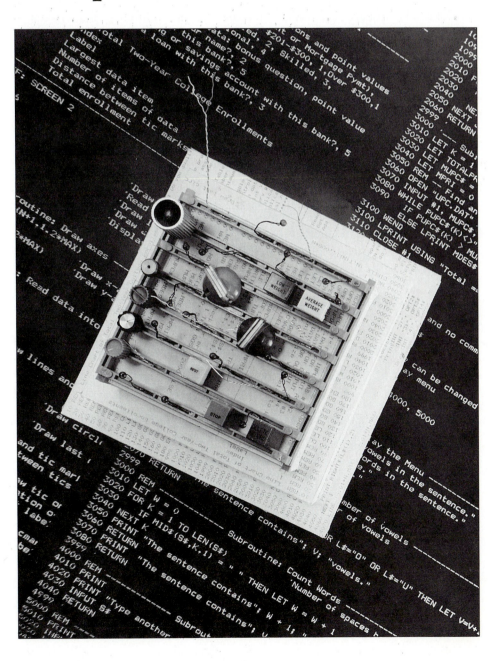

1.1 AN INTRODUCTION TO COMPUTERS

An Introduction to Programming Using Visual Basic is a book about problem solving with computers. The programming language used is Visual Basic, but the principles taught apply to many modern structured programming languages. The examples and exercises present a sampling of the ways that computers are used in society.

Computers are so common today that you certainly have seen them in use and heard some of the terminology applied to them. Here are some of the questions that you might have about computers and programming.

Question: What is meant by personal computer?

Answer: The word personal does not mean that the computer is intended for personal, as opposed to business, purposes. Rather, it indicates that the machine is operated by one person at a time instead of by many people.

Question: What are the main components of a personal computer?

Answer: The visible components are shown in Figure 1.1. Instructions are entered into the computer by typing them on the keyboard or by reading them from a diskette in a diskette drive or from a hard disk. Characters normally appear on the monitor as they are typed. Information processed by the computer can be displayed on the monitor, printed on the printer, or recorded on a diskette or hard drive. Hidden from view inside the system unit are the microprocessor and the memory of the computer. The microprocessor, which can be thought of as the brain of the computer, carries out all computations. The memory stores the instructions and data that are processed by the computer.

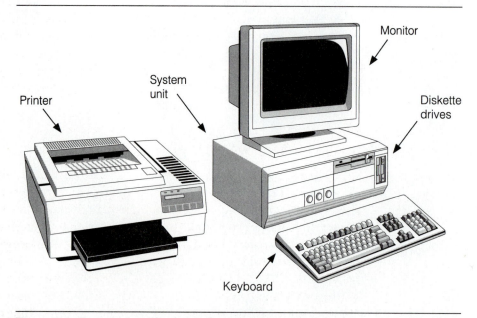

Figure 1.1 Components of a personal computer.

Question: What are some uses of computers in our society?

Answer: Whenever we make a phone call, a computer determines how to route the call and calculates the cost of the call. Banks store all customer transactions on computers and process these data to revise the balance for each customer. Airlines record all reservations into computers. This information, which is said to form a database, can be accessed to determine the status of any flight. NASA uses computers to calculate the trajectories of satellites. Business analysts use computers to create pie and bar charts that give visual impact to data.

Question: What are some topics covered in this text that students can use immediately?

Answer: Computer files can be created to hold lists of names, addresses, and phone numbers, which can be alphabetized and printed in entirety or selectively. Line graphs or attractive tables can be created to enhance the data in a term paper. Mathematical computations can be carried out for science, business, and engineering courses. Personal financial transactions, such as bank deposits and loans, can be recorded, organized, and analyzed.

Question: How do we communicate with the computer?

Answer: There are many languages that are used to communicate with the computer. At the lowest level, there is machine language, which is understood directly by the microprocessor, but is awkward for humans. Visual Basic is an example of a higher-level language. It consists of instructions to which people can relate, such as Print, Let, and Do. The Visual Basic software translates Visual Basic programs into machine language programs.

Question: How do we get computers to perform complicated tasks?

Answer: Tasks are broken down into a sequence of instructions that can be expressed in a computer language. (This text uses the language Visual Basic.) The sequence of instructions is called a program. Programs range in size from two or three instructions to tens of thousands of instructions. Instructions are typed on the keyboard and stored in the computer's memory. (They can also be stored permanently on a diskette or hard disk.) The process of executing the instructions is called running the program.

Question: Are there certain features that all programs have in common?

Answer: Most programs do three things: take in data, manipulate it, and give desired information. These operations are referred to as input, processing, and output. The input data might be held in a portion of the program, reside on a diskette or hard drive, or be provided by the computer operator in response to requests made by the computer while the program is running. The processing of the input data takes place inside the computer and can take from a fraction of a second to many hours. The output data are either displayed on the screen, printed on the printer, or recorded onto a disk. As a simple example, consider a program that computes sales tax. An item of input data is the cost of the thing purchased. The processing consists of multiplying the cost by a certain percentage. An item of output data is the resulting product, the amount of sales tax to be paid.

Question: What are the meanings of the terms hardware and software?

Answer: The term **hardware** refers to the physical components of the computer, including all peripherals, data terminals, disk drives, and all mechanical and electrical devices. Programs are referred to as **software**.

Question: What are the meanings of the terms programmer and user?

Answer: A **programmer** is a person who solves problems by writing programs on a computer. After analyzing the problem and developing a plan for solving it, he or she writes and tests the program that instructs the computer how to carry out the plan. The program might be run many times, either by the programmer or by others. A **user** is any person who uses a program. While working through this text, you will function both as a programmer and a user.

Question: What is meant by problem solving?

Answer: Problems are solved by carefully reading them to determine what data are given and what outputs are requested. Then a step-by-step procedure is devised to process the given data and produce the requested output. This procedure is called an **algorithm**. Finally, a computer program is written to carry out the algorithm. Algorithms are discussed in Section 2.2.

Question: What types of problems are solved in this text?

Answer: Carrying out business computations, creating and maintaining records, alphabetizing lists, and drawing line graphs are some of the types of problems we will solve.

Question: What is the difference between standard BASIC and Visual Basic?

Answer: In the early 1960s, two mathematics professors at Dartmouth College developed BASIC to provide their students with an easily learned language that could tackle complicated programming projects. As the popularity of BASIC grew, refinements were introduced that permitted so-called structured programming (discussed in Chapter 2), which increases the reliability of programs. Visual Basic is a version of BASIC that was written by the Microsoft Corporation to incorporate structured programming into BASIC and to allow easy development of Windows applications.

1.2   USING DISKETTES AND DOS

Modern computers have a hard disk and at least one diskette drive. The hard disk is permanently housed in a drive inside the computer. Most diskette drives accommodate the type of diskette shown in Figure 1.2. This diskette has a plastic jacket and measures $3\frac{1}{2}''$ on each side.

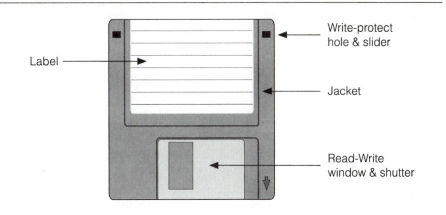

Figure 1.2 $3\frac{1}{2}''$ diskette.

When the diskette is inserted into a drive, the shutter slides to the right and exposes the read-write window. The diskette drive records and reads data through the read-write window. The write-protect hole is normally covered. When the write-protect hole is uncovered by sliding the slider on the back of the diskette, nothing can be erased from or recorded on the diskette. To insert a diskette, hold the diskette with the label facing up and the read/write window pointing toward the diskette drive. You insert the diskette by just pushing it into the drive until you hear a click. You remove it by pressing the button on the drive.

When handling a diskette, be careful not to touch the exposed surface in the read-write window. Also, do not remove a diskette from a diskette drive while the little light on the diskette drive is lit.

We use the word **disk** to refer to either the hard disk or to a diskette. Each disk drive is identified by a letter. Normally the hard drive is designated the C drive. If there is only one diskette drive, it is called the A drive. When two diskette drives are present, they are usually named the A and B drives.

Currently each computer comes with a set of DOS (Disk Operating System) programs on the hard disk. The DOS programs carry out disk operations. After the computer has been turned on, but before Windows is invoked, we say that the computer is in the DOS environment. After Windows has been invoked, we say that the computer is in the Windows environment. To return to the DOS environment from Windows, either exit from Windows or double-click on the "MS-DOS Prompt" icon in the "Main" window of Windows' Program Manager.

At any time, one of the drives, called the **current drive** or **default drive**, is given preferential treatment. When DOS is first invoked, normally the prompt C> appears and the C drive is the default drive. To change the default drive to A, enter A:. The prompt will change to A>.

Files and Directories

Disks hold not only programs but also collections of data stored in **data files**. The term file refers to either a data file or a program file. We create a data file in Section 1.3 and a program file in Section 3.1. Each file has a name consisting of a base name of at most eight characters followed by an optional extension consisting of a period and at most three characters. Letters, digits, and a few other assorted characters (see Comment 1) can be used in either the base name or the extension. Blank spaces are not allowed. Some examples of file names are INCOME.94, CUSTOMER.TXT, and FORT500.

Since a disk is capable of storing thousands of files, locating a specific file can be quite time consuming. Therefore, related files are grouped into directories.

Think of a disk as a large envelope, called the root envelope, which contains several smaller envelopes, each with its own name. (The naming of envelopes follows the same rule as the naming of files.) Each of these smaller envelopes can contain yet other named envelopes. Each envelope is identified by listing its name preceded by the names of the successively larger envelopes that contain it, with each envelope name preceded by a backslash. Such a sequence is called a **path**. For instance, the path \SALES\NY.90\JULY identifies the envelope JULY, contained in the envelope NY.90, which in turn is contained in the envelope SALES.

Think of a file name as written on a slip of paper that can be placed into either the root envelope or one of the smaller envelopes. At any time, we can select one of the envelopes. The selected envelope is called the **current** envelope. All commands to place a slip of paper into an envelope or list the contents of an envelope refer to the current envelope unless a path leading to another envelope is specified. In the language of directories, the root envelope is the **root directory**, the other envelopes are **subdirectories**, and the current envelope is the **current directory**.

When DOS is first invoked, the root directory of the current drive is the current directory. The command

```
CD pathname
```

tells DOS to change the current directory to the directory at the end of the named path. (To execute a DOS command, type in the command and then press the Enter key.) The command

```
CD \
```

makes the root directory the current directory.

The command

```
MD directoryname
```

tells DOS to create a new subdirectory with the specified name in the current directory of the current drive.

The command

```
RD directoryname
```

tells DOS to remove the specified subdirectory from the current directory of the current drive. A subdirectory can be removed only if it has no files or subdirectories. The current directory cannot be removed.

The combination of a drive letter followed by a colon, a path, and a file name is called a **filespec**, an abbreviation of "file specification." Some examples of filespecs are C:\VBPRIMER\VB.EXE and A:\PERSONAL\INCOME94.TXT. The drive (along with the colon) or the path may be omitted. If so, the file is assumed to reside in the current drive or the current directory, respectively.

Other DOS Commands

Some other commands that can be executed in DOS are FORMAT, DIR, COPY, ERASE, and RENAME.

FORMAT

The first time a blank diskette is used, it must be formatted for the computer. The formatting process is analogous to preparing graph paper by drawing grid lines. Let's assume the unformatted diskette is in the A drive, and the current drive is C. To format the diskette, enter

```
FORMAT A:
```

and then follow the directions displayed on the screen. While the formatting is taking place, the light on the A drive will be on, the blank diskette will spin, and the percentage of the diskette formatted will be displayed. After about one minute, the message "Format complete" will appear on the screen, and you will be prompted for a volume label. A volume label is a name (consisting of 1 to 11 characters) for your diskette. You can decline to specify a volume label by pressing the Enter key. You will be informed of the amount of space on the diskette, and the statement "Format another (Y/N)?" will be displayed. Answer the question by pressing either the Y or N key and then the Enter key. If the answer is N, the DOS prompt will appear and await your next command. If the answer is Y, the steps above will be repeated.

Caution: Formatting any disk destroys all its existing files. The hard disk is formatted when the computer is first readied for use, so never enter FORMAT C:.

DIR

The command

```
DIR
```

displays the names of the files and subdirectories in the current directory. (Periods are omitted and the base names are separated from the extensions.)
    If the disk has more than a screen full of files, enter the command

```
DIR /P
```

which makes the computer display just a screen full of files at a time.
    The command

```
DIR *.TXT
```

displays only files with the extension TXT. To generalize, the command

```
DIR *.ext
```

displays only files with the specified extension and the command

```
DIR basename.*
```

displays only files with the specified base name.

COPY

The command COPY is used to make a second copy of a file. The command

```
COPY filespec  A:
```

copies the specified file to the current directory of the diskette in drive A. In general, the command

```
COPY filespec driveletter:
```

copies the specified file to the current directory of the specified drive.

ERASE

The command

```
ERASE filespec
```

removes the specified file from the disk. For instance, the command ERASE B:\ACCOUNTS.TXT deletes the file ACCOUNTS.TXT from the root directory of the diskette in drive B.

RENAME

The command

```
RENAME filename1 filename2
```

changes the name of the file identified as filename1 to the new name filename2. The new name must be different from the name of any file in the current directory.

Comments:

1. File names can consist of digits, letters of the alphabet, and the characters & ! _ @ ' ` ~ ( ) { } – # % $. Spaces are not allowed in file names.

2. Neither DOS nor Visual Basic distinguishes between upper and lower case letters in file names. For instance, the names COSTS95.TXT, Costs95.Txt, and costs95.txt are equivalent. DOS always displays file names with uppercase characters.

3. The asterisk used with the DIR command is called a wildcard character. It also can be used with COPY or ERASE to apply the command to many files at once. For instance, COPY *.TXT A: copies files with extension .TXT to the A drive, ERASE TEMP.* erases files with base name TEMP, and COPY *.* B: copies all files in the current directory of the current drive to drive B.

PRACTICE PROBLEMS 1.2

(Solutions to practice problems always follow the exercises.)

1. What is the difference between the following two statements?

```
MD \SALES
MD sales
```

2. Suppose the current directory is named 1995 and is a direct subdirectory of the root directory. Then suppose the statement MD SALES is executed and several files are placed in the new directory. What command displays the files in the directory SALES, no matter what directory is the current directory?

EXERCISES 1.2

In Exercises 1 through 9, give the DOS command that accomplishes the stated task.

1. Reproduce a file on another disk.

2. Delete a file from a disk.

3. Change the name of a file.

4. Prepare a new diskette for use.

5. List the files in the current directory.

6. Change the current disk drive to drive B.

7. Create a new subdirectory of the current directory.

8. Change the current directory.

9. Remove a subdirectory of the current directory.

10. Which of the following are valid file names or filespecs?

    (a) ACCOUNTS.REC   (d) 123.TXT
    (b) B:SALES.87   (e) INVENTORY.TXT
    (c) QUESTION.???   (f) A:PRINT

11. What is wrong with each of the following filespecs?

    (a) COUNTRIES.TXT   (d) DAN@UCB.GAME
    (b) A:/GAMES/CHESS.TXT   (e) JAN*FEB.INC
    (c) <12-2-3>.DOC   (f) 12:00.AM

12. Suppose your computer has just one diskette drive. How could you use the commands discussed in this section to copy all the files in the root directory of a diskette onto another diskette?

SOLUTIONS TO PRACTICE PROBLEMS 1.2

1. If the root directory is the current directory, then the two statements are equivalent. Otherwise, the "\" symbol in the first statement creates a subdirectory of the root directory named SALES, whereas the second statement creates a subdirectory of the current directory named SALES. *Note:* The capitalization is of no consequence and is ignored by DOS.

2. DIR \1995\SALES

1.3 USING WINDOWS

Programs such as Visual Basic, which are designed for Microsoft Windows, are supposed to be easy to use—and they are once you learn a little jargon and a few basic techniques. This section explains the jargon, giving you enough of an understanding of Windows to get you started in Visual Basic. Although Windows may seem intimidating if you've never used it before, you only need to learn a few basic techniques, which are covered right here.

Mice Pointers

When you use Windows, think of yourself as the conductor and Windows as the orchestra. The conductor in an orchestra points to various members, does something with his or her baton, and then the orchestra members respond in certain ways. For a Windows user, the baton is called the **pointing device**; most often it is a **mouse**. The idea is that as you move the mouse across your desk, a pointer moves along the screen in sync with your movements. Two basic types of mouse pointers you will see in Windows are an arrow and an hourglass.

The **arrow** is the ordinary mouse pointer you use to point at various Windows objects before activating them. You will usually be instructed to "Move the pointer to . . . ." This really means "Move the mouse around your desk until the mouse pointer is at . . . ."

The **hourglass** mouse pointer pops up whenever Windows is saying: "Wait a minute; I'm thinking." This pointer still moves around when you move the mouse, but you can't tell Windows to do anything until it finishes what it's doing and the mouse pointer no longer resembles an hourglass. (Sometimes you can press the Esc key to tell Windows to stop what it is doing.)

Note: The mouse pointer can take on many other shapes, depending on which document you are using and what task you are performing. For instance, when entering text in a word processor or Visual Basic, the mouse pointer appears as a thin, large, uppercase I (referred to as an I-Beam).

Mouse Actions

After you move the (arrow) pointer to a place where you want something to happen, you need to do something with the mouse. There are four basic things you can do with a mouse—point, click, double-click, and drag.

Tip: You can pick the mouse up off your desk and replace it without moving the mouse pointer. This is useful, for example, when the mouse pointer is in the center of the screen but the mouse is about to fall off your desk!

Pointing means moving your mouse across your desk until the mouse pointer is over the desired object on the screen.

Clicking (sometimes people say single-clicking) means pressing and releasing the left mouse button once. Whenever a sentence begins "Click on . . . ," you need to

1. Move the mouse pointer until it is at the object you are supposed to click on.

2. Press and release the left mouse button.

An example of a sentence using this jargon might be "Click on the button marked Yes." You also will see sentences that begin "Click inside the . . ." This means to move the mouse pointer until it is inside the boundaries of the object, and then click.

Double-clicking means clicking the left mouse button twice in quick succession (that is, pressing it, releasing it, pressing it, and releasing it again *quickly* so that Windows doesn't think you single-clicked twice). Whenever a sentence begins "Double-click on . . . ," you need to

1. Move the mouse pointer until it is at the object you are supposed to double-click on.

2. Press and release the left mouse button twice in quick succession.

For example, you might be instructed to "Double-click on the little box at the far left side of your screen."

Note: An important Windows convention is that clicking selects an object so you can give Windows or the document further directions about it, but double-clicking tells Windows (or the document) to do something.

Dragging usually moves a Windows object. If you see a sentence that begins "Drag the . . . ," you need to

1. Move the mouse pointer until it is at the object.

2. Press the left mouse button and hold it down.

3. Now move the mouse pointer until the object moves to where you want it to be.

4. Finally, release the mouse button.

Sometimes this whole activity is called *drag and drop*.

Starting Windows

It's possible that, when you turn on your computer, Windows starts without your needing to do anything. If this is the case, you'll see a Windows copyright notice, an hourglass pointer while you wait, and then either the Program Manager icon (see Figure 1.3) or the Program Manager window (possibly looking something like Figure 1.4) will be displayed on the screen. If your screen shows the Program Manager icon, double-click on the icon to obtain the Program Manager window. (Your screen will look a little different from Figure 1.4 because one exciting feature of Windows is that you can change the way it looks to reflect *your* way of working. What should remain the same is that the top line of your screen will say "Program Manager.")

Figure 1.3 Program Manager icon.

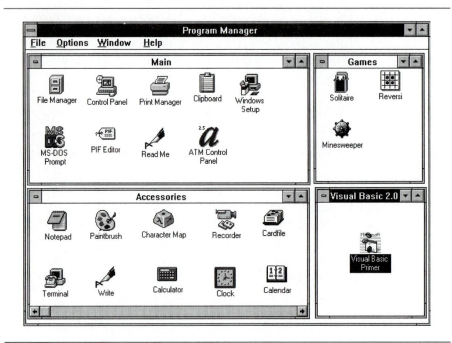

Figure 1.4 Program Manager window.

If Windows does not start automatically, you will see something that looks like this:

C>

meaning that you are at the (infamous) C prompt. This means that DOS is in control. Type WIN and press the Enter key to start Windows. If your machine responds with something like "Bad Command," Windows may not be installed on your machine, in which case you'll need to get it installed before you can continue. If you know Windows is installed on your system and the above didn't work, then consult the documentation that came with it—or the guru who decided to set Windows up in a nonstandard way.

Windows and Its Little Windows

Windows gets its name from the way it organizes your screen into rectangular regions. Each rectangular region in the Program Manager is called a **program**

group window. The whole region is called the **Windows desktop**. When you run a program, the program runs inside a bordered rectangular box. Unfortunately Windows jargon calls all of these windows, so there's only a lower case "w" to distinguish them from the program called Windows.

Think of a program group window as analogous to organizing your desk efficiently by grouping related piles together—as opposed to keeping all your papers in one unwieldy mess. The Program Manager in the Windows desktop starts out with four program group windows. When you install a program like Visual Basic, the installation procedure will usually add another program group window to the Program Manager for the program and its files.

Each rectangular program group window contains little **icons**. These icons represent files stored on your computer and are usually called **program items**. Some of these icons represent programs that you can run, and some represent data stored in your computer. You manipulate a window or the objects represented by the icons inside of it by various combinations of clicking, double-clicking, and dragging. Here are some important icons.

Starting Programs from the Program Manager

The general rule in Windows is that double-clicking on the icon that represents a program starts the program.

When Windows' attentions are focused on a specific window, the bar at the top of the window is highlighted and the window is said to be **active**. The active window is the only one that can be affected by your actions. An example of a sentence you might see is "Make the window active." This means if the title bar of the window is not already highlighted, click inside the window. At this point the (new) window will be responsive to your actions.

Finding Program Groups from the Program Manager's Window Menu

As you install more Windows programs, you may no longer be able to see the program group window that contains the program you want to work with. There is a surefire method of finding a program group window—if you remember its name:

1. Choose <u>W</u>indow from the Program Manager's main menu bar. (You can do this by pressing Alt and then W.) This drops down a (long) list of items.

2. If the program group is listed on the drop-down list, click on it or type the number to the left of its name. If not, click on the More Windows item and look through the next list (and so on as needed) until you find the program group you want. Windows opens the program group window for the item you selected.

Starting Programs from the Program Manager's File Menu

If you are unable to locate the icon for a program, but you know the base name of the file used to start the program, you can invoke the program from the Program Manager's File menu. To do this, open the File menu in the Program Manager and choose Run. (Press Alt then F then R.) This opens a little dialog box. Now type the name of the document in the box labeled Command Line and click on the OK button. (You will usually need the full name of the document in order for this to work; for Visual Basic Primer Edition this is most likely C:\VBPRIMER\VB.)

Using the Notepad

We will explore the Windows application Notepad in detail to illustrate the Windows environment. The Notepad is used extensively in this text to create data files for documents. Most of the concepts learned here carry over to Visual Basic and other Windows applications.

Go into Program Manager by holding down the Alt key, repeatedly pressing the Tab key until the words "Program Manager" appear, and releasing the Alt key. Then double-click on the Notepad icon in the Accessories window. The Notepad window shown in Figure 1.5 will appear.

Note: If the Notepad icon is not visible in the Accessories window, click on the maximize button in the upper-right corner of the Accessories window. If there is no Accessories window showing, double-click on the Accessories icon. If there is no Accessories icon, click on the word Window in the Program Manager title bar and then double-click on the word Accessories.

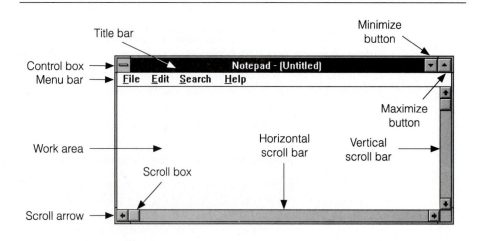

Figure 1.5 The Notepad window.

As its name suggests, Notepad is an elementary word processor. You can type text into the Notepad window, edit the text, print the text on the printer, and save the text for later recall.

The blinking vertical line is called the **cursor**. Each letter you type will appear at the cursor. The Notepad window is divided into four parts. The part containing the cursor is called the **Work area**. It is the largest and most important part of the window since documents are typed into this window.

The **Title bar** at the top of the screen holds the name of the document currently being written. Until the document is given a name, the document is called "Untitled." The two small buttons on the right end are referred to as the **Minimize** and **Maximize** buttons and the one small button on the left end is referred to as the **Control box**. You can click on the maximize button to make the Notepad window fill the entire screen (maximize the window), click on the minimize button to change the Notepad window into an icon (minimize the window), or double-click on the control box to exit Notepad. As long as a window isn't maximized, you can usually move it around the screen by dragging its title bar. (Recall that this means to move the mouse pointer until it is in the title bar, hold down the left mouse button, move the mouse until the window is where you want it to be, and then release the mouse button.) **Note 1:** If you have maximized a window, the Maximize button changes to a double-headed arrow called the **Restore button**. Click on this button to return the window to its previous size. **Note 2:** If the Notepad window has been minimized, it can be restored to its previous size by double-clicking on the icon that was created when the Minimize button was clicked. However, the icon may be hidden behind other windows. If so, you can restore the Notepad window by holding down the Alt key and repeatedly pressing the Tab key until the word Notepad appears.

You can change the size of a window by maximizing or restoring it. In addition, you can change the size of most windows to exactly suit your needs. To adjust the size of a nonmaximized window,

1. Move the mouse pointer until it is at the place on the boundary you want to adjust. The mouse pointer changes to a double-headed arrow.

2. Drag the border to the left or right or up or down to make it smaller or larger.

3. When you are satisfied with the new size of the window, release the left mouse button.

If the work area contains more information than can fit on the screen, you need a way to move through this information so you can see it all. For example, you will certainly be writing instructions in Visual Basic that are longer than one screen. You can use the mouse to march through your instructions with small steps or giant steps. A **vertical Scroll bar** lets you move from the top to the bottom of the window; a **horizontal Scroll bar** lets you move within the left and right margins of the window. Use this Scroll bar when the contents of the window are too wide to fit on the screen. Figure 1.5 shows both vertical and horizontal Scroll bars.

As you can see, a Scroll bar has two arrows at the end of a channel that also contains a little box (usually called the **Scroll box**). The Scroll box is the key to moving rapidly; the arrows are the key to moving in smaller increments. Dragging the Scroll box enables you to quickly move long distances to an approximate location in your document. For example, if you drag the Scroll box to the middle of the channel, you'll scroll to approximately the middle of your document.

The **Menu bar** just below the Title bar is used to call up menus, or lists of tasks. Several of these tasks are described in this section.

Documents are created from the keyboard in much the same way they would be written with a typewriter. In computerese, writing a document is referred to as editing the document; therefore, the Notepad is called a **text editor**. Before discussing editing, we must first examine the workings of the keyboard.

There are several different styles of keyboards. Figure 1.6 contains a typical keyboard. The keyboard is divided into several parts. The largest portion looks and functions like an ordinary typewriter keyboard. The row of keys above this portion consists of twelve keys labeled F1 through F12, called the **function keys**. (On many keyboards, the function keys are located on the left side.) Function keys are used to perform certain tasks with a single keystroke. For instance, pressing the function key F5 displays the time and date. The right portion of the keyboard, called the **numeric keypad**, is used either to move the cursor or to enter numbers. Press the **Num Lock** key a few times and notice the tiny light labeled NUM LOCK blink on and off. When the light is on, the numeric keypad produces numbers; otherwise, it moves the cursor. The Num Lock key is called a toggle key since it "toggles" between two states. When the numeric keypad is in the cursor-moving state, the four arrow keys each move the cursor around the existing document.

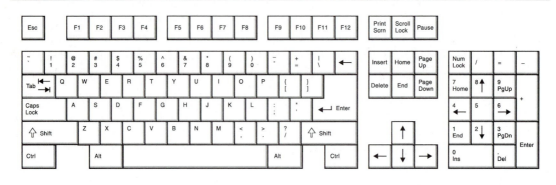

Figure 1.6 IBM PC keyboard.

Two very important keys may not have names printed on them. The **Enter** key is the key with the hooked arrow (and/or the word Enter). It is used to start a new line of a document. The Enter key corresponds to the carriage return on a typewriter. The **Backspace** key is the gray key with the left-pointing arrow located above the Enter key. It moves the cursor one space to the left and erases any character in that location.

After the Notepad has been invoked, the following routine will introduce you to the keyboard.

1. Click on the Work area of the Notepad.

2. Type a few words into the Notepad.

3. Use the right and left cursor-moving keys on the numeric keypad to move the cursor.

4. Press the **Home** key to move the cursor back to the beginning of the line. In general, the Home key moves the cursor to the beginning of the line on which it currently is located.

5. Now press the **End** key (on the numeric keypad). The cursor will move to the end of the line.

6. Type some letters using the central typewriter portion of the keyboard. The two **Shift** keys are used to obtain uppercase letters or the upper character of keys showing two characters.

7. Press the **Caps Lock** key and then type some letters. The letters will appear in uppercase. We say the computer is in uppercase mode. To toggle back to lowercase mode, press the Caps Lock key again. Only alphabetic keys are affected by Caps Lock. *Note:* When the Notepad is in the uppercase state, the tiny light labeled CAPS LOCK on the keyboard is lit.

8. Hold down the **Ctrl** key (Ctrl stands for "Control") and press the **Y** key. This combination erases the line containing the cursor. We describe this combination as **Ctrl + Y**. (The plus sign indicates that the Ctrl key is to be held down while pressing the Y key.) There are many useful key combinations like this.

9. Type some letters and then press the Backspace key a few times. It will erase letters one at a time. Another method of deleting a letter is to move the cursor to that letter and press the **Del** key. (Del stands for "Delete.") The backspace key erases the character to the left of the cursor, and the Del key erases the character at the cursor.

10. Type a few letters and use the appropriate cursor-moving key to move the cursor under one of the letters. Now type any letter and notice that it is inserted at the cursor position and that the letters following it move to the right. This is because the Notepad uses **insert mode**. Visual Basic has an additional mode, called **overwrite mode**, in which a typed letter overwrites the letter located at the cursor position. In Visual Basic, overwrite mode is invoked by pressing the **Ins** key. (Ins stands for "Insert.") Pressing this toggle key again reinstates insert mode. The cursor size indicates the active mode; a large cursor means overwrite mode.

11. The key to the left of the Q key is called the **Tab** key. It is marked with a pair of arrows, the upper one pointing to the left and the lower one pointing to the right. At the beginning of the line, pressing the Tab key indents the cursor several spaces.

12. Type more characters than can fit on one line of the screen. Notice that the leftmost characters scroll off the screen to make room for the new characters.

13. The Enter key is used to begin a new line on the screen in much the same way the carriage return lever is used on a manual typewriter.

14. The **Alt** key activates the Menu bar. Then, pressing one of the highlighted letters, such as F, E, S, or H, selects a menu. (A menu can also be selected by pressing the right-arrow key to highlight the name and then pressing the

Enter key.) As shown in Figure 1.7, after opening a menu, each option has one letter underlined. Pressing the underlined letter selects the option. (Underlined letters are called **Access** keys or **Hot** keys.) For instance, pressing A from the file menu selects the option "Save As." Selections also can be made with the cursor-moving keys and the Enter key. **Note 1:** You can select menus and options without the use of keys by clicking on them with the mouse. **Note 2:** You can close a menu, without making a selection, by clicking anywhere outside the menu, or pressing the Esc key.

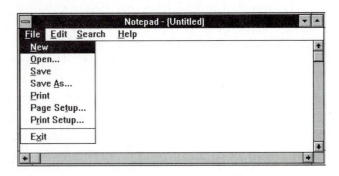

Figure 1.7 A menu and its options.

15. The **Esc** key (Esc stands for "Escape") is used to return to the Work area.

16. Press and release Alt, then press and release F, and then press N. (This key combination is abbreviated Alt/File/New or Alt/F/N.) The dialog box in Figure 1.8 will appear and ask you if you want to save the current document. Decline by pressing N or clicking on the No button.

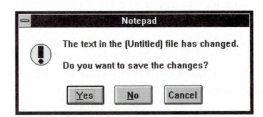

Figure 1.8 A "Do you want to save the changes?" dialog box.

17. Type the following information into the Notepad. (It gives the names of employees, their hourly wages, and the number of hours worked in the past week.) This document is used in Section 3.5. **Note:** We follow the convention of surrounding words with quotation marks to distinguish words from numbers, which are written without quotation marks.

"Mike Jones", 7.35, 35
"John Smith", 6.75, 33

18. Let's store the document as a file on a disk. To save the document, press Alt/File/Save As. The dialog box in Figure 1.9 appears to request a file name for the document.

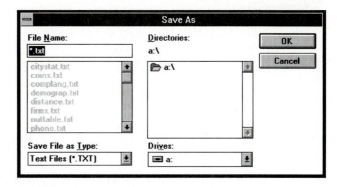

Figure 1.9 A Save As dialog box.

Type a drive letter, a colon, and a name containing at most eight letters and digits (no spaces), and then press the Enter key or click on OK. For instance, you might type A:PERSONEL. The document will then be stored on drive A. This process is called **saving** the document. Notepad automatically adds a period and the suffix TXT to the name. Therefore, the complete file name is PERSONEL.TXT on the disk and in the Title bar. *Note:* If you want to save the document in a specific subdirectory of the disk, also type the subdirectory. For instance, you might type A:\MYFILES\PERSONEL.

19. Press the key combination Alt/File/New to clear PERSONEL.TXT from Notepad.

20. Restore PERSONEL.TXT as the document in the Notepad by pressing Alt/File/Open, typing PERSONEL (possibly preceded by a drive letter and a colon, such as A:, and a subdirectory) at the cursor position, and then pressing the Enter key.

21. Press Alt/File/Exit to exit Notepad and return to Program Manager.

Ending Windows

To close Windows from Program Manager, hold down the Alt key and then press the F4 function key. (That is, press Alt+F4.) You are presented with a message box that looks like Figure 1.10.

Figure 1.10 Dialog box for ending Windows.

Click on the **OK button** if you want to shut down Windows, or click on the button marked Cancel (or press Esc) if you don't want to leave Windows.
    Caution: It is a bad idea to end Windows by just shutting off your machine.

Comments:

1. The key sequences discussed in this section have the form key1+key2 or key1/key2. The plus sign (+) instructs you to hold down key1 and then press key2. The slash symbol (/) tells you to release key1 before pressing key2. Some useful key combinations that we have not discussed yet are the following:

   (a) Ctrl+Home: moves the cursor to the beginning of the document
   (b) Ctrl+End: moves the cursor to the end of the document
   (c) Alt/F/P/Enter: prints a copy of the current document on the printer

2. When the work area is completely filled with lines of text, the document scrolls upward to accommodate additional lines. The lines that have scrolled off the top can be viewed again by pressing the **PgUp** key. The **PgDn** key moves farther down the document.

3. There are two methods to clear the work area. You can either erase the lines one at a time with Ctrl+Y or erase all lines simultaneously and begin a new document with Alt/F/N. With the second method, a dialog box may query you about saving the current document. In this case, use Tab to select the desired option and press the Enter key. The document name in the Title bar might change to Untitled.

4. Notepad can perform many of the tasks of word processors, such as search and block operations. However, these features needn't concern us presently. A discussion of them can be found in Appendix B, under "HOW TO: Use the Editor."

5. TXT is the default extension for files created with Notepad.

6. Refer to step 18 at the bottom of page 18, and suppose you typed A:\MYFILES\ PERSONEL into the "File Name:" box. The disk drive and directory could have been specified with other parts of the dialog box with the following steps.

   (a) Press Tab four times to activate the "Drives:" box, and then type A. (Alternatively, click on the "Drives:" box, click on the arrow to the right of the box, and click on "a:".)
   (b) Hold down the Shift key and press Tab twice to activate the "Directories:" box. Then type in the name of the subdirectory, say MYFILES. (Alternatively, click on the "Directories:" box, and then select the desired subdirectory from the displayed list.)
   (c) Return to the "File Name:" box and type PERSONEL.
   (d) Press the Enter key or click on OK.

   The line under the word "Directories:" contains a path for the drive listed in the "Drives:" box. The large box on the left, the File Name list box, lists all .txt files in the subdirectory at the end of the path. The path can be changed by double-clicking on the appropriate subdirectories in the "Directories:" box. The file icon next to a subdirectory is shown as open if the subdirectory is part of the path. You can have a whole chain of open directories. Notepad automatically updates the File Name list whenever you move up the directory tree by double-clicking or change drives via the "Drives:" drop-down list box. **Note:** In step 20, after you have selected the drive and directory, you can click once to select a file in this list box (it will then fill the box marked "File Name:"), or you can double-click on a filename to open the file.

There are many uses of dialog boxes. For instance, they pop up to report errors in a Visual Basic document. In general, the Tab key is used to move around inside a dialog box and the Enter key makes a selection. Although dialog boxes often have a cancel rectangle, the Esc key also can be used to remove the dialog box from the screen.

PRACTICE PROBLEMS 1.3

Assume you are using Windows' Notepad.

1. Give two ways to open the Edit menu.

2. Assume the Edit menu has been opened. Give three ways to pick a menu item.

EXERCISES 1.3

1. What does an hourglass icon mean?

2. Describe "clicking" in your own words.

3. Describe "double-clicking" in your own words.

4. Describe "dragging" in your own words.

5. How do you invoke Windows from DOS?

6. How can you tell when a window is active?

7. What is the difference between "Windows" and "windows"?

8. How do you open Notepad when the Notepad icon is visible?

9. What is the purpose of the vertical scroll bar in Notepad?

10. By what name is a Notepad document known before it is named as part of being saved on disk?

11. What is the small blinking dash called, and what is its purpose?

12. What is a toggle key?

Figure 1.11 shows many of the special keys on the keyboard. In Exercises 13 through 37 select the key (or key combination) that performs the task in Windows' Notepad.

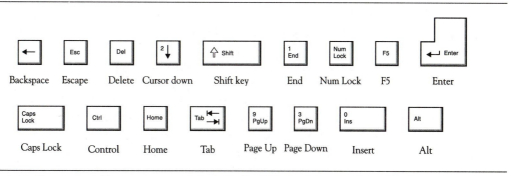

Figure 1.11 Some special keys.

13. Erase the line containing the cursor.

14. Erase the character to the left of the cursor.

15. Exit Windows.

16. Toggle the numeric keypad between states.

17. Erase the character at the cursor.

18. Toggle the case for alphabetic characters.

19. Move the cursor to the beginning of the line containing the cursor.

20. Move the cursor to the end of the line containing the cursor.

21. Display the time and date.

22. Cause the upper character of a double-character key to be displayed.

23. Move the cursor down to the next row of the screen.

24. Print a copy of the current document on the printer.

25. Exit Notepad.

26. Move the cursor to the beginning of the document.

27. Move the cursor to the end of the document.

28. Move the cursor from the Work area to the Menu bar.

29. Cancel a dialog box.

30. Move from the Menu bar to the Work area.

31. Move from one option rectangle of a dialog box to another rectangle.

32. Save the current document on a diskette.

33. Clear the current document from the Work area and start a new document.

34. Create a blank line in the middle of a document.

35. Remove a pull-down menu from the screen.

36. Scroll the document to view a higher part.

37. Scroll the document to view a lower part.

SOLUTIONS TO PRACTICE PROBLEMS 1.3

1. Press Alt/Edit or click on the word Edit in the toolbar to display the Edit menu. The jargon says the menu is "dropped down" or "pulled down."

2. Press the Down arrow key to highlight the item and then press the Enter key, press the underlined letter in the name of the item, or click on the item.

1.4 AN INTRODUCTION TO VISUAL BASIC

Visual Basic is the most exciting development in programming in many years. Visual Basic is the next generation of BASIC and is designed to make user-friendly programs easier to develop.

Prior to the invention of Visual Basic, developing a friendly user interface usually required teams of programmers using arcane languages like "C" that came in 10-pound boxes with thousands of pages of documentation. Now they can be done by a few people using a language that is a direct descendent of BASIC—the language most accessible to beginning programmers.

Visual Basic comes in two "flavors," one for ordinary DOS programs and the other for Microsoft Windows. Since Microsoft Windows is becoming more and more the dominant environment for PC's, we have chosen to show you the version of Visual Basic developed for Windows programming. Although you don't need to be an expert user of Microsoft Windows, you do need to know the basics before you can master Visual Basic—that is, you need to be comfortable with manipulating a mouse, and you need to know how to manipulate a window and how to use the Notepad and Program Manager built into Microsoft Windows. However, there is no better way to master Microsoft Windows than to write applications for it—and that is what Visual Basic is all about.

Why Windows and Why Visual Basic?

What people call **Graphical User Interfaces**, or GUIs (pronounced "gooies"), have revolutionized the microcomputer industry. Instead of the cryptic C:\> prompt that DOS users have long seen (and that some have long feared), users are presented with a desktop filled with little pictures called icons. Icons provide a visual guide to what the program can do.

Similarly, along with the revolution in how programs look was a revolution in how they feel. Consider a program that requests information for a database. Figure 1.12 shows how such a DOS-based BASIC program gets its information. The program requests the six pieces of data one at a time, with no opportunity to go back and alter previously entered information. After the program requests the six pieces of data, the screen clears and the six inputs are again requested one at a time. Figure 1.13 shows how an equivalent Visual Basic program gets its information. The boxes may be filled in any order. When the user clicks on a box with the mouse, the cursor moves to that box. The user can either type in new information or edit the existing information. When the user is satisfied that all the information is correct, he or she just clicks on the Write to Database button. The boxes will clear and the data for another person can be entered. After all names have been entered, the user clicks on the Exit button. In Figure 1.12 the program is in control; in Figure 1.13 the user is in control!

```
Enter Name (Enter EOD to terminate): Bill Clinton
Enter Address: 1600 Pennsylvania Avenue
Enter City: Washington
Enter State: DC
Enter Zipcode: 20500
Enter Phone Number: 202-395-3000
```

Figure 1.12 Input screen of a BASIC program to create a database.

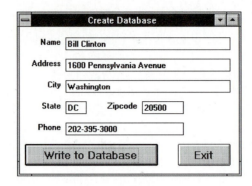

Figure 1.13 Input screen of a Visual Basic program to create a database.

How You Develop a Visual Basic Application

One of the key elements of planning a Visual Basic application is deciding what the user sees—in other words, designing the screen. What data will he or she be entering? How large a window should the application use? Where will you place the command buttons, the "buttons" the user clicks on to activate the applications? Will the applications have places to enter text (text boxes) and places to display output? What kind of warning boxes (message boxes) should the application use? In Visual Basic, the responsive controls a program designer places on windows are called *objects*.

Two features make Visual Basic different from almost any other programming tool:

1. You literally draw the user interface, much like using a paint program. Next, and perhaps more importantly,

2. When you're done drawing the interface, the command buttons, text boxes, and other objects that you have placed in a blank window will automatically recognize user actions such as mouse movements and button clicks. That is, the sequence of procedures executed in your program is controlled by "events" that the user initiates, rather than by a predetermined sequence of procedures in your program.

In any case, only after you design the interface does anything like traditional programming occur. Objects in Visual Basic recognize events like mouse clicks; how the objects respond to them depends on the instructions you write. You always need to write instructions in order to make controls respond to events. This makes Visual Basic programming fundamentally different from conventional programming.

Programs in conventional programming languages run from the top, down. For older programming languages, execution starts from the first line and moves with the flow of the program to different parts as needed. A Visual Basic program works completely differently. The core of a Visual Basic program is a set of independent groups of instructions that are activated by the events they have been told to recognize. This is a fundamental shift. Instead of designing a program to do what the programmer thinks should happen, the user is in control.

Most of the programming instructions in Visual Basic that tell your program how to respond to events like mouse clicks occur in what Visual Basic calls *event procedures*. Essentially, everything executable in a Visual Basic program is either in an event procedure or is used by an event procedure to help the procedure carry out its job. In fact, to stress that Visual Basic is fundamentally different from ordinary programming languages, Microsoft uses the term *project*, rather than *program*, to refer to the combination of programming instructions and user interface that makes a Visual Basic application possible.

Here is a summary of the steps you take to design a Visual Basic application:

1. Decide how the windows that the user sees will look.

2. Determine which events the objects on the window should recognize.

3. Write the event procedures for those events.

Now here is what happens when the program is running:

1. Visual Basic monitors the window and the objects in the window to detect any event that an object can recognize (mouse movements, clicks, keystrokes, and so on).

2. When Visual Basic detects an event, it examines the program to see if you've written an event procedure for that event.

3. If you have written an event procedure, Visual Basic executes the instructions that make up that event procedure and goes back to step 1.

4. If you have not written an event procedure, Visual Basic waits for the next event and goes back to step 1.

These steps cycle continuously until the application ends. Usually, an event must happen before Visual Basic will do anything. Event-driven programs are reactive more than active—and that makes them more user-friendly.

The Different Versions of Visual Basic

Visual Basic 1.0 first appeared in 1991. It was followed by version 2.0 in 1992, and version 3.0 in 1993. Since Microsoft has publicly announced that Visual Basic is a key product for them, Microsoft will continue to add further enhancements to the language. For example, Microsoft plans to use versions of Visual Basic to control all its applications, such as Word and Excel. Master Visual Basic and you will be well-prepared for almost any office computer environment in the 1990s!

Visual Basic 2.0 comes in three editions—Standard, Professional, and Primer. Whereas the Standard and Professional editions must be purchased from Microsoft or from a software dealer, the Primer Edition may be freely copied for demonstration purposes. You can use any edition of Visual Basic 2.0 or later with this textbook, although some of the screens may differ slightly from those shown in this text.

1.5 BIOGRAPHICAL HISTORY OF COMPUTING

The following people made important contributions to the evolution of the computer and the principles of programming.

1800s

George Boole: a self-taught British mathematician; devised an algebra of logic that later became a key tool in computer design. The logical operators presented in Section 5.1 are also known as Boolean operators.

Charles Babbage: a British mathematician and engineer; regarded as the father of the computer. Although the mechanical "analytical engine" that he conceived was never built, it influenced the design of modern computers. It had units for input, output, memory, arithmetic, logic, and control. Algorithms were intended to be communicated to the computer via punched cards, and numbers were to be stored on toothed wheels.

Augusta Ada Byron: a mathematician and colleague of Charles Babbage; regarded as the first computer programmer. She encouraged Babbage to modify the design based on programming considerations. Together they developed the concepts of decision structures, loops, and a library of procedures. Decision structures, loops, and procedures are presented in Chapters 5, 6, and 4 of this text, respectively.

Herman Hollerith: the founder of a company that was later to become IBM; at the age of 20 he devised a computer that made it possible to process the data for the U.S. Census of 1890 in one-third the time required for the 1880 census. His electromagnetic "tabulating machine" passed metal pins through holes in punched cards and into mercury-filled cups to complete an electronic circuit. Each location of a hole corresponded to a characteristic of the population.

1930s

Alan Turing: a gifted and far-sighted British mathematician; made fundamental contributions to the theory of computer science, assisted in the construction of some of the early large computers, and proposed a test for detecting intelligence within a machine. His theoretical "Turing machine" laid the foundation for the development of general purpose programmable computers. He changed the course of the second world war by breaking the German "Enigma" code, thereby making secret German messages comprehensible to the Allies.

John V. Atanasoff: a mathematician and physicist at Iowa State University; declared by a federal court in Minnesota to be the inventor of the first electronic digital special-purpose computer. Designed with the assistance of his graduate assistant, Clifford Berry, this computer used vacuum tubes (instead of the less efficient relays) for storage and arithmetic functions.

1940s

Howard Aiken: a professor at Harvard University; built the Mark I, a large-scale digital computer functionally similar to the "analytical engine" proposed by

Babbage. This computer, which took five years to build and used relays for storage and computations, was technologically obsolete before it was completed.

Grace M. Hopper: retired in 1986 at the age of 79 as a rear admiral in the United States Navy; wrote the first major subroutine (a procedure used to calculate sin x on the Mark I computer) and one of the first assembly languages. In 1945 she found that a moth fused into a wire of the Mark I was causing the computer to malfunction, thus the origin of the term "debugging" for finding errors. As an administrator at Remington Rand in the 1950s, Dr. Hopper pioneered the development and use of COBOL, a programming language for the business community written in English-like notation.

John Mauchley and J. Presper Eckert: electrical engineers working at the University of Pennsylvania; built the first large-scale electronic digital general-purpose computer to be put into full operation. The ENIAC used 18,000 vacuum tubes for storage and arithmetic computations, weighed 30 tons, and occupied 1500 square feet. It could perform 300 multiplications of 2 10-digit numbers per second, whereas the Mark I required 3 seconds to perform a single multiplication. Later they designed and developed the UNIVAC I, the first commercial electronic computer.

John von Neumann: a mathematical genius and member of the Institute of Advanced Studies in Princeton, New Jersey; developed the stored program concept used in all modern computers. Prior to this development, instructions were programmed into computers by manually rewiring connections. Along with Hermann H. Goldstein, he wrote the first paper on the use of flowcharts.

Stanislaw Ulam: American research mathematician and educator; pioneered the application of random numbers and computers to the solution of problems in mathematics and physics. His techniques, known as Monte Carlo methods or computer simulation, are used to determine the likelihoods of various outcomes of games of chance and to analyze business operations.

Maurice V. Wilkes: an electrical engineer at Cambridge University in England and student of von Neumann; built the EDSAC, the first computer to use the stored program concept. Along with D.J. Wheeler and S. Gill, he wrote the first computer programming text, *The Preparation of Programs for an Electronic Digital Computer* (Addison-Wesley, 1951), which dealt in depth with the use and construction of a versatile subroutine library.

John Bardeen, Walter Brattain, and William Shockley: physicists at Bell Labs; developed the transistor, a miniature device that replaced the vacuum tube and revolutionized computer design. It was smaller, lighter, more reliable, and cooler than the vacuum tube.

1950s

John Backus: a programmer for IBM; in 1953 headed a small group of programmers who wrote the most extensively used early interpretive computer system, the IBM 701 Speedcoding System. An interpreter translates a high-level language program into machine language one statement at a time as the program is executed. In 1957, Backus and his team produced the compiled language Fortran, which soon became the primary academic and scientific language. A compiler translates an entire program into efficient machine language before the program is executed. Visual Basic combines the best of both worlds. It has the power and speed of a compiled language and the ease of use of an interpreted language.

Donald L. Shell: in 1959, the year that he received his Ph.D. in mathematics from the University of Cincinnati, published an efficient algorithm for ordering (or sorting) lists of data. Sorting has been estimated to consume nearly one-quarter of the running time of computers. The Shell sort is presented in Chapter 7 of this text.

1960s

John G. Kemeny and Thomas E. Kurtz: professors of mathematics at Dartmouth College and the inventors of BASIC; led Dartmouth to national leadership in the educational uses of computing. Kemeny's distinguished career included serving as an assistant to both John von Neumann and Albert Einstein, serving as president of Dartmouth College, and chairing the commission to investigate the Three Mile Island accident. In recent years, Kemeny and Kurtz have devoted considerable energy to the promotion of structured BASIC.

Corrado Bohm and Guiseppe Jacopini: two European mathematicians; proved that any program can be written with the three structures discussed in Section 2.2: sequences, decisions, and loops. This result led to the systematic methods of modern program design known as structured programming.

Edsger W. Dijkstra: professor of computer science at the Technological University at Eindhoven, The Netherlands; stimulated the move to structured programming with the publication of a widely read article, "Go To Statement Considered Harmful." In that article he proposes that GOTO statements be abolished from all high-level languages such as BASIC. The modern programming structures available in Visual Basic do away with the need for GOTO statements.

Harlan B. Mills: IBM Fellow and Professor of Computer Science at the University of Maryland; has long advocated the use of structured programming. In 1969, Mills was asked to write a program creating an information database for the New York *Times*, a project that was estimated to require thirty man-years with traditional programming techniques. Using structured programming techniques, Mills single-handedly completed the project in six months. The methods of structured programming are used throughout this text.

Donald E. Knuth: Professor of Computer Science at Stanford University; is generally regarded as the preeminent scholar of computer science in the world. He is best known for his monumental series of books, *The Art of Computer Programming*, the definitive work on algorithms.

Ted Hoff, Stan Mazer, Robert Noyce, and Federico Faggin: engineers at the Intel Corporation; developed the first microprocessor chip. Such chips, which serve as the central processing units for microcomputers, are responsible for the extraordinary reduction in the size of computers. A computer with greater power than the ENIAC can now be held in the palm of the hand.

1970s

Paul Allen and Bill Gates: cofounders of Microsoft Corporation; developed languages and the operating system for the IBM PC. The operating system, known as MS-DOS, is a collection of programs that manage the operation of the computer. In 1974, Gates dropped out of Harvard after one year, and Allen left a programming job with Honeywell to write software together. Their initial project was a version of BASIC for the Altair, the first microcomputer. Microsoft is one of the most highly respected software companies in the United States and a leader in the development of programming languages.

Stephen Wozniak and Stephen Jobs: cofounders of Apple Computer Inc.; started the microcomputer revolution. The two had met as teenagers while working summers at Hewlett-Packard. Another summer, Jobs worked in an orchard, a job that inspired the names of their computers. Wozniak designed the Apple computer in Jobs' parents' garage, and Jobs promoted it so successfully that the company was worth hundreds of millions of dollars when it went public. Both men resigned from the company in 1985.

Dan Bricklin and Dan Fylstra: cofounders of Software Arts; wrote VisiCalc, the first electronic spreadsheet program. An electronic spreadsheet is a worksheet divided into rows and columns, which analysts use to construct budgets and estimate costs. A change made in one number results in the updating of all numbers derived from it. For instance, changing a person's housing expenses will immediately produce a change in his total expenses. Bricklin got the idea for an electronic spreadsheet after watching one of his professors at the Harvard Business School struggle while updating a spreadsheet at the blackboard. VisiCalc became so popular that many people bought personal computers just so they could run the program. A simplified spreadsheet is developed as a case study in Section 7.6 of this text.

Robert Barnaby: a dedicated programmer; best known for writing WordStar, one of the most popular word processors. Word processing programs account for thirty percent of all software sold in the United States. The Visual Basic editor uses WordStar-like commands.

1980s

William L. Sydnes: manager of the IBM Entry Systems Boca engineering group; headed the design team for the IBM Personal Computer. Shortly after its introduction in 1981, the IBM PC dominated the microcomputer field. Visual Basic runs on IBM Personal Computers and compatibles.

Mitchell D. Kapor: cofounder of Lotus Corporation; wrote the business software program 1-2-3, the most successful piece of software for personal computers. Lotus 1-2-3 is an integrated program consisting of a spreadsheet, a database manager, and a graphics package. Databases are studied in Chapters 8 and 9 of this text and graphics in Chapter 10.

Tom Button: group product manager for applications programmability at Microsoft; headed the team that developed QuickBasic, QBasic, and Visual Basic. These modern, yet easy-to-use languages, have greatly increased the productivity of programmers.

Alan Cooper: director of applications software for Coactive Computing Corporation; is considered the father of Visual Basic. In 1987 he wrote a program called Ruby that delivered visual programming to the average user. A few years later, Ruby was combined with QuickBasic to produce Visual Basic, the remarkably successful language that allows Windows programs to be written from within Windows easily and efficiently.

2

Problem Solving

2.1 PROGRAM DEVELOPMENT CYCLE

We learned in the first chapter that hardware refers to the machinery in a computer system (such as the monitor, keyboard, and CPU) and software refers to a collection of instructions, called a **program** (or **project**), that directs the hardware. Programs are written to solve problems or perform tasks on a computer. Programmers translate the solutions or tasks into a language the computer can understand. As we write programs, we must keep in mind that the computer will only do what we instruct it to do. Because of this, we must be very careful and thorough with our instructions.

Performing a Task on the Computer

The first step in writing instructions to carry out a task is to determine what the **output** should be, that is, exactly what the task should produce. The second step is to identify the data, or **input**, necessary to obtain the output. The last step is to determine how to **process** the input to obtain the desired output, that is, to determine what formulas or ways of doing things can be used to obtain the output.

This problem-solving approach is the same as that used to solve word problems in an algebra class. For example, consider the following algebra problem:

How fast is a car traveling if it goes 50 miles in 2 hours?

The first step is to determine the type of answer requested. The answer should be a number giving the rate of speed in miles per hour (the output). The information needed to obtain the answer is the distance and time the car has traveled (the input). The formula

$$rate = distance \: / \: time$$

is used to process the distance traveled and the time elapsed in order to determine the rate of speed. That is,

$$rate = 50 \: miles \: / \: 2$$
$$= 25 \: miles \: / \: hour$$

A pictorial representation of this problem-solving process is

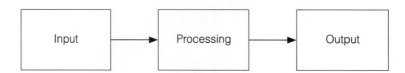

We determine what we want as output, get the needed input, and process the input to produce the desired output.

In the following chapters, we discuss how to write programs to carry out the above operations. But first, we look at the general process of writing programs.

Program Planning

A recipe provides a good example of a plan. The ingredients and the amounts are determined by what is to be baked. That is, the *output* determines the *input* and the *processing*. The recipe, or plan, reduces the number of mistakes you might make if you tried to bake with no plan at all. While it's difficult to imagine an architect building a bridge or a factory without a detailed plan, many programmers (particularly students in their first programming course) frequently try to write programs without first making a careful plan. The more complicated the problem, the more complex the plan must be. You will spend much less time working on a program if you devise a carefully thought out step-by-step plan and test it before actually writing the program.

Many programmers plan their programs using a sequence of steps, referred to as the **program development cycle**. The following step-by-step process will enable you to use your time efficiently and help you design error-free programs that produce the desired output.

1. ***Analyze:*** Define the problem.

   Be sure you understand what the program should do, that is, what the output should be. Have a clear idea of what data (or input) are given and the relationship between the input and the desired output.

2. ***Design:*** Plan the solution to the problem.

   Find a logical sequence of precise steps that solve the problem. Such a sequence of steps is called an **algorithm**. Every detail, including obvious steps, should appear in the algorithm. In the next section, we discuss three popular methods used to develop the logic plan: flowcharts, pseudocode, and top-down charts. These tools help the programmer break a problem into a sequence of small tasks the computer can perform to solve the problem.

   Planning also involves using representative data to test the logic of the algorithm by hand to ensure that it is correct.

3. ***Choose the Interface:*** Select the objects (text boxes, command buttons, etc.).

   Determine how the input will be obtained and how the output will be displayed. Then create objects to receive the input and display the output. Also, create appropriate command buttons to allow the user to control the program.

4. ***Code:*** Translate the algorithm into a programming language.

   Coding is the technical word for writing the program. During this stage, the program is written in Visual Basic and entered into the computer. The programmer uses the algorithm devised in Step 2 along with a knowledge of Visual Basic.

5. ***Test and debug:*** Locate and remove any errors in the program.

   Testing is the process of finding errors in a program, and **debugging** is the process of correcting errors found during the testing process. (An error in a program is called a **bug**.) As the program is typed, Visual Basic points out certain types of program errors. Other types of errors will be detected by Visual Basic when the program is executed; however, many errors due to typing mistakes, flaws in the algorithm, or incorrect usages of the Visual Basic language rules can only be uncovered and corrected by careful detective work. An example of such an error would be using addition when multiplication was the proper operation.

6. *Complete the documentation:* Organize all the material that describes the program.

Documentation is intended to allow another person, or the programmer at a later date, to understand the program. Internal documentation consists of statements in the program that are not executed, but point out the purposes of various parts of the program. Documentation might also consist of a detailed description of what the program does and how to use the program (for instance, what type of input is expected). For commercial programs, documentation includes an instruction manual. Other types of documentation are the flowchart, pseudocode, and top-down chart that were used to construct the program. Although documentation is listed as the last step in the program development cycle, it should take place as the program is being coded.

2.2 PROGRAMMING TOOLS

This section discusses some specific algorithms and develops three tools used to convert algorithms into computer programs: flowcharts, pseudocode, and hierarchy charts.

You use algorithms every day to make decisions and perform tasks. For instance, whenever you mail a letter, you must decide how much postage to put on the envelope. One rule of thumb is to use one stamp for every five sheets of paper or fraction thereof. Suppose a friend asks you to determine the number of stamps to place on an envelope. The following algorithm will accomplish the task.

1. Request the number of sheets of paper, call it Sheets.   *(input)*

2. Divide Sheets by 5.   *(processing)*

3. Round the quotient up to the next highest whole number,
   call it Stamps.   *(processing)*

4. Reply with the number Stamps.   *(output)*

The algorithm above takes the number of sheets (Sheets) as input, processes the data, and produces the number of stamps needed (Stamps) as output. We can test the algorithm for a letter with 16 sheets of paper.

1. Request the number of sheets of paper, Sheets = 16.

2. Dividing 5 into 16 gives 3.2.

3. Rounding 3.2 up to 4 gives Stamps = 4.

4. Reply with the answer, 4 stamps.

This problem-solving example can be pictured by

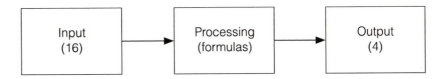

Of the program design tools available, the three most popular are the following:

Flowcharts: Graphically depict the logical steps to carry out a task and show how the steps relate to each other.

Pseudocode: Uses English-like phrases with some Visual Basic terms to outline the task.

Hierarchy charts: Show how the different parts of a program relate to each other.

Flowcharts

A flowchart consists of special geometric symbols connected by arrows. Within each symbol is a phrase presenting the activity at that step. The shape of the symbol indicates the type of operation that is to take place. For instance, the parallelogram denotes input or output. The arrows connecting the symbols, called **flowlines**, show the progression in which the steps take place. Flowcharts should "flow" from the top of the page to the bottom. Although the symbols used in flowcharts are standardized, no standards exist for the amount of detail required within each symbol.

Below is a table of the flowchart symbols adopted by the American National Standards Institute (ANSI). Figure 2.1 contains the flowchart for the Postage Stamp problem.

Symbol	Name	Meaning
→	*Flowline*	Used to connect symbols and indicate the flow of logic.
⬭	*Terminal*	Used to represent the beginning (Start) or the end (End) of a task.
▱	*Input/Output*	Used for input and output operations, such as reading and printing. The data to be read or printed are described inside.
▭	*Processing*	Used for arithmetic and data-manipulation operations. The instructions are listed inside the symbol.
◇	*Decision*	Used for any logic or comparison operations. Unlike the input/output and processing symbols, which have one entry and one exit flowline, the decision symbol has one entry and two exit paths. The path chosen depends on whether the answer to a question is "yes" or "no."

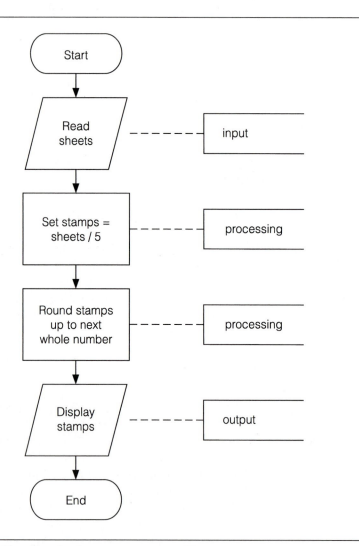

◯	**Connector**	Used to join different flowlines.
	Offpage Connector	Used to indicate that the flowchart continues to a second page.
	Predefined Process	Used to represent a group of statements that perform one processing task.
	Annotation	Used to provide additional information about another flowchart symbol.

Figure 2.1 Flowchart for the postage stamp problem.

The main advantage of using a flowchart to plan a task is that it provides a pictorial representation of the task, which makes the logic easier to follow. We can clearly see every step and how each step is connected to the next. The major disadvantage with flowcharts is that when a program is very large, the flowcharts may continue for many pages, making them hard to follow and modify.

Pseudocode

Pseudocode is an abbreviated version of actual computer code (hence, *pseudocode*). The geometric symbols used in flowcharts are replaced by English-like statements that outline the process. As a result, pseudocode looks more like computer code than does a flowchart. Pseudocode allows the programmer to focus on the steps required to solve a problem rather than on how to use the computer language. The programmer can describe the algorithm in Visual Basic-like form without being restricted by the rules of Visual Basic. When the pseudocode is completed, it can be easily translated into the Visual Basic language.

The following is pseudocode for the Postage Stamp problem:

> **Program:** Determine the proper number of stamps for a letter
>
> Read Sheets   *(input)*
> Set the number of stamps to sheets / 5   *(processing)*
> Round the number of stamps up to the next whole number   *(processing)*
> Display the number of stamps   *(output)*

Pseudocode has several advantages. It is compact and probably will not extend for many pages as flowcharts commonly do. Also, the plan looks like the code to be written and so is preferred by many programmers.

Hierarchy Chart

The last programming tool we'll discuss is the **hierarchy chart**, which shows the overall program structure. Hierarchy charts are also called structure charts, HIPO (Hierarchy plus Input-Process-Output) charts, top-down charts, or VTOC (Visual Table of Contents) charts. All these names refer to planning diagrams that are similar to a company's organization chart.

Hierarchy charts depict the organization of a program but omit the specific processing logic. They describe what each part, or **module**, of the program does and they show how the modules relate to each other. The details on how the modules work, however, are omitted. The chart is read from top to bottom and from left to right. Each module may be subdivided into a succession of submodules that branch out under it. Typically, after the activities in the succession of submodules are carried out, the module to the right of the original module is considered. A quick glance at the hierarchy chart reveals each task performed in the program and where it is performed. Figure 2.2 contains a hierarchy chart for the Postage Stamp problem.

The main benefit of hierarchy charts is in the initial planning of a program. We break down the major parts of a program so we can see what must be done in general. From this point, we can then refine each module into more detailed plans using flowcharts or pseudocode. This process is called the **divide-and-conquer** method.

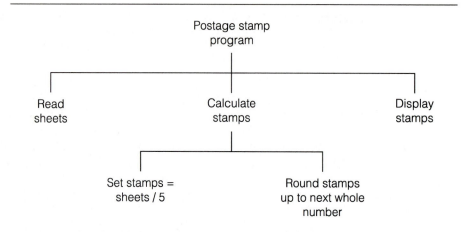

Figure 2.2 Hierarchy chart for the postage stamp problem.

The Postage Stamp problem was solved by a series of instructions to read data, perform calculations, and display results. Each step was in a sequence; that is, we moved from one line to the next without skipping over any lines. This kind of structure is called a **sequence structure**. Many problems, however, require a decision to determine whether a series of instructions should be executed. If the answer to a question is "Yes," then one group of instructions is executed. If the answer is "No," then another is executed. This structure is called a **decision structure**. Figure 2.3 contains the pseudocode and flowchart for a decision structure.

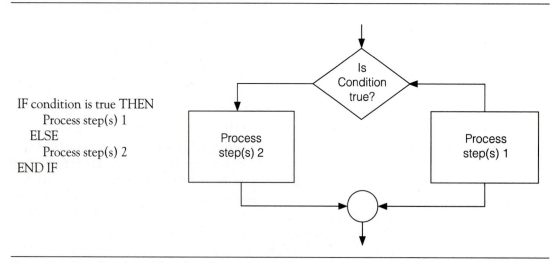

```
IF condition is true THEN
      Process step(s) 1
   ELSE
      Process step(s) 2
END IF
```

Figure 2.3 Pseudocode and flowchart for a decision structure.

The sequence and decision structures are both used to solve the following problem.

Direction of Numbered New York Streets Algorithm

Problem: Given a street number of a one-way street in New York, decide the direction of the street, either eastbound or westbound.

Discussion: There is a simple rule to tell the direction of a one-way street in New York: Even numbered streets run eastbound.

Input: Street number

Processing: Decide if street number is divisible by 2.

Output: "Eastbound" or "Westbound"

Figures 2.4 through 2.6 contain the flowchart, pseudocode, and hierarchy chart for the New York numbered streets problem.

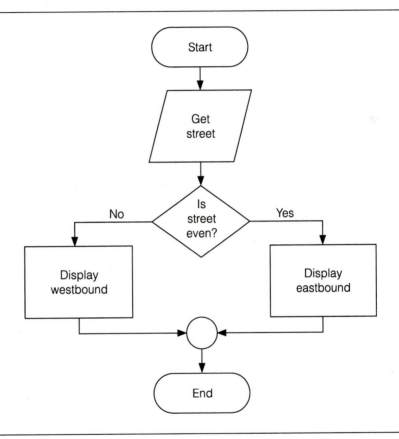

Figure 2.4 Flowchart for the New York numbered streets problem.

Program: Determine the direction of a numbered NYC street

```
Get Street
IF Street is even THEN
     Display Eastbound
   ELSE
     Display Westbound
END IF
```

Figure 2.5 Pseudocode for the New York numbered streets problem.

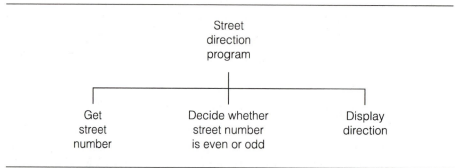

Figure 2.6 Hierarchy chart for the New York numbered streets problem.

The solution to the next problem requires the repetition of a series of instructions. A programming structure that executes instructions many times is called a **loop structure**.

We need a test (or decision) to tell when the loop should end. Without an exit condition, the loop would repeat endlessly (an infinite loop). One way to control the number of times a loop repeats (often referred to as the number of passes or iterations) is to check a condition before each pass through the loop and continue executing the loop so long as the condition is true.

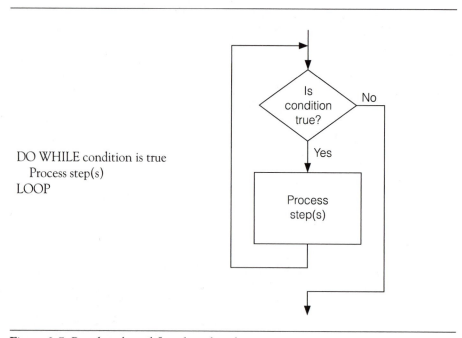

Figure 2.7 Pseudocode and flowchart for a loop.

Class Average Algorithm

Problem: Calculate and report the grade-point average for a class.

Discussion: The average grade equals the sum of all grades divided by the number of students. We need a loop to read and then add (accumulate) the grades for each student in the class. Inside the loop we also need to total (count) the number of students in the class. See Figures 2.8 through 2.10.

Input: Student grades

Processing: Find the sum of the grades; count the number of students; calculate average grade = sum of grades / number of students.

Output: Average grade

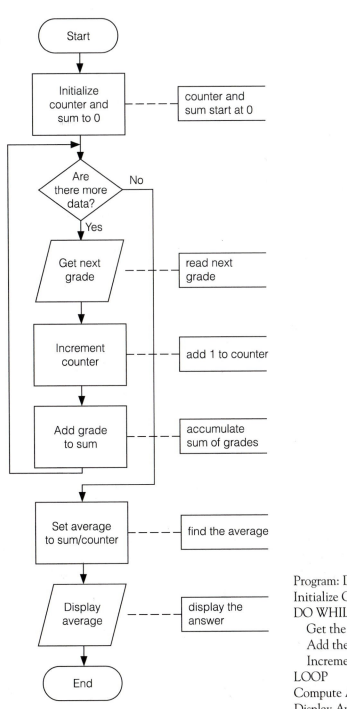

Program: Determine the average grade of a class
Initialize Counter and Sum to 0
DO WHILE there are more data
    Get the next Grade
    Add the Grade to the Sum
    Increment the Counter
LOOP
Compute Average = Sum / Counter
Display Average

Figure 2.8 Flowchart for the class average problem.

Figure 2.9 Pseudocode for the class average problem.

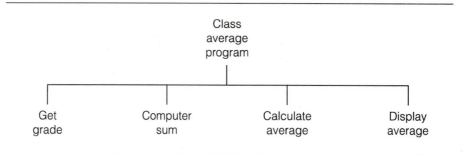

Figure 2.10 Hierarchy chart for the class average problem.

Comments:

1. Tracing a flowchart is like playing a board game. We begin at the Start symbol and proceed from symbol to symbol until we reach the End symbol. At any time we will be at just one symbol. In a board game, the path taken depends on the result of spinning a spinner or rolling a pair of dice. The path taken through a flowchart depends on the input.

2. The algorithm should be tested at the flowchart stage before being coded into a program. Different data should be used as input and the output checked. This process is known as **desk-checking**. The test data should include nonstandard data as well as typical data.

3. Flowcharts, pseudocode, and hierarchy charts are universal problem-solving tools. They can be used to construct programs in any computer language, not just Visual Basic.

4. Flowcharts are used throughout this text to provide a visualization of the flow of certain programming tasks and Visual Basic control structures. Major examples of pseudocode and hierarchy charts appear in the case studies.

5. There are four primary logical programming constructs: sequence, decision, loop, and unconditional branch. Unconditional branch, which appears in some languages as Goto statements, involves jumping from one place in a program to another. Structured programming uses the first three constructs, but forbids the fourth. One advantage of pseudocode over flowcharts is that pseudocode has no provision for unconditional branching and thus forces the programmer to write structured programs.

6. Flowcharts are time consuming to write and update. For this reason, professional programmers are more likely to favor pseudocode and hierarchy charts. Since flowcharts so clearly illustrate the logical flow of programming techniques, however, they are a valuable tool in the education of programmers.

7. There are many styles of pseudocode. Some programmers use an outline form, whereas others use a form that looks almost like a programming language. The pseudocode appearing in the case studies of this text focuses on the primary tasks to be performed by the program and leaves many of the routine details to be completed during the coding process. Several Visual Basic keywords, such as, Print, If, Do, and While, are used extensively in the pseudocode appearing in this text.

8. Many people draw rectangles around each item in a hierarchy chart. In this text, rectangles are omitted to encourage the use of hierarchy charts by making them easier to draw.

3

Fundamentals of Programming in Visual Basic

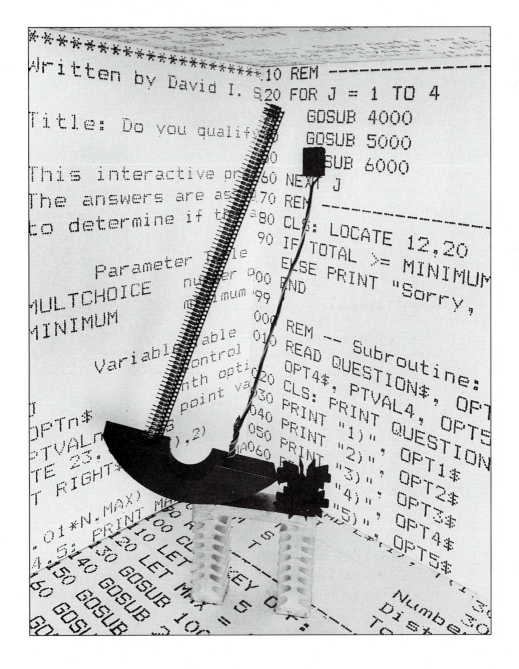

3.1 VISUAL BASIC OBJECTS

Visual Basic programs display a Windows style screen (called a **form**) with boxes into which users type (and edit) information and buttons which they click to initiate actions. The boxes and buttons are referred to as **controls**. Forms and controls are called **objects**. In this section, we examine forms and four of the most useful Visual Basic controls.

Note: If Visual Basic has not been installed on your computer, you can install it by following the steps outlined on the first page of Appendix B.

Invoking Visual Basic: To invoke Visual Basic, double-click on the Visual Basic icon. If you are unable to locate the icon, see "Starting Programs from the Program Manager's File Menu" in Section 1.3.

Figure 3.1 shows an initial Visual Basic screen. The appearance of this screen varies slightly with different versions of Visual Basic.

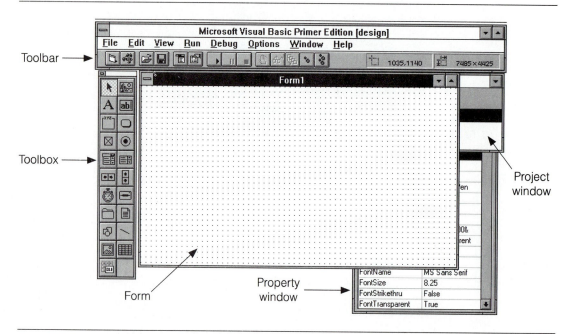

Figure 3.1 The initial Visual Basic screen.

The Toolbar is a collection of fourteen icons that carry out standard operations when clicked. For example, clicking the fourth icon, that looks like a diskette, can be used to save the current program to a disk.

The large stippled Form window, or *form* for short, becomes a Windows' window when a program is executed. All information displayed by the program appears on the form. The information is displayed either directly on the form or in controls that have been placed on the form.

The partially hidden **Project window** is seldom needed for our purposes. The partially hidden **Properties window** is used to change how objects look and react. Press F4 to uncover the Properties window (or just click on any part of that window). Click anywhere on the form to restore the screen to its original layout.

The icons in the **Toolbox** represent objects that can be placed on the form. The four objects discussed in this chapter are text boxes, labels, command buttons, and picture boxes.

Text boxes: You use a text box primarily to get information, referred to as **input**, from the user.

Labels: A label is placed next to a text box to tell the user what type of information to enter into the text box.

Command buttons: The user clicks a command button to initiate an action.

Picture boxes: You use a picture box to display text or graphics.

A Text Box Walkthrough

1. Double-click on the text box icon. (The text box icon consists of the bold letters **ab** and a vertical bar cursor inside a rectangle and is the second icon in the right column of the Toolbox). A rectangle with eight small squares, called **sizing handles**, appears at the center of the screen. See Figure 3.2.

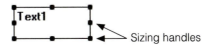

Figure 3.2 A text box with sizing handles.

2. Click anywhere on the form outside the rectangle to remove the handles.

3. Click on the rectangle to restore the handles. An object showing its handles is (said to be) **active**. An active object can have its size altered, location changed, and other properties modified.

4. Move the mouse arrow to the handle in the center of the right side of the text box. The arrow should change to a double arrow ($\Leftrightarrow$). Hold down the left mouse button and move the mouse to the right. The text box is stretched to the right. Similarly, grabbing the text box by one of the other handles and moving the mouse stretches the text box in another direction. For instance, you use the handle in the upper-left corner to stretch the text box up and to the left. Handles also can be used to make the text box smaller.

5. Move the mouse arrow to any point of the text box other than a handle, hold down the left mouse button, and move the mouse. You can now drag the text box to a new location. Using steps 4 and 5, you can place a text box of any size anywhere on the form.

   Note: The text box should now be active; that is, its sizing handles should be showing. If not, click anywhere inside the text box to make it active.

6. Press the delete key, Del, to remove the text box from the form. Step 7 gives an alternative way to place a text box of any size at any location on the form.

7. Click on the text box icon in the Toolbox. Then move the mouse pointer to any place on the form. (When over the form, the mouse pointer becomes

a pair of crossed thin lines.) Hold down the left mouse button and move the mouse on a diagonal to generate a rectangle. Release the mouse button to obtain an active text box. You can now alter the size and location as before.

Note: The text box should now be active; that is, its sizing handles should be showing. If not, click anywhere inside the text box to make it active.

8. Press F4 to uncover the properties window. (You can also uncover the properties window by clicking on it.) See Figure 3.3. The first line of the properties box reads "Text1 TextBox". Text1 is the current name of the text box. Ignore the second line for a moment. Lines 3 and on contain the 37 different properties that can be set for the text box. Press Tab if the cursor is on the second line. Use the up- and down-arrow keys (or the up- and down-scroll arrows) to glance through the list. The left column gives the property and the right column gives the current setting of the property. We discuss four properties in this walkthrough.

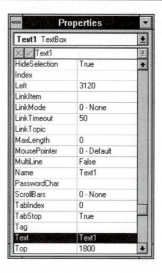

Figure 3.3 Text box properties window.

9. Move to the Text property with the up- and down-arrow keys. (Alternatively, scroll until the property is visible and click on the property.) The Text property is now highlighted. The Text property determines the words in the text box. Currently the words are "Text1". Notice that "Text1" also appears in the second line of the Properties window, known as the **Settings box**.

10. Type your first name. As you type, your name replaces "Text1" in both the settings box and the text box.

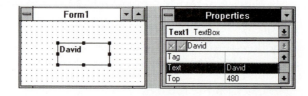

Figure 3.4 Setting the text property to David.

11. Click at the beginning of your name in the settings box and add your title, such as Mr., Ms., or The Honorable. (If you mistyped your name, you can easily correct it now.)

12. Press Shift+Ctrl+F to move to the first property that begins with the letter F. Now use the down-arrow key or the mouse to highlight the property ForeColor. The foreground color is the color of the text.

13. Click on the ellipsis (. . .) box in the right part of the settings box to display a selection of colors. Click on one of the solid colors, such as blue or red. Notice the change in the color of your name.

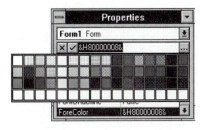

Figure 3.5 Setting the ForeColor property.

14. Highlight the FontSize property with a single click of the mouse. The current font size is 8.25.

15. Double-click on the FontSize property. The size becomes 9.75 and your name gets larger. Keep double-clicking until the size cycles through the different possibilities and returns to 8.25. (An alternative way to change the font size is to click on the underlined down arrow at the right of the settings box and select a size from the pull-down list.)

16. Click on the text box and resize it to be about three inches wide and one inch high.

Visual Basic programs consist of three parts—interface, values of properties, and code. Our interface consists of a form with a single object, a text box. We have set a couple of properties for the text box—the text (namely, your name), the foreground color, and the font size. In the next section we see how to place code into a program. Visual Basic endows certain capabilities to programs that are independent of any code. We will now run the existing codeless program and experience these capabilities.

17. Press F5 to run the program. (Alternatively, a program can be run from the menu by pressing Alt/R/S or by clicking on the Run icon ▶, the seventh icon on the Toolbar.) Notice that the dots have disappeared from the form.

18. The cursor is at the beginning of your name. Press the End key to move the cursor to the end of your name. Now type in your last name, and then keep typing. Eventually the words will scroll to the left.

19. Press Home to return to the beginning of the text. You have a full-fledged word processor at your disposal. You can place the cursor anywhere you like to add or delete text. You can drag the cursor across text to create a block, place a copy of the block in the clipboard with Ctrl+Ins, and then duplicate it anywhere with Shift+Ins.

20. To terminate the program, press Alt+F4. Alternatively, you can end a program by clicking on the End icon ■, the ninth icon on the Toolbar.

21. Activate the text box, uncover the Properties window, and double-click on the MultiLine property. The MultiLine property has been changed from False to True.

22. Run the program and type in the text box. Notice that now words wrap around when the end of a line is reached. Also, text will scroll up when it reaches the bottom of the text box.

23. End the program.

24. Press Alt/F/V to save the work done so far. A Save File As dialog box appears. Visual Basic creates two disk files to store a program. The first, with the extension .frm, is entered into the Save File As dialog box and the second, with the extension .mak, into a Save Project As dialog box. As noted earlier, Visual Basic refers to programs as **projects**.

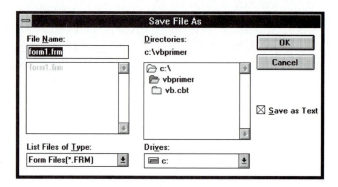

Figure 3.6 The Save File As dialog box.

25. Type a file name, such as *testprog* into the File Name box. The extension .frm automatically will be appended to the name. Do not press the Enter key yet. (Pressing the Enter key has the same effect as clicking OK.) The Directories and Drives boxes tell where your program will be saved. Alter these as desired. (**Suggestion:** If you are using a computer in a campus computer lab, you probably should use a diskette to save your work. If so, place the diskette in a drive, say the A drive, and select a: in the Drives box.)

26. Click the OK button when you are ready to go on. (Alternatively, press Tab several times until the OK button is highlighted and then press Enter.) The Save Project As dialog box appears.

27. Type a file name into the File Name box. You can use the same name, such as *testprog*, as before. Then proceed as in steps 25 and 26.

28. Press Alt/F/N to begin a new program.

29. Place three text boxes on the form. (Move each text box out of the center of the form before creating the next.) Notice that they have the names Text1, Text2, and Text3.

30. Run the program. Notice that the cursor is in Text1. We say that Text1 has the **focus**. Any text typed will display in that text box.

31. Press Tab once. Now, Text2 has the focus. When you type, the characters appear in Text2.

32. Press Tab several times and then press Shift+Tab a few times. With Tab the focus cycles through the objects on the form in the order the objects were created. With Shift+Tab, the focus cycles in the reverse order.

33. End the program.

34. Press Alt/F/O to reload your first program. When a dialog box asks if you want to save your changes, click the No button or press N. An Open File dialog box appears on the screen. The name of your first program should appear in the second box in the left column.

35. Click on the name of your first program and then click on the OK button. Alternatively, double-click on the name. (You also have the option of typing the name into the File Name box and then clicking the OK button.)

36. Click the View Form button on the Project window.

A Command Button Walkthrough

1. Press Alt/F/N to start anew. There is no need to save anything.

2. Double-click on the command button icon to place a command button in the center of the form. (The rounded rectangle shaped command button icon is the third icon in the right column of the Toolbox.)

3. Uncover the Properties window, highlight the Caption property, and type "Please Push Me." See Figure 3.7. Notice that the letters appear on the command button as they are typed. This phrase is a little too long to fit on the command button.

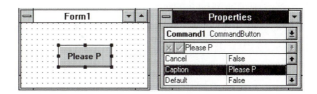

Figure 3.7 Setting the caption property.

4. Click on the command button to make it active and then enlarge it to accommodate the phrase "Please Push Me."

5. Run the program and click on the command button. The command button appears to move in and then out. In Section 3.2 we write code that is activated when a command button is pushed.

6. End the program.

7. From the Properties window, edit the Caption setting by inserting an ampersand (&) before the first letter, P. Notice that the ampersand does not show on the button. However, the letter following the ampersand is now underlined. See Figure 3.8. Pressing Alt+P while the program is running triggers the same event as clicking the command button. Here, the letter P is referred to as the **access key** for the command button. (The access key is always the key following the ampersand.)

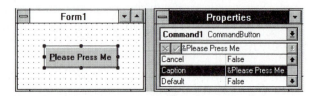

Figure 3.8 Designating P as an access key.

8. End the program.

A Label Walkthrough

1. Press Alt/F/N to start anew. There is no need to save anything.

2. Double-click on the label icon to place a label in the center of the form. (The label icon, a large letter A, is the second icon in the left column of the Toolbox.)

3. Uncover the Properties window, highlight the Caption property and type "Phone Number." Such a label would be placed next to a text box into which the user will enter a phone number.

4. Click on the label to make it active and then widen it until both words are on the same line.

5. Make the label narrower until the words occupy two lines.

6. Uncover the Properties window and double-click on the Alignment property. Double-click two more times. The combination of sizing and alignment permits you to design a label easily.

7. Run the program. Nothing happens, even if you click on the label. Labels just sit there. The user cannot change what a label displays unless you write code to allow the change.

8. End the program.

A Picture Box Walkthrough

1. Press Alt/F/N to start anew. There is no need to save anything.

2. Double-click on the picture box icon to place a picture box in the center of the form. (The picture box icon is the first icon in the right column of the Toolbox. It contains a picture of the sun shining over a desert.)

3. Enlarge the picture box.

4. Run the program. Nothing happens and nothing will, no matter what you do. Although picture boxes look like text boxes, you can't type in them. However, you can display text in them with statements discussed later in this chapter, you can draw lines and circles in them with statements discussed in Chapter 10, and you can insert pictures into them.

5. End the program and click the picture box to make it active.

6. Uncover the Properties window and double-click on the Picture property. A Load Picture dialog box appears. See Figure 3.9.

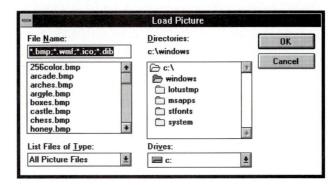

Figure 3.9 The Load Picture dialog box.

7. Look for the Windows directory in the directories box. (You may have to change the drive and also do some searching to find it.) Double-click on the Windows directory. A list of pictures stored in the Windows directory appears in the files box, the large box on the left.

8. Double-click on one of the files in the files box. Two good candidates are chess.bmp, shown in Figure 3.10, or winlogo.bmp. (You must scroll down in the files box to see the name winlogo.bmp.)

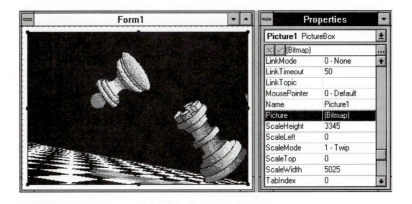

Figure 3.10 A picture box filled with the chess.bmp picture from Windows.

9. If part of the picture is hidden, enlarge the picture box to reveal more of the picture.

10. Press Del to remove the picture box.

Comments:

1. When selecting from a list, double-clicking has the same effect as clicking once and pressing Enter.

2. On a form, the Tab key cycles through the objects that can get the focus, and in a dialog box, it cycles through the items.

3. The form itself is also an object and has properties. For instance, you can change the text in the title bar with the Caption property. Although an active form does not have sizing handles, you can size an active form by grabbing it by one of its corners, bottom edge, or sides and dragging the mouse. You can move the form by dragging its title bar.

4. The name of an object is used in code to refer to the object. By default, objects are given names like Text1 and Text2. You can use the Properties window to change the Name property of an object to a more suggestive name. For instance, if the text boxes are intended to hold addresses and zip codes, suitable names are txtAddress and txtZip. In this book, we use the suggestive names in all case studies.

5. Changing the caption on a command button does not alter the name of the command button. The name remains something like Command1 unless the Name property setting is changed.

6. The color settings appear as strings of digits and letters preceded by &H and trailed with &. Don't concern yourself with the notation at this time.

7. Here are some fine points on the use of the Properties window.

   (a) Press Shift+Ctrl+*letterkey* to highlight the first property that begins with that letter. Successive pressings highlight successive properties that begin with that letter.
   (b) To change the active object from the Properties window, click on the underlined down-arrow icon at the right of the top box of the Properties window. Then select the new object from the pull-down list.
   (c) The x and check marks on the left side of the settings box are clicked to reject or confirm the shown setting. (The setting is usually also confirmed by clicking anywhere outside the settings box.)
   (d) There are three techniques used to set a property. For a given property, one or more of them work.
       (i) Highlight the property and then edit the words in the setting window.
       (ii) Double-click on the property.
       (iii) Highlight the property, click the underlined down-arrow or the ellipsis at the right of the settings box, and select a setting. (To select a setting, either double-click on it or highlight it and press Enter.)

8. Some useful properties that have not been discussed are the following:

   (a) BorderStyle: Setting the BorderStyle to 0 – None, removes the border from an object. Also, BorderStyle can be used to create a thicker border.
   (b) Visible: Setting the Visible property to False hides an object when the program is run. The object can be made to reappear with code.

(c) BackColor: Specifies the background color for a text box, label, picture box, or form. When a program is run, an active command button has a dotted ring of the complementary color of BackColor around the caption.

(d) BackStyle: The BackStyle property of a label is opaque by default. The rectangular region associated with the label is filled with the label's background color and caption. Setting the background style of a label to transparent causes whatever is behind the label to remain visible; the background color of the label essentially becomes "see through."

(e) FontBold: When set to True, text appears boldfaced.

(f) FontItalic: When set to True, text appears italicized.

(g) FontName: Can be set to any of Windows' fonts, such as Courier and Times Roman. Two unusual fonts are Symbols and Wingdings. For instance, with the Wingdings font, pressing the keys for %, &, ', and J yield a bell, a book, a candle, and a smiling face, respectively. To view the characters in the different Windows' fonts,

  (i) Open Program Manager

  (ii) Open the Accessories window

  (iii) Open Character Map

  (iv) After selecting a font, hold down the left mouse button on any character to enlarge the character and obtain the keystroke that produces that character.

9. Objects can be grouped together by attaching them to a picture box. (To attach an object to a picture box, click on the icon in the Toolbox, move the mouse to a point inside the picture box, and drag the mouse until the object has the shape you want. Do not use the double-click method to create the object.)

10. Most properties can be set or altered with code as the program is running instead of being preset from the Properties window. For instance, a command button can be made to disappear with a line such as Let Command1.Visible = False. See Section 3.2 for details.

11. The BorderStyle and MultiLine properties of a text box can only be set from the Properties window. You cannot alter them during run time.

12. Of the objects discussed in this section, only command buttons have true access keys.

13. If you inadvertently double-click an object in a form, a window containing the word Sub will appear. This is a code window and is discussed in the next section. To remove this window, double-click on the button in the upper-left corner of the window.

14. Appendix C provides a quick reference to many Visual Basic properties.

15. Visual Basic Standard Edition has an extensive Help system that is discussed in Appendix B.

PRACTICE PROBLEMS 3.1

1. What is the difference between the Caption and the Name of a command button?

2. Suppose in an earlier session you created an object that looks like an empty rectangle. It might be a picture box, a text box with Text property set to nothing (blanked out by deleting all characters), or a label with a blank caption and BorderStyle property set to Fixed Single. How might you determine which it is?

EXERCISES 3.1

1. Why are command buttons sometimes called "push buttons"?

2. How can you tell if a program is running by looking at the screen?

3. Create a form with two command buttons, run the program, and click on each button. Do you notice anything different about a button after it has been clicked?

4. Design an experiment to convince yourself that picture boxes can get the focus, but labels cannot.

5. Place three command buttons vertically on a form with Command3 above Command2, and Command2 above Command1. Then run the program and successively press Tab. Notice that the command buttons receive the focus from bottom to top. Experiment with various configurations of command buttons and text boxes to convince yourself that objects get the focus in the order in which they were created.

6. While a program is running, an object is said to **lose focus** when the focus moves from that object to another object. In what three ways can the user cause an object to lose focus?

In Exercises 7 through 28, carry out the task. Use a new form for each exercise.

7. Place CHECKING ACCOUNT in the title bar of a form.

8. Create a text box containing the words PLAY IT, SAM in blue letters.

9. Create an empty text box with a yellow background.

10. Create a text box containing the word HELLO in large italic letters.

11. Create a text box containing the sentence "After all is said and done, more is said than done." The sentence should occupy three lines and each line should be centered in the text box.

12. Create a borderless text box containing the words VISUAL BASIC in bold white letters on a red background.

13. Create a text box containing the words VISUAL BASIC in Courier font.

14. Create a command button containing the word PUSH.

15. Create a command button containing the word PUSH in large italic letters.

16. Create a command button containing the word PUSH in nonbold letters with the letter P underlined.

17. Create a command button containing the word PUSH with the letter H as access key.

18. Create a command button containing the word PUSH that will have a green dotted ring around PUSH when it becomes active during run time. **Note:** Green is the complement of purple.

19. Create a label containing the word ALIAS.

20. Create a label containing the word ALIAS in white on a blue background.

21. Create a label with a border containing the centered italicized word ALIAS.

22. Create a label containing VISUAL on the first line and BASIC on the second line. Each word should be right justified.

23. Create a label containing a picture of a diskette. (**Hint:** Use the Wingdings character <.) Make the diskette as large as possible.

24. Create a label with a border containing the bold word ALIAS in the Terminal font.

25. Create a picture box with a yellow background.

26. Create a picture box with no border and a red background.

27. Create a picture box containing two command buttons.

28. Create a picture box with a blue background containing a picture box with a white background.

In Exercises 29 through 36, create the interface shown in the figure. (These exercises give you practice creating objects and assigning properties. The interfaces do not necessarily correspond to actual programs.)

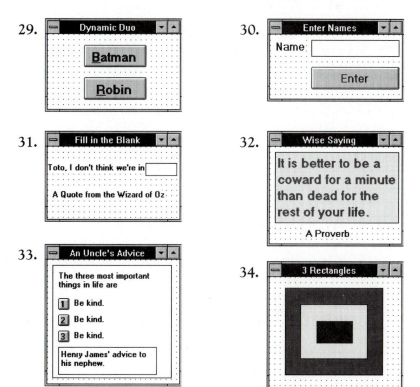

35.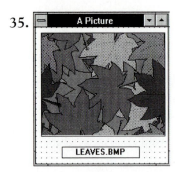

36.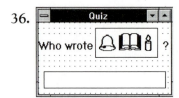

37. Create a replica of your bank check on a form. Words common to all checks, such as PAY TO THE ORDER OF, should be contained in labels. Items specific to your checks, such as your name at the top left, should be contained in text boxes. Make the check on the screen resemble your check as much as possible.

38. Create a replica of your campus ID on a form. Words that are on all student IDs, such as the name of the college, should be contained in labels. Information specific to your ID, such as your name and social security number, should be contained in text boxes. Simulate your picture with a text box containing a smiling face—a size 24 Wingdings J.

39. If you are familiar with Paintbrush (one of Windows' Accessories), use Paintbrush to make a drawing and then save it as a .bmp file. In Visual Basic, create a picture box containing the picture.

SOLUTIONS TO PRACTICE PROBLEMS 3.1

1. The Caption is the text appearing on the command button, whereas the Name is the designation used to refer to the command button. Initially, they have the same value, such as Command1. However, they can both be changed independently of each other.

2. Click on the object to make it active and then press F4 to display its properties box. The first line gives the Name of the object (in bold letters) and its type, such as Label, TextBox, or PictureBox.

We have examined only four of the objects from the Toolbox. To determine the type of one of the other objects, double-click it and then press F4.

3.2 VISUAL BASIC EVENTS

When a Visual Basic program is run, a form and its controls appear on the screen. Normally, nothing happens until the user takes an action, such as clicking a control or pressing the Tab key. Such an action is called an **event**.

The three steps to creating a Visual Basic program are

1. Create the interface; that is, generate, position, and size the objects.

2. Set properties; that is, set relevant properties for the objects.

3. Write code.

This section is devoted to step 3.

Code consists of statements that carry out tasks. Visual Basic has a repertoire of nearly 200 statements and we will use many of them in this text. In this section we limit ourselves to statements that change properties of objects while a program is running.

Properties of an object are changed in code with statements of the form

```
Let objectName.property = setting
```

where *objectName* is the name of the form or a control, *property* is one of the properties of the object, and *setting* is a valid setting for that object. Here are three such statements.

The statement

```
Let Text1.FontSize = 12
```

sets the size of the characters in the text box Text1 to 12.

The statement

```
Let Text1.FontBold = True
```

converts the characters in the text box Text1 to boldface.

The statement

```
Let Text1.Text = ""
```

clears the contents of the text box Text1; that is, it invokes the blank setting.

Most events are associated with objects. The event *clicking Command1* is different from the event *clicking Picture1*. These two events are specified Command1_Click and Picture1_Click. The statements to be executed when an event occurs are written in a block of code called an **event procedure**. The structure of an event procedure is

```
Sub objectName_event ()
  statements
End Sub
```

The word Sub in the first line signals the beginning of the event procedure, and the first line identifies the object and the event occurring to that object. The last line signals the termination of the event procedure. The statements to be executed appear between these two lines. (**Note:** The word *Sub* is an abbreviation of *Subprogram*.) For instance, the event procedure

```
Sub Command1_Click ()
  Let Text1.Text = ""
End Sub
```

clears the contents of the text box when the command button is clicked.

An Event Procedure Walkthrough

The form in Figure 3.11 contains the text box Text1 and the command button Command1. The following walkthrough creates the three event procedures Text1_LostFocus, Text1_GotFocus, and Command1_Click.

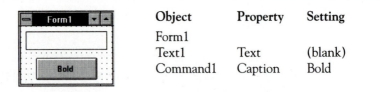

Object	Property	Setting
Form1		
Text1	Text	(blank)
Command1	Caption	Bold

Figure 3.11 The interface for the event procedure walkthrough.

1. Create the interface in Figure 3.11. The Text property for Text1 should be made blank and the Caption property for Command1 should be set to Bold.

2. Double-click on the text box. A window, called a **code window**, appears. (See Figure 3.12) The box marked **Object:** shows Text1, the current object. The box marked **Proc:** shows Change. ("Proc" is short for "Procedure.")

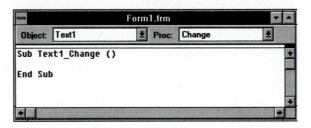

Figure 3.12 A code window.

3. Click on the underlined down-arrow icon to the right of the Proc box. The pull-down menu contains a list of all possible event procedures associated with text boxes. See Figure 3.13.

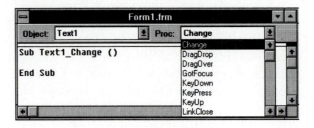

Figure 3.13 Pull-down menu of event procedures.

4. Scroll down the list of event procedures and click on LostFocus. (LostFocus is the last event procedure.) The lines

```
Sub Text1_LostFocus ()

End Sub
```

appear in the code window with a blinking cursor poised at the beginning of the blank line.

5. Type the line

```
Let Text1.FontSize = 12
```

between the existing two lines. (We usually indent lines containing code.) The screen appears as in Figure 3.14. We have now created an event procedure that is activated whenever the text box loses the focus.

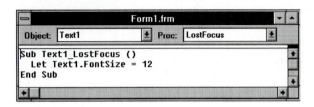

Figure 3.14 A LostFocus event procedure.

6. Let's create another event procedure for the text box. Click on the underlined down-arrow icon to the right of the Proc box, scroll up the list of event procedures, and click on GotFocus. Then type the lines

```
Let Text1.FontSize = 8.5
Let Text1.FontBold = False
```

between the existing two lines. See Figure 3.15.

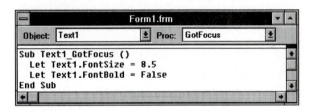

Figure 3.15 A GotFocus event procedure.

7. Let's now create an event procedure for the command button. Click on the underlined down-arrow icon to the right of the Object box. The pull-down menu contains a list of the objects, along with a mysterious object called (general). See Figure 3.16. (We'll discuss (general) later in this chapter.)

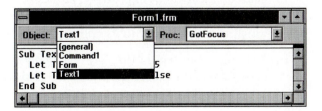

Figure 3.16 List of objects.

8. Click on Command1. The event procedure Command1_Click is displayed. Type in the line

```
Let Text1.FontBold = True
```

9. Now run the program by pressing F5.

10. Type something into the text box. In Figure 3.17 the words "Hello Friend" have been typed.

Figure 3.17 Text box containing input.

11. Press the Tab key. The contents of the text box will be enlarged as in Figure 3.18. When Tab was pressed, the text box lost the focus; that is, the event LostFocus happened to Text1. Thus the event procedure Text1_LostFocus was called and the code inside the procedure was executed.

Figure 3.18 Text box after it has lost the focus.

12. Click on the command button. This calls the event procedure Command1_Click, which converts the text to boldface. See Figure 3.19.

Figure 3.19 Text box after the command button has been clicked.

13. Click on the text box or press the Tab key to move the cursor (and therefore the focus) to the text box. This calls the event procedure Text1_GotFocus, which restores the text to its original state.

14. You can repeat steps 10 through 13 as many times as you like. When you are finished, end the program with Alt+F4 or the End icon from the Toolbar.

15. Double-click on any of the objects to obtain a code window.

16. Press F2 to obtain a View Procedures window. See Figure 3.20. Ignore the upper list headed by Modules. The lower list, headed Procedures, enumerates the event procedures in alphabetical order. The list includes the mysterious procedure (declarations). Ignore (declarations) for now. Select one of the event procedures by highlighting it and pressing the Enter key, or by double-clicking on it.

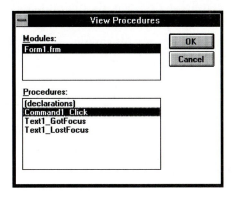

Figure 3.20 A View Procedures window.

17. Repeatedly press Ctrl+Down Arrow to see each code window one after the other.

Comments:

1. Pressing F2 to obtain a View Procedures dialog box or pressing Ctrl+Down Arrow to cycle through the procedures only works when a code window is currently open.

2. The form is the default object in Visual Basic code. That is, code such as

```
Let Form1.property = setting
```

can be written as

```
Let property = setting
```

Also, event procedures associated with Form1 appear as

```
Form_event ()
```

rather than

```
Form1_event ().
```

3. The Primer edition of Visual Basic allows a program only to have one form. Although the complete edition of Visual Basic permits multiple forms, the programs in Chapters 3 through 10 are limited to a single form. Multiple forms are discussed in Chapter 11.

4. Another useful command is SetFocus. The statement

```
object.SetFocus
```

moves the focus to the object.

5. We have ended our programs by clicking the End icon or pressing Alt+F4. A more elegant technique is to create a command button, call it Command2, with caption Quit and the event procedure:

```
Sub Command2_Click ()
  End
End Sub
```

6. Certain words, such as Sub, End, and Let have special meanings in Visual Basic and are referred to as **reserved words** or **keywords**. The Visual Basic editor automatically capitalizes the first letter of a reserved word and displays the word in blue.

7. Visual Basic can detect certain types of errors. For instance, consider the line

```
Let Text1.FontSize = 12
```

from the walkthrough. Suppose you neglected to type the number 12 to the right of the equal sign before pressing the Enter key. Visual Basic would tell you something was missing by displaying the message box on the left below. On the other hand, suppose you misspell the keyword Let. You might notice something is wrong when Let doesn't turn blue. If not, you will certainly know about the problem when the program is run because Visual Basic will display the message box on the right below. After you click on OK, the cursor will be on the offending line.

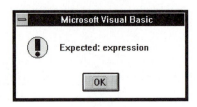

8. Each color can be identified by a sequence of digits and letters beginning with &H. The common colors and their identifying sequences are red (&HFF&), green (&HFF00&), blue (&HFF0000&), yellow (&HFFFF&), black (&H0&), and white (&HFFFFFF&). Whereas these sequences are not required when assigning colors from the properties window, they are necessary when assigning colors at run time. For instance, the statement

```
Let Picture1.BackColor = &HFFFF&
```

gives Picture1 a yellow background.

9. For statements of the form Let *object.property* = *setting*, with properties Caption, Text, or FontName, the setting must be surrounded by quotes. (For instance, Let Label2.Caption = "Name", Let Text1.Text = "45", and Let Picture1.FontName = "Courier".)

PRACTICE PROBLEM 3.2

1. The methods in Steps 16 and 17 of the event procedure walkthrough provide two ways to select a code window for viewing. Give another way.

EXERCISES 3.2

In Exercises 1 through 6, describe the string displayed in the text box when the command button is clicked.

1.
```
Sub Command1_Click ()
    Let Text1.Text = "Hello"
End Sub
```

2.
```
Sub Command1_Click ()
    Let Text1.ForeColor = &HFF&
    Let Text1.Text = "Hello"
End Sub
```

3.
```
Sub Command1_Click ()
    Let Text1.FontItalic = True
    Let Text1.Text = "Hello"
End Sub
```

4.
```
Sub Command1_Click ()
    Let Text1.FontSize = 24
    Let Text1.Text = "Hello"
End Sub
```

5.
```
Sub Command1_Click ()
    Let Text1.Text = "Hello"
    Let Text1.Visible = False
End Sub
```

6.
```
Sub Command1_Click ()
    Let Text1.FontBold = True
    Let Text1.Text = "Hello"
End Sub
```

In Exercises 7 through 10, assume the three objects on the form were created in the order Text1, Text2, and Label1. Also assume that Text1 has the focus. Determine the output displayed in Label1 when Tab is pressed.

7.
```
Sub Text1_LostFocus ()
    Let Label1.ForeColor = &HFF00&
    Let Label1.Caption = "Hello"
End Sub
```

8.
```
Sub Text1_LostFocus ()
    Let Label1.Caption = "Hello"
End Sub
```

9.
```
Sub Text2_GotFocus ()
    Let Label1.FontName = "Courier"
    Let Label1.FontSize = 24
    Let Label1.Caption = "Hello"
End Sub
```

10.
```
Sub Text2_GotFocus ()
    Let Label1.FontItalic = True
    Let Label1.Caption = "Hello"
End Sub
```

In Exercises 11 through 16, determine the errors.

11.
```
Sub Command1_Click ()
    Let Form1 = "Hello"
End Sub
```

12.
```
Sub Command1_Click ()
    Let Text1.ForeColor = "red"
End Sub
```

13.
```
Sub Command1_Click ()
    Let Text1.Caption = "Hello"
End Sub
```

14.
```
Sub Command1_Click ()
    Let Label2.Text = "Hello"
End Sub
```

15.
```
Sub Command1_Click ()
    Let Label2.BorderStyle = 2
End Sub
```

16.
```
Sub Command1_Click ()
    Let Text1.MultiLine = True
End Sub
```

In Exercises 17 through 32, write a line (or lines) of code to carry out the task.

17. Display "E.T. phone home." in Label2.

18. Display "Play it, Sam." in Label2.

19. Display "The stuff that dreams are made of." in red letters in Text1.

20. Display "Life is like a box of chocolates." in Courier font in Text1.

21. Delete the contents of Text1.

22. Delete the contents of Label2.

23. Make Label2 disappear.

24. Remove the border from Label2.

25. Give Picture1 a blue background.

26. Place a bold red "Hello" in Label2.

27. Place a bold italics "Hello" in Text1.

28. Make Picture1 disappear.

29. Give the focus to Command1.

30. Remove the border from Picture1.

31. Place a border around Label2 and center its contents.

32. Give the focus to Text2.

33. Describe the GotFocus event in your own words.

34. Describe the LostFocus event in your own words.

35. Labels and picture boxes have an event called DblClick that responds to a double-clicking of the left mouse button. Write a simple program to test this event. Determine whether or not you can trigger the DblClick event without also triggering the Click event.

36. Why do you think that text boxes do not support the Click event?

In Exercises 37 through 42, the interface and initial properties are specified. Write the code to carry out the stated task.

37. When one of the three command buttons is pressed, the words on the command button are displayed in the label with the stated alignment.

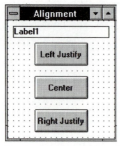

Object	Property	Setting
Form1	Caption	Alignment
Label1		
Command1	Caption	Left Justify
Command2	Caption	Center
Command3	Caption	Right Justify

38. When one of the command buttons is pressed, the face changes to a smiling face (Wingdings character "J") or a frowning face (Wingdings character "L").

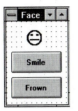

Object	Property	Setting
Form1	Caption	Face
Label1	FontName	Wingdings
	Caption	K
	FontSize	24
Command1	Caption	Smile
Command2	Caption	Frown

39. Pressing the command buttons alters the background and foreground colors in the text box.

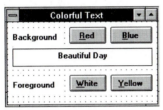

Object	Property	Setting
Form1	Caption	Colorful Text
Label1	Caption	Background
Command1	Caption	&Red
Command2	Caption	&Blue
Text1	Text	Beautiful Day
	MultiLine	True
	Alignment	2 – Center
Label2	Caption	Foreground
Command3	Caption	&White
Command4	Caption	&Yellow

40. While one of the three text boxes has the focus, its text is bold. When it loses the focus, it ceases to be bold. The command buttons enlarge text (FontSize = 12) or return text to normal size (FontSize = 8.25).

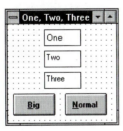

Object	Property	Setting
Form1	Caption	One, Two, Three
Text1	Text	One
	FontBold	False
Text2	Text	Two
	FontBold	False
Text3	Text	Three
	FontBold	False
Command1	Caption	&Big
Command2	Caption	&Normal

41. When you click on one of the three small text boxes at the bottom of the form, an appropriate saying is displayed in the large text box. Use the sayings "I like life, it's something to do.", "The future isn't what it used to be."; and "Tell the truth and run."

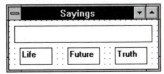

Object	Property	Setting
Form1	Caption	Sayings
Text1	Text	(blank)
Text2	Text	Life
Text3	Text	Future
Text4	Text	Truth

42. After the user types something into the text box, the user can change the font by clicking on one of the command buttons.

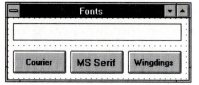

Object	Property	Setting
Form1	Caption	Fonts
Text1	Text	(blank)
Command1	Caption	Courier
Command2	Caption	MS Serif
Command3	Caption	Wingdings

In Exercises 43 through 48, write a program with a Windows-style interface to carry out the task.

43. Allow the user to click on command buttons to change the size of the text in a text box and alter its appearance between bold and italics.

44. A form contains two text boxes and one large label between them with no caption. When the focus is on the first text box the label reads. "Enter your full name." When the focus is on the second text box the label reads "Enter your phone number, including area code."

45. Use the same form and properties as in Exercise 38, with the captions for the command buttons replaced with Vanish and Reappear. Clicking a button should produce the stated result.

46. Simulate a traffic light with three small square picture boxes placed vertically on a form. Initially the bottom picture is solid green and the other picture boxes are white. When the Tab key is pressed, the middle picture box turns yellow and the bottom picture box turns white. The next time Tab is pressed, the top picture box turns red and the middle picture box turns white. Subsequent pressing of the Tab key cycles through the three colors. **Hint:** First place the bottom picture box on the form, then the middle picture box, and finally the top picture box.

47. The form contains four square buttons arranged in a rectangular array. Each button has the caption "Push Me." When you click on a button, the button disappears and the other three become visible.

48. The form contains two text boxes into which the user types information. When the user clicks on one of the text boxes, it becomes blank and its contents are displayed in the other text box.

SOLUTION TO PRACTICE PROBLEM 3.2

1. With any code window open, click on the arrow to the right of the Object window and then select the desired object. Then click on the arrow to the right of the Proc window and select the desired event procedure.

3.3 NUMBERS

Much of the data processed by computers consists of numbers. In "computer-ese," numbers are often called **numeric constants**. This section discusses the operations that are performed with numbers and the ways numbers are displayed.

Arithmetic Operations

The five arithmetic operations are addition, subtraction, multiplication, division, and exponentiation. (Since exponentiation is not as familiar as the others, it is reviewed in detail in Comment 10.) Addition, subtraction, and division are denoted in Visual Basic by the standard symbols +, −, and /. However, the notations for multiplication and exponentiation differ from the customary mathematical notations.

Mathematical Notation	Visual Basic Notation
$a \cdot b$ or $a \times b$	$a * b$
a^r	$a \wedge r$

(The asterisk [*] is the upper character of the 8 key on the top row of the keyboard. The caret [^] is the upper character of the 6 key at the top of the keyboard.) **Note:** In this book, the proportional font used for text differs from the monospaced font used for programs. In the program font, the asterisk appears as a five-pointed star (*).

A common way to show a number on the screen is to display it in a picture box. If n is a number, then the instruction

```
Picture1.Print n
```

displays the number n in the picture box. If the Picture1.Print instruction is followed by a combination of numbers and arithmetic operations, it carries out the operations and displays the result. Print is a reserved word and the Print operation is called a **method**. Another important method is Cls. The statement

```
Picture1.Cls
```

erases all text and graphics from the picture box Picture1.

EXAMPLE 1   The following program applies each of the five arithmetic operations to the numbers 3 and 2. Notice that 3 / 2 is displayed in decimal form. Visual Basic never displays numbers as common fractions. **Note 1:** The star in the fifth and eighth lines is the computer font version of the asterisk. **Note 2:** The word Run in the phrasing [Run ...] indicates that F5 should be pressed to execute the program.

Below is the form design and a table showing the names of the objects on the form and the settings, if any, for properties of these objects. This form design is also used in the discussion and examples in the remainder of this section.

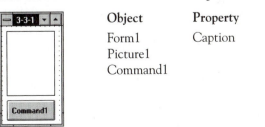

Object	Property	Setting
Form1	Caption	3-3-1
Picture1		
Command1		

```
Sub Command1_Click ()
  Picture1.Cls
  Picture1.Print 3 + 2
  Picture1.Print 3 - 2
  Picture1.Print 3 * 2
  Picture1.Print 3 / 2
  Picture1.Print 3 ^ 2
  Picture1.Print 2 * (3 + 4)
End Sub
```

[Run and then click the command button.]

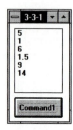

Scientific Notation

Let us review powers of 10 and scientific notation. Our method of decimal notation is based on a systematic use of exponents.

$$10^1 = 10 \qquad\qquad 10^{-1} = 1/10 = .1$$
$$10^2 = 100 \qquad\qquad 10^{-2} = .01$$
$$10^3 = 1000 \qquad\qquad 10^{-3} = .001$$
$$\vdots \qquad\qquad\qquad\qquad \vdots$$
$$\vdots \qquad\qquad\qquad\qquad \vdots$$
$$10^n = \underbrace{1000...0}_{n \text{ zeros}} \qquad\qquad 10^{-n} = \underbrace{.000...01}_{n \text{ digits}}$$

Scientific notation provides a convenient way of writing numbers by using powers of 10 to stand for zeros. Numbers are written in the form $b \cdot 10^r$, where b is a number from 1 up to (but not including) 10, and r is an integer. For example, it is much more convenient to write the diameter of the sun (1,400,000,000 meters) in scientific notation: $1.4 \cdot 10^9$ meters. Similarly, rather than write .0000003 meters for the diameter of a bacterium, it is simpler to write $3 \cdot 10^{-7}$ meters.

Any acceptable number can be entered into the computer in either standard or scientific notation. The form in which Visual Basic displays a number depends on many factors, with size being an important consideration. In Visual Basic, $b \cdot 10^r$ is usually written as $b\text{E}r$. (The letter E is an abbreviation for *exponent.*) The following forms of the numbers mentioned above are equivalent.

1.4 * 10^9	1.4E+09	1.4E+9	1.4E9	1400000000
3 * 10^–7	3E–07	3E–7	.0000003	

The computer displays r as a two-digit number, preceded by a plus sign if r is positive and a minus sign if r is negative.

EXAMPLE 2   The following program illustrates scientific notation. The computer's choice of whether to display a number in scientific or standard form depends on the magnitude of the number.

```
Sub Command1_Click ()
  Picture1.Cls
  Picture1.Print 1.2 * 10 ^ 34
  Picture1.Print 1.2 * 10 ^ 8
  Picture1.Print 1.2 * 10 ^ 3
  Picture1.Print 10 ^ -20
  Picture1.Print 10 ^ -2
End Sub
```

[Run and then click the command button.]

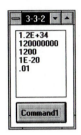

Variables

In applied mathematics problems, quantities are referred to by names. For instance, consider the following high school algebra problem. "If a car travels at 50 miles per hour, how far will it travel in 14 hours? Also, how many hours are required to travel 410 miles?" The solution to this problem uses the well-known formula

$$\text{distance} = \text{rate} \times \text{time elapsed}$$

Here's how this problem would be solved with a computer program.

```
Sub Command1_Click ()
  Picture1.Cls
  Let rate = 50
  Let timeElapsed = 14
  Let distance = rate * timeElapsed
  Picture1.Print distance
  Let distance = 410
  Let timeElapsed = distance / rate
  Picture1.Print timeElapsed
End Sub
```

[Run and then click the command button. The following is displayed in the picture box.]

```
700
8.2
```

The third line of the event procedure sets the rate to 50 and the fourth line sets the time elapsed to 14. The fifth line multiplies the value for the rate by the value for the time elapsed and sets the distance to this product. The next line displays the answer to the first question. The last three lines before the End Sub statement answer the second question in a similar manner.

The names *rate*, *timeElapsed*, and *distance*, which hold numbers, are referred to as **variables**. Consider the variable *timeElapsed*. In the fourth line its value was set to 14. In the eighth line its value was changed as the result of a computation. On the other hand, the variable *rate* had the same value, 50, throughout the program.

In general, a variable is a name that is used to refer to an item of data. The value assigned to the variable may change during the execution of the program. In Visual Basic, variable names can be up to forty characters long, must begin with a letter, and can consist only of letters, digits, and underscores. (The shortest variable names consist of a single letter.) Visual Basic does not distinguish between upper and lowercase letters used in variable names. Some examples of variable names are *total*, *numberOfCars*, *taxRate_1994*, and *n*. As a convention, we write variable names in lowercase letters except for the first letters of additional words (as in *numberOfCars*). Let statements assign values to variables and Print methods display the values of variables.

If *var* is a variable and num is a constant, then the statement

```
Let var = num
```

assigns the number *num* to the variable *var*. Actually, the computer sets aside a location in memory with the name *var*, and places the number *num* in it. The statement

```
Picture1.Print var
```

looks into this memory location for the value of the variable and displays the value in the picture box.

A combination of constants, variables, and arithmetic operations that can be evaluated to yield a number is called a **numeric expression**. Expressions are evaluated by replacing each variable by its value and carrying out the arithmetic. Some examples of expressions are 2 * distance + 7, n + 1, and (a + b) / 3.

EXAMPLE 3   The following program displays the value of an expression.

```
Sub Command1_Click ()
  Picture1.Cls
  Let a = 5
  Let b = 4
  Picture1.Print a * (2 + b)
End Sub
```

[Run and then click the command button. The following is displayed in the picture box.]

If *var* is a variable, then the statement

```
Let var = expression
```

first evaluates the expression on the right and *then* assigns its value to the variable. For instance, the event procedure in Example 3 can be written as

```
Sub Command1_Click ()
  Picture1.Cls
  Let a = 5
  Let b = 4
  Let c = a * (2 + b)
  Picture1.Print c
End Sub
```

The expression a * (2 + b) is evaluated to 30 and then this value is assigned to the variable c.

Since the expression in a Let statement is evaluated before an assignment is made, a statement such as

```
Let n = n + 1
```

is meaningful. It first evaluates the expression on the right (that is, it adds 1 to the original value of the variable n), and then assigns this sum to the variable n. The effect is to increase the value of the variable n by 1. In terms of memory locations, the statement retrieves the value of n from n's memory location, uses it to compute n + 1, and then places the sum in n's memory location.

Print Method

Consider the following event procedure.

```
Sub Command1_Click ()
  Picture1.Cls
  Picture1.Print 3
  Picture1.Print -3
End Sub
```

[Run and then click the command button.]

Notice that the negative number −3 begins directly at the left margin, whereas the positive number 3 begins one space to the right. The Print method always displays nonnegative numbers with a leading space. The Print method also displays a trailing space after every number. Although the trailing spaces are not apparent here, we will soon see evidence of their presence.

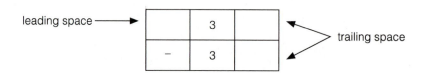

The Print methods used so far only display one number per line. After displaying a number, the cursor moves to the leftmost position and down a line for the next display. Borrowing from typewriter terminology, we say that the computer performs a carriage return and a line feed after each number is displayed. The carriage return and line feed, however, can be suppressed by placing a semicolon at the end of the Print method.

EXAMPLE 4   The following program illustrates the use of semicolons in Print methods. The output reveals the presence of the space trailing each number. For instance, the space trailing –3 combines with the leading space of 99 to produce two spaces between the numbers.

```
Sub Command1_Click ()
  Picture1.Cls
  Picture1.Print 3;
  Picture1.Print -3;
  Picture1.Print 99;
  Picture1.Print 100
End Sub
```

[Run and then click the command button.]

Semicolons can be used to display several numbers with one Print method. If m, n, and r are numbers, a line of the form

```
Picture1.Print m; n; r;
```

or

```
Picture1.Print m; n; r
```

displays the three numbers, one after another, separated only by their leading and trailing spaces. For instance, the Print methods in Example 4 above can be replaced by the single line

```
Picture1.Print 3; -3; 99; 100
```

Comments:

1. Numbers must not contain commas, dollar signs, or percent signs. Also, mixed numbers, such as 8 1/2, are not allowed.

2. In this text we use lowercase letters for variable names. For names such as *interestRate*, however, we capitalize the first letter of the second word to improve readability. Visual Basic allows any type of capitalization you like and helps you to be consistent with the use of uppercase letters in a variable name. For instance, if you use the variable name *interestRate* in a program and later enter a line using *InterestRate*, the appearance of the first variable name will automatically be changed to *InterestRate* by Visual Basic.

3. Some people think of the equals sign (=) in a Let statement as an arrow pointing to the left. This stresses the fact that the value on the right is assigned to the variable on the left.

4. Parentheses should be used when necessary to clarify the meaning of an expression. When there are no parentheses, the arithmetic operations are performed in the following order: (1) exponentiations; (2) multiplications and divisions; (3) additions and subtractions. In the event of ties, the leftmost operation is carried out first. Table 3.1 summarizes these rules.

( )	Inner to outer, left to right
∧	Left to right in expression
* /	Left to right in expression
+ −	Left to right in expression

Table 3.1 Level of precedence for arithmetic operations.

5. Visual Basic statements and certain other words that have a specific meaning in the Visual Basic language cannot be used as names of variables. For instance, the statements Let print = 99 and Let end = 99 are not valid. These words are called **reserved words**. Some reserved words that are most likely to be used inadvertently are Color, Error, Height, Name, Select, Time, Val, Width, and Year. Most of the items in Appendix C, other than properties, are reserved words.

6. Grammatical errors, such as misspellings or incorrect punctuations, are called **syntax errors**. Certain types of syntax errors are spotted by the smart editor when they are entered, whereas others are not detected until the program is executed. When Visual Basic spots an error, it displays a dialog box. Some incorrect statements and their errors are given below.

Statement	Reason for Error
Picture1.Primt 3	Misspelling of keyword
Picture1.Print 2 +	No number follows the plus sign
Let 9W = 5	9W is not a valid variable name

7. Numeric variables that have not been assigned values by Let statements have the value 0. We say that the **default value** is 0.

```
Sub Command1_Click ()
  Picture1.Cls
  Let a = 5
  Picture1.Print a + b; b
End Sub
```

[Run and then click the command button. The following is displayed in the picture box.]

```
5  0
```

8. The omission of the asterisk to denote multiplication is a common error. For instance, the expression a(b + c) is not valid. It should read a * (b + c).

9. The largest number the numeric variables considered in this text can represent is 3.402823E+38. Attempting to generate larger values produces the message "Overflow." The numbers generated by the programs in this text usually have a maximum of seven digits.

10. *A Review of Exponents.* The expression 2^3 means $2 \cdot 2 \cdot 2$, the product of three 2's. The number 3 is called the **exponent**, and the number 2 is called the **base**. In general, if r is a positive integer and a is a number, then a^r is defined as follows:

$$a^r = \underbrace{a \cdot a \ldots a.}_{r \text{ factors}}$$

The process of calculating a^r is called *raising a to the rth power.* Some other types of exponents are the following:

$$a^{1/2} = \sqrt{a}$$
$$a^{1/n} = \sqrt[n]{a} \quad n \text{ positive integer} \qquad\qquad 9^{1/2} = 3$$
$$16^{1/4} = 2$$
$$a^{m/n} = (\sqrt[n]{a})^m \quad m, n \text{ positive integers} \qquad 8^{2/3} = (\sqrt[3]{8})^2 = 4$$
$$a^{-r} = 1/a^r \quad a \neq 0 \qquad\qquad 10^{-2} = .01$$

11. More than one statement can be placed on a single line of a program provided the statements are separated by colons. For instance, the code inside the event procedure in Example 3 can be written as

```
Picture1.Cls: Let a = 5: Let b = 4: Picture1.Print a * (2 + b)
```

In general, though, programs are much easier to follow if just one statement appears on each line. In this text we almost always use single-statement lines.

PRACTICE PROBLEMS 3.3

1. Evaluate 2 + 3 * 4.

2. Complete the table by filling in the value of each variable after each line is executed.

	a	b	c
Sub Command1_Click ()			
Let a = 3	3	0	0
Let b = 4	3	4	0
Let c = a + b			
Let a = c * a			
Picture1.Print a - b			
Let b = b * b			
End Sub			

EXERCISES 3.3

In Exercises 1 through 6, evaluate the numeric expression.

1. $3 * 4$

2. $7 \wedge 2$

3. $1 / (2 \wedge 5)$

4. $3 + (4 * 5)$

5. $(5 - 3) * 4$

6. $3 * ((-2) \wedge 5)$

In Exercises 7 through 10, write the number in scientific notation as it might be displayed by the computer.

7. 3 billion

8. 12,300,000

9. $4 / (10 \wedge 8)$

10. $32 * (10 \wedge 20)$

In Exercises 11 through 16, determine whether or not the name is a valid variable name.

11. balance

12. room&Board

13. fOrM_1040

14. 1040B

15. expenses?

16. INCOME 1987

In Exercises 17 through 22, evaluate the numeric expression where a = 2, b = 3, and c = 4.

17. $(a * b) + c$

18. $a * (b + c)$

19. $(1 + b) * c$

20. $a \wedge c$

21. $b \wedge (c - a)$

22. $(c - a) \wedge b$

In Exercises 23 through 28, write an event procedure to calculate and display the value of the expression.

23. $7 \cdot 8 + 5$

24. $(1 + 2 \cdot 9)^3$

25. 5.5% of 20

26. $15 - 3(2 + 3^4)$

27. $17 (3 + 162)$

28. $4 \ 1/2 - 3 \ 5/8$

In Exercises 29 and 30, complete the table by filling in the value of each variable after each line is executed.

29.

	x	y
Sub Command1_Click ()		
Let x = 2		
Let y = 3 * x		
Let x = y + 5		
Picture1.Cls		
Picture1.Print x + 4		
Let y = y + 1		
End Sub		

30.

	bal	inter	withDr
Sub Command1_Click ()			
Let bal = 100			
Let inter = .05			
Let withDr = 25			
Let bal = bal + inter * bal			
Let bal = bal - withDr			
End Sub			

In Exercises 31 through 38, determine the output displayed in the picture box by the lines of code.

31.
```
Let amount = 10
Picture1.Print amount - 4
```

32.
```
Let a = 4
Let b = 5 * a
Picture1.Print a + b; b - a
```

33.
```
Picture1.Print 1; 2;
Picture1.Print 3; 4
Picture1.Print 5 + 6
```

34.
```
Let number = 5
Let number = 2 * number
Picture1.Print number
```

35.
```
Picture1.Print a
Let a = 4
Let b = a ^ 2
Picture1.Print a * b
```

36.
```
Let tax = 200
Let tax = 25 + tax
Picture1.Print tax
```

37.
```
Let x = 3
Picture1.Print x ^ x; x + 3 * x
```

38.
```
Let n = 2
Picture1.Print 3 * n
Let n = n + n
Picture1.Print n + n
```

In Exercises 39 through 42, identify the errors.

39.
```
Let a = 2
Let b = 3
Let a + b = c
Picture1.Print c
```

40.
```
Let a = 2
Let b = 3
Let c = d = 4
Picture1.Print 5((a + b) / (c + d)
```

41.
```
Let balance = 1,234
Let deposit = $100
Picture1.Print balance + deposit
```

42.
```
Let .05 = interest
Let balance = 800
Picture1.Print interest * balance
```

In Exercises 43 and 44, rewrite the code with fewer lines.

43.
```
Picture1.Print 1;
Picture1.Print 2;
Picture1.Print 1 + 2
```

44.
```
Let a = 1
Let b = a + 2
Picture1.Print b
```

In Exercises 45 through 52, write code starting with Sub Command1_Click () and Picture1.Cls statements, ending with an End Sub statement, and having one line for each step. Lines that display data should use the given variable names.

45. The following steps calculate a company's profit.

(a) Assign the value 98456 to the variable *revenue*.
(b) Assign the value 45000 to the variable *costs*.
(c) Assign to the variable *profit*, the difference between the variables *revenue* and *costs*.
(d) Display the value of the variable *profit* in a picture box.

46. The following steps calculate the amount of a stock purchase.

(a) Assign the value 25.625 to the variable *costPerShare*.
(b) Assign the value 400 to the variable *numberOfShares*.
(c) Assign the product of *costPerShare* and *numberOfShares* to the variable *amount*.
(d) Display the value of the variable *amount* in a picture box.

47. The following steps calculate the price of an item after a 30% reduction.

    (a) Assign the value 19.95 to the variable *price*.
    (b) Assign the value 30 to the variable *discountPercent*.
    (c) Assign the value of (*discountPercent* divided by 100) times *price* to the variable *markDown*.
    (d) Decrease price by *markDown*.
    (e) Display the value of *price* in a picture box.

48. The following steps calculate a company's break-even point, the number of units of goods the company must manufacture and sell in order to break even.

    (a) Assign the value 5000 to the variable *fixedCosts*.
    (b) Assign the value 8 to the variable *pricePerUnit*.
    (c) Assign the value 6 to the variable *costPerUnit*.
    (d) Assign the value *fixedCosts* divided by the difference of *pricePerUnit* and *costPerUnit* to the variable *breakEvenPoint*.
    (e) Display the value of the variable *breakEvenPoint* in a picture box.

49. The following steps calculate the balance after three years when $100 is deposited in a savings account at 5% interest compounded annually.

    (a) Assign the value 100 to the variable *balance*.
    (b) Increase the variable *balance* by 5% of its value.
    (c) Increase the variable *balance* by 5% of its value.
    (d) Increase the variable *balance* by 5% of its value.
    (e) Display the value of the variable *balance* in a picture box.

50. The following steps calculate the balance after three years when $100 is deposited at the beginning of each year in a savings account at 5% interest compounded annually.

    (a) Assign the value 100 to the variable *balance*.
    (b) Increase the variable *balance* by 5% of its value and add 100.
    (c) Increase the variable *balance* by 5% of its value and add 100.
    (d) Increase the variable *balance* by 5% of its value and add 100.
    (e) Display the value of the variable *balance* in a picture box.

51. The following steps calculate the balance after ten years when $100 is deposited in a savings account at 5% interest compounded annually.

    (a) Assign the value 100 to the variable *balance*.
    (b) Multiply the variable *balance* by 1.05 raised to the 10th power.
    (c) Display the value of the variable *balance* in a picture box.

52. The following steps calculate the percentage profit from the sale of a stock.

    (a) Assign the value 10 to the variable *purchasePrice*.
    (b) Assign the value 15 to the variable *sellingPrice*.
    (c) Assign to the variable *percentProfit*, one hundred times the value of the difference between *sellingPrice* and *purchasePrice* divided by *purchasePrice*.
    (d) Display the value of the variable *percentProfit* in a picture box.

In Exercises 53 through 58, write an event procedure to solve the problem and display the answer in a picture box. The program should use variables for each of the quantities.

53. Suppose each acre of farmland produces 18 tons of corn. How many tons of corn can be produced on a 30-acre farm?

54. Suppose a ball is thrown straight up in the air with an initial velocity of 50 feet per second and an initial height of 5 feet. How high will the ball be after 3 seconds? **Note:** The height after t seconds is given by the expression $-16t^2 + v_0t + h_0$, where v_0 is the initial velocity and h_0 is the initial height.

55. If a car left Washington, D.C., at two o'clock and arrived in New York at seven o'clock, what was its average speed? **Note:** New York is 233 miles from Washington.

56. A motorist wants to determine her gas mileage. At 23,340 miles (on the odometer), the tank is filled. At 23,695 miles, the tank is filled with 14.1 gallons. How many miles per gallon did the car average between the two fillings?

57. A U.S. geological survey showed that Americans use an average of 1600 gallons of water per person per day, including industrial use. How many gallons of water are used each year in the United States? **Note:** The current population of the U.S. is about 260 million people.

58. According to FHA specifications, each room in a house should have a window area equal to at least 10 percent of the floor area of the room. What is the minimum window area for a 14-ft by 16-ft room?

SOLUTIONS TO PRACTICE PROBLEMS 3.3

1. 14. Multiplications are performed before additions. If the intent is for the addition to be performed first, the expression should be written (2 + 3) * 4.

2.

	a	b	c
Sub Command1_Click ()			
Let a = 3	3	0	0
Let b = 4	3	4	0
Let c = a + b	3	4	7
Let a = c * a	21	4	7
Picture1.Print a - b	21	4	7
Let b = b * b	21	16	7
End Sub			

Each time a Let statement is executed, only one variable has its value changed (the variable to the left of the equals sign).

3.4 STRINGS

There are two primary types of data that can be processed by Visual Basic: numbers and strings. Sentences, phrases, words, letters of the alphabet, names, phone numbers, addresses, and dates are all examples of strings. Formally, a **string constant** is a sequence of characters that is treated as a single item. Strings can be assigned names with Let statements, can be displayed with Print methods, and there is an operation called concatenation (denoted by +) for combining strings.

Variables and Strings

A **string variable** is a name used to refer to a string. The allowable names of string variables are identical to those of numeric variables. The value of a string variable is assigned or altered with Let statements and displayed with Print methods just like the value of a numeric variable.

EXAMPLE 1   The following code shows how Let and Print are used with strings. The string variable *today* is assigned a value by the fourth line and this value is displayed by the fifth line. The quotation marks surrounding each string constant are not part of the constant and are not displayed by the Print method. (The form design for Examples 1 through 6 consists of a command button and picture box as shown in Example 1 of the previous section.)

```
Sub Command1_Click ()
  Picture1.Cls
  Picture1.Print "hello"
  Let today = "9/17/95"
  Picture1.Print today
End Sub
```

[Run and then click the command button. The following is displayed in the picture box.]

```
hello
9/17/95
```

If x, y, ..., z are characters and *strVar1* is a string variable, then the statement

```
Let strVar1 = "xy...z"
```

assigns the string constant $xy...z$ to the variable, and the statement

```
Picture1.Print "xy...z"
```

or

```
Picture1.Print strVar1
```

displays the string *xy...z* in a picture box. If *strVar2* is another string variable, then the statement

```
Let strVar2 = strVar1
```

assigns the value of the variable *strVar1* to the variable *strVar2*. (The value of *strVar1* will remain the same.) String constants used in Let or Picture1.Print statements must be surrounded by quotation marks, but string variables are never surrounded by quotation marks.

   As with numbers, semicolons can be used with strings in Picture1.Print statements to suppress carriage returns and line feeds. However, Picture1.Print statements do not display leading or trailing spaces along with strings.

EXAMPLE 2   The following program illustrates the use of the Let and Picture1.Print statements.

```
Sub Command1_Click ()
  Picture1.Cls
  Let phrase = "win or lose that counts."
  Picture1.Print "It's not whether you "; phrase
  Picture1.Print "It's whether I "; phrase
End Sub
```

[Run and then click the command button. The following is displayed in the picture box.]

```
It's not whether you win or lose that counts.
It's whether I win or lose that counts.
```

Concatenation

Two strings can be combined to form a new string consisting of the strings joined together. The joining operation is called **concatenation** and is represented by a plus sign (+). For instance, "good" + "bye" is "goodbye". A combination of strings and plus signs that can be evaluated to form a string is called a **string expression**. The Let and Picture1.Print statements evaluate expressions before assigning them to variables or displaying them.

EXAMPLE 3   The following program illustrates concatenation.

```
Sub Command1_Click ()
  Picture1.Cls
  Let quote1 = "The ballgame isn't over, "
  Let quote2 = "until it's over."
  Let quote = quote1 + quote2
  Picture1.Print quote + "   Yogi Berra"
End Sub
```

[Run and then click the command button. The following is displayed in the picture box.]

```
The ballgame isn't over, until it's over.   Yogi Berra
```

EXAMPLE 4   The following program has strings and numbers occurring together in a Picture1.Print instruction.

```
Sub Command1_Click ()
  Picture1.Cls
  Let interestRate = .0655
  Let principal = 100
  Let phrase = "The balance after a year is"
  Picture1.Print phrase; (1 + interestRate) * principal
End Sub
```

[Run and then click the command button. The following is displayed in the picture box.]

```
The balance after a year is 106.55
```

Declaring Variable Types

So far, we have not distinguished between variables that hold strings and variables that hold numbers. There are several advantages to specifying the type of values, string or numeric, that can be assigned to a variable. A statement of the form

```
Dim variableName As String
```

specifies that only strings can be assigned to the named variable. A statement of the form

```
Dim variableName As Single
```

specifies that only numbers can be assigned to the named variable. **Note:** The term Single derives from *single-precision real number*.

A Dim statement is said to **declare** a variable. From now on we will declare all variables. However, all the programs will run correctly even if the Dim statements are omitted. Declaring variables is regarded as good programming practice since it makes programs easier to read and helps prevent certain types of errors.

EXAMPLE 5   The following rewrite of Example 4 declares all variables.

```
Sub Command1_Click ()
  Dim interestRate As Single
  Dim principal As Single
  Dim phrase As String
  Picture1.Cls
  Let interestRate = .0655
  Let principal = 100
  Let phrase = "The balance after a year is"
  Picture1.Print phrase; (1 + interestRate) * principal
End Sub
```

Several Dim statements can be combined into one. For instance, the first three lines of Example 5 can be replaced by

```
Dim interestRate As Single, principal As Single, phrase As String
```

The dollar sign provides an alternative way to identify a variable as being a string variable. A statement of the form

```
Dim var As String
```

can be replaced by

```
Dim var$
```

In the event you do not declare a variable with a Dim statement, you can still designate a type for it by appending a special character, called a **type declaration tag** to the end of the variable name. Use an exclamation mark for a numeric variable (that is, a single-precision variable) and a dollar sign for a string variable. For instance, a program can contain lines such as the following:

```
Let price! = 65.99
Let nom$ = "John"
```

Visual Basic actually has several different types of numeric variables. So far, we have used only single-precision numeric variables. Single-precision numeric variables can hold numbers of magnitude from as small as 1.4×10^{-45} to as large as 3.4×10^{38}. Another type of numeric variable, called **Integer**, can only hold whole numbers from -32768 to 32767. Integer type variables are declared with a statement of the form

```
Dim intVar As Integer
```

The type declaration tag for Integer variables is the percent symbol. The Integer data type uses less memory than the Single data type and statements using the Integer type execute faster. (This is only useful in programs with many calculations, such as the programs in later chapters that use For...Next loops.) Of course, Integer variables are limited since they cannot hold decimals or large numbers. We will use Integer variables extensively with For...Next loops in Chapter 6 and occasionally when the data clearly consists of small whole numbers.

Other types of numeric variables are Long Integer, Double-precision, and Currency. We do not use them in this text. If you want to learn about them, consult Appendix C. In this text, whenever we refer to a numeric variable without mentioning a type, we mean type Single.

Using Text Boxes For Input and Output

The contents of a text box is always a string. Therefore, statements such as

```
Let strVar = Text1.Text
```

and

```
Let Text1.Text = strVar
```

can be used to assign the contents of the text box to the string variable *strVar* and vice versa.

Numbers are stored in text boxes as strings. Therefore, they must be converted to numbers before being assigned to numeric variables. If *str* is a string representation of a number, then Val(*str*) is that number. Conversely, if *num* is a number, then Str$(*num*) is a string representation of the number. Therefore, statements such as

```
Let numVar = Val(Text1.Text)
```

and

```
Let Text1.Text = Str$(numVar)
```

can be used to assign the contents of the text box to the numeric variable *numVar* and vice versa. **Note:** When a nonnegative number is converted to a string with Str$, its first character (but not its last character) is a blank space.

EXAMPLE 6 The following program converts miles to furlongs and vice versa. **Note:** A furlong is 1/8th of a mile.

Object	Property	Setting
Form1	Caption	Convertor
Label1	Alignment	1 – Right Justify
	Caption	Miles
txtMile	Text	(blank)
Label2	Alignment	1 – Right Justify
	Caption	Furlongs
txtFurlong	Text	(blank)

The two text boxes have been named txtMile and txtFurlong. With the Event procedures shown, typing a number into a text box and pressing Tab results in the converted number being displayed in the other text box.

```
Sub txtMile_LostFocus ()
  Let txtFurlong.Text = Str$(8 * Val(txtMile.Text))
End Sub

Sub txtFurlong_LostFocus ()
  Let txtMile.Text = Str$(Val(txtMile.Text) / 8)
End Sub
```

ANSI Character Set

Each of the 47 different keys in the center typewriter portion of the keyboard can produce two characters, for a total of 94 characters. Adding 1 for the space character produced by the space bar makes 95 characters. These characters have numbers ranging from 32 to 126 associated with them. These values, called the ANSI (or ASCII) values of the characters, are given in Appendix A. Table 3.2 shows a few of the values.

32 (space)	48 0	66 B	122 z
33 !	49 1	90 Z	123 {
34 "	57 9	97 a	125 }
35 #	65 A	98 b	126 ~

Table 3.2 A few ANSI values.

Most of the best-known fonts, such as Ariel, Courier, Helvetica, and Times Roman, are essentially governed by the ANSI standard, which assigns characters to the numbers from 32 to 255. Table 3.3 shows a few of the higher ANSI values.

162 ¢	177 ±	181 μ	190 $\frac{3}{4}$
169 ©	178 ^{2}	188 $\frac{1}{4}$	247 ÷
176 °	179 ^{3}	189 $\frac{1}{2}$	248 φ

Table 3.3 A few higher ANSI values.

If n is a number between 32 and 255, then

```
Chr$(n)
```

is the string consisting of the character with ANSI value n. If str is any string, then

```
Asc(str)
```

is the ANSI value of the first character of str. For instance, the statement

```
Let Text1.Text = Chr$(65)
```

displays the letter A in the text box and the statement

```
Picture1.Print Asc("Apple")
```

displays the number 65 in the picture box.

Concatenation can be used with Chr$ to obtain strings using the higher ANSI characters. For instance, with one of the fonts that conforms to the ANSI standard, the statement

```
Let Text1.Text = "32" + Chr$(176) + " Fahrenheit"
```

displays 32° Fahrenheit in the text box.

The KeyPress Event Procedure

When a text box has the focus and the user presses a key, the KeyPress event procedure identifies the key pressed. When a key is pressed, the event procedure assigns the ANSI value of the key to an Integer variable called *KeyAscii*. The general form of the procedure is

```
Sub ControlName_KeyPress (KeyAscii As Integer)
  statements
End Sub
```

The statements usually involve the variable *KeyAscii*. Also, a character does not appear in the text box until End Sub is reached. At that time, the character with ANSI value *KeyAscii* is displayed.

EXAMPLE 7   The following program allows the user to determine the ANSI values of the standard (typewriter) keys of the keyboard. The statement Let Text1.Text = "" removes any previously typed characters from the text box.

Object	Property	Setting
Form1	Caption	ANSI Values
Label1	Caption	Press any key
Text1	Text	(blank)
Picture1		

```
Sub Text1_KeyPress (KeyAscii As Integer)
  Let Text1.Text = ""
  Picture1.Cls
  Picture1.Print Chr$(KeyAscii); " has ANSI value"; KeyAscii
End Sub
```

[Run and then press a key. For instance, if A is pressed, the following is displayed in the picture box.]

```
A has ANSI value 65
```

The KeyPress procedure can alter the character typed into the text box. For instance, if the statement

```
Let KeyAscii = 65
```

is placed in a KeyPress event procedure, the letter A is displayed when any standard key is pressed. In Chapter 5 we use a decision structure to prevent the user from typing unwanted keys. For instance, if we want the user to enter a number into a text box, we can intercept and discard any key presses that are not digits. The statement

```
Let KeyAscii = 0
```

placed in a KeyPress event procedure, discards the key pressed. Finally, a program can be made more friendly by letting the Enter key (ANSI value 13) move the focus in the same way that the Tab key moves the focus. This requires having a KeyPress event procedure for each object that is to respond to the Enter key and then setting the focus to the next object when the value of *KeyAscii* is 13.

Comments:

1. The string "", which contains no characters, is called the **null string** or the **empty string**. It is different from " ", the string consisting of a single space. String variables that have not been assigned values by Let statements initially have "" as their default values.

2. The statement Picture1.Print, with no string or number, simply skips a line in the picture box.

3. Assigning string values to numeric variables or numeric values to string variables results in the error message "Type mismatch."

4. In Visual Basic, the maximum allowable number of characters in a string is 32,767.

5. The quotation mark character (") can be placed into a string constant by using CHR$(34). For example, after the statement

```
Let Text1.Text = "George " + Chr$(34) + "Babe" + Chr$(34) + " Ruth"
```

is executed, the text box contains

```
George "Babe" Ruth
```

6. Most major programming languages require that all variables be declared before they can be used. Although declaring variables with Dim statements is optional in Visual Basic, you can tell Visual Basic to make declaration mandatory. The steps are as follows:

   (a) From any code window, click on the down-arrow to the right of the box labeled "Object:" and select (general). A clear code window will appear.
   (b) Type

   ```
   Option Explicit
   ```

   into this code window.

   Then, if you use a variable without first declaring it in a Dim statement, the message "Variable not defined" will appear as soon as you attempt to run the program. One big advantage of using Option Explicit is that mistypings of variable names will be detected. Otherwise, malfunctions due to typing errors are often difficult to detect.

7. If you are using Visual Basic version 3.0 or later, you can have Visual Basic automatically place Option Explicit in every program you write. The steps are as follows:

   (a) Press Alt/O/E to invoke the Environment Options.
   (b) Move to the second entry in the list, "Require Variable Declarations."
   (c) If "No" appears in the right column, double-click on the line to change it to "Yes."

8. Val can be applied to strings containing nonnumeric characters. If the beginning of the string *str* represents a number, then Val(*str*) is that number; otherwise, it is 0. For instance, Val("123Blastoff") is 123, and Val("abc") is 0.

9. The KeyPress event also applies to command buttons and picture boxes.

10. If Val is omitted from the statement

```
Let numVar = Val(Text1.Text)
```

or Str$ is omitted from the statement

```
Let Text1.Text = Str$(numVar)
```

Visual Basic does not complain, but simply makes the conversion for you. However, errors can arise from omitting Val and Str$. For instance, if the contents of Text1.Text is 34 and the contents of Text2.Text is 56, then the statement

```
Let numVar = Text1.Text + Text2.Text
```

assigns the number 3456 rather than 90 to *numVar*. We follow the standards of good programming practice by always using Val and Str$ to convert values between text boxes and numeric variables. Similar considerations apply to conversions involving label captions.

PRACTICE PROBLEMS 3.4

1. Compare the two statements below, where *phrase* is a string variable and *balance* is a numeric variable.

```
Picture1.Print "It's whether I "; phrase
Picture1.Print "The balance is"; balance
```

Why is the space preceding the second quote mark necessary for the first Picture1.Print statement, but not necessary for the second Picture1.Print statement?

2. A label's caption is a string and can be assigned a value with a statement of the form

```
Let Label1.Caption = strVar
```

What is one advantage to using a label for output as opposed to a text box?

3. Write code to add the numbers in Text1 and Text2 and place the sum in Label3.

EXERCISES 3.4

In Exercises 1 through 14, determine the output displayed in the picture box by the lines of code.

1.
```
Picture1.Print "Hello"
Picture1.Print "12" + "34"
```

2.
```
Picture1.Print "Welcome; my friend."
Picture1.Print "Welcome"; "my friend."
```

3.
```
Picture1.Print "12"; 12; "TWELVE"
```

4.
```
Picture1.Print Chr$(104) + Chr$(105)
```

5. ```
Dim r As String, b As String
Let r = "A ROSE"
Let b = " IS "
Picture1.Print r; b; r; b; r
```

6. ```
Dim n As Single, x As String
Let n = 5
Let x = "5"
Picture1.Print n
Picture1.Print x
```

7. ```
Dim houseNumber As Single
Dim street As String
Let houseNumber = 1234
Let street = "Main Street"
Picture1.Print houseNumber; street
```

8. ```
Dim p As String, word As String
Let p = "f"
Let word = "lute"
Picture1.Print p + word
```

9. ```
Dim quote As String, person As String, qMark As String
Let quote = "We're all in this alone."
Let person = "Lily Tomlin"
Let qMark = Chr$(34)
Picture1.Print qMark + quote + qMark + " " + person
```

10. ```
Dim letter As String
Let letter = "D"
Picture1.Print letter; " is the"; Asc(letter) - Asc("A") + 1;
Picture1.Print "th letter of the alphabet."
```

11. ```
Picture1.Print Str$(17); Val("2B")
Picture1.Print Str$(-20); Val("$16.00")
```

12. ```
Dim a As Single, b As Single
Let a = 1
Let b = 2
Picture1.Print Val(Str$(a)); Str$(a + b)
Picture1.Print Str$(4 - a)
```

13. ```
Dim num1 As Single, num2 As Single
Let num1 = 3567
Let num2 = Len(Str$(num1))
Picture1.Print "The number of digits in 3567 is"; num2 - 1
```

14. ```
Dim address As String
Let address = "1600 Pennsylvania Avenue"
Picture1.Print "Bill, your house number is"; Val(address)
```

In Exercises 15 through 20, identify the errors.

15. ```
Dim phone As Single
Let phone = "234-5678"
Picture1.Print "My phone number is "; phone
```

16. ```
Dim x As String, y As Single
Let x = "2"
Let y = 3
Picture1.Print x + y
```

17. ```
Dim quote As String
Let quote = I came to Casablanca for the waters.
Picture1.Print quote; " "; "Bogart"
```
```

18.
```
Dim strVar As String
Let strVar = Str$(23Skidoo)
Picture1.Print strVar
```

19.
```
Dim end As String
Let end = "happily ever after."
Picture1.Print "They lived "; end
```

20.
```
Dim hi-Yo As String
Let hi-Yo = Silver
Picture1.Print "Hi-Yo "; hi-Yo
```

21. Write an event procedure that allows the user to press a command button by pressing any key while the focus is on the command button.

22. Describe the KeyPress event in your own words.

In Exercises 23 through 26, write code starting with Sub Command1_Click () and Picture1.Cls statements, ending with an End Sub statement, and having one line for each step. Lines that display data should use the given variable names.

23. The following steps give the name and birth year of a famous inventor.

    (a) Declare all variables used in the steps below.
    (b) Assign "Thomas" to the variable *firstName*.
    (c) Assign "Alva" to the variable *middleName*.
    (d) Assign "Edison" to the variable *lastName*.
    (e) Assign 1847 to the variable *yearOfBirth*.
    (f) Display the inventor's full name followed by a comma and his year of birth.

24. The following steps compute the price of ketchup.

    (a) Declare all variables used in the steps below.
    (b) Assign "ketchup" to the variable *item*.
    (c) Assign 1.80 to the variable *regularPrice*.
    (d) Assign .27 to the variable *discount*.
    (e) Display the phrase "1.53 is the sale price of ketchup."

25. The following steps display a copyright statement.

    (a) Declare all variables used in the steps below.
    (b) Assign "Prentice-Hall, Inc" to the variable *publisher*.
    (c) Display the phrase "© Prentice-Hall, Inc."

26. The following steps give advice.

    (a) Declare all variables used in the steps below.
    (b) Assign "Fore" to the variable *prefix*.
    (c) Display the phrase "Forewarned is Forearmed."

In Exercises 27 through 32, the interface and initial properties are specified. Write the code to carry out the stated task.

27. After values are placed in the x and y text boxes, pressing Compute Sum places x + y in the sum picture box.

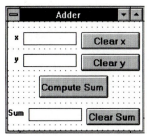

Object	Property	Setting
Form1	Caption	Adder
Label1	Caption	x
Text1	Text	(blank)
Command1	Caption	Clear x
Label2	Caption	y
Text2	Text	(blank)
Command2	Caption	Clear y
Command3	Caption	Compute Sum
Label3	Caption	Sum
Picture1		
Command4	Caption	Clear Sum

28. When Command1 is pressed, the temperature is converted from Fahrenheit to Celsius, the title bar changes to Celsius, Command1 is hidden, and Command2 becomes visible. If Command2 is now pressed, the temperature is converted from Celsius to Fahrenheit, the title bar reverts to Fahrenheit, Command2 is hidden, and Command1 becomes visible. Of course, the user can change the temperature in the text box at any time. (**Note:** The conversion formulas are C = (5/9)*(F – 32) and F = (9/5)*C + 32.)

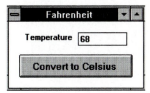

Object	Property	Setting
Form1	Caption	Fahrenheit
Label	Caption	Temperature
Text1	Text	0
Command1	Caption	Convert to Celsius
Command2	Caption	Convert to Fahrenheit
	Visible	False

29. If *n* is the number of seconds between lightning and thunder, the storm is *n*/5 miles away. Write a program that requests the number of seconds between lightning and thunder and reports the distance of the storm.

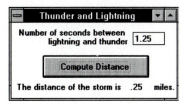

Object	Property	Setting
Form1	Caption	Thunder and Lightning
Label1	Caption	Number of seconds between lightning and thunder
Text1	Text	(blank)
Command1	Caption	Compute Distance
Label2	Caption	The distance of the storm is
Label3	Caption	(blank)
Label4	Caption	miles.

30. Write a program to request the name of a baseball team, the number of games won, and the number of games lost as input, and then display the percentage of games won.

Object	Property	Setting
Form1	Caption	Baseball
Label1	Caption	Team
Text1	Text	(blank)
Label2	Caption	Games Won
Text2	Text	(blank)
Label3	Caption	Games Lost
Text3	Text	(blank)
Command1	Caption	Compute Percentage
Picture1		

31. The number of calories burned per hour by bicycling, jogging, and swimming are 200, 475, and 275 respectively. A person loses one pound of weight for each 3500 calories burned. Write a program that allows the user to input the number of hours spent at each activity, and then calculates the number of pounds worked off.

Object	Property	Setting
Form1	Caption	Triathalon
Label1	Caption	Number of Hours Cycling
Text1	Text	(blank)
Label2	Caption	Number of Hours Running
Text2	Text	(blank)
Label3	Caption	Number of Hours Swimming
Text3	Text	(blank)
Command1	Caption	Compute Weight Loss
Picture1		

32. The American College of Sports Medicine recommends that you maintain your *training heart rate* during an aerobic workout. Your training heart rate is computed as $.7 * (220 - a) + .3 * r$ where a is your age and r is your resting heart rate (your pulse when you first awaken). Write a program to request a person's age and resting heart rate and then calculate the training heart rate. (Determine *your* training heart rate.)

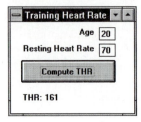

Object	Property	Setting
Form1	Caption	Training Heart Rate
Label1	Caption	Age
Text1	Text	(blank)
Label2	Caption	Resting Heart Rate
Text2	Text	(blank)
Command1	Caption	Compute THR
Label3	Caption	(blank)

In Exercises 33 through 37, write a program with a Windows-style interface to carry out the task. The program should use variables for each of the quantities and display the outcome with a complete explanation, as in Example 4.

33. If a company's annual revenue is $550,000 and its expenses are $410,000, what is its net income (revenue minus expenses)?

34. If the price of a 17-ounce can of corn is 68 cents, what is the price per ounce?

35. If a company earns $5.25 per share for the year and the price of one share of stock is $68.25, what is the company's price to earnings ratio (that is, price/earnings)?

36. If the radius of the earth is 6170 kilometers, what is the volume of the earth? **Note:** The volume of a sphere of radius r is $(4/3) * (3.14159) * r^3$.

37. How many pounds of grass seed are needed to seed a lawn 40 feet by 75 feet if 40 ounces are recommended for 2000 square feet? **Note:** There are 16 ounces in a pound.

38. A store manager needs three shelf signs. Write a program to produce the output shown below. The words "SALE! Everything on this shelf" and "% off!" should appear only once in the program.

SALE! Everything on this shelf 10% off!
SALE! Everything on this shelf 30% off!
SALE! Everything on this shelf 50% off!

39. Write a program that displays a command button and a label on the screen, with the label initially containing 0. Each time the command button is pressed the number in the label should increase by 1.

40. Allow the user to enter any number of positive numbers. As each number is entered, display the sum of the numbers and the number of numbers entered. The user should be able to start anew at any time.

41. Calculate the amount of a waiter's tip, given the amount of the bill and the percentage tip. (Test the program with $20 and 15%.)

SOLUTIONS TO PRACTICE PROBLEMS 3.4

1. In the second Picture1.Print statement, the item following the second quotation mark is a positive number, which is displayed with a leading space. Since the corresponding item in the first Picture1.Print statement is a string, which is *not* displayed with a leading space, a space had to be inserted before the quotation mark.

2. The user cannot enter data into a label from the keyboard. Therefore, if a control is to be used for output only, a label is preferred. **Note:** When using a label for output, you might want to set its BorderStyle property to "1-Fixed Single."

3. `Label3.Caption = Str$(Val(Text1.Text) + Val(Text2.Text))`

3.5 INPUT AND OUTPUT

So far we have relied on the Let statement to assign values to variables. Data can also be stored in files and accessed through Input# statements, or data can be supplied by the user in a text box or input box. The Print method, with a little help from commas and the Tab and Spc functions, can spread out and align the display of data in a picture box or on a printer. Message boxes grab the user's attention and display temporary messages.

Reading Data from Files

In Chapter 1 we saw how to create data files with the Windows' Notepad. (As a rule of thumb, and simply as a matter of style, we enclose each string in quotation marks.) A file can have either one item per line, or many items (separated by commas) can be listed on the same line. Usually, related items are grouped together on a line. For instance, if a file consisted of payroll information, each line would contain the name of a person, that person's hourly wage, and the number of hours that person worked during the week as shown in Figure 3.21.

```
"Mike Jones", 7.35, 35
"John Smith", 6.75, 33
```

Figure 3.21 Contents of PERSONEL.TXT

The items of data will be assigned to variables one at a time in the order they appear in the file. That is, "Mike Jones" will be the first value assigned to a variable. After all the items from the first line have been assigned to variables, subsequent requests for values will be read from the next line.

Data stored in a file can be read in order (that is, sequentially) and assigned to variables with the following steps.

1. Choose a number from 1 to 255 to be the **reference number** for the file.

2. Execute the statement

```
Open "filespec" For Input As #n
```

where *n* is the reference number. This procedure is referred to as **Opening a file for input**. It establishes a communications link between the computer and the disk drive for reading data *from* the disk. Data can then be input from the specified file and assigned to variables in the program.

3. Read items of data in order, one at a time, from the file with Input# statements. The statement

```
Input #n, var
```

causes the program to look in the file for the next available item of data and assign it to the variable *var*. In the file, individual items are separated by commas or line breaks. The variable in the Input# statement should be the same type (that is, string versus numeric) as the data to be assigned to it from the file.

4. After the desired items have been read from the file, close the file with the statement

```
Close #n
```

EXAMPLE 1   Write a program that uses a file for input and produces the same output as the code below. (The form design for all examples in this section consists of a command button and a picture box.)

```
Sub Command1_Click ()
  Dim houseNumber As Single, street As String
  Picture1.Cls
  Let houseNumber = 1600
  Let street = "Pennsylvania Ave."
  Picture1.Print "The White House is located at"; houseNumber; street
End Sub
```

[Run and then click the command button. The following is displayed in the picture box.]

```
The White House is located at 1600 Pennsylvania Ave.
```

SOLUTION   Use Windows' Notepad to create the file DATA.TXT containing the following two lines:

1600
"Pennsylvania Ave"

In the following code, the fifth line looks for the first item of data, 1600, and assigns it to the numeric variable *houseNumber*. (Visual Basic records that this piece of data has been used.) The sixth line looks for the next available item of data, "Pennsylvania Ave.", and assigns it to the string variable *street*.

```
Sub Command1_Click ()
  Dim houseNumber As Single, street As String
  Picture1.Cls
  Open "DATA.TXT" For Input As #1
  Input #1, houseNumber
  Input #1, street
  Picture1.Print "The White House is located at"; houseNumber; street
  Close #1
End Sub
```

A single Input# statement can assign values to several different variables. For instance, the two Input# statements in the solution of Example 1 can be replaced by the single statement

```
    Input #1, houseNumber, street
```

In general, a statement of the form

```
    Input #n, var1, var2, ..., varj
```

has the same effect as the sequence of statements

```
    Input #n, var1
    Input #n, var2
       .
       .
       .
    Input #n, varj
```

EXAMPLE 2 The following program uses the file PERSONEL.TXT in Figure 3.21 to compute weekly pay. Notice that the variables in the Input# statement are the same types (string, numeric, numeric) as the constants in each line of the file.

```
Sub Command1_Click ()
  Dim nom As String, wage As Single, hrs As Single
  Picture1.Cls
  Open "PERSONEL.TXT" For Input As #1
  Input #1, nom, wage, hrs
  Picture1.Print nom; hrs * wage
  Input #1, nom, wage, hrs
  Picture1.Print nom; hrs * wage
  Close #1
End Sub
```

[Run and then click the command button. The following will be displayed in the picture box.]

```
Mike Jones 257.25
John Smith 222.75
```

In certain situations, we must read the data in a file more than once. This is accomplished by closing the file and reopening it. After a file is closed and then reopened, subsequent Input# statements begin reading from the first entry of the file.

EXAMPLE 3 The following program takes the average annual amounts of money spent by college graduates for several categories and converts these amounts to percentages. The data are read once to compute the total amount of money spent and then read again to calculate the percentage for each category. The purpose of the fifth line is to initialize the numeric variable *total*, which keeps a running total of the amounts. **Note:** These figures were compiled for the year 1990 by the Bureau of Labor Statistics.

COSTS.TXT consists of the following four lines:

```
"Transportation", 7232
"Housing", 14079
"Food", 5649
"Other", 15833
```

```
Sub Command1_Click ()
  Dim total As Single, category As String, amount As Single
  Open "COSTS.TXT" For Input As #1
  Picture1.Cls
  Let total = 0
  Input #1, category, amount
  Let total = total + amount
  Input #1, category, amount
  Let total = total + amount
```

```
   Input #1, category, amount
   Let total = total + amount
   Input #1, category, amount
   Let total = total + amount
   Close #1
   Open "COSTS.TXT" For Input As #1
   Input #1, category, amount
   Picture1.Print category; amount / total
   Input #1, category, amount
   Picture1.Print category; amount / total
   Input #1, category, amount
   Picture1.Print category; amount / total
   Input #1, category, amount
   Picture1.Print category; amount / total
   Close #1
End Sub
```

[Run and then click the command button. The following is displayed in the picture box.]

```
Transportation .1689996
Housing .3290024
Food .1320076
Other .3699904
```

Input from an Input Box

Normally a text box is used to obtain input described by a label. Sometimes we want just one piece of input and would rather not have a text box and label stay on the screen forever. The problem can be solved with an **input box**. When a statement of the form

```
   Let stringVar = InputBox$(message)
```

is executed, an input box similar to the one shown in Figure 3.22 pops up on the screen. After the user types a response into the rectangle at the bottom of the screen and presses Enter (or clicks OK), the response is assigned to the string variable. The message to be displayed can consist of any string.

Figure 3.22 Sample input box.

EXAMPLE 4   Rewrite the solution to Example 1 with the file name provided by the user in an input box.

```
Sub Command1_Click ()
  Dim fileName As String, message As String
  Dim houseNumber As Single, street As String
  Picture1.Cls
  Let message = "Enter the name of the file containing the information."
  Let fileName = InputBox$(message)
  Open fileName For Input As #1
  Input #1, houseNumber
  Input #1, street
  Picture1.Print "The White House is located at"; houseNumber; street
  Close #1
End Sub
```

[Run and then click the command button. The input box of Figure 3.22 appears on the screen. Type DATA.TXT into the input box and click on OK. The input box disappears and the following appears in the picture box.]

```
The White House is located at 1600 Pennsylvania Ave.
```

The response typed into an input box is treated as a single string value, no matter what is typed. (Quotation marks are not needed, and if included, are considered as part of the string.) Numeric data typed into an input box should be converted to a number with Val before it can be assigned to a numeric variable or used in a calculation.

Formatting Output with Print Zones

Each line in a picture box can be thought of as being subdivided into zones as shown in Figure 3.23. Each zone contains 14 positions, where the width of a position is the average width of the characters in the font.

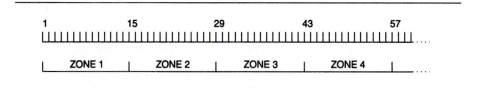

Figure 3.23 Print zones.

We have seen that when the Print method is followed by several items separated by semicolons, the items are displayed one after another. When commas are used instead of semicolons, the items are displayed in consecutive zones. For instance, if the FontName property of Picture1 is set to Courier, when the motto of the state of Alaska is displayed with the statements

```
Picture1.Print "North", "to", "the", "future."
Picture1.Print "12345678901234567890123456789012345678901234567890"
```

the resulting picture box is

```
North          to          the          future.
12345678901234567890123456789012345678901234567890
```

where each word is in a separate print zone. This same output can be achieved with the code

```
Dim a As String, b As String, c As String, d As String
Let a = "North"
Let b = "to"
Let c = "the"
Let d = "future."
Picture1.Print a, b, c, d
Picture1.Print "12345678901234567890123456789012345678901234567890"
```

EXAMPLE 5   The following program uses Print zones to organize expenses for public and private schools into columns. The data represent the average expenses for 1991–92. (The FontName for Picture1 is the default font MS Sans Serif.)

```
Sub Command1_Click ()
  Picture1.Cls
  Picture1.Print " ", "Pb 2-yr", "Pr 2-yr", "Pb 4-yr", "Pr 4-yr"
  Picture1.Print
  Picture1.Print "Tuit & Fees", 1022, 5290, 2137, 10017
  Picture1.Print "Bks & Suppl", 480, 476, 485, 508
  Picture1.Print "Board", 1543, 1529, 1468, 1634
  Picture1.Print "Other Exp", 966, 925, 1153, 1029
  Picture1.Print "Trans", 902, 786, 793, 795
  Picture1.Print " ", "----------", "----------", "----------", "----------"
  Picture1.Print "Total", 4913, 9006, 6036, 13983
End Sub
```

[Run and then click the command button. The resulting picture box is shown below.]

	Pb 2-yr	Pr 2-yr	Pb 4-yr	Pr 4-yr
Tuit & Fees	1022	5290	2137	10017
Bks & Suppl	480	476	485	508
Board	1543	1529	1468	1634
Other Exp	966	925	1153	1029
Trans	902	786	793	795
	----------	----------	----------	----------
Total	4913	9006	6036	13983

Tab Function

If an item appearing in a Print statement is preceded by

```
Tab(n);
```

where n is a positive integer, that item will be displayed (if possible) beginning at the nth position of the line. (Exceptions are discussed in Comment 8.)

EXAMPLE 6   The following program uses the Tab function to organize data into columns. The data represent the number of bachelor's degrees conferred (in units of 1000). (*Source:* National Center of Educational Statistics. Data for 1990-91 are projections.)

```
Sub Command1_Click ()
  Picture1.Cls
  Picture1.Print Tab(10); "1970-71"; Tab(20); "1980-81"; Tab(30); "1990-91"
  Picture1.Print
  Picture1.Print "Male"; Tab(10); 476; Tab(20); 470; Tab(30); 490
  Picture1.Print "Female"; Tab(10); 364; Tab(20); 465; Tab(30); 560
  Picture1.Print "Total"; Tab(10); 840; Tab(20); 935; Tab(30); 1050
End Sub
```

[Run and then click the command button. The resulting picture box is shown below.]

	1970-71	1980-81	1990-91
Male	476	470	490
Female	364	465	560
Total	840	935	1050

Spc Function

A statement of the form

```
Picture1.Print item1; Spc(n); item2
```

inserts *n* spaces between the two items. The width of each space is the average width of the characters in the font. For example, the statement

```
Picture1.Print "North"; Spc(5); "to"; Spc(10); "the"; Spc(5); "future."
```

results in the output

```
North        to          the      future.
```

Using a Message Box for Output

Sometimes you want to grab the user's attention with a brief message such as "Correct" or "Nice try, but no cigar." You want this message only to appear on the screen until the user has read it. This mission is easily accomplished with a **message box** such as the one shown in Figure 3.24. When a statement of the form

```
MsgBox message, , ""
```

is executed, where *message* is a string, a message box with *message* displayed appears and stays on the screen until the user presses Enter or clicks OK. For instance, the statement MsgBox "Nice try, but no cigar.", , "" produces Figure 3.24. The double quotations in the statement clear the title bar. If you replace it with a string, that string will appear in the title bar.

Figure 3.24 Sample message box.

Output to the Printer

You print text on a sheet of paper in the printer in much the same way you display text in a picture box. Visual Basic treats the printer as an object named Printer. If *expr* is a string or numeric expression, then the statement

```
Printer.Print expr
```

sends *expr* to the printer in exactly the same way Picture1.Print sends output to a picture box. You can use semicolons, commas for print zones, Tab and Spc.

Font properties can be set with statements like

```
Let Printer.FontName = "Script"
Let Printer.FontBold = True
Let Printer.FontSize = 12
```

Another useful printer command is

```
Printer.NewPage
```

which starts a new page.

The Windows' Print Manager usually waits until an entire page has been completed before starting to print. To avoid losing information, execute the statement

```
Printer.EndDoc
```

when you are finished printing.

The statement

```
PrintForm
```

performs a screen dump, that is, prints the content of the screen.

Rem Statement

Now that we have the capability to write more complicated programs, we must concern ourselves with program documentation. **Program documentation** is the inclusion of comments that specify the intent of the program, the purpose of the variables, the nature of the data in the files, and the tasks performed by individual portions of the program. If *text* is any information whatsoever, then the statement

```
Rem text
```

is completely ignored when the program is executed. Program documentation appears whenever the program is displayed or printed. Also, a line can be documented by adding 'text

to the end of the line.

EXAMPLE 7   Document the program in Example 2.

SOLUTION   In the following program, the first Rem statement describes the entire program, the three apostrophes precede the meanings of the variables, and the second Rem statement tells the nature of the items in each line of the file.

```
Sub Command1_Click ()
  Rem Compute weekly pay
  Dim nom As String      'Employee name
  Dim wage As Single     'Hourly pay
  Dim hrs As Single       'Number of hours worked during week
  Picture1.Cls
  Open "PERSONEL.TXT" For Input As #1
  Rem person's name, person's wage, person's hours worked
  Input #1, nom, wage, hrs
  Picture1.Print nom; hrs * wage
  Input #1, nom, wage, hrs
  Picture1.Print nom; hrs * wage
  Close #1
End Sub
```

Some of the benefits of documentation are as follows:

1. Other people can easily comprehend the program.

2. The program can be understood when read later.

3. Long programs are easier to read since the purposes of individual pieces can be determined at a glance.

Comments:

1. The text box and input box provide a whole new dimension to the capabilities of a program. The user, rather than the programmer, can provide the data to be processed.

2. A string used in a file does not have to be enclosed by quotation marks. The only exceptions are strings containing commas or leading and trailing spaces.

3. If an Input# statement looks for a string and finds a number, it will treat the number as a string. Suppose the first two entries in the file DATA.TXT are the numbers 2 and 3.

```
Sub Command1_Click ()
  Dim a As String, b As String
  Picture1.Cls
  Open "DATA.TXT" For Input As #1
  Input #1, a, b
  Picture1.Print a + b
  Close #1
End Sub
```

[Run and then click the command button. The following is displayed in the picture box.]

```
23
```

4. If an Input# statement looks for a number and finds a string, the Input# statement will assign the value 0 to the numeric variable. For instance, suppose the first two entries in the file DATA.TXT are "ten" and 10. Then after the statement

```
Input #1, num1, num2
```

is executed, where *num1* and *num2* are numeric variables, the values of these variables will be 0 and 10.

5. If all the data in a file have been read by Input# statements and another item is requested by an Input# statement, a box will appear displaying the message "Input past end of file."

6. Numeric data in a text box, input box, or file must be a constant. It *cannot* be a variable or an expression. For instance, num, 1 / 2, and 2 + 3 are not acceptable.

7. To skip a Print zone, just include two consecutive commas.

8. The Tab function cannot be used to move the cursor to the left. If the position specified in a Tab function is to the left of the current cursor position, the cursor will move to that position on the next line. For instance, the line

```
Picture1.Print "hello"; Tab(3); "good-bye"
```

results in the output

```
hello
  good-bye
```

9. Rem statements that apply to an entire program, rather than a single-event procedure can be placed in the (declarations) section of (general).

10. The statement Close, without any reference number, closes all open files.

11. Windows allows you to alternate between Visual Basic and Notepad without exiting either application. To invoke Notepad without exiting Visual Basic, go into Program Manager by holding down the Alt key, repeatedly pressing the Tab key until the words "Program Manager" appear, and releasing the Alt key. Then double-click on the Notepad icon in the Accessories window. Now that both Visual Basic and Notepad have been invoked, you can go from one application to the other by holding down the Alt key and repeatedly pressing the Tab key until the name of the other application appears. When the Alt key is released, the named application becomes active.

PRACTICE PROBLEMS 3.5

1. What is the difference in the outcomes of the following sets of lines of code?

```
Input #1, num1, num2
Picture1.Print num1 + num2


Input #1, num1
Input #1, num2
Picture1.Print num1 + num2
```

2. What is the difference in the outcomes of the following sets of lines of code?

```
Let strVar = InputBox$("How old are you?")
Let numVar = Val(strVar)
Picture1.Print numVar

Let numVar = Val(InputBox$("How old are you?"))
Picture1.Print numVar
```

EXERCISES 3.5

In Exercises 1 through 14, assume that the file DATA.TXT (shown to the right of the code) has been opened for input with reference number 1. Determine the output displayed in the picture box by the lines of code.

1.
```
Dim num As Single
Input #1, num
Picture1.Print num * num
```
DATA.TXT
4

2.
```
Dim word As String
Input #1, word
Picture1.Print "un" + word
```
DATA.TXT
"speakable"

3.
```
Dim str1 As String, str2 As String
Input #1, str1, str2
Picture1.Print str1; str2
```
DATA.TXT
"base"
"ball"

4.
```
Dim num1 As Single, num2 As Single
Dim num3 As Single
Input #1, num1, num2, num3
Picture1.Print (num1 + num2) * num3
```
DATA.TXT
3
4
5

5.
```
Dim yrOfBirth As Single, curYr As Single
Input #1, yrOfBirth
Input #1, curYr       'Current year
Picture1.Print "Age:"; curYr - yrOfBirth
```
DATA.TXT
1976
1996

6.
```
Dim str1 As String, str2 As String
Input #1, str1
Input #1, str2
Picture1.Print str1 + str2
```
DATA.TXT
"A, my name is "
"Alice"

7.
```
Dim word1 As String, word2 As String
Input #1, word1
Input #1, word2
Picture1.Print word1 + word2
```
DATA.TXT
"set", "up"

8.
```
Dim num As Single, sum As Single
Let sum = 0
Input #1, num
Let sum = sum + num
Input #1, num
Let sum = sum + num
Picture1.Print "Sum:"; sum
```
DATA.TXT
123, 321

9.
```
Dim building As String
Dim numRooms As Single
Input #1, building, numRooms
Picture1.Print "The "; building;
Picture1.Print " has" numRooms; "rooms."
```
DATA.TXT
"White House", 132

10.
```
Dim nom As String        'Name of student
Dim grade1 As Single     'Grade on 1st exam
Dim grade2 As Single     'Grade on 2nd exam
Dim average As Single    'Ave of grades
Input #1, nom, grade1, grade2
Let average = (grade1 + grade2) / 2
Picture1.Print nom; " ======> "; average
Input #1, nom, grade1, grade2
Let average = (grade1 + grade2) / 2
Picture1.Print nom; " ======> "; average
```
DATA.TXT
"Al Adams", 72, 88
"Betty Brown", 76, 82

11.
```
Dim num1 As Single, num2 As Single
Dim str1 As String, str2 As String
Input #1, num1, str1
Input #1, str2, num2
Picture1.Print num1; str1; str2; num2
Close #1
Open "DATA.TXT" For Input As #1
Picture1.Print num2
Input #1, num2
Picture1.Print num2
```
DATA.TXT
1, "One", "Two", 2

12.
```
Dim num As Integer, str As String
Input #1, num, str
Picture1.Print num; str
Close #1
Open "DATA.TXT" For Input As #1
Input #1, num, str
Picture1.Print num, str
```
DATA.TXT
4, "calling birds"
3, "French hens"

13.
```
Dim college As String
Dim yrFounded As Single
Dim yrStr As String, yr As Single
Input #1, college, yrFounded
Let yrStr = InputBox$("What is the current year?")
Let yr = Val(yrStr)
Picture1.Print college; " is";
Picture1.Print yr - yrFounded; "years old."
```
DATA.TXT
"Harvard University", 1636

(Assume that the response is *1996.*)

14.
```
Dim hourlyWage As Single, nom As String
Dim hoursWorked As Single, message As String
Input #1, hourlyWage, nom
Let message = "Hours worked by " + nom + ":"
Let hoursWorked = Val(InputBox$(message))
Picture1.Print "Pay for "; nom; " is";
Picture1.Print hoursWorked * hourlyWage
```
DATA.TXT
7.50, "Joe Smith"

(Assume that the response is *10.*)

In Exercises 15 through 28, determine the output displayed in the picture box by the following lines of code.

15.
```
Dim bet As Single      'Amount bet at roulette
Let bet = Val(InputBox$("How much do you want to bet?"))
Picture1.Print "You might win"; 36 * bet; "dollars."
```

(Assume that the response is 5.)

16.
```
Dim word As String
Let word = InputBox$("Word to negate:")
Picture1.Print "un"; word
```

(Assume that the response is *tied.*)

17.
```
Dim lastName As String, message As String, firstName As String
Let lastName = "Jones"
Let message = "What is your first name Mr. " + lastName
Let firstName = InputBox$(message)
Picture1.Print "Hello "; firstName; " "; lastName
```

(Assume that the response is *John.*)

18.
```
Dim rate As Single  'Current interest rate
Let rate = Val(InputBox$("Current interest rate?"))
Picture1.Print "At the current interest rate, ";
Picture1.Print "your money will double in";
Picture1.Print 72 / rate; "years."
```

(Assume that the response is 6.)

19.
```
Picture1.Print 1; "one", "won"
```

20.
```
Picture1.Print 1, 2; 3
```

21.
```
Picture1.Print "one",
Picture1.Print "two"
```

22.
```
Picture1.Print "one", , "two"
```

23.
```
Let Picture1.FontName = "Courier"     'Fixed-width font
Picture1.Print "1234567890"
Picture1.Print Tab(4); 5
```

24.
```
Let Picture1.FontName = "Courier""     'Fixed-width font
Picture1.Print "1234567890"
Picture1.Print "Hello"; Tab(3); "Good-bye"
```

25.
```
Let Picture1.FontName = "Courier"
Picture1.Print "1234567890"
Picture1.Print "one", Tab(12); "two"
```

26.
```
Let Picture1.FontName = "Courier"
Picture1.Print "1234567890"
Picture1.Print Tab(3); "one"
Picture1.Print Spc(3); "two"
```

27.
```
Let Picture1.FontName = "Courier"
Picture1.Print "1234567890"
Picture1.Print Spc(2); "one"; Tab(8); "two"
```

28.
```
Let Picture1.FontName = "Courier"
    Picture1.Print "1234567890"
    Picture1.Print Spc(1); "1"; Spc(2); "2"
    Picture1.Print 1; 2
```

In Exercises 29 through 40, assume that the file DATA.TXT (shown to the right of the code) has been opened for input with reference number 1. Identify the errors.

29.
```
Dim str1 As String, str2 As String
    Input #1, str1, str2
    Picture1.Print "Hello "; str1
```

DATA.TXT
John Smith

30.
```
Dim num As Single
    Input #1, num
    Picture1.Print 3 * num
```

DATA.TXT
1 + 2

31.
```
Rem  Each line of DATA.TXT contains
    Rem  building, height, # of stories
    Dim building As String
    Dim ht As Single
    Input #1, building, ht
    Picture1.Print building, ht
    Input #1, building, ht
    Picture1.Print building, ht
```

DATA.TXT
"World Trade Center", 1350, 110
"Sears Tower", 1454, 110

32.
```
Dim num As Single
    Let num = InputBox$("Pick a number from 1 to 10.")
    Picture1.Print "Your number is; num
```

33.
```
Dim statePop As Single
    Let statePop = Val(InputBox$("State Population?"))
    Printer1.Print "The population should grow to";
    Picture1.Print 1.01 * statePop; "by next year."
```

(Assume that the response is 8,900,000)

34. `Let info = InputBox$()`

35. `Let Printer.Font = Courier`

36. `Let Text1.Text = "one", "two"`

37. `Let Label2.Caption = 1, 2`

38. `Printer.Print "Hello"; Tab(200); "Good-bye"`

39. `Let Form.Caption = "one"; Spc(5); "two"`

40.
```
Dim rem As Single  'Number to remember
    Input #1, rem
    Picture1.Print "Don't forget to ";
    Picture1.Print "remember the number"; rem
```

DATA.TXT
4

41. Fill in the table with the value of each variable after each line is executed. Assume the file DATA.TXT consists of the two lines

"phone", 35.25
"postage", 14.75

Event Procedure	category	amount	total
Sub Command1_Click ()			
Dim category As String			
Dim amount As Single			
Dim total As Single			
Open "DATA.TXT" For Input As #1			
Input #1, category, amount			
Let total = total + amount			
Input #1, category, amount			
Let total = total + amount			
Picture1.Print total			
Close #1			
End Sub			

42. Fill in the table with the value of each variable after each line is executed. Assume the file DATA.TXT consists of the single line

2, 3, 5

Event Procedure	a	b	c
Sub Command1_Click ()			
Dim num1 As Single, num2 As Single			
Dim num3 As Single			
Open "DATA.TXT" For Input As #1			
Input #1, num1, num2, num3			
Let num1 = num2 + num3			
Close #1			
Open "DATA.TXT" For Input As #2			
Input #2, num1, num3			
Let num3 = num3 + 1			
Close #2			
End Sub			

In Exercises 43 through 46, write code starting with Sub Command1_Click () and Picture1.Cls statements, ending with an End Sub statement, and having one line for each step. Lines that display data should use the given variable names.

43. The following steps display the increase in the enrollment in selected courses taken by high school graduates. Assume the file DATA.TXT consists of the two lines

   "Algebra I", 65.1, 77.2
   "Geometry", 45.7, 61.0

   (a) Declare all variables used in the steps below.
   (b) Use an Input# statement to assign values to the variables *course*, *percent1982*, and *percent1987*.
   (c) Display a sentence giving the percentage change in enrollment from 1982 to 1987.
   (d) Repeat steps (b) and (c).

44. The following steps display information about Americans' eating habits. Assume the file DATA.TXT consists of the single line

   "soft drinks", "million gallons", 23

   (a) Declare all variables used in the steps below.
   (b) Open the file DATA.TXT for input.
   (c) Use an Input# statement to assign values to the variables *food*, *units*, and *quantityPerDay*.
   (d) Display a sentence giving the quantity of a food item consumed by Americans in one day.

45. The following steps calculate the percent increase in a typical grocery basket of goods.

   (a) Declare all variables used in the steps below.
   (b) Assign 200 to the variable *begOfYearPrice*.
   (c) Request the price at the end of the year with an input box and assign it to the variable *endOfYearPrice*.
   (d) Assign 100 * (*endOfYearPrice* − *begOfYearPrice*) / *begOfYearPrice* to the variable *percentIncrease*.
   (e) Display a sentence giving the percent increase for the year.

   (Test the program with a $215 end-of-year price.)

46. The following steps calculate the amount of money earned in a walk-a-thon.

   (a) Declare all variables used in the steps below.
   (b) Request the amount pledged per mile from an input box and assign it to the variable *pledge*.
   (c) Request the number of miles walked from an input box and assign it to the variable *miles*.
   (d) Display a sentence giving the amount to be paid.

   (Test the program with a pledge of $2.00 and a 15-mile walk.)

In Exercises 47 and 48, write a line of code to carry out the task.

47. Pop up a message box stating "The future isn't what it used to be."

48. Pop up a message box with "Taking Risks Proverb" in the title bar and the message "You can't steal second base and keep one foot on first."

49. Table 3.4 summarizes the month's activity of three checking accounts. Write a program that displays the account number and the end-of-month balance for each account, and then displays the total amount of money in the three accounts. Assume the data is stored in a data file.

Account Number	Beginning of Month Balance	Deposits	Withdrawals
AB4057	1234.56	345.67	100.00
XY4321	789.00	120.00	350.00
GH2222	321.45	143.65	0.00

Table 3.4 Checking account activity.

50. Table 3.5 contains a list of colleges with their student enrollments and faculty sizes. Write a program to display the names of the colleges and their student/faculty ratios, and the ratio for the total collection of students and faculty. Assume the data for the colleges is stored in a data file.

	Enrollment	Faculty
Ohio State	54313	3900
Univ. of MD, College Park	34623	2631
Princeton	6412	890

Table 3.5 Colleges.
Source: World Almanac, 1993.

51. Write a program to compute semester averages. Each line in a data file should contain a student's social security number and the grades for three hourly exams and the final exam. (The final exam counts as two hourly exams.) The program should display each student's social security number and semester average, and then the class average. Use the data in Table 3.6.

Soc. Sec. No.	Exam 1	Exam 2	Exam 3	Final Exam
123-45-6789	67	85	90	88
111-11-1111	93	76	82	80
123-32-1234	85	82	89	84

Table 3.6 Student grades.

52. Table 3.7 gives the 1991 populations of three New England states. Write a program that calculates the average population and then displays the name of each state and the difference between its population and the average population. The states and their populations should be stored in a data file.

Maine	1235
Massachusetts	5996
Connecticut	3291

Table 3.7 1991 Population (in thousands) of three New England states.

53. Write a program to produce Table 3.8. (The amounts are given in millions of dollars.) For each person, the name, sport, salary or winnings, and other income should be contained in a data file. The totals should be computed by the program.

Athlete	Sport	Salary or winnings	Other income	Total
M. Jordan	basketball	2.1	6	8.1
A. Agassi	tennis	1	4.5	5.5
J. Montana	football	1.4	3	4.4

Table 3.8 Estimated 1990 earnings of athletes.

54. Write a program to calculate the amount of a waiter's tip given the amount of the bill and the percentage tip. The output should be a complete sentence that reiterates the inputs and gives the resulting tip. For example, if $20 and 15% are the inputs, then the output might read "A 15% tip on 20 dollars is 3 dollars."

55. Design a form with two text boxes labeled "Name" and "Phone number." Then write an event procedure that shows a message box stating "Be sure to include the area code!" when the second text box receives the focus.

In Exercises 56 and 57, write lines of code corresponding to the given flowchart. Assume that the data needed are contained in a file.

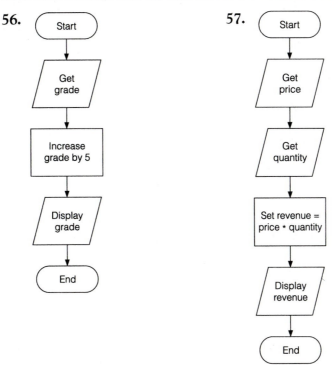

56.

Start → Get grade → Increase grade by 5 → Display grade → End

57.

Start → Get price → Get quantity → Set revenue = price * quantity → Display revenue → End

SOLUTIONS TO PRACTICE PROBLEMS 3.5

1. The outputs are identical. In this text we tend to use a single Input# statement for each line of the file.

2. The outputs are identical. In this text we use the second style.

3.6 BUILT-IN FUNCTIONS

Visual Basic has a number of built-in functions that greatly extend its capability. These functions perform such varied tasks as taking the square root of a number, counting the number of characters in a string, and capitalizing letters. Functions associate with one or more values, called the *input*, a single value called the *output*. The function is said to **return** the output value. The two functions considered below have numeric input and output.

Numeric Functions: Sqr, Int

The function Sqr calculates the square root of a number. The function Int finds the greatest integer less than or equal to a number. Therefore, Int discards the decimal part of positive numbers. Some examples follow:

```
Sqr(9) is 3.              Int(2.7) is 2.
Sqr(0) is 0.              Int(3) is 3.
Sqr(2) is 1.414214.       Int(-2.7) is -3.
```

The terms inside the parentheses can be either numbers (as above), numeric variables, or numeric expressions. Expressions are first evaluated to produce the input.

EXAMPLE 1   The following program evaluates each of the functions for a specific input given by the value of the variable *n*.

```
Sub Command1_Click ()
  Dim n As Single
  Rem Evaluate functions at a variable
  Picture1.Cls
  Let n = 6.25
  Picture1.Print Sqr(n); Int(n)
End Sub
```

[Run and then click the command button. The following is displayed in the picture box.]

```
2.5  6
```

EXAMPLE 2   The following program evaluates each of the functions above at an expression.

```
Sub Command1_Click ()
  Dim a As Single, b As Single
  Rem Evaluate functions at expressions
  Picture1.Cls
  Let a = 2
  Let b = 3
  Picture1.Print Sqr(5 * b + 1); Int(a ^ b)
End Sub
```

[Run and then click the command button. The following is displayed in the picture box.]

    4 8

EXAMPLE 3   The following program shows an application of the Sqr function.

```
Sub Command1_Click ()
  Dim leg1 As Single, leg2 As Single, hyp As Single
  Rem  Find the length of the hypotenuse of a right triangle
  Picture1.Cls
  Let leg1 = Val(Text1.Text)
  Let leg2 = Val(Text2.Text)
  Let hyp = Sqr(leg1 ^ 2 + leg2 ^ 2)
  Picture1.Print "The length of the hypotenuse is"; hyp
End Sub
```

[Run, type 3 and 4 into the text boxes, then click the command button.]

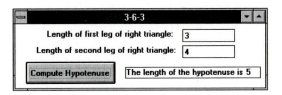

EXAMPLE 4   The following program rounds a positive number to the nearest integer.

```
Sub Command1_Click ()
  Dim n As Single, r As Single
  Rem Round positive number to nearest integer
  Picture1.Cls
  Let n = Val(Text1.Text)
  Let r = Int(n + .5)
  Picture1.Print "The rounded value of"; n; "is"; r
End Sub
```

[Run, type 3.6 into the text box, and then click the command button.]

[Run, type 2.4 into the text box, and then click the command button.]

The idea in Example 4 can be extended to round a number to two decimal places, an essential task for financial applications. Just replace the sixth line by

```
Let r = Int(100 * n + .5) / 100
```

Then, substitute some different values for *n* and carry out the computation to check that the formula works.

EXAMPLE 5   The following program shows how Int is used to carry out long division. When the integer *m* is divided into the integer *n* with long division, the result is a quotient and a remainder. (See Figure 3.25.)

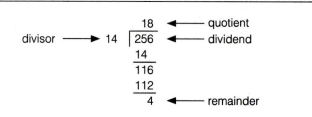

Figure 3.25 Long division.

```
Sub Command1_Click ()
  Dim divisor As Single, dividend As Single
  Dim quotient As Single, remainder As Single
  Rem Long division
  Picture1.Cls
  Let divisor = Val(Text1.Text)
  Let Dividend = Val(Text2.Text)
  Let quotient = Int(dividend / divisor)
  Let remainder = dividend - Int(dividend / divisor) * divisor
  Picture1.Print "The quotient is"; quotient
  Picture1.Print "The remainder is"; remainder
End Sub
```

[Run, type 14 and 256 into the text boxes, and then click the command button.]

String Functions: Left$, Mid$, Right$, UCase$, Trim$

The functions Left$, Mid$, and Right$ are used to extract characters from the left end, middle, and right end of a string. Suppose *str* is a string and *m* and *n* are positive integers. Then Left$(*str, n*) is the string consisting of the first *n* characters of *str* and Right$(*str, n*) is the string consisting of the last *n* characters of *str*. Mid$(*str, m, n*) is the string consisting of *n* characters of *str*, beginning with the *m*th character. UCase$(*str*) is the string *str* with all of its lowercase letters capitalized. Trim$(*str*) is the string *str* with all leading and trailing spaces removed. Some examples are as follows:

```
Left$("fanatic", 3) is "fan".        Right$("fanatic", 3) is "tic".
Left$("12/15/93", 2) is "12".        Right$("12/15/93", 2) is "93".
Mid$("fanatic", 5, 1) is "t".        Mid$("12/15/93", 4, 2) is "15".
UCase$("Disk") is "DISK".            UCase$("12three") is "12THREE".
Trim$("  1  2  ") is "1  2".         Trim$("-12 ") is "-12".
```

The strings produced by Left$, Mid$, and Right$ are referred to as **substrings** of the strings from which they were formed. For instance, "fan" and "t" are substrings of "fanatic". The substring "fan" is said to begin at position 1 of "fanatic" and the substring "t" is said to begin at position 5.

Like the numeric functions discussed above, Left$, Mid$, Right$, UCase$, and Trim$ also can be evaluated for variables and expressions.

EXAMPLE 6 The following program evaluates the functions above for variables and expressions. Note that spaces are counted as characters.

```
Sub Command1_Click ()
  Dim str1 As String, str2 As String
  Rem Evaluate functions at variables and expressions.
  Picture1.Cls
  Let str1 = "Quick as "
  Let str2 = "a wink"
  Picture1.Print Left$(str1, 7)
  Picture1.Print Mid$(str1 + str2, 7, 6)
  Picture1.Print UCase$(str1 + str2)
  Picture1.Print "The average "; Right$(str2, 4); " lasts .1 second."
  Picture1.Print Trim$(str1); str2
End Sub
```

[Run and then click the command button. The following is displayed in the picture box.]

```
Quick a
as a w
QUICK AS A WINK
The average wink lasts .1 second.
Quick asa wink
```

String-Related Numeric Functions: Len, Instr

The functions Len and Instr operate on strings, but produce numbers. The function Len gives the number of characters in a string. The function Instr searches for the first occurrence of one string in another and gives the position at which the string is found. Suppose *str1* and *str2* are strings. The value of Len(*str1*) is the number of characters in *str1*. The value of Instr(*str1*, *str2*) is 0 if *str2* is not a substring of *str1*. Otherwise, its value is the first position of *str2* in *str1*. Some examples of Len and Instr follow:

```
Len("Shenandoah") is 10.          Instr("Shenandoah", "nand") is 4.
Len("Just a moment") is 13.       Instr("Just a moment", " ") is 5.
Len(" ") is 1.                    Instr("Croissant", "ist") is 0.
```

EXAMPLE 7 The following program evaluates functions at variables and expressions. The ninth line locates the position of the space separating the two names. The first name will end one position to the left of this position and the last name will consist of all but the first n characters of the full name.

```
Sub Command1_Click ()
    Dim nom As String      'Name
    Dim n As Integer       'Location of space
    Dim first As String    'First name
    Dim last As String     'Last name
    Rem Evaluate functions at variables and expressions.
    Picture1.Cls
    Let nom = Text1.Text
    Let n = Instr(nom, " ")
    Let first = Left$(nom, n - 1)
    Let last = Right$(nom, Len(nom) - n)
    Picture1.Print "Your first name is "; first
    Picture1.Print "Your last name has"; Len(last); "letters."
End Sub
```

[Run, type John Doe into the text box, and then click the command button.]

Format$ Function

The Visual Basic function Format$ is used to display numbers and dates in familiar forms and to right-justify numbers. We will look at just a few variations of this versatile function. (See the discussion of Format$ in Appendix C for more nuances.)

Here are some examples of how numbers are converted to convenient strings with Format$.

Function	String Value
Format$(12345.628, "Standard")	12,345.62
Format$(12345.628, "Currency")	$12,345.62
Format$(12345.628, "#,0")	12,346
Format$(12345.628, "Percent")	1234562.80%
Format$(12345.628, "Scientific")	1.23E+04

The strings "Currency", "Standard", "#,0", "Percent", and "Scientific" are referred to as format strings. If *num* is a number, a numeric expression, or the string representation of a number, and *fmt* is a format string, then

    Format$(*num*, *fmt*)

is a string consisting of a formatted version of the number.

The format strings "Standard" and "Currency" convert numbers to string representations having two decimal places and commas every three digits to the left of the decimal point. Numbers less than 1 in magnitude have a zero to the left of the decimal point. "Currency" attaches a leading dollar sign and encloses negative numbers in parentheses. Accountants normally use parentheses to denote negative numbers.

Function	String Value
Format$(1 / 4, "Standard")	0.25
Format$(2 + 3.759, "Currency")	$5.76
Format$(-1234, "Standard")	-1,234.00
Format$(-1234, "Currency")	($1,234.00)
Format$(".2", "Currency")	$0.20

The format string "#,0" rounds numbers to whole numbers and places commas every three digits to the left of the decimal point. The format strings "Percent" and "Scientific" convert numbers to string representations consisting of percentages and scientific notation, respectively. Both forms include two decimal places. The scientific notations consist of a number between 1 and 9.99 followed by an exponent and possibly preceded by a minus sign.

Function	String Value
Format$(-3.6, "#,0")	-4
Format$(.06265, "Percent")	6.27%
Format$(1 / 8, "Percent")	12.50%
Format$(-600.228, "Scientific")	-6.00E+02
Format$(1 / 8, "Scientific")	1.25E-01

If *dateString* represents a date in a form such as 7/4/96 and *fmt* is a format string, then

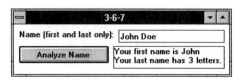

    Format$(*dateString*, *fmt*)

is a string consisting of a formatted version of the date. Two useful format strings are "Long Date" and "Medium Date", which produce the results implied by their names.

Function	String Value
Format$("7/4/96", "Long Date")	Thursday, July 4, 1996
Format$("7/4/96", "Medium Date")	04-Jul-96

Format$ can be used with fixed-width fonts, such as Courier or Terminal, to display columns of numbers so that the decimal points are lined up. If *num* is a number, a numeric expression, or a string representation of a number, and *fmt* is a string of *n* "at" symbols then

Format$(*num*, *fmt*)

is a string of *n* characters with the number right-justified in a field of *n* spaces. Actually, if *num* is any string, such as a string produced by a Format$ function, then the value of Format$(num, fmt) contains the string right-justified in a field of *n* spaces. In the following table, each string value has length 10. For instance, in the second example, the string value consists of seven spaces followed by the string "123".

Function	String Value
Format$(1234567890, "@@@@@@@@@@")	1234567890
Format$(123, "@@@@@@@@@@")	123
Format$("1234.56", "@@@@@@@@@@")	1234.56
Format$("$1,234.56", "@@@@@@@@@@")	$1,234.56

EXAMPLE 8   The following program produces the first two columns of the table in Example 5 of the previous section. However, Format$ is used to right justify the expense categories and to align the numbers.

Object	Property	Setting
Form1	Caption	Public 2-year College Expenses
Command1	Caption	Display Expenses
Picture1	FontName	Courier

```
Sub Command1_Click ()
  Dim fmt1 As String, fmt2 As String, fmt3 As String
  Dim col1 As String, col2 As String
  Rem Average expenses of commuter students (1991-92)
  Picture1.Cls
  Picture1.Print Tab(19); "Pb 2-yr"
  Picture1.Print
  Let fmt1 = "@@@@@@@@@@@@@@@@@"
  Let fmt2 = "#,0"
  Let fmt3 = "@@@@@@"
  Let col1 = Format$("Tuition & Fees", fmt1)
  Let col2 = Format$(1022, fmt2)
  Let col2 = Format$(col2, fmt3)
  Picture1.Print col1; Tab(19); col2
  Let col1 = Format$("Books & Supplies", fmt1)
  Let col2 = Format$(480, fmt2)
  Let col2 = Format$(col2, fmt3)
  Picture1.Print col1; Tab(19); col2
  Let col1 = Format$("Board", fmt1)
  Let col2 = Format$(1543, fmt2)
  Let col2 = Format$(col2, fmt3)
  Picture1.Print col1; Tab(19); col2
  Let col1 = Format$("Other Expenses", fmt1)
  Let col2 = Format$(966, fmt2)
  Let col2 = Format$(col2, fmt3)
```

```
    Picture1.Print col1; Tab(19); col2
    Let col1 = Format$("Transportation", fmt1)
    Let col2 = Format$(902, fmt2)
    Let col2 = Format$(col2, fmt3)
    Picture1.Print col1; Tab(19); col2
    Picture1.Print Tab(19); "------"
    Let col1 = Format$("Total", fmt1)
    Let col2 = Format$(4913, fmt2)
    Let col2 = Format$(col2, fmt3)
    Picture1.Print col1; Tab(19); col2
End Sub
```

[Run and then click the command button.]

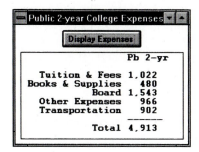

Generating Random Numbers: Rnd

Consider a specific collection of numbers. We say that a process selects a number at **random** from this collection if any number in the collection is just as likely to be selected as any other and the number cannot be predicted in advance. Some examples follow:

Collection	Process
1, 2, 3, 4, 5, 6	toss a die
0 or 1	toss a coin: 0 = tails, 1 = heads
–1, 0, 1, . . . , 36	spin a roulette wheel (interpret –1 as 00)
1, 2, . . . , n	write numbers on slips of paper, pull one from hat
numbers from 0 to 1	flip the spinner in Figure 3.26

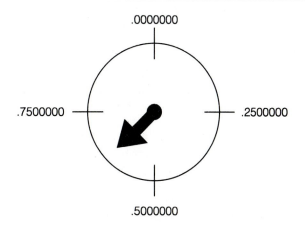

Figure 3.26 Spinner to randomly select a number between 0 and 1.

The function Rnd, which acts like the spinner in Figure 3.26, returns a random number. The statement

```
Picture1.Print Rnd
```

randomly displays a number from 0 up to (but not including) 1. The statement

```
Let numVar = Rnd
```

randomly assigns a number between 0 and 1 to the variable *numVar*. A different number will be assigned each time Rnd is called in the program, and any number greater than or equal to 0 and less than 1 is just as likely to be generated as any other. Therefore, although Rnd looks like a numeric variable, it does not act at all like a variable.

With appropriate scaling, the Rnd function can generate random numbers from other collections. The statement

```
Picture1.Print Int(6 * Rnd) + 1;
```

displays a number from the set 1, 2, 3, 4, 5, 6. Since Rnd always has a value from 0 to 1, excluding 1, 6 * Rnd has a value from 0 to 6 (excluding 6), and Int(6 * Rnd) has one of the values 0, 1, 2, 3, 4, 5. Adding 1 shifts the resulting number into the desired range.

Suppose the statement above is repeated many times. The integers generated should exhibit no apparent pattern. They should look very much like a sequence of integers obtained from successively rolling a die. For instance, each of the six integers should appear about one-sixth of the time and be reasonably spread out in the sequence. The longer the sequence, the more likely this is to occur.

Rnd normally generates the same sequence of numbers each time a program is run. However, Visual Basic has another function, Randomize Timer, that changes the sequence of numbers generated by Rnd. This statement will be used in all programs in this text.

EXAMPLE 9   The DC Lottery number is obtained by selecting a Ping-Pong ball from each of three separate bowls. Each ball is numbered with an integer from 0 through 9. Write a computer program to produce a lottery number. (Such a program is said to **simulate** the selection of Ping-Pong balls.)

SOLUTION   The value of Int(10 * Rnd) will be an integer from 0 through 9, and each of these integers has the same likelihood of occurring. Repeating the process three times produces the requested digits.

```
Sub Command1_Click ()
  Rem Display a lottery number
  Picture1.Cls
  Randomize Timer
  Picture1.Print Int(10 * Rnd);
  Picture1.Print Int(10 * Rnd);
  Picture1.Print Int(10 * Rnd)
End Sub
```

[Run and then click the command button. One possible output to be displayed in the picture box is as follows.]

8   3   9

Comments:

1. Requesting the square root of a negative number terminates the execution of the program and gives the error message "Illegal function call."

2. If n is greater than the length of *str*, then the value of Left\$(*str*, n) will be the entire string *str*. A similar result holds for Mid\$ and Right\$.

3. Visual Basic has a function called LCase\$ that is analogous to UCase\$. LCase\$ converts all uppercase letters in a string to lowercase letters.

4. The names of the functions Left\$, Mid\$, Right\$, UCase\$, and Format\$ are followed by dollar signs since their values are strings. They are referred to as **string-valued functions**.

5. Mid\$ is an important function. It will be used several times in this book to examine each letter of a string.

6. Trim\$ is useful when reading data from a text box. Sometimes users type spaces at the end of input. Unless the spaces are removed, they can cause havoc elsewhere in the program. Also, Trim\$ is useful in trimming the leading spaces from numbers that have been converted to strings with Str\$.

7. The Instr function has a useful extension. The value of Instr(n, *str1*, *str2*) is the position of the first occurrence of *str2* in *str1* in position n or greater. For instance, Instr(5, "Mississippi", "ss") is 6.

8. In Example 5, we found that 4 is the remainder when 256 is divided by 14. Mathematicians say "4 = 256 modulo 14." Visual Basic has an operation, Mod, that performs this calculation directly. If m and n are positive integers, then n Mod m is the remainder when n is divided by m. Visual Basic also has an operation called **integer division**, denoted by \, which gives the quotient portion of a long division problem.

9. Recall that the function Mid\$ has the form Mid\$(*str*, m, n) and returns the substring of *str* starting with position m and having length n. Visual Basic does its best to please for unexpected values of m and n. If m is greater than the length of the string or n is 0, then the empty string is returned. If $m + n$ is greater than the length of the string, then Mid\$(*str*, m, n) is the right part of the string beginning with the mth character. For instance, the value of Mid\$("abcdef", 3, 9) is "cdef".

10. When Format\$ is used with the "Currency" format string, negative numbers are indicated by parentheses instead of minus signs. If you prefer minus signs, use the format string "\$0,0.00" instead. For instance, the value of Format\$ (−1234, "\$0,0.00") is "−\$1,234.00".

11. When Format\$ is used with the "#,0" format string, commas are placed every three positions to the left of the decimal point. If you prefer to omit the commas, use the format string "0" instead. For instance, the value of Format\$(1234.6, "0") is 1235.

12. Each time the function Rnd appears in a program, it will be reassigned a value. For instance, the task attempted (but not accomplished) by the first set of lines below is achieved by the second set of lines. Since each of the Rnd's in the first set of lines will assume a different value, it is highly unlikely that the square of the first one will equal the product of the last two.

```
Rem Generate the square of a randomly chosen number
Randomize Timer
Picture1.Print The square of"; Rnd; "is"; Rnd * Rnd

Rem Generate the square of a randomly chosen number
Randomize Timer
Let numVar = Rnd
Picture1.Print "The square of"; numVar; "is"; numVar * numVar
```

PRACTICE PROBLEMS 3.6

1. What is the value of Instr("Computer", "E")?

2. What is the value of Sqr(12 * Len("WIN"))?

3. Write an expression that will randomly select an uppercase letter from the alphabet.

4. When will Int(n / 2) be the same as n / 2?

EXERCISES 3.6

In Exercises 1 through 18, find the value of the given function.

1. UCase$("McD's")

2. Sqr(64)

3. Int(10.75)

4. Left$("harp", 2)

5. Sqr(3 * 12)

6. Int(9 - 2)

7. Left$("ABCD", 2)

8. Mid$("ABCDE", 2, 3)

9. Mid$("shoe", 4, 1)

10. UCase$("2$ bill")

11. Len("shoe")

12. Instr("shoe", "h")

13. Instr("shoe", "f")

14. Len("s" + Left$("help", 2))

15. Right$("snow", 3)

16. Right$("123", 1)

17. Len(Trim$(Str$(32)))

18. Len(Trim$(Str$(-32)))

In Exercises 19 through 35, find the value of the given function where a and b are numeric variables, c and d are string variables; $a = 5, b = 3, c = $ "Lullaby", and $d = $ "lab".

19. Len(d)

20. Sqr(4 + a)

21. Int(-a / 2)

22. UCase$(d)

23. Sqr(a - 5)

24. Int(b * .5)

25. `Left$(c, Len(d))`   **26.** `Mid$(c, a, 3)`

27. `Mid$(c, a - b, 2 * a)`   **28.** `Left$(d, b - 2)`

29. `UCase$(c)`   **30.** `Instr(c, d)`

31. `Instr(c, "r")`   **32.** `Len(c + Left$(d, 2))`

33. `Right$(c, 2)`   **34.** `Right$("Sky" + d, 5)`

35. `Trim$(Str$(a + b)) + d`

In Exercises 36 through 43, determine the output produced by the lines of code.

36.
```
Let numVar = 3.67
Picture1.Print Int(10 * numVar + .5) / 10;
Let numVar = 7.345
Picture1.Print Int(10 * numVar + .5) / 10
```

37.
```
Let week = "SunMonTueWedThuFriSat"
Let strVar = InputBox$("Day of week (1 to 7)")
Picture1.Print "Today is "; Mid$(week, 3 * Val(strVar) - 2, 3)
```

(Assume that the response is *5.*)

38.
```
Let today = InputBox$("Date (mm/dd/yy)")
Picture1.Print "The year is 19" + Mid$(today, 7, 2)
```

(Assume that the response is *10/23/96.*)

39.
```
Let word = "Hello"
Picture1.Print Mid$(word, Len(word), 1)
```

40.
```
Let nom = Text1.Text
Picture1.Print Left$(nom, 1) + Mid$(nom, Instr(nom, " ") + 1, 1)
```

(Assume that Text1.Text is *Bill Clinton.*)

41.
```
Let response = InputBox$("Do you like jazz (yes or no)")
Let num = Int(Instr("YyNn", Left$(response, 1)) / 2 + .5)
Let response = Mid$("yesno ", 3 * num - 2, 3)
Picture1.Print "I guess your answer is "; response
```

(Assume that the response is *yup* or *Yeah.*)

42.
```
Let num = 123
Let strVar = Str$(num)
Picture1.Print "xxx"; Right$(strVar, Len(strVar) - 1)
```

43.
```
Let numStr = Trim$(Str$(37))
Let strVar = " Yankees"
Picture1.Print "19"; numStr; UCase$(strVar)
```

In Exercises 44 through 77, determine the output displayed in the text box by the following lines of code.

44. `Let Text1.Text = Format$(7654.321, "Standard")`

45. `Let Text1.Text = Format$(3.2E+05, "Standard")`

46. `Let Text1.Text = Format$(-.0005, "Standard")`

47. Let Text1.Text = Format$(32, "Standard")

48. Let Text1.Text = Format$(58 + 2, "Standard")

49. Let Text1.Text = Format$(3E-2, "Standard")

50. Let Text1.Text = Format$(7654.3, "Currency")

51. Let Text1.Text = Format$(-23, "Currency")

52. Let Text1.Text = Format$(".25", "Currency")

53. Let Text1.Text = Format$(3 / 4, "Currency")

54. Let Text1.Text = Format$(-5555555.555, "Currency")

55. Let Text1.Text = Format$((1 + .05) * 10, "Currency")

56. Let Text1.Text = Format$(12345.8, "#,0")

57. Let Text1.Text = Format$(.43, "#,0")

58. Let Text1.Text = Format$(-.249, "#,0")

59. Let Text1.Text = Format$(-2345.256, "0")

60. Let Text1.Text = Format$(1000 * Sqr(9), "0")

61. Let Text1.Text = Format$(-Sqr(2), "#,0")

62. Let Text1.Text = Format$(.05, "Percent")

63. Let Text1.Text = Format$(.06253, "Percent")

64. Let Text1.Text = Format$(1 / 4, "Percent")

65. Let Text1.Text = Format$(1, "Percent")

66. Let Text1.Text = Format$(-Sqr(2), "Percent")

67. Let Text1.Text = Format$(.005 + .02002, "Percent")

68. Let Text1.Text = Format$(5.5 * 10 ^ 5, "Scientific")

69. Let Text1.Text = Format$(.0002, "Scientific")

70. Let Text1.Text = Format$(-23E+04, "Scientific")

71. Let Text1.Text = Format$(34 + 66, "Scientific")

72. Let Text1.Text = Format$(12.345, "Scientific")

73. Let Text1.Text = Format$(-Sqr(2), "Scientific")

74. Let Text1.Text = Format$("12/31/99", "Long Date")

(**Note:** The year 1999 ends on a Friday.)

75. Let Text1.Text = Format$("1/1/2000", "Long Date")

76. Let Text1.Text = Format$("12/13/99", "Medium Date")

77. Let Text1.Text = Format$("1/2/2000", "Medium Date")

In Exercises 78 through 81, what will be displayed in the picture box by the following statements?

78. `Picture1.Print "Pay to France "; Format$(27267622, "Currency")`

79. `Picture1.Print "Manhattan", Format$(24, "Currency")`

80. `Picture1.Print "Name"; Tab(10); "Salary"`
    `Picture1.Print "Bill"; Tab(10); Format$(123000, "Currency")`

81. `Picture1.Print "Name"; Tab(10); Format$("Salary", "@@@@@@@@@@@")`
    `Let strVar = Format$(123000, "Currency")`
    `Picture1.Print "Bill"; Tab(10); Format$(strVar, "@@@@@@@@@@@")`

    (Assume that the setting for FontName is "Courier.")

In Exercises 82 through 89, determine the format string, *fmt*, for which the lines of code on the left produce the output shown on the right. Assume that the setting for FontName is "Courier".

82. `Picture1.Print "1234567890"`   Output: 1234567890
    `Picture1.Print Format$(98765.123, fmt)`   98,765.12

83. `Picture1.Print "1234567890"`   Output: 1234567890
    `Picture1.Print Format$("2.5", fmt)` $2.50

84. `Picture1.Print "1234567890"`   Output: 1234567890
    `Picture1.Print Format$(.0125, fmt)`   1.25%

85. `Picture1.Print "1234567890"`   Output: 1234567890
    `Picture1.Print Format$(123, fmt)`   123

86. `Picture1.Print "1234567890"`   Output: 1234567890
    `Picture1.Print Format$(-123.459, fmt)`   ($123.46)

87. `Picture1.Print "1234567890"`   Output: 1234567890
    `Picture1.Print Format$(201.3, fmt)`   2.01E+02

88. `Picture1.Print "1234567890"`   Output: 1234567890
    `Picture1.Print Tab(2); Format$(.3, fmt)`   0

89. `Picture1.Print "1234567890"`   Output: 1234567890
    `Picture1.Print Spc(3); Format$(23, fmt)`   23.00

In Exercises 90 through 95, determine the output displayed on the printer by the following lines of code.

90. `Let Printer.FontName = "Courier"     'Fixed-width font`
    `Printer.Print "1234567890"`
    `Printer.Print Format$(123, "@@@@@@@@@@")`

91. `Let Printer.FontName = "Courier"     'Fixed-width font`
    `Printer.Print "1234567890"`
    `Printer.Print Format$("abcd", "@@@@@@@@@@")`

92. `Let Printer.FontName = "Courier"     'Fixed-width font`
    `Printer.Print "1234567890"`
    `Printer.Print Format$("$1,234.56", "@@@@@@@@@@")`

93.
```
Let Printer.FontName = "Courier"     'Fixed-width font
Printer.Print "1234567890"
Let strVar = Str$(1234.559)
Printer.Print Format$(strVar, "@@@@@@@@@@")
```

94.
```
Let Printer.FontName = "Courier"     'Fixed-width font
Printer.Print "1234567890"
Printer.Print Format$(1 / 4, "@@@@@@@@@@")
```

95.
```
Let Printer.FontName = "Courier"     'Fixed-width font
Printer.Print "1234567890"
Let numVar = 25
Let strVar = Format$(numVar, "Currency")
Printer.Print Format$(strVar, "@@@@@@@@@@")
```

In Exercises 96 through 103, determine the errors.

96.
```
Let strVar = "Thank you"
Picture1.Print Instr(strVar, k)
```

97.
```
Picture1.Print Mid$(1980, 3, 2)
```

98.
```
Let firstName = InputBox$("Enter your first name.")
Picture1.Print "Your first name is "; firstName
```

(Assume that the response is Left$("John Doe", 4).)

99.
```
Let num1 = 7
Let num2 = 5
Picture1.Print Sqr(num1 - 2 * num2)
```

100.
```
Dim numStr As String
Let numString = 123
Picture1.Print 2 * Val(numString)
```

101. `Picture1.Print Format$(123.45, Standard)`

102. `Let Text1.Text = Format$($7654.3, "Currency")`

103. `Let Text1.Text = (1,234.568, "Standard")`

104. `Is Str$(Val("32")) the same string as "32"?`

105. `Is Trim$(Str$(Val("32"))) the same string as "32"?`

In Exercises 106 through 111, determine the range of values that can be generated by the given expression.

106. `Int(38 * Rnd) - 1`

107. `Int(10 * Rnd) + 10`

108. `2 * Rnd`

109. `Int(52 * Rnd) + 1`

110. `Chr$(Int(3 * Rnd) + 65)`

111. `Chr$(Int(26 * Rnd) + 97)`

In Exercises 112 through 117, write an expression that will randomly select a value from the given range.

112. An integer from 1 through 100

113. A number from 2 through 4 (excluding 4)

114. An even integer from 2 through 100

115. Either 0 or 1

116. The answer to a multiple-choice question, where the answers range from a to d

117. A white piano key from an octave; that is, one of the letters A through G

118. Suppose Text1.Text contains a positive number. Write code to replace this number with its units digit.

119. Suppose a text box contains a (complete) phone number. Write code to display the area code.

120. The formula $s = \sqrt{24d}$ gives an estimate of the speed of a car in miles per hour that skidded d feet on dry concrete when the brakes were applied. Write a program that requests the distance skidded and then displays the estimated speed of the car. (Try the program for a car that skids 54 feet.)

121. A college graduation is to be held in an auditorium with 2000 seats available for the friends and relatives of the graduates. Write a program that requests the number of graduates as input and then displays the number of tickets to be distributed to each graduate. Assume each graduate receives the same number of tickets. (Try the program for 325 graduates.)

122. Suppose you decide to give three pieces of Halloween candy to each trick-or-treater. Write a program that requests the number of pieces of candy you have and displays the number of children you can treat. (Try the program for 101 pieces of candy.)

123. The optimal inventory size for a specific item is given by the formula $s = \sqrt{2qh/c}$, where q is the quantity to be sold each year, h is the cost of placing an order, and c is the annual cost of stocking one unit of the item. Write a program that requests the quantity, ordering cost, and storage cost as input, and displays the optimum inventory size. (Use the program to compute the optimal inventory size for an item selling 3025 units during the year, where placing an order costs $50, and stocking a unit for one year costs $25.)

124. Write a program that requests a whole number of inches and converts it to feet and inches. (Try the program with 72, 53, and 8 inches.)

125. Write a program that requests a number and the number of decimal places to which the number should be rounded, and then displays the rounded number.

126. Write a program that requests a letter, converts it to uppercase and gives its first position in the sentence "THE QUICK BROWN FOX JUMPS OVER A LAZY DOG." For example, if the user responds by typing *b* into the text box, then the message *B first occurs in position 11* is displayed.

127. Write a program that requests an amount of money between 1 and 99 cents and gives the number of quarters to be used when making that amount of change. (Try each of the amounts 85, 43, and 15 as input.)

128. Write a program that requests a day of the week (Sunday, Monday, . . . , Saturday) and gives the numerical position of that day in the week. For example, if the user responds by typing *Wednesday* into the text box, then the message *Wednesday is day number 4* is displayed.

129. On the nautical clock, hours of the day are numbered from 0 to 23, beginning at midnight. Write a program to convert nautical hours to standard hours. For example, if the user responds by typing *17* into the text box, then the message *The standard hour is 5* is displayed. **Note:** Let 12 o'clock in standard hours appear as 0.

130. Write a program that requests a sentence, a word in the sentence, and another word, and then displays the sentence with the first word replaced by the second. For example, if the user responds by typing "What you don't know won't hurt you" into the first text box and *know* and *owe* into the second and third text boxes, then the message "What you don't owe won't hurt you" is displayed.

131. Write a program that requests a positive number containing a decimal point as input, and then displays the number of digits to the left of the decimal point and the number of digits to the right of the decimal point.

132. When *P* dollars are deposited in a savings account at interest rate *r* compounded annually, the balance after *n* years is $P(1 + r)^n$. Write a program to request the principal *P* and the interest rate *r* as input, and compute the balance after ten years, as shown in the sample output on the left below.

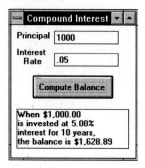
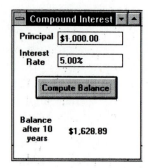

133. Redo Exercise 132 to achieve the output shown on the right above. The principal and interest should be entered as 1000 and .05, but should be converted to nice forms when the button is pressed. (The balance is displayed in a label.) Also, the two text boxes should become empty when they receive the focus to allow for additional computations.

134. Write a program to generate a rent receipt. The program should request the person's name, amount received, and the current date in text boxes and print a receipt of the type shown on the right below.

Received from Jane Smith the sum of $645.50

Signed _____
Wednesday, April 2, 1997

```
Receipt for Payment
Name   Jane Smith
Amount 645.50
Date   4/2/97
      Print Receipt
```

135. Write a program to produce Table 3.9 on the printer. (The population is for 1992, the area is given in square miles, and the density is in people per square mile.) For each state, the name, capital, population, and area should be contained in a file. The densities should be computed by the program.

State	Capital	Population	Area	Density
Alaska	Juneau	570,000	570,374	1.00
New York	Albany	18,058,000	47,224	82.39
Texas	Austin	17,349,000	261,914	66.24

Table 3.9 State Data
Source: Statistical Abstract of the United States, 1992

136. Table 3.10 provides approximate information about certain occupations and projects the percent change in job openings from 1990 to 2005. Write a program to produce this table on the printer. Place the data in a file. Notice that the names of the occupations and the numbers are right-justified.

Occupation	Current Number of Jobs	% Change	Weekly Median Earning
Computer programmer	565,000	63	$653
Teacher, Secondary School	1,280,000	45	$648
Physician	580,000	41	$2,996

Table 3.10 Job openings to 2005 and 1990 earnings
Source: Bureau of Labor Statistics.

137. Write a program to randomly select a month and year during the 1990s. A typical outcome is 6 / 1997.

138. Write a program to randomly select one of the 64 squares on a chess board. **Note:** Each square is represented by a letter (from *a* to *h*, giving the column starting from white's left) and a number (from 1 to 8, giving the row starting from white's side). A typical outcome is d5.

139. Write an event procedure to drive the user crazy. Assume that the focus is on a text box. Each time the user presses a key, have a randomly selected letter from A to Z appear in the text box.

SOLUTIONS TO PRACTICE PROBLEMS 3.6

1. 0. There is no uppercase letter E in the string "Computer". Instr distinguishes between upper- and lowercase.

2. 6. Len("WIN") is 3, 12 * 3 is 36, and Sqr(36) is 6. This expression is an example of function composition. The inner function will be evaluated first.

3. Chr$(Int(26 * Rnd) + 65). Uppercase letters have the 26 ANSI values ranging from 65 to 90. The value of 26 * Rnd is a number from 0 through 26 (excluding 26). The value of Int(26 * Rnd) is a whole number from 0 to 25, and therefore the value of Int(26 * Rnd) + 65 is a whole number from 65 to 90.

4. When n / 2 is an integer, that is, when n is an even number. (This idea will be used later in the text to determine whether an integer is even.)

Chapter 3
Summary

1. The Visual Basic screen consists of a collection of objects for which various properties can be set. Some examples of *objects* are text boxes, labels, command buttons, picture boxes, and the form itself. Objects placed on the form are called *controls*. Some useful properties are Text (set the text displayed by a text box), Caption (set the title of a form, the contents of a label, or the words on a command button), FontSize (set the size of the characters displayed), Alignment (set the placement of the contents of a label), MultiLine (text box to display text on several lines), Picture (display drawing in picture box), ForeColor (set foreground color), BackColor (set background color), Visible (show or hide object), BorderStyle (alter and possibly remove border), FontBold (display boldface text), and FontItalic (displays italic text).

2. An event procedure is called when a specific event occurs to a specified object. Some event procedures are *object*_Click (*object* is clicked), *object*_Lost-Focus (*object* loses the focus), *object*_GotFocus (*object* receives the focus), and *object*_KeyPress (a key is pressed while *object* has the focus).

3. Visual Basic methods such as Print and Cls are applied to objects and are coded as *object*.Print and *object*.Cls.

4. Two types of *constants* can be stored and processed by computers, *numbers* and *strings*.

5. The arithmetic *operations* are +, −, *, /, and ^. The only string operation is +, concatenation. An *expression* is a combination of constants, variables, functions, and operations that can be evaluated.

6. A *variable* is a name used to refer to data. Variable names can be up to 40 characters long, must begin with a letter, and may contain letters, digits, and underscores. Variables may be *declared* using Dim statements.

7. Values are assigned to variables by Let and Input# statements. The values assigned by Let statements can be constants, variables, or expressions. Input#

statements look to data files for constants. String constants used in Let statements must be surrounded by quotation marks, whereas quotation marks are optional for string constants input with Input#. InputBox$ can be used to request that the user type in a constant.

8. The Print method displays information in a picture box or on the printer. *Semicolons, commas,* and *Tab* and *Spc* control the placement of the items on a particular line. A temporary message can be displayed on the screen using the MsgBox statement.

9. You control the printer with the Printer object and write to it with statements of the form Printer.Print *expression*. You set properties with statements of the form Let Printer.*property* = *setting*. Printer.NewPage starts a new page and PrintForm does a screen dump. A series of commands to the Printer object must end with EndDoc which actually produces the final printed page.

10. The Format$ function provides detailed control of how numbers, dates, and strings are displayed. Numbers can be made to line up uniformly and be displayed with dollar signs, commas, and a specified number of decimal places. Dates can be converted to a long or medium form. Strings can be right justified.

11. *Functions* can be thought of as accepting numbers or strings as input and returning numbers or strings as output.

Function	Input	Output
Asc	string	number
Chr$	number	string
Instr	string, string	number
Int	number	number
LCase$	string	string
Left$	string, number	string
Len	string	number
Mid$	string, number, number	string
Right$	string, number	string
Rnd		number
Sqr	number	number
Str$	number	string
Trim$	string	string
UCase$	string	string
Val	string	number

Chapter 3
Programming Projects

1. Write a program that allows the user to specify two numbers and then adds, subtracts, or multiplies them when the user clicks on the appropriate command button. The output should give the type of arithmetic performed and the result.

2. Suppose automobile repair customers are billed at the rate of $35 per hour for labor. Also, costs for parts and supplies are subject to a 5 percent sales tax. Write a program to print out a simplified bill. The customer's name, the number of hours of labor, and the cost of parts and supplies should be entered into the program via text boxes. When a command button is clicked, the customer's name (indented) and the three costs should be displayed in a picture box as shown in the sample run in Figure 3.27.

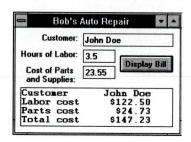

Figure 3.27 Sample run for Programming Project 2.

3. Write a program to generate the personalized form letter shown below. The person's name and address should be read from text boxes.

```
Mr. John Jones
123 Main Street
Juneau, Alaska  99803

Dear Mr. Jones,

    The Jones family has been selected as the
first family on Main Street to have the opportunity
to purchase an Apex solar-powered flashlight. Due to limited
supply, only 1000 of these amazing inventions will be available
in the entire state of Alaska. Don't delay. Order today.

                        Sincerely,
                        Cuthbert J. Twillie
```

4. At the end of each month, a credit card company constructs the table in Figure 3.28 to summarize the status of the accounts. Write a program to produce this table. The first four pieces of information for each account should be read from a data file. The program should compute the finance charges (1.5 percent of the unpaid past due amount) and the current amount due. Format the last column to be aligned right.

```
Account   Past Due   Payments   Purchases   Finance   Current
Number    Amount                            Charges   Amt Due

123-AB    123.45     10.00      934.00      1.70      $1,049.15
456-CD    134.56     134.56     300.00      0.00        $300.00
```

Figure 3.28 Status of credit card accounts.

5. Table 3.11 gives the distribution of the U.S. population (in thousands) by age group and sex. Write a program to produce the table shown in Figure 3.29. For each age group, the column labeled %Males gives the percentage of the people in that age group that are male, similarly for the column labeled %Females. The last column gives the percentage of the total population in each age group. (**Note:** Store the information in Table 3.11 in a data file. For instance, the first line in the file should be "Under 20", 36743, 34993. Read and add up the data once to obtain the total population, then read the data again to produce the table.)

Age Group	Males	Females
Under 20	36,743	34,993
20–64	72,003	73,893
Over 64	12,854	15,818

Table 3.11 U.S. resident population (1990).

U.S. Population (in thousands)					
Age Group	Males	Females	%Males	%Females	%Total
Under 20	36,743	34,993	51.22%	48.78%	29.12%
20 - 64	72,003	73,893	49.35%	50.65%	59.23%
Over 64	12,854	15,818	44.83%	55.17%	11.64%

Figure 3.29 Output of Programming Project 5.

6. Write a program to convert a U.S. Customary System length in miles, yards, feet, and inches to a Metric System length in kilometers, meters, and centimeters. A sample run is shown in Figure 3.30. After the number of miles, yards, feet, and inches are read from the text boxes, the length should be converted entirely to inches and then divided by 39.37 to obtain the value in meters. The Int function should be used to break the total number of meters into a whole number of kilometers and meters. The number of centimeters should be displayed to one decimal place. Some of the needed formulas are as follows:

total inches = 63360 * miles + 36 * yards + 12 * feet + inches
total meters = total inches / 39.37
kilometers = Int(meters / 1000)

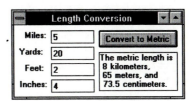

Figure 3.30 Sample run for Programming Project 6.

4

Procedures

4.1 SUBPROGRAMS, PART I

Structured program design requires that problems be broken into small problems to be solved one at a time. Visual Basic has two devices, subprograms and functions, that are used to break problems into manageable chunks. Subprograms and functions are known as **procedures**. To distinguish them from event procedures, subprograms and functions are referred to as *general procedures*. Procedures also eliminate repetitive code, can be reused in other programs, and allow a team of programmers to work on a single program.

In this section, we show how subprograms are defined and used. The programs in this section are designed to demonstrate the use of subprograms rather than to accomplish sophisticated programming tasks. Later chapters of the book use procedures for more substantial programming efforts.

A **subprogram** is a part of a program that performs one or more related tasks, has its own name, is written as a separate part of the program, and is accessed via a Call statement. The simplest type of subprogram has the form

```
Sub SubprogramName ()
    statement(s)
End Sub
```

Consider the following program that calculates the sum of two numbers. This program will be revised to incorporate subprograms.

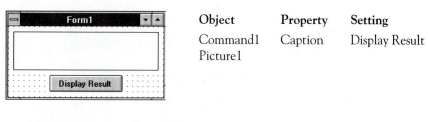

Object	Property	Setting
Command1	Caption	Display Result
Picture1		

```
Sub Command1_Click()
    Dim num1 As Single, num2 As Single
    Rem Display the sum of two numbers
    Picture1.Cls
    Picture1.Print "This program displays a sentence "
    Picture1.Print "identifying two numbers and their sum."
    Picture1.Print
    Let num1 = 2
    Let num2 = 3
    Picture1.Print "The sum of"; num1; "and"; num2; "is"; num1 + num2
End Sub
```

[Run and then click the command button. The following is displayed in the picture box.]

```
This program displays a sentence
identifying two numbers and their sum.

The sum of 2 and 3 is 5
```

The tasks performed by this program can be summarized as follows:

Explain purpose of program.

Display numbers and their sum.

Subprograms allow us to write and read the program in such a way that we first focus on the tasks and later on how to accomplish each task.

EXAMPLE 1   The following program uses a subprogram to accomplish the first task of the program above. When the statement Call ExplainPurpose is reached, execution jumps to the Sub ExplainPurpose statement. The lines between Sub ExplainPurpose and End Sub are executed, and then execution continues with the line following the Call statement. *Note:* Do not type this program into the computer until you have read the two paragraphs following the example.

```
Sub Command1_Click()
  Dim num1 As Single, num2 As Single
  Rem Display the sum of two numbers
  Picture1.Cls
  Call ExplainPurpose
  Picture1.Print
  Let num1 = 2
  Let num2 = 3
  Picture1.Print "The sum of"; num1; "and"; num2; "is"; num1 + num2
End Sub

Sub ExplainPurpose ()
  Rem Explain the task performed by the program
  Picture1.Print "This program displays a sentence"
  Picture1.Print "identifying two numbers and their sum."
End Sub
```

Subprograms are not typed into event procedure windows. Instead, a separate window is created to hold each subprogram. The steps for creating a subprogram are as follows.

1. Activate a code window if one is not already active.

2. Select New Procedure from the View menu with the mouse or the key combination Alt/V/N.

3. The word Sub should appear selected in the Type box. If not, click on the circle to the left of the word Sub.

4. Type in the name of the subprogram and then press the Enter key or click the OK button.

5. A special window has been created for the subprogram. The line Sub *SubName* ( ) appears at the top of the window, and the cursor appears on a blank line just above the words End Sub.

6. Type the statements of the subprogram into this window.

7. To return directly to another procedure, press F2 to obtain a View Procedures dialog box and select the desired procedure from the list of procedures. To return to the form, just click on it.

Notes: General procedures are stored in the location denoted as (general), which is listed along with the objects. The list of procedures in the View Procedures dialog box contains "(declarations)" as its first entry. The (declarations) window is used to declare special types of variables and will be discussed later.

The second task performed by the addition program also can be handled by a subprogram. The values of the two numbers, however, must be transmitted to the subprogram. This transmission is called **passing**.

EXAMPLE 2   The following revision of the program in Example 1 uses a subprogram to accomplish the second task. The statement Call Add(2, 3) causes execution to jump to the Sub Add (num1 As Single, num2 As Single) statement, which assigns the number 2 to *num1* and the number 3 to *num2*.

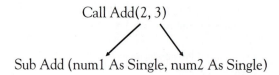

After the lines between Sub Add (num1 As Single, num2 As Single) and End Sub are executed, execution continues with the line following Call Add(2, 3), namely the End Sub statement in the event procedure. **Note:** When you create the subprogram Add, you can type in (num1 As Single, num2 As Single) either before or after leaving the New Procedure dialog box. Notice that the subprograms are listed in alphabetical order. This is the way they are listed when F2 is pressed.

```
Sub Command1_Click()
  Rem Display the sum of two numbers
  Picture1.Cls
  Call ExplainPurpose
  Picture1.Print
  Call Add(2, 3)
End Sub

Sub Add (num1 As Single, num2 As Single)
  Rem Display numbers and their sum
  Picture1.Print "The sum of"; num1; "and"; num2; "is"; num1 + num2
End Sub

Sub ExplainPurpose ()
  Rem Explain the task performed by the program
  Picture1.Print "This program displays a sentence"
  Picture1.Print "identifying two numbers and their sum."
End Sub
```

Subprograms make a program easy to read, modify, and debug. The event procedure gives an unencumbered description of what the program does and the subprograms fill in the details. Another benefit of subprograms is that they can be called several times during the execution of the program. This feature is especially useful when there are many statements in the subprogram.

EXAMPLE 3   The following extension of the program in Example 2 displays several sums.

```
Sub Command1_Click()
  Rem Display the sums of several pairs of numbers
  Picture1.Cls
  Call ExplainPurpose
  Picture1.Print
  Call Add(2, 3)
  Call Add(4, 6)
  Call Add(7, 8)
End Sub

Sub Add (num1 As Single, num2 As Single)
  Rem Display numbers and their sum
  Picture1.Print "The sum of"; num1; "and"; num2; "is"; num1 + num2
End Sub

Sub ExplainPurpose ()
  Rem Explain the task performed by the program
  Picture1.Print "This program displays sentences"
  Picture1.Print "identifying pairs of numbers and their sums."
End Sub
```

[Run and then click the command button. The following is displayed in the picture box.]

```
This program displays sentences
identifying pairs of numbers and their sums.

The sum of 2 and 3 is 5
The sum of 4 and 6 is 10
The sum of 7 and 8 is 15
```

The variables *num1* and *num2* appearing in the subprogram Add are called **parameters**. They are merely temporary place holders for the numbers passed to the subprogram; their names are not important. The only essentials are their type, quantity, and order. In the Add subprogram, the parameters must be numeric variables and there must be two of them. For instance, the subprogram could have been written

```
  Sub Add (this As Single, that As Single)
    Rem Display numbers and their sum
    Picture1.Print "The sum of"; this; "and"; that; "is"; this + that
  End Sub
```

A string also can be passed to a subprogram. In this case, the receiving parameter in the subprogram must be followed by the declaration As String.

EXAMPLE 4   The following program passes a string and two numbers to a subprogram. When the subprogram is first called, the string parameter *state* is assigned the string constant "Hawaii", and the numeric parameters *pop* and *area* are assigned the numeric constants 1134750 and 6471, respectively. The subprogram then uses these parameters to carry out the task of producing the population density of Hawaii. The second Call statement assigns different values to the parameters.

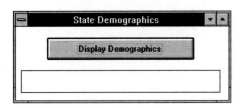

Object	Property	Setting
Form1	Caption	State Demographics
Command1	Caption	Display Demographics
Picture1		

```
Sub Command1_Click()
  Rem Calculate the population densities of states
  Picture1.Cls
  Call ProduceDensity("Hawaii", 1134750, 6471)
  Call ProduceDensity("Alaska", 570345, 591000)
End Sub

Sub ProduceDensity (state As String, pop As Single, area As Single)
  Dim rawDensity As Single, density As Single
  Rem  The density (number of people per square mile)
  Rem  will be displayed rounded to a whole number
  Let rawDensity = pop / area
  Let density = Int(rawDensity + .5)   'round to whole number
  Picture1.Print "The density of "; state; " is"; density;
  Picture1.Print " people per square mile."
End Sub
```

[Run and then click the command button. The following is displayed in the picture box.]

```
The density of Hawaii is 175 people per square mile.
The density of Alaska is 1 people per square mile.
```

The parameters in the density program can have any names, as with the parameters in the addition program of Example 3. The only restriction is that the first parameter be a string variable and that the last two parameters be numeric variables. For instance, the subprogram could have been written

```
Sub ProduceDensity (x As String, y As Single, z As Single)
  Dim rawDensity As Single, density As Single
  Rem The density (number of people per square mile)
  Rem will be rounded to a whole number
  Let rawDensity = y / z
  Let density = Int(rawDensity + .5)
  Picture1.Print "The density of "; x; " is"; density;
  Picture1.Print "people per square mile."
End Sub
```

When nondescriptive names are used, the subprogram should contain Rem statements giving the meanings of the variables. Possible Rem statements for the program above are

```
Rem x    name of the state
Rem y    population of the state
Rem z    area of the state
```

Variables and Expressions as Arguments

The items appearing in the parentheses of a Call statement are called **arguments**. These should not be confused with parameters, which appear in the heading of a subprogram. In Example 3, the arguments of the Call Add statements were constants. These arguments also could have been variables or expressions. For instance, the event procedure could have been written as follows. (See Figure 4.1.)

```
Sub Command1_Click()
  Dim x As Single, y As Single, z As Single
  Rem Display the sum of two numbers
  Picture1.Cls
  Call ExplainPurpose
  Picture1.Print
  Let x = 2
  Let y = 3
  Call Add(x, y)
  Call Add(x + 2, 2 * y)
  Let z = 7
  Call Add(z, z + 1)
End Sub
```

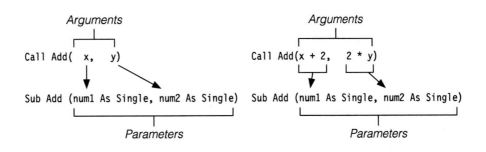

Figure 4.1 Passing arguments to parameters.

This feature allows values obtained as input from the user to be passed to a subprogram.

EXAMPLE 5   The following variation of the addition program requests the two numbers as input from the user. Notice that the names of the arguments, *x* and *y*, are different than the names of the parameters. The names of the arguments and parameters may be the same or different; what matters is that the order, number, and types of the arguments and parameters match.

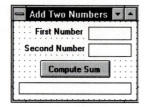

Object	Property	Setting
Form1	Caption	Add Two Numbers
Label1	Caption	First Number
Text1	Text	(blank)
Label2	Caption	Second Number
Text2	Text	(blank)
Command1	Caption	Compute Sum
Picture1		

```
Sub Command1_Click ()
  Dim x As Single, y As Single
  Rem This program requests two numbers and
  Rem displays the two numbers and their sum.
  Let x = Val(Text1.Text)
  Let y = Val(Text2.Text)
  Call Add(x, y)
End Sub

Sub Add (num1 As Single, num2 As Single)
  Rem Display numbers and their sum
  Picture1.Cls
  Picture1.Print "The sum of"; num1; "and"; num2; "is"; num1 + num2
End Sub
```

[Run, type 23 and 67 into the text boxes, and then click the command button.]

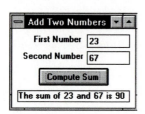

EXAMPLE 6   The following variation of Example 4 obtains its input from the file DEMO-GRAP.TXT. The second Call statement uses different variable names for the arguments to show that using the same argument names is not necessary. (See Figure 4.2.)

DEMOGRAP.TXT contains the following two lines:

"Hawaii", 1134750, 6471
"Alaska", 570345, 591000

```
Sub Command1_Click()
  Dim state As String, pop As Single, area As Single
  Dim s As String, p As Single, a As Single
  Rem Calculate the population densities of states
  Picture1.Cls
  Open "DEMOGRAP.TXT" For Input As #1
  Input #1, state, pop, area
  Call ProduceDensity(state, pop, area)
  Input #1, s, p, a
  Call ProduceDensity(s, p, a)
  Close #1
End Sub
```

```
Sub ProduceDensity (state As String, pop As Single, area As Single)
  Dim rawDensity As Single, density As Single
  Rem The density (number of people per square mile)
  Rem will be rounded to a whole number
  Let rawDensity = pop / area
  Let density = Int(rawDensity + .5)
  Picture1.Print "The density of "; state; " is "; density;
  Picture1.Print " people per square mile."
End Sub
```

[Run and then click the command button. The following is displayed in the picture box.]

```
The density of Hawaii is 175 people per square mile.
The density of Alaska is 1 people per square mile.
```

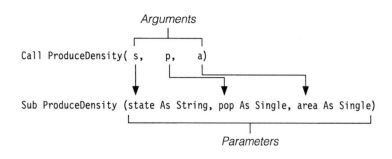

Figure 4.2 Passing arguments to parameters in Example 6.

Arguments and parameters also can be used to pass values from subprograms back to event procedures or other subprograms. This important property of subprograms is explored in detail in the next section.

Comments:

1. In this text, subprogram names begin with uppercase letters in order to distinguish them from variable names. Like variable names, however, they can be written with any combination of uppercase and lowercase letters. To improve readability, the Visual Basic editor will automatically ensure that the capitalization of a subprogram name is consistent throughout a program. For instance, if you type Call SubPROGRAMNAME and later type Call SubprogramName, the first name will be changed to match the second. **Note:** Parameters appearing in a Sub statement are not part of the subprogram name.

2. The rules for naming subprograms are identical to the rules for naming numeric variables. The name chosen for a subprogram should describe the task it performs.

3. Subprograms allow programmers to focus on the main flow of the program and defer the details of implementation. Modern programs use subprograms liberally. An event procedure acts as a supervisor, delegating tasks to the subprograms. This method of program construction is known as **modular** or **top-down** design.

4. As a rule, a subprogram should perform only one task, or several closely related tasks, and should be kept relatively small.

5. Pressing F2 to obtain a View Procedures dialog box only works when a code window is currently active. So doing produces a list of all subprograms (in alphabetical order) followed by a list of all event procedures (in alphabetical order). Double-click on a subprogram or event procedure to select it.

6. An alternative way to view the subprograms and event procedures from an active code window is to repeatedly press Ctrl+Down Arrow.

7. To delete a subprogram, erase every line of the subprogram.

8. In this text, the first line inside a subprogram is often a Rem statement describing the task performed by the subprogram. If necessary, several Rem statements are devoted to this purpose. Conventional programming practice also recommends that all variables used by the subprogram be listed in Rem statements with their meanings. In this text, we give several examples of this practice, but only adhere to it when the variables are especially numerous or lack descriptive names.

9. Although both constants and expressions can be used as arguments in Call statements, only variables can be used as parameters in Sub statements.

10. A subprogram can call another subprogram. If so, after the End Sub of the called subprogram is reached, execution continues with the line in the calling subprogram that follows the Call statement.

11. An alternative method of creating a subprogram window is to move the cursor to a blank line of any code window, type Sub *SubName*, and press the Enter key.

12. When you write a subprogram without parameters, Visual Basic automatically adds a pair of empty parentheses at the end of the subprogram name. However, Call statements should not use the empty parentheses.

13. The first lines of event procedures and subprograms end with a pair of parentheses. With the event procedures we have discussed the parentheses are usually empty, whereas with subprograms the parentheses often contain parameters.

PRACTICE PROBLEMS 4.1

1. What is displayed in the picture box by the following code when the command button is clicked?

```
Sub Command1_Click ()
  Rem Demonstrate subprograms calling other subprograms
  Call FirstPart
  Picture1.Print 4;
End Sub

Sub FirstPart ()
  Picture1.Print 1;
  Call SecondPart
  Picture1.Print 3;
End Sub
```

```
Sub SecondPart
  Picture1.Print 2;
End Sub
```

2. What is wrong with the following code?

```
Sub Command1_Click
  Dim phone As String
  Let phone = Text1.Text
  Call AreaCode(phone)
End Sub


Sub AreaCode ()
  Picture1.Print "Your area code is "; Left$(phone, 3)
End Sub
```

EXERCISES 4.1

In Exercises 1 through 34, determine the output displayed in the picture box when the command button is clicked.

1.
```
Sub Command1_Click ()
  Rem Quote from Kermit
  Call Quotation
  Picture1.Print "          Kermit the frog"
End Sub


Sub Quotation ()
  Rem Display a quotation
  Picture1.Print "It isn't easy being green."
End Sub
```

2.
```
Sub Command1_Click ()
  Picture1.Print "Today ";
  Call WhatDay
  Picture1.Print "of the rest of your life."
End Sub


Sub WhatDay ()
  Picture1.Print "is the first day ";
End Sub
```

3.
```
Sub Command1_Click ()
  Call Question
  Call Answer
End Sub


Sub Answer ()
  Picture1.Print "Because they were invented in the northern"
  Picture1.Print "hemisphere where sundials move clockwise."
End Sub


Sub Question ()
  Picture1.Print "Why do clocks run clockwise?"
End Sub
```

4.
```
Sub Command1_Click ()
    Call FirstName
    Picture1.Print "How are you today?"
End Sub

Sub FirstName ()
    Dim nom As String
    Let nom = InputBox$("What is your first name?")
    Picture1.Print "Hello " + UCase$(nom)
End Sub
```

(Assume that the response is *Bill.*)

5.
```
Sub Command1_Click ()
    Rem The fates of Henry the Eighth's six wives
    Call CommonFates
    Picture1.Print "died;"
    Call CommonFates
    Picture1.Print "survived."
End Sub

Sub CommonFates ()
    Rem The most common fates
    Picture1.Print "Divorced, beheaded, ";
End Sub
```

6.
```
Sub Command1_Click ()
    Picture1.Print "A rose";
    Call Rose
    Call Rose
    Picture1.Print "."
End Sub

Sub Rose ()
    Picture1.Print ", is a rose";
End Sub
```

7.
```
Sub Command1_Click ()
    Rem Good advice to follow
    Call Advice
End Sub

Sub Advice ()
    Picture1.Print "Keep cool, but don't freeze."
    Call Source
End Sub

Sub Source ()
    Picture1.Print "Source: A jar of mayonnaise."
End Sub
```

8.
```
Sub Command1_Click ()
    Call Answer
    Call Question
End Sub
```

```
Sub Answer ()
  Picture1.Print "The answer is 9W."
  Picture1.Print "What is the question?"
End Sub

Sub Question ()
  Rem Note: "Wagner" is pronounced "Vagner"
  Picture1.Print
  Picture1.Print "Do you spell your name with a V, Mr. Wagner?"
End Sub
```

9.
```
Sub Command1_Click ()
  Call Piano(88)
End Sub

Sub Piano(num As Integer)
  Picture1.Print num; "keys on a piano"
End Sub
```

10.
```
Sub Command1_Click ()
  Rem Opening line of Moby Dick
  Call FirstLine("Ishmael")
End Sub

Sub FirstLine (nom As String)
  Rem Display first line
  Picture1.Print "Call me "; nom
End Sub
```

11.
```
Sub Command1_Click ()
  Rem Opening line of Tale of Two Cities
  Call Times("best")
  Call Times("worst")
End Sub

Sub Times (word As String)
  Rem Display first line
  Picture1.Print "It was the "; word; " of times."
End Sub
```

12.
```
Sub Command1_Click ()
  Call Potato(1)
  Call Potato(2)
  Call Potato(3)
  Picture1.Print 4
End Sub

Sub Potato (quantity As Integer)
  Picture1.Print quantity; "potato,";
End Sub
```

13.
```
Command1_Click ()
    Dim nom As String
    Rem Analyze a name
    Let nom = "Gabriel"
    Call AnalyzeName(nom)
End Sub


Sub AnalyzeName (nom As String)
  Rem Display length and first letter
  Picture1.Print "Your name has"; Len(nom); "letters."
  Picture1.Print "The first letter is "; Left$(nom, 1)
End Sub
```

14.
```
Sub Command1_Click ()
    Dim color As String
    Let color = InputBox$("What is your favorite color?")
    Call Flattery(color)
End Sub


Sub Flattery (color As String)
  Picture1.Print "You look dashing in "; color
End Sub
```

(Assume that the response is *blue*.)

15.
```
Sub Command1_Click ()
    Dim num As Single
    Let num = Val(InputBox$("Give a number from 1 to 26."))
    Call Alphabet(num)
End Sub


Sub Alphabet (num As Single)
  Picture1.Print Left$("abcdefghijklmnopqrstuvwxyz", num)
End Sub
```

(Assume that the response is *5*.)

16.
```
Sub Command1_Click ()
    Dim size As Single
    Let size = 435
    Call House(size)
    Picture1.Print "of Representatives"
End Sub


Sub House (size As Single)
  Picture1.Print size; "members in the House ";
End Sub
```

17.
```
Sub Command1_Click ()
    Dim num As Single
    Let num = 144
    Call Gross(num)
End Sub


Sub Gross (amount As Single)
  Picture1.Print amount; "items in a gross"
End Sub
```

18.
```
Sub Command1_Click ()
    Dim a As String
    Let a = "mile"
    Call Acres(a)
End Sub

Sub Acres (length As String)
    Picture1.Print "640 acres in a square "; length
End Sub
```

19.
```
Sub Command1_Click ()
    Dim candy As String
    Let candy = "M&M's Plain Chocolate Candies"
    Call Brown(candy)
End Sub

Sub Brown (item As String)
    Picture1.Print "30% of "; item; " are brown."
End Sub
```

20.
```
Sub Command1_Click ()
    Dim annualRate As Single
    Let annualRate = .08
    Call Balance(annualRate)
End Sub

Sub Balance (r As Single)
    Dim p As Single
    p = InputBox$("What is the principal?")
    Picture1.Print "The balance after 1 year is"; (1 + r) * p
End Sub
```

(Assume that the response is *100*.)

21.
```
Sub Command1_Click ()
    Dim hours As Single
    Let hours = 24
    Call Minutes(60 * hours)
End Sub

Sub Minutes (num As Single)
    Picture1.Print num; "minutes in a day"
End Sub
```

22.
```
Sub Command1_Click ()
    Dim a As String, b As String
    Let a = "United States"
    Let b = "acorn"
    Call Display(Left$(a, 3) + Mid$(b, 2, 4))
End Sub

Sub Display (word As String)
    Picture1.Print word
End Sub
```

23.
```
Sub Command1_Click ()
    Dim word As String
    Let word = InputBox$("Enter a word.")
    Call T(Instr(word, "t"))
End Sub

Sub T (num As Integer)
    Picture1.Print "t is the"; num; "th letter of the word."
End Sub
```

(Assume that the response is *computer*.)

24.
```
Sub Command1_Click ()
    Dim states As Single, senators As Single
    Let states = 50
    Let senators = 2
    Call Senate(states * senators)
End Sub

Sub Senate (num As Single)
    Picture1.Print "The number of members of the U.S. Senate is"; num
End Sub
```

25.
```
Sub Command1_Click ()
    Call DisplaySource
    Call Language("BASIC", 22)
    Call Language("Assembler", 16)
    Call Language("C", 15)
    Call Language("Pascal", 13)
End Sub

Sub DisplaySource
    Picture1.Print "According to a poll in the May 31, 1988"
    Picture1.Print "issue of PC Magazine, 75% of the people polled"
    Picture1.Print " write programs for their companies."
    Picture1.Print "The four most popular languages used are as follows."
End Sub

Sub Language(nom As String, users As Single)
    Picture1.Print users; "percent of the respondents use "; nom
End Sub
```

26.
```
Sub Command1_Click ()
    Rem Sentence using number, thing, and place
    Call Sentence(168, "hour", "a week")
    Call Sentence(76, "trombone", "the big parade")
End Sub

Sub Sentence (num As Single, thing As String, where As String)
    Picture1.Print num; thing; "s in "; where
End Sub
```

27.
```
Sub Command1_Click ()
    Dim pres As String, college As String
    Open "CHIEF.TXT" For Input As #1
    Input #1, pres, college
    Call PresAlmaMater(pres, college)
    Input #1, pres, college
    Call PresAlmaMater(pres, college)
    Close #1
End Sub

Sub PresAlmaMater (pres As String, college As String)
    Picture1.Print "President "; pres; " is a graduate of "; college
End Sub
```

(Assume that the file CHIEF.TXT contains the following two lines)

"Bush", "Yale University"
"Clinton", "Georgetown University"

28.
```
Sub Command1_Click ()
    Dim nom As String, yob As Integer
    Let nom = InputBox$("Name?")
    Let yob = Val(InputBox$( "Year of birth?"))
    Call AgeIn2000(nom, yob)
End Sub

Sub AgeIn2000 (nom As String, yob As Integer)
    Picture1.Print nom; ", in the year 2000 your age will be"; 2000 - yob
End Sub
```

(Assume that the responses are *Gabriel* and *1980*.)

29.
```
Sub Command1_Click ()
    Dim word As String, num As Integer
    Let word = "Visual Basic"
    Let num = 6
    Call FirstPart(word, num)
End Sub

Sub FirstPart (term As String, digit As Integer)
    Picture1.Print "The first"; digit; "letters are ";
    Picture1.Print Left$(term, digit)
End Sub
```

30.
```
Sub Command1_Click ()
    Dim object As String, tons As Single
    Let object = "The Statue of Liberty"
    Let tons = 250
    Call HowHeavy(object, tons)
End Sub

Sub HowHeavy (what As String, weight As Single)
    Picture1.Print what; " weighs"; weight; "tons"
End Sub
```

31.
```
Sub Command1_Click ()
    Dim word As String
    Let word = "worldly"
    Call Negative("un" + word, word)
End Sub

Sub Negative (neg As String, word As String)
    Picture1.Print "The negative of "; word; " is "; neg
End Sub
```

32.
```
Sub Command1_Click ()
    Dim age As Integer, yrs As Integer, major As String
    Let age = Val(InputBox$("How old are you?"))
    Let yrs = Val(InputBox$("In how many years will you graduate?"))
    Let major=InputBox$("What sort of major do you have(Arts or Sciences)?")
    Call Graduation(age + yrs, Left$(major, 1))
End Sub

Sub Graduation (num As Integer, letter As String)
    Picture1.Print "You will receive a B"; UCase$(letter);
    Picture1.Print " degree at age"; num
End Sub
```

(Assume that the responses are *19*, *3*, and *arts*.)

33.
```
Sub Command1_Click ()
    Call HowMany(24)
    Picture1.Print "a pie."
End Sub

Sub HowMany (num As Integer)
    Call What(num)
    Picture1.Print " baked in ";
End Sub

Sub What (num As Integer)
    Picture1.Print num; "blackbirds";
End Sub
```

34.
```
Sub Command1_Click ()
    Picture1.Print "All's";
    Call PrintWell
    Call PrintWords(" that ends")
    Picture1.Print "."
End Sub

Sub PrintWell
    Picture1.Print " well";
End Sub

Sub PrintWords (words As String)
    Picture1.Print words;
    Call PrintWell
End Sub
```

In Exercises 35 through 38, find the errors.

35.
```
Sub Command1_Click ()
    Dim n As Integer
    Let n = 5
    Call Alphabet
End Sub

Sub Alphabet (n As Integer)
    Picture1.Print Left$("abcdefghijklmnopqrstuvwxyz", n)
End Sub
```

36.
```
Sub Command1_Click ()
    Dim word As String, number As Single
    Let word = "seven"
    Let number = 7
    Call Display(word, number)
End Sub

Sub Display (num As Single, term As String)
    Picture1.Print num; term
End Sub
```

37.
```
Sub Command1_Click ()
    Dim nom As String
    Let nom = InputBox$("Name")
    Call Print(nom)
End Sub

Sub Print (handle As String)
    Picture1.Print "Your name is "; handle
End Sub
```

38.
```
Sub Command1_Click ()
    Dim num As Integer
    Let num = 2
    Call Tea(num)
End Sub

Sub Tea ()
    Picture1.Print "Tea for"; num
End Sub
```

In Exercises 39 through 42, rewrite the program so the output is performed by calls to a subprogram.

39.
```
Sub Command1_Click ()
    Dim num As Integer
    Rem Display a lucky number
    Picture1.Cls
    Let num = 7
    Picture1.Print num; "is a lucky number."
End Sub
```

40.
```
Sub Command1_Click ()
    Dim nom As String
    Rem Greet a friend
    Picture1.Cls
    Let nom = "Jack"
    Picture1.Print "Hi, "; nom
End Sub
```

41.
```
Sub Command1_Click ()
    Dim tree As String, ht As Single
    Rem Information about trees
    Picture1.Cls
    Open "TREES.TXT" For Input As #1
    Input #1, tree, ht
    Picture1.Print "The tallest "; tree; " in the U.S. is"; ht; "feet."
    Input #1, tree, ht
    Picture1.Print "The tallest "; tree; " in the U.S. is"; ht; "feet."
    Close #1
End Sub
```

(Assume that the file TREES.TXT contains the following two lines.)

"redwood", 362
"pine", 223

42.
```
Sub Command1_Click ()
    Dim major As String, enrolled As Single
    Rem Undergraduate majors at U of MD, College Park
    Picture1.Cls
    Open "MAJORS.TXT" For Input As #1
    Input #1, major, enrolled
    Picture1.Print "In 1992, the University of Maryland had";
    Picture1.Print enrolled; major; " majors."
    Input #1, major, enrolled
    Picture1.Print "In 1992, the University of Maryland had";
    Picture1.Print enrolled; major; " majors."
    Close #1
End Sub
```

(Assume that the file MAJORS.TXT contains the following two lines.)

"computer science", 914
"economics", 556

43. Write a program that requests a number as input and displays three times the number. The output should be produced by a call to a subprogram named Triple.

44. Write a program that requests a word as input and displays the word followed by the number of letters in the word. The output should be produced by a call to a subprogram named Length.

45. Write a program that requests a word and a column number from 1 through 10 as input and displays the word tabbed over to the column number. The output should be produced by a call to a subprogram named PlaceNShow.

46. Write a program that requests three numbers as input and displays the average of the three numbers. The output should be produced by a call to a subprogram named Average.

In Exercises 47 through 50, write a program that, when Command1 is clicked, will display in Picture1 the output shown. The last two lines of the output should be displayed by one or more subprograms using data passed by variables from an event procedure.

47. (Assume that the following is displayed.)

```
According to a 1991 survey of college freshmen
taken by the Higher Educational Research Institute:

18 percent said they intend to major in business
2 percent said they intend to major in computer science
```

48. (Assume that the current date is 12/31/1995, the label for Text1 reads "What is your year of birth?", and the user types 1976 into Text1 before Command1 is clicked.)

```
You are now 19 years old.
You have lived for more than 6935 days.
```

49. (Assume that the label for Text1 reads "What is your favorite number?" and the user types 7 into Text1 before Command1 is clicked.)

```
The sum of your favorite number with itself is 14
The product of your favorite number with itself is 49
```

50. (Assume that the following is displayed.)

```
In the year 1990,
533,600 college students took a course in Spanish
272,600 college students took a course in French
```

51. Write a program to display four verses of *Old McDonald Had a Farm*. The primary verse, with variables substituted for the animals and sounds, should be contained in a subprogram. The program should use the file FARM.TXT.

FARM.TXT contains the following four lines:

"lamb", "baa"
"firefly", "blink"
"chainsaw", "brraap"
"computer", "beep"

The first verse of the output should be

```
Old McDonald had a farm. Eyi eyi oh.
And on his farm he had a lamb. Eyi eyi oh.
With a baa baa here and a baa baa there.
Here a baa, there a baa, everywhere a baa baa.
Old McDonald had a farm. Eyi eyi oh.
```

52. Write a program that displays the word WOW vertically in large letters. Each letter should be drawn in a subprogram. For instance, the subprogram for the letter W is shown below.

```
Sub DrawW ()
  Rem Draw the letter W
  Picture1.Print "**            **"
  Picture1.Print " **          **"
  Picture1.Print "  **  **  **"
  Picture1.Print "   **    **"
  Picture1.Print
End Sub
```

53. Write a program to display the data from Table 4.1. The occupations and numbers of people for 1982 and 1991 should be contained in a file. A subprogram, to be called three times, should read the three pieces of data for an occupation, calculate the percent change from 1982 to 1991, and display the four items. **Note:** The percent change is calculated as 100 * (1991 value – 1982 value) / (1982 value).

Occupation	1982	1991	Percent Change
Computer analysts, programmers	719	1321	84%
Data processing equipment repairers	98	152	55%
Social workers	407	603	48%

Table 4.1 Occupations experiencing the greatest growth from 1982 to 1991 (numbers in thousands).

Source: Bureau of Labor Statistics

54. Write a program to compute tips for services rendered. The program should request the person's occupation, the amount of the bill, and the percentage tip as input and pass this information to a subprogram to display the person and the tip. A sample run is shown below.

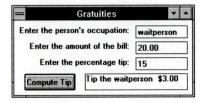

SOLUTIONS TO PRACTICE PROBLEMS 4.1

1. 1 2 3 4

After the subprogram Second is called, execution continues with the remaining statements in the subroutine First before returning to the event procedure.

2. The statement Sub AreaCode ( ) must be replaced by Sub AreaCode (phone As String). Whenever a value is passed to a subprogram, the Sub statement must provide a parameter to receive the value.

4.2 SUBPROGRAMS, PART II

The previous section introduced the concept of a subprogram, but left some questions unanswered. Why can't the value of a variable be passed from an event procedure to a subprogram by just using the variable in the subprogram? How do subprograms pass values back to an event procedure? The answers to these questions provide a deeper understanding of the workings of subprograms and reveal their full capabilities.

Passing Values Back from Subprograms

Suppose a variable, call it *arg*, appears as an argument in a Call statement, and its corresponding parameter in the Sub statement is *par*. After the subprogram is executed, *arg* will have whatever value *par* had in the subprogram. Hence, not only is the value of *arg* passed to *par*, but the value of *par* is passed back to *arg*.

EXAMPLE 1   The following program illustrates the transfer of the value of a parameter to its calling argument.

```
Sub Command1_Click ()
  Dim amt As Single
  Rem Illustrate effect of value of parameter on value of argument
  Picture1.Cls
  Let amt = 2
  Picture1.Print amt;
  Call Triple(amt)
  Picture1.Print amt
End Sub

Sub Triple (num As Single)
  Rem Triple a number
  Picture1.Print num;
  Let num = 3 * num
  Picture1.Print num;
End Sub
```

[Run and then click the command button. The following is displayed in the picture box.]

```
2  2  6  6
```

Although this feature may be surprising at first glance, it provides a vehicle for passing values from a subprogram back to the place from which the subprogram was called. Different names may be used for an argument and its corresponding parameter, but only one memory location is involved. Initially, the Command1_Click( ) event procedure allocates a memory location to hold the value of *amt* (Figure 4.3(a)). When the subprogram is called, the parameter *num* becomes the subprograms's name for this memory location (Figure 4.3(b)). When the value of *num* is tripled, the value in the memory location becomes 6 (Figure 4.3(c)). After the completion of the procedure, the parameter name *num* is forgotten; however, its value lives on in *amt* (Figure 4.3(d)). The variable *amt* is said to be **passed by reference**.

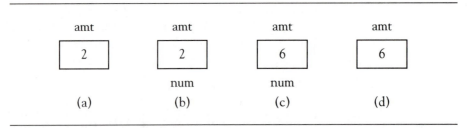

Figure 4.3 Passing a variable by reference to a subprogram.

Passing by reference has a wide variety of uses. In the next example, it is used as a vehicle to transport a value from a subprogram back to an event procedure.

EXAMPLE 2   The following variation of the addition program from the previous section uses a subprogram to acquire the input. The variables *x* and *y* are not assigned values prior to the execution of the first Call statement. Therefore, before the Call statement is executed, they have the value 0. After the Call statement is executed, however, they have the values 2 and 3. These values then are passed by the second Call statement to the subprogram Add.

Object	Property	Setting
Form1	Caption	Add Two Numbers
Label1	Caption	First Number
Text1	Text	(blank)
Label2	Caption	Second Number
Text2	Text	(blank)
Command1	Caption	Compute Sum
Picture1		

```
Sub Command1_Click ()
  Dim x As Single, y As Single
  Rem Display the sum of the two numbers
  Call GetNumbers(x, y)
  Call Add(x, y)
End Sub

Sub Add (num1 As Single, num2 As Single)
  Dim sum As Single
  Rem Display numbers and their sum
  Picture1.Cls
  Let sum = num1 + num2
  Picture1.Print "The sum of"; num1; "and"; num2; "is"; sum
End Sub

Sub GetNumbers (num1 As Single, num2 As Single)
  Rem Record the two numbers in the text boxes
  Let num1 = Val(Text1.Text)
  Let num2 = Val(Text2.Text)
End Sub
```

[Run, type 2 and 3 into the text boxes, and then click the command button.]

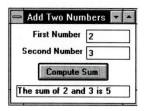

In most situations, a variable with no preassigned value is used as an argument of a Call statement for the sole purpose of carrying back a value from the subprogram.

EXAMPLE 3   The following variation of Example 2 allows the Command1_Click event procedure to be written in the input-process-output style.

```
Sub Command1_Click ()
  Dim x As Single, y As Single, s As Single
  Rem Display the sum of two numbers
  Call GetNumbers(x, y)
  Call CalculateSum(x, y, s)
  Call DisplayResult(x, y, s)
End Sub

Sub CalculateSum (num1 As Single, num2 As Single, sum As Single)
  Rem Add the values of num1 and num2
  Rem and assign the value to sum
  Let sum = num1 + num2
End Sub

Sub DisplayResult (num1 As Single, num2 As Single, sum As Single)
  Rem Display a sentence giving the two numbers and their sum
  Picture1.Cls
  Picture1.Print "The sum of"; num1; "and"; num2; "is"; sum
End Sub

Sub GetNumbers (num1 As Single, num2 As Single)
  Rem Record the two numbers in the text boxes
  Let num1 = Val(Text1.Text)
  Let num2 = Val(Text2.Text)
End Sub
```

Local Variables

When the same variable name appears in two different subprograms or in a subprogram and an event procedure, Visual Basic gives the variables separate identities and treats them as two different variables. A value assigned to a variable in one part of the program will not affect the value of the like-named variable in the other part of the program, unless, of course, the values are passed by a Call statement. Also, each time a subprogram is called, all variables that are not parameters assume their default values, either zero or the empty string. The variables in a subprogram are said to be **local** to the subprogram in which they reside.

EXAMPLE 4   The following program illustrates the fact that each time a subprogram is called, its variables are set to their default values; that is, numerical variables are set to 0 and string variables are set to the empty string.

```
Sub Command1_Click ()
   Rem  Demonstrate that variables in a subprogram do
   Rem  not retain their values in subsequent calls
   Picture1.Cls
   Call Three
   Call Three
End Sub

Sub Three ()
   Dim num As Single
   Rem Display the value of num and assign it the value 3
   Picture1.Print num;
   Let num = 3
End Sub
```

[Run and then click the command button. The following is displayed in the picture box.]

```
0  0
```

EXAMPLE 5   The following program illustrates the fact that variables are local to the part of the program in which they reside. The variable x in the event procedure and the variable x in the subprogram are treated as different variables. Visual Basic handles them as if their names were separate, such as *xCommand1_Click.* and *xTrivial.* Also, each time the subprogram is called, the value of variable x inside the subprogram is reset to 0.

```
Sub Command1_Click ()
   Dim x As Single
   Rem Demonstrate the local nature of variables
   Picture1.Cls
   Let x = 2
   Picture1.Print x;
   Call Trivial
   Picture1.Print x;
   Call Trivial
   Picture1.Print x;
End Sub

Sub Trivial ()
   Dim x As Single
   Rem Do something trivial
   Picture1.Print x;
   Let x = 3
   Picture1.Print x;
End Sub
```

[Run and then click the command button. The following is displayed in the picture box.]

```
2  0  3  2  0  3  2
```

Form-level Variables

Visual Basic provides a way to make a variable visible to *every* procedure in the form without being passed. Such a variable is called a **form-level variable**. Form-level variables are declared in the (declarations) section of (general) with the following steps.

    1. Invoke a code window if one is not already active.

    2. Click on the down-arrow to the right of the object list box.

    3. Double-click on (general).

    4. Type in a declaration statement, such as Dim strVar As String.

When a form-level variable is assigned a value by a procedure, it retains that value when the procedure is exited. In this text, we rarely use form-level variables until Chapter 7.

EXAMPLE 6   The following demonstration program contains the form-level variables *num1* and *num2*. Their Dim statement does not appear inside a procedure.

```
Dim num1 As Single, num2 As Single     'In (declarations) section of (general)

Sub Command1_Click()
  Rem Display the sum of two numbers
  Let num1 = 2
  Let num2 = 3
  Picture1.Cls
  Call AddAndIncrement
  Picture1.Print
  Picture1.Print "num1 = "; num1
  Picture1.Print "num2 = "; num2
End Sub

Sub AddAndIncrement ()
  Rem Display numbers and their sum
  Picture1.Print "The sum of"; num1; "and"; num2; "is"; num1 + num2
  Let num1 = num1 + 1
  Let num2 = num2 + 1
End Sub
```

[Run and click the command button. The following is displayed in the picture box.]

```
The sum of 2 and 3 is 5

num1 = 3
num2 = 4
```

In the above example we had to click a command button to assign values to the form-level variables. In some situations we want to assign a value immediately to a form-level variable, without requiring the user to perform some specific action. Visual Basic has a special event procedure called Form_Load that is automatically activated as soon as the program is run, even before the form is created. The Form_Load template is invoked by double-clicking on the form itself.

EXAMPLE 7   The following program demonstrates the use of Form_Load.

```
Dim pi As Single    'In (declarations) section of (general)

Sub Form_Load ()
  Rem  Assign a value to pi
  Let pi = 3.14159
End Sub

Sub Command1_Click()
  Rem Display the area a circle of radius 5
  Picture1.Cls
  Picture1.Print "The area of a circle of radius 5 is"; pi * 5 ^ 2
End Sub
```

[Run and then click the command button. The following is displayed in the picture box.]

```
The area of a circle of radius 5 is 78.53975
```

Comments:

1. In addition to the reasons presented earlier, some other reasons for using subprograms follow:

   (a) Programs with subprograms are easier to debug. Each subprogram can be checked individually before being placed into the program.
   (b) The task performed by a subprogram might be needed in another program. The subprogram can be reused with no changes. Programmers refer to the collection of their most universal subprograms as a **library** of subprograms. (The fact that variables appearing in subprograms are local to the subprograms is quite helpful when reusing subprograms in other programs. There is no need to worry if a variable in the subprogram is used for a different purpose in another part of the program.)
   (c) Often, programs are written by a team of programmers. After a problem has been broken into distinct and manageable tasks, each programmer is assigned a single subprogram to write.
   (d) Subprograms make large programs easier to understand. Some programming standards insist that each subprogram be at most two pages long.

(e) Subprograms permit the following program design, which provides a built-in outline of an event procedure. A reader can focus on the main flow first, and then go into the specifics of accomplishing the secondary tasks.

```
Sub Object_Event ()
   Rem An event procedure written entirely as subprograms
   Call FirstSubprogram      'Perform first task
   Call SecondSubprogram     'Perform second task
   Call ThirdSubprogram      'Perform third task
End Sub
```

2. Subprograms can call other subprograms. In such cases, the calling subprogram plays the role of the event procedure with respect to the called subprogram. Complex problems are thereby broken into simpler tasks, which are then broken into still more elementary tasks. This approach to problem solving is called **top-down design**.

3. In Appendix D, the section "Stepping Through a Program Containing a Procedure: Chapter 4" uses the Visual Basic debugger to trace the flow through a program and observe the interplay between arguments and parameters.

4. The Form_Load event procedure is activated just before the form and its controls appears on the screen. Therefore, it cannot contain statements such as

```
Picture1.Print "Hello".
```

PRACTICE PROBLEMS 4.2

1. What does the following code display in the picture box when the command button is clicked?

```
Sub Command1_Click ()
   Dim b As Integer, c As Integer
   Let b = 1
   Let c = 2
   Call Rhyme
   Picture1.Print b; c
End Sub

Sub Rhyme ()
   Dim b As Integer, c As Integer
   Picture1.Print b; c; "buckle my shoe."
   Let b = 3
End Sub
```

2. When a variable appears as a parameter in the top line of a subprogram, how do we know if its role is to receive a value from an event procedure or to pass a value back to an event procedure, or both?

EXERCISES 4.2

In Exercises 1 through 18, determine the output displayed in the picture box when the command button is clicked.

1.
```
Sub Command1_Click ()
    Dim num As Single
    Let num = 7
    Call AddTwo(num)
    Picture1.Print num
End Sub

Sub AddTwo (num As Single)
    Let num = num + 2
End Sub
```

2.
```
Sub Command1_Click ()
    Dim term As String
    Let term = "Fall"
    Call Plural(term)
    Picture1.Print term
End Sub

Sub Plural (term As String)
    Let term = term + "s"
End Sub
```

3.
```
Sub Command1_Click ()
    Dim dance As String
    Let dance = "Can "
    Call Twice(dance)
    Picture1.Print dance
End Sub

Sub Twice (dance As String)
    Let dance = dance + dance
End Sub
```

4.
```
Sub Command1_Click ()
    Dim num As Single, fmt As String
    Let num = 1234.967
    Call GetFormatString(fmt)
    Picture1.Print "The number is "; Format$(num, fmt)
End Sub

Sub GetFormatString (formatString As String)
    Let formatString = "currency"
End Sub
```

5.
```
Sub Command1_Click ()
    Dim a As Single
    Let a = 5
    Call Square(a)
    Picture1.Print a
End Sub

Sub Square (num As Single)
    Let num = num * num
End Sub
```

6.
```
Sub Command1_Click ()
    Dim state As String
    Let state = "NEBRASKA"
    Call Abbreviate(state)
    Picture1.Print state
End Sub

Sub Abbreviate (a As String)
    Let a = Left$(a, 2)
End Sub
```

7.
```
Sub Command1_Click ()
    Dim word As String
    Call GetWord(word)
    Picture1.Print "Less is "; word
End Sub
```

```
Sub GetWord (w As String)
  Let w = "more"
End Sub
```

8.
```
Sub Command1_Click ()
    Dim hourlyWage As Single, annualWage As Single
    Let hourlyWage = 10
    Call CalculateAnnualWage(hourlyWage, annualWage)
    Picture1.Print "Approximate Annual Wage:"; annualWage
End Sub

Sub CalculateAnnualWage (hWage As Single, aWage As Single)
  Let aWage = 2000 * hWage
End Sub
```

9.
```
Sub Command1_Click ()
    Dim nom As String, yob As Integer
    Call GetVita(nom, yob)
    Picture1.Print nom; " was born in the year"; yob
End Sub

Sub GetVita (nom As String, yob As Integer)
  Let nom = "Gabriel"         'name
  Let yob = 1980              'year of birth
End Sub
```

10.
```
Sub Command1_Click ()
    Dim word1 As String, word2 As String
    Let word1 = "fail"
    Let word2 = "plan"
    Picture1.Print "If you ";
    Call Sentence(word1, word2)
    Call Exchange(word1, word2)
    Picture1.Print " then you ";
    Call Sentence(word1, word2)
End Sub

Sub Exchange (word1 As String, word2 As String)
  Dim temp As String
  Let temp = word1
  Let word1 = word2
  Let word2 = temp
End Sub

Sub Sentence (word1 As String, word2 As String)
  Picture1.Print word1; " to "; word2;
End Sub
```

11.
```
Sub Command1_Click ()
    Dim state As String
    Let state = "Ohio "
    Call Team
End Sub

Sub Team
    Dim state As String
    Picture1.Print state;
    Picture1.Print "Buckeyes"
End Sub
```

12.
```
Sub Command1_Click ()
    Dim a As Single
    Let a = 5
    Call Multiply(7)
    Picture1.Print a * 7
End Sub

Sub Multiply (num As Single)
    Dim a As Single
    Let a = 11
    Picture1.Print a * num
End Sub
```

13.
```
Sub Command1_Click ()
    Dim a As Single
    Let a = 5
    Call Multiply(7)
End Sub

Sub Multiply (num As Single)
    Dim a As Single
    Picture1.Print a * num
End Sub
```

14.
```
Sub Command1_Click ()
    Dim nom As String, n As String
    Let nom = "Ray"
    Call Hello(nom)
    Picture1.Print n; " and "; nom
End Sub

Sub Hello (nom As String)
    Dim n As String
    Let n = nom
    Let nom = "Bob"
    Picture1.Print "Hello "; n; " and "; nom
End Sub
```

15.
```
Sub Command1_Click ()
    Dim num As Single
    Let num = 1
    Call Amount(num)
    Call Amount(num)
End Sub

Sub Amount (num As Single)
    Dim total As Single
    Let total = total + num
    Picture1.Print total;
End Sub
```

16.
```
Sub Command1_Click ()
    Dim river As String
    Let river = "Wabash"
    Call Another
    Picture1.Print river
    Call Another
End Sub

Sub Another ()
    Dim river As String
    Picture1.Print river;
    Let river = "Yukon"
End Sub
```

17.
```
Sub Command1_Click ()
    Dim explorer As String
    Let explorer = "de Leon"
    Call Place(explorer)
End Sub

Sub Place (nom As String)
    Picture1.Print explorer; " discovered Florida"
End Sub
```

18.
```
Sub Command1_Click ()
    Dim tax As Single, price As Single, total As Single
    Let tax = .05
    Call GetPrice("bicycle", price)
    Call ProcessItem(price, tax, total)
    Call DisplayResult(total)
End Sub

Sub DisplayResult (total As Single)
    Picture1.Print "With tax, the price is "; Format$(total, "currency")
End Sub

Sub GetPrice (item As String, price As Single)
    Dim strVar As String
    Let strVar = InputBox$("What is the price of a " + item + "?")
    Let price = Val(strVar)
End Sub

Sub ProcessItem (price As Single, tax As Single, total As Single)
    Let total = (1 + tax) * price
End Sub
```

(Assume that the cost of the bicycle is $200.)

In Exercises 19 and 20, find the errors.

19.
```
Sub Command1_Click ()
    Dim a As Single, b As Single, c As Single
    Let a = 1
    Let b = 2
    Call Sum(a, b, c)
    Picture1.Print "The sum is"; c
End Sub

Sub Sum (x As Single, y As Single)
    Dim c As Single
    Let c = x + y
End Sub
```

20.
```
Sub Command1_Click ()
    Dim ano As String
    Call GetYear(ano)
    Picture1.Print ano
End Sub

Sub GetYear (yr As Single)
    Let yr = 1995
End Sub
```

In Exercises 21 through 24, rewrite the program so input, processing, and output are each performed by Calls to subprograms.

21.
```
Sub Command1_Click ()
    Dim price As Single, tax As Single, cost As Single
    Rem Calculate sales tax
    Picture1.Cls
    Let price = InputBox$("Enter the price of the item:")
    Let tax = .05 * price
    Let cost = price + tax
    Picture1.Print "Price: "; price
    Picture1.Print "Tax: "; tax
    Picture1.Print "-----------"
    Picture1.Print "Cost: "; cost
End Sub
```

22.
```
Sub Command1_Click ()
    Dim nom As String, n As Integer, firstName As String
    Rem Letter of acceptance
    Picture1.Cls
    Let nom = InputBox$("What is your full name?")
    Let n = InStr(nom, " ")
    Let firstName = Left$(nom, n - 1)
    Picture1.Print "Dear "; firstName; ","
    Picture1.Print "We are proud to accept you to Gotham College."
End Sub
```

23.
```
Sub Command1_Click ()
    Dim length As Single, wdth As Single, area As Single
    Rem Determine the area of a rectangle
    Picture1.Cls
    Let length = Val(Text1.Text)
    Let wdth = Val(Text2.Text)
    Let area = length * wdth
    Picture1.Print "The area of the rectangle is"; area
End Sub
```

24.
```
Sub Command1_Click ()
    Dim a As String, feet As Single, inches As Single
    Dim totalInches As Single, centimeters As Single
    Rem Convert feet and inches to centimeters
    Picture1.Cls
    Let a =  "Give the length in feet and inches."
    Let feet = InputBox$(a + "Enter the number of feet.")
    Let inches = InputBox$(a + "Enter the number of inches. ")
    Let totalInches = 12 * feet + inches
    Let centimeters = 2.54 * totalInches
    Picture1.Print "The length in centimeters is"; centimeters
End Sub
```

In Exercises 25 and 26, write a line of code to carry out the task. Specify where in the program the line of code would occur.

25. Declare the variable *nom* as a string variable visible to all parts of the program.

26. Declare the variable *nom* as a string variable visible only to the Form_Click event.

In Exercises 27 through 32, write a program to perform the stated task. The input, processing, and output should be performed by calls to subprograms.

27. Request a person's first name and last name as input and display the corresponding initials.

28. Request the amount of a restaurant bill as input and display the amount, the tip (15 percent), and the total amount.

29. Request the cost and selling price of an item of merchandise as input and display the percentage markup. Test the program with a cost of $4 and a selling price of $6. **Note:** The percentage markup is 100 * ((selling price − cost) / cost).

30. Read the number of students in public colleges (10.8 million) and private colleges (3.1 million) from a file, and display the percentage of college students attending public colleges.

31. Read a baseball player's name (Sheffield), times at bat (557), and hits (184) from a file and display his name and batting average. **Note:** Batting average is calculated as (hits)/(times at bat).

32. Request three numbers as input and then calculate and display the average of the three numbers.

33. The Hat Rack is considering locating its new branch store in one of three malls. The file below gives the monthly rent per square foot and the total square feet available at each of the three locations. Write a program to display a table exhibiting this information along with the total monthly rent for each mall.

    MALLS.TXT contains the following three lines:

    "Green Mall", 6.50, 583
    "Red Mall", 7.25, 426
    "Blue Mall", 5.00, 823

34. Write a program that uses the data in file CHARGES.TXT below to display the end-of-month credit card balances of three people. (Each line gives a person's name, beginning balance, purchases during month, and payment for the month.) The end-of-month balance is calculated as [finance charges] + [beginning-of-month balance] + [purchases] − [payment], where the finance charge is 1.5 percent of the beginning-of-month balance.

    CHARGES.TXT contains the following three lines:

    "John Adams", 125.00, 60.00, 110.00
    "Sue Jones", 0, 117.25, 117.25
    "John Smith", 350.00, 200.50, 300.00

35. Write a program to produce a sales receipt. Each time the user clicks on a command button, an item and its price should be read from a pair of text boxes and displayed in a picture box. Use a form-level variable to track the sum of the prices. When the user clicks on a second command button (after all the entries have been made), the program should display the sum of the prices, the sales tax (5 percent of total), and the total amount to be paid. Figure 4.4 shows a sample output of the program.

```
Light bulbs    2.65
Soda           3.45
Soap           1.15
               --------
Sum            7.25
Tax            0.36
Total          7.61
```

Figure 4.4 Sales receipt for Exercise 35.

SOLUTIONS TO PRACTICE PROBLEMS 4.2

1. `0  0 buckle my shoe.`
   `1  2`

   This program illustrates the local nature of the variables in a subprogram. Notice that the variables *b* and *c* appearing in the subprogram have no relationship whatsoever to the variables of the same name in the event procedure. In a certain sense, the variables inside the subprogram can be thought of as having alternate names, such as *bRhyme* and *cRhyme*.

2. You cannot determine this by simply looking at the arguments and the parameters. The code of the subprogram must be examined.

4.3 FUNCTIONS

Visual Basic has many built-in functions. In one respect, functions are like miniature programs. They use input, they process the input, and they have output. Some functions we encountered earlier are listed in Table 4.2.

Function	Example	Input	Output
Int	Int(2.6) is 2	number	number
Chr$	Chr$(65) is "A"	number	string
Len	Len("perhaps") is 7	string	number
Mid$	Mid$("perhaps",4,2) is "ha"	string,number,number	string
InStr	InStr("to be"," ") is 3	string,string	number

Table 4.2 Some Visual Basic built-in functions.

Although the input can involve several values, the output always consists of a single value. The items inside the parentheses can be constants (as above), variables, or expressions. The type of output can be determined by looking at the name of the function. For instance, if the name is followed by a dollar sign, then the output is a string.

In addition to using built-in functions, we can define functions of our own. These new functions, called **user-defined functions**, are defined in much the same way as subprograms and are used in the same way as built-in functions. Like built-in functions, user-defined functions have a single output which can be string or numeric. User-defined functions can be used in expressions in exactly the same way as built-in functions. Programs refer to them as if they were constants, variables, or expressions. Functions are defined by function blocks of the form

```
Function FunctionName (var1 As Type1, var2 As Type2, ...) As dataType
  statement(s)
  FunctionName = expression
End Function
```

The variables in the top line are called **parameters** and variables inside the function block that are not parameters are local. Function names should be suggestive of the role performed and must conform to the rules for naming variables. The type *dataType* will be one of String, Integer, Single, and so on. In the general code above, the next-to-last line assigns the output, which must be of type *dataType*, to the function name. When the output of a function is a string, the As String may be dropped if a dollar signed is added to the end of the function name. Two examples of functions are as follows:

```
Function FtoC (t As Single) As Single
  Rem Convert Fahrenheit temperature to Celsius
  FtoC = (5 / 9) * (t - 32)
End Function

Function FirstName$ (nom As String)
  Dim firstSpace As Integer
  Rem Extract the first name from the full name nom
  Let firstSpace = InStr(nom, " ")
  FirstName$ = Left$(nom, firstSpace - 1)
End Function
```

In each of the preceding functions, the value of the function is assigned by a statement of the form *FunctionName = expression*. (Such a statement can also be written as Let *FunctionName = expression*.) The variables *t* and *nom* appearing in the functions above are parameters. They can be replaced with any variable of the same type without affecting the function definition. For instance, the function FtoC could have been defined as

```
Function FtoC (temp As Single) As Single
  Rem Convert Fahrenheit temperature to Celsius
  FtoC = (5 / 9) * (temp - 32)
End Function
```

Like subprograms, functions are created with **Alt/V/N**. The only difference is that the circle next to the word Function should be selected. After the name is typed and the OK button is clicked, the lines Function *FunctionName* ( ) and End Function will automatically be placed (separated by a blank line) in the function window.

EXAMPLE 1   The following program uses the function FtoC.

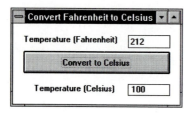

Object	Property	Setting
Form1	Caption	Convert Fahrenheit to Celsius
Label1	Caption	Temperature (Fahrenheit)
Text1	Text	(blank)
Command1	Caption	Convert to Celsius
Label2	Caption	Temperature (Celsius)
Picture1		

```
Sub Command1_Click ()
  Picture1.Cls
  Picture1.Print FtoC(Val(Text1.Text))
End Sub


Function FtoC (t As Single) As Single
  Rem Convert Fahrenheit temperature to Celsius
  FtoC = (5 / 9) * (t - 32)
End Function
```

[Run, type 212 into the text box, and then click the command button.]

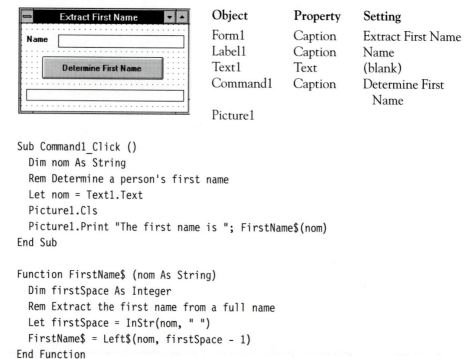

EXAMPLE 2   The following program uses the function FirstName$.

Object	Property	Setting
Form1	Caption	Extract First Name
Label1	Caption	Name
Text1	Text	(blank)
Command1	Caption	Determine First Name
Picture1		

```
Sub Command1_Click ()
  Dim nom As String
  Rem Determine a person's first name
  Let nom = Text1.Text
  Picture1.Cls
  Picture1.Print "The first name is "; FirstName$(nom)
End Sub


Function FirstName$ (nom As String)
  Dim firstSpace As Integer
  Rem Extract the first name from a full name
  Let firstSpace = InStr(nom, " ")
  FirstName$ = Left$(nom, firstSpace - 1)
End Function
```

[Run, type Thomas Woodrow Wilson into the text box, and then click the command button.]

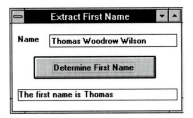

The input to a user-defined function can consist of one or more values. Two examples of functions with several parameters are shown below. One-letter variable names have been used so the mathematical formulas will look familiar and be readable. Since the names are not descriptive, the meanings of these variables are carefully stated in Rem statements.

```
Function Hypotenuse (a As Single, b As Single) As Single
   Rem  Calculate the hypotenuse of a right triangle
   Rem  having sides of lengths a and b
   Hypotenuse = Sqr(a ^ 2 + b ^ 2)
End Function

Function FVal (p As Single,r As Single,c As Single,n As Single) As Single
   Dim i As Single, m As Single
   Rem Find the future value of a bank savings account
   Rem p  principal, the amount deposited
   Rem r  annual rate of interest
   Rem c  number of times interest is compounded per year
   Rem n  number of years
   Rem i  interest per period
   Rem m  total number of times interest is compounded
   Let i = r / c
   Let m = c * n
   FVal = p * ((1 + i) ^ m)
End Function
```

EXAMPLE 3 The following program uses the Hypotenuse function.

Object	Property	Setting
Form1	Caption	Right Triangle
Label1	Caption	Length of one side
Text1	Text	(blank)
Label2	Caption	Length of other side
Text2	Text	(blank)
Command1	Caption	Calculate Hypotenuse
Label3	Caption	Length of one side
Picture1		

```
Sub Command1_Click ()
  Dim a As Single, b As Single
  Rem Calculate length of the hypotenuse of a right triangle
  Let a = Val(Text1.Text)
  Let b = Val(Text2.Text)
  Picture1.Cls
  Picture1.Print Hypotenuse(a, b)
End Sub

Function Hypotenuse (a As Single, b As Single) As Single
  Rem Calculate the hypotenuse of a right triangle
  Rem having sides of lengths a and b
  Hypotenuse = Sqr(a ^ 2 + b ^ 2)
End Function
```

[Run, type 3 and 4 into the text boxes, and then click the command button.]

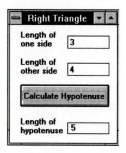

EXAMPLE 4 The following program uses the future value function. With the responses shown, the program computes the balance in a savings account when $100 is deposited for 5 years at 4 percent interest compounded quarterly. Interest is earned 4 times per year at the rate of 1 percent per interest period. There will be 4 * 5 or 20 interest periods.

Object	Property	Setting
Form1	Caption	Bank Deposit
Label1	Caption	Amount of bank deposit
Text1	Text	(blank)
Label2	Caption	Annual rate of interest
Text2	Text	(blank)
Label3	Caption	Number of times interest is com- pounded per year
Text3	Text	(blank)
Label4	Caption	Number of years
Text4	Text	(blank)
Command1	Caption	Compute Balance
Label5	Caption	Balance
Picture1		

```
Sub Command1_Click ()
  Dim p As Single, r As Single, c As Single, n As Single
  Rem Find the future value of a bank deposit
  Call InputData(p, r, c, n)
  Call DisplayBalance(p, r, c, n)
End Sub

Sub DisplayBalance (p As Single, r As Single, c As Single, n As Single)
  Dim balance As Single
  Rem Display the balance in the picture box
  Picture1.Cls
  Let balance = FVal(p, r, c, n)
  Picture1.Print Format$(balance, "currency")
End Sub

Function FVal (p As Single, r As Single, c As Single, n As Single) As Single
  Dim i As Single, m As Single
  Rem Find the future value of a bank savings account
  Rem p   principal, the amount deposited
  Rem r   annual rate of interest
  Rem c   number of times interest is compounded per year
  Rem n   number of years
  Rem i   interest per period
  Rem m   total number of times interest is compounded
  Let i = r / c
  Let m = c * n
  FVal = p * ((1 + i) ^ m)
End Function

Sub InputData (p As Single, r As Single, c As Single, n As Single)
  Rem Get the four values from the text boxes
  Let p = Val(Text1.Text)
  Let r = Val(Text2.Text)
  Let c = Val(Text3.Text)
  Let n = Val(Text4.Text)
End Sub
```

[Run, type 100, .04, 4, and 5 into the text boxes, then click the command button.]

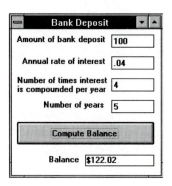

EXAMPLE 5   Some computer languages have a useful built-in function called Ceil that is similar to the function Int, except that it rounds noninteger numbers up to the next integer. For instance, Ceil(3.2) is 4 and Ceil(–1.6) is –1. The following program creates Ceil in Visual Basic as a user-defined function.

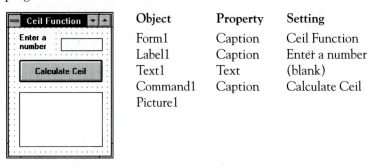

Object	Property	Setting
Form1	Caption	Ceil Function
Label1	Caption	Enter a number
Text1	Text	(blank)
Command1	Caption	Calculate Ceil
Picture1		

```
Function Ceil (x As Single) As Single
  Rem Round nonintegers up
  Ceil = -Int(-x)
End Function

Sub Command1_Click ()
 Rem Demonstrate the Ceil function
 Picture1.Print "Ceil("; Text1.Text; ") ="; Ceil(Val(Text1.Text))
End Sub
```

[Run, type 4.3 into the text box, click the command button, type 4 into the text box, and then click the command button again.]

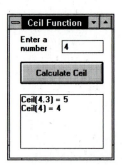

There are many reasons for employing user-defined functions.

1. User-defined functions are consistent with the modular approach to program design. Once we realize a particular function is needed, we can give it a name but save the task of figuring out the computational details until later.

2. Sometimes a single formula must be used several times in a program. Specifying the formula as a function saves repeated typing of the same formula, improves readability, and simplifies debugging.

3. Functions written for one program can be used in other programs. Programmers maintain a collection, or library, of functions that might be needed.

Comments:

1. The word **procedure** refers to either a function or a subprogram.

2. Functions can perform the same tasks as subprograms. For instance, they can request input and display text; however, they are primarily used to calculate a single value. Normally, subprograms are used to carry out other tasks.

3. Functions differ from subprograms in the way they are accessed. Subprograms are invoked with Call statements, whereas functions are invoked by placing them where you would otherwise expect to find a constant, variable, or expression.

4. Functions can invoke other functions or subprograms.

5. Functions, like subprograms, need not have any parameters. Unlike subprograms, when a parameterless function is used, the function name must be followed by an empty set of parentheses. The following program uses a "parameterless" function.

```
Sub Command1_Click ()
  Rem Request and display a saying
  Picture1.Cls
  Picture1.Print Saying$()
End Sub

Function Saying$ ()
  Rem Retrieve a saying from the user
  Saying$ = InputBox$("What is your favorite saying?")
End Function
```

[Run, click the command button, and then type *Less is more.* into the message box.]

The saying *Less is more.* is displayed in the picture box.

6. An alternative method of creating a function window is to move the cursor to a blank line of any code window, type Function *FunctionName*, and press the Enter key.

PRACTICE PROBLEMS 4.3

1. Suppose a program contains the lines

```
Dim n As Single, x As String
Picture1.Print a$(n, x)
```

What types of inputs and output (numeric or string) does the function a$ have?

2. What is displayed in the picture box when Command1 is clicked?

```
Sub Command1_Click ()
  Dim gallonsPerBushel As Single, apples As Single
  Rem How many gallons of apple cider can we make?
  Call GetData(gallonsPerBushel, apples)
  Call DisplayNumOfGallons(gallonsPerBushel, apples)
End Sub

Function Cider (g As Single, x As Single) As Single
  Cider = g * x
End Function

Sub DisplayNumOfGallons (galPerBu As Single, apples As Single)
  Picture1.Cls
  Picture1.Print "You can make"; Cider(galPerBu, apples);
  Picture1.Print "gallons of cider."
End Sub

Sub GetData (gallonsPerBushel As Single, apples As Single)
  Rem  gallonsPerBushel    Number of gallons of cider one bushel
  Rem                      of apples makes
  Rem  apples              Number of bushels of apples available
  Let gallonsPerBushel = 3
  Let apples = 9
End Sub
```

EXERCISES 4.3

In Exercises 1 through 10, determine the output displayed in the picture box when the command button is clicked.

1.
```
Sub Command1_Click ()
  Dim temp As Single
  Rem Convert Celsius to Fahrenheit
  Let temp = 95
  Picture1.Print CtoF(temp)
End Sub

Function CtoF (t As Single) As Single
  CtoF = (9 / 5) * t + 32
End Function
```

2.
```
Sub Command1_Click ()
  Dim acres As Single
  Rem  acres    Number of acres in a parking lot
  Let acres = 5
  Picture1.Print "You can park about"; Cars(acres); "cars."
End Sub

Function Cars (x As Single) As Single
  Rem Parking cars
  Cars = 100 * x
End Function
```

3.
```
Sub Command1_Click ()
    Dim p As Single
    Rem Rule of 72
    Let p = Val(Text1.Text)        'Population growth as a percent
    Picture1.Print "The population will double in"
    Picture1.Print DoublingTime(p); "years."
End Sub

Function DoublingTime (x As Single) As Single
    Rem Estimate time required for a population to double
    Rem at a growth rate of x percent
    DoublingTime = 72 / x
End Function
```

(Assume that the text box contains the number 3.)

4.
```
Sub Command1_Click ()
    Dim initVel As Single, initHt As Single
    Rem Calculate max. ht. of a ball thrown straight up in the air
    Let initVel = Val(Text1.Text)    'Initial velocity of ball
    Let initHt = Val(Text2.Text)     'Initial height of ball
    Picture1.Print MaximumHeight(initVel, initHt)
End Sub

Function MaximumHeight (v As Single, h As Single) As Single
    MaximumHeight = h + v ^ 2 / 64
End Function
```

(Assume that the text boxes contain the values 96 and 256.)

5.
```
Sub Command1_Click ()
    Dim r As Single, h As Single
    Rem Compute volume of a cylinder
    Let r = 1
    Let h = 2
    Call DisplayVolume(r, h)
    Let r = 3
    Let h = 4
    Call DisplayVolume(r, h)
End Sub

Function Area (r As Single) As Single
    Rem Compute area of a circle of radius r
    Area = 3.14159 * r ^ 2
End Function

Sub DisplayVolume (r As Single, h As Single)
    Picture1.Print "Volume of cylinder having base area"; Area(r)
    Picture1.Print "and height"; h; "is"; h * Area(r)
End Sub
```

6.
```
Sub Command1_Click ()
    Dim days As String, num As Integer
    Rem Determine the day of the week from its number
    Let days = "SunMonTueWedThuFriSat"
    Let num = Val(InputBox$("Enter the number of the day"))
    Picture1.Print "The day is "; DayOfWeek$(days, num)
End Sub

Function DayOfWeek$ (x As String, n As Integer)
    Dim position As Integer
    Rem x    string containing 3-letter abbreviations of days of the week
    Rem n    the number of the day
    Let position = 3 * n - 2
    DayOfWeek$ = Mid$(x, position, 3)
End Function
```

(Assume that the response is 4.)

7.
```
Sub Command1_Click ()
    Dim a As String
    Rem Demonstrate local variables
    Let a = "Choo "
    Picture1.Print TypeOfTrain$()
End Sub

Function TypeOfTrain$ ()
    Dim a As String
    Let a = a + a
    TypeOfTrain$ = a + "train"
End Function
```

8.
```
Sub Command1_Click ()
    Dim num As Single
    Rem Triple a number
    Let num = 5
    Picture1.Print Triple(num);
    Picture1.Print num
End Sub

Function Triple (x As Single) As Single
    Dim num As Single
    Let num = 3
    Triple = num * x
End Function
```

9.
```
Sub Command1_Click ()
    Dim word As String
    Let word = "moral"
    Call Negative(word)
    Let word = "political"
    Call Negative(word)
End Sub

Function AddA$ (word As String)
    AddA$ = "a" + word
End Function
```

```
Sub Negative (word As String)
  Picture1.Print word; " has the negative "; AddA$(word)
End Sub
```

10.
```
Sub Command1_Click ()
  Dim city As String, pop As Single, shrinks As Single
  Open "DOCS.TXT" For Input as #1
  Input #1, city, pop, shrinks
  Call DisplayData(city, pop, shrinks)
  Input #1, city, pop, shrinks
  Call DisplayData(city, pop, shrinks)
  Close #1
End Sub

Sub DisplayData (city As String, pop As Single, shrinks As Single)
  Picture1.Print city; " has"; ShrinkDensity(pop, shrinks);
  Picture1.Print "psychiatrists per 100,000 people."
End Sub

Function ShrinkDensity (pop As Single, shrinks As Single) As Integer
  ShrinkDensity = Int(100000 * (shrinks / pop))
End Function
```

(Assume that the file DOCS.TXT contains the following two lines.)

"Boston", 2824000, 8602
"Denver", 1633000, 3217

In Exercises 11 and 12, identify the errors.

11.
```
Sub Command1_Click ()
  Dim answer As Single
  Rem Select a greeting
  Let answer = Val(InputBox$("Enter 1 or 2."))
  Picture1.Print Greeting$(answer)
End Sub

Function Greeting (x As Single) As Single
  Greeting$ = Mid$("hellohi ya", 5 * x - 4, 5)
End Function
```

12.
```
Sub Command1_Click ()
  Dim word As String
  Let word = InputBox$("What is your favorite word?")
  Picture1.Print "When the word is written twice,";
  Picture1.Print Twice (word); "letters are used."
End Sub

Function Twice (w As String) As Single
  Rem Compute twice the length of a string
  Twice(w) = 2 * Len(w)
End Function
```

In Exercises 13 through 21, construct user-defined functions to carry out the primary task(s) of the program.

13. To determine the number of square centimeters of tin needed to make a tin can, add the square of the radius of the can to the product of the radius and height of the can, then multiply this sum by 6.283. Write a program that requests the radius and height of a tin can in centimeters as input and displays the number of square centimeters required to make the can.

14. According to Plato, a man should marry a woman whose age is half his age plus seven years. Write a program that requests a man's age as input and gives the ideal age of his wife.

15. Write a program that accepts a number (m) and a small positive integer (n) as input and rounds m to n decimal places.

16. In order for exercise to be beneficial to the cardiovascular system, the heart rate (number of heart beats per minute) must exceed a value called the training heart rate, THR. A person's THR can be calculated from his age and resting heart rate (pulse when first awakening) as follows:

    (a) Calculate the maximum heart rate as 220 – age.
    (b) Subtract the resting heart rate from the maximum heart rate.
    (c) Multiply the result in step (b) by 60 percent and then add the resting heart rate.

    Write a program to request a person's age and resting heart rate as input and display her THR. (Test the program with an age of 20 and a resting heart rate of 70, then determine *your* training heart rate.)

17. The three ingredients for a serving of popcorn at a movie theater are popcorn, butter substitute, and a bucket. Write a program that requests the cost of these three items and the price of the serving as input and then displays the profit. (Test the program where popcorn costs 5 cents, butter substitute costs 2 cents, the bucket costs 25 cents, and the selling price is $2.)

18. Rewrite the population density program from Example 4 of Section 4.1 using a function to calculate the population density.

19. The original cost of airmail letters was 5 cents for the first ounce and 10 cents for each additional ounce. Write a program to compute the cost of a letter whose weight is given by the user in a text box. **Hint:** Use the function Ceil discussed in Example 5. (Test the program with the weights 4, 1, 2.5, and .5 ounces.)

20. Suppose a fixed amount of money is deposited at the beginning of each month into a savings account paying 6% interest compounded monthly. After each deposit is made, [new balance] = 1.005*[previous balance one month ago] + [fixed amount]. Write a program that requests the fixed amount of the deposits as input and displays the balance after each of the first four deposits. Below is a sample outcome when 800 is typed into the text box for the amount deposited each month.

```
Month 1    800.00
Month 2   1604.00
Month 3   2412.02
Month 4   3224.08
```

21. Write a program to request the name of a United States senator as input and display the address and greeting for a letter to the senator. Assume the name has two parts and use a function to determine the senator's last name. Below is a sample outcome when Robert Smith is typed into the text box holding the senator's name.

```
The Honorable Robert Smith
United States Senate
Washington, DC 20001

Dear Senator Smith,
```

SOLUTIONS TO PRACTICE PROBLEMS 4.3

1. Since the name of the function is followed by a dollar sign, the output will be a string. The first argument, n, takes numeric values and the second argument, x, takes string values; therefore, the input consists of a number and a string.

2. You can make 27 gallons of cider. In this program, the function was used by a subprogram rather than by an event procedure.

4.4 MODULAR DESIGN

Top-Down Design

Large problems usually require large programs. One method programmers use to make a large problem more understandable is to divide it into smaller, less complex subproblems. Repeatedly using a "divide-and-conquer" approach to break up a large problem into smaller subproblems is called **stepwise refinement**. Stepwise refinement is part of a larger methodology of writing programs known as **top-down design**. The term top-down refers to the fact that the more general tasks occur near the top of the design and tasks representing their refinement occur below. Top-down design and structured programming emerged as techniques to enhance programming productivity. Their use leads to programs that are easier to read and maintain. They also produce programs containing fewer initial errors, with these errors being easier to find and correct. When such programs are later modified, there is a much smaller likelihood of introducing new errors.

The goal of top-down design is to break a problem into individual tasks, or modules, that can easily be transcribed into pseudocode, flowcharts, or a program. First, a problem is restated as several simpler problems depicted as modules. Any modules that remain too complex are broken down further. The process of refining modules continues until the smallest modules can be coded directly.

Each stage of refinement adds a more complete specification of what tasks must be performed. The main idea in top-down design is to go from the general to the specific. This process of dividing and organizing a problem into tasks can be pictured using a hierarchy chart. When using top-down design, certain criteria should be met:

1. The design should be easily readable and emphasize small module size.

2. Modules proceed from general to specific as you read down the chart.

3. The modules, as much as possible, should be single-minded. That is, they should only perform a single well-defined task.

4. Modules should be as independent of each other as possible, and any relationships among modules should be specified.

This process is illustrated with the following example.

EXAMPLE 1   Write a hierarchy chart for a program that gives certain information about a car loan. The amount of the loan, the duration (in years), and the interest rate should be input. The output should consist of the monthly payment and the amount of interest paid during the first month.

SOLUTION   In the broadest sense, the program calls for obtaining the input, making calculations, and displaying the output. Figure 4.5 shows these tasks as the first row of a hierarchy chart.

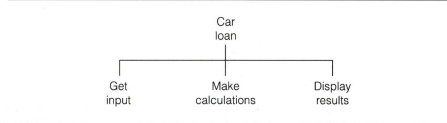

Figure 4.5 Beginning of a hierarchy chart for the car loan program.

Each of these tasks can be refined into more specific subtasks. (See Figure 4.6 for the final hierarchy chart.) Most of the subtasks in the second row are straightforward and so do not require further refinement. For instance, the first month's interest is computed by multiplying the amount of the loan by one-twelfth of the annual rate of interest. The most complicated subtask, the computation of the monthly payment, has been broken down further. This task is carried out by applying a standard formula found in finance books; however, the formula requires the number of payments.

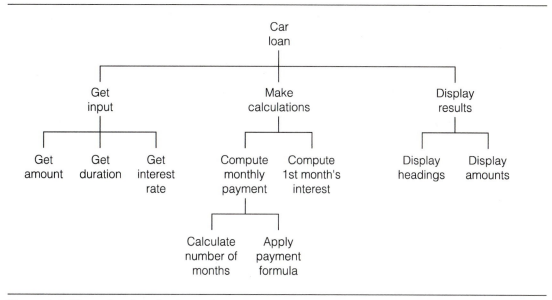

Figure 4.6 Hierarchy chart for the car loan program.

It is clear from the hierarchy chart that the top modules manipulate the modules beneath them. While the higher-level modules control the flow of the program, the lower-level modules do the actual work. By designing the top modules first, specific processing decisions can be delayed.

Structured Programming

A program is said to be **structured** if it meets modern standards of program design. Although there is no formal definition of the term **structured program**, computer scientists are in uniform agreement that such programs should have modular design and use only the three types of logical structures discussed in Chapter 2: sequences, decisions, and loops.

Sequences: Statements are executed one after another.

Decisions: One of two blocks of program code is executed based on a test for some condition.

Loops (iteration): One or more statements are executed repeatedly as long as a specified condition is true.

Chapters 5 and 6 are devoted to decisions and loops, respectively.

One major shortcoming of the earliest programming languages was their reliance on the GoTo statement. This statement was used to branch (that is, jump) from one line of a program to another. It was common for a program to be composed of a convoluted tangle of branchings that produced confusing code referred to as *spaghetti code*. At the heart of structured programming is the assertion of E. W. Dijkstra that GoTo statements should be eliminated entirely since they lead to complex and confusing programs. Two Italians, C. Bohm and G. Jacopini, were able to prove that GoTo statements are not needed and that any program can be written using only the three types of logic structures discussed above.

Structured programming requires that all programs be written using sequences, decisions, and loops. Nesting of such statements is allowed. All other logical constructs, such as GoTos, are not allowed. The logic of a structured program can be pictured using a flowchart that flows smoothly from the top to the bottom without unstructured branching (GoTos). The portion of a flowchart shown in Figure 4.7(a) contains the equivalent of a GoTo statement and, therefore, is not structured. A correctly structured version of the flowchart in which the logic flows from the top to the bottom appears in Figure 4.7(b).

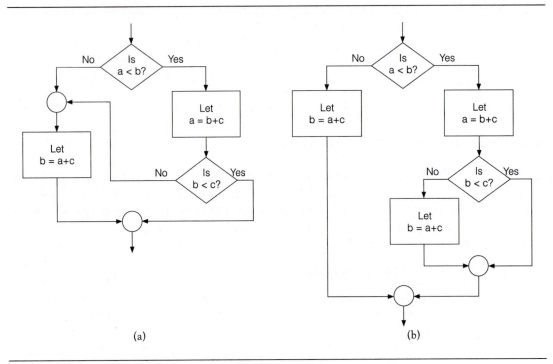

Figure 4.7 Flowcharts illustrating the removal of a GoTo statement.

Advantages of Structured Programming

The goal of structured programming is to create correct programs that are easy to write, understand, and change. Let us now take a closer look at the way modular design, along with a limited number of logical structures, contributes to attaining these goals.

1. *Easy to write.*

Modular design increases the programmer's productivity by allowing him or her to look at the big picture first and focus on the details later. During the actual coding, the programmer works with a manageable chunk of the program and does not have to think about an entire complex program.

Several programmers can work on a single large program, each taking responsibility for a specific module.

Studies have shown structured programs require significantly less time to write than standard programs.

Often, procedures written for one program can be reused in other programs requiring the same task. Not only is time saved in writing a program, but reliability is enhanced because reused procedures will already be tested and debugged. A procedure that can be used in many programs is said to be **reusable**.

2. *Easy to debug.*

Since each procedure is specialized to perform just one task, a procedure can be checked individually to determine its reliability. A dummy program, called a **driver**, is set up to test the procedure. The driver contains the minimum definitions needed to call the procedure to be tested. For instance, if the procedure to be tested is a function, the driver program assigns diverse values to the arguments and then examines the corresponding function value. The arguments should contain both typical and special-case values.

The program can be tested and debugged as it is being designed with a technique known as **stub programming**. In this technique, the key event procedures and perhaps some of the smaller procedures are coded first. Dummy procedures, or stubs, are written for the remaining procedures. Initially, a stub procedure might consist of a Print method to indicate that the procedure has been called, and thereby confirm that the procedure was called at the right time. Later, a stub might simply display values passed to it in order to confirm not only that the procedure was called, but also that it received the correct values from the calling procedure. A stub also can assign new values to one or more of its parameters to simulate either input or computation. This provides greater control of the conditions being tested. The stub procedure is always simpler than the actual procedure it represents. Although the stub program is only a skeleton of the final program, the program's structure can still be debugged and tested. (The stub program consists of some coded procedures and the stub procedures.)

Old-fashioned unstructured programs consist of a sequence of instructions that are not grouped for specific tasks. The logic of such a program is cluttered with details and therefore difficult to follow. Needed tasks are easily left out and crucial details easily neglected. Tricky parts of the program cannot be isolated and examined. Bugs are difficult to locate since they might be present in any part of the program.

3. *Easy to understand.*

The interconnections of the procedures reveal the modular design of the program.

The meaningful procedure names, along with relevant comments, identify the tasks performed by the modules.

The meaningful variable names help the programmer to recall the purpose of each variable.

4. *Easy to change.*

Since a structured program is self-documenting, it can easily be deciphered by another programmer.

Modifying a structured program often amounts to inserting or altering a few procedures rather than revising an entire complex program. The programmer does not even have to look at most of the program. This is in sharp contrast to the situation with unstructured programs that require an understanding of the entire logic of the program before any changes can be made with confidence.

Chapter 4
Summary

1. A *general procedure* is a portion of a program that resides in its own window and is accessed by event procedures or another general procedure. The two types of general procedures are *subprograms* and *user-defined functions*.

2. Subprograms are defined in blocks beginning with Sub statements and ending with End Sub statements. They are accessed by Call statements.

3. User-defined functions are defined in blocks beginning with Function statements and ending with End Function statements. A function is activated by a reference in an expression and returns a value.

4. In any procedure, the arguments appearing in the calling statement must match the parameters of the Sub or Function statement in number, type, and order. They need not match in name.

5. A variable declared in the (declarations) section of (general) is *form-level*. Such a variable is available to every procedure in the program and retains its value from one procedure invocation to the next. Form-level variables are often initialized in the Form_Load event procedure.

6. A variable appearing inside a procedure is *local* to the procedure if it is declared in a Dim statement within the procedure or if it is not a form-level variable and does not appear in the parameter list. The values of these variables are reinitialized each time the procedure is called. A variable with the same name appearing in another part of the program is treated as a different variable.

7. Structured programming uses modular design to refine large problems into smaller subproblems. Programs are coded using the three logical structures of sequences, decisions, and loops.

Chapter 4
Programming Projects

1. The numbers of calories per gram of carbohydrate, fat, and protein are 4, 9, and 4, respectively. Write a program that requests the nutritional content of a 1-ounce serving of food and displays the number of calories in the serving.

The input and output should be handled by subprograms and the calories computed by a function. A sample run for a typical breakfast cereal is shown in Figure 4.8.

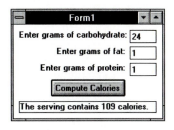

Figure 4.8 Sample run for Programming Project 1.

2. About eighteen million PCs were sold during 1994. Table 4.3 gives the market share for the four largest vendors. Write a program that displays the number of computers sold by each of the Big Four. The input and output should be handled by subprograms and the number of computers calculated by a function.

Company	Market Share
Compaq	12.8%
Apple	12.2%
Packard Bell	10.8%
IBM	10.2%

Table 4.3 Market shares of leading PC companies.

3. Table 4.4 gives the revenues (in millions of dollars) of several major beverage companies. Write a program that displays the percentage growth for each company. Subprograms should be used for input and output and the percentage growth should be computed with a function. **Note:** The percentage growth is 100 * ([1992 revenues] – [1991 revenues]) / [1991 revenues].

Company	1991 Revenues	1992 Revenues
PepsiCo	19,292	21,970
Coca-Cola Company	11,572	13,074
A&W Brands	123	130
Snapple Beverage Corp.	95	232

Table 4.4 Growth of beverage companies.
Source: Nordby International (*Beverage World*, July 1993)

4. A fast-food vendor sells pizza slices ($1.25), fries ($1.00), and soft drinks ($.75). Write a program to compute a customer's bill. The program should request the quantity of each item ordered in a subprogram, calculate the total cost with a function, and use a subprogram to display an itemized bill. A sample output is shown in Figure 4.9.

Figure 4.9 Sample run for Programming Project 4.

5. Write a program to generate a Business Travel Expense attachment for an income tax return. The program should request as input the name of the organization visited, the date and location of the visit, and the expenses for meals and entertainment, airplane fare, lodging, and taxi fares. (Only 50% of the expenses for meals and entertainment are deductible.) A possible form layout and run is shown in Figures 4.10 and 4.11. Subprograms should be used for the input and output.

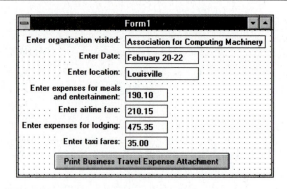

Figure 4.10 Form with sample data for Programming Project 5.

```
Business Travel Expense

Trip to attend meeting of
Association for Computing Machinery
February 20-22 in Louisville

Meals and entertainment      $190.10
Airplane fare                $210.15
Lodging                      $475.35
Taxi fares                    $35.00


Total other than Meals and Entertainment: $720.50

50% of Meals and Entertainment: $95.05
```

Figure 4.11 Output on printer for sample run of Programming Project 5.

5

Decisions

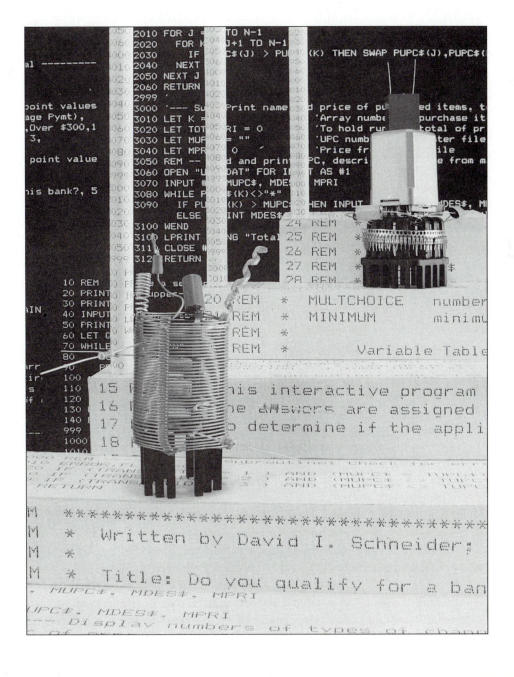

5.1 RELATIONAL AND LOGICAL OPERATORS

A **condition** is an expression involving relational operators (such as < and =) that is either true or false when evaluated. Conditions also may incorporate logical operators (such as And, Or, and Not).

The relational operator *less than* (<) can be applied to both numbers and strings. The number a is said to be less than the number b if a lies to the left of b on the number line. For instance, $2 < 5$, $-5 < -2$, and $0 < 3.5$.

The string a is said to be less than the string b if a precedes b alphabetically when using the ANSI (or ASCII) table to alphabetize their values. For instance, "cat" < "dog", "cart" < "cat", and "cat" < "catalog". Digits precede uppercase letters, which precede lowercase letters. Two strings are compared working from left to right, character by character, to determine which one should precede the other. Therefore, "9W" < "bat", "Dog" < "cat", and "Sales-89" < "Sales-retail".

Table 5.1 shows the different mathematical relational operators, their representations in Visual Basic, and their meanings.

Mathematical Notation	Visual Basic Notation	Numeric Meaning	String Meaning
=	=	equal to	identical to
≠	<>	unequal to	different from
<	<	less than	precedes alphabetically
>	>	greater than	follows alphabetically
≤	<=	less than or equal to	precedes alphabetically or is identical to
≥	>=	greater than or equal to	follows alphabetically or is identical to

Table 5.1 Relational operators.

EXAMPLE 1 Determine whether each of the following conditions is true or false.

(a) 1 <= 1

(b) 1 < 1

(c) "car" < "cat"

(d) "Dog" < "dog"

SOLUTION (a) True. The notation <= means "less than *or* equal to." That is, the condition is true provided either of the two circumstances holds. The second one (equal to) holds.

(b) False. The notation < means "strictly less than" and no number can be strictly less than itself.

(c) True. The characters of the strings are compared one at a time working from left to right. Since the first two match, the third character decides the order.

(d) True. Since uppercase letters precede lowercase letters in the ANSI table, the first character of "Dog" precedes the first character of "dog."

Conditions also can involve variables, numeric operators, and functions. To determine whether a condition is true or false, first compute the numeric or string values and then decide if the resulting assertion is true or false.

EXAMPLE 2 Suppose the numeric variables *a* and *b* have values 4 and 3, and the string variables *c* and *d* have values "hello" and "bye". Are the following conditions true or false?

(a) (a + b) < 2 * a
(b) (Len(c) – b) = (a / 2)
(c) c < ("good" + d)

SOLUTION (a) The value of a + b is 7 and the value of 2 * a is 8. Since 7 < 8, the condition is true.
(b) True, since the value of Len(c) – b is 2, the same as (a / 2).
(c) The condition "hello" < "goodbye" is false since "h" follows "g" in the ANSI table.

Logical Operators

Programming situations often require more complex conditions than those considered so far. For instance, suppose we would like to state that the value of a numeric variable, *n*, is strictly between 2 and 5. The proper Visual Basic condition is

$$(2 < n) \text{ And } (n < 5)$$

The condition (2 < n) And (n < 5) is a combination of the two conditions 2 < n and n < 5 with the logical operator And.

The three main logical operators are And, Or, and Not. If *cond1* and *cond2* are conditions, then the condition

```
cond1 And cond2
```

is true if both *cond1* and *cond2* are true. Otherwise, it is false. The condition

```
cond1 Or cond2
```

is true if either *cond1* or *cond2* (or both) is true. Otherwise, it is false. The condition

```
Not cond1
```

is true if *cond1* is false, and is false if *cond1* is true.

EXAMPLE 3 Suppose the numeric variable *n* has value 4 and the string variable *answ* has value "Y". Determine whether each of the following conditions is true or false.

(a) (2 < n) And (n < 6)
(b) 2 < n) Or (n = 6)
(c) Not (n < 6)
(d) (answ = "Y") Or (answ = "y")
(e) (answ = "Y") And (answ = "y")
(f) Not (answ = "y")
(g) ((2 < n) And (n = 5 + 1)) Or (answ = "No")
(h) ((n = 2) And (n = 7)) Or (answ = "Y")
(i) (n = 2) And ((n = 7) Or (answ = "Y"))

SOLUTION (a) True, since the conditions (2 < 4) and (4 < 6) are both true.

(b) True, since the condition (2 < 4) is true. The fact that the condition (4 = 6) is false does not affect the conclusion. The only requirement is that at least one of the two conditions be true.

(c) False, since (4 < 6) is true.

(d) True, since the first condition becomes ("Y" = "Y") when the value of *answ* is substituted for *answ*.

(e) False, since the second condition is false. Actually, this compound condition is false for every value of *answ*.

(f) True, since ("Y" = "y") is false.

(g) False. In this logical expression, the compound condition ((2 < n) And (n = 5 + 1)) and the simple condition (answ = "No") are joined by the logical operator Or. Since both of these conditions are false, the total condition is false.

(h) True, because the second Or clause is true.

(i) False. Comparing (h) and (i) shows the necessity of using parentheses to specify the intended grouping.

The use of parentheses with logical operators improves readability; however, they can be omitted sometimes. Visual Basic has an operator hierarchy for deciding how to evaluate logical expressions without parentheses. First, all arithmetic operations are carried out, and then all expressions involving >, <, and = are evaluated to true or false. The logical operators are next applied, in the order Not, then And, and finally Or. For instance, the logical expression in part (g) of Example 3 could have been written 2 < n And n = 5 + 1 Or answ = "No". In the event of a tie, the leftmost operator is applied first.

EXAMPLE 4 Place parentheses in the following condition to show how it would be evaluated by Visual Basic.

a < b + c Or d < e And Not f = g

SOLUTION ((a <(b + c)) Or ((d < e) And (Not (f = g))))

The step-by-step analysis of the order of operations is

a < (b + c)	Or	d < e	And	Not f = g	arithmetic operation
(a < (b + c))	Or	(d < e)	And	Not (f = g)	relational expressions
(a < (b + c))	Or	(d < e)	And	(Not (f = g))	Not
(a < (b + c))	Or	((d < e)	And	(Not (f = g)))	And
((a < (b + c))	Or	((d < e)	And	(Not (f = g))))	Or

Comments:

1. A condition involving numeric variables is different from an algebraic truth. The assertion (a + b) < 2 ∗ a, considered in Example 2, is not a valid algebraic truth since it isn't true for all values of *a* and *b*. When encountered in a Visual Basic program, however, it will be considered true if it is correct for the current values of the variables.

2. Conditions evaluate to either true or false. These two values often are called the possible **truth values** of the condition.

3. A condition such as 2 < n < 5 should never be used, since Visual Basic will not evaluate it as intended. The correct condition is (2 < n) And (n < 5).

4. A common error is to replace condition Not (2 < 3) by condition (3 > 2). The correct condition is (3 >= 2).

PRACTICE PROBLEMS 5.1

1. Is the condition "Hello " = "Hello" true or false?

2. Complete Table 5.2.

cond1	cond2	cond1 And cond2	cond1 Or cond2	Not cond2
true	true	true		
true	false		true	
false	true			false
false	false			

Table 5.2 Truth values of logical operators.

EXERCISES 5.1

In Exercises 1 through 12, determine whether the condition is true or false. Assume a = 2 and b = 3.

1. 3 * a = 2 * b

2. (5 – a) * b < 7

3. b <= 3

4. a ^ b = b ^ a

5. a ^ (5 – 2) > 7

6. 3E–02 < .01 * a

7. (a < b) Or (b < a)

8. (a * a < b) Or Not (a * a < a)

9. Not ((a < b) And (a < (b + a)))

10. Not (a < b) Or Not (a < (b + a))

11. ((a = b) And (a * a < b * b)) Or ((b < a) And (2 * a < b))

12. ((a = b) Or Not (b < a)) And ((a < b) Or (b = a + 1))

In Exercises 13 through 24, determine whether the condition is true or false.

13. "9W" <> "9w"

14. "Inspector" < "gadget"

15. "Car" < "Train"

16. "J" >= "J"

17. "99" > "ninety-nine"

18. "B" > "?"

19. ("Duck" < "pig") And ("pig" < "big")

20. "Duck" < "Duck" + "Duck"

21. Not (("B" = "b") Or ("Big" < "big"))

22. Not ("B" = "b") And Not ("Big" < "big")

23. (("Ant" < "hill") And ("mole" > "hill")) Or Not (Not ("Ant" < "hill") Or Not ("Mole" > "hill"))

24. (7 < 34) And ("7" > "34")

In the Exercises 25 through 34, determine whether or not the two conditions are equivalent, that is, whether they will be true or false for exactly the same values of the variables appearing in them.

25. a <= b; (a < b) Or (a = b)

26. Not (a < b); a > b

27. (a = b) And (a < b); a <> b

28. Not ((a = b) Or (a = c)); (a <> b) And (a <> c)

29. (a < b) And ((a > d) Or (a > e)); ((a < b) And (a > d)) Or ((a < b) And (a > e))

30. Not ((a = b + c) Or (a = b)); (a <> b) Or (a <> b + c)

31. (a < b + c) Or (a = b + c); Not ((a > b) Or (a > c))

32. Not (a >= b); (a <= b) Or Not (a = b)

33. Not (a >= b); (a <= b) And Not (a = b)

34. (a = b) And ((b = c) Or (a = c)); (a = b) Or ((b = c) And (a = c))

In Exercises 35 through 39, write a condition equivalent to the negation of the given condition. (For example, a <> b is equivalent to the negation of a = b.)

35. a > b   **36.** (a = b) Or (a = d)

37. (a < b) And (c <> d)   **38.** Not ((a = b) Or (a > b))

39. (a <> "") And (a < b) And (Len(a) < 5)

SOLUTIONS TO PRACTICE PROBLEMS 5.1

1. False. The first string has six characters, whereas the second has five. Two strings must be 100 percent identical to be called equal.

2.

cond1	cond2	cond1 And cond2	cond1 Or cond2	Not cond2
true	true	true	true	false
true	false	false	true	true
false	true	false	true	false
false	false	false	false	true

5.2 IF BLOCKS

An If block allows a program to decide on a course of action based on whether a certain condition is true or false. A block of the form

```
If condition Then
    action1
  Else
      action2
End If
```

causes the program to take *action1* if *condition* is true and *action2* if *condition* is false. Each action consists of one or more Visual Basic statements. After an action is taken, execution continues with the line after the If block. Figure 5.1 contains the pseudocode and flowchart for an If block.

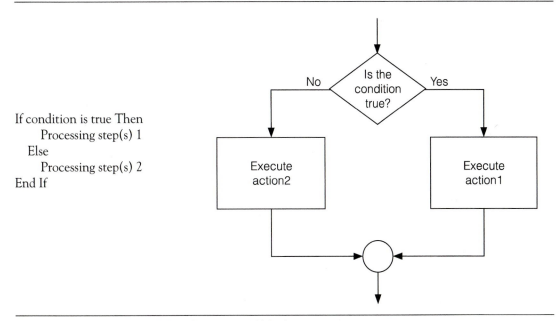

If condition is true Then
      Processing step(s) 1
  Else
      Processing step(s) 2
End If

Figure 5.1 Pseudocode and flowchart for an If block.

EXAMPLE 1   Write a program to find the larger of two numbers input by the user.

SOLUTION   In the following program, the condition is Val(Text1.Text) > Val(Text2.Text), and each action consists of a single Let statement. With the input 3 and 7, the condition is false and so the second action is taken.

Object	Property	Setting
Form1	Caption	Maximum
Label1	Caption	First Number
	Alignment	Right Justify
Text1	Text	(blank)
Label2	Caption	Second Number
	Alignment	Right Justify
Text2	Text	(blank)
Command1	Caption	Find Larger Number
Picture1		

```
Sub Command1_Click ()
  Dim largerNum As Single
  Picture1.Cls
  If Val(Text1.Text) > Val(Text2.Text) Then
      Let largerNum = Val(Text1.Text)
    Else
      Let largerNum = Val(Text2.Text)
  End If
  Picture1.Print "The larger number is"; largerNum
End Sub
```

[Run, type 3 and 7 into the text boxes, and press the command button.]

EXAMPLE 2   Write a program that requests the costs and revenue for a company and displays the message "Break even" if the costs and revenue are equal or otherwise displays the profit or loss.

SOLUTION   In the following program, action2 is another If block.

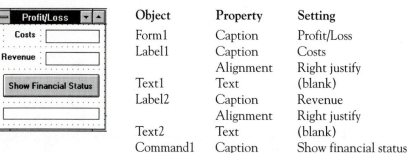

Object	Property	Setting
Form1	Caption	Profit/Loss
Label1	Caption	Costs
	Alignment	Right justify
Text1	Text	(blank)
Label2	Caption	Revenue
	Alignment	Right justify
Text2	Text	(blank)
Command1	Caption	Show financial status
Picture1		

```
Sub Command1_Click ()
  Dim costs As Single, revenue As Single, profit As Single
  Let costs = Val(Text1.Text)
  Let revenue = Val(Text2.Text)
  Picture1.Cls
  If costs = revenue Then
      Picture1.Print "Break even"
    Else
      If costs < revenue Then
          Let profit = revenue - costs
          Picture1.Print "Profit is "; Format$(profit, "currency")
        Else
          Let loss = costs - revenue
          Picture1.Print "Loss is "; Format$(loss, "currency")
      End If
  End If
End Sub
```

[Run, type 9500 and 8000 into the text boxes, and press the command button.]

EXAMPLE 3   The If block in the following program has a logical operator in its condition.

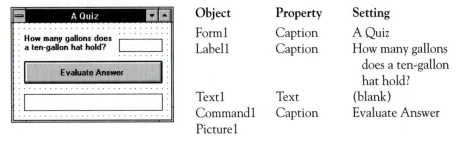

Object	Property	Setting
Form1	Caption	A Quiz
Label1	Caption	How many gallons does a ten-gallon hat hold?
Text1	Text	(blank)
Command1	Caption	Evaluate Answer
Picture1		

```
Sub Command1_Click ()
  Dim answer As Single
  Rem Evaluate answer
  Picture1.Cls
  Let answer = Val(Text1.Text)
  If (.5 <= answer) And (answer <= 1) Then
      Picture1.Print "Good, ";
    Else
      Picture1.Print "No, ";
  End If
  Picture1.Print "it holds about 3/4 of a gallon."
End Sub
```

[Run, type 10 into the text box, and press the command button.]

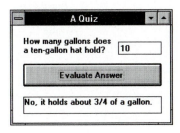

The Else part of an If block can be omitted. In its absence, a false condition causes execution to continue with the statement after the If block. This important type of If block appears in the next example.

EXAMPLE 4   The following program offers assistance to the user before presenting a quotation.

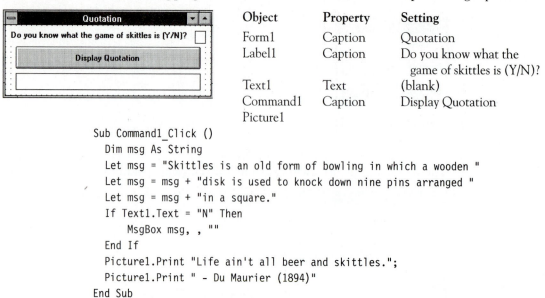

Object	Property	Setting
Form1	Caption	Quotation
Label1	Caption	Do you know what the game of skittles is (Y/N)?
Text1	Text	(blank)
Command1	Caption	Display Quotation
Picture1		

```
Sub Command1_Click ()
  Dim msg As String
  Let msg = "Skittles is an old form of bowling in which a wooden "
  Let msg = msg + "disk is used to knock down nine pins arranged "
  Let msg = msg + "in a square."
  If Text1.Text = "N" Then
      MsgBox msg, , ""
  End If
  Picture1.Print "Life ain't all beer and skittles.";
  Picture1.Print " - Du Maurier (1894)"
End Sub
```

[Run, type N into the text box, and press the command button.]

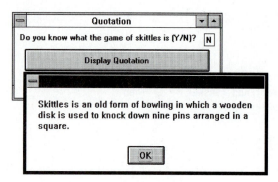

[Press OK.]

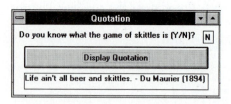

An extension of the If block allows for more than two possible alternatives with the inclusion of ElseIf clauses. A typical block of this type is

```
If condition1 Then
    action1
  ElseIf condition2 Then
    action2
  ElseIf condition3 Then
    action3
  Else
    action4
End If
```

This block searches for the first true condition, carries out its action, and then skips to the statement following End If. If none of the conditions are true, then Else's action is carried out. Execution then continues with the statement following the block. In general, an If block can contain any number of ElseIf clauses. As before, the Else clause is optional.

EXAMPLE 5   Redo Example 1 so that if the two numbers are equal, the program so reports.

SOLUTION
```
Sub Command1_Click ()
    Picture1.Cls
    If Val(Text1.Text) > Val(Text2.Text) Then
        Picture1.Print "The larger number is"; Text1.Text
      ElseIf Val(Text2.Text) > Val(Text1.Text) Then
        Picture1.Print "The larger number is"; Text2.Text
      Else
        Picture1.Print "The two numbers are equal."
    End If
End Sub
```

[Run, type 7 into both text boxes, and press the command button.]

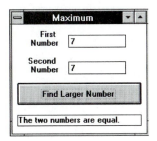

If blocks allow us to define functions whose values are not determined by a simple formula. The function in Example 6 uses an If block.

EXAMPLE 6   The Social Security or FICA tax has two components—the Social Security benefits tax, which in 1995 is 6.2 percent on the first $61,200 of earnings for the year, and the Medicare tax, which is 1.45 percent of earnings. Write a program to calculate an employee's FICA tax for a specific paycheck.

SOLUTION

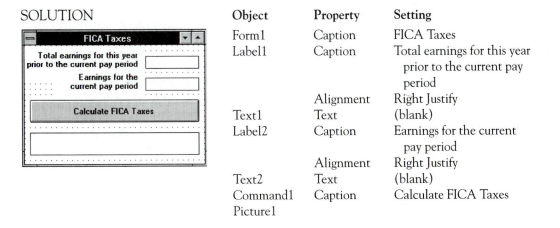

Object	Property	Setting
Form1	Caption	FICA Taxes
Label1	Caption	Total earnings for this year prior to the current pay period
	Alignment	Right Justify
Text1	Text	(blank)
Label2	Caption	Earnings for the current pay period
	Alignment	Right Justify
Text2	Text	(blank)
Command1	Caption	Calculate FICA Taxes
Picture1		

```
Sub Command1_Click ()
  Dim FicaTaxes As Single
  Let FicaTaxes = FICA(Val(Text1.Text), Val(Text2.Text))
  Picture1.Cls
  Picture1.Print "Your FICA taxes for the current"
  Picture1.Print "pay period are "; Format$(FicaTaxes, "currency")
End Sub

Function FICA (ytdEarnings As Single, curEarnings As Single) As Single
  Dim socialSecurityBenTax As Single, medicare As Single
  Rem  Calculate Social Security benefits tax and Medicare tax
  Rem  for a single pay period
  Let socialSecurityBenTax = 0
  If (ytdEarnings + curEarnings) <= 61200 Then
      Let socialSecurityBenTax = .062 * curEarnings
    ElseIf ytdEarnings < 61200 Then
      Let socialSecurityBenTax = .062 * (61200 - ytdEarnings)
  End If
  Let medicare = .0145 * curEarnings
  FICA = socialSecurityBenTax + medicare
End Function
```

[Run, type 12345.67 and 543.21 into the text boxes, and press the command button.]

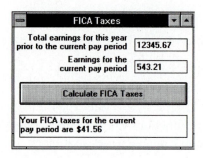

Comments:

1. The actions of an If block and the words Else and ElseIf do not have to be indented. For instance, the If block of Example 1 can be written

```
If Val(Text1.Text) > Val(Text2.Text) Then
Let largerNum = Val(Text1.Text)
Else
Let largerNum = Val(Text2.Text)
End If
```

However, since indenting improves the readability of the block, it is regarded as good programming style. As soon as you see the word If, your eyes can easily scan down the program to find the matching End If and the enclosed Else and ElseIf clauses. You then immediately have a good idea of the size and complexity of the block.

2. Constructs in which an If block is contained inside another If block are referred to as **nested** If blocks.

3. Care should be taken to make If blocks easy to understand. For instance, in Figure 5.2, the block on the left is difficult to follow, and should be replaced by the clearer block on the right.

```
If cond1 Then                    If cond1 And cond2 Then
    If cond2 Then                    action
        action                   End If
    End If
End If
```

Figure 5.2 A confusing If block and an improvement.

4. Some programs call for selecting among many possibilities. Although such tasks can be accomplished with complicated nested If blocks, the Select Case block (discussed in the next section) is often a better alternative.

5. In Appendix D, the section "Stepping Through Programs Containing Decision Structures: Chapter 5" uses the Visual Basic debugging tools to trace the flow through an If block.

6. Visual Basic also has a single-line If statement of the form

```
If condition Then action1 Else action2
```

which is a holdover from earlier, unstructured versions of BASIC; it is not used in this text.

7. Another holdover from unstructured versions of BASIC is the controversial GoTo statement which is commonly used along with If. Although this statement is not needed in structured versions of BASIC, there are some rare situations in which it provides the clearest way to handle a task. Visual Basic has a device called a label, which is a name (of the same type as a variable name) followed by a colon, that is placed on its own line preceding a line of a program. The statement GoTo *label* causes execution to jump to the line following *label*. As an alternative to a label, a line of a program can be preceded by a positive integer, called a **line number**. In this case, the statement GoTo *lineNumber* causes that line to be the next line executed. The GoTo statement is not used in this text.

PRACTICE PROBLEMS 5.2

1. Suppose the user is asked to input a number into Text1 for which the square root is to be taken. Fill in the If block so that the lines of code below either will display the message "Number can't be negative" or will display the square root of the number.

```
Sub Command1_Click ()
    Dim num As Single
    Rem Check reasonableness of data
    Let num = Val(Text1.Text)
    If

    End If
End Sub
```

2. Improve the block

```
If a < b Then
    If c < 5 Then
        Picture1.Print "hello"
    End If
End If
```

EXERCISES 5.2

In Exercises 1 through 12, determine the output displayed in the picture box when the command button is clicked.

1.
```
Sub Command1_Click ()
    Dim i As Single
    Let i = 4
    If i <= 9 Then
        Picture1.Print "Less than ten"
      Else
        If i = 4 Then
            Picture1.Print "Equal to four"
        End If
    End If
End Sub
```

2.
```
Sub Command1_Click ()
    Dim gpa As Single
    Let gpa = 3.49
    If gpa >= 3.5 Then
        Picture1.Print "Honors ";
    End If
    Picture1.Print "Student"
End Sub
```

3.
```
Sub Command1_Click ()
    Dim a As Single
    Let a = 5
    If 3 * a - 4 < 9 Then
        Picture1.Print "Remember, "
    End If
    Picture1.Print "Tomorrow is another day."
End Sub
```

4.
```
Sub Command1_Click ()
    Dim change As Single
    Let change = 356          'Amount of change in cents
    If change >= 100 Then
        Picture1.Print "Your change contains";
        Picture1.Print Int(change / 100); "dollars."
      Else
        Picture1.Print "Your change contains no dollars."
    End If
End Sub
```

5.
```
Sub Command1_Click ()
    Dim a As Single, b As Single, c As Single
    Let a = 2
    Let b = 3
    Let c = 5
    If a * b < c Then
        Let b = 7
      Else
        Let b = c * a
    End If
    Picture1.Print b
End Sub
```

6.
```
Sub Command1_Click ()
    Dim a As Single, b As Single
    Let a = Val(InputBox$("Enter a number."))
    Let b = Val(InputBox$("Enter another number."))
    If a > b Then
        Let a = a + 1
      Else
        Let b = b + 1
    End If
    Picture1.Print a; b
End Sub
```

(Assume that the responses are *7, 11.*)

7.
```
Sub Command1_Click ()
    Dim length As Single
    Rem Cost of phone call from NY to LA
    Call InputLength(length)
    Call DisplayCost(length)
End Sub

Function Cost (length As Single) As Single
    If length < 1 Then
        Let Cost = .46
      Else
        Let Cost = .46 + (length - 1) * .36
    End If
End Function

Sub DisplayCost (length As Single)
    Rem Display the cost of a call
    Picture1.Print "Cost of call: "; Format$(Cost(length), "currency")
End Sub

Sub InputLength (length As Single)
    Rem Request the length of a phone call
    Let length = Val(InputBox$("Duration of the call in minutes?"))
End Sub
```

(Assume that the response is *31.*)

8.
```
Sub Command1_Click ()
    Dim letter As String
    Let letter = InputBox$("Enter A, B, or C.")
    If letter = "A" Then
        Call DisplayAmessage
      ElseIf letter = "B" Then
        Call DisplayBmessage
      ElseIf letter = "C" Then
        Call DisplayCmessage
      Else
        Picture1.Print "Not a valid letter"
    End If
End Sub

Sub DisplayAmessage ()
  Picture1.Print "A, my name is Alice."
End Sub

Sub DisplayBmessage ()
  Picture1.Print "To be or not to be."
End Sub

Sub DisplayCmessage ()
  Picture1.Print "Oh, say can you see."
End Sub
```

(Assume that the response is *B*.)

9.
```
Sub Command1_Click ()
    Dim vowels As Integer
    Let vowels = 0      'Number of vowels
    Call ExamineLetter(vowels)
    Call ExamineLetter(vowels)
    Call ExamineLetter(vowels)
    Picture1.Print "The number of vowels is"; vowels
End Sub

Sub ExamineLetter (vowels As Integer)
  Dim ltr As String
  Let ltr = InputBox$("Enter a letter.")
  Let ltr = UCase$(ltr)
  If ltr = "A" Or ltr = "E" Or ltr = "I" Or ltr = "O" Or ltr = "U" Then
      Let vowels = vowels + 1
  End If
End Sub
```

(Assume that the three responses are *U*, *b*, and *a*.)

10.
```
Sub Command1_Click ()
    Dim a As Single
    Let a = 5
    If (a > 2) And (a = 3 Or a < 7) Then
        Picture1.Print "Hi"
    End If
End Sub
```

11.
```
Sub Command1_Click ()
    Dim num As Single
    Let num = 5
    If num < 0 Then
        Picture1.Print "neg"
      Else
        If num = 0 Then
            Picture1.Print "zero"
          Else
            Picture1.Print "positive"
        End If
    End If
End Sub
```

12.
```
Sub Command1_Click ()
    Dim msg As String, age As Integer
    Let msg = "You are eligible to vote"
    Let age = Val(InputBox$("Enter your age."))
    If age >= 18 Then
        Picture1.Print msg
      Else
        Picture1.Print msg + " in"; 18 - age; "years"
    End If
End Sub
```

(Assume that the response is *16*.)

In Exercises 13 through 20, identify the errors.

13.
```
Sub Command1_Click ()
    Dim num As Single
    Let num = .5
    If 1 < num < 3 Then
        Picture1.Print "Number is between 1 and 3."
    End If
End Sub
```

14.
```
Sub Command1_Click ()
    Dim num As Single
    Let num = 6
    If num > 5 And < 9 Then
        Picture1.Print "Yes"
      Else
        Picture1.Print "No"
    End If
End Sub
```

15.
```
Sub Command1_Click ()
    If 2 <> 3
        Picture1.Print "Numbers are not equal"
    End If
End Sub
```

16.
```
Sub Command1_Click ()
    Dim major As String
    If major = "Business" Or "Computer Science" Then
        Picture1.Print "Yes"
    End If
End Sub
```

17.
```
Sub Command1_Click ()
    Dim numName As String, num As Single
    Let numName = "Seven"
    Let num = Val(InputBox$("Enter a number."))
    If num < numName Then
        Picture1.Print "Less than"
      Else
        Picture1.Print "Greater than"
    End If
End Sub
```

18.
```
Sub Command1_Click ()
    Dim switch As String
    Rem Change switch from "on" to "off", or from "off" to "on"
    Let switch = InputBox$("Enter on or off.")
    If switch = "off" Then
        Let switch = "on"
    End If
    If switch = "on" Then
        Let switch = "off"
    End If
End Sub
```

19.
```
Sub Command1_Click ()
    Dim j As Single, k As Single
    Rem Display "OK" if either j or k equals 4
    Let j = 2
    Let k = 3
    If j Or k = 4 Then
        Picture1.Print "OK"
    End If
End Sub
```

20.
```
Sub Command1_Click ()
    Dim query As String, answer1 As String, answer2 As String
    Rem Is your program correct?
    Let query = "Are you certain everything in your program is correct?"
    Let answer1 = InputBox$(query)
    Let answer1 = UCase$(Left$(answer1, 1))
    If answer1 = "N" Then
        Picture1.Print "Don't patch bad code, rewrite it."
      Else
        Let query = "Does your program run correctly"
        Let answer2 = InputBox$(query)
        Let answer2 = UCase$(Left$(answer2, 1))
```

```
             If answer2 = "Y" Then
                 Picture1.Print "Congratulations"
               Else
                 Picture1.Print "One of the things you are certain"
                 Picture1.Print "about is wrong."
             End If
     End Sub
```

In Exercises 21 through 26, simplify the code.

21.
```
If a = 2 Then
    Let a = 3 + a
  Else
    Let a = 5
End If
```

22.
```
If Not (answer <> "y") Then
    Picture1.Print "YES"
  Else
    If (answer = "y") Or (answer = "Y") Then
        Picture1.Print "YES"
    End If
End If
```

23.
```
If j = 7 Then
    Let b = 1
  Else
    If j <> 7 Then
        Let b = 2
    End If
End If
```

24.
```
If a < b Then
    If b < c Then
        Picture1.Print b; "is between"; a; "and"; c
    End If
End If
```

25.
```
Let message = "Is Alaska bigger than Texas and California combined?"
Let answer = InputBox$(message)
If Left$(answer, 1) = "Y" Then
    Let answer = "YES"
End If
If Left$(answer, 1) = "y" Then
    Let answer = "YES"
End If
If answer = "YES" Then
    Picture1.Print "Correct"
  Else
    Picture1.Print "Wrong"
End If
```

```
26. Let msg = "How tall (in feet) is the Statue of Liberty?"
    Let feet = Val(InputBox$(msg))
    If feet <= 141 Then
        Picture1.Print "Nope"
    End If
    If feet > 141 Then
        If feet < 161 Then
            Picture1.Print "Close"
        Else
            Picture1.Print "Nope"
        End If
    End If
    Picture1.Print "The Statue of Liberty is 151.08 feet"
    Picture1.Print "from base to torch."
```

27. Write a program to determine how much to tip the waiter in a fine restaurant. The tip should be 15 percent of the check with a minimum of $1.

28. Write a quiz program to ask "Who was the first Ronald McDonald?" The program should display "Correct" if the answer is Willard Scott and otherwise should display "Nice try."

29. A computer store sells diskettes at $1 each for small orders or at 70 cents apiece for orders of 25 diskettes or more. Write a program that requests the number of diskettes ordered and displays the total cost. (Test the program for purchases of 5, 25, and 35 diskettes.)

30. A copying center charges 5 cents per copy for the first 100 copies and 3 cents per copy for each additional copy. Write a program that requests the number of copies as input and displays the total cost. (Test the program with the quantities 25 and 125.)

31. Write a Text1_KeyPress event procedure that allows the user to type only digits into the text box.

32. Suppose a program has a command button with the caption "Quit." Suppose also that the name property of this command button is cmdQuit. Write a cmdQuit_Click event procedure that gives the user a second chance before ending the program. The procedure should use an input box to request that the user confirm that the program should be terminated, and then only end the program if the user responds in the affirmative.

33. Write a program to handle a savings account withdrawal. The program should request the current balance and the amount of the withdrawal as input and then display the new balance. If the withdrawal is greater than the original balance, the program should display "Withdrawal denied." If the new balance is less than $150, the message "Balance below $150" should be displayed.

34. Write a program that requests three scores as input and displays the average of the two highest scores. The input and output should be handled by subprograms and the average should be determined by a function.

35. A lottery drawing produces three digits. Write a program that uses Rnd to generate three digits and then displays "Lucky seven" if two or more of the digits are 7.

36. Federal law requires hourly employees be paid "time-and-a-half" for work in excess of 40 hours in a week. For example, if a person's hourly wage is $8 and he works 60 hours in a week, his gross pay should be

$$(40 \times 8) + (1.5 \times 8 \times (60 - 40)) = \$560.$$

Write a program that requests as input the number of hours a person works in a given week and his hourly wage, and then displays his gross pay.

37. Write a program that requests a word (with lowercase letters) as input and translates the word into pig latin. The rules for translating a word into pig latin are as follows:

(a) If the word begins with a consonant, move the first letter to the end of the word and add *ay*. For instance, *chip* becomes *hipcay*.

(b) If the word begins with a vowel, add *way* to the end of the word. For instance, *else* becomes *elseway*.

38. The current calendar, called the Gregorian calendar, was introduced in 1582. Every year divisible by 4 was declared to be a leap year with the exception of the years ending in 00 (that is, those divisible by 100) and not divisible by 400. For instance, the years 1600 and 2000 are leap years, but 1700, 1800, and 1900 are not. Write a program that requests a year as input and states whether or not it is a leap year. (Test the program on the years 1994, 1995, 1900, and 2000.)

39. Create a form with a picture box and two command buttons captioned Bogart and Raines. When Bogart is first pressed, the sentence "I came to Casablanca for the waters." is displayed in the picture box. The next time Bogart is pressed, the sentence "I was misinformed." is displayed. When Raines is pressed, the sentence "But we're in the middle of the desert." is displayed. Run the program and then press Bogart, Raines, Bogart to obtain a dialogue.

40. Write a program that allows the user to use one command button to toggle the appearance of the text in a text box between bold and italics and use another pair of command buttons to increase or decrease the size of the text to the next available point size. (Point sizes available in the default MS Sans Serif font are 8.25, 9.75, 12, 13.5, 18, and 24.)

41. Write a program that allows the user 10 tries to answer the question "Which U.S. President was born on July 4?" After three incorrect guesses the program should pop-up the hint, "He once said, 'If you don't say anything, you won't be called upon to repeat it.' " in a message box. After seven incorrect guesses, the program should give the hint, "His nickname was 'Silent Cal.' " The number of guesses should be displayed in a label. **Note:** Calvin Coolidge was born on July 4, 1872.

42. Write a program that reads a test score from a text box each time a command button is clicked and then displays the two highest scores whenever a second command button is clicked. Use two form-level variables to track the two highest scores.

43. The flowchart in Figure 5.3 calculates New Jersey state income tax. Write a program corresponding to the flowchart. (Test the program with taxable incomes of $15,000, $30,000, and $60,000.)

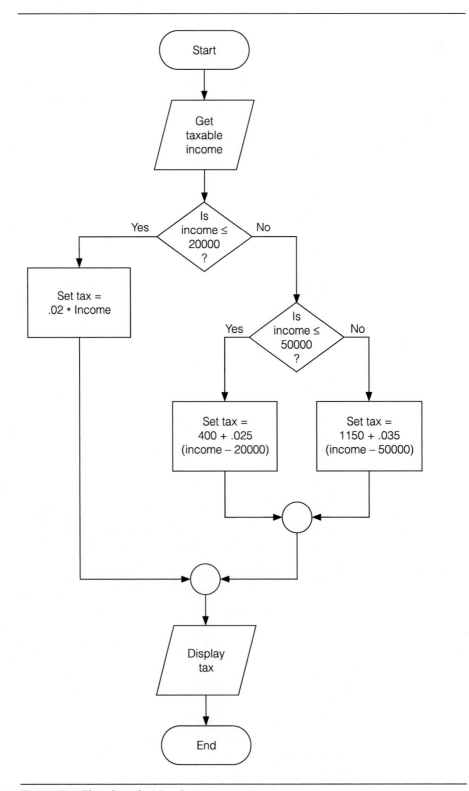

Figure 5.3 Flowchart for New Jersey state income tax program.

44. Write a program to play "Hide and Seek" with the chess picture that follows (or any other picture of your choosing). When the command button is pressed, the picture should disappear and the caption on the button should change to Show Picture. The next time the button is pressed, the picture should reappear and the caption revert to Hide Picture, and so on.

Object	Property	Setting
Form1	Caption	Chess Hide and Seek
Picture1	Picture	chess.bmp
Command1	Caption	Hide Picture

SOLUTIONS TO PRACTICE PROBLEMS 5.2

1.
```
If num < 0 Then
    MsgBox "Number can't be negative.", , "Input Error"
    Text1.Text = ""
    Text1.SetFocus
  Else
    Picture1.Print Sqr(num)
End If
```

2. The Print method will be executed when a < b is true and c < 5 is also true. That is, it will be executed when both of these two conditions are true. The clearest way to write the block is

```
If (a < b) And (c < 5) Then
    Picture1.Print "hello"
End If
```

5.3 SELECT CASE BLOCKS

A Select Case block is an efficient decision-making structure that simplifies choosing among several actions. It avoids complex nested If constructs. If blocks make decisions based on the truth value of a condition; Select Case choices are determined by the value of an expression called a **selector**. Each of the possible actions is preceded by a statement of the form

```
Case valueList
```

where *valueList* itemizes the values of the selector for which the action should be taken.

EXAMPLE 1   The following program converts the finishing position in a horse race into a descriptive phrase. After the variable *position* is assigned a value from Text1, the computer searches for the first Case statement whose value list contains that value and executes the succeeding statement. If the value of *position* is greater than 5, then the statement following Case Else is executed.

Object	Property	Setting
Form1	Caption	Horse Race
Label1	Caption	Finishing position (1, 2, 3, . . .)
Text1	Text	(blank)
Command1	Caption	Describe Position
Picture1		

```
Sub Command1_Click ()
  Dim position As Integer
  Let position = Val(Text1.Text)
  Picture1.Cls
  Select Case position
    Case 1
      Picture1.Print "Win"
    Case 2
      Picture1.Print "Place"
    Case 3
      Picture1.Print "Show"
    Case 4, 5
      Picture1.Print "You almost placed"
      Picture1.Print "in the money."
    Case Else
      Picture1.Print "Out of the money."
  End Select
End Sub
```

[Run, type 2 into the text box, and press the command button.]

EXAMPLE 2   In the following variation of Example 1, the value lists specify ranges of values. The first value list provides another way to specify the numbers 1, 2, and 3. The second value list covers all numbers from 4 on.

```
Sub Command1_Click ()
  Dim position As Integer
  Rem Describe finishing positions in a horse race
  Picture1.Cls
  Let position = Val(Text1.Text)
```

```
    Select Case position
      Case 1 To 3
        Picture1.Print "In the money."
        Picture1.Print "Congratulations"
      Case Is > 3
        Picture1.Print "Not in the money."
    End Select
End Sub
```

[Run, type 2 into the text box, and press the command button.]

The general form of the Select Case block is

```
Select Case selector
  Case valueList1
    action1
  Case valueList2
    action2
      .

      .
  Case Else
    action of last resort
End Select
```

where Case Else (and its action) is optional, and each value list contains one or more of the following types of items separated by commas:

1. a constant

2. a variable

3. an expression

4. an inequality sign preceded by Is and followed by a constant, variable, or expression

5. a range expressed in the form a To b, where a and b are either constants, variables, or expressions.

Different items appearing in the same list must be separated by commas. Each action consists of one or more statements. After the selector is evaluated, the computer looks for the first value list item containing the value of the selector and carries out its associated action. Figure 5.4 contains the flowchart for a Select Case block. The pseudocode for a Select Case block is the same as for the equivalent If block.

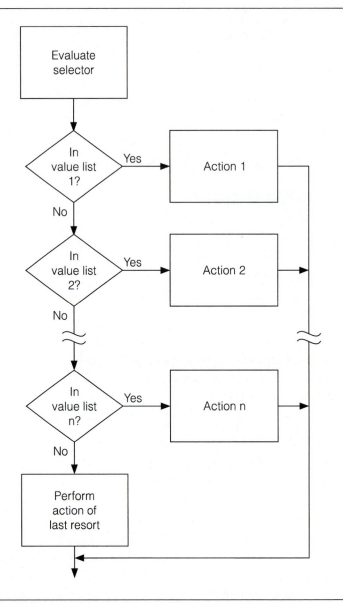

Figure 5.4 Flowchart for a Select Case block.

EXAMPLE 3 The following program illustrates several different types of value lists. With the response shown, the first action was selected because the value of y − x is 1.

Object	Property	Setting
Form1	Caption	One, Two, Buckle My Shoe
Label1	Caption	Enter a number from 1 to 10
Text1	Text	(blank)
Command1	Caption	Interpret Number
Picture1		

```
Sub Command1_Click ()
  Dim x As Integer, y As Integer, num As Integer
  Rem One, Two, Buckle My Shoe
  Picture1.Cls
  Let x = 2
  Let y = 3
  Let num = Val(Text1.Text)
  Select Case num
    Case y - x, x
      Picture1.Print "Buckle my shoe."
    Case Is <= 4
      Picture1.Print "Shut the door."
    Case x + y To x * y
      Picture1.Print "Pick up sticks."
    Case 7, 8
      Picture1.Print "Lay them straight."
    Case Else
      Picture1.Print "Start all over again."
  End Select
End Sub
```

[Run, type 4 into the text box, and press the command button.]

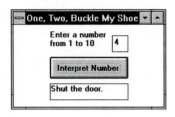

In each of the three preceding examples, the selector was a numeric variable; however, the selector also can be a string variable or an expression.

EXAMPLE 4   The following program has the string variable *firstName* as a selector.

Object	Property	Setting
Form1	Caption	Quiz
Label1	Caption	"What was President Wilson's first name ?"
Text1	Text	(blank)
Command1	Caption	Interpret Answer
Picture1		

```
Sub Command1_Click ()
  Dim firstName As String
  Rem Quiz
  Picture1.Cls
  Let firstName = Text1.Text
  Select Case firstName
    Case "Thomas"
      Picture1.Print "Correct."
```

```
      Case "Woodrow"
        Picture1.Print "Sorry, his full name was"
        Picture1.Print "Thomas Woodrow Wilson."
      Case "President"
        Picture1.Print "Are you for real?"
      Case Else
        Picture1.Print "Nice try, but no cigar."
    End Select
End Sub
```

[Run, type Woodrow into the text box, and press the command button.]

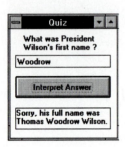

EXAMPLE 5 The following program has the selector Left$(anyString, 1), a string expression. In the sample run, only the first action was carried out even though the value of the selector was in both of the first two value lists. The computer stops looking as soon as it finds the value of the selector.

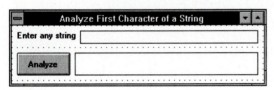

Object	Property	Setting
Form1	Caption	Analyze First Character of a String
Label1	Caption	Enter any string
Text1	Text	(blank)
Command1	Caption	Analyze
Picture1		

```
Sub Command1_Click ()
  Dim anyString As String
  Rem Analyze the first character of a string
  Picture1.Cls
  Let anyString = UCase$(Text1.Text)
  Select Case Left$(anyString, 1)
    Case "S", "Z"
      Picture1.Print "The string begins with a sibilant."
    Case "A" To "Z"
      Picture1.Print "The string begins with a nonsibilant."
    Case "0" To "9"
      Picture1.Print "The string begins with a digit."
    Case Is < "0"
      Picture1.Print "The string begins with a character of ANSI"
      Picture1.Print " value less than 48 (e.g. +, &, #, or %)."
    Case Else
      Picture1.Print "The string begins with one of the following:"
      Picture1.Print "      :  ;  <  =  >  ?  @  [  /  ]  ^  _  '"
  End Select
End Sub
```

[Run, type Sunday into the text box, and press the command button.]

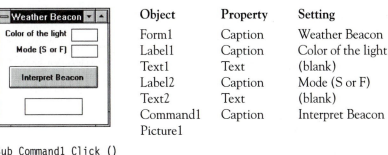

EXAMPLE 6   The color of the beacon light atop Boston's John Hancock Building forecasts the weather according to the rhyme below. Write a program that requests a color (blue or red) and a mode (steady or flashing) as input and displays the weather forecast. The program should contain a Select Case block with a string variable as selector.

Steady blue, clear view.
Flashing blue, clouds due.
Steady red, rain ahead.
Flashing red, snow instead.

SOLUTION

Object	Property	Setting
Form1	Caption	Weather Beacon
Label1	Caption	Color of the light
Text1	Text	(blank)
Label2	Caption	Mode (S or F)
Text2	Text	(blank)
Command1	Caption	Interpret Beacon
Picture1		

```
Sub Command1_Click ()
  Dim color As String, mode As String
  Rem Interpret a weather beacon
  Picture1.Cls
  Let color = Text1.Text
  Let mode = Text2.Text
  Select Case UCase$(mode) + UCase$(color)
    Case "SBLUE"
      Picture1.Print "CLEAR VIEW"
    Case "FBLUE"
      Picture1.Print "CLOUDS DUE"
    Case "SRED"
      Picture1.Print "RAIN AHEAD"
    Case "FRED"
      Picture1.Print "SNOW AHEAD"
  End Select
End Sub
```

[Run, type red and S into the text boxes, and press the command button.]

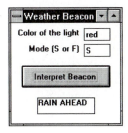

EXAMPLE 7 Select Case is useful in defining functions that are not determined by a formula. The following program assumes the current year is not a leap year.

Object	Property	Setting
Form 1	Caption	Seasons
Label1	Caption	Season
Text1	Text	(blank)
Command1	Caption	Number of Days
Picture1		

```
Sub Command1_Click ()
  Dim season As String
  Rem Determine the number of days in a season
  Picture1.Cls
  Let season = Text1.Text
  Picture1.Print season; " has"; NumDays(season); "days."
End Sub

Function NumDays (season As String) As Integer
  Rem Look up the number of days in a given season
  Select Case UCase$(season)
    Case "WINTER"
      NumDays = 87
    Case "SPRING"
      NumDays = 92
    Case "SUMMER", "AUTUMN", "FALL"
      NumDays = 93
  End Select
End Function
```

[Run, type Summer into the text box, and press the command button.]

Comments:

1. Some programming languages do not allow a value to appear in two different value lists; Visual Basic does. If a value appears in two different value lists, the action after the first value list will be carried out.

2. In Visual Basic, if the value of the selector does not appear in any of the value lists and there is no Case Else clause, execution of the program will continue with the statement following the Select Case block.

3. The Case statements and their actions do not have to be indented; however, since indenting improves the readability of the block, it is regarded as good programming style. As soon as you see the words Select Case, your eyes can

easily scan down the block to find the matching End Select statement. You immediately know the number of different cases under consideration.

4. The items in the value list must evaluate to a constant of the same type, string or numeric, as the selector. For instance, if the selector evaluates to a string value, as in

```
Dim firstName As String
Let firstName = Text1.Text
Select Case firstName
```

then the clause

```
Case Len(firstName)
```

produces the run-time error message "Type mismatch."

5. If the word Is, which should precede an inequality sign in a value list, is accidentally omitted, the smart editor will automatically insert it upon checking the line.

6. A Case clause of the form Case b To c selects values from *b* to *c* inclusive. However, the extreme values can be excluded by placing the action inside an If block beginning with If (*selector* <> b) And (*selector* <> c) Then.

7. The value of *b* must be less than or equal to the value of *c* in a Case clause of the form Case b To c.

8. Every Select Case block can be replaced by an If block. Select Case is preferable to an If block when the possible choices have more or less the same importance.

9. In Appendix D, the section "Stepping Through Programs Containing Selection Structures: Chapter 5" uses the Visual Basic debugging tools to trace the flow through a Select Case block.

PRACTICE PROBLEMS 5.3

1. Suppose the selector of a Select Case block is the numeric variable *num*. Determine whether each of the following Case clauses is valid.

    (a) `Case 1, 4, Is < 10`

    (b) `Case Is < 5, Is >= 5`

    (c) `Case "2"`

2. Do the two programs below always produce the same output for a whole number grade from 0 to 100?

```
Let grade = Val(Text1.Text)        Let grade = Val(Text1.Text)
Select Case grade                  Select Case grade
  Case Is >= 90                      Case Is >= 90
    Picture1.Print "A"                 Picture1.Print "A"
  Case Is >= 60                      Case 60 To 89
    Picture1.Print "Pass"              Picture1.Print "Pass"
  Case Else                          Case 0 To 59
    Picture1.Print "Fail"              Picture1.Print "Fail"
End Select                         End Select
```

EXERCISES 5.3

In Exercises 1 through 8, for each of the responses shown in the parentheses, determine the output displayed in the picture box when the command button is clicked.

1.
```
Sub Command1_Click ()
    Dim age As Single
    Let age = Val(InputBox$("What is your age?"))
    Select Case age
      Case Is < 6
        Let price = 0
      Case 6 To 17
        Let price = 3.75
      Case Is > 17
        Let price = 5
    End Select
    Picture1.Print "The price is "; Format$(price, "currency")
End Sub
```

(8.5, 17)

2.
```
Sub Command1_Click ()
    Dim n As Single
    Let n = Val(InputBox$("Enter a number from 5 to 12"))
    Select Case n
      Case 5
        Picture1.Print "case 1"
      Case 5 To 7
        Picture1.Print "case 2"
      Case 7 To 12
        Picture1.Print "case 3"
    End Select
End Sub
```

(7, 5, 11.2)

3.
```
Sub Command1_Click ()
    Dim age As Integer
    Let age = Val(InputBox$("Enter age (in millions of years)"))
    Select Case age
      Case Is < 70
        Picture1.Print "Cenozoic Era"
      Case Is < 225
        Picture1.Print "Mesozoic Era"
      Case Is <= 600
        Picture1.Print "Paleozoic Era"
      Case Else
        Picture1.Print "?"
    End Select
End Sub
```

(100, 600, 700)

4.
```
Sub Command1_Click ()
    Dim yearENIAC As Integer
    Call AskQuestion(yearENIAC)
    Call ProcessAnswer(yearENIAC)
End Sub

Sub AskQuestion (yearENIAC As Integer)
  Dim msg As String
  Rem Ask question and obtain answer
  Let msg = "In what year was the ENIAC computer completed?"
  Let yearENIAC = Val(InputBox$(msg))
End Sub

Sub ProcessAnswer (yearENIAC As Integer)
  Rem Respond to answer
  Select Case yearENIAC
    Case 1945
      Picture1.Print "Correct"
    Case 1943 To 1947
      Picture1.Print "Close, 1945."
    Case Is < 1943
      Picture1.Print "Sorry, 1945. Work on the ENIAC began ";
      Picture1.Print "in June 1943."
    Case Is > 1947
      Picture1.Print "No, 1945. By then IBM had built a stored-program ";
      Picture1.Print "computer."
  End Select
End Sub
```

(1940, 1945, 1950)

5.
```
Sub Command1_Click ()
    Dim nom As String
    Let nom = InputBox$("Who developed the stored program concept")
    Select Case UCase$(nom)
      Case "JOHN VON NEUMANN", "VON NEUMANN"
        Picture1.Print "Correct"
      Case "JOHN MAUCHLY", "MAUCHLY", "J. PRESPER ECKERT", "ECKERT"
        Picture1.Print "He worked with the developer, von Neumann, on the ENIAC."
      Case Else
        Picture1.Print "Nope"
    End Select
End Sub
```

(Grace Hopper, Eckert, John von Neumann)

6.
```
Sub Command1_Click ()
    Dim msg As String, a As Single, b As Single, c As Single
    Let msg = "Analyzing solutions to the quadratic equation "
    Let msg = msg + "A*X^2 + B*X + C = 0.  Enter the value for "
    Let a = Val(InputBox$(msg + "A"))
    Let b = Val(InputBox$(msg + "B"))
    Let c = Val(InputBox$(msg + "C"))
```

```
      Select Case b * b - 4 * a * c
        Case < 0
          Picture1.Print "The equation has no real solutions."
        Case 0
          Picture1.Print "The equation has exactly one solution."
        Case > 0
          Picture1.Print "The equation has two solutions."
      End Select
    End Sub
```

(1,2,3; 1,5,1; 1,2,1)

7.
```
Sub Command1_Click ()
    Dim num1 As Single, word As String, num2 As Single
    Rem State a quotation
    Let num1 = 3
    Let word = "hello"
    Let num2 = Val(InputBox$("Enter a number"))
    Select Case 2 * num2 - 1
      Case num1 * num1
        Picture1.Print "Less is more."
      Case Is > Len(word)
        Picture1.Print "Time keeps everything from happening at once."
      Case Else
        Picture1.Print "The less things change, the more they remain the same."
    End Select
  End Sub
```

(2, 5, 6)

8.
```
Sub Command1_Click ()
    Dim whatever As Single
    Let whatever = Val(InputBox$("Enter a number"))
    Select Case whatever
      Case Else
        Picture1.Print "Hi"
    End Select
  End Sub
```

(7, −1)

In Exercises 9 through 16, identify the errors.

9.
```
Sub Command1_Click ()
    Dim num As Single
    Let num = 2
    Select Case num
      Picture1.Print "Two"
    End Select
  End Sub
```

10.
```
Sub Command1_Click ()
    Dim num1 As Single, num2 As Single
    Let num1 = 5
    Let num2 = 7
    Select Case num1
      Case 3 <= num1 <= 10
        Picture1.Print "Between 3 and 10"
      Case num2 To 5; 4
        Picture1.Print "Near 5"
    End Select
  End Sub
```

11.
```
Sub Command1_Click ()
    Dim a As String
    Let a = "12BMS"
    Select Case a
      Case 0 To 9
        Picture1.Print "Begins with a digit"
      Case Else
    End Select
End Sub
```

12.
```
Sub Command1_Click ()
    Dim word As String
    Let word = "hello"
    Select Case Left$(word, 1)
      Case h
        Picture1.Print "Begins with h"
    End Select
End Sub
```

13.
```
Sub Command1_Click ()
    Dim word As String
    Let word = InputBox$("Enter a word from the United States motto")
    Select Case UCase$(word)
      Case "E"
        Picture1.Print "This is the first word of the motto."
      Case Left$(word, 1) = "P"
        Picture1.Print "The second word is PLURIBUS."
      Case Else
        Picture1.Print "The third word is UNUM."
    End Select
End Sub
```

14.
```
Sub Command1_Click ()
    Dim num As Single
    Let num = 5
    Select Case num
      Case 5, Is <> 5
        Picture1.Print "Five"
      Case Is > 5
        Picture1.Print "Greater than 5"
End Sub
```

15.
```
Sub Command1_Click ()
    Dim a As Single
    Let a = 3
    Select Case a * a < 9
      Case "true"
        Picture1.Print "true"
      Case "false"
        Picture1.Print "false"
    End Select
End Sub
```

16.
```
Sub Command1_Click ()
    Dim purchase As Single
    Let purchase = Val(InputBox$("Quantity purchased?"))
    Select Case purchase
      Case Is < 10000
        Picture1.Print "Five dollars per item."
      Case Is 10000 To 30000
        Picture1.Print "Four dollars per item."
      Case Is > 30000
        Picture1.Print "Three dollars per item."
    End Select
End Sub
```

In Exercises 17 through 22, suppose the selector of a Select Case block, *word*, evaluates to a string value. Determine whether the Case clause is valid.

17. `Case "un" + "til"`

18. `Case "hello", Is < "goodbye"`

19. `Case 0 To 9`

20. `Case word <> "No"`

21. `Case Left$("abc", 1)`

22. `Case word Then`

In Exercises 23 through 26, rewrite the code using a Select Case block.

23.
```
If a = 1 Then
    Picture1.Print "one"
Else
    If a > 5 Then
        Picture1.Print "two"
    End If
End If
```

24.
```
If a = 1 Then
        Picture1.Print "lambs"
End If
If a <= 3 And a < 4 Then
        Picture1.Print "eat"
End If
If a = 5 Or a > 7 Then
        Picture1.Print "ivy"
End If
```

25.
```
If a < 5 Then
    If a = 2 Then
        Picture1.Print "yes"
    Else
        Picture1.Print "no"
    End If
Else
    If a = 2 Then
        Picture1.Print "maybe"
    End If
End If
```

26.
```
If a = 3 Then
    Let a = 1
End If
If a = 2 Then
    Let a = 3
End If
If a = 1 Then
    Let a = 2
End If
```

27. Table 5.3 gives the terms used by the National Weather Service to describe the degree of cloudiness. Write a program that requests the percentage of cloud cover as input and then displays the appropriate descriptor.

Percentage of Cloud Cover	Descriptor
0–30	clear
31–70	partly cloudy
71–99	cloudy
100	overcast

Table 5.3 Cloudiness descriptors.

28. Table 5.4 shows the location of books in the library stacks according to their call numbers. Write a program that requests the call number of a book as input and displays the location of the book.

Call Numbers	Location
100 to 199	basement
200 to 500 and over 900	main floor
501 to 900 except 700 to 750	upper floor
700 to 750	archives

Table 5.4 Location of library books.

29. Write an interactive program that requests a month of the year and then gives the number of days in the month. If the response is February, the user should be asked whether or not the current year is a leap year. The first request should be made in a subprogram and the computation should be carried out in a function.

30. Figure 5.5 shows some geometric shapes and formulas for their areas. Write a program that requests the user to select one of the shapes, requests the appropriate lengths, and then gives the area of the figure. Input and output should be handled by subprograms, and the areas should be computed by functions.

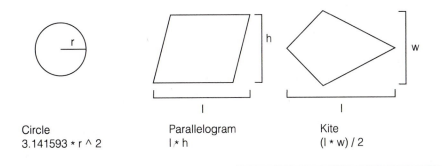

Figure 5.5 Areas of geometric shapes.

31. Write an interactive program that requests an exam score and assigns a letter grade with the scale 90–100 (A), 80–89 (B), 70–79 (C), 60–69 (D), 0–59 (F). The input should be accomplished by a subprogram and the computation carried out in a function. (Test the program with the grades 84, 100, and 57.)

32. (Computerized quiz show.) Write a program that asks the contestant to select one of the numbers 1, 2, or 3 and then calls a subprogram that asks the question. Another subprogram should then request the answer as input and tell the contestant if the answer is correct. Use the following three questions:

1. Who was the only living artist to have his work displayed in the Grand Gallery of the Louvre?
2. Who said "Computers are useless. They can only give you answers."?
3. By what name is Pablo Blasio better known?

Note: These questions have the same answer, Pablo Picasso.

33. IRS informants are paid cash awards based on the value of the money recovered. If the information was specific enough to lead to a recovery, the informant receives 10 percent of the first $75,000, 5 percent of the next $25,000, and 1 percent of the remainder, up to a maximum award of $50,000. Write a program that requests the amount of the recovery as input and displays the award. (Test the program on the amounts $10,000, $125,000, and $10,000,000.) **Note:** The source of this formula is *The Book of Inside Information*, Boardroom Books, 1993.

34. Table 5.5 contains information on several states. Write a program that requests a state and category (flower, motto, and nickname) as input and displays the requested information. If the state or category requested is not in the table, the program should so inform the user.

State	Flower	Nickname	Motto
California	Golden poppy	Golden State	Eureka
Indiana	Peony	Hoosier State	Crossroads of America
Mississippi	Magnolia	Magnolia State	By valor and arms
New York	Rose	Empire State	Ever upward

Table 5.5 State flowers, nicknames, and mottos.

35. Write a program which, given the last name of one of the four most recent Presidents, displays his state and a colorful fact about him.

    Note: Carter: Georgia, The only soft drink served in the Carter White House was Coca-Cola.; Reagan: California, His secret service code name was Rawhide.; Bush: Texas, He was the third left-handed president.; Clinton: Arkansas, In college he did a good imitation of Elvis Presley.

36. Table 5.6 contains the meanings of some abbreviations doctors often use for prescriptions. Write a program that requests an abbreviation and gives its meaning. The user should be informed if the meaning is not in the table.

Abbreviation	Meaning
ac	before meals
ad lib	freely as needed
bid	twice daily
gtt	a drop
hs	at bedtime
qid	four times a day

Table 5.6 Physicians' abbreviations.

37. The user enters a number into a text box and then clicks on the appropriate command button to have either one of three pieces of humor or one of three insults displayed in the large label below the buttons. Place the humor and insults in general procedures, with Select Case statements in each to display the appropriate phrase. Also, if the number entered is not between 1 and 3, the text box should be cleared.

Note: Some possible bits of humor are "I can resist everything except temptation.", "I just heard from Bill Bailey. He's not coming home.", and "I have enough money to last the rest of my life, unless I buy something." Some possible insults are "How much would you charge to haunt a house?", "I bet you have no more friends than an alarm clock.", and "When your IQ rises to 30, sell."

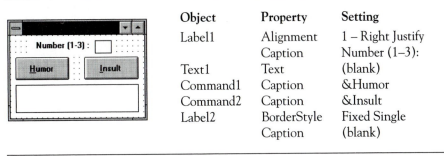

Object	Property	Setting
Label1	Alignment	1 – Right Justify
	Caption	Number (1–3):
Text1	Text	(blank)
Command1	Caption	&Humor
Command2	Caption	&Insult
Label2	BorderStyle	Fixed Single
	Caption	(blank)

Form for Exercise 37   Objects and Properties for Exercise 37

SOLUTIONS TO PRACTICE PROBLEMS 5.3

1. (a) Valid. These items are redundant since 1 and 4 are just special cases of Is < 10. However, this makes no difference in Visual Basic.

   (b) Valid. These items are contradictory. However, Visual Basic looks at them one at a time until it finds an item containing the value of the selector. The action following this Case clause will always be carried out.

   (c) Not valid. "2" is a string and the selector has numeric type.

2. Yes. However, the program on the right is clearer and therefore preferable.

5.4 A CASE STUDY: WEEKLY PAYROLL

This case study processes a weekly payroll using the 1994 Employer's Tax Guide. Table 5.7 shows typical data used by a company's payroll office. These data are processed to produce the information in Table 5.8 that is supplied to each employee along with his or her paycheck. The program should request the data from Table 5.7 for an individual as input and produce output similar to that in Table 5.8.

The items in Table 5.8 should be calculated as follows:

Current Earnings: Hourly wage times hours worked (with time-and-a-half after 40 hours)

Year-to-Date Earnings: Previous year-to-date earnings plus current earnings

FICA Tax: Sum of 6.2 percent of first $60,600 of earnings (Social Security benefits tax) and 1.45 percent of total wages (Medicare tax)

Federal Income Tax Withheld: Subtract $47.12 from the current earnings for each withholding exemption and use Table 5.9 or Table 5.10, depending on marital status

Check Amount: [Current earnings] − [FICA taxes] − [Income tax withheld]

Name	Hourly Wage	Hours Worked	Withholding Exemptions	Marital Status	Previous Year-to-Date Earnings
Al Johnson	26.25	38	4	Married	$59,865.00
Ann Jones	14.00	35	3	Married	$21,840.50
John Smith	7.95	50	1	Single	$12,900.15
Sue Williams	27.50	43	2	Single	$41,890.50

Table 5.7 Employee data.

Name	Current Earnings	Yr. to Date Earnings	FICA Taxes	Income Tax Wh.	Check Amount
Al Johnson	997.50	60,862.50	60.03	103.45	834.02

Table 5.8 Payroll information.

Adjusted Weekly Income	Income Tax Withheld
$0 to $50	0
Over $50 to $463	15% of amount over $50
Over $463 to $968	$61.95 + 28% of amount over $463
Over $968 to $2,238	$203.35 + 31% of amount over $968
Over $2,238 to $4,834	$597.05 + 36% of amount over $2,238
Over $4,834	$1,531.61 + 39.6% of amount over $4,834

Table 5.9 1994 federal income tax withheld for a single person.

Adjusted Weekly Income	Income Tax Withheld
$0 to $122	0
Over $122 to $806	15% of amount over $122
Over $806 to $1,606	$102.60 + 28% of amount over $806
Over $1,606 to $2,767	$326.60 + 31% of amount over $1,606
Over $2,767 to $4,883	$686.51 + 36% of amount over $2,767
Over $4,883	$1,448.27 + 39.6% of amount over $4,883

Table 5.10 1994 federal income tax withheld for a married person.

Designing the Weekly Payroll Program

After the data for an employee have been gathered from the text boxes, the program must compute the five items appearing in Table 5.8 and then display the payroll information. The five computations form the basic tasks of the program.

1. Compute current earnings.

2. Compute year-to-date earnings.

3. Compute FICA tax.

4. Compute federal income tax withheld.

5. Compute paycheck amount (that is, take-home pay).

Tasks 1, 2, 3, and 5 are fairly simple. Each involves applying a formula to given data. (For instance, if hours worked is at most 40, then Current Earnings = Hourly Wage times Hours Worked.) Thus, we won't break down these tasks any further. Task 4 is more complicated, so we continue to divide it into smaller subtasks.

4. *Compute Federal Income Tax Withheld.* First the employee's pay is adjusted for exemptions, and then the amount of income tax to be withheld is computed. The computation of the income tax withheld differs for married and single individuals. Task 4 is, therefore, divided into the following subtasks:

4.1 Compute pay adjusted by exemptions.
4.2 Compute income tax withheld for single employee.
4.3 Compute income tax withheld for married employee.

The hierarchy chart in Figure 5.6 shows the stepwise refinement of the problem.

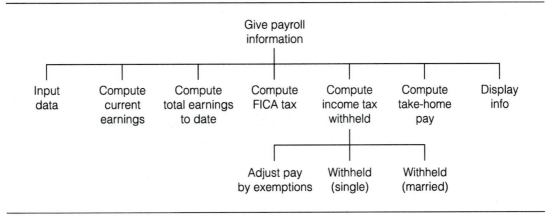

Figure 5.6 Hierarchy chart for the weekly payroll program.

Pseudocode for the Display Payroll Event

INPUT employee data (Subprogram InputData)
COMPUTE CURRENT GROSS PAY (Function Gross_Pay)
COMPUTE TOTAL EARNINGS TO DATE (Function Total_Pay)
COMPUTE FICA TAX (Function FICA_Tax)
COMPUTE FEDERAL TAX (Function Fed_Tax)
   Adjust pay for exemptions
   IF employee is single THEN
       COMPUTE INCOME TAX WITHHELD from adjusted pay using tax
       brackets for single taxpayers (Function TaxSingle)
     ELSE
       COMPUTE INCOME TAX WITHHELD from adjusted pay using tax
       brackets for married taxpayers (Function TaxMarried)
   END IF
COMPUTE CHECK (Function Net_Check)
Display payroll information (Subprogram ShowPayroll)

Writing the Weekly Payroll Program

The cmdDisplay event procedure calls a sequence of seven subprograms. Table 5.11 shows the tasks and the procedures that perform the tasks.

Task	Procedure
0. Input employee data.	InputData
1. Compute current earnings.	Gross_Pay
2. Compute year-to-date earnings.	Total_Pay
3. Compute FICA tax.	FICA_Tax
4. Compute federal income tax withheld.	Fed_Tax
4.1 Compute adjusted pay.	Fed_Tax
4.2 Compute amount withheld for single employee.	TaxSingle
4.3 Compute amount withheld for married employee.	TaxMarried
5. Compute paycheck amounts.	Net_Check
6. Display payroll information.	ShowPayroll

Table 5.11 Tasks and their procedures.

The User Interface

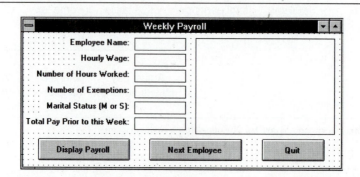

Figure 5.7 Template for entering payroll data.

Object	Property	Setting
Form1	Caption	Weekly Payroll
lblName	Alignment	1 – Right Justify
	Caption	Employee Name
txtName	Text	(blank)
lblWage	Alignment	1 – Right Justify
	Caption	Hourly Wage
txtWage	Text	(blank)
lblHours	Alignment	1 – Right Justify
	Caption	Number of Hours Worked
txtHours	Text	(blank)
lblExempts	Alignment	1 – Right Justify
	Caption	Number of Exemptions
txtExempts	Text	(blank)
lblMarital	Alignment	1 – Right Justify
	Caption	Marital Status (M or S)
txtMarital	Text	(blank)
lblPriorPay	Alignment	1– Right Justify
	Caption	Total Pay Prior to this Week
txtPriorPay	Text	(blank)
cmdDisplay	Caption	Display Payroll
cmdNext	Caption	Next Employee
cmdQuit	Caption	Quit
picResults		

Table 5.12 Objects and initial properties for the weekly payroll program.

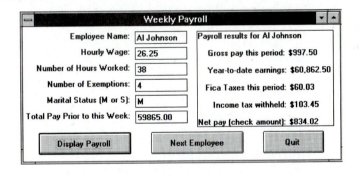

Figure 5.8 Sample run of weekly payroll.

```
Rem Program to compute employees' weekly payroll
Rem
Rem ****************************************************************
Rem *            Variable Table                                  *
Rem *                                                            *
Rem *    exempts          Number of exemptions for employee       *
Rem *    fedTax           Federal income tax withheld this week    *
Rem *    ficaTax          FICA taxes for this week                 *
Rem *    hrsWorked        Hours worked this week                   *
Rem *    hrWage           Hourly wage                              *
Rem *    medicare         Medicare tax for this week               *
Rem *    mStatus          Marital status: S for Single; M for Married *
Rem *    empName          Name of employee                         *
```

```
Rem *   grossPay       This week's pay before taxes          *
Rem *   check          Paycheck this week (take-home pay)     *
Rem *   prevPay        Total pay for year excluding this week *
Rem *   socialSecurity Social Security tax for this week      *
Rem *   totalPay       Total pay for year including this week *
Rem ***********************************************************

Sub cmdDisplay_Click ()
  Dim empName As String, hrWage As Single, hrsWorked As Single
  Dim exempts As Single, mStatus As String, prevPay As Single
  Dim grossPay As Single, totalPay As Single, ficaTax As Single
  Dim fedTax As Single, check As Single
  Rem Obtain data, compute payroll, display results
  Call InputData(empName,hrWage,hrsWorked,exempts,mStatus,prevPay)
  Let grossPay = Gross_Pay(hrWage, hrsWorked)
  Let totalPay = Total_Pay(prevPay, grossPay)
  Let ficaTax = FICA_Tax(grossPay, prevPay, totalPay)
  Let fedTax = Fed_Tax(grossPay, exempts, mStatus)
  Let check = Net_Check(grossPay, ficaTax, fedTax)
  Call ShowPayroll(empName, grossPay, totalPay, ficaTax, fedTax, check)
End Sub

Sub cmdNext_Click ()
  Rem Clear all text boxes for next employee's data
  Let txtName.Text = ""
  Let txtWageEarn.Text = ""
  Let txtHrsYtd.Text = ""
  Let txtExempFica.Text = ""
  Let txtMarTax.Text = ""
  Let txtPayChk.Text = ""
  Picture1.Cls
End Sub

Sub cmdQuit_Click ()
  End
End Sub

Function Net_Check (pay As Single, ficaTax As Single, fedTax As Single)
  Rem Compute amount of money given to employee
  Net_Check = pay - ficaTax - fedTax
End Function

Function Fed_Tax (pay As Single,exempts As Single,mStatus As String)
  Dim adjPay As Single
  Rem Compute federal income tax
  Let adjPay = pay - (47.12 * exempts)
  If adjPay < 0 Then
      Let adjPay = 0
  End If
  If mStatus = "S" Then
      Fed_Tax = TaxSingle(adjPay)
    Else
      Fed_Tax = TaxMarried(adjPay)
  End If
End Function
```

```
Function FICA_Tax (pay As Single, prevPay As Single, totalPay As Single)
  Dim socialSecurity As Single, medicare As Single
  Rem Compute social security and medicare tax
  Let socialSecurity = 0
  If totalPay <= 60600 Then
      Let socialSecurity = .062 * pay
    ElseIf prevPay < 60600 Then
      Let socialSecurity = .062 * (60600 - prevPay)
  End If
  Let medicare = .0145 * pay
  FICA_Tax = socialSecurity + medicare
End Function

Function Gross_Pay (hrWage As Single, hrsWorked As Single)
  Rem Compute weekly pay before taxes
  If hrsWorked <= 40 Then
      Gross_Pay = hrsWorked * hrWage
    Else
      Gross_Pay = 40 * hrWage + (hrsWorked - 40) * 1.5 * hrWage
  End If
End Function

Function Total_Pay (prevPay As Single, pay As Single)
  Rem Compute total pay before taxes
  Total_Pay = prevPay + pay
End Function

Sub InputData (empName As String, hrWage As Single, hrsWorked As Single,
                      exempts As Single, mStatus As String, prevPay As Single)
  Rem Enter above two lines as one
  Rem Get payroll data for employee
  Let empName = txtName.Text
  Let hrWage = Val(txtWageEarn.Text)
  Let hrsWorked = Val(txtHrsYtd.Text)
  Let exempts = Val(txtExempFica.Text)
  Let mStatus = Left$(UCase$(txtMarTax.Text), 1) 'M or S
  Let prevPay = Val(txtPayChk.Text)
End Sub

Sub ShowPayroll (empName As String, pay As Single, totalPay As Single,
                      ficaTax As Single, fedTax As Single, check As Single)
  Rem Enter above two lines as one
  Rem Display results of payroll computations
  Picture1.Cls
  Picture1.Print "Payroll results for "; empName
  Picture1.Print
  Picture1.Print "    Gross pay this period: "; Format$(pay, "Currency")
  Picture1.Print
  Picture1.Print "    Year-to-date earnings: "; Format$(totalPay, "Currency")
  Picture1.Print
  Picture1.Print "   Fica Taxes this period: "; Format$(ficaTax, "Currency")
  Picture1.Print
  Picture1.Print "     Income tax withheld: "; Format$(fedTax, "Currency")
  Picture1.Print
  Picture1.Print "Net pay (check amount): "; Format$(check, "Currency")
End Sub
```

```
Function TaxMarried (adjPay As Single)
  Rem Compute federal tax for married person based on adjusted pay
  Select Case adjPay
    Case 0 To 122
      TaxMarried = 0
    Case 122 To 806
      TaxMarried = .15 * (adjPay - 122)
    Case 806 To 1606
      TaxMarried = 102.6 + .28 * (adjPay - 806)
    Case 1606 To 2767
      TaxMarried = 326.6 + .31 * (adjPay - 1606)
    Case 2767 To 4883
      TaxMarried = 686.51 + .36 * (adjPay - 2767)
    Case Is > 4883
      TaxMarried = 1448.27 + .396 * (adjPay - 4883)
  End Select
End Function

Function TaxSingle (adjPay As Single)
  Rem Compute federal tax for single person based on adjusted pay
  Select Case adjPay
    Case 0 To 50
      TaxSingle = 0
    Case 50 To 463
      TaxSingle = .15 * (adjPay - 50)
    Case 463 To 968
      TaxSingle = 61.95 + .28 * (adjPay - 463)
    Case 968 To 2238
      TaxSingle = 203.35 + .31 * (adjPay - 968)
    Case 2238 To 4834
      TaxSingle = 597.05 + .36 * (adjPay - 2238)
    Case Is > 4834
      TaxSingle = 1531.61 + .396 * (adjPay - 4834)
  End Select
End Function
```

Comments:

1. In ComputeFICATax, care has been taken to avoid computing social security benefits tax on income in excess of $60,600 per year. The logic of the program makes sure an employee whose income crosses the $60,600 threshold during a given week is only taxed on the difference between $60,600 and his previous year-to-date income.

2. The two functions TaxMarried and TaxSingle use Select Case to incorporate the tax brackets given in Tables 5.9 and 5.10 for the amount of federal income tax withheld. The upper limit of each Case clause is the same as the lower limit of the next Case clause. This ensures fractional values for adjPay, such as 50.50 in the TaxSingle function, will be properly treated as part of the higher salary range.

Chapter 5
Summary

1. The *relational operators* are <, >, =, <>, <=, and >=.

2. The principal *logical operators* are And, Or, and Not.

3. A *condition* is an expression involving constants, variables, functions, and operators (arithmetic, relational, and/or logical) that can be evaluated to either true or false.

4. An If block decides what action to take depending upon the truth values of one or more conditions. To allow several courses of action, the If and Else parts of an If statement can contain other If statements.

5. A Select Case block selects one of several actions depending on the value of an expression, called the *selector*. The entries in the *value* lists must have the same type (string or numeric) as the selector.

Chapter 5
Programming Projects

1. Table 5.13 gives the price schedule for Eddie's Equipment Rental. Full-day rentals cost one-and-a-half times half-day rentals. Write a program that displays Table 5.13 in a picture box when an appropriate command button is clicked and displays a bill in another picture box based on the item number and time period chosen by a customer. The bill should include a $30.00 deposit.

Piece of Equipment	Half-Day	Full-Day
1. Rug cleaner	$16.00	$24.00
2. Lawn mower	$12.00	$18.00
3. Paint sprayer	$20.00	$30.00

Table 5.13 Price schedule for Eddie's Equipment Rental.

A possible form layout and sample run is shown in Figure 5.9.

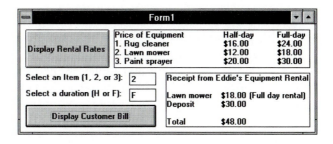

Figure 5.9 Form layout and sample run for Programming Project 1.

2. The American Heart Association suggests that at most 30% of the calories in our diet come from fat. Whereas food labels give the number of calories and amount of fat per serving, they often do not give the percentage of calories from fat. This percentage can be calculated by multiplying the number of grams of fat in one serving by 9, dividing that number by the total number of calories per serving, and multiplying the result by 100. Write a program that requests the name, number of calories per serving, and the grams of fat per serving as input, and tells us whether the food meets the American Heart Association recommendation. A sample run is as follows:

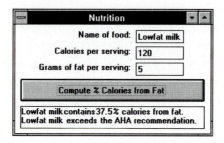

3. Table 5.14 gives the 1994 federal income tax rate schedule for single taxpayers. Write a program that requests the taxable income calculates the federal income tax. Use a subprogram for the input and a function to calculate the tax.

Taxable Income Over	But Not Over	Your Tax Is	Of Amount Over
$0	$22,750	15%	$0
$22,750	$55,100	$3,412.50 + 28%	$22,750
$55,100	$115,000	$12,470.50 + 31%	$55,100
$115,000	$250,000	$31,039.50 + 36%	$115,000
$250,000		$79,639.50 + 39.6%	$250,000

Table 5.14 1994 federal income tax rates for single taxpayers.

4. Write a program to determine the real roots of the quadratic equation $ax^2 + bx + c = 0$ (where $a \neq 0$) after requesting the values of a, b, and c. Use a subprogram to insure that a is nonzero. **Note:** The equation has 2, 1, or 0 solutions depending upon whether the value of $b^2 - 4*a*c$ is positive, zero, or negative. In the first two cases the solutions are given by the quadratic formula $(-b \pm Sqr(b^2 - 4*a*c))/(2*a)$.

5. Table 5.15 contains seven proverbs and their truth values. Write a program that presents these proverbs one at a time and asks the user to evaluate them as true or false. The program should then tell the user how many questions were answered correctly and display one of the following evaluations: Perfect (all correct), Excellent (5 or 6 correct), You might consider taking Psychology 101 (less than 5 correct).

Proverb	Truth Value
The squeaky wheel gets the grease.	True
Cry and you cry alone.	True
Opposites attract.	False
Spare the rod and spoil the child.	False
Actions speak louder than words.	True
Familiarity breeds contempt.	False
Marry in haste, repent at leisure.	True

Table 5.15 Seven proverbs.

Source: "You Know What They Say . . .", by Alfie Kohn, *Psychology Today*, April 1988.

6. Write a program to find the day of the week for any date after 1582, the year our current calendar was introduced. The program should

   (a) Request the year and the number of the month as input.
   (b) Determine the number of days in the month. **Note:** All years divisible by 4 are leap years, with the exception of those years divisible by 100 and not by 400. For instance, 1600 and 2000 are leap years, but 1700, 1800, and 1900 are not.
   (c) Request the number of the day as input. The prompt should list the possible range for the number.
   (d) Determine the day of the week with the following algorithm.
      (1) Treat January as the 13th month and February as the 14th month of the previous year. For example 1/23/1986 should be converted to 13/23/1985 and 2/6/1987 should be converted to 14/6/1986.
      (2) Denote the number of the day, month, and year by d, m, and y. Compute

$$w = d + 2*m + \text{Int}(.6 * (m+1)) + y + \text{Int}(y/4) - \text{Int}(y/100) + \text{Int}(y/400) + 2$$

      (3) The remainder when w is divided by 7 is the day of the week of the given date, with Saturday as the zeroth day of the week, Sunday the first day of the week, Monday the second, and so on.

   A sample run of the program for a famous date in U.S. history is shown below.

Test the program with the following memorable dates in the history of the U.S. space program.

On Tuesday, February 20, 1962, John Glenn became the first American to orbit the earth.

On Sunday, July 20, 1969, Neil Armstrong became the first person to set foot on the moon.

On Saturday, June 18, 1983, Sally Ride became the first American woman to travel in space.

7. Write a program to analyze a mortgage. The user should enter the amount of the loan, the annual rate of interest, and the duration of the loan in months. When the user clicks on the command button, the information that was entered should be checked to make sure it is reasonable. If bad data have been supplied, the user should be so advised. Otherwise, the monthly payment and the total amount of interest paid should be displayed. The formula for the monthly payment is

```
payment = p * r / (1 - (1 + r) ^ (-n))
```

where *p* is the amount of the loan, *r* is the monthly interest rate (annual rate divided by 12) given as a number between 0 (for 0 percent) and 1 (for 100 percent), and *n* is the duration of the loan. The formula for the total interest paid is

```
total interest = n * payment - p
```

8. Write a program using the form in Figure 5.10. Each time the command button is pressed, Rnd is used to simulate a coin toss and the values are updated. The figure shows the status after 10 coin tosses. **Note:** You can produce tosses quickly by just holding down the Enter key. Although the percentage of heads initially will fluctuate considerably, it should stay close to 50% after many (say 1000) tosses.

Figure 5.10 Form for Programming Project 8.

6

Repetition

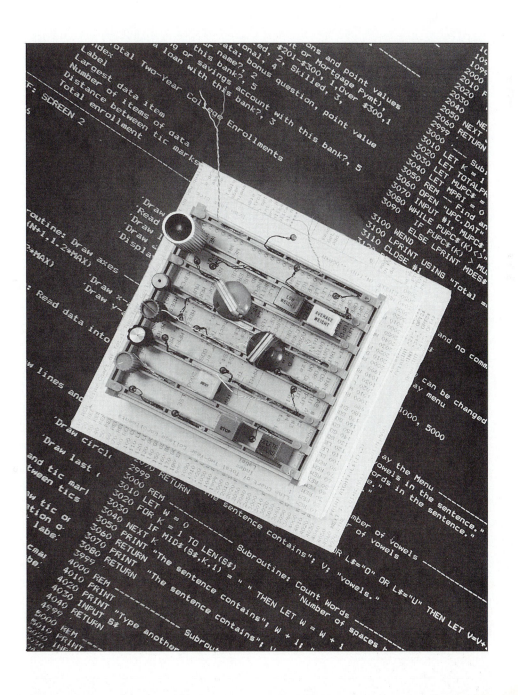

6.1 DO LOOPS

A **loop**, one of the most important structures in Visual Basic, is used to repeat a sequence of statements a number of times. At each repetition, or **pass**, the statements act upon variables whose values are changing.

The **Do loop** repeats a sequence of statements either as long as or until a certain condition is true. A Do statement precedes the sequence of statements and a Loop statement follows the sequence of statements. The condition, along with either the word While or Until, follows the word Do or the word Loop. When Visual Basic executes a Do loop of the form

```
Do While condition
    statement(s)
Loop
```

it first checks the truth value of *condition*. If *condition* is false, then the statements inside the loop are not executed and the program continues with the line after the Loop statement. If *condition* is true, then the statements inside the loop are executed. When the statement Loop is encountered, the entire process is repeated beginning with the testing *condition* in the Do While statement. In other words, the statements inside the loop are repeatedly executed as long as the condition is true. Figure 6.1 contains the pseudocode and flowchart for this loop.

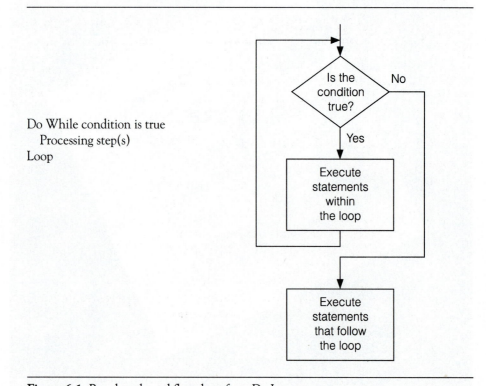

```
Do While condition is true
    Processing step(s)
Loop
```

Figure 6.1 Pseudocode and flowchart for a Do Loop.

EXAMPLE 1 Write a program that displays the numbers from 1 through 10.

SOLUTION The condition in the Do loop is "num <= 10".

```
Sub Command1_Click ()
  Dim num As Integer
  Rem Display the numbers from 1 to 10
  Let num = 1
  Do While num <= 10
    Picture1.Print num;
    Let num = num + 1
  Loop
End Sub
```

[Run and click the command button. The following is displayed in the picture box.]

```
1  2  3  4  5  6  7  8  9  10
```

Do loops are commonly used to insure that a proper response is received from the InputBox$ function.

EXAMPLE 2 The following program requires the user to give a password before a secret file can be accessed.

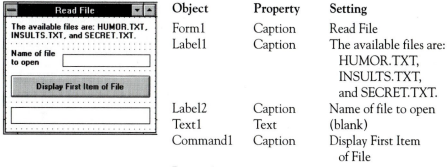

Object	Property	Setting
Form1	Caption	Read File
Label1	Caption	The available files are: HUMOR.TXT, INSULTS.TXT, and SECRET.TXT.
Label2	Caption	Name of file to open
Text1	Text	(blank)
Command1	Caption	Display First Item of File
Picture1		

```
Sub Command1_Click ()
  Dim passWord As String, info As String
  If UCase$(Text1.Text) = "SECRET.TXT" Then
      Let passWord = ""
      Do While passWord <> "SHAZAM"
        Let passWord = InputBox$("What is the password?")
        Let passWord = UCase$(passWord)
      Loop
  End If
  Open Text1.Text For Input As #1
  Input #1, info
  Picture1.Print info
  Close #1
End Sub
```

[Run, type SECRET.TXT into the text box, and click the command button.]

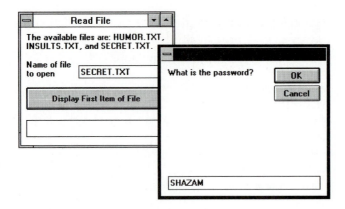

Note: If a file other than SECRET.TXT is requested, the statements inside the loop are not executed.

In Examples 1 and 2, the condition was checked at the top of the loop, that is, before the statements were executed. Alternatively, the condition can be checked at the bottom of the loop when the statement Loop is reached. When Visual Basic encounters a Do loop of the form

```
Do
    statement(s)
Loop Until condition
```

it executes the statements inside the loop and then checks the truth value of *condition*. If *condition* is true, then the program continues with the line after the Loop statement. If *condition* is false, then the entire process is repeated beginning with the Do statement. In other words, the statements inside the loop are executed at least once and then are repeatedly executed until the condition is true. Figure 6.2 shows the pseudocode and flowchart for this type of Do loop.

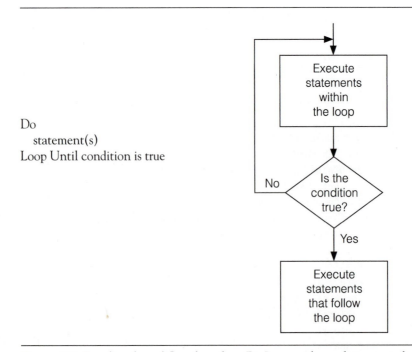

Do
    statement(s)
Loop Until condition is true

Figure 6.2 Pseudocode and flowchart for a Do Loop with condition tested at the bottom.

EXAMPLE 3   The following program is equivalent to Example 2, except that the condition is tested at the bottom of the loop.

```
Sub Command1_Click ()
  Dim passWord As String, info As String
  If UCase$(Text1.Text) = "SECRET.TXT" Then
      Do
        Let passWord = InputBox$("What is the password?")
        Let passWord = UCase$(passWord)
      Loop Until passWord = "SHAZAM"
  End If
  Open Text1.Text For Input As #1
  Input #1, info
  Picture1.Print info
  Close #1
End Sub
```

Do loops allow us to calculate useful quantities for which we might not know a simple formula.

EXAMPLE 4   Suppose you deposit $100 into a savings account and let it accumulate at 7 percent interest compounded annually. The following program determines when you will be a millionaire.

Object	Property	Setting
Form1	Caption	7% Interest
Label1	Caption	Amount Deposited
Text1	Text	(blank)
Command1	Caption	Years to become a millionaire
Picture1		

```
Sub Command1_Click ()
  Dim balance As Single, numYears As Integer
  Rem Compute years required to become a millionaire
  Picture1.Cls
  Let balance = Val(Text1.Text)
  Let numYears = 0
  Do While balance < 1000000
    Let balance = balance + .07 * balance
    Let numYears = numYears + 1
  Loop
  Picture1.Print "In"; numYears; "years you will have a million dollars."
End Sub
```

[Run, type 100 into the text box, and press the command button.]

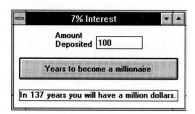

Comments:

1. Be careful to avoid infinite loops, that is, loops that are never exited. The following loop is infinite since the condition "num < > 0" will always be true. **Note:** The loop can be terminated by pressing Ctrl+Break.

```
Sub Command1_Click ()
   Dim num As Single
   Rem An infinite loop
   Let num = 7
   Do While num <> 0
      Let num = num - 2
   Loop
End Sub
```

   Notice that this slip-up can be avoided by changing the condition to "num >= 0".

2. The statements between Do and Loop do not have to be indented. However, since indenting improves the readability of the program, it is regarded as good programming style. As soon as you see the word Do, your eyes can easily scan down the program to find the matching Loop statement. You know immediately the size of the loop.

3. Visual Basic allows the use of the words While and Until either at the top or bottom of a Do loop. In this text, the usage of these words is restricted for the following reasons.

   (a) Since any While statement can easily be converted to an Until statement and vice versa, the restriction produces no loss of capabilities and the programmer has one less matter to think about.
   (b) Restricting the use simplifies reading the program. The word While proclaims testing at the top and the word Until proclaims testing at the bottom.
   (c) Certain other major structured languages, such as Pascal, only allow While at the top and Until at the bottom of a loop. Therefore, following this convention will make life easier for people already familiar with Pascal or planning to learn it.
   (d) Standard pseudocode uses the word While to denote testing a loop at the top and the word Until to denote testing at the bottom.

4. Good programming practice requires that all variables appearing in a Do loop be assigned values before the loop is entered, rather than relying on default values. For instance, the code on the left below should be replaced with the code on the right below.

```
Rem Add 1 through 10          Rem Add 1 through 10
Do While num < 10            Let num = 0
   Let num = num + 1         Let sum = 0
   Let sum = sum + num       Do While num < 10
Loop                            Let num = num + 1
                                Let sum = sum + num
                             Loop
```

PRACTICE PROBLEMS 6.1

1. How do you decide whether a condition should be checked at the top of a loop or at the bottom?

2. Change the following loop so it will be executed at least once.

```
Do While continue = "Yes"
   Let answer = InputBox$("Do you want to continue (Y or N)")
   If UCase$(answer) = "Y" Then
       Let continue = "Yes"
     Else
       Let continue = "No"
   End If
Loop
```

EXERCISES 6.1

In Exercises 1 through 6, determine the output displayed in the picture box when the command button is clicked.

1. ```
Sub Command1_Click ()
   Dim q As Single
   Let q = 3
   Do While q < 15
     Let q = 2 * q - 1
   Loop
   Picture1.Print q
End Sub
```

2. ```
Sub Command1_Click ()
   Dim balance As Single, interest As Single, n As Integer
   Let balance = 1000
   Let interest = .1
   Let n = 0                'Number of years
   Do
     Picture1.Print n; balance
     Let balance = (1 + interest) * balance
     Let n = n + 1
   Loop Until balance > 1200
   Picture1.Print n
End Sub
```

3.
```
Sub Command1_Click ()
    Dim num As Single, msg As String
    Rem Display a message
    Let num = 4
    Do
      Select Case num
        Case 1
          Let msg = "grammer!"
          Let num = -1
        Case 2
          Let msg = "re a su"
          Let num = (5 - num) * (3 - num)
        Case 3
          Let msg = "per pro"
          Let num = 4 - num
        Case 4
          Let msg = "You a"
          Let num = 2 * num - 6
      End Select
      Picture1.Print msg;
    Loop Until num = -1
End Sub
```

4.
```
Sub Command1_Click ()
    Dim prompt As String, firstYear As Integer
    Rem Computer-assisted instruction
    Let prompt = "In what year was the IBM PC first produced?"
    Do
      Let firstYear = Val(InputBox$(prompt))
      Select Case firstYear
        Case 1981
          Picture1.Print "Correct. The computer was an instant"
          Picture1.Print "success. By the end of 1981, there was"
          Picture1.Print "such a backlog of orders that customers"
          Picture1.Print "had a three-month waiting period."
        Case Is < 1981
          Picture1.Print "Later. The Apple II computer, which"
          Picture1.Print "preceded the IBM PC, appeared in 1977."
        Case Is > 1981
          Picture1.Print "Earlier. The first successful IBM PC clone,"
          Picture1.Print "the Compaq Portable, appeared in 1983."
      End Select
      Picture1.Print
    Loop Until firstYear = 1981
End Sub
```

(Assume that the first response is *1980* and the second response is *1981*.)

5.
```
Sub Command1_Click ()
    Rem Calculate the remainder in long division
    Picture1.Print Remainder(3, 17)
End Sub
```

```
Function Remainder (divisor As Single, dividend As Single) As Single
   Dim sum As Single
   Let sum = 0
   Do While sum <= dividend
     Let sum = sum + divisor
   Loop
     Remainder = dividend - sum + divisor
 End Function
```

6.
```
Sub Command1_Click ()
   Dim info As String, counter As Integer, letter As String
   Rem Simulate Instr; search for the letter t
   Let info = "Potato"
   Let counter = 0
   Let letter = ""
   Do While (letter <> "t") And (counter < Len(info))
     Let counter = counter + 1
     Let letter = Mid$(info, counter, 1)
     If letter = "t" Then
         Picture1.Print counter
     End If
   Loop
   If letter <> "t" Then
       Picture1.Print 0
   End If
 End Sub
```

In Exercises 7 through 10, identify the errors.

7.
```
Sub Command1_Click ()
   Dim q As Single
   Let q = 1
   Do While q > 0
     Let q = 3 * q - 1
     Picture1.Print q;
   Loop
 End Sub
```

8.
```
Sub Command1_Click ()
   Dim num As Integer
   Rem Display the numbers from 1 to 5
   Do While num <> 5
     Let num = 1
     Picture1.Print num;
     Let num = num + 1
   Loop
 End Sub
```

9.
```
Sub Command1_Click ()
   Dim answer As String
   Rem Repeat until a yes response is given
   Loop
     Let answer = InputBox$("Did you chop down the cherry tree (Y/N)?")
   Do Until UCase$(answer) = "Y"
 End Sub
```

10.
```
Sub Command1_Click ()
    Dim n As Integer, answer As String
    Rem Repeat as long as desired
    Do
      Let n = n + 1
      Picture1.Print n
      Let answer = InputBox$("Do you want to continue (Y/N)?")
    Until UCase$(answer) = "Y"
End Sub
```

In Exercises 11 through 20, replace each phrase containing Until with an equivalent phrase containing While, and vice versa. For instance, the phrase Until sum = 100 would be replaced by While sum < > 100.

11. `Until num < 7`

12. `Until nom = "Bob"`

13. `While response = "Y"`

14. `While total = 10`

15. `While nom <> ""`

16. `Until balance >= 100`

17. `While (a > 1) And (a < 3)`

18. `Until (ans = "") Or (n = 0)`

19. `Until Not (n = 0)`

20. `While (ans = "Y") And (n < 7)`

In Exercises 21 and 22, write simpler and clearer code that performs the same task as the given code.

21.
```
Sub Command1_Click ()
    Dim nom As String
    Let nom = InputBox$("Enter a name:")
    Picture1.Print nom
    Let nom = InputBox$("Enter a name:")
    Picture1.Print nom
    Let nom = InputBox$("Enter a name:")
    Picture1.Print nom
End Sub
```

22.
```
Sub Command1_Click ()
    Dim loopNum As Integer, answer As String
    Let loopNum = 0
    Do
      If loopNum >= 1 Then
          Let answer = InputBox$("Do you want to continue (Y/N)?")
          Let answer = UCase$(answer)
        Else
          Let answer = "Y"
      End If
      If (answer = "Y") Or (loopNum = 0) Then
          Let loopNum = loopNum + 1
          Picture1.Print loopNum
      End If
    Loop Until answer <> "Y"
End Sub
```

23. Write a program that displays a Celsius-to-Fahrenheit conversion table. Entries in the table should range from –40 to 40 degrees Celsius in units of 5 degrees. **Note:** The formula f = (9 / 5) * c + 32 converts Celsius to Fahrenheit.

24. World population doubled from 2.7 billion in 1951 to 5.4 billion in 1991. If we assume that the world population has been doubling every 40 years, write a program to determine in what year the world population would have been less than 4.

25. Recall that the function Rnd has a random value between 0 and 1 (excluding 1), and so the expression Int(6*Rnd)+1 has a random whole number value between 1 and 6. Write a program which repeatedly "throws" a pair of dice and tallies the number of tosses and the number of those tosses that total (lucky) seven. The program should stop when 100 lucky sevens have been tossed. The program should then report the approximate odds of tossing a lucky seven. (The odds will be "1 in" followed by the result of dividing the number of tosses by the number of tosses that came up lucky sevens.)

26. Write a program to display all the numbers between 1 and 100 that are perfect squares. (A perfect square is an integer that is the square of another integer; 1, 4, and 16 are examples of perfect squares.)

27. Write a program to display all the numbers between 1 and 100 that are part of the Fibonaci sequence. The Fibonaci sequence begins 1, 1, 2, 3, 5, 8, . . . , where each new number in the sequence is found by adding up the previous two numbers in the sequence.

28. The population of Mexico City in 1994 was 23 million people and was growing at the rate of 3 percent each year. Write a program to determine when the population will reach 30 million.

29. An old grandfather clock reads 6:00 p.m. Somewhere not too long after 6:30 p.m. the minute hand will pass directly over the hour hand. Write a program using a loop to make better and better guesses as to what time it is when the hands exactly overlap. Keep track of the positions of both hands using the minutes at which they are pointing. (At 6:00 p.m. the minute hand points at 0 while the hour hand points at 30.) You will need to use the fact that when the minute hand advances m minutes, the hour hand advances $m/12$ minutes. (For example, when the minute hand advances 60 minutes, the hour hand advances 5 minutes from one hour mark to the next.) To make an approximation, record how far the minute hand is behind the hour hand, then advance the minute hand by this much and the hour hand by 1/12 this much. The loop should terminate when the resulting positions of the minute and hour hands differ by less than .0001 minutes. (The exact answer is 32 and 8/11 minutes after 6.)

30. Write a program that requests a word containing the two letters r and n as input and determines which of the two letters appears first. If the word does not contain both of the letters, the program should so advise the user. (Test the program with the words *colonel* and *merriment*.)

31. The coefficient of restitution of a ball, a number between 0 and 1, specifies how much energy is conserved when a ball hits a rigid surface. A coefficient of .9, for instance, means a bouncing ball will rise to 90 percent of its initial height after each bounce. Write a program to input a coefficient of restitution and a height in meters and report how many times a ball bounces before it rises to a height of less than 10 centimeters. Also report the total distance traveled by the ball before this point. The coefficients of restitution of a tennis ball, basketball, super ball, and softball are .7, .75, .9, and .3, respectively.

In Exercises 32 through 35, write a program to solve the stated problem.

32. *Savings Account.* $15,000 is deposited into a savings account paying 5 percent interest and $1000 is withdrawn from the account at the end of each year. Approximately how many years are required for the savings account to be depleted?

33. Rework Exercise 32 for the case where the amount of money deposited initially is input by the user and the program computes the number of years required to deplete the account. **Note:** Be careful to avoid infinite loops.

34. $1000 is deposited into a savings account, and an additional $1000 is deposited at the end of each year. If the money earns interest at the rate of 5 percent, how long will it take before the account contains at least $1 million?

35. A person born in 1980 can claim, "I will be x years old in the year x squared." Write a program to determine the value of x.

36. Illustrate the growth of money in a savings account. When the user presses the command button, values for Amount and Interest Rate are obtained from text boxes and used to calculate the number of years until the money doubles and the number of years until the money reaches a million dollars. Use the form design shown below. **Notes:** The balance at the end of each year is $(1 + r)$ times the previous balance, where r is the annual rate of interest in decimal form. Use Do loops to determine the number of years.

Object	Property	Setting
Form1	Caption	Compound Interest
Label1	Alignment	1 – Right Justify
	Caption	Amount
Text1	Text	(blank)
Label2	Alignment	1 – Right Justify
	Caption	Interest Rate (Annual)
Text2	Text	(blank)
Command1	Caption	Determine Years
Label3	Alignment	1 – Right Justify
	Caption	Doubling Time (Years)
Picture1		
Label4	Alignment	1 – Right Justify
	Caption	Reach a Million (Years)
Picture2		

Form for Exercise 36   Objects and Properties for Exercise 36

37. Allow the user to enter a sentence. Then, depending on which command button the user clicks, display the sentence entirely in capital letters or with just the first letter of each word capitalized.

In Exercises 38 and 39, write a program corresponding to the flowchart.

38. The flowchart in Figure 6.3 requests an integer greater than 1 as input, and factors it into a product of prime numbers. (**Note:** A number is prime if its only factors are 1 and itself. Test the program with the numbers 660 and 139.)

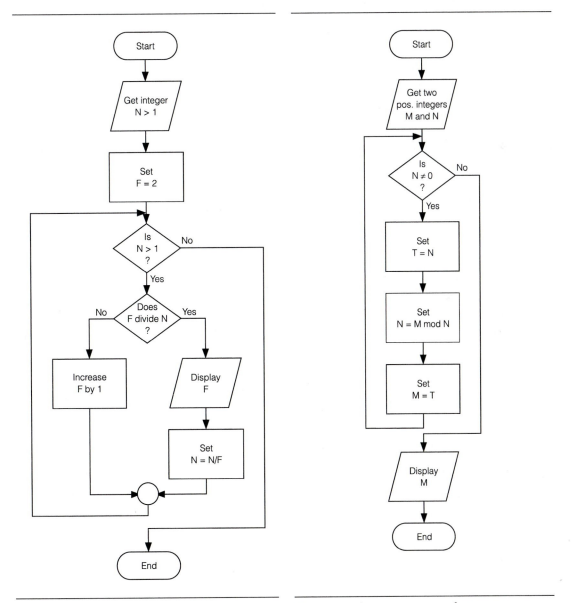

Figure 6.3 Prime factors.

Figure 6.4 Greatest common divisor.

39. The flowchart in Figure 6.4 finds the greatest common divisor of two positive integers input by the user. (The greatest common divisor of two positive integers is the largest integer that divides both of the numbers.) Write a program that corresponds to the flowchart.

1. As a rule of thumb, the condition is checked at the bottom if the loop should be executed at least once.

2. Either precede the loop with the statement Let continue = "Yes" or change the first line to Do and replace the Loop statement with Loop Until continue <> "Yes".

6.2 PROCESSING LISTS OF DATA WITH DO LOOPS

One of the main applications of programming is the processing of lists of data. Do loops are used to display all or selected items from lists, search lists for specific items, and perform calculations on the numerical entries of a list. This section introduces several devices that facilitate working with lists. **Counters** calculate the number of elements in lists, **accumulators** sum numerical values in lists, **flags** record whether certain events have occurred, and the **EOF function** indicates the end of a file. **Nested loops** add yet another dimension to repetition.

EOF Function

Data to be processed are often retrieved from a file by a Do loop. Visual Basic has a useful function, EOF, that tells us if we have reached the end of the file from which we are reading. Suppose a file has been opened with reference number n. At any time, the condition

```
EOF(n)
```

will be true if the end of the file has been reached, and false otherwise.

One of the first programs I wrote when I got my computer stored a list of names and phone numbers and printed a phone directory. I first had the program display the directory on the screen and later changed the Picture1.Print statements to Printer.Print statements to produce a printed copy. I stored the names in a file so I could easily add, change, or delete entries.

EXAMPLE 1 The following program displays the contents of a telephone directory. The names and phone numbers are contained in the file PHONE.TXT. The loop will repeat as long as the end of the file is not reached.

PHONE.TXT contains the following four lines:

"Bert", "123-4567"
"Ernie", "987-6543"
"Grover", "246-8321"
"Oscar", "135-7900"

Object	Property	Setting
Form1	Caption	Directory
Command1	Caption	Display Phone Numbers
Picture1		

```
Sub Command1_Click ()
  Dim nom As String, phoneNum As String
  Picture1.Cls
  Open "PHONE.TXT" For Input As #1
  Do While Not EOF(1)
    Input #1, nom, phoneNum
    Picture1.Print nom, phoneNum
  Loop
  Close #1
End Sub
```

[Run and press the command button.]

The program in Example 1 illustrates the proper way to process a list of data contained in a file. The Do loop should be tested at the top with an end-of-file condition. (If the file is empty, no attempt is made to input data from the file.) The first set of data should be input *after* the Do statement and then the data should be processed. Figure 6.5 contains the pseudocode and flowchart for this technique.

Do While there are still data in the file
    Get an item of data
    Process the item
Loop

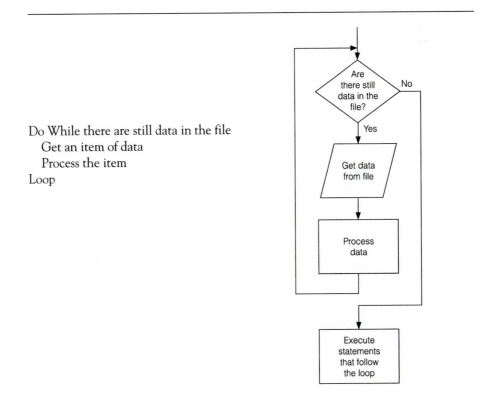

Figure 6.5 Pseudocode and flowchart for processing data from a file.

Sequential files can be quite large. Rather than list the entire contents, we typically search the file for a specific piece of information.

EXAMPLE 2 Modify the program in Example 1 to search the telephone directory for a name specified by the user. If the name does not appear in the directory, so notify the user.

SOLUTION We want to keep searching as long as there is no match *and* we have not reached the end of the list. Therefore, the condition for the Do While statement is a compound logical expression with the operator And. After the last pass through the loop, we will know whether the name was found and be able to display the requested information.

Object	Property	Setting
Form1	Caption	Phone Number
Label1	Caption	Name to look up
Text1	Text	(blank)
Command1	Caption	Display Phone Number
Picture1		

```
Sub Command1_Click ()
   Dim nom As String, phoneNum As String
   Open "PHONE.TXT" For Input As #1
   Do While (nom <> Text1.Text) And (Not EOF(1))
     Input #1, nom, phoneNum
   Loop
   Close #1
   Picture1.Cls
   If nom = Text1.Text Then
       Picture1.Print nom, phoneNum
     Else
       Picture1.Print "Name not found."
   End If
End Sub
```

[Run, type Grover into the text box, and press the command button.]

Counters and Accumulators

A **counter** is a numeric variable that keeps track of the number of items that have been processed. An **accumulator** is a numeric variable that totals numbers.

EXAMPLE 3   The following program counts and finds the value of coins listed in a file. COINS.TXT contains the following entries:

1, 1, 5, 10, 10, 25

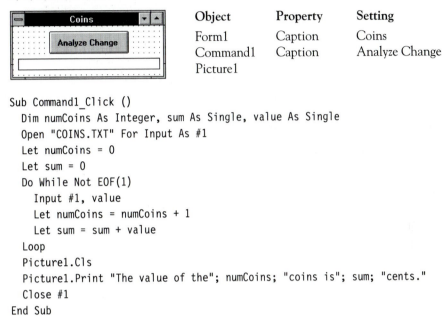

Object	Property	Setting
Form1	Caption	Coins
Command1	Caption	Analyze Change
Picture1		

```
Sub Command1_Click ()
  Dim numCoins As Integer, sum As Single, value As Single
  Open "COINS.TXT" For Input As #1
  Let numCoins = 0
  Let sum = 0
  Do While Not EOF(1)
    Input #1, value
    Let numCoins = numCoins + 1
    Let sum = sum + value
  Loop
  Picture1.Cls
  Picture1.Print "The value of the"; numCoins; "coins is"; sum; "cents."
  Close #1
End Sub
```

[Run and press the command button.]

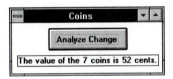

The value of the counter, *numCoins*, was initially 0 and changed on each execution of the loop to 1, 2, 3, 4, 5, and finally 6. The accumulator, *sum*, initially had the value 0 and increased with each execution of the loop to 1, 2, 7, 17, 27, and finally 52.

Flags

A **flag** is a variable that keeps track of whether a certain event has occurred. Typically, it is initialized with the value 0 and then assigned a nonzero value when the event occurs. It is used within a loop to provide information that will be taken into consideration after the loop has terminated. The flag also provides an alternative method of terminating a loop.

EXAMPLE 4   The following program counts the number of words in the file WORDS.TXT and then reports whether the words are in alphabetical order. In each execution of the loop, a word is compared to the next word in the list. The flag variable, called *orderFlag*, is initially assigned the value 0 and is set to 1 if a pair of adjacent words is out of order. The technique used in this program will be used in Chapter 7 when we study sorting. **Note:** The statement in line 7, Let word1 = "", is a device to get things started. Each word must first be read into the variable *word2*.

WORDS.TXT contains the following winning words from the U.S. National Spelling Bee:

"cambist", "croissant", "deification"
"hydrophyte", "incisor", "maculature"
"macerate", "narcolepsy", "shallon"

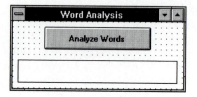

Object	Property	Setting
Form1	Caption	Word Analysis
Command1	Caption	Analyze Words
Picture1		

```
Sub Command1_Click ()
   Dim orderFlag As Integer, wordCounter As Integer
   Dim word1 As String, word2 As String
   Rem Count words.  Are they in alphabetical order?
   Let orderFlag = 0
   Let wordCounter = 0
   Let word1 = ""
   Open "WORDS.TXT" For Input As #1
   Do While Not EOF(1)
     Input #1, word2
     Let wordCounter = wordCounter + 1
     If word1 > word2 Then
         Let orderFlag = 1
     End If
     Let word1 = word2
   Loop
   Close #1
   Picture1.Print "The number of words is"; wordCounter
   If orderFlag = 0 Then
       Picture1.Print "The words are in alphabetical order."
     Else
       Picture1.Print "The words are not in alphabetical order."
   End If
End Sub
```

[Run and press the command button.]

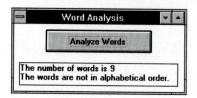

Nested Loops

The statements inside of a Do loop can consist of another Do loop. Such a configuration is referred to as a **nested loop** and is useful in repeating a single data processing routine several times.

EXAMPLE 5   Modify the program in Example 2 to allow the user to look through several lists of names. Suppose we have several different phone directories, the names of which are listed in the file LISTS.TXT. (For instance, the file LISTS.TXT might contain the entries CLIENTS.TXT, FRIENDS.TXT, and KINFOLK.TXT.) A sought-after name might be in any one of the files.

SOLUTION   The statements in the inner Do loop will be used to look up names as before. At least one pass through the outer Do loop is guaranteed and passes will continue as long as the name is not found and phone lists remain to be examined.

```
Sub Command1_Click ()
  Dim foundFlag As String, fileName As String
  Dim nom As String, phoneNum As String
  Open "LISTS.TXT" For Input As #1
  Let foundFlag = "no"
  Let nom = ""
  Do While (foundFlag = "no") And (Not EOF(1))
    Input #1, fileName
    Open fileName For Input As #2
    Do While (nom <> Text1.Text) And (Not EOF(2))
      Input #2, nom, phoneNum
    Loop
    Close #2
    Picture1.Cls
    If nom = Text1.Text Then
        Picture1.Print nom, phoneNum
        Let foundFlag = "yes"
    End If
  Loop
  Close #1
  If foundFlag = "no" Then
      Picture1.Print "Name not found."
  End If
End Sub
```

Comment:

1. In Appendix D, the section "Stepping Through a Program Containing a Do Loop: Chapter 6" uses the Visual Basic debugging tools to trace the flow through a Do loop.

PRACTICE PROBLEMS 6.2

1. Determine the output of the following program, where the file SCORES.TXT contains the three scores 150, 200, and 300.

```
Sub Command1_Click ()
  Dim sum As Single, score As Single
  Rem Find the sum of a collection of bowling scores
  Let sum = 0
  Open "SCORES.TXT" For Input As #1
  Input #1, score
  Do While Not EOF(1)
    Let sum = sum + score
    Input #1, score
  Loop
  Close #1
  Picture1.Print sum
End Sub
```

2. Why didn't the program above produce the intended output?

3. Correct the program above so it has the intended output.

EXERCISES 6.2

In Exercises 1 through 10, determine the output displayed in the picture box when the command button is clicked.

1.
```
Sub Command1_Click ()
  Dim total As Single, num As Single
  Let total = 0
  Open "DATA.TXT" For Input As #1
  Do While Not EOF(1)
    Input #1, num
    Let total = total + num
  Loop
  Close #1
  Picture1.Print total
End Sub
```

(Assume that the file DATA.TXT contains the following entries.)

5, 2, 6

2.
```
Sub Command1_Click ()
  Dim nom As String
  Open "DATA.TXT" For Input As #1
  Do While Not EOF(1)
    Input #1, nom
    Picture1.Print nom
  Loop
  Close #1
End Sub
```

(Assume that the file DATA.TXT contains the following entries.)

"Lisa", "Michael"

3. ```
Sub Command1_Click ()
    Dim dessert As String
    Rem Display list of desserts
    Open "DESSERTS.TXT" For Input As #1
    Do While Not EOF(1)
      Input #1, dessert
      Picture1.Print dessert
    Loop
    Close #1
End Sub
```

(Assume that the file DESSERTS.TXT contains the following entries.)

"pie", "cake", "melon"

**4.** ```
Sub Command1_Click ()
    Dim city As String, pop As Single
    Open "CITYPOPS.TXT" For Input As #1
    Do While Not EOF(1)
      Input #1, city, pop
      If pop >= 7 Then
          Picture1.Print city, pop
      End If
    Loop
    Close #1
End Sub
```

(Assume that the file CITYPOPS.TXT contains the following four lines that give a city and its population in millions.)

"San Francisco", 5.6
"Boston", 4
"Chicago", 8
"New York", 17.7

5. ```
Sub Command1_Click ()
    Dim firstLetter As String, fruit As String
    Let firstLetter = ""
    Open "FRUITS.TXT" For Input As #1
    Do While Not EOF(1)
      Input #1, fruit
      If Left$(fruit, 1) <> firstLetter Then
          If firstLetter <> "" Then
              Picture1.Print
          End If
          Let firstLetter = Left$(fruit, 1)
          Picture1.Print Tab(3); firstLetter
      End If
      Picture1.Print fruit
    Loop
    Close #1
End Sub
```

(Assume that the file FRUITS.TXT contains the following entries.)

"Apple", "Apricot", "Avocado", "Banana", "Blueberry", "Grape", "Lemon", "Lime"
```

6.
```
Sub Command1_Click ()
    Dim num As Single
    Rem Display list of numbers
    Open "DATA.TXT" For Input As #1
    Input #1, num
    Do While Not EOF(1)
      Picture1.Print num;
      Input #1, num
    Loop
    Close #1
End Sub
```

(Assume that the file DATA.TXT contains the following entries.)

2, 3, 8, 5

7.
```
Sub Command1_Click ()
    Dim animal As String, groupName As String
    Call InputAnimal(animal)
    If animal <> "" Then
        Call SearchList(animal, groupName)
        Call DisplayResult(animal, groupName)
    End If
End Sub


Sub DisplayResult (anml As String, gName As String)
  If gName = "" Then
      Picture1.Print "Animal not found."
    Else
      Picture1.Print "A group of "; anml; "s is called a "; gName
  End If
End Sub


Sub InputAnimal (anml As String)
  Rem Request the name of an animal as input
  Let anml = InputBox$("Please enter the name of an animal")
End Sub


Sub SearchList (anml As String, gName As String)
  Dim creature As String, groupName As String
  Let creature = ""
  Open "ANIMALS.TXT" For Input As #1
  Do While (creature <> anml) And Not EOF(1)
    Input #1, creature, groupName
  Loop
  If EOF(1) Then
      Let gName = ""
    Else
      Let gName = groupName
  End If
  Close #1
End Sub
```

(Assume that the file ANIMALS.TXT contains the following three lines that give an animal and the name of a group of those animals. Assume the response is *duck*.)

"lion", "pride"
"duck", "brace"
"bee", "swarm"

8.
```
Sub Command1_Click ()
   Dim s As String
   Let s = "I think I can. "
   Call Duplicate30(s)
   Let s = "We're off to see the wizard, the wonderful wizard of OZ."
   Call Duplicate30(s)
End Sub

Sub Duplicate30 (sentence As String)
   Dim flag As Integer
   Let flag = 0     'flag tells whether loop has been executed
   Do While Len(sentence) < 30
     Let flag = 1
     Let sentence = sentence + sentence
   Loop
   If flag = 1 Then
       Picture1.Print sentence
     Else
       Picture1.Print "Loop not executed."
   End If
End Sub
```

9.
```
Sub Command1_Click ()
   Dim word As String, cWord As String
   Open "WORDS.TXT" For Input As #1
   Do While Not EOF(1)
     Input #1, word
     If Left$(word, 1) = "c" Then
         Let cWord = word
     End If
   Loop
   Close #1
   Picture1.Print cWord
End Sub
```

(Assume that the file WORDS.TXT contains the following saying data.)

"time", "is", "a", "child", "idly", "moving", "counters", "in", "a", "game",
"Heraclitus"

10.
```
Sub Command1_Click ()
   Dim max As Single, value As Single, rowMax As Single
   Let max = 0
   Open "DATA.TXT" For Input As #1
   Do While Not EOF(1)
     Input #1, value
     Let rowMax = 0
```

```
        Do While value <> -2
          If value > rowMax Then
              Let rowMax = value
          End If
          Input #1, value
        Loop
        Picture1.Print rowMax
        If rowMax > max Then
            Let max = rowMax
        End If
      Loop
      Close #1
      Picture1.Print max
    End Sub
```

(Assume that the file DATA.TXT contains the following entries.)

5, 7, 3, –2, 10, 12, 6, 4, –2, 1, 9, –2

In Exercises 11 through 14, identify the errors.

11.
```
Sub Command1_Click ()
    Dim num As Single
    Open "DATA.TXT" For Input As #1
    Do While (Not EOF(1)) And (num > 0)
      Input #1, num
      Picture1.Print num
    Close #1
End Sub
```

(Assume that the file DATA.TXT contains the following entries.)

7, 6, 0, –1, 2

12.
```
Sub Command1_Click ()
    Dim flag As Integer, num As Single
    Let flag = 0
    Do While flag <> 1
      Let num = Val(InputBox$("Enter a number"))
      If num * num < 0 Then
          Let flag = 1
      End If
    Loop
End Sub
```

13.
```
Sub Command1_Click ()
    Dim president As String
    Rem Display names of some U.S. Presidents
    Open "PRES.TXT" For Input As #1
    Input #1, president
    Do
      Picture1.Print president
      Input #1, president
    Loop Until EOF(1)
    Close #1
End Sub
```

(Assume that the file PRES.TXT contains the following entries.)

"Lincoln", "Washington", "Kennedy", "Clinton"

14.
```
Sub Command1_Click ()
    Dim num As Single
    Open "DATA.TXT" For Input As #1
    If EOF(1) Then
        Let num = 0
      Else
        Input #1, num
    End If
    Do While 1 < num < 5
      Picture1.Print num
      If EOF(1) Then
          Let num = 0
        Else
          Input #1, num
      End If
    Loop
    Close #1
End Sub
```

(Assume that the file DATA.TXT contains the following entries)

3, 2, 4, 7, 2

15. Write a program to find and display the largest of a collection of positive numbers contained in a data file. (Test the program with the collection of numbers 89, 77, 95, and 86.)

16. Write a program to find and display those names that are repeated in a data file. Assume the file has already been sorted into alphabetical order. When a name is found to be repeated, only display it once.

17. Suppose the file GRADES.TXT contains student grades on a final exam. Write a program that displays the average grade on the exam and the percentage of grades that are above average.

18. Suppose the file BIDS.TXT contains a list of bids on a construction project. Write a program to analyze the list and report the two highest bids.

19. Suppose the file USPRES.TXT contains the names of the United States Presidents in order from Washington to Clinton. Write a program that asks the user to type a number from 1 to 42 into a text box, and then, when a command button is clicked, displays the name of the President corresponding to that number.

20. Table 6.1 shows the different grades of eggs and the minimum weight required for each classification. Write a program that processes a data file that lists the weights of a sample of eggs. The program should report the number of eggs in each grade and the weight of the lightest and heaviest egg in the sample. (**Note:** Eggs weighing less than 1.5 ounces cannot be sold in supermarkets.) Figure 6.6 shows a sample output of the program.

Grade	Weight (in ounces)
Jumbo	2.5
Extra Large	2.25
Large	2
Medium	1.75
Small	1.5

25 Jumbo eggs
132 Extra Large eggs
180 Large eggs
150 Medium eggs
95 Small eggs
Lightest egg: 1.52 ounces
Heaviest egg: 2.72 ounces

Table 6.1 Grades of eggs.

Figure 6.6 Output for Exercise 20.

21. Write a program to request a positive integer as input and carry out the following algorithm. If the number is even, divide it by 2. Otherwise, multiply the number by 3 and add 1. Repeat this process with the resulting number and continue repeating the process until the number 1 is reached. After the number 1 is reached, the program should display how many iterations were required. *Note:* A number is even if Int(num / 2) = num / 2. (Test the program with the numbers 9, 21, and 27.)

22. Suppose the file USPRES.TXT contains the names of all United States Presidents, and the file USSENATE.TXT contains the names of all former and present U.S. Senators. Write a program with nested loops that uses these files to display the names of all Presidents who served in the Senate.

23. Suppose the file SONNET.TXT contains Shakespeare's Sonnet #18. Each entry in the file consists of a line of the sonnet enclosed in quotes. Write a program using nested loops to analyze this file line by line and report the average number of words in a line and the average length of a word in the sonnet.

24. Suppose the file SALES.TXT contains information on the sales during the past week at a new car dealership. Assume the file begins as shown in Figure 6.7. The file contains the following for each salesperson at the dealership: the name of the salesperson, pairs of numbers giving the final sales price and the dealer cost for each sale made by that salesperson, a pair of zeros to indicate the end of data for that salesperson. Write a program to display the name of each salesperson and the commission earned for the week. Assume the commission is 15% of the profit on each sale.

"Tom Jones"
18100, 17655
22395, 21885
15520, 14895
0,0
"Bill Smith"
16725, 16080
.
.
.

Figure 6.7 Sales data file for Exercise 24.

25. Write a program to do the following. (The program should use a flag.)

   (a) Ask the user to input a sentence that possibly contains one pair of parentheses.
   (b) Display the sentence with the parentheses and their contents removed.

   Test the program with the following sentence as input: BASIC (Beginners All-purpose Symbolic Instruction Code) is the world's most widely known computer language.

26. The salespeople at a health club keep track of the members who have joined in the last month. Their names and types of membership, Bronze, Silver, or Gold, are stored in the data file NEWMEMBS.TXT. Write a program that displays all the Bronze members, then the Silver members, and finally the Gold members.

27. Table 6.2 gives the prices of various liquids. Write a program that requests an amount of money as input and displays the names of all liquids for which a gallon could be purchased with that amount of money. The information from the table should be recovered from a data file. As an example, if the user has $2.35, then the following should be displayed in the picture box:

   You can purchase one gallon of any of the following liquids.

   Bleach
   Gasoline
   Milk

Liquid	Price	Liquid	Price
Apple Cider	2.60	Milk	.30
Beer	6.00	Gatorade	4.20
Bleach	1.40	Perrier	6.85
Coca Cola	2.55	Pancake Syrup	15.50
Gasoline	1.30	Spring Water	4.10

Table 6.2 Some comparative prices per gallon of various liquids.

SOLUTIONS TO PRACTICE PROBLEMS 6.2

1. 350

2. When the third score was read from the file, EOF(1) became true. With EOF(1) true the loop terminated and the third score was never added to *sum*. In addition, if the data file had been empty or contained only one piece of data, then the error message "Input past end of file" would have been displayed.

3.
```
Sub Command1_Click ()
    Dim sum As Single, score As Single
    Rem Find the sum of a collection of bowling scores
    Let sum = 0
    Open "SCORES.TXT" For Input As #1
    Do While Not EOF(1)
      Input #1, score
      Let sum = sum + score
    Loop
    Close #1
    Picture1.Print sum
End Sub
```

6.3 FOR...NEXT LOOPS

When we know exactly how many times a loop should be executed, a special type of loop, called a For...Next loop, can be used. For...Next loops are easy to read and write, and have features that make them ideal for certain common tasks. The following code uses a For...Next loop to display a table.

```
Sub Command1_Click ()
  Dim i As Integer
  Rem Display a table of the first 5 numbers and their squares
  Picture1.Cls
  For i = 1 To 5
    Picture1.Print i; i ^ 2
  Next i
End Sub
```

[Run and click on Command1. The following is displayed in the picture box.]

```
1   1
2   4
3   9
4   16
5   25
```

The equivalent program written with a Do loop is as follows.

```
Sub Command1_Click ()
  Dim i As Integer
  Rem Display a table of the first 5 numbers and their squares
  Picture1.Cls
  Let i = 1
  Do While i <= 5
    Picture1.Print i; i ^ 2
    Let i = i + 1
  Loop
End Sub
```

In general, a portion of a program of the form

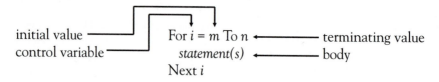

$$\text{initial value} \longrightarrow \quad \text{For } i = m \text{ To } n \longleftarrow \text{terminating value}$$
$$\text{control variable} \longrightarrow \quad statement(s) \longleftarrow \text{body}$$
$$\text{Next } i$$

constitutes a For...Next loop. The pair of statements For and Next cause the statements between them to be repeated a specified number of times. The For statement designates a numeric variable, called the **control variable**, that is initialized and then automatically changes after each execution of the loop. Also, the For statement gives the range of values this variable will assume. The Next statement increments the control variable. If $m > n$, then i is assigned the values $m, m + 1, ..., n$ in order, and the body is executed once for each of these values. If $m > n$, then execution continues with the statement after the For loop.

When program execution reaches a For...Next loop such as the one shown above, the For statement assigns to the control variable i the initial value m and checks to see whether i is greater than the terminating value n. If so, then execution jumps to the line following the Next statement. If $i <= n$, the statements inside the loop are executed. Then, the Next statement increases the value of i by 1 and checks this new value to see if it exceeds n. If not, the entire process is repeated until the value of i exceeds n. When this happens, the program moves to the line following the loop. Figure 6.8 contains the pseudocode and flowchart of a For...Next loop.

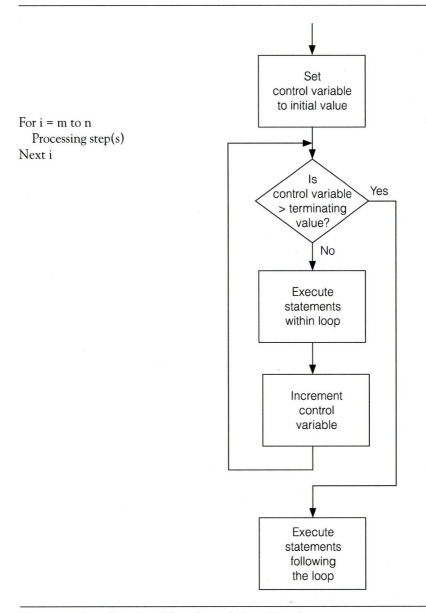

For i = m to n
    Processing step(s)
Next i

Figure 6.8 Pseudocode and flowchart of a For...Next loop.

The control variable can be *any* numeric variable. The most common single letter names are i, j, and k; however, if appropriate, the name should suggest the purpose of the control variable.

EXAMPLE 1 Suppose the population of a city is 300,000 in the year 1990 and is growing at the rate of 3 percent per year. The following program displays the projected population each year until 1995.

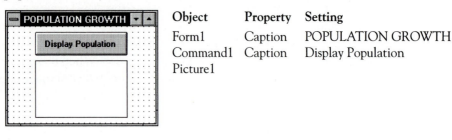

Object	Property	Setting
Form1	Caption	POPULATION GROWTH
Command1	Caption	Display Population
Picture1		

```
Sub Command1_Click ()
  Dim pop As Single, yr As Integer
  Rem Display population from 1990 to 1995
  Picture1.Cls
  Let pop = 300000
  For yr = 1990 To 1995
    Picture1.Print yr, Format$(pop, "#,#")
    Let pop = pop + .03 * pop
  Next yr
End Sub
```

[Run and click the command button.]

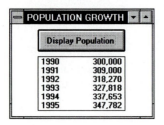

The initial and terminating values can be constants, variables, or expressions. For instance, the For statement in the program above can be replaced by

```
Let firstYr = 1990
Let lastYr = 1995
For yr = firstYr To lastYr
```

In Example 1, the control variable was increased by 1 after each pass through the loop. A variation of the For statement allows any number to be used as the increment. The statement

```
For i = m To n Step s
```

instructs the Next statement to add s to the control variable instead of 1. The numbers m, n, and s do not have to be whole numbers. The number s is called the **step value** of the loop.

EXAMPLE 2   The following program displays the values of the index of a For...Next loop for terminating and step values input by the user.

Object	Property	Setting
Form1	Caption	For index = 0 To n Step s
Label1	Caption	n:
Text1	Text	(blank)
Label2	Caption	s:
Text2	Text	(blank)
Command1	Caption	Display Values of index!
Picture1		

```
Sub Command1_Click ()
  Dim n As Single, s As Single, index As Single
  Rem Display values of index ranging from 0 to n Step s
  Picture1.Cls
  Let n = Val(Text1.Text)
  Let s = Val(Text2.Text)
  For index = 0 To n Step s
    Picture1.Print index;
  Next index
End Sub
```

[Run, type 3.2 and .5 into the text boxes, and click the command button.]

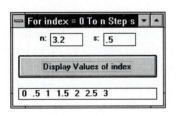

In the examples considered so far, the control variable was successively increased until it reached the terminating value. However, if a negative step value is used and the initial value is greater than the terminating value, then the control value is decreased until reaching the terminating value. In other words, the loop counts backward or downward.

EXAMPLE 3   The following program accepts a word as input and displays it backwards.

Object	Property	Setting
Form1	Caption	Write Backwards
Label1	Caption	Enter Word
Text1	Text	(blank)
Command1	Caption	Reverse Letters
Picture1		

```
Sub Command1_Click ()
  Picture1.Cls
  Picture1.Print Reverse$((Text1.Text))
End Sub
```

```
Function Reverse$ (info As String)
  Dim m As Integer, j As Integer, temp As String
  Let m = Len(info)
  Let temp = ""
  For j = m To 1 Step -1
    Let temp = temp + Mid$(info, j, 1)
  Next
  Reverse$ = temp
End Function
```

[Run, type SUEZ into the text box, and click the command button.]

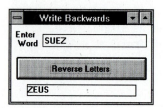

Note: The initial and terminating values of a For...Next loop can be expressions. For instance, the third and fifth lines of the function in Example 3 can be consolidated to

```
For j = Len(info) To 1 Step -1
```

The body of a For...Next loop can contain *any* sequence of Visual Basic statements. In particular, it can contain another For...Next loop. However, the second loop must be completely contained inside the first loop and must have a different control variable. Such a configuration is called **nested loops**. Figure 6.9 shows several examples of valid nested loops.

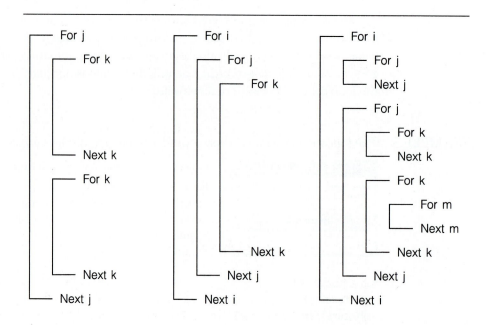

Figure 6.9 Nested loops.

EXAMPLE 4   Write a program to display the products of the integers from 1 to 4.

SOLUTION   In the following program, *j* denotes the left factors of the products and *k* denotes the right factors. Each factor takes on values from 1 to 4. The values are assigned to *j* in the outer loop and to *k* in the inner loop. Initially, *j* is assigned the value 1 and then the inner loop is traversed four times to produce the first row of products. At the end of these four passes, the value of *j* will still be 1 and the value of *k* will have been incremented to 5. The Picture1.Print statement just before Next j guarantees that no more products will be displayed in that row. The first execution of the outer loop is then complete. Following this, the statement Next j increments the value of *j* to 2. The statement beginning For k is then executed. It resets the value of *k* to 1. The second row of products is displayed during the next four executions of the inner loop, and so on.

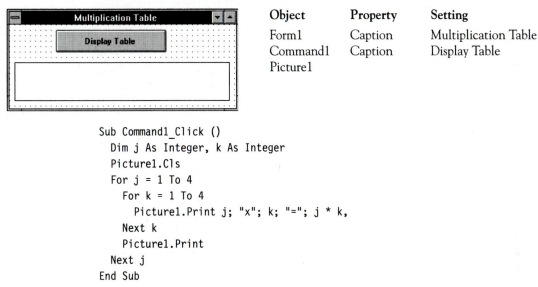

Object	Property	Setting
Form1	Caption	Multiplication Table
Command1	Caption	Display Table
Picture1		

```
Sub Command1_Click ()
  Dim j As Integer, k As Integer
  Picture1.Cls
  For j = 1 To 4
    For k = 1 To 4
      Picture1.Print j; "x"; k; "="; j * k,
    Next k
    Picture1.Print
  Next j
End Sub
```

[Run and press the command button.]

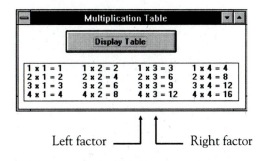

Left factor ⎯⎯⎯ ⎿ Right factor

Comments:

1. The body of a For...Next loop need not be indented. However, since indenting improves the readability of the program, it is good programming style. As soon as you see the word For, your eyes can easily scan down the program to find the matching Next statement. You then know two facts immediately: the number of statements in the body of the loop and the number of passes that will be made through the loop.

2. For and Next statements must be paired. If one is missing, the program will generate the error message "For without Next" or "Next without For."

3. Consider a loop beginning with For *i* = *m* To *n* Step *s*. The loop will be executed once if *m* equals *n*. The loop will not be executed at all if *m* is greater than *n* and *s* is positive, or if *m* is less than *n* and *s* is negative.

4. The value of the control variable should not be altered within the body of the loop; doing so might cause the loop to repeat indefinitely or have an unpredictable number of repetitions.

5. Noninteger step values can lead to roundoff errors with the result that the loop is not executed the intended number of times. For instance, a loop beginning with For i = 1 To 2 Step .1 will be executed only 10 times instead of the intended 11 times. It should be replaced with For i = 1 To 2.01 Step .1.

PRACTICE PROBLEMS 6.3

1. Why won't the following lines of code work as intended?

```
For i = 15 To 1
  Picture1.Print i;
Next i
```

2. When is a For...Next loop more appropriate than a Do loop?

EXERCISES 6.3

In Exercises 1 through 12, determine the output displayed in the picture box when the command button is clicked.

```
1. Sub Command1_Click ()
     Dim i As Integer
     For i = 1 To 4
       Picture1.Print "Pass #"; i
     Next i
   End Sub
```

```
2. Sub Command1_Click ()
     Dim i As Integer
     For i = 3 To 6
       Picture1.Print 2 * i;
     Next i
   End Sub
```

```
3. Sub Command1_Click ()
     Dim j As Integer
     For j = 2 To 8 Step 2
       Picture1.Print j;
     Next j
     Picture1.Print "Who do we appreciate?"
   End Sub
```

```
4. Sub Command1_Click ()
     Dim countdown As Integer
     For countdown = 10 To 1 Step -1
       Picture1.Print countdown;
     Next countdown
     Picture1.Print "blastoff"
   End Sub
```

5.
```
Sub Command1_Click ()
  Dim num As Integer, i As Integer
  Let num = 5
  For i = num To 2 * num + 3
    Picture1.Print i;
  Next i
End Sub
```

6.
```
Sub Command1_Click ()
  Dim i As Single
  For i = 3 To 5 Step .25
    Picture1.Print i;
  Next i
  Picture1.Print i
End Sub
```

7.
```
Sub Command1_Click ()
  Dim recCount As Integer, miler As Integer
  Dim nom As String, mileTime As String
  Rem First entry in data file is number of records in file
  Open "MILER.TXT" For Input As #1
  Input #1, recCount
  For miler = 1 To recCount
    Input #1,  nom, mileTime
    Picture1.Print nom, mileTime
  Next miler
  Close #1
End Sub
```

(Assume that the file MILER.TXT contains the following four lines.)

3
"Steve Cram", "3:46.31"
"Steve Scott", "3:51.6"
"Mary Slaney", "4:20.5"

8.
```
Sub Command1_Click ()
  Dim recCount As Integer, total As Integer
  Dim i As Integer, score As Integer
  Rem First entry in data file is number of records in file
  Open "SCORES.TXT" For Input As #1
  Input #1, recCount
  Let total = 0
  For i = 1 To recCount
    Input #1, score
    Let total = total + score
  Next i
  Close #1
  Picture1.Print "Average ="; total / recCount
End Sub
```

(Assume that the file SCORES.TXT contains the following entries.)

4, 89, 85, 88, 98

9.
```
Sub Command1_Click ()
  Dim i As Integer, j As Integer
  For i = 0 To 2
    For j = 0 To 3
      Picture1.Print i + 3 * j + 1; "  ";
    Next j
    Picture1.Print
  Next i
End Sub
```

10.
```
Sub Command1_Click ()
    Dim i As Integer, j As Integer
    For i = 1 To 5
      For j = 1 To i
        Picture1.Print "*";
      Next j
      Picture1.Print
    Next i
End Sub
```

11.
```
Sub Command1_Click ()
    Dim word As String, num1 As Integer, num2 As Integer
    Let word = InputBox$("Please enter a word")
    Let num1 = Int((20 - Len(word)) / 2)
    Let num2 = 20 - num1 - Len(word)
    Call Asterisks(num1)
    Picture1.Print word;
    Call Asterisks(num2)
End Sub

Sub Asterisks (num As Integer)
  Dim i As Integer
  Rem Display num asterisks
  For i = 1 To num
    Picture1.Print "*";
  Next i
End Sub
```

(Assume that the response is *Hooray*.)

12.
```
Sub Command1_Click ()
    Dim info As String, i As Integer, letter As String
    Rem Display an array of letters
    Let info = "DATA"
    For i = 1 To Len(info)
      Let letter = Mid$(info, i, 1)
      Call DisplayFive(letter)
      Picture1.Print        'Move to next line
    Next i
  End Sub

Sub DisplayFive (letter As String)
  Dim i As Integer
  Rem Display letter five times
  For i = 1 To 5
    Picture1.Print letter;
  Next i
End Sub
```

In Exercises 13 through 16, identify the errors.

13.
```
Sub Command1_Click ()
    Dim j As Single
    For j = 1 To 25.5 Step -1
        Picture1.Print j
    Next j
End Sub
```

14.
```
Sub Command1_Click ()
    Dim i As Integer
    For i = 1 To 3
        Picture1.Print i; 2 ^ i
End Sub
```

15.
```
Sub Command1_Click ()
    Dim i As Integer
    For i = 1 To 99
        If i Mod 2 = 0 Then
            Next i
        Else
            Picture1.Print i
        End If
    Next i
End Sub
```

16.
```
Sub Command1_Click ()
    Dim i As Integer, j As Integer
    For i = 1 To 6
        For j = 1 To 3
            Picture1.Print i / j;
        Next i
    Next j
End Sub
```

In Exercises 17 and 18, rewrite the program using a For...Next loop.

17.
```
Sub Command1_Click ()
    Dim num As Integer
    Let num = 1
    Do While num <= 10
        Picture1.Print num
        Let num = num + 2
    Loop
End Sub
```

18.
```
Sub Command1_Click ()
    Picture1.Print "hello"
    Picture1.Print "hello"
    Picture1.Print "hello"
    Picture1.Print "hello"
End Sub
```

In Exercises 19 through 37, write a program to complete the stated task.

19. Display a row of 10 stars (asterisks).

20. Request a number from 1 to 20 and display a row of that many stars (asterisks).

21. Display a 10-by-10 square of stars.

22. Request a number and call a subprogram to display a square having that number of stars on each side.

23. Find the sum $1 + 1/2 + 1/3 + 1/4 + \ldots + 1/100$.

24. Find the sum of the odd numbers from 1 through 99.

25. You are offered two salary options for ten days of work. Option 1: $100 per day. Option 2: $1 the first day, $2 the second day, $4 the third day, and so on, with the amount doubling each day. Write a program to determine which option pays better.

26. When $1000 is deposited at 5 percent simple interest, the amount grows by $50 each year. When money is invested at 5 percent compound interest, then the amount at the end of each year is 1.05 times the amount at the beginning of that year. Write a program to display the amounts for ten years for a $1000 deposit at 5 percent simple and compound interest. The first few lines displayed in the picture box should appear as in Figure 6.10.

Years	Amount Simple Interest	Amount Compound Interest
1	$1,050.00	$1,050.00
2	$1,100.00	$1,102.50
3	$1,150.00	$1,157.63

Figure 6.10 Growth of $1000 at simple and compound interest.

27. According to researchers at Stanford Medical School (as cited in *Medical Self Care*), the ideal weight for a woman is found by multiplying her height in inches by 3.5 and subtracting 108. The ideal weight for a man is found by multiplying his height in inches by 4 and subtracting 128. Request a lower and upper bound for heights and then produce a table giving the ideal weights for women and men in that height range. For example, when a lower bound of 62 and an upper bound of 65 are specified, Figure 6.11 shows the output displayed in the picture box:

Height	Wt - Women	Wt - Men
62	109	120
63	112.5	124
64	116	128
65	119.5	132

Figure 6.11 Output for Exercise 27.

28. Table 6.3 contains statistics on professional quarterbacks. Read this information from a data file and generate an extended table with two additional columns, Pct Comp (Percent Completions) and Avg Gain (Average Gain per Completed Pass).

Name	Att	Comp	Yards
Young	279	180	2517
Rypien	421	249	3564
Bono	237	141	1617
Aikman	363	237	2754

Table 6.3 1991 Passing statistics (attempts, completions, yards gained).

29. Request a sentence and display the number of sibilants (that is, letters S or Z) in the sentence. The counting should be carried out by a function.

30. Request a number, *n*, from 1 to 30 and one of the letters *S* or *P*. Then calculate the sum or product of the numbers from 1 to *n* depending upon whether *S* or *P* was selected. The calculations should be carried out with functions.

31. Suppose $800 is deposited into a savings account earning 4 percent interest compounded annually, and $100 is added to the account at the end of each year. Calculate the amount of money in the account at the end of 10 years. (Determine a formula for computing the balance at the end of one year based on the balance at the beginning of the year. Then write a program that starts with a balance of $800 and makes 10 passes through a loop containing the formula to produce the final answer.)

32. A TV set is purchased with a loan of $563 to be paid off with 5 monthly payments of $116. The interest rate is 1 percent per month. Display a table giving the balance on the loan at the end of each month.

33. *Radioactive Decay.* Cobalt 60, a radioactive form of cobalt used in cancer therapy, decays or dissipates over a period of time. Each year, 12 percent of the amount present at the beginning of the year will have decayed. If a container of cobalt 60 initially contains 10 grams, determine the amount remaining after 5 years.

34. *Supply and Demand.* This year's level of production and price for most agricultural products greatly affects the level of production and price next year. Suppose the current crop of soybeans in a certain country is 80 million bushels and experience has shown that for each year,

[price this year] = 20 – .1 * [quantity this year]

[quantity next year] = 5 * [price this year] –10

where quantity is measured in units of millions of bushels. Generate a table to show the quantity and price for each of the next 12 years.

35. Request a number greater than 3 and display a hollow rectangle of stars (asterisks) with each outer row and column having that many stars. Use a fixed-width font such as Courier or Terminal so that the space and asterisk will have the same width. (See Figure 6.12(a).)

Figure 6.12 Outputs for Exercises 35 and 36.

36. Request an odd number and display a triangle similar to the one in Figure 6.12(b) with the input number of stars in the top row.

37. Allow any two integers, *m* and *n*, between 2 and 12 to be specified and then generate an *m* by *n* multiplication table. Figure 6.13 shows the output when *m* is 5 and *n* is 7. To obtain a nicely lined up table, use a fixed-space font such as Courier or Terminal together with the following function which right justifies a value in a field 6 spaces wide.

```
Function RightJustify6$ (what As Integer)
  Dim s As String
  Let s = Format$(what, "#")
  RightJustify$ = Format$(s, "@@@@@@")
End Function
```

1	2	3	4	5	6	7
2	4	6	8	10	12	14
3	6	9	12	15	18	21
4	8	12	16	20	24	28
5	10	15	20	25	30	35

Figure 6.13 Output for Exercise 37.

38. Write a program to create the histogram in Figure 6.14. A data file should hold the years and values. The first entry in the data file could be used to hold the title for the histogram.

```
1987 *** 3
1988 *** 3
1989 ***** 5
1990 ********* 9
1991 ****************** 19
```

Market Value of Microsoft Stock (in billions of dollars)

Figure 6.14 Histogram for Exercise 38.

39. A man pays $1 to get into a gambling casino. He loses half of his money there and then has to pay $1 to leave. He goes to a second casino, pays another $1 to get in, loses half his money again and then pays another $1 to leave. Then, he goes to a third casino, pays another $1 to get in, loses half of his money again, and then pays another $1 to get out. After this, he's broke. Write a program to determine the amount of money he began with by testing $5, then $6, and so on.

40. Write a program to estimate how much a young worker will make before retiring at age 65. Request the worker's name, age, and starting salary as input. Assume the worker receives a 5 percent raise each year. For example, if the user enters Helen, 25, and 20000, then the picture box should display the following:

Helen will earn about $2,415,995.00

Exercises 41–44 require the Rnd function presented in Section 3.6.

41. Write a program that selects a word at random from among 20 words in a file.

42. Write a program to simulate the tossing of a coin 100 times and display the numbers of "heads" and "tails" that occur.

43. A company has a sequential file containing the names of people who have qualified for a drawing to win an IBM Personal Computer. Write a program to select a name at random from the file. Assume the file contains at most 1000 names. Test your program on a file consisting of 5 names.

44. A club has 20 members. Write a program to select two different people at random to serve as president and treasurer. (The names of the members should be contained in a file.)

SOLUTIONS TO PRACTICE PROBLEMS 6.3

1. The loop will never be entered since 15 is greater than 1. The intended first line might have been

```
For i = 15 To 1 Step -1
```

or

```
For i = 1 To 15
```

2. If the exact number of times the loop will be executed is known before entering the loop, then a For...Next loop should be used. Otherwise, a Do loop is more appropriate.

6.4 A CASE STUDY: ANALYZE A LOAN

This case study develops a program to analyze a loan. Assume the loan is repaid in equal monthly payments and interest is compounded monthly. The program should request the amount (principal) of the loan, the annual rate of interest, and the number of years over which the loan is to be repaid. The four options to be provided by command buttons are as follows.

1. Calculate the monthly payment. The formula for the monthly payment is

$$\text{payment} = p * r / (1 - (1 + r) \wedge (-n))$$

where p is the principal of the loan, r is the monthly interest rate (annual rate divided by 12) given as a number between 0 (for 0 percent) and 1 (for 100 percent), and n is the number of months over which the loan is to be repaid. Since a payment computed in this manner can be expected to include fractions of a cent, the value should be rounded UP to the next nearest cent. This corrected payment can be achieved using the formula

$$\text{correct payment} = -\text{Int}(-100*\text{payment}) / 100$$

2. Display an amortization schedule, that is, a table showing the balance on the loan at the end of each month for any year over the duration of the loan.

Also show how much of each monthly payment goes toward interest and how much is used to repay the principal. Finally, display the total interest paid over the duration of the loan. The balances for successive months are calculated with the formula

$$\text{balance} = (1 + r) * b - m$$

where r is the monthly interest rate (annual rate / 12, a fraction between 0 and 1), b is the balance for the preceding month (amount of loan left to be paid), and m is the monthly payment.

3. Show the effect of changes in the interest rate. Display a table giving the monthly payment for each interest rate from 1 percent below to 1 percent above the specified annual rate in steps of one-eighth of a percent.

4. Quit

Designing the Analyze a Loan Program

For each of the tasks described in options 1 to 4 above, the program must first look at the text boxes to obtain the particulars of the loan to be analyzed. Thus, the first division of the problem is into the following tasks:

1. Input principal, interest, duration.

2. Calculate monthly payment.

3. Calculate amortization schedule.

4. Display the effects of interest rate changes.

5. Quit.

Task 1 is a basic input operation and task 2 involves applying the formula given in step 1; therefore, these tasks need not be broken down any further. The demanding work of the program is done in tasks 3 and 4, which can be divided into smaller subtasks.

3. *Calculate amortization schedule.* This task involves simulating the loan month by month. First, the monthly payment must be computed. Then, for each month, the new balance must be computed together with a decomposition of the monthly payment into the amount paid for interest and the amount going toward repaying the principal. That is, task 3 is divided into the following subtasks:

3.1 Calculate monthly payment.
3.2 Calculate new balance.
3.3 Calculate amount of monthly payment for interest.
3.4 Calculate amount of monthly payment for principal.

4. *Display the effects of interest rate changes.* A table is needed to show the effects of changes in the interest rate on the size of the monthly payment. First the interest rate is reduced by one percentage point and the new monthly payment is computed. Then the interest rate is increased by regular increments until it reaches one percentage point above the original rate, with new monthly payment amounts computed for each intermediate interest rate. The subtasks for this task are then:

4.1 Reduce interest rate by 1 percent.
4.2 Calculate monthly payment.
4.3 Increase interest rate by 1/8 percent.

The hierarchy chart in Figure 6.15 shows the stepwise refinement of the problem.

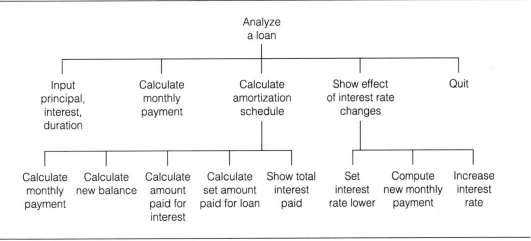

Figure 6.15 Hierarchy chart for the Analyze a Loan Program.

The User Interface

Figure 6.16 shows a possible form design. Figures 6.17 through 6.18 show possible runs of the program for each task available through the command buttons. The width and height of the picture box were adjusted by trial and error to handle the extensive output generated.

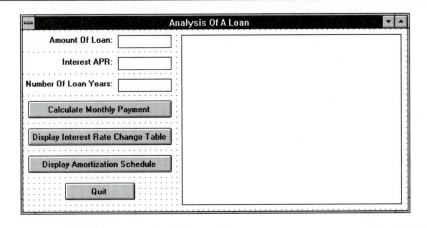

Figure 6.16 Template for loan analysis.

Object	Property	Setting
Form1	Caption	Analysis of a Loan
lblAmt	Alignment	1 – Right Justify
	Caption	Amount of Loan:
txtAmt	Text	(blank)
lblApr	Alignment	1 – Right Justify
	Caption	Interest APR:
txtApr	Text	(blank)
lblYrs	Alignment	1 – Right Justify
	Caption	Number of Loan Years
txtYrs	Text	(blank)
cmdPayment	Caption	Calculate Monthly Payment
cmdRateTable	Caption	Display Interest Rate Change Table
cmdAmort	Caption	Display Amortization Schedule
cmdQuit	Caption	Quit
picDisp		

Table 6.5 Objects and initial properties for the loan analysis program.

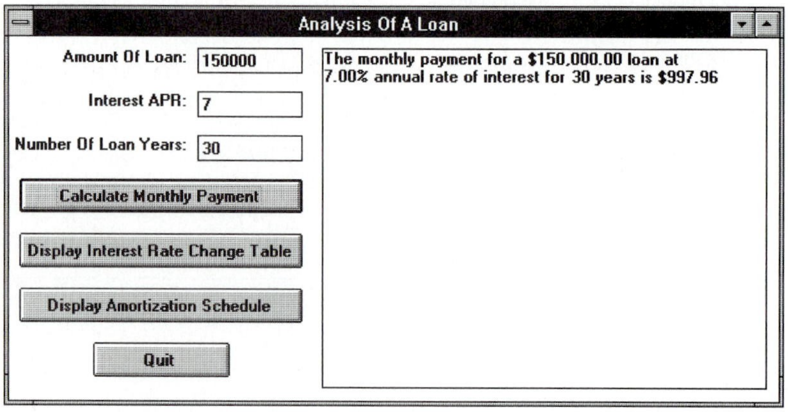

Figure 6.17 Monthly payment on a 30-year loan.

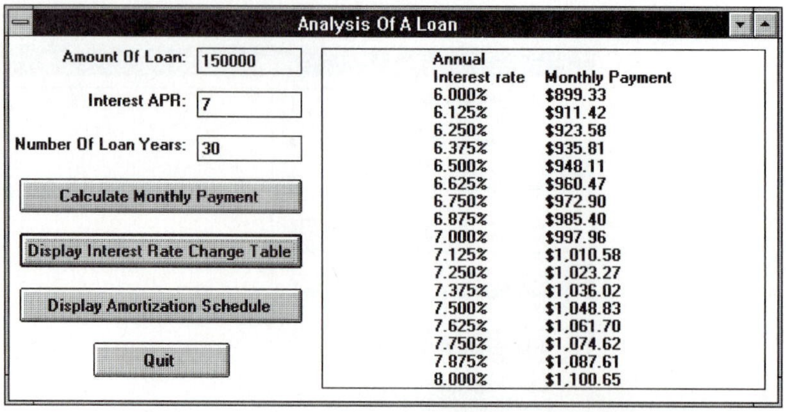

Figure 6.18 Interest rate change table for a 30-year loan.

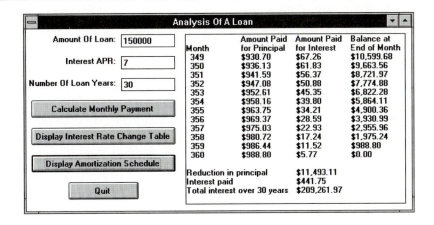

Figure 6.19 Amortization of year 30 of a loan.

Writing the Analyze a Loan Program

Table 6.4 shows each task discussed above and the procedure that carries out the task.

Pseudocode for the Analyze a Loan Program

Calculate Monthly Payment command button:
    INPUT LOAN DATA (Subprogram InputData)
    COMPUTE MONTHLY PAYMENT (Function Payment)
    DISPLAY MONTHLY PAYMENT (Subprogram ShowPayment)

Display Interest Rate Change Table command button:
    INPUT LOAN DATA (Subprogram InputData)
    Decrease annual rate by .01
    DO
        Compute monthly interest rate
        COMPUTE MONTHLY PAYMENT (Function Payment)
        Increase annual rate by .00125
    LOOP UNTIL annual rate > original annual rate + .01

Display Amortization Schedule command button:
    INPUT LOAN DATA (Subproram InputData)
    DISPLAY AMORTIZATION SCHEDULE (Subprogram ShowAmortSched)
    Compute monthly interest rate
    COMPUTE MONTHLY PAYMENT (Function Payment)
    Display amortization table
    Display total interest paid

Task	Procedure
1. Input principal, interest, duration.	InputData
2. Calculate monthly payment.	ShowPayment
3. Calculate amortization schedule.	ShowAmortSched
3.1 Calculate monthly payment.	Payment
3.2 Calculate new balance.	Balance
3.3 Calculate amount paid for loan.	ShowAmortSched
3.4 Calculate amount paid for interest.	ShowAmortSched
4. Show effect of interest rate changes.	ShowInterestChanges
4.1 Reduce interest rate.	ShowInterestChanges
4.2 Compute new monthly payment.	Payment
4.3 Increase interest rate.	ShowInterestChanges

Table 6.4 Tasks and their procedures.

```
Rem Analyze a loan
Rem
Rem ****************************************************
Rem *                                                  *
Rem *           Variable Table                         *
Rem *                                                  *
Rem *                                                  *
Rem * numMonths         Number of months to pay loan   *
Rem * principal         Amount of loan                 *
Rem * yearlyRate        Yearly interest rate           *
Rem *                                                  *
Rem ****************************************************
Rem


Function Balance(mPayment As Single,prin As Single,mRate As Single) As Single
  Dim newBal As Single
  Rem Compute balance at end of month
  Let newBal = (1 + mRate) * prin
  If newBal <= mPayment Then
      Let mPayment = newBal
      Balance = 0
    Else
      Balance = newBal - mPayment
  End If
End Function


Sub cmdAmort_Click ()
  Dim principal As Single, yearlyRate As Single
  Dim numMonths As Integer
  Call InputData(principal, yearlyRate, numMonths)
  Call ShowAmortSched(principal, yearlyRate, numMonths)
End Sub


Sub cmdPayment_Click ()
  Dim principal As Single, yearlyRate As Single
  Dim numMonths As Integer
  Call InputData(principal, yearlyRate, numMonths)
  Call ShowPayment(principal, yearlyRate, numMonths)
End Sub
```

```
Sub cmdQuit_Click ()
  End
End Sub

Sub cmdRateTable_Click ()
  Dim principal As Single, yearlyRate As Single
  Dim numMonths As Integer
  Call InputData(principal, yearlyRate, numMonths)
  Call ShowInterestChanges(principal, yearlyRate, numMonths)
End Sub

Sub InputData (prin As Single, yearlyRate As Single, numMs As Integer)
  Dim percentageRate As Single, numYears As Integer
  Rem Input the loan amount, yearly rate of interest, and duration
  Let prin = Val(txtAmt.Text)
  Let percentageRate = Val(txtApr.Text)
  Let numYears = Val(txtYrs.Text)
  Let yearlyRate = percentageRate / 100
  Let numMs = numYears * 12
End Sub

Function Payment(prin As Single, mRate As Single, numMs As Integer) As Single
  Dim payEst As Single
  If numMs = 0 Then
      Let payEst = prin
    ElseIf mRate = 0 Then
      Let payEst = prin / numMs
    Else
      Let payEst = prin * mRate / (1 - (1 + mRate) ^ (-numMs))
  End If
  Payment = -Int(-payEst * 100) / 100   'round up to nearest cent
End Function

Sub ShowAmortSched (prin As Single, yearlyRate As Single, numMs As Integer)
  Dim msg As String, startMonth As Integer, mRate As Single
  Dim monthlyPayment As Single, totalInterest As Single
  Dim yearInterest As Single, oldBalance As Single
  Dim monthNum As Integer, newBalance As Single
  Dim principalPaid As Single, interestPaid As Single
  Dim reducPrin As Single, loanYears As String
  Rem Display amortization schedule
  Let msg = "Please enter year (1-" + Str$(numMs / 12)
  Let msg = msg + ") for which amorization is to be shown:"
  Let startMonth = 12 * Val(InputBox$(msg)) - 11
  picDisp.Cls
  picDisp.Print "", "Amount Paid ",
  picDisp.Print "Amount Paid", "Balance at"
  picDisp.Print "Month", "for Principal",
  picDisp.Print "for Interest", "End of Month"
  Let mRate = yearlyRate / 12   'monthly rate
  Let monthlyPayment = Payment(prin, mRate, numMs)
  Let totalInterest = 0
  Let yearInterest = 0
  Let oldBalance = prin
  For monthNum = 1 To numMs
```

```
            Let newBalance = Balance(monthlyPayment, oldBalance, mRate)
            Let principalPaid = oldBalance - newBalance
            Let interestPaid = monthlyPayment - principalPaid
            Let totalInterest = totalInterest + interestPaid
            If monthNum >= startMonth And monthNum <= startMonth + 11 Then
                picDisp.Print Tab(2); Format$(monthNum, "#"),
                picDisp.Print Format$(principalPaid, "Currency"),
                picDisp.Print Format$(interestPaid, "Currency"),
                picDisp.Print Format$(newBalance, "Currency")
                Let yearInterest = yearInterest + interestPaid
            End If
            Let oldBalance = newBalance
        Next monthNum
        Let reducPrin = 12 * monthlyPayment - yearInterest
        Let loanYears = Str(numMs / 12)
        picDisp.Print
        picDisp.Print "Reduction in principal",
        picDisp.Print Format$(reducPrin, "Currency")
        picDisp.Print "Interest paid", ,
        picDisp.Print Format$(yearInterest, "Currency")
        picDisp.Print "Total interest over" + loanYears + " years",
        picDisp.Print Format$(totalInterest, "Currency")
    End Sub


    Sub ShowInterestChanges(prin As Single,yearlyRate As Single,numMs As Integer)
        Dim newRate As Single, mRate As Single, py As Single
        Dim pymnt As String
        Rem Display affect of interest changes
        picDisp.Cls
        picDisp.Print , "Annual"
        picDisp.Print , "Interest rate", "Monthly Payment"
        Let newRate = yearlyRate - .01
        Do
          Let mRate = newRate / 12   'monthly rate
          Let py = Payment(prin, mRate, numMs)
          Let pymnt = Format$(py, "currency")
          picDisp.Print , Format$(newRate * 100, "#.000") + "%", pymnt
          Let newRate = newRate + .00125
        Loop Until newRate > yearlyRate + .01
    End Sub


    Sub ShowPayment (prin As Single, yearlyRate As Single, numMs As Integer)
        Dim mRate As Single, prn As String, apr As String
        Dim yrs As String, pay As Single, pymnt As String
        Rem Display monthly payment amount
        Let mRate = yearlyRate / 12   'monthly rate
        Let prn = Format$(prin, "Currency")
        Let apr = Format$(yearlyRate * 100, "#.00")
        Let yrs = Format$(numMs / 12, "#")
        Let pay = Payment(prin, mRate, numMs)
        Let pymnt = Format$(pay, "Currency")
        picDisp.Cls
        picDisp.Print "The monthly payment for a " + prn + " loan at "
        picDisp.Print apr + "% annual rate of interest for ";
        picDisp.Print yrs + " years is " + pymnt
    End Sub
```

Comments:

1. Tasks 3.1 and 3.2 are performed by functions. Using functions to compute these quantities simplifies the computations in ShowAmortSched.

2. Since the payment was rounded up to the nearest cent, it is highly likely that the payment needed in the final month to pay off the loan will be less than the normal payment. For this reason, ShowAmortSched checks if the balance of the loan (including interest due) is less than the regular payment, and if so, makes appropriate adjustments.

3. The standard formula for computing the monthly payment cannot be used if either the interest rate is zero percent or the loan duration is zero months. Although both of these situations do not represent reasonable loan parameters, provisions are made in the function Payment so that the program can handle these esoteric situations.

Chapter 6
Summary

1. A Do loop repeatedly executes a block of statements either as long as or until a certain condition is true. The condition can be checked either at the top of the loop or at the bottom.

2. The EOF function tells us if we have read to the end of a file.

3. As various items of data are processed by a loop, a *counter* can be used to keep track of the number of items and an *accumulator* can be used to sum numerical values.

4. A *flag* is a variable used to indicate whether or not a certain event has occurred.

5. A For...Next loop repeats a block of statements a fixed number of times. The *control variable* assumes an initial value and increments by one after each pass through the loop until it reaches the terminating value. Alternative increment values can be specified with the Step keyword.

Chapter 6
Programming Projects

1. Write a program to display a company's payroll report in a picture box. The program should read each employee's name, hourly rate, and hours worked from a file and produce a report in the form of the sample run shown in Figure 6.20. Employees should be paid time-and-a-half for hours in excess of 40.

```
        Payroll Report for Week ending 3/15/95

        Employee      Hourly Rate   Hours Worked  Gross Pay

        Al Adams      $6.50         38            $247.00
        Bob Brown     $5.70         50            $313.50
        Carol Coe     $7.00         40            $280.00

        Final Total   $840.50
```

Figure 6.20 Sample output from Programming Project 1.

2. Table 6.6 shows the standard prices for items in a department store. Suppose prices will be reduced for the annual George Washington's Birthday Sale. The new price will be computed by reducing the old price by 10 percent, rounding up to the nearest dollar, and subtracting one cent. If the new price is greater than the old price, the old price is used as the sale price. Write a program to display in a picture box the output shown in Figure 6.21.

Item	Original Price
GumShoes	39.00
SnugFoot Sandals	21.00
T-Shirt	7.75
Maine Handbag	33.00
Maple Syrup	6.75
Flaked Vest	24.00
Nightshirt	26.00

Table 6.6 Washington's Birthday sale.

```
                      Sale
Item                  Price
GumShoes              35.99
SnugFoot Sandals      18.99
T-Shirt                6.99
Maine Handbag         29.99
Maple Syrup            6.75
Flaked Vest           21.99
Nightshirt            23.99
```

Figure 6.21 Output of Project 2.

3. The Rule of 72 is used to make a quick estimate of the time required for prices to double due to inflation. If the inflation rate is r percent, then the Rule of 72 estimates that prices will double in $72/r$ years. For instance, at an inflation rate of 6 percent, prices double in about 72/6 or 12 years. Write a program to test the accuracy of this rule. The program should display a table showing, for each value of r from 1 to 20, the rounded value of $72/r$ and the actual number of years required for prices to double at an r percent inflation rate. (Assume prices increase at the end of each year.) Figure 6.22 shows the first few rows of the output.

```
    Interest      Rule
    Rate (%)      of 72      Actual
        1          72          70
        2          36          36
        3          24          24
```

Figure 6.22 Rule of 72.

4. Table 6.7 shows the number of bachelor degrees conferred in 1980 and 1989 in certain fields of study. Tables 6.8 and 6.9 show the percentage change and a histogram of 1989 levels, respectively. Write a program that allows the user to display any one of these tables as an option and quit as a fourth option.

Field of Study	1980	1989
Business and management	185,361	246,659
Computer and info. science	11,154	30,637
Education.	118,169	96,988
Engineering	68,893	85,273
Social sciences	103,519	107,714

Table 6.7 Bachelor degrees conferred in certain fields.

Source: U.S. National Center of Educational Statistics

Field of Study	% Change (1980–1989)
Business and management	33.1
Computer and info. science	174.7
Education	–17.9
Engineering	23.8
Social sciences	4.1

Table 6.8 Percentage change in bachelor degrees conferred.

Business and management	************************	246,659
Computer and info. science	***	30,637
Education	**********	96,988
Engineering	*********	85,273
Social sciences	**********	107,714

Table 6.9 Bachelor degrees conferred in 1989 in certain fields.

5. *Least Squares Approximation.* Table 6.10 shows the 1988 price of a gallon of fuel and the consumption of motor fuel for several countries. Figure 6.23 displays the data as points in the xy-plane. For instance, the point with coordinates (1, 1400) corresponds to the USA. Figure 6.23 also shows the straight line that best fits these data in the least squares sense. (The sum of the squares of the distances of the eleven points from this line is as small as possible.) In general, if $(x_1, y_1), (x_2, y_2), \ldots, (x_n, y_n)$ are n points in the xy-coordinate system, then the least squares approximation to these points is the line $y = mx + b$, where

$$m = \frac{n*(\text{sum of } x_i*y_i) - (\text{sum of } x_i)*(\text{sum of } y_i)}{n*(\text{sum of } x_i*x_i) - (\text{sum of } x_i)^2}$$

and

$$b = ((\text{sum of } y_i) - m*(\text{sum of } x_i))/n$$

Write a program that calculates and displays the equation of the least squares line, then allows the user to enter a fuel price and uses the equation of the line to predict the corresponding consumption of motor fuel. (Place the numeric data from the table in a data file.) A sample run is shown in Figure 6.24.

Country	Price per gallon in US dollars	Tons of oil per 1000 persons	Country	Price per gallon in US dollars	Tons of oil per 1000 persons
USA	$1.00	1400	France	$3.10	580
W.Ger.	$2.20	620	Norway	$3.15	600
England	$2.60	550	Japan	$3.60	410
Austria	$2.75	580	Denmark	$3.70	570
Sweden	$2.80	700	Italy	$3.85	430
Holland	$3.00	490			

Table 6.10 A comparison of 1988 fuel prices and per capita motor fuel use.

Source: World Resources Institute

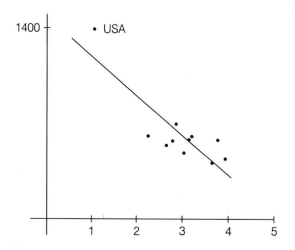

Figure 6.23 Least-squares fit to data from Table 6.10.

Figure 6.24 Sample run of Programming Project 5.

6. Write a program to provide information on the height of a ball thrown straight up into the air. The program should request the initial height, *h* feet, and the initial velocity, *v* feet per second, as input. The four options to be provided by command buttons are as follows:

(a) Determine the maximum height of the ball. **Note:** The ball will reach its maximum height after *v*/32 seconds.

(b) Determine approximately when the ball will hit the ground. **Hint:** Calculate the height after every .1 seconds and observe when the height is no longer a positive number.

(c) Display a table showing the height of the ball every quarter second for 5 seconds, or until it hits the ground.

(d) Quit.

The formula for the height of the ball after *t* seconds, $h + v*t - 16*t*t$, should be specified in a user-defined function. (Test the program with *v* = 148 and *h* = 0. This velocity is approximately the top speed clocked for a ball thrown by a professional baseball pitcher.)

7. *Depreciation to a Salvage Value of 0.* For tax purposes an item may be depreciated over a period of several years, *n*. With the *straight-line* method of depreciation, each year the item depreciates by 1/*n*th of its original value. With the *double-declining* balance method of depreciation, each year the item depreciates by 2/*n*ths of its value at the *beginning* of that year. (In the last year it is depreciated by its value at the beginning of the year.) Write a program that

(a) Requests a description of the item, the year of purchase, the cost of the item, the number of years to be depreciated (estimated life), and the method of depreciation. The method of depreciation should be chosen by clicking one of two command buttons.

(b) Displays a depreciation schedule for the item similar to the schedule shown in Figure 6.25.

```
Description: Computer
Year of purchase: 1994
Cost: $2000.00
Estimated life: 5
Method of depreciation: double-declining balance
```

Year	Value at Beg of Yr	Amount Deprec During Year	Total Depreciation to End of Year
1994	2,000.00	800.00	800.00
1995	1,200.00	480.00	1,280.00
1996	720.00	288.00	1,568.00
1997	432.00	172.80	1,740.80
1998	259.20	259.20	2,000.00

Figure 6.25 Depreciation schedule.

8. *The Twelve Days of Christmas* Each year, Provident National Bank of Phila-
delphia publishes a Christmas price list. See Table 6.11. Write a program
that requests an integer from 1 through 12 and then lists the gifts for that
day along with that day's cost. On the *n*th day, the *n* gifts are 1 partridge in
a pear tree, 2 turtle doves, . . . *n* of the *n*th item. The program also should
give the total cost of all twelve days. As an example, Figure 6.26 shows the
output in the picture box when the user enters 3.

Item	Cost	Item	Cost
partridge in a pear tree	27.50	swan-a-swimming	1000.00
turtle dove	25.00	maid-a-milking	4.25
French hen	5.00	lady dancing	289.50
calling bird	70.00	lord-a-leaping	292.50
gold ring	60.00	piper piping	95.75
geese-a-laying	25.00	drummer drumming	95.00

Table 6.11 Christmas price index.

```
The gifts for day 3 are
 1 partridge in a pear tree
 2 turtle doves
 3 French hens
Cost:    $92.50

Total cost for the twelve days: $71,613.50
```

Figure 6.26 Sample output for Programming Project 8.

7

Arrays

7.1 CREATING AND ACCESSING ARRAYS

A **variable** (or simple variable) is a name to which the computer can assign a single value. An **array variable** is a collection of simple variables of the same type to which the computer can efficiently assign a list of values.

Consider the following situation. Suppose you want to evaluate the exam grades for 30 students. Not only do you want to compute the average score, but you also want to display the names of the students whose scores are above average. You might place the 30 pairs of student names and scores in a data file and run the program outlined below.

```
Sub Command1_Click ()
    Dim student1 As String, score1 As Single
    Dim student2 As String, score2 As Single
    Dim student3 As String, score3 As Single
      .
      .
      .
    Dim student30 As String, score30 As Single
    Rem Analyze exam grades
    Open "SCORES.TXT" For Input As #1
    Input #1, student1, score1
    Input #1, student2, score2
    Input #1, student3, score3
      .
      .
      .
    Input #1, student30, score30
    Rem Compute the average grade
      .
      .
      .
    Rem Display names of above average students
      .
      .
      .
End Sub
```

This program is going to be uncomfortably long. What's most frustrating is that the thirty Dim statements and thirty Input# statements are very similar and look as if they should be condensed into a short loop. A shorthand notation for the many related variables would be welcome. It would be nice if we could just write

```
For i = 1 To 30
    Input #1, studenti, scorei
Next i
```

Of course, this will not work. The computer will treat *studenti* and *scorei* as two variables and keep reassigning new values to them. At the end of the loop they will have the values of the thirtieth student.

Visual Basic provides a data structure called an **array** that lets us do what we tried to accomplish in the loop. The variable names will be similar to those in the Input statement. They will be

```
student(1), student(2), student(3), ..., student(30)
```

and

```
score(1), score(2), score(3), ..., score(30).
```

We refer to these collections of variables as the array variables *student( )* and *score( )*. The numbers inside the parentheses of the individual variables are called **subscripts**, and each individual variable is called a **subscripted variable** or **element**. For instance, *student*(3) is the third subscripted variable of the array *student( )*, and *score*(20) is the 20th subscripted variable of the array *score( )*. The elements of an array are assigned successive memory locations. Figure 7.1 shows the memory locations for the array *score( )*.

	score(1)	score(2)	score(3)	. . .	score(30)
score( )				. . .	

Figure 7.1 The array *score( )*.

Array variables have the same kinds of names as simple variables. If *arrayName* is the name of an array variable and *n* is a whole number, then the statement

```
Dim arrayName(1 To n) As varType
```

placed in the (declarations) section of (general) reserves space in memory to hold the values of the subscripted variables *arrayName*(1), *arrayName*(2), *arrayName*(3), . . . , *arrayName*(*n*). (Recall from Chapter 3 that the (declarations) section of (general) is accessed from any code window by pressing F2 and then double-clicking on (declarations) in the procedures list.) The spread of the subscripts specified by the Dim statement is called the **range** of the array, and the Dim statement is said to **dimension** the array. In particular, the statements

```
Dim student(1 To 30) As String
Dim score(1 To 30) As Integer
```

dimension the arrays needed for the program above. An array holds either all string values or all numeric values, depending on whether *varType* is String or one of the numeric type names.

As with any variable created in the (declarations) section of (general), these array variables are form-level as discussed in Chapter 4. Recall that form-level variables can be accessed from any procedure in the program and continue to exist and retain their values as long as the program is running.

Values can be assigned to subscripted variables with Let statements and displayed with Print methods. The statement

```
Dim score(1 To 30) As Integer
```

sets aside a portion of memory for the numeric array *score( )* and places the default value 0 in each element.

	score(1)	score(2)	score(3)	. . .	score(30)
score( )	0	0	0	. . .	0

The statements

```
Let score(1) = 87
Let score(3) = 92
```

assign values to the first and third elements.

	score(1)	score(2)	score(3)	. . .	score(30)
score( )	87	0	92	. . .	0

The statements

```
For i = 1 To 4
  Picture1.Print score(i);
Next i
```

then produce the output   87   0   92   0   in Picture1.

EXAMPLE 1   The following program creates a string array consisting of the names of the first five World Series winners. Figure 7.2 shows the array created by the program.

```
Rem Create array for five strings
Dim teamName(1 To 5) As String    'in (declarations) section of (general)

Sub Command1_Click ()
  Dim n As Integer
  Rem Fill array with World Series Winners
  Let teamName(1) = "Red Sox"
  Let teamName(2) = "Giants"
  Let teamName(3) = "White Sox"
  Let teamName(4) = "Cubs"
  Let teamName(5) = "Cubs"
  Rem Access array of five strings
  Let n = Val(Text1.Text)
  Picture1.Cls
  Picture1.Print "The "; teamName(n); " won World Series number"; n
End Sub
```

[Run, type 2 into the text box, and click the command button.]

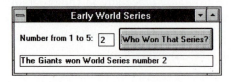

	teamName(1)	teamName(2)	teamName(3)	teamName(4)	teamName(5)
teamName( )	Red Sox	Giants	White Sox	Cubs	Cubs

Figure 7.2 The array *teamName( )* of Example 1.

In Example 1, the array *teamName* was assigned values within the Command1_Click event procedure. Every time the command button is clicked, the values are reassigned to the array. This manner of assigning values to an array can be very inefficient, especially in programs with large arrays where the task of the program (in Example 1, looking up a fact) may be repeated numerous times for different user input. When, as in Example 1, the data to be placed in an array is known at the time the program first begins to run, a more efficient location for the statements that fill the array is in Visual Basic's Form_Load event procedure. The Form_Load event procedure is executed by Visual Basic only once, and this execution is guaranteed to occur before the execution of any other event or general procedure in the program. Example 2 uses the Form_Load procedure to improve on Example 1.

EXAMPLE 2   Modify Example 1 to request the name of a baseball team as input and search the array to determine whether or not the team name appears in the array. Load the array values only once.

```
Rem Create array for five strings
Dim teamName(5) As String  'in (declarations) section of (general)

Sub Command1_Click ()
  Dim team As String, foundFlag As Integer, n As Integer
  Rem Search for an entry in a list of strings
  Let team = Text1.Text
  Let foundFlag = 0
  Let n = 0
  Do
    Let n = n + 1
    If UCase$(teamName(n)) = UCase$(team) Then
        Let foundFlag = 1
    End If
  Loop Until (foundFlag = 1) Or (n = 5)
  Picture1.Cls
  If foundFlag = 0 Then
      Picture1.Print "The "; team; " did not win any";
      Picture1.Print " of the first five World Series."
    Else
      Picture1.Print "The "; teamName(n); " won World Series number"; n
  End If
End Sub

Sub Form_Load ()
  Rem Fill array with World Series winners
  Let teamName(1) = "Red Sox"
  Let teamName(2) = "Giants"
  Let teamName(3) = "White Sox"
  Let teamName(4) = "Cubs"
  Let teamName(5) = "Cubs"
End Sub
```

[Run, type White Sox into the text box, and click the command button.]

```
┌─────────────────────────────────────────────────────────┐
│  ▄  Early World Series Winners  ▼ ▲                      │
│                                                           │
│  Name of baseball team: White Sox      │ Did they win? │ │
│                                                           │
│  The White Sox won World Series number 3                 │
└─────────────────────────────────────────────────────────┘
```

We could have written the program in Example 2 with a For...Next loop beginning For *n* = 1 To 5. However, such a loop would unnecessarily search the entire list when the sought-after item is found early. The wasted time could be significant for a large array.

In some applications, arrays are only needed temporarily to help a procedure complete a task. Visual Basic also allows us to create array variables that are local to a specific procedure and that exist temporarily while the procedure is executing. If the statement

```
ReDim arrayName(1 To n) As varType
```

is placed inside an event procedure or general procedure, then space for *n* subscripted variables is set aside in memory each time the procedure is invoked and released when the procedure is exited.

In Example 1, values were assigned to the elements of the array with Let statements. However, data for large arrays are more often stored in a data file and read with Input# statements. Example 3 uses this technique. Also, since the task of the program is likely to be performed only once during a run of the program, a local array is utilized.

EXAMPLE 3   Table 7.1 gives names and test scores from a mathematics contest given in 1953. Write a program to display the names of the students scoring above the average for these eight students.

Richard Dolen	135	Paul H. Monsky	150
Geraldine Ferraro	114	Max A. Plager	114
James B. Fraser	92	Robert A. Schade	91
John H. Maltby	91	Barbara M. White	124

Table 7.1 The top scores on the Fourth Annual Mathematics Contest Sponsored by the Metropolitan NY section of the MAA.

Source: The Mathematics Teacher, February, 1953

SOLUTION   The following program creates a string array to hold the names of the contestants and a numeric array to hold the scores. The first element of each array holds data for the first contestant, the second element of each array holds data for the second contestant, and so on. See Figure 7.3. Note that the two arrays can be dimensioned in a single ReDim statement by placing a comma between the array declarations.

```
Sub Command1_Click ()
  Dim Total As Integer, student As Integer, average As Single
  Rem Create arrays for names and scores
  ReDim nom(1 To 8) As String, score(1 To 8) As Integer
  Rem Assume the data has been placed in the file "SCORES.TXT"
  Rem (The first line of the file is "Richard Dolen", 135)
  Open "SCORES.TXT" For Input As #1
  For student = 1 To 8
    Input #1, nom(student), score(student)
  Next student
  Close #1
  Rem Analyze exam scores
  Let Total = 0
  For student = 1 To 8
    Let Total = Total + score(student)
  Next student
  Let average = Total / 8
  Rem Display all names with above average grades
  Picture1.Cls
  For student = 1 To 8
    If score(student) > average Then
        Picture1.Print nom(student)
    End If
  Next student
End Sub
```

[Run and click the command button.]

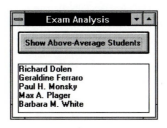

---

	nom(1)	nom(2)	. . .	nom(8)
nom( )	Richard Dolen	Geraldine Ferraro	. . .	Barbara M. White

	score(1)	score(2)	. . .	score(8)
score( )	135	114	. . .	124

Figure 7.3 Arrays created by Example 3.

In Example 3, the number of students to be processed had to be known at the time the program was written. In actual practice, the amount of data that a program will be processing is not known in advance. Programs should be flexible and incorporate a method for handling varying amounts of data. Visual Basic makes this possible by allowing ReDim statements to use variables or expressions when indicating the subscript range.

EXAMPLE 4   The following program reworks Example 3 for the case where the amount of data is not known in advance.

```
Sub Command1_Click ()
  Dim numStudents As Integer, nTemp As String, sTemp As Integer
  Dim student As Integer, Total As Integer, average As Single
  Rem Determine amount of data to be processed
  Let numStudents = 0
  Open "SCORES.TXT" For Input As #1
  Do While Not EOF(1)
    Input #1, nTemp, sTemp
    Let numStudents = numStudents + 1
  Loop
  Close #1
  Rem Create arrays for names and scores
  ReDim nom(1 To numStudents) As String, score(1 To numStudents) As Integer
  Open "SCORES.TXT" For Input As #1
  For student = 1 To numStudents
    Input #1, nom(student), score(student)
  Next student
  Close #1
  Rem Analyze exam scores
  Let Total = 0
  For student = 1 To numStudents
    Let Total = Total + score(student)
  Next student
  Let average = Total / numStudents
  Rem Display all names with above average grades
  Picture1.Cls
  For student = 1 To numStudents
    If score(student) > average Then
        Picture1.Print nom(student)
    End If
  Next student
End Sub
```

An alternative approach to program flexibility that does not require reading the data file twice is to require that the data file begin with a line that holds the number of records to be processed. If SCORES.TXT is modified by adding a new first line that gives the number of students, then the fourth through eighteenth lines of Example 4 can be replaced with

```
    Rem Create arrays for names and scores
    Open "SCORES.TXT" For Input As #1
    Input #1, numStudents
    ReDim nom(1 To numStudents) As String, score(1 To numStudents) As Integer
```

```
For student = 1 To numStudents
  Input #1, nom(student), score(student)
Next student
Close #1
```

In Example 4, the ReDim statement allowed us to create arrays whose size was not known before the program was run. On the other hand, the arrays that were created were local to the event procedure Command1_Click. Many applications require form-level arrays whose size is not known in advance. Unfortunately, Dim statements in the (declaration) section of (general) cannot use variables or expressions to specify the subscript range. The solution offered by Visual Basic is to allow the (declarations) section of (general) to contain Dim statements of the form

```
Dim arrayName() As varType
```

where no range for the subscripts of the array is specified. An array created in this manner will be form-level, but cannot be used until a ReDim statement is executed in a procedure to establish the range of subscripts. It is important to note that both the Dim statement and the ReDim statement must include identical "As *varType*" clauses.

EXAMPLE 5 Suppose the data file WINNERS.TXT contains the names of the teams who have won each of the World Series, with the first line of the file giving the number of World Series that have been played. Write a program that displays the numbers, if any, of the World Series that were won by the team specified by the user.

```
Rem Create form-level array
Dim teamName() As String
Dim seriesCount As Integer

Sub Command1_Click ()
  Dim teamToFind As String, numWon As Integer, series As Integer
  Rem Search for World Series won by user's team
  Let teamToFind = Text1.Text
  Let numWon = 0
  Picture1.Cls
  For series = 1 To seriesCount
    If UCase$(teamName(series)) = UCase$(teamToFind) Then
        Let numWon = numWon + 1
        If numWon = 1 Then
            Picture1.Print "The "; teamName(series);
            Picture1.Print " won the following World Series: ";
          Else
            Rem Separate from previous
            Picture1.Print ",";  'comma here; space before number from Str$
            If (numWon = 5) Or (numWon = 16) Then
                Rem Start a new line at 5th and 16th win
                Picture1.Print
            End If
        End If
    End If
```

```
          Rem First world series played in 1903
            Picture1.Print Str$(series + 1902);  'leading space helps separate
        End If
      Next series
      If numWon = 0 Then
          Picture1.Print "The "; teamToFind; " did not win any World Series."
      End If
  End Sub

  Sub Form_Load ()
    Dim series As Integer
    Rem Fill array with World Series winners
    Open "WINNERS.TXT" For Input As #1
    Input #1, seriesCount
    ReDim teamName(1 To seriesCount) As String
    For series = 1 To seriesCount
      Input #1, teamName(series)
    Next series
    Close #1
  End Sub
```

[Run, type Yankees into the text box, and click the command button.]

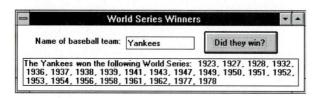

The range of an array need not just begin with 1. A statement of the form

```
Dim arrayName(m To n) As varType
```

where *m* is less than or equal to *n*, creates an array with elements *arrayName*(*m*), *arrayName*(*m* + 1), *arrayName*(*m* + 2), . . . , *arrayName*(*n*).

EXAMPLE 6   The following program segment stores the names of the 40th, 41st, and 42nd presidents in the array pictured in Figure 7.4.

```
Rem Place names of last three presidents in an array
Dim pres(40 To 42) As String

Sub Form_Load ()
  Let pres(40) = "Ronald Reagan"
  Let pres(41) = "George Bush"
  Let pres(42) = "Bill Clinton"
End Sub
```

	pres(40)	pres(41)	pres(42)
pres( )	Ronald Reagan	George Bush	Bill Clinton

Figure 7.4 The array created by Example 6.

An array can be used as either a checklist or frequency table, as in the next example. The function Asc associates each character with its position in the ANSI table.

EXAMPLE 7   The following program requests a sentence as input and records the number of occurrences of each letter of the alphabet. The array *count*( ) has range Asc("A") To Asc("Z"); that is, 65 To 90. The number of occurrences of each letter is stored in the element whose subscript is the ANSI value of the uppercase letter.

```
Sub Command1_Click ()
  Dim index As Integer, letterNum As Integer, sentence As String
  Dim letter As String, column As Integer
  Rem Count occurrences of different letters in a sentence
  ReDim charCount(Asc("A") To Asc("Z")) As Integer
  For index = Asc("A") To Asc("Z")
    Let charCount(index) = 0
  Next index
  Rem Consider and tally each letter of sentence
  Let sentence = UCase$(Text1.Text)
  For letterNum = 1 To Len(sentence)
    Let letter = Mid$(sentence, letterNum, 1)
    If (letter >= "A") And (letter <= "Z") Then
        Let index = Asc(letter)
        Let charCount(index) = charCount(index) + 1
    End If
  Next letterNum
  Rem List the tally for each letter of alphabet
  Let Picture1.Font = "Courier"
  Picture1.Cls
  Let column = 1    'Next column at which to display letter & count
  For letterNum = Asc("A") To Asc("Z")
    Let letter = Chr$(letterNum)
    Picture1.Print Tab(column); letter;
    Picture1.Print Tab(column + 1); charCount(letterNum);
    Let column = column + 6
    If column > 42 Then    'only room for 7 sets of data in a line
        Picture1.Print
        Let column = 1
    End If
  Next letterNum
End Sub
```

[Run, type in the given sentence, and click the command button.]

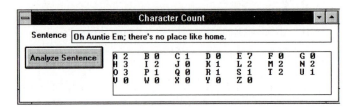

Comments:

1. Arrays must be dimensioned in a Dim or ReDim statement before they are used. If a statement such as Let $a(6) = 3$ appears without a previous Dim or ReDim of the array $a(\ )$, then the error message "Array not defined" will be displayed when an attempt is made to run the program. **Note:** Good programming practice dictates that all ReDim statements appear near the beginning of procedures. A person maintaining the program can then conveniently determine the existing arrays and their ranges.

2. Subscripts in ReDim statements can be numeric expressions. Subscripts whose values are not whole numbers are rounded to the nearest whole number. Subscripts outside the range of the array produce an error message as shown below when t has the value 6 in the For...Next loop.

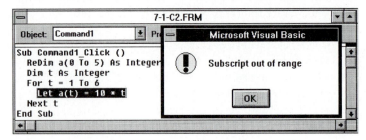

3. The two arrays in Example 3 are referred to as **parallel arrays** because subscripted variables having the same subscript are related.

4. The integers m and n in the statement Dim *arrayName*(m To n) As *varType* can be positive, negative, or zero. The only restriction is that m cannot be greater than n. The same holds true for ReDim statements.

5. Until a value is assigned to an element of an array, the element has its default value. Numeric variables have a default value of 0, and string variables have the default value "", the empty string.

6. The statement Dim *arrayName*(0 To n) As *varType* can be replaced by the statement Dim *arrayName*(n) As *varType*. The same holds for the ReDim statement.

PRACTICE PROBLEMS 7.1

1. When should arrays be used to hold data?

2. (a) Give an appropriate Dim statement to declare a string array to hold the names of the Time Magazine "Man of the Year" awards for the years 1980 through 1989.

(b) Write a statement to assign to the array element for 1982 the name of that year's winner, "The Computer".

EXERCISES 7.1

In Exercises 1 through 6, determine the output displayed in the picture box when the command button is clicked. All Dim statements for arrays are in the (declarations) section of (general).

1.
```
Dim a(1 To 20) As Integer

Sub Command1_Click ()
  Let a(5) = 1
  Let a(10) = 2
  Let a(15) = 7
  Picture1.Print a(5) + a(10);
  Picture1.Print a(5 + 10);
  Picture1.Print a(20)
End Sub
```

2.
```
Dim sq(1 To 5) As Integer

Sub Command1_Click ()
  Dim i As Integer
  For i = 1 To 5
    Let sq(i) = i * i
  Next i
  Picture1.Print sq(3)
  Let t = 3
  Picture1.Print sq(5 - t)
End Sub
```

3.
```
Dim fh(1 To 4) As String

Sub Command1_Click ()
  Dim i As Integer, n As Integer
  Open "HORSEMEN.TXT" For Input As #1
  For i = 1 To 4
    Input #1, fh(i)
  Next i
  Picture1.Print fh(4)
  Let n = 1
  Picture1.Print fh(2 * n + 1)
  Close #1
End Sub
```

(Assume that the file HORSEMEN.TXT contains the following entries.)

"Miller", "Layden", "Crowley", "Stuhldreher"

4.
```
Dim s(1 To 4) As Integer

Sub Command1_Click ()
  Dim t As Integer, k As Integer
  Open "DATA.TXT" For Input As #1
  Let t = 0
  For k = 1 To 4
    Input #1, s(k)
    Let t = t + s(k)
  Next k
  Picture1.Print t
  Close #1
End Sub
```

(Assume that the file DATA.TXT contains the following entries.)

3, 5, 2, 1

5. `Dim p(1 To 6) As Integer`

```
Sub Command1_Click ()
  Dim k As Integer
  Open "DATA.TXT" For Input As #1
  For k = 1 To 6
    Input #1, p(k)
  Next k
  For k = 6 To 1 Step -1
    Picture1.Print p(k);
  Next k
End Sub
```

(Assume that the file DATA.TXT contains the following entries.)

4, 3, 11, 9, 2, 6

6. `Dim a(1 To 4) As Integer`
`Dim b(1 To 4) As Integer`
`Dim c(1 To 4) As Integer`

```
Sub Command1_Click ()
  Dim i As Integer
  Open "DATA.TXT" For Input As #1
  For i = 1 To 4
    Input #1, a(i), b(i)
  Next i
  For i = 1 To 4
    Let c(i) = a(i) * b(i)
    Picture1.Print c(i);
  Next i
End Sub
```

(Assume that the file DATA.TXT contains the following entries.)

2, 5, 3, 4, 1, 3, 7, 2

In Exercises 7 through 12, identify the errors.

7. `Dim companies(1 To 100) As String`

```
Sub Form_Load ()
  Dim recCount As Integer, i As Integer
  Open "COMPLIST.TXT" For Input As #1
  Input #1, recCount
  ReDim companies(1 To RecCount) As String
  For i = 1 To recCount
    Input #1, companies(i)
  Next i
  Close #1
End Sub
```

8. `Dim p(1 To 100) As Single`

```
Sub Command1_Click ()
  Dim i As Integer
  For i = 1 To 200
    Let p(i) = i / 2
  Next i
End Sub
```

9. `Dim a(1 To 10) As Integer`

```
Sub Command1_Click ()
  Dim i As Integer, k As Integer
  Open "DATA.TXT" For Input As #1
  For i = 1 To 9
    Input #1, a(i)
  Next i
  Close #1
  For k = 1 To 9
    Let a(k) = a(5 - k)
  Next k
End Sub
```

(Assume that the file DATA.TXT contains the following entries.)

1, 2, 3, 4, 5, 6, 7, 8, 9

10. `Let maxRecords = 100`
`Dim patients(1 To maxRecords) As String`

```
Sub Command1_Click ()
  Dim recCount As Integer, i As Integer
  Open "PATIENTS.TXT" For Input As #1
  Let recCount = 0
  Do While (Not EOF(1)) And (recCount < maxRecords)
    Let recCount = recCount + 1
    Input #1, patients(recCount)
  Loop
  Close #1
  Picture1.Cls
  Picture1.Print recCount; "records were read"
End Sub
```

11. `Dim b(2 To 8 Step 2) As Integer`

```
Sub Command1_Click ()
  Dim t As Integer
  Open "DATA.TXT" For Input As #1
  For t = 2 To 8 STEP 2
    Input #1, b(t)
  Next t
  Close #1
End Sub
```

(Assume that the file DATA.TXT contains the following entries.)

1, 4, 8, 19

12.
```
Dim names()

Sub Form_Load
  Dim i As Integer, recCount As Integer
  Open "DATA.TXT" For Input As #1
  Input #1, recCount
  ReDim names(1 to recCount) As String
  For i = 1 to recCount
    Input #1, names(i)
  Next i
  Close #1
End Sub
```

(Assume that the file DATA.TXT contains the following entries.)

3, "Tom", "Dick", "Harry"

13. Assuming the array *river*( ) is as shown below, fill in the empty rectangles to show the progressing status of *river*( ) after the execution of each program segment.

	river(1)	river(2)	river(3)	river(4)	river(5)
river( )	Nile	Ohio	Amazon	Volga	Thames

```
Let temp = river(1)
Let river(1) = river(5)
Let river(5) = temp
```

	river(1)	river(2)	river(3)	river(4)	river(5)
river( )					

```
Let temp = river(1)
For i = 1 To 4
  Let river(i) = river(i + 1)
Next i
Let river(5) = temp
```

	river(1)	river(2)	river(3)	river(4)	river(5)
river( )					

14. Assuming the array *cat*( ) is as shown below, fill in the empty rectangles to show the final status of *cat*( ) after executing the nested loops.

	cat(1)	cat(2)	cat(3)	cat(4)
cat( )	Morris	Garfield	Socks	Felix

```
For i = 1 To 3
  For j = 1 To 4 - i
    If cat(j) > cat(j + 1) Then
        Let temp = cat(j)
        Let cat(j) = cat(j + 1)
        Let cat(j + 1) = temp
    End If
  Next j
Next I
```

	cat(1)	cat(2)	cat(3)	cat(4)
cat( )				

15. The subscripted variables of the array $a(\ )$ have the following values: $a(1) = 6$, $a(2) = 3$, $a(3) = 1$, $a(4) = 2$, $a(5) = 5$, $a(6) = 8$, $a(7) = 7$. Suppose $i = 2$, $j = 4$, and $k = 5$. What values are assigned to n when the following Let statements are executed?

   (a) `Let n = a(k) - a(i)`   (c) `Let n = a(k) * a(i + 2)`
   (b) `Let n = a(k - i) + a(k - j)`   (d) `Let n = a(j - i) * a(i)`

16. The array *monthName( )* holds the following three-character strings.

    `monthName(1)="Jan", monthName(2)="Feb", ..., monthName(12)="Dec"`

   (a) What is displayed by the following statement?

       `Picture1.Print monthName(4), monthName(9)`

   (b) What value is assigned to *winter* by the following statement?

       `Let winter = monthName(12) + "," + monthName(1) + "," + monthName(2)`

17. Modify the program in Example 3 to display each student's name and the number of points his or her score differs from the average.

18. Modify the program in Example 3 to display only the name(s) of the student(s) with the highest score.

In Exercises 19 through 30, write a line of code or program segment to complete the stated task.

19. Inside a procedure, dimension the string array *bestPicture( )* to have subscripts ranging from 1975 to 1995.

20. In the (declarations) section of (general), dimension the string array *info( )* to have subscripts ranging from 10 to 100.

21. Dimension the string array *marx( )* with subscripts ranging from 1 to 4 so that the array is visible to all parts of the program. Assign the four values Chico, Harpo, Groucho, and Zeppo to the array as soon as the program is run.

22. Dimension the string array *stooges( )* with subscripts ranging from 1 to 3 so that the array is visible only to the event procedure Command1_Click. Assign the three values Moe, Larry, Curly to the array as soon as a command button is clicked.

23. The arrays $a(\ )$ and $b(\ )$ have been dimensioned to have range 1 to 4, and values have been assigned to $a(1)$ through $a(4)$. Reverse the order of these values and store them in $b(\ )$.

24. Given two arrays, $p(\ )$ and $q(\ )$, each with range 1 to 20, compute the sum of the products of the corresponding array elements; that is

```
p(1)*q(1) + p(2)*q(2) + ... + p(20)*q(20)
```

25. Display the values of the array $a(\ )$ of range 1 to 30 in five columns as shown below.

```
a(1)     a(2)     a(3)     a(4)     a(5)
  .        .        .        .        .
  .        .        .        .        .
  .        .        .        .        .
a(26)    a(27)    a(28)    a(29)    a(30)
```

26. A list of 20 integers, all between 1 and 10, is contained in a data file. Determine how many times each integer appears and have the program display the frequency of each integer.

27. Compare two arrays $a(\ )$ and $b(\ )$ of range 1 to 10 to see if they hold identical values, that is, if $a(i) = b(i)$ for all i.

28. Calculate the sum of the entries with odd subscripts in an array $a(\ )$ of range 1 to 9.

29. Twelve exam grades are stored in the array $grades(\ )$. Curve the grades by adding 7 points to each grade.

30. Read 10 numbers contained in a data file into an array and then display three columns as follows: Column 1 should contain the original 10 numbers, column 2 should contain these numbers in reverse order, and column 3 should contain the averages of the corresponding numbers in columns 1 and 2.

31. Thirty scores, each lying between 0 and 49, are given in a data file. These scores are used to create an array $frequency(\ )$ as follows:

frequency(1) = # of scores < 10
frequency(2) = # of scores such that 10 <= score < 20
frequency(3) = # of scores such that 20 <= score < 30
frequency(4) = # of scores such that 30 <= score < 40
frequency(5) = # of scores such that 40 <= score < 50.

Write a program to display the results in tabular form as follows:

Interval	Frequency
0 to 10	frequency(1)
10 to 20	frequency(2)
20 to 30	frequency(3)
30 to 40	frequency(4)
40 to 50	frequency(5)

32. Given the following flight schedule,

Flight #	Origin	Destination	Departure Time
117	Tucson	Dallas	8:45 a.m.
239	LA	Boston	10:15 a.m.
298	Albany	Reno	1:35 p.m.
326	Houston	New York	2:40 p.m.
445	New York	Tampa	4:20 p.m.

write a program to load this information into four arrays of range 1 to 5, *flightNum*( ), *orig*( ), *dest*( ), and *deptTime*( ), and ask the user to request a flight number. Have the computer find the flight number and display the information corresponding to that flight. Account for the case where the user requests a nonexistent flight.

33. Table 7.2 contains the names and number of stores of the top 10 pizza chains in 1993. Write a program to place these data into a pair of parallel arrays, compute the total number of stores for these 10 chains, and display a table giving the name and percentage of total stores for each of the companies.

Name	Stores	Name	Stores
1. Pizza Hut	7264	6. S'Barro	490
2. Domino's	5120	7. Godfather's	514
3. Little Caesar's	3650	8. Pizza Inn	375
4. Round Table	571	9. Papa Gino's	218
5. Showbiz/Chuck E. Cheese	264	10. Pizzeria Uno	96

Table 7.2 Top 10 pizza chains for 1993 (and numbers of stores).

Source: Pizza Today magazine

34. A retail store has five bins, numbered 1 to 5, each containing a different commodity. At the beginning of a particular day, each bin contains 45 items. Table 7.3 below shows the cost per item for each of the bins and the quantity sold during that day.

Bin	Cost per Item	Quantity Sold
1	3.00	10
2	12.25	30
3	37.45	9
4	7.49	42
5	24.95	17

Table 7.3 Costs of items and quantities sold for Exercise 34.

Write a program to

(a) place the cost per item and the quantity sold from each bin into parallel arrays.

(b) display a table giving the inventory at the end of the day and the amount of revenue obtained from each bin.

(c) compute the total revenue for the day.

(d) list the number of each bin that contains fewer than 20 items at the end of the day.

35. Write a program that asks the user for a month by number, and then displays the name of that month. For instance, if the user inputs 2, the program should display February. *Hint:* Create an array of 12 strings, one for each month of the year.

Exercises 36 and 37 require the Rnd function presented in Section 3.6.

36. Write a program to select the winning lottery numbers. The selection should consist of six randomly chosen whole numbers from 1 through 40 (with no repeats).

37. Write a program to simulate 1000 rolls of a die and report the number of times each integer occurs.

SOLUTIONS TO PRACTICE PROBLEMS 7.1

1. Arrays should be used when

(a) several pieces of data of the same type will be entered by the user

(b) computations must be made on the items in a data file *after* all of the items have been read

(c) lists of corresponding data are being analyzed.

2. (a) `Dim manOfTheYear(1980 To 1989)`

(b) `Let manOfTheYear(1982) = "The Computer"`

7.2 USING ARRAYS

This section considers three aspects of the use of arrays: processing ordered arrays, reading part of an array, and passing arrays to procedures.

Ordered Arrays

An array is said to be ordered if its values are in either ascending or descending order. The arrays below illustrate the different types of ordered and unordered arrays. In an ascending ordered array, the value of each element is less than or equal to the value of the next element. That is,

[each element] ≤ [next element].

For string arrays, the ANSI table is used to evaluate the "less than or equal to" condition.

Ordered Ascending Numeric Array

dates( )	1492	1776	1812	1929	1969

Ordered Descending Numeric Array

discov( )	1610	1541	1513	1513	1492

Ordered Ascending String Array

king( )	Edward	Henry	James	John	Kong

Ordered Descending String Array

lake( )	Superior	Ontario	Michigan	Huron	Erie

Unordered Numeric Array

rates( )	8.25	5.00	7.85	8.00	6.50

Unordered String Array

char( )	G	R	E	A	T

Ordered arrays can be searched more efficiently than unordered arrays. In this section we use their order to shorten the search. The technique used here is applied to searching sequential files in Chapter 8.

EXAMPLE 1 The following program places an ordered list of names into an array, requests a name as input, and informs the user if the name is in the list. Since the list is ordered, the search of the array ends when an element is reached whose value is greater than or equal to the input name. On average, only half the ordered array will be searched. Figure 7.5 shows the flowchart for this search.

```
Rem Create array to hold 10 strings
Dim nom(1 To 10) As String

Sub Command1_Click ()
  Dim n As Integer, name2Find As String
  Rem Search for a name in an ordered list
  Let name2Find = UCase$(Trim$(Text1.Text))
  Let n = 0    'n is the subscript of the array
  Do
    Let n = n + 1
  Loop Until (nom(n) >= name2Find) Or (n = 10)
  Rem Interpret result of search
  Picture1.Cls
  If nom(n) = name2Find Then
      Picture1.Print "Found."
    Else
      Picture1.Print "Not found."
  End If
End Sub
```

```
Sub Form_Load ()
  Rem Place the names into the array
  Rem All names must be in uppercase
  Let nom(1) = "AL"
  Let nom(2) = "BOB"
  Let nom(3) = "CARL"
  Let nom(4) = "DON"
  Let nom(5) = "ERIC"
  Let nom(6) = "FRED"
  Let nom(7) = "GREG"
  Let nom(8) = "HERB"
  Let nom(9) = "IRA"
  Let nom(10) = "JUDY"
End Sub
```

[Run, type Don into the text box, and click the command button.]

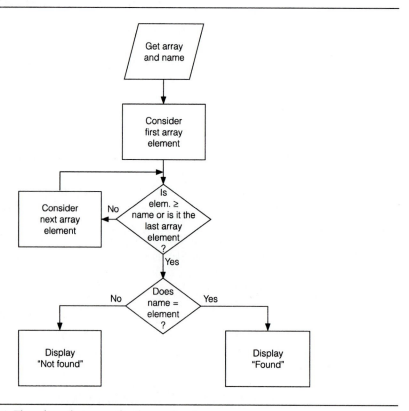

Figure 7.5 Flowchart for a search of an ordered array.

Using Part of an Array

In some programs, we must dimension an array before knowing how many pieces of data are to be placed into the array. In these cases, we dimension the array large enough to handle all reasonable contingencies. For instance, if the array is to hold exam grades and class sizes vary from 5 to 100 students, we would use a statement such as Dim grades(1 To 100) As Integer. In such situations, we must employ a **counter variable** to keep track of the number of values actually stored in the array. We create this counter variable using a Dim statement in the (declarations) section of (general) so that all procedures will have access to it.

EXAMPLE 2 The following program requests a list of companies and then displays them along with a count.

```
Rem Demonstrate using only part of an array
Dim stock(1 To 100) As String
Dim counter As Integer

Sub Command1_Click ()
  If (counter < 100) Then
      Let counter = counter + 1
      Let stock(counter) = Text1.Text
      Let Text1.Text = ""
      Text1.SetFocus
    Else
      MsgBox "No space to record additional companies.", , ""
      Let Text1.Text = ""
      Command2.SetFocus
  End If
End Sub

Sub Command2_Click ()
  Dim i As Integer
  Rem List stock company that have been recorded
  Picture1.Cls
  Picture1.Print "You own the following"; counter; "stocks."
  For i = 1 To counter
    Picture1.Print stock(i) + "  ";
  Next i
End Sub

Sub Form_Load ()
  Rem Initialize count of companies
  Let counter = 0
End Sub
```

[Run, type in IBM, press Record Name, type in Texaco, press Record Name, type in Exxon, press Record Name, press Summarize.]

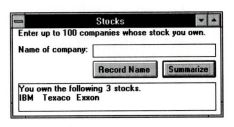

Suppose you have two ordered lists of customers (possibly with some customers on both lists) and you want to consolidate them into a single ordered list. The technique for creating the third list, called the **merge algorithm**, is as follows.

1. Compare the two names at the top of the first and second lists.

   (a) If one name alphabetically precedes the other, copy it onto the third list and cross it off its original list.

   (b) If the names are the same, copy the name onto the third list and cross out the name from the first and second lists.

2. Repeat step 1 with the current top names until you reach the end of either list.

3. Copy the names from the remaining list onto the third list.

EXAMPLE 3   The following program stores two lists of names in arrays and merges them into a third list. Although at most 10 names will be placed into the third array, duplications will reduce this number. Since the variable r identifies the next position to insert a name in the third array, $r - 1$ is the number of names in the array.

```
Rem Create arrays to hold list of names
Dim list1(1 To 5) As String, list2(1 To 5) As String
Dim newList(1 To 10) As String

Sub Command1_Click ()
  Dim m As Integer, n As Integer, r As Integer
  Dim numNames As Integer, i As Integer
  Rem Merge two lists of names
  Let m = 1    'Subscript for first array
  Let n = 1    'Subscript for second array
  Let r = 1    'Subscript and counter for third array
  Do While (m <= 5) And (n <= 5)
    Select Case list1(m)
      Case Is < list2(n)
        Let newList(r) = list1(m)
        Let m = m + 1
      Case Is > list2(n)
        Let newList(r) = list2(n)
        Let n = n + 1
      Case list2(n)
        Let newList(r) = list1(m)
        Let m = m + 1
        Let n = n + 1
    End Select
    Let r = r + 1
  Loop
  Rem At most one of the following two loops will be executed
  Do While m <= 5        'Copy rest of first array into third
    Let newList(r) = list1(m)
    Let r = r + 1
    Let m = m + 1
  Loop
```

```
    Do While n <= 5        'Copy rest of second array into third
      Let newList(r) = list2(n)
      Let r = r + 1
      Let n = n + 1
    Loop
    Let numNames = r - 1
    Rem Show result of merging lists
    Picture1.Cls
    For i = 1 To numNames
      Picture1.Print newList(i) + "  ";
    Next i
End Sub

Sub Form_Load ()
  Rem Fill list1 with names
  Let list1(1) = "Al"
  Let list1(2) = "Carl"
  Let list1(3) = "Don"
  Let list1(4) = "Greg"
  Let list1(5) = "Judy"
  Rem Fill list2 with names
  Let list2(1) = "Bob"
  Let list2(2) = "Carl"
  Let list2(3) = "Eric"
  Let list2(4) = "Greg"
  Let list2(5) = "Herb"
End Sub
```

[Run and click the command button.]

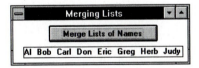

Passing Arrays Between Procedures

An array that is not dimensioned in the (declarations) section of (general) but rather is declared in a procedure with a ReDim statement is local to that procedure and unknown in all other procedures. However, an entire local array can be passed to another procedure. The name of the array, followed by an empty set of parentheses, must appear as an argument in the calling statement, and an array variable name of the same type must appear as a corresponding parameter in the procedure definition of the procedure that is to receive the array.

EXAMPLE 4   The following program illustrates passing an array to both a subprogram and a function.

```
Sub Command1_Click ()
  Rem Pass array to subprogram and function
  ReDim score(1 To 10) As Integer
  Call FillArray(score())
  Picture1.Cls
  Picture1.Print "The average score is"; Sum(score()) / 10
End Sub

Sub FillArray (s() As Integer)
  Rem Fill array with scores
  Let s(1) = 85
  Let s(2) = 92
  Let s(3) = 75
  Let s(4) = 68
  Let s(5) = 84
  Let s(6) = 86
  Let s(7) = 94
  Let s(8) = 74
  Let s(9) = 79
  Let s(10) = 88
End Sub

Function Sum (s() As Integer) As Integer
  Dim total As Integer, index As Integer
  Rem Add up scores
  Let total = 0
  For index = 1 To 10
    Let total = total + s(index)
  Next index
  Sum = total
End Function
```

[Run and click the command button.]

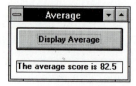

Sometimes it is also necessary to pass a form-level array from one procedure to another. For example, you might have a sorting procedure (discussed in Section 7.3) and three form-level arrays to be sorted. The sorting procedure would be called three times, each time passing a different form-level array. The method for passing a form-level array to another procedure is the same as the method for passing a local array.

EXAMPLE 5   The following program incorporates all three topics discussed in this section. It reads an ordered list of computer languages and spoken languages into form-level arrays, requests a new language as input, and inserts the language into its proper array position (avoiding duplication). The language arrays are dimensioned to hold up to 20 names; the variables *numCompLangs* and *numSpokLang* record the actual number of languages in each of the ordered arrays. The original contents of the data files are

COMPLANG.TXT: ADA, C, Cobol, Fortran, Pascal, Visual Basic
SPOKLANG.TXT: Cantonese, English, French, Mandarin, Russian, Spanish

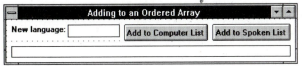

Object	Property	Setting
Form1	Caption	Adding to an Ordered Array
Label1	Caption	New language
Text1	Text	(blank)
Command1	Caption	Add to Computer List
Command2	Caption	Add to Spoken List
Picture1		

```
Dim compLang(1 To 20) As String
Dim spokLang(1 To 20) As String
Dim numCompLangs As Integer
Dim numSpokLangs As Integer

Sub AddALang (lang() As String, langCount As Integer)
  Dim language As String, n As Integer, i As Integer
  Rem Insert a language into an ordered array of languages
  Let language = Trim$(Text1.Text)
  Let n = 0
  Do
    Let n = n + 1
  Loop Until (UCase$(lang(n)) >= UCase$(language)) Or (n = langCount)
  If UCase$(lang(n)) < UCase$(language) Then      'Insert new language at end
      Let lang(langCount + 1) = language
      Let langCount = langCount + 1
    ElseIf UCase$(lang(n)) > UCase$(language) Then      'Insert before item n
      For i = langCount To n Step -1
        Let lang(i + 1) = lang(i)
      Next i
      Let lang(n) = language
      Let langCount = langCount + 1
  End If
End Sub

Sub Command1_Click ()
  Rem Insert language into ordered array of computer languages
  Call AddALang(compLang(), numCompLangs)
  Call DisplayArray(compLang(), numCompLangs)
End Sub

Sub Command2_Click ()
  Rem Insert language into ordered array of spoken languages
  Call AddALang(spokLang(), numSpokLangs)
  Call DisplayArray(spokLang(), numSpokLangs)
End Sub
```

```
Sub DisplayArray (lang() As String, howMany As Integer)
  Dim i As Integer
  Rem Display the languages in the array
  Picture1.Cls
  For i = 1 To howMany
    Picture1.Print lang(i) + "  ";
  Next i
End Sub

Sub Form_Load ()
  Rem Fill computer language array from COMPLANG.TXT
  Let numCompLangs = 0
  Open "COMPLANG.TXT" For Input As #1
  Do While (Not EOF(1)) And (numCompLangs < 20)
    Let numCompLangs = numCompLangs + 1
    Input #1, compLang(numCompLangs)
  Loop
  Close #1
  Rem Fill spoken language array from SPOKLANG.TXT
  Let numSpokLangs = 0
  Open "SPOKLANG.TXT" For Input As #1
  Do While (Not EOF(1)) And (numSpokLangs < 20)
    Let numSpokLangs = numSpokLangs + 1
    Input #1, spokLang(numSpokLangs)
  Loop
  Close #1
End Sub
```

[Run, type in German, and click Add to Spoken List.]

[Run, type in FORTRAN, and click Add to Computer List.]

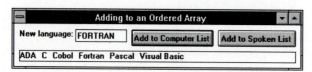

Comments:

1. In Examples 1 and 5 we searched successive elements of an ordered list beginning with the first element. This is called a **sequential search**. An efficient alternative to the sequential search is the **binary search** considered in the next section.

2. A single element of an array can be passed to a procedure just like any ordinary numeric or string variable.

```
Sub Command1_Click ()
  ReDim num(1 TO 20) As Integer
  Let num(5) = 10
  Picture1.Print Triple(num(5))
End Sub

Function Triple (x As Integer)
  Triple = 3 * x
End Function
```

When the program is run and the command button clicked, 30 will be displayed.

3. Visual Basic provides two functions that simplify working with arrays that have been passed to a procedure. If an array has been dimensioned with the range *m* To *n*, then the values of the functions LBound(*arrayName*) and UBound(*arrayName*) are *m* and *n*.

```
Sub Command1_Click ()
  ReDim pres(40 To 42) As String
  Let pres(40) = "Reagan"
  Let pres(41) = "Bush"
  Let pres(42) = "Clinton"
  Call Display(pres())
End Sub

Sub Display (a() As String)
  Dim i As Integer
  For i = LBound(a) To UBound(a)
    Picture1.Print a(i) + "  ";
  Next i
End Sub
```

When the program is run and the command button clicked, "Reagan Bush   Clinton" will be displayed.

PRACTICE PROBLEMS 7.2

1. Can an array be in both ascending and descending order at the same time?

2. How can the Select Case block in Example 3 be changed so all entries of both arrays (including duplicates) are merged into the third array?

EXERCISES 7.2

In Exercises 1 and 2, decide if the array is ordered.

1.   month()

January	February	March	April	May

2.   pres()

Adams	Adams	Bush	Johnson	Johnson

In Exercises 3 through 8, determine the output displayed in the picture box when the command button is clicked.

3.
```
Sub Command1_Click ()
    ReDim lake(1 To 5) As String
    Let lake(3) = "Michigan"
    Call DisplayThird(lake())
End Sub

Sub DisplayThird (lake() As String)
  Rem Display the third element of an array
    Picture1.Print lake(3)
End Sub
```

4.
```
Sub Command1_Click ()
    Dim i As Integer, num As Integer
    ReDim square(1 To 20)
    Let num = Val(InputBox$("Enter a number from 1 to 20:"))
    For i = 1 To num
      Let square(i) = i ^ 2
    Next i
    Call Total(square(), num)
End Sub

Sub Total (array() As Integer, n As Integer)
  Dim sum As Integer
  Let sum = 0
  For i = 1 To n
    Let sum = sum + array(i)
  Next i
  Picture1.Print "The sum of the first"; n; "elements is"; sum
End Sub
```

(Assume that the response is 4.)

5.
```
Sub Command1_Click ()
    Dim i As Integer
    ReDim value(1 To 5) As Integer
    Call FillArray(value())
    For i = 1 To 4
      Select Case value(i)
        Case Is < value(i + 1)
          Picture1.Print "less than"
        Case Is > value(i + 1)
          Picture1.Print "greater than"
        Case Else
          Picture1.Print "equals"
      End Select
    Next i
End Sub
```

```
Sub FillArray (array() As Integer)
  Rem Place values into an array of five elements
  Open "DATA.TXT" For Input As #1
  For i = 1 To 5
    Input #1, array(i)
  Next i
  Close #1
End Sub
```

(Assume that the file DATA.TXT contains the following entries.)

3, 7, 1, 1, 17

6.
```
Sub Command1_Click ()
  ReDim ocean(1 To 5) As String
  Let ocean(1) = "Pacific"
  Call Musical(ocean(1))
End Sub
```

```
Sub Musical (sea As String)
  Picture1.Print "South "; sea
End Sub
```

7.
```
Sub Command1_Click ()
  ReDim rainfall(1 To 12) As Single
  Let rainfall(1) = 2.4
  Let rainfall(2) = 3.6
  Let rainfall(3) = 4.0
  Picture1.Print "The total rainfall for the first quarter is";
  Picture1.Print Total(rainfall(),3)
End Sub
```

```
Function Total (rainfall() As Single, n As Integer)
  Dim sum As Single, i As Integer
  Let sum = 0
  For i = 1 To n
    Let sum = sum + rainfall(i)
  Next i
  Total = sum
End Function
```

8.
```
Sub Command1_Click ()
  Dim i As Integer
  ReDim num(1 To 8) As Integer
  Open "DATA.TXT" For Input As #1
  For i = 1 To 8
    Input #1, num(i)
  Next i
  Close #1
  Picture1.Print "The array has"; Nonzero(num()); "nonzero entries."
End Sub
```

```
Function Nonzero (digit() As Integer)
  Dim count As Integer, i As Integer
  Let count = 0
  For i = 1 To 8
    If digit(i) <> 0 Then
        Let count = count + 1
    End If
  Next i
  Nonzero = count
End Function
```

(Assume that the file DATA.TXT contains the following entries.)

5, 0, 2, 1, 0, 0, 7, 7

In Exercises 9 through 12, identify the error.

9.
```
Sub Command1_Click ()
    Dim city(1 To 3) As String
    Call Assign(city())
    Picture1.Print city(1)
End Sub


Sub Assign (town() As String)
  Let town(1) = "Chicago"
End Sub
```

10.
```
Sub Command1_Click ()
    ReDim planet(1 To 9) As String
    Call Assign(planet)
    Picture1.Print planet(1)
End Sub


Sub Assign (planet As String)
  Let planet(1) = "Venus"
End Sub
```

11.
```
Sub Command1_Click ()
    Dim prompt As String, n As Integer
    Dim number As Single, product As Single, i As Integer
    Rem Multiply several numbers together
    ReDim num(1 To 5) As Single
    Let prompt = "Enter a positive number to multiply by, or, to see the "
    Let prompt = prompt + "product, press Enter without giving a number. "
    Let prompt = prompt + "(Five numbers maximum can be specified.)"
    Let n = 0
    Do
      Let n = n + 1
      Let number = Val(InputBox$(prompt))
      If number > 0 Then
          Let num(n) = number
      End If
```

```
      Loop Until (number <= 0) Or (n = 5)
      Let product = 1
      For i = 1 To n
        Let product = product * num(i)
      Next i
      Picture1.Print "The product of the numbers entered is "; product
    End Sub
```

12.
```
    Sub Command1_Click ()
      ReDim hue(0 To 15) As String
      Let hue(1) = "Blue"
      Call Favorite(hue())
    End Sub

    Sub Favorite (tone() As String)
      Let tone(1) = hue(1)
      Picture1.Print tone
    End Sub
```

In Exercises 13 and 14, find the error in the program and rewrite the program to correctly perform the intended task.

13.
```
    Sub Command1_Click ()
      Dim i As Integer
      ReDim a(1 To 10) As Integer
      ReDim b(1 To 10) As Integer
      For i = 1 To 10
        Let a(i) = i ^ 2
      Next i
      Call CopyArray(a(), b())
      Picture1.Print b(10)
    End Sub

    Sub CopyArray (a() As Integer, b() As Integer)
      Rem Place a's values in b
      Let b() = a()
    End Sub
```

14.
```
    Sub Command1_Click ()
      Dim a(1 To 3) As Integer
      Let a(1) = 42
      Let a(2) = 7
      Let a(3) = 11
      Call FlipFirstTwo(a())
      Picture1.Print a(1); a(2); a(3)
    End Sub

    Sub FlipFirstTwo (a() As Integer)
      Rem Swap first two elements
      Let a(2) = a(1)
      Let a(1) = a(2)
    End Sub
```

Suppose an array has been dimensioned in the (declarations) section of (general) with the statement Dim scores(1 To 50) As Single and numbers assigned to each element by the Form_Load event procedure. In Exercises 15 through 18, write a procedure to perform the stated task.

15. Determine if the array is in ascending order.

16. Determine if the array is in descending order.

17. With a single loop, determine if the array is in ascending order, descending order, both, or neither.

18. Assuming the array is in ascending order, count the numbers that appear more than once in the array.

In Exercises 19 and 20, suppose arrays a( ), b( ), and c( ) are form-level and that arrays a( ) and b( ) have each been assigned 20 numbers in ascending order (duplications may occur) by a Form_Load event procedure. For instance, array a( ) might hold the numbers 1, 3, 3, 3, 9, 9, ...

19. Write a procedure to place all the 40 numbers from arrays a( ) and b( ) into c( ) so that c( ) is also ordered. The array c( ) could contain duplications.

20. Write a procedure to place the numbers from a( ) and b( ) into c( ) so that c( ) is ordered but contains no duplications.

21. Write a program to dimension an array with the statement Dim state(1 To 50) As String and maintain a list of certain states. The list of states should always be in alphabetical order and occupy consecutive elements of the array. The command buttons in the program should give the user the following options:

   (a) Take the state specified by the user in Text1 and insert it into its proper position in the array. (If the state is already in the array, so report.)
   (b) Take the state specified by the users in Text1 and delete it from the array. (If the state is not in the array, so report.)
   (c) Display the states in the array.
   (d) Quit.

22. Write a program that requests a sentence one word at a time from the user and then checks whether the sentence is a *word palindrome*. A word palindrome sentence reads the same, word by word, backward and forward (ignoring punctuation and capitalization). An example is "You can cage a swallow, can't you, but you can't swallow a cage, can you?" The program should hold the words of the sentence in an array and use procedures to obtain the input, analyze the sentence, and declare whether the sentence is a word palindrome. (Test the program with the sentences, "Monkey see, monkey do." and "I am; therefore, am I?")

23. Write a program to display average score and the number of above average scores on an exam. Each time the user clicks a "record score" command button, a grade should be read from a text box. The average score and number of above average scores should be displayed in a picture box whenever the user clicks on a "show average" command button. (Assume the class contains at most 100 students.) Use a function to calculate the average and another

function to determine the number of scores above average. **Note:** Pass the functions two parameters, an array parameter for the grades and a numeric parameter for the number of elements of the array that have been assigned values.

24. Suppose an array of 1000 names is in ascending order. Write a procedure to search for a name input by the user. If the first letter of the name is N through Z, then the search should begin with the 1000th element of the array and proceed backwards.

Exercises 25 and 26 require the Rnd function presented in Section 3.6.

25. Write a program to randomly select 50 different people from a group of 100 people whose names are contained in a data file. **Hint:** Use an array of 100 elements to keep track of whether or not a person has been selected.

26. *The Birthday Problem.* Given a random group of 23 people, how likely is it that two people have the same birthday? To answer this question, write a program that creates an array of range 1 To 23, randomly assigns to each subscripted variable one of the integers from 1 through 365, and checks to see if any of the subscripted variables have the same value. (Make the simplifying assumption that no birthdays occur on February 29.) Now expand the program to repeat the process 100 times and determine the percentage of the time that there is a match. **Note:** This program may take a few minutes to run.

SOLUTIONS TO PRACTICE PROBLEMS 7.2

1. Yes, provided each element of the array has the same value.

2. The third Case tests for duplicates and only assigns one array element to the third array if duplicates are found in the two arrays. Thus, we remove the third Case and change the first Case so it will process any duplicates. A situation where you would want to merge two lists while retaining duplications is the task of merging two ordered arrays of test scores.

```
Select Case first(m)
  Case Is <= second(n)
    Let third(r) = first(m)
    Let m = m + 1
  Case Is > second(n)
    Let third(r) = second(n)
    Let n = n + 1
End Select
```

7.3 CONTROL ARRAYS

We have seen many examples of the usefulness of subscripted variables. They are essential for writing concise solutions to many programming problems. Because of the great utility that subscripts provide, Visual Basic also provides a means of constructing arrays of text boxes, labels, command buttons, and so on. Since text boxes, labels, and command buttons are referred to generically in Visual Basic as controls, arrays of these objects are called **control arrays**.

Unlike variable arrays, which can only be created by Dim statements once a program is running, at least one element of a control array must be created when the form is designed. The remaining elements can be created either during form design, or, perhaps more typically, with the Load statement when the program is running.

To create the first element of an array of text boxes, create an ordinary text box, then access the Properties window and select the property called Index. By default this property is blank. Change the Index property to 0 (zero). Your text box is now the first element in a subscripted control array. To avoid confusion, it is also a good idea to change the Name property for the text box to a meaningful name rather than using the default value of Text1. If the name of a text box is *txtBox* and its Index property is 0, then assigning a value to the text box during run-time requires a statement of the form

```
Let txtBox(0).Text = value
```

Arrays are not of much use if they contain only a single element. To create additional elements of the *txtBox*( ) control array during form design, make sure that the element you just created is active by clicking on it. Next, press Ctrl+C (or open the Edit menu and select Copy). Visual Basic has now recorded all the properties associated with *txtBox*(0) and is ready to reproduce as many copies as you desire. To create a copy, press Ctrl+V (or open the Edit menu and select Paste). The copy of *txtBox*(0) appears in the upper-left corner of the form. The value of the Index property for this new text box is 1; thus the text box is referred to as *txtBox*(1). Move this text box to the desired position. Press Ctrl+V again and another copy of *txtBox*(0) appears in the upper left corner of the form. Its Index property is 2. Move *txtBox*(2) to an appropriate position. Continue copying *txtBox*(0) in this manner until all desired controls have been created.

It is important to note that all properties of *txtBox*(0) are being passed to the other elements of the *txtBox*( ) control array, with the exception of the Index, Top, and Left properties. Thus, as a matter of efficiency, before you begin copying *txtBox*(0), set all properties that you want carried over to all elements of *txtBox*( ). For example, if you desire to have the Text property blank for all *txtBox*( ) elements, set the Text property of *txtBox*(0) to (blank) before starting the copying process.

The discussion above gave a process for creating an array of text boxes. This same process applies to creating arrays of labels or any other control. In summary, the following steps create an array of controls while designing a form:

1. Add one instance of the desired control to the form.

2. Set the Index property of this control to 0.

3. Set any other properites of the control that will be common to all elements of the array.

4. Click on the control and then press Ctrl+C to prepare to make a copy of the control.

5. Press Ctrl+V to create a copy of the control. Position this control as desired.

6. Repeat Step 5 until all desired elements of the control array have been created.

EXAMPLE 1   A department store has five departments. Write a program to request the amount of sales for each department and display the total sales.

SOLUTION   We use a control array of five labels and a control array of five text boxes to handle the input. For the label captions we use "Department 1", "Department 2", and so on. Since these labels are the same except for the number, we wait until run-time and use a For...Next loop inside the Form_Load ( ) event procedure to assign the captions to each element of the *lblDepart*( ) control array. At design-time, before making copies of *lblDepart*(0), we set the Alignment property to "1 – Right Justify" so that all elements of the array inherit this property. Similarly, the Text property of *txtSales*(0) is set to (blank) before copying.

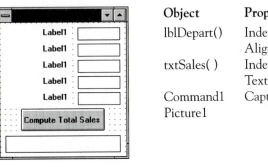

Object	Property	Setting
lblDepart()	Index	0 to 4
	Alignment	1 – Right Justify
txtSales( )	Index	0 to 4
	Text	(blank)
Command1	Caption	Compute Total Sales
Picture1		

```
Sub Form_Load ()
  Dim depNum As Integer
  For depNum = 0 To 4
    Let lblDepart(depNum).Caption = "Department" + Str$(depNum + 1)
  Next depNum
End Sub

Sub Command1_Click ()
  Dim depNum As Integer, sales As Single
  For depNum = 0 To 4
    Let sales = sales + Val(txtSales(depNum).Text)
  Next depNum
  Picture1.Cls
  Picture1.Print "Total sales were " + Format$(sales, "Currency")
End Sub
```

[Run, type the data below into the text boxes, and click the command button.]

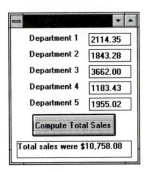

Control Array Event Procedures

In Chapter 3 we discussed several events related to text boxes. One example was the GotFocus event procedure. If *txtBox* is an ordinary text box, then the GotFocus event procedure begins with the statement

```
Sub txtBox_GotFocus ()
```

If, on the other hand, we make *txtBox* a control array, the GotFocus event procedure begins with the statement

```
Sub txtBox_GotFocus (Index As Integer)
```

Two points should be noted. First, even though we may have a dozen or more elements in the *txtBox*( ) control array, we will have just one txtBox_GotFocus event procedure to deal with. Second, Visual Basic passes to this one event procedure the value of the Index property for the element of the control array that has the focus. We may wish to respond in the same manner whenever any element of *txtBox*( ) has the focus, in which case we simply ignore the value of *Index*. If, on the other hand, we wish to respond in different ways depending on which element has the focus, then we write the GotFocus event procedure in the form

```
Sub txtBox_GotFocus (Index As Integer)
  Select Case Index
    Case 0
      action when txtBox(0) gets the focus
    Case 1
      action when txtBox(1) gets the focus
      .
      .
      .
  End Select
End Sub
```

In general, all event procedures for a control array have the additional parameter Index As Integer. This additional parameter can be used, if desired, to base the action taken by the event procedure on which element of the control array underwent the event.

EXAMPLE 2   Create an electronic dialing pad.

SOLUTION   The form below contains a control array of ten command buttons. Each time a command button is clicked, the Index parameter conveys the digit to be added onto the phone number. This program illustrates using the Index parameter without employing a Select Case statement.

Object	Property	Setting
cmdDigit( )	Index	0 to 9
	Caption	(same as Index)
lblPhoneNum	BorderStyle	1 – Fixed Single
	Caption	(blank)

```
Sub cmdDigit_Click (Index As Integer)
  Let lblPhoneNum.Caption = lblPhoneNum.Caption + Format$(Index, "0")
  If Len(lblPhoneNum.Caption) = 3 Then
      Let lblPhoneNum.Caption = lblPhoneNum.Caption + "-"
    ElseIf Len(lblPhoneNum.Caption) = 8 Then
      MsgBox "Dialing ...", , ""
      Let lblPhoneNum.Caption = ""
  End If
End Sub
```

Creating Control Arrays at Run-Time

We have discussed the process for creating an entire control array while designing a form, that is, at design-time. However, copying and positioning control array elements can become tedious if the number of elements is large. Also, the actual number of elements needed in a control array may not be known until a response from the user is processed at run-time. In light of these concerns, Visual Basic provides a solution via the Load statement that only requires us to create the first element of a control array during design-time. The remaining elements are then created as needed at run-time. Before we discuss creating arrays at run-time, we must consider a preliminary topic—the Left, Top, Width, and Height properties of controls. These properties specify the location and size of controls.

The standard unit of measurement in Visual Basic is called a *twip*. There are 1440 twips to the inch. When a control is active, the two panels on the right side of the toolbar give the location and size of the control, respectively. Figure 7.6(a) shows an active text box, named Text1. The first panel says that the left side of the text box is 960 twips from the left side of the form, and the top of the text box is 720 twips down from the title bar of the form. In terms of properties, Text1.Left is 960, and Text1.Top is 720. Similarly, the numbers 1935 and 975 in the second panel give the width and height of the text box in twips. In terms of properties, Text1.Width is 1935 and Text1.Height is 975. Figure 7.6(b) shows the meanings of these four properties.

The location and size properties of a control can be altered at run-time with statements such as

```
Let Text1.Left = 480
```

which moves the text box to the left or

```
Let Text2.Top = Text1.Top + 1.5 * Text1.Height
```

which places Text2 a comfortable distance below Text1. As a result of the second statement, the distance between the two text boxes will be half the height of Text1.

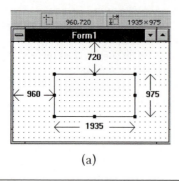 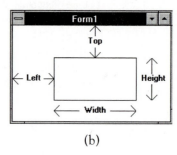

Figure 7.6 The location and size of a control.

If *controlName* is the name of a control whose Index property was assigned a value during form design (thus creating the beginnings of a control array) and *num* is a whole number that has not yet been used as an index for the *control-Name*( ) array, then the statement

```
Load controlName(num)
```

copies all the properties of *controlName*(0), including the Top and Left properties, and creates the element *controlName*(*num*) of the *controlName*( ) array. The only property of *controlName*(*num*) that may differ from that of *controlName*(0) is the Visible property. The Load statement always sets the Visible property of the created element to False. After creating a new element of a control array, you will want to adjust the Top and Left properties so that the new element has its own unique location on the form, and then set the Visible property of the new element to True.

EXAMPLE 3 Write a program to create a control array of 12 labels and a control array of 12 text boxes. Position the labels and text boxes so that they form two columns, with the labels to the left of the text boxes and the text boxes one immediately below the other. Use text boxes whose height is as small as possible. Use labels whose height is just large enough to display a single line. Assign the captions Jan, Feb, and so on, to the labels.

SOLUTION When designing the form, we place the first label to the left of the first text box and set the Index property of both controls to 0. The height of the shortest text box is 285 units while the height of a label just tall enough for a single line is 255 units. We use the text box's Height property as the unit of vertical spacing for both the new text box elements and the new label elements. Below is the form at design-time and at run-time.

Object	Property	Setting
lblMonth	Index	0
	Caption	Jan
txtInfo	Index	0
	Text	(blank)

```
Sub Form_Load ()
  Dim i As Integer, monthNames As String
  Let monthNames = "FebMarAprMayJunJulAugSepOctNovDec"
  For i = 1 To 11
    Load lblMonth(i)
    Load txtInfo(i)
    Let lblMonth(i).Top = lblMonth(i - 1).Top + txtInfo(0).Height
    Let txtInfo(i).Top = txtInfo(i - 1).Top + txtinfo(0).Height
    Let lblMonth(i).Caption = Mid$(monthNames, 3 * i - 2, 3)
    Let lblMonth(i).Visible = True
    Let txtInfo(i).Visible = True
  Next i
End Sub
```

Comments:

1. In the discussion and examples of control arrays, the initial index was always 0. For a particular application it may be more natural to have the lowest index of a control array be 1 or even 1995. To achieve this when creating just the first element at design-time and the remaining controls at run-time, set the Index property of the first element to the desired lowest index value at design-time, then Load the other elements using the desired indexes at run-time. (The Load statement copies the properties of the element with the lowest index, whatever that lowest index may be.) For example, at design-time you might create *txtSales*(1995) and then at run-time execute the statements

```
For yearNum = 1996 to 2005
  Load txtSales(yearNum)
Next yearNum
```

To create an entire control array at design-time with indexes starting at a value other than 0, first create the control array using an initial index of 0. Once all elements have been created, use the Properties window to adjust the index of each element of the control array, starting with the element having the highest index.

PRACTICE PROBLEMS 7.3

1. Suppose an event procedure has the first line

```
Sub txtBox_GotFocus ()
```

How do you know whether txtBox is the name of an ordinary control or a control array?

2. Assume element 0 of the txtBox control array was created during design-time. What is the shortcoming of the following event procedure?

```
Sub Form_Load ()
  Load txtBox(1)
  Let txtBox(1).Visible = True
End Sub
```

3. What is the effect of adding the following line to the event procedure in Problem 2?

```
Let txtBox(1).Top = txtBox(0).Top + 2 * txtBox(0).Height
```

EXERCISES 7.3

In Exercises 1 to 4, design the given form using the indicated number and type of controls.

1. A control array of four text boxes, a command button, and a picture box.

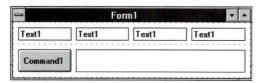

2. A control array of three command buttons and a picture box.

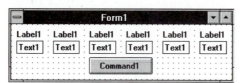

3. A contol array of six labels, a control array of six text boxes, and a command button.

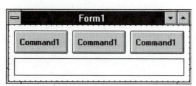

4. Two control arrays of four text boxes each and a control array of four command buttons.

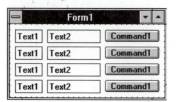

In Exercises 5 to 10, give the effect of the statement.

5. `Let Text1.Width = .5 * Text1.Width`

6. `Let Text1.Top = .5 * Text1.Height`

7. `Let Text1.Left = Text1.Top`

8. `Let Text1.Width = Text1.Height`

9. `Let Text1.Width = Form.Width`

10. `Let Text1.Width = .5 * Form.Width`

In Exercises 11 through 18, suppose the control array cmdButton( ) consists of the two command buttons cmdButton(0) and cmdButton(1) placed vertically, and write an event procedure to carry out the indicated task.

11. When a button is clicked on, it disappears.

12. Whan a button is clicked on, it moves 100 twips to the right.

13. When the button is clicked, its caption turns italic and the caption of the other button turns non-italic.

14. When a button is clicked, the other button assumes the caption of the clicked on button, but with the letters reversed.

15. When a button is clicked, it moves 100 twips to the right of the other button.

16. When a button is clicked, it moves 100 twips below the other button.

17. When a button is clicked, it doubles in width.

18. When a button is clicked, it becomes twice the width of the other button.

In Exercises 19 and 20, write lines of code to carry out the given tasks.

19. Suppose the text box txtBox with index 0 was created at design-time. Create a new text box at run-time and place it 100 twips below the original text box.

20. Suppose the text box txtBox with index 0 was created at design-time. Create two additional text boxes at run-time and place them below the original text box. Then italicize the contents of a text box when the text box is clicked on.

In Exercises 21 through 24, identify the error.

21.
```
Sub cmdButton(1)_Click
    Let cmdButton(1).ForeColor = &HFFFF&
End Sub
```

22.
```
Load cmdButton(Index As Integer)
```

23.
```
Sub Form_Load ()
    Dim i As Integer
    For i = 0 To 5
      Load lbl(i)
      Let lbl(i).Caption = Str$(1995 + i)
      Let lbl(i).Top = lbl(i - 1).Top + lbl(i - 1).Height
      Let lbl(i).Visible = True
    Next i
End Sub
```

24.
```
Sub Form_Load ()
    Dim i As Integer
    For i = 1 To 12
      Load txt(i)
      Let txt.Text(i) = ""
      Let txt.Left(i) = txt.Left(i - 1) + txt.TextWidth(i - 1)
    Next i
    Let txt.Visible(i - 1) = True
End Sub
```

In Exercises 25 through 28, use the form below (already filled in by the user) to determine the output displayed in the picture box when the command button is clicked. The text boxes on the form consist of four control arrays—*txtWinter*( ), *txtSpring*( ), *txtSummer*( ), and *txtFall*( )—with each control array having indexes ranging from 1 to 4.

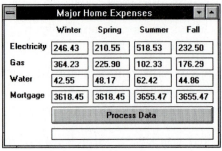

25.
```
Sub Command1_Click ()
    Dim itemNum As Integer, total As Single
    Let total = 0
    For itemNum = 1 to 4
      Let total = total + Val(txtWinter(itemNum).Text)
    Next itemNum
    Picture1.Print "Home expenses for winter were ";
    Picture1.Print Format$(total, "Currency")
End Sub
```

26.
```
Sub Command1_Click ()
    Dim total As Single
    Let total = 0
    Let total = total + Val(txtWinter(3).Text)
    Let total = total + Val(txtSpring(3).Text)
    Let total = total + Val(txtSummer(3).Text)
    Let total = total + Val(txtFall(3).Text)
    Picture1.Print "Annual water bill was ";
    Picture1.Print Format$(total, "Currency")
End Sub
```

27.
```
Sub Command1_Click ()
    Dim itemNum As Integer, diff As Single, total As Single
    Let total = 0
    For itemNum = 1 To 4
      Let diff = Val(txtSummer(itemNum).Text) - Val(txtWinter(itemNum).Text)
      Let total = total + diff
    Next itemNum
    Picture1.Print "Summer bills exceeded winter by ";
    Picture1.Print Format$(total, "Currency")
End Sub
```

28.
```
Sub Command1_Click ()
    Dim itemNum As Integer, total As Single
    Let total = 0
    For itemNum = 1 To 4
      Let total = total + TotalCateg(itemNum)
    Next itemNum
    Picture1.Print "Total major expenses were ";
    Picture1.Print Format$(total, "Currency")
End Sub
```

```
Function TotalCateg (itemNum As Integer) As Single
  Dim total As Single
  Let total = 0
  Let total = total + Val(txtWinter(itemNum).Text)
  Let total = total + Val(txtSpring(itemNum).Text)
  Let total = total + Val(txtSummer(itemNum).Text)
  Let total = total + Val(txtFall(itemNum).Text)
  TotalCateg = total
End Function
```

For Exercises 29 through 32, the design-time appearance of a form is given below along with the properties assigned to the controls. Determine the appearance of the form after the given program segment is executed.

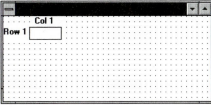

Object	Property	Setting
Form1	Caption	(blank)
lblSide	Index	1
	Caption	Row 1
lblTop	Index	1
	Caption	Col 1
txtInfo	Index	1
	Text	(blank)

29.
```
Dim itemNum As Integer
For itemNum = 2 To 4
  Load lblSide(itemNum)
  Load txtInfo(itemNum)
  Let lblSide(itemNum).Top=lblSide(itemNum-1).Top + 1.5*txtInfo(1).Height
  Let txtInfo(itemNum).Top=txtInfo(itemNum-1).Top + 1.5*txtInfo(1).Height
  Let lblSide(itemNum).Caption = "Row" + Str$(itemNum)
  Let lblSide(itemNum).Visible = True
  Let txtInfo(itemNum).Visible = True
Next itemNum
```

30.
```
Dim itemNum As Integer
For itemNum = 2 To 4
  Load lblTop(itemNum)
  Load txtInfo(itemNum)
  Let lblTop(itemNum).Left=lblTop(itemNum-1).Left + 1.5*txtInfo(1).Width
  Let txtInfo(itemNum).Left=txtInfo(itemNum-1).Left + 1.5*txtInfo(1).Width
  Let lblTop(itemNum).Caption = "Col" + Str$(itemNum)
  Let lblTop(itemNum).Visible = True
  Let txtInfo(itemNum).Visible = True
Next itemNum
```

31.
```
Dim itemNum As Integer
For itemNum = 2 To 4
  Load lblTop(itemNum)
  Load txtInfo(itemNum)
  Let lblTop(itemNum).Left = lblTop(itemNum - 1).Left + txtInfo(1).Width
  Let txtInfo(itemNum).Left = txtInfo(itemNum - 1).Left + txtInfo(1).Width
  Let lblTop(itemNum).Caption = "Col" + Str$(itemNum)
  Let lblTop(itemNum).Visible = True
  Let txtInfo(itemNum).Visible = True
Next itemNum
```

32.
```
Dim itemNum As Integer
For itemNum = 2 To 4
   Load lblTop(itemNum)
   Load lblSide(itemNum)
   Load txtInfo(itemNum)
   Let lblTop(itemNum).Left = lblTop(itemNum - 1).Left + txtInfo(1).Width
   Let lblSide(itemNum).Top = lblSide(itemNum - 1).Top + txtInfo(1).Height
   Let txtInfo(itemNum).Left = txtInfo(itemNum - 1).Left + txtInfo(1).Width
   Let txtInfo(itemNum).Top = txtInfo(itemNum - 1).Top + txtInfo(1).Height
   Let lblTop(itemNum).Caption = "Col" + Str$(itemNum)
   Let lblSide(itemNum).Caption = "Row" + Str$(itemNum)
   Let lblTop(itemNum).Visible = True
   Let lblSide(itemNum).Visible = True
   Let txtInfo(itemNum).Visible = True
Next itemNum
```

33. Modify the form given for Exercises 25 through 28 by deleting the command button and picture box and adding a row of labels below the row of Mortgage text boxes (use a control array named *lblQuarterTot*) and a column of labels to the right of the Fall text boxes (use a control array named *lblCategTot*). The purpose of these new labels is to hold the totals of each column and each row. Write an event procedure that updates the totals displayed on these new labels whenever the cursor is moved from one text box to another.

34. Write a program to compute a student's grade point average. The program should use InputBox$ in the Form_Load event procedure to request the number of courses to be averaged and then create elements in two text box control arrays to hold the grade and semester hours credit for each course. After the student fills in these text boxes and clicks on a command button, the program should use a function to compute the grade point average. Another subprogram should display the GPA and then display one of two messages. A student with a GPA of 3 or more should be informed that he has made the honor roll. Otherwise, the student should be congratulated on having completed the semester. In either case, the student should be wished a merry vacation.

35. Simulate a traffic light with a control array consisting of three small square picture boxes placed vertically on a form. Initially, the bottom picture box is solid green and the other picture boxes are white. When the Tab key is pressed, the middle picture box turns yellow and the bottom picture box turns white. The next time Tab is pressed, the top picture box turns red and the middle picture box turns white. Subsequent pressing of the Tab key cycles through the three colors. **Hint:** First place the bottom picture box on the form, then the middle picture box, and finally the top picture box.

36. (A primitive typewriter.) Create a form containing a picture box and a control array of twenty-six small command buttons, each having one of the letters of the alphabet as its caption. When a command button is pressed, its letter should be added to the text in the picture box.

37. *Multiple-choice Quiz.* Write a program to ask multiple-choice questions with four possible answers. Figure 7.7 shows a typical question. The user selects an answer by clicking on a command button and is informed as to the correctness of the answer by a message box. When the user gives a correct answer, a new question is presented. The program ends when all questions have been presented or when the user clicks on the quit command button. Questions and correct answers should be read from a data file. The numbered command buttons should be elements of a command button control array. The question and answers should be displayed using a five-element control array of labels.

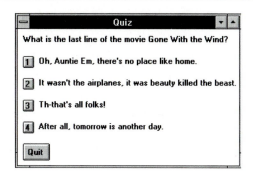

Figure 7.7 A typical question for Exercise 37.

38. Table 7.4 gives the U.S. Census Bureau projections for the populations (in millions) of the states predicted to be the most populous in the year 2010. Write a program that stores the 2010 data in an array and provides a control array of text boxes for the input of the current population of each of these states. When a command button is clicked, the percentage population growth for each state should be displayed in a control array of labels. In a picture box below these five values, the program should display the average percentage population growth for the five states. (Figure 7.8 shows a possible form design and run with sample data for 1990.) The growth is calculated using the formula

$$growth = (projected \ pop. - current \ pop.) \ / \ current \ pop.$$

Percentage growth can be obtained using Format$(growth, "Percentage"). Test the program with the current populations shown in Figure 7.8.

State	Population in 2010
California	36.9
Texas	21.4
New York	20.3
Illinois	13.5
Florida	13.0

Table 7.4 State popuations in the Year 2010.

Figure 7.8 Sample run for Exercise 38.

SOLUTIONS TO PRACTICE PROBLEMS 7.3

1. It is an ordinary array. If it were a control array, the parentheses at the end of the line would contain the word "Index As Integer."

2. The new text box will be placed in the exact same location as the original text box. An additional line, like the one in Practice Problem 3, is needed.

3. The new text box will be placed below the original text box, with space between them equal to the height of the text boxes.

7.4 SORTING AND SEARCHING

A **sort** is an algorithm for ordering an array. Of the many different techniques for sorting an array, we discuss two, the **bubble sort** and the **Shell sort**. Both sorts require the interchange of values stored in a pair of variables. If *var1*, *var2*, and *temp* are all variables of the same type (that is, all numeric or all string), then the statements

```
Let temp = var1
Let var1 = var2
Let var2 = temp
```

assign *var1*'s value to *var2*, and *var2*'s value to *var1*.

EXAMPLE 1   Write a program to alphabetize two words supplied in text boxes.

SOLUTION
```
Sub Command1_Click ()
    Dim firstWord As String, secondWord As String, temp As String
    Rem Alphabetize two words
    Let firstWord = Text1.Text
    Let secondWord = Text2.Text
    If firstWord > secondWord Then
        Let temp = firstWord
        Let firstWord = secondWord
        Let secondWord = temp
    End If
    Picture1.Cls
    Picture1.Print firstWord; " before "; secondWord
End Sub
```

[Run, type the text shown below into the text boxes, and click the command button.]

Bubble Sort

The bubble sort is an algorithm that compares adjacent items and swaps those that are out of order. If this process is repeated enough times, the list will be ordered. Let's carry out this process on the list Pebbles, Barney, Wilma, Fred, Dino. The steps for each pass through the list are as follows:

1. Compare the first and second items. If they are out of order, swap them.

2. Compare the second and third items. If they are out of order, swap them.

3. Repeat this pattern for all remaining pairs. The final comparison and possible swap is between the second-to-last and last elements.

The first time through the list, this process is repeated to the end of the list. This is called the first pass. After the first pass, the last item (Wilma) will be in its proper position. Therefore, the second pass does not have to consider it and so requires one less comparison. At the end of the second pass, the last two items will be in their proper position. (The items that must have reached their proper position have been underlined.) Each successive pass requires one less comparison. After four passes, the last four items will be in their proper positions and, hence, the first will be also.

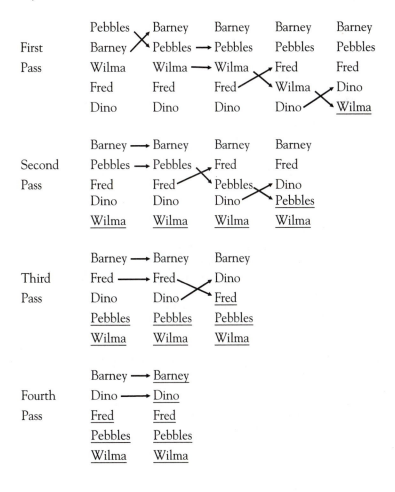

EXAMPLE 2 Write a program to alphabetize the names Pebbles, Barney, Wilma, Fred, Dino.

SOLUTION Sorting the list requires a pair of nested loops. The inner loop performs a single pass and the outer loop controls the number of passes.

```
Dim nom(1 To 5) As String

Sub Command1_Click ()
  Dim passNum As Integer, i As Integer, temp As String
  Rem Bubble sort names
  For passNum = 1 To 4     'Number of passes is 1 less than number of items
    For i = 1 To 5 - passNum            'Each pass needs 1 less comparison
      If nom(i) > nom(i + 1) Then
          Let temp = nom(i)
          Let nom(i) = nom(i + 1)
          Let nom(i + 1) = temp
      End If
    Next i
  Next passNum
  Rem Display alphabetized list
  Picture1.Cls
  For i = 1 To 5
    Picture1.Print nom(i),
  Next i
End Sub

Sub Form_Load ()
  Rem Fill array with names
  Let nom(1) = "Pebbles"
  Let nom(2) = "Barney"
  Let nom(3) = "Wilma"
  Let nom(4) = "Fred"
  Let nom(5) = "Dino"
End Sub
```

[Run and click the command button.]

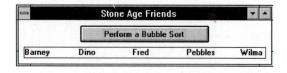

EXAMPLE 3 Table 7.5 contains facts about the ten most populous metropolitan areas with listings in ascending order by city name. Sort the table in descending order by population.

Metro Area	Population in Millions	Median Income per Household	% Native to State	% Advanced Degree
Boston	4.2	$40,666	73	12
Chicago	8.1	$35,918	73	8
Dallas	3.9	$32,825	64	8
Detroit	4.7	$34,729	76	7
Houston	3.7	$31,488	67	8
Los Angeles	14.5	$36,711	59	8
New York	18.1	$38,445	73	11
Philadelphia	5.9	$35,797	70	8
San Francisco	6.3	$41,459	60	11
Washington	3.9	$47,254	32	17

Note: Column 4 gives the percentage of residents who were born in their current state of residence. Column 5 gives the percentage of residents age 25 or older with a graduate or professional degree.

Table 7.5 The ten most populous metropolitan areas.

Source: The 1990 Census

SOLUTION   Data are read from a file into parallel arrays by the Form_Load event procedure. When Command1 is clicked, the collection of parallel arrays is sorted based on the array *pop*( ). Each time two items are interchanged in the array *pop*( ), the corresponding items are interchanged in each of the other arrays. This way, for each city, the items of information remain linked by a common subscript.

```
Dim city(1 To 10) As String,pop(1 To 10) As Single,income(1 To 10) As Single
Dim natives(1 To 10) As Single, advDeg(1 To 10) As Single

Sub Command1_Click ()
  Call SortData
  Call ShowData
End Sub

Sub Form_Load ()
  Dim i As Integer
  Rem Assume the data for city name, population, medium income, % native,
  Rem and % advanced degree have been placed in the file "CITYSTAT.TXT"
  Rem (First line of file is "Boston", 4.2, 4066, 73, 12)
  Open "CITYSTAT.TXT" For Input As #1
  For i = 1 To 10
    Input #1, city(i), pop(i), income(i), natives(i), advDeg(i)
  Next i
  Close #1
End Sub

Sub ShowData ()
  Dim i As Integer
  Rem Display ordered table
  Picture1.Cls
  Picture1.Print , "Pop. in", "Med. income", "% Native", "% Advanced"
  Picture1.Print "Metro Area", "millions", "per hsd", "to State", "Degree"
  Picture1.Print
```

```
    For i = 1 To 10
      Picture1.Print city(i); Tab(16); pop(i), income(i), natives(i), advDeg(i)
    Next i
End Sub

Sub SortData ()
  Dim passNum As Integer, index As Integer
  Rem Bubble sort table in descending order by population
  For passNum = 1 To 9
    For index = 1 To 10 - passNum
      If pop(index) < pop(index + 1) Then
          Call SwapData(index)
      End If
    Next index
  Next passNum
End Sub

Sub SwapData (index As Integer)
  Rem Swap entries
  Call SwapStr(city(index), city(index + 1))
  Call SwapNum(pop(index), pop(index + 1))
  Call SwapNum(income(index), income(index + 1))
  Call SwapNum(natives(index), natives(index + 1))
  Call SwapNum(advDeg(index), advDeg(index + 1))
End Sub

Sub SwapNum (a As Single, b As Single)
  Dim temp As Single
  Rem Interchange values of a and b
  Let temp = a
  Let a = b
  Let b = temp
End Sub

Sub SwapStr (a As String, b As String)
  Dim temp As String
  Rem Interchange values of a and b
  Let temp = a
  Let a = b
  Let b = temp
End Sub
```

[Run and click the command button.]

Metro Area	Pop. in millions	Med. income per hsd	% Native to State	% Advanced Degree
New York	18.1	38445	73	11
Los Angeles	14.5	36711	59	8
Chicago	8.1	35918	73	8
San Francisco	6.3	41459	60	11
Philadelphia	5.9	35797	70	8
Detroit	4.7	34729	76	7
Boston	4.2	40666	73	12
Dallas	3.9	32825	64	8
Washington	3.9	47254	32	17
Houston	3.7	31488	67	8

Display Statistics on 10 Most Populous Metropolitan Areas (Metropolitan Statistics window)

Shell Sort

The bubble sort is easy to understand and program. However, it is too slow for really long lists. The Shell sort, named for its inventor, Donald L. Shell, is much more efficient in such cases. It compares distant items first and works its way down to nearby items. The interval separating the compared items is called the **gap**. The gap begins at one-half the length of the list and is successively halved until eventually each item is compared with its neighbor as in the bubble sort. The algorithm for a list of n items is as follows.

1. Begin with a gap of $g = \text{Int}(n / 2)$.

2. Compare items 1 and $1 + g$, 2 and $2 + g$, . . . , $n - g$ and n. Swap any pairs that are out of order.

3. Repeat step 2 until no swaps are made for gap g.

4. Halve the value of g.

5. Repeat steps 2, 3, and 4 until the value of g is 0.

The Shell sort is illustrated below. Crossing arrows indicate that a swap occurred.

Initial Gap = Int([Number of Items] / 2) = Int(5 / 2) = 2

First Pass

Pebbles → Pebbles	Pebbles	Pebbles
Barney	Barney → Barney	Barney
Wilma → Wilma	Wilma	Dino
Fred	Fred → Fred	Fred
Dino	Dino	Dino	Wilma

Since there was a swap, use the same gap for the second pass.

Second Pass

Pebbles	Dino	Dino	Dino
Barney	Barney → Barney	Barney
Dino	Pebbles	Pebbles → Pebbles
Fred	Fred → Fred	Fred
Wilma	Wilma	Wilma → Wilma

Again, there was a swap, so keep the current gap.

Third Pass

Dino → Dino	Dino	Dino
Barney	Barney → Barney	Barney
Pebbles → Pebbles	Pebbles → Pebbles
Fred	Fred → Fred	Fred
Wilma	Wilma	Wilma → Wilma

There were no swaps for the current gap of 2 so,

Next Gap = Int([Previous Gap] / 2) = Int(2 / 2) = 1

Fourth
Pass

Dino	Barney	Barney	Barney	Barney
Barney	Dino →	Dino	Dino	Dino
Pebbles	Pebbles →	Pebbles	Fred	Fred
Fred	Fred	Fred	Pebbles →	Pebbles
Wilma	Wilma	Wilma	Wilma →	Wilma

Since there was a swap (actually two swaps), keep the same gap.

Fifth
Pass

Barney →	Barney	Barney	Barney	Barney
Dino →	Dino →	Dino	Dino	Dino
Fred	Fred →	Fred →	Fred	Fred
Pebbles	Pebbles	Pebbles →	Pebbles →	Pebbles
Wilma	Wilma	Wilma	Wilma →	Wilma

Since there were no swaps for the current gap, then

Next Gap = Int([Previous Gap] / 2) = Int(1 / 2) = 0

and the Shell sort is complete.

Notice that the Shell sort required 14 comparisons to sort the list whereas the bubble sort required only 10 comparisons for the same list. This illustrates the fact that for very short lists, the bubble sort is preferable; however, for lists of 30 items or more, the Shell sort will consistently outperform the bubble sort. Table 7.6 shows the average number of comparisons required to sort arrays of varying sizes.

Array Elements	Bubble Sort Comparisons	Shell Sort Comparisons
5	10	15
10	45	57
15	105	115
20	190	192
25	300	302
30	435	364
50	1225	926
100	4950	2638
500	124,750	22,517
1000	499,500	58,460

Table 7.6 Efficiency of bubble and Shell sorts.

EXAMPLE 4   Use the Shell sort to alphabetize the parts of a running shoe (see Figure 7.9).

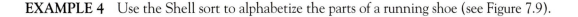

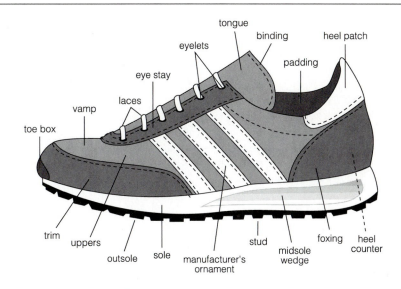

Figure 7.9 Running shoe.

SOLUTION   In the following program, the data are read into an array that has been dimensioned so as to guarantee more than enough space. In the event procedure Form_Load, the variable *numParts* provides the subscripts for the array and serves as a counter. The final value of *numParts* is available to all subprograms since the variable was created in the (declarations) section of (general). The subprogram SortData uses a flag to indicate if a swap has been made during a pass.

```
Dim part(1 To 50) As String
Dim numParts As Integer

Sub Command1_Click ()
  Rem Sort and display parts of running shoe
  Call SortData
  Call ShowData
End Sub

Sub Form_Load ()
  Rem Read part names
  Let numParts = 0      'Number of parts
  Open "SHOEPART.TXT" For Input As #1
  Do While (Not EOF(1)) And (numParts < UBound(part))
    Let numParts = numParts + 1
    Input #1, part(numParts)
  Loop
  Close #1
End Sub

Sub ShowData ()
  Dim i As Integer
  Rem Display sorted list of parts
  Picture1.Cls
```

```
    For i = 1 To numParts
      Picture1.Print part(i),
      If i Mod 5 = 0 Then   'only put 5 items per line
          Picture1.Print
      End If
    Next i
End Sub

Sub SortData ()
  Dim gap As Integer, doneFlag As Integer
  Dim index  As Integer, temp As String
  Rem Shell sort shoe parts
  Let gap = Int(numParts / 2)
  Do While gap >= 1
    Do
      Let doneFlag = 1
      For index = 1 To numParts - gap
        If part(index) > part(index + gap) Then
            Let temp = part(index)
            Let part(index) = part(index + gap)
            Let part(index + gap) = temp
            Let doneFlag = 0
        End If
      Next index
    Loop Until doneFlag = 1
    Let gap = Int(gap / 2)          'Halve the length of the gap
  Loop
End Sub
```

[Run and click the command button.]

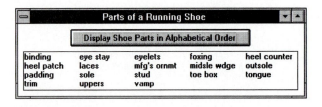

Searching

Suppose we had an array of 1000 names in alphabetical order and wanted to
locate a specific person in the list. One approach would be to start with the first
name and consider each name until a match was found. This process is called a
sequential search. We would find a person whose name begins with "A" rather
quickly, but 1000 comparisons might be necessary to find a person whose name
begins with "Z." For much longer lists, searching could be a time-consuming
matter. However, when the list has already been sorted into either ascending or
descending order, there is a method, called a **binary search**, that shortens the
task considerably.

Let us refer to the sought item as *quarry*. The binary search looks for *quarry*
by determining in which half of the list it lies. The other half is then discarded
and the retained half is temporarily regarded as the entire list. The process is
repeated until the item is found. A flag can indicate if *quarry* has been found.

The algorithm for a binary search of an ascending list is as follows (Figure 7.10 contains the flowchart for a binary search):

1. At each stage, denote the subscript of the first item in the retained list by *first* and the subscript of the last item by *last*. Initially, the value of *first* is 1, the value of *last* is the number of items in the list, and the value of *flag* is 0.

2. Look at the middle item of the current list, the item having the subscript *middle* = Int((*first* + *last*) / 2).

3. If the middle item is *quarry*, then *flag* is set to 1 and the search is over.

4. If the middle item is greater than *quarry*, then *quarry* should be in the first half of the list. So the subscript of *quarry* must lie between *first* and *middle* – 1. That is, the new value of *last* is *middle* – 1.

5. If the middle item is less than *quarry*, then *quarry* should be in the second half of the list of possible items. So the subscript of *quarry* must lie between *middle* + 1 and *last*. That is, the new value of *first* is *middle* + 1.

6. Repeat steps 2 through 5 until *quarry* is found or until the halving process uses up the entire list. (When the entire list has been used up, *first* > *last*.) In the second case, *quarry* was not in the original list.

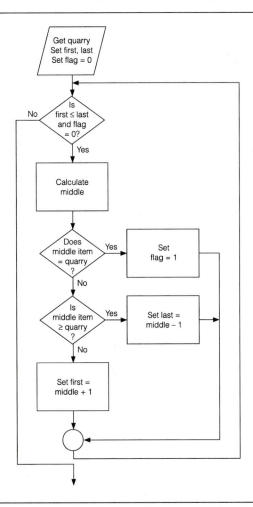

Figure 7.10 Flowchart for a binary search.

EXAMPLE 5   Assume the array *firm*( ) contains the alphabetized names of 100 corporations. Write a program that requests the name of a corporation as input and uses a binary search to determine whether or not the corporation is in the array.

SOLUTION

```
Dim firm(100) As String
Dim numFirms As Integer

Sub BinarySearch (corp As String, result As String)
  Dim foundFlag As Integer
  Dim first As Integer, middle As Integer, last As Integer
  Rem Array firm() assumed already ordered alphabetically
  Rem Binary search of firm() for corp
  Let foundFlag = 0                    '1 indicates corp found
  Let first = 1
  Let last = numFirms
  Do While (first <= last) And (foundFlag = 0)
    Let middle = Int((first + last) / 2)
    Select Case UCase$(firm(middle))
      Case corp
        Let foundFlag = 1
      Case Is > corp
        Let last = middle - 1
      Case Is < corp
        Let first = middle + 1
    End Select
  Loop
  If foundFlag = 1 Then
      Let result = "found"
    Else
      Let result = "not found"
  End If
End Sub

Sub Command1_Click ()
  Dim corp As String, result As String
  Let corp = UCase$(Trim$(Text1.Text))
  Call BinarySearch(corp, result)
  Rem Display results of search
  Picture1.Cls
  Picture1.Print corp; " "; result
End Sub

Sub Form_Load ()
  Rem Fill array with data from FIRMS.TXT
  Open "FIRMS.TXT" For Input As #1
  Let numFirms = 0
  Do While (Not EOF(1)) And (numFirms < UBound(firm))
    Let numFirms = numFirms + 1
    Input #1, firm(numFirms)
  Loop
End Sub
```

[Run, type IBM into the text box, and click the command button.]

Suppose the corporation input in Example 5 is in the second half of the array. On the first pass, *middle* would be assigned Int((1 + 100)/2) = Int(50.5) = 50 and then *first* would be altered to 50 + 1 = 51. On the second pass, *middle* would be assigned Int((51 + 100))/2 = Int(75.5) = 75. If the corporation is not the array element with subscript 75, then either *last* would be assigned 74 or *first* would be assigned 76 depending upon whether the corporation appears before or after the 75th element. Each pass through the loop halves the range of subscripts containing the corporation until the corporation is located.

In Example 5, the binary search merely reported whether or not an array contained a certain item. After finding the item, its array subscript was not needed. However, if related data are stored in parallel arrays (as in Table 7.5), the subscript of the found item can be used to retrieve the related information in the other arrays. This process, called a **table lookup**, is used in the following example.

EXAMPLE 6   Use a binary search procedure to locate the data for a city from Example 3 requested by the user.

SOLUTION   The program below does not include a sort of the data file CITYSTAT.TXT since the file is already ordered alphabetically.

```
Dim city(1 To 10) As String,pop(1 To 10) As Single,income(1 To 10) As Single
Dim natives(1 To 10) As Single, advDeg(1 To 10) As Single

Sub Command1_Click ()
  Dim searchCity As String, result As Integer
  Rem Search for city in the metropolitan areas table
  Call GetCityName(searchCity)
  Call FindCity(searchCity, result)
  Picture1.Cls
  If result > 0 Then
      Call ShowData(result)
    Else
      Picture1.Print searchCity + " not in file"
  End If
End Sub

Sub FindCity (searchCity As String, result As Integer)
  Dim first As Integer, middle As Integer, last As Integer
  Dim foundFlag As Integer
  Rem Binary search table for city name
  Let first = 1
  Let last = 10
```

```
      Do While (first <= last) And (foundFlag = 0)
        Let middle = Int((first + last) / 2)
        Select Case UCase$(city(middle))
          Case searchCity
            Let foundFlag = 1
          Case Is > searchCity
            Let last = middle - 1
          Case Is < searchCity
            Let first = middle + 1
        End Select
      Loop
      If foundFlag = 1 Then
          Let result = middle
        Else
          Let result = 0
      End If
  End Sub


  Sub Form_Load ()
    Dim i As Integer
    Rem Assume that the data for city name, population, medium income, % native,
    Rem and % advanced degree have been placed in the file "CITYSTAT.TXT"
    Rem (First line of file is "Boston", 4.2, 4066, 73, 12)
    Open "CITYSTAT.TXT" For Input As #1
    For i = 1 To 10
      Input #1, city(i), pop(i), income(i), natives(i), advDeg(i)
    Next i
    Close #1
  End Sub


  Sub GetCityName (searchCity As String)
    Rem Request name of city as input
    Let searchCity = UCase$(Trim$(Text1.Text))
  End Sub


  Sub ShowData (index As Integer)
    Rem Display city and associated information
    Picture1.Print , "Pop. in", "Med. income", "% Native", "% Advanced"
    Picture1.Print "Metro Area", "millions", "per hsd", "to State", "Degree"
    Picture1.Print
    Picture1.Print city(index), pop(index), income(index),
    Picture1.Print natives(index), advDeg(index)
  End Sub
```

[Run, type San Francisco into the text box, and click the command button.]

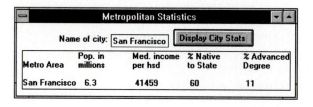

Comments:

1. Suppose our bubble sort algorithm is applied to an ordered list. The algorithm will still make $n - 1$ passes through the list. The process could be shortened for some lists by flagging the presence of out-of-order items as in the Shell sort. It may be preferable not to use a flag since for greatly disordered lists, the flag would slow down an already sluggish algorithm.

2. In Example 3, parallel arrays already ordered by one field were sorted by another field. Usually, parallel arrays are sorted by the field to be searched when accessing the file. This field is called the **key field**.

3. Suppose an array of 2000 items is searched sequentially; that is, one item after another, in order to locate a specific item. The number of comparisons would vary from 1 to 2000, with an average of 1000. With a binary search, the number of comparisons would be at most 11, since $2^{11} > 2000$.

4. The built-in function UCase$ converts all the characters in a string to uppercase. UCase$ is useful in sorting and searching arrays when the alphabetic case (upper or lower) is unimportant. For instance, Examples 5 includes UCase$ in the Select Case comparisons, and so the binary search will locate "Mobil" in the array even if the user entered "MOBIL".

5. The Visual Basic function Timer can be used to determine the speed of a sort. Precede the sort with the statement Let t = Timer. After the sort has executed, the statement Picture1.Print Timer – t will display the duration of the sort in seconds.

PRACTICE PROBLEMS 7.4

1. The pseudocode for a bubble sort of an array of *n* items is given below. Why is the terminating value of the outer loop $n - 1$ and the terminating value of the inner loop $n - j$?

```
For j = 1 To n - 1
  For k = 1 To n - j
    If [kth and (k+1)st items are out of order] Then [interchange them]
  Next k
Next j
```

2. Complete the table by filling in the values of each variable after successive passes of a binary search of a list of 20 items, where the sought item is in the 13th position.

First	Last	Middle
1	20	10
11	20	

EXERCISES 7.4

In Exercises 1 through 4, determine the output displayed in the picture box when the command button is clicked.

1.
```
Sub Command1_Click ()
    Dim p As Integer, q As Integer, temp As Integer
    Let p = 100
    Let q = 200
    Let temp = p
    Let p = q
    Let q = temp
    Picture1.Print p; q
End Sub
```

2.
```
Dim gag(1 To 2) As String

Sub Command1_Click ()
    If gag(2) < gag(1) Then
        Let temp = gag(2)
        Let gag(2) = gag(1)
        Let gag(1) = temp
    End If
    Picture1.Print gag(1), gag(2)
End Sub

Sub Form_Load ()
    Open "DATA.TXT" For Input As #1
    Input #1, gag(1), gag(2)
    Close #1
End Sub
```

(Assume that the file DATA.TXT contains the following entries.)

"Stan", "Oliver"

3.
```
Sub Command1_Click ()
    Dim x As Single, y As Single, temp As Single
    Dim swappedFlag As Integer
    Open "DATA.TXT" For Input As #1
    Input #1, x, y
    Close #1
    Let swappedFlag = 0
    If y > x Then
        Let temp = x
        Let x = y
        Let y = temp
        Let swappedFlag = 1
    End If
    Print x; y;
    If swappedFlag = 1 Then
        Picture1.Print "Numbers interchanged."
    End If
End Sub
```

(Assume that the file DATA.TXT contains the following entries.)

7, 11

4. `Dim a(1 To 3) As Integer`

```
Sub Command1_Click ()
  Dim j As Integer, k As Integer, temp As Integer
  For j = 1 To 2
    For k = 1 To 3 - j
      If a(k) > a(k + 1) Then
          Let temp = a(k)
          Let a(k) = a(k + 1)
          Let a(k + 1) = temp
      End If
    Next k
  Next j
  For j = 1 To 3
    Picture1.Print a(j);
  Next j
End Sub

Sub Form_Load ()
  Dim j As Integer
  Open "DATA.TXT" For Input As #1
  For j = 1 To 3
    Input #1, a(j)
  Next j
  Close #1
End Sub
```

(Assume that the file DATA.TXT contains the following entries.)

7, 4, 3

In Exercises 5 and 6, identify the errors.

5. `Dim c(1 To 4) As Integer, d(1 To 4) As String`

```
Sub Command1_Click ()
  Dim temp As Integer
  Let temp = c(4)
  Let c(4) = d(4)
  Let d(4) = temp
End Sub

Sub Form_Load ()
  Dim i As Integer
  Open "DATA.TXT" For Input As #1
  For i = 1 To 4
    Input #1, c(i), d(i)
  Next i
  Close #1
End Sub
```

(Assume that the file DATA.TXT contains the following entries.)

1, 2, 3, 4, 5, 6, 7, 8

6. `Dim a(1 To 3) As Integer, b(1 To 3) As Integer`

```
Sub Command1_Click ()
  ReDim temp(1 To 3) As Integer
  Let temp() = a()
  Let a() = b()
  Let b() = temp()
End Sub

Sub Form_Load ()
  Dim i As Integer
  Open "DATA.TXT" For Input As #1
  For i = 1 To 3
    Input #1, a(i), b(i)
  Next i
  Close #1
End Sub
```

(Assume that the file DATA.TXT contains the following entries.)

1, 3, 5, 7, 9, 11

7. Which type of search would be best for the array shown below?

1	2	3	4	5
Paul	Ringo	John	George	Pete

8. Which type of search would be best for the array shown below?

1	2	3	4	5
Beloit	Green Bay	Madison	Milwaukee	Oshkosh

9. Consider the items Tin Man, Dorothy, Scarecrow, and Lion, in that order. After how many swaps in a bubble sort will the list be in alphabetical order?

10. How many comparisons will be made in a bubble sort of six items?

11. How many comparisons will be made in a bubble sort of n items?

12. Modify the program in Example 2 so that it will keep track of the number of swaps and comparisons and display these numbers before ending.

13. Rework Exercise 9 using the Shell sort.

14. How many comparisons would be made in a Shell sort of six items if the items were originally in descending order and were sorted in ascending order?

15. If a list of six items is already in the proper order, how many comparisons will be made by a Shell sort?

16. The following subprogram fills an array of 200 integers with values between 0 and 63 that are in need of sorting. Write a program that uses the subprogram and sorts the array *nums( )* with a bubble sort. Run the program and time the execution. Do the same for the Shell sort.

```
Sub FillArray (nums() As Integer)
  Rem Generate numbers from 0 to 63 and place in array
  Let nums(1) = 5
  For i = 2 To 200
    Let nums(i) = (9 * nums(i - 1) + 7) Mod 64
  Next i
End Sub
```

17. Suppose a list of 5000 numbers is to be sorted, but the numbers consist of only 1, 2, 3, and 4. Describe a method of sorting the list that would be much faster than either the bubble or Shell sort.

18. The bubble sort gets its name from the fact that in an ascending sort successive passes cause "lighter" items to rise to the top like bubbles in water. How did the Shell sort get its name?

19. What is the maximum number of comparisons required to find an item in a sequential search of 16 items? What is the average number of comparisons? What is the maximum number of comparisons required to find an item in a binary search of 16 items?

20. Redo Exercise 19 with 2^n items, where n is any positive integer.

In Exercises 21 through 32, write a short program (or procedure) to complete the stated task.

21. Exchange the values of the variables x, y, and z so that x has y's value, y has z's value, and z has x's value.

22. Display the names of the seven dwarfs in alphabetical order. For the contents of a data file use

    Doc, Grumpy, Sleepy, Happy, Bashful, Sneezy, Dopey

23. Table 7.7 lists the top 10 most attended exhibits in the history of the National Gallery of Art. Read the data into a pair of parallel arrays and display a similar table with the exhibit names in alphabetical order.

Exhibit	Attendance (in thousands)
Rodin Rediscovered	1053
Treasure Houses of Britain	999
Treasures of Tutankhamen	836
Chinese Archaeology	684
Ansel Adams	652
Splendor of Dresden	617
Wyeth's Helga Pictures	558
Post-Impressionism	558
Matisse in Nice	537
John Hay Whitney Collection	513

Table 7.7 National Gallery of Art's greatest hits.

24. Table 7.8 presents statistics on the five leading athletic footwear brands. Read the data into three parallel arrays and display a similar table with sales in descending order.

Brand	Sales ($ millions)	Ad Spending ($ millions)
Converse	400	22
Keds	690	11
L.A. Gear	984	24
Nike	3386	120
Reebok	2672	78

Table 7.8 Leading athletic footwear brands.
Source: The 1994 Information Please Business Almanac

25. Accept 10 words to be input in alphabetical order and store them in an array. Then accept an 11th word as input and store it in the array in its correct alphabetical position.

26. An airline has a list of 200 flight numbers in an ascending ordered array. Accept a number as input and do a binary search of the list to determine if the flight number is valid.

27. Modify the program in Exercise 16 to compute and display the number of times each of the numbers from 0 through 63 appears.

28. Allow a number *n* to be input by the user. Then accept as input a list of *n* numbers. Place the numbers into an array and apply a bubble sort.

29. Write a program that accepts a word as input and converts it into Morse code. The dots and dashes corresponding to each letter of the alphabet are as follows:

A ._	H	O _ _ _	V ..._
B _...	I ..	P ._ _.	W ._ _
C _._.	J ._ _ _	Q _ _._	X _.._
D _..	K _._	R ._.	Y _._ _
E .	L ._..	S ...	Z _ _ ..
F .._.	M _ _	T _	
G _ _.	N _.	U .._	

30. Write a program that accepts an American word as input and performs a binary search to translate it into its British equivalent. Use the following list of words for data and account for the case when the word requested is not in the list.

American	British	American	British
attic	loft	ice cream	ice
business suit	lounge suit	megaphone	loud hailer
elevator	lift	radio	wireless
flashlight	torch	sneakers	plimsolls
french fries	chips	truck	lorry
gasoline	petrol	zero	nought

31. Write a program that accepts a student's name and seven test scores as input and calculates the average score after dropping the two lowest grades.

32. Suppose letter grades are assigned as follows:

97 and above	A+	74–76	C
94–96	A	70–73	C–
90–93	A–	67–69	D+
87–89	B+	64–66	D
84–86	B	60–63	D–
80–83	B–	0–59	F
77–79	C+		

Write a program that accepts a grade as input and displays the corresponding letter. **Hint:** This problem shows that when you search an array, you don't always look for equality. Set up an array *range*( ) containing the values 97, 94, 90, 87, 84, . . . , 59 and the parallel array *letter*( ) containing A+, A, A–, B+, . . . , F. Next, perform a sequential search to find the first i such that *range*(i) is less than or equal to the input grade.

33. The *median* of a set of n measurements is a number such that half the n measurements fall below the median and half fall above. If the number of measurements n is odd, the median is the middle number when the measurements are arranged in ascending or descending order. If the number of measurements n is even, the median is the average of the two middle measurements when the measurements are arranged in ascending or descending order. Write a program that requests a number n and a set of n measurements as input and then displays the median.

34. Write a program with two command buttons labeled Ascending Order and Descending Order that displays the eight vegetables in V8 in either ascending or descending alphabetic order. The vegetables (tomato, carrot, celery, beet, parsley, lettuce, watercress, and spinach) should be stored in a form-level array.

SOLUTIONS TO PRACTICE PROBLEMS 7.4

1. The outer loop controls the number of passes, one less than the number of items in the list. The inner loop performs a single pass, and the jth pass consists of $n - j$ comparisons.

2.

First	Last	Middle
1	20	10
11	20	15
11	14	12
13	14	13

7.5 TWO-DIMENSIONAL ARRAYS

Each array discussed so far held a single list of items. Such array variables are called **single-subscripted variables**. An array can also hold the contents of a table with several rows and columns. Such arrays are called **two-dimensional arrays** or **double-subscripted variables**. Two tables are shown below. Table 7.9 gives the road mileage between certain cities. It has four rows and four columns. Table 7.10 shows the leading universities in three disciplines. It has three rows and five columns.

	Chicago	Los Angeles	New York	Philadelphia
Chicago	0	2054	802	738
Los Angeles	2054	0	2786	2706
New York	802	2786	0	100
Philadelphia	738	2706	100	0

Table 7.9 Road mileage between selected U.S. cities.

	1	2	3	4	5
Business	U of PA	MIT	U of IN	U of MI	UC Berk
Comp Sc.	MIT	Cng-Mellon	UC Berk	Cornell	U of IL
Engr/Gen.	UCLA	U of IL	U of MD	U of OK	Stevens I.T.

Table 7.10 University rankings.

Source: A Rating of Undergraduate Programs in American and International Universities, Dr. Jack Gourman, 1993

Two-dimensional array variables store the contents of tables. They have the same types of names as other array variables. The only difference is that they have two subscripts, each with its own range. The range of the first subscript is determined by the number of rows in the table, and the range of the second subscript is determined by the number of columns. The statement

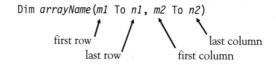

```
Dim arrayName(m1 To n1, m2 To n2)
```
first row   last column
        last row   first column

placed in the (declarations) section of (general), dimensions an array corresponding to a table with rows labeled from *m1* To *n1* and columns labeled from *m2* To *n2*. The entry in the *j*th row, *k*th column is *arrayName*(*j,k*). For instance, the data in Table 7.9 can be stored in an array named *rm*( ). The statement

```
Dim rm(1 To 4, 1 To 4)
```

will dimension the array. Each element of the array has the form *rm*(*row, column*). The entries of the array are

rm(1,1)=0	rm(1,2)=2054	rm(1,3)=802	rm(1,4)=738
rm(2,1)=2054	rm(2,2)=0	rm(2,3)=2786	rm(2,4)=2706
rm(3,1)=802	rm(3,2)=2786	rm(3,3)=0	rm(3,4)=100
rm(4,1)=738	rm(4,2)=2706	rm(4,3)=100	rm(4,4)=0

As with one-dimensional arrays, when a two-dimensional array is created using Dim in the (declarations) section of (general), the array becomes a form-level subscripted variable, and is therefore accessible in all event procedures and general procedures and retains whatever values are assigned until the program is terminated. Two-dimensional arrays also can be created that are local to a procedure and cease to exist once the procedure is exited. The proper statement to use within a procedure to create such an array is

```
ReDim arrayName(m1 To n1, m2 To n2)
```

The data in Table 7.10 can be stored in a two-dimensional string array named *univ*( ). The statement

```
Dim univ(1 To 3, 1 To 5) As String
```

will dimension the array as form-level. Some of the entries of the array are

univ(1,1) = "U of PA"
univ(2,3) = "UC Berk"
univ(3,5) = "Stevens I.T."

EXAMPLE 1   Write a program to store and access the data from Table 7.9.

SOLUTION   Data are read from the data file DISTANCE.TXT into a two-dimensional form-level array using a pair of nested loops. The outer loop controls the rows and the inner loop controls the columns.

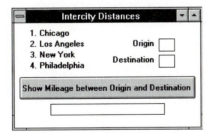

Object	Property	Setting
Form1	Caption	Intercity Distances
Label1	Caption	1. Chicago
Label2	Caption	2. Los Angeles
Label3	Caption	3. New York
Label4	Caption	4. Philadelphia
Label5	Caption	Origin
Text1	Text	(blank)
Label6	Caption	Destination
Text2	Text	(blank)
Command1	Caption	Show Mileage between Origin and Destination

Picture1

```
Dim rm(1 To 4, 1 To 4) As Single  'In (declarations) section of (general)

Sub Command1_Click ()
  Dim row As Integer, col As Integer
  Rem Determine road mileage between cities
  Let row = Val(Text1.Text)
  Let col = Val(Text2.Text)
```

```
      If (row >= 1 And row <= 4) And (col >= 1 And col <= 4) Then
          Call ShowMileage(rm(), row, col)
        Else
          MsgBox "Origin and Destination must be numbers from 1 to 4", , "Error"
      End If
      Text1.SetFocus
  End Sub

  Sub Form_Load ()
    Dim row As Integer, col As Integer
    Rem Fill two-dimensional array with intercity mileages
    Rem Assume the data has been placed in the file "DISTANCE.TXT"
    Rem (First line of the file is 0,2054,802,738)
    Open "DISTANCE.TXT" For Input As #1
    For row = 1 To 4
      For col = 1 To 4
        Input #1, rm(row, col)
      Next col
    Next row
    Close #1
  End Sub

  Sub ShowMileage (rm() As Single, row As Integer, col As Integer)
    Rem Display mileage between cities
    Picture1.Cls
    Picture1.Print "The road mileage is"; rm(row, col)
  End Sub
```

[Run, type 3 into the Origin box, type 1 into the Destination box, and click the command button.]

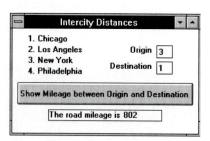

So far, two-dimensional arrays have only been used to store data for convenient lookup. In the next example, an array is used to make a valuable computation.

EXAMPLE 2   The Center for Science in the Public Interest publishes *The Nutrition Scorebook*, a highly respected rating of foods. The top two foods in each of five categories are shown in Table 7.11 along with some information on their composition. Write a program to compute the nutritional content of a meal. The table should be read into an array and then the program should request the quantities of each food item that is part of the meal. The program should then compute the amounts of each nutritional component consumed by summing each column with each entry weighted by the quantity of the food item.

	Calories	Protein (grams)	Fat (grams)	Vit A (IU)	Calcium (mg)
spinach (1 cup)	23	3	0.3	8100	93
sweet potato (1 med.)	160	2	1	9230	46
yogurt (8 oz.)	230	10	3	120	343
skim milk (1 cup)	85	8	0	500	302
whole wheat bread (1 slice)	65	3	1	0	24
brown rice (1 cup)	178	3.8	0.9	0	18
watermelon (1 wedge)	110	2	1	2510	30
papaya (1 lg.)	156	2.4	0.4	7000	80
tuna in water (1 lb.)	575	126.8	3.6	0	73
lobster (1 med.)	405	28.8	26.6	984	190

Table 7.11 Composition of ten top-rated foods.

SOLUTION   Coding is simplified by using a control array of labels to hold the food names and a control array of text boxes to hold the amount input by the user. In the template below, the label captions have been assigned an initial value of "(food name)" so that the labels can be seen. The five nutrients of interest and the actual names and nutrient values of the foods to be used in building a meal are read from the data file NUTTABLE.TXT.

Object	Property	Setting
Form1	Caption	Nutrition in a Meal
lblFood	Caption	(food name)
	Index	0 – 9
Label2	Caption	Quantity in Meal
txtQnty	Text	(blank)
	Index	0 – 9
Command1	Caption	Analyze Meal Nutrition
Picture1		

```
Dim nutName(1 To 5) As String          'nutrient names
Dim nutTable(1 To 10, 1 To 5) As Single 'nutrient values for each food

Sub Command1_Click ()
  Rem Determine the nutritional content of a meal
  ReDim quantity(1 To 10) As Single 'amount of food in meal
  Call GetAmounts(quantity())
  Call ShowData(quantity())
End Sub

Sub Form_Load ()
  Dim i As Integer, j As Integer, foodName As String
  Rem Fill arrays; assign label captions
  Open "NUTTABLE.TXT" For Input As #1
  For i = 1 To 5
    Input #1, nutName(i)
  Next i
```

```
    For i = 1 To 10
      Input #1, foodName
      Let lblFood(i - 1).Caption = foodName
      For j = 1 To 5
        Input #1, nutTable(i, j)
      Next j
    Next i
    Close #1
End Sub

Sub GetAmounts (quantity() As Single)
  Dim i As Integer
  Rem Obtain quantities of foods consumed
  For i = 1 To 10
    Let quantity(i) = Val(txtQnty(i - 1).Text)
  Next i
End Sub

Sub ShowData (quantity() As Single)
  Dim col As Integer, row As Integer
  Dim amount As Single, nutWid As Single
  Rem Display amount of each component
  Picture1.Cls
  Picture1.Print "This meal contains the"
  Picture1.Print "following quantities"
  Picture1.Print "of these nutritional"
  Picture1.Print "components:"
  Picture1.Print
  For col = 1 To 5
    Let amount = 0
    For row = 1 To 10
      Let amount = amount + quantity(row) * nutTable(row, col)
    Next row
    Picture1.Print nutName(col) + ":"; Tab(16); amount
  Next col
End Sub
```

[Run, type the quantities below into each text box, and click the command button.]

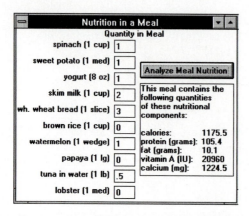

Comments:

1. A two-dimensional array variable created using an "As *varType*" clause can only hold data of the specified type; in particular, it cannot hold string data in some rows/columns and numeric data in other rows/columns.

2. Three- (or higher) dimensional arrays can be defined by statements similar to those used for two-dimensional arrays. A three-dimensional array uses three subscripts, and the assignment of values requires a triple-nested loop. As an example, a meteorologist might use a three-dimensional array to record temperatures for various dates, times, and elevations. The array might be created by the statement

```
Dim temps(1 To 31, 1 To 24, 0 To 14) As Single
```

PRACTICE PROBLEMS 7.5

1. Consider the road mileage program in Example 1. How can the program be modified so the actual names of the cities can be supplied by the user?

2. In what types of problems are two-dimensional arrays superior to parallel arrays?

EXERCISES 7.5

In Exercises 1 through 8, determine the output displayed in the picture box when the command button is clicked. All Dim statements for arrays are in the (declarations) section of (general).

1.
```
Dim a(1 To 20, 1 To 30) As Single

Sub Command1_Click ()
  Let a(3, 5) = 6
  Let a(5, 3) = 2 * a(3, 5)
  Picture1.Print a(5, 3)
End Sub
```

2.
```
Dim years(1 To 100, 1 To 50) As Single

Sub Command1_Click ()
  Dim x As Single, y As Single
  Let x = 7
  Let y = 8
  Let years(x, y) = 1937
  Picture1.Print years(7, 8) + 50
End Sub
```

3.
```
Dim w(1 To 10, 1 To 15) As String

Sub Command1_Click ()
  Dim d As String, n As Integer
  Let d = "Dorothy"
  Let w(1, 1) = d
  Let n = 1
  Picture1.Print w(n, n)
End Sub
```

4. `Dim actor(1 To 5, 1 To 5) As String`

```
Sub Command1_Click ()
  Dim a As Integer, b As Integer, temp As Integer
  Let a = 2
  Let b = 3
  Let actor(a, b) = "Bogart"
  Let temp = a
  Let a = b
  Let b = temp
  Picture1.Print "1. "; actor(a, b)
  Picture1.Print "2. "; actor(b, a)
End Sub
```

5. `Dim a()`

```
Sub Command1_Click ()
  Dim p As Integer, q As Integer
  Dim j As Integer, k As Integer
  Open "DATA.TXT" For Input As #1
  Input #1, p, q
  ReDim a(1 To p, 1 To q) As Single
  For j = 1 To p
    For k = 1 To q
      Input #1, a(j, k)
      Picture1.Print a(j, k);
    Next k
    Picture1.Print
  Next j
  Close #1
End Sub
```

(Assume that the file DATA.TXT contains the following entries.)

2, 3, 4, 1, 6, 5, 8, 2

6. `Dim a(1 To 4, 1 To 5) As Integer`

```
Sub Command1_Click ()
  Dim j As Integer, k As Integer
  For j = 1 To 4
    For k = 1 To 5
      Let a(j, k) = (j - k) * j
      Picture1.Print a(j, k);
    Next k
    Picture1.Print
  Next j
End Sub
```

7. `Dim s(1 To 3, 1 To 3)`

```
Sub Command1_Click ()
  Dim j As Integer, k As Integer
  Open "DATA.TXT" For Input As #1
```

```
     For j = 1 To 3
       For k = 1 To 3
         Input #1, s(j, k)
       Next k
     Next j
     Close #1
     For j = 1 To 3
       Picture1.Print s(j, j);
     Next j
   End Sub
```

(Assume that the file DATA.TXT contains the following entries.)

1, 2, 3, 4, 3, 2, 3, 4, 5

8. `Dim m() As Integer`

```
   Sub Command1_Click ()
     Dim x As Integer, y As Integer
     Dim j As Integer, k As Integer
     Open "DATA.TXT" For Input As #1
     Input #1, x, y
     ReDim m(1 To x, 1 To y) As Integer
     For j = 1 To x
       For k = 1 To y - j
         Input #1, m(j, k)
         Picture1.Print m(j, k) - k;
       Next k
       Picture1.Print
     Next j
     Close #1
   End Sub
```

(Assume that the file DATA.TXT contains the following entries.)

2, 3, 6, 3, 2, 1, 3, 4, 9, 8

In Exercises 9 and 10, identify the errors.

9. `Dim a(1 To 3, 1 To 4) As Integer`

```
   Sub Command1_Click ()
     Dim j As Integer, k As Integer
     Rem Fill an array
     Open "DATA.TXT" For Input As #1
     For j = 1 To 4
       For k = 1 To 3
         Input #1, a(j, k)
       Next k
     Next j
     Close #1
   End Sub
```

(Assume that the file DATA.TXT contains the following entries.)

1, 2, 3, 4, 5, 6, 7, 8, 9, 0, 1, 2

10. ```
Dim score(1 To 3, 1 To 3) As Integer

Sub Form_Load ()
  Dim j As Integer, k As Integer, student As Integer
  Rem Fill array from data file
  Open "SCORES.TXT" For Input As #1
  For j = 1 To 3
    Input #1, student
    For k = 1 To 3
      Input #1, score(k, j)
    Next k
  Next j
End Sub

Sub Command1_Click ()
  Dim student As Integer, exam As Integer
  Rem Report individual scores
  Let student = Val(Text1.Text)
  Let exam = Val(Text2.Text)
  If (student >= 1 And student <= 3) And (exam >= 1 And exam <= 3) Then
    Picture1.Print score(student, exam)
  End If
End Sub
```

(Assume that the file SCORES.TXT contains the following three lines.)

1, 80, 85, 90
2, 72, 80, 88
3, 87, 93, 90

**In Exercises 11 through 14, write a procedure to perform the stated task.**

11. Given an array dimensioned with the statement Dim a(1 To 10, 1 To 10) As Single, set the entries in the jth column to j (for j = 1, ... , 10).

12. Given an array dimensioned with the statement Dim a(1 To 10, 1 To 10) As Single, and values assigned to each entry, compute the sum of the values in the 10th row.

13. Given an array dimensioned with the statement Dim a(1 To 10, 1 To 10) As Single, and values assigned to each entry, interchange the values in the second and third rows.

14. Given an array dimensioned with the statement Dim a(1 To 3, 1 To 45) As Single, and values assigned to each entry, find the greatest value and the locations (possibly more than one) at which it occurs.

**In Exercises 15 through 24, write a program to perform the stated task.**

15. A company has two stores (1 and 2), and each store sells three items (1, 2, and 3). The tables below give the inventory at the beginning of the day and the amount of each item sold during that day.
```

| | Item | | |
Store	1	2	3
1	25	64	23
2	12	82	19

Beginning Inventory

| | Item | | |
Store	1	2	3
1	7	45	11
2	4	24	8

Sales for Day

(a) Record the values of each table in an array.

(b) Adjust the values in the first array to hold the inventories at the end of the day and display these new inventories.

(c) Calculate and display the total number of items in the store at the end of the day.

16. Table 7.12 gives the results of a survey on the uses of computers in the workplace. Each entry shows the percentage of respondents from the educational attainment category that use the computer for the indicated purpose.

(a) Place the data from the table in an array.

(b) Determine the average of the percentages in the Inventory Control column.

Educational Attainment	Word Processing	Book–keeping	Inventory Control	Communi–cations	Databases
Not a high school graduate	17.7	20.0	37.4	13.2	11.7
High school graduate	32.2	27.7	29.7	21.0	20.0
Some college	40.0	28.2	27.3	26.7	27.2
Four years of college	46.5	26.6	22.7	29.8	32.6
More than 4 yrs of college	57.4	22.5	15.9	31.3	37.7

Table 7.12 Computer use on the job by educational attainment, 1989.

Source: U.S. Center of Educational Statistics

17. A university offers ten courses at each of three campuses. The number of students enrolled in each is presented in Table 7.13.

| | | Course | | | | | | | | | |
		1	2	3	4	5	6	7	8	9	10
	1	5	15	22	21	12	25	16	11	17	23
Campus	2	11	23	51	25	32	35	32	52	25	21
	3	2	12	32	32	25	26	29	12	15	11

Table 7.13 Number of students enrolled in courses.

(a) Find the total number of course enrollments on each campus.

(b) Find the total number of students taking each course.

18. Table 7.14 gives the number of stores for 1991 and 1992 for the five leading retail franchises.

(a) Place the data into an array.
(b) Calculate the total change in the number of stores for these five companies.

	1991	1992
1. 7–Eleven	6500	6395
2. True Value	7000	6800
3. Ace Hardware	5200	5200
4. ServiStar	4500	4500
5. Radio Shack	6746	6756

Table 7.14 Number of stores for leading retail franchises.
Source: Stores, May 1993

19. The scores for the top three golfers at the 1992 PGA Championship are shown in Table 7.15.

(a) Place the data into an array.
(b) Compute the total score for each player.
(c) Compute the average score for each round.

	Round			
	1	2	3	4
Nick Price	70	70	68	70
Jim Gallagher, Jr.	72	66	72	70
John Cook	71	72	67	71

Table 7.15 1992 PGA championship leaders.

20. Table 7.16 contains part of the pay schedule for federal employees. Table 7.17 gives the number of employees of each classification in a certain division. Place the data from each table into an array and compute the amount of money this division pays for salaries during the year.

	Step			
	1	2	3	4
GS–1	12,806	13,234	13,659	14,084
GS–2	14,398	14,741	15,219	15,623
GS–3	15,711	16,235	16,760	17,284
GS–4	17,637	18,225	18,812	19,400
GS–5	19,732	20,390	21,049	22,707
GS–6	21,995	22,728	23,461	24,194
GS–7	24,441	25,255	26,069	26,884

Table 7.16 1995 pay schedule for federal white-collar workers.

	1	2	3	4
GS–1	0	0	2	1
GS–2	2	3	0	1
GS–3	4	2	5	7
GS–4	12	13	8	3
GS–5	4	5	0	1
GS–6	6	2	4	3
GS–7	8	1	9	2

Table 7.17 Number of employees in each category.

21. Consider Table 7.10, the rankings of three university departments. Write a program that places the data into an array, allows the name of a college to be input, and gives the categories in which it appears. Of course, a college might appear more than once or not at all.

22. Table 7.18 gives the monthly precipitation for a typical Nebraska city during a five-year period.

	Jan.	Feb.	Mar.	Apr.	May	June	July	Aug.	Sept.	Oct.	Nov.	Dec.
1986	0.88	1.11	2.01	3.64	6.44	5.58	4.23	4.34	4.00	2.05	1.48	0.77
1987	0.76	0.94	2.09	3.29	4.68	3.52	3.52	4.82	3.72	2.21	1.24	0.80
1988	0.67	0.80	1.75	2.70	4.01	3.88	3.72	3.78	3.55	1.88	1.21	0.61
1989	0.82	0.80	1.99	3.05	4.19	4.44	3.98	4.57	3.43	2.32	1.61	0.75
1990	0.72	0.90	1.71	2.02	2.33	2.98	2.65	2.99	2.55	1.99	1.05	0.92

Table 7.18 Monthly precipitation (in inches) for a typical Nebraska city.

Write a program that reads the table from a data file into an array and then displays in a picture box the output shown below.

```
Total precipitation for each year
 1986  36.53
 1987  31.59
 1988  28.56
 1989  31.96
 1990  22.81

Average precipitation for each month
Jan  Feb  Mar  Apr  May  Jun  Jul  Aug  Sep  Oct  Nov  Dec
0.77 0.91 1.91 2.94 4.33 4.08 3.62 4.10 3.50 2.09 1.32 0.77
```

23. Suppose a course has 15 students enrolled and five exams were given during the semester. Write a program that accepts each student's name and grades as input and places the names in a one-dimensional array and the grades in a two-dimensional array. The program should then display each student's name and semester average. Also, the program should display the median for each exam. (For an odd number of grades, the median is the middle grade. For an even number of grades it is the average of the two middle grades.)

24. An n-by-n array is called a magic square if the sums of each row, each column, and each diagonal are equal. Write a program to determine if an array is a magic square and use it to determine if either of the arrays below is a magic square. **Hint**: If at any time one of the sums is not equal to the others, the search is complete.

(a)
1	15	15	4
12	6	7	9
8	10	11	5
13	3	2	16

(b)
11	10	4	23	17
18	12	6	5	24
25	19	13	7	1
2	21	20	14	8
9	3	22	16	15

25. A company has three stores (1, 2, and 3), and each store sells five items (1, 2, 3, 4, and 5). The tables below give the number of items sold by each store and category on a particular day, and the cost of each item.

(a) Place the data from the left-hand table in a two-dimensional array and the data from the right-hand table in a one-dimensional array.

(b) Compute and display the total dollar amount of sales for each store and for the entire company.

			Item				Item	Cost
		1	**2**	**3**	**4**	**5**	1	$12.00
	1	25	64	23	45	14	2	$17.95
Store	2	12	82	19	34	63	3	$95.00
	3	54	22	17	43	35	4	$86.50
							5	$78.00

Number of Items Sold During Day   **Cost per Item**

SOLUTIONS TO PRACTICE PROBLEMS 7.5

1. The function FindCityNum can be used to determine the subscript associated with each city. This function and the modified event procedure Command1_Click are as follows:

```
Function FindCityNum (city As String)
  Select Case UCase$(city)
    Case "CHICAGO"
      FindCityNum = 1
    Case "LOS ANGELES"
      FindCityNum = 2
    Case "NEW YORK"
      FindCityNum = 3
    Case "PHILADELPHIA"
      FindCityNum = 4
    Case Else
      FindCityNum = 0
  End Select
End Function

Sub Command1_Click ()
  Dim orig As String, dest As String
  Dim row As Integer, col As Integer
  Rem Determine road mileage between cities
  Let orig = Text1.Text
  Let dest = Text2.Text
  Let row = FindCityNum(orig)
  Let col = FindCityNum(dest)
  If (row < 1 Or row > 4) Then
      MsgBox "City of origin not available", , "Error"
    ElseIf (col < 1 Or col > 4) Then
      MsgBox "Destination city not available", , "Error"
    Else
      Call ShowMileage(rm(), row, col)
  End If
  Text1.SetFocus
End Sub
```

2. Both parallel arrays and two-dimensional arrays are used to hold related data. If some of the data are numeric and some are string, then parallel arrays must be used since all entries of an array must be of the same type. Parallel arrays should also be used if the data will be sorted. Two-dimensional arrays are best suited to tabular data.

7.6 A CASE STUDY: CALCULATING WITH A SPREADSHEET

Spreadsheets are one of the most popular types of software used on personal computers. A spreadsheet is a financial planning tool in which data are analyzed in a table of rows and columns. Some of the items are entered by the user and other items, often totals and balances, are calculated using the entered data. The outstanding feature of electronic spreadsheets is their ability to recalculate an entire table after changes are made in some of the entered data, thereby allowing the user to determine the financial implications of various alternatives. This is called "What if?" analysis.

The Design of the Program

Figure 7.11 contains an example of a spreadsheet used to analyze a student's financial projections for the four quarters of a year. Column F holds the sum of the entries in columns B through E, rows 6 and 14 hold sums of the entries in rows 3 through 5 and 9 through 13, respectively, and row 16 holds the differences of the entries in rows 6 and 14. Since the total balance is negative, some of the amounts in the spreadsheet must be changed and the totals and balances recalculated.

	A	B Fall	C Winter	D Spring	E Summer	F Total
1		Fall	Winter	Spring	Summer	Total
2	**Income**					
3	Job	1000	1300	1000	2000	5300
4	Parents	200	200	200	0	600
5	Scholarship	150	150	150	0	450
6	**Total**	1350	1650	1350	2000	6350
7						
8	**Expenses**					
9	Tuition	400	0	400	0	800
10	Food	650	650	650	650	2600
11	Rent	600	600	600	400	2200
12	Books	110	0	120	0	230
13	Misc	230	210	300	120	860
14	**Total**	1990	1460	2070	1170	6690
15						
16	**Balance**	–640	190	–720	830	–340

Figure 7.11 Spreadsheet for student's financial projections.

The 96 locations in the spreadsheet that hold information are called **cells**. Each cell is identified by its row number and column letter. For instance, the cell 14, C contains the amount 1460. For programming purposes, each column is identified by a number, starting with 1 for the leftmost column. Thus cell 14, C above will be cell 14, 3 in our program.

This case study develops a program to produce a spreadsheet with the five columns of numbers shown in Figure 7.11, three user-specified categories of income, and five user-specified categories of expenses. The following tasks are to be selected by command buttons:

1. Start a new spreadsheet. All current category names and values are erased and the cursor is placed in the text box of the first income category.

2. Quit.

Three additional tasks need to be performed as the result of other events:

1. Create the spreadsheet when the form is loaded.

2. Limit the user to editing category names and quarterly values.

3. Display totals after a change is made in the spreadsheet.

The User Interface

Each cell in the spreadsheet will be an element of a text box control array. A control array of labels is needed for the numeric labels to the left of each row and another control array of labels for the alphabetic labels at the top of each column. Finally, two command buttons are required. The task of controlling which cells the user can edit will be handled by a GotFocus event. The task of updating the totals will be handled by a LostFocus event. Figure 7.12 shows one possible form design with all control elements loaded. For this application of a spreadsheet, the headings that have been assigned to cells in rows 1, 2, 6, 8, 14, and 16 are fixed; the user will not be allowed to edit them. The other entries in column A, the category names, may be edited by the user, but we have provided the set from Figure 7.11 as the default.

	A	B	C	D	E	F
1		Fall	Winter	Spring	Summer	Total
2	Income					
3	Job					
4	Parents					
5	Scholarship					
6	Total					
7						
8	Expenses					
9	Tuition					
10	Food					
11	Rent					
12	Books					
13	Misc					
14	Total					
15						
16	Balance					

Figure 7.12 Template for spreadsheet.

Since processing the totals for the spreadsheet involves adding up columns and rows of cells, coding is simplified by using a control array of text boxes so that an index in a For...Next loop can step through a set of cells. A two-dimensional array of text boxes seems natural for the spreadsheet. Unfortunately, only a single index is available for control arrays in Visual Basic. However, a single dimensional array of text boxes can be used without much difficulty if we define a function Indx that connects a pair of row (1 to 16) and column (1 to 6) values to a unique index (1 to 96) value. An example of such a rule would be Indx(row,column)=(row−1)*6+column. Successive values of this function are generated by going from left to right across row 1, then left to right across row 2, and so on.

A solution to the spreadsheet problem that uses one control array of text boxes and two control arrays of labels is presented below. The text box control array *txtCell*( ) provides the 96 text boxes needed for the spreadsheet cells. Since the proposed Indx function advances by one as we move from left to right across a row of cells, the cells must be positioned in this order as they are loaded. The label control array *lblRowLab*( ) provides a label for each of the rows of cells, while label control array *lblColLab*( ) provides a label for each column of cells. Figure 7.13 shows the layout of the form at design-time. The properties for the controls are given in Table 7.19. The Height and Width properties given for the text box will assure enough room on the screen for all 96 cells. These dimensions can be obtained by creating a normal size text box, then reducing its width by one set of grid marks and its height by two sets of grid marks.

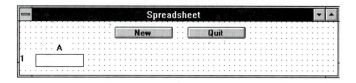

Figure 7.13 Controls at design-time.

Object	Property	Setting
Form1	Caption	Spreadsheet
cmdNew	Caption	New
cmdQuit	Caption	Quit
lblRowLab	Caption	1
	Index	1
lblColLab	Caption	A
	Index	1
txtCell	Text	(blank)
	Index	1
	Height	1095
	Width	285

Table 7.19 Objects and their properties.

Coding the Program

The top row of Figure 7.14 shows the different events to which the program must respond. Table 7.20 identifies the corresponding event procedures and the general procedures they call. Let's examine each event procedure.

1. **Form_Load** assigns the number of rows (16) and columns (6) in our spreadsheet to the form-level variables *maxRow* and *maxCol*. Form_Load then calls three general procedures to create and initialize the spreadsheet.

The procedure CreateSpreadsheet loads each element of the *txtCell( )* control array in order from left to right, top to bottom. Cell 1, which is to be the first cell in the first row, is not loaded since it was created at design time. The Top property of a new cell is set so that the top edge of the new cell overlaps the bottom edge of the previous cell in the column. The Top property of the first cell in a column is not modified, and so the value of the Top property is the same as cell 1. Similarly, the Left property of a new cell is set so that the left edge of the new cell overlaps the right edge of the previous cell in the row. The Left property of the first cell in a row is not modified, and so the value of the Left property is the same as cell 1. CreateSpreadsheet also loads the additional row and column label elements and assigns an appropriate caption. CreateSpreadsheet's final task is to set the Height and Width properties of Form1 to accommodate all the objects that have been loaded. The numbers 500 and 200, which appear in these statements, were obtained by trial and error and are necessary to account for the space used by the form caption and borders.

The procedure SetStructure assigns heading values to various cells of the spreadsheet in accordance with the specific application we were asked to program. The user will not be able to alter the value in these cells, since the rules for which cells are to be totaled, and where these totals are to be placed are "hard wired" into the program and cannot be changed by the user. SetStructure also assigns values to a set of form-level variables so that other procedure in the program can be coded using meaningful names rather than possibly obscure numbers. Besides Form_Load, SetStructure is also called by the cmdNew_Click event procedure.

The procedure SetDefaults assigns the income and expense category headings shown in Figure 7.11 to the appropriate cells. The user may change these headings at any time, and must supply them if the "New" command is issued.

2. **txtCell_GotFocus** checks to see if the cell that has received the focus may, according to the rules of this application, be edited by the user. The row and column numbers for the cell are computed from the cell's index. If the cell that has received the focus is in a column after *stopCol*, the last editable column, then the column to be edited is changed to *startCol*, the first editable column, and the row to be edited is advanced by one. If the row to be edited does not contain any editable cells, then the row to be edited is advanced to the next row containing editable cells. (When the focus goes past the last row of editable cells, the next editable row is the first editable row, that is, *incStartRow*.) Finally, focus is set to the adjusted row and column, but only if an adjustment has been made. If the test Indx(row,col)<>Index were not made and focus were reset to a cell that already had the focus, then the GotFocus event procedure would be invoked again as a result of the Set-Focus, and then again as a result of the SetFocus performed by this invocation of GotFocus, and so on, resulting in an infinite loop.

3. **txtCell_LostFocus** invokes the general procedure DisplayTotals when the cursor leaves one of the spreadsheet cells. DisplayTotals in turn invokes five general procedures that each compute one set of needed totals and display the results by assigning values to appropriate text boxes. TotalIncome adds up the income for each quarter and saves the results in the array *iTot*( ). Similarly, TotalExpenses adds up the expenses for each quarter and saves the results in the array *eTot*( ). ComputeBalances takes the results stored in *iTot*( ) and *eTot*( ) and subtracts them to determine the balance for each quarter. TotalRows adds up the four quarters for each category and assigns the results to the text boxes at the right end of each row. Finally, Determine-GrandTotals adds up the values in *iTot*( ) and *eTot*( ) to determine the values for the right end of the "balance" row and each "total" row.

4. **cmdNew_Click** prepares for the entry of a new spreadsheet by setting the Text property of each element of the control array *txtCell*( ) to the null string and then setting focus to the first cell in the spreadsheet.

5. **cmdQuit_Click** ends the program.

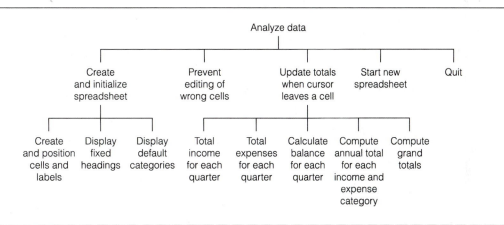

Figure 7.14 Hierarchy chart for spreadsheet program.

1. Create & Initialize spreadsheet	Form_Load
1.1 Create & position cells & labels	CreateSpreadsheet
1.2 Display fixed headings	SetStructure
1.3 Display default categories	SetDefaults
2. Prevent editing of wrong cells	txtCell_GotFocus
3. Update totals when cursor leaves a cell	txtCell_LostFocus (DisplayTotals)
3.1 Total income each quarter	TotalIncome
3.2 Total expenses each quarter	TotalExpenses
3.3 Compute balances each quarter	ShowBalances
3.4 Total each income & expense category	TotalRows
3.5 Determine grand totals	ShowGrandTotals
4. Start a new spreadsheet	cmdNew_Click
5. End program	cmdQuit_Click

Table 7.20 Tasks and their procedures.

```
Rem Spreadsheet Program
Rem ***********************************************************************
Rem *                                                                     *
Rem *           Variable Table                                            *
Rem *                                                                     *
Rem *   txtCell()              Control array for data cells               *
Rem *   lblRowLab()            Control array for numeric row labels       *
Rem *   lblColLab()            Control array for alphabetic column labels *
Rem *   maxCol                 Number of columns in spreadsheet           *
Rem *   maxRow                 Number of rows in spreadsheet              *
Rem *   incStartRow            Row where income categories begin          *
Rem *   incStopRow             Row where income categories end            *
Rem *   incTotRow              Row where income total is displayed        *
Rem *   expStartRow            Row where expense categories begin         *
Rem *   expStopRow             Row where expense categories end           *
Rem *   expTotRow              Row where expense total is displayed       *
Rem *   balRow                 Row where balance is displayed             *
Rem *   startCol               Column where numeric data begins           *
Rem *   stopCol                Column where numeric data ends             *
Rem *   totCol                 Column where total for each row is displayed *
Rem *                                                                     *
Rem ***********************************************************************
Dim maxCol As Integer
Dim maxRow As Integer
Dim incStartRow As Integer
Dim incStopRow As Integer
Dim incTotRow As Integer
Dim expStartRow As Integer
Dim expStopRow As Integer
Dim expTotRow As Integer
Dim balRow As Integer
Dim startCol As Integer
Dim stopCol As Integer
Dim totCol As Integer

Sub cmdNew_Click ()
  Dim row As Integer, col As Integer
  Rem Clear all data and total text boxes
  For col = 1 To maxCol
    For row = 1 To maxRow
      Let txtCell(Indx(row, col)).Text = ""
    Next row
  Next col
  Call SetStructure
  Rem Place cursor in first data txtCell
  txtCell(Indx(1, 1)).SetFocus
End Sub

Sub cmdQuit_Click ()
  End
End Sub

Sub CreateSpreadsheet ()
  Dim row As Integer, col As Integer, i As Integer
  Dim cellHeight As Single, cellWidth As Single
```

```
    Dim cellTop As Single, cellLeft As Single
    Let cellHeight = txtCell(1).Height
    Let cellWidth = txtCell(1).Width
    Rem Create cells
    For row = 1 To maxRow
      For col = 1 To maxCol
        Let i = Indx(row, col)
        If Not (col = 1 And row = 1) Then
            Load txtCell(i)
        End If
        If row > 1 Then
            Let cellTop = txtCell(Indx(row - 1, col)).Top
            Let txtCell(i).Top = cellTop + cellHeight
        End If
        If col > 1 Then
            Let cellLeft = txtCell(Indx(row, col - 1)).Left
            Let txtCell(i).Left = cellLeft + cellWidth
        End If
        Let txtCell(i).Visible = True
      Next col
    Next row
    Rem Create Row Labels
    For row = 2 To maxRow
      Load lblRowLab(row)
      Let lblRowLab(row).Top = lblRowLab(row - 1).Top + cellHeight
      Let lblRowLab(row).Caption = Format$(row, "0")
      Let lblRowLab(row).Visible = True
    Next row
    Rem Create Column Labels
    For col = 2 To maxCol
      Load lblColLab(col)
      Let lblColLab(col).Left = lblColLab(col - 1).Left + cellWidth
      Let lblColLab(col).Caption = Chr$(col + 64)
      Let lblColLab(col).Visible = True
    Next col
    Rem Set form height and width to accommodate all objects
    Let i = Indx(maxRow, maxCol)
    Let form1.Height = txtCell(i).Top + cellHeight + 500
    Let form1.Width = txtCell(i).Left + cellWidth + 200
End Sub

Sub DisplayTotals ()
  ReDim itot(startCol To stopCal) As Single
  ReDim etot(startCol To stopCal)  As Single
  Rem Calculate and show totals for Income each quarter
  Call TotalIncome(itot())
  Rem Calculate and show totals for Expenses each quarter
  Call TotalExpenses(etot())
  Rem Calculate and show Balances for each quarter
  Call ShowBalances(itot(), etot())
  Rem Calculate and show the Total of each Income & Expense category
  Call TotalRows
  Rem Calculate and show grand totals of quarter totals and balances
  Call ShowGrandTotals(itot(), etot())
End Sub
```

```
Sub Form_Load ()
  Rem Establish number of rows and columns. Trial and error show
  Rem that a maximum of 20 rows and 8 columns will fit the screen.
  Rem For this particular application, 16 rows an 6 columns is adequate.
  Let maxRow = 16
  Let maxCol = 6
  Call CreateSpreadsheet
  Call SetStructure
  Call SetDefaults
End Sub

Function Indx (row As Integer, col As Integer) As Integer
  Indx = (row - 1) * maxCol + col
End Function

Sub SetDefaults ()
  Rem Set default values specific to this application
  Let txtCell(Indx(3, 1)).Text = "Job"
  Let txtCell(Indx(4, 1)).Text = "Parents"
  Let txtCell(Indx(5, 1)).Text = "Scholarship"
  Let txtCell(Indx(9, 1)).Text = "Tuition"
  Let txtCell(Indx(10, 1)).Text = "Food"
  Let txtCell(Indx(11, 1)).Text = "Rent"
  Let txtCell(Indx(12, 1)).Text = "Books"
  Let txtCell(Indx(13, 1)).Text = "Misc"
End Sub

Sub SetStructure ()
  Let txtCell(Indx(1, 2)).Text = "Fall"
  Let txtCell(Indx(1, 3)).Text = "Winter"
  Let txtCell(Indx(1, 4)).Text = "Spring"
  Let txtCell(Indx(1, 5)).Text = "Summer"
  Let txtCell(Indx(1, 6)).Text = "Total"
  Let txtCell(Indx(1, 6)).ForeColor = QBColor(2)
  Let txtCell(Indx(2, 1)).Text = "Income"
  Let txtCell(Indx(2, 1)).ForeColor = QBColor(5)
  Let txtCell(Indx(6, 1)).Text = "Total"
  Let txtCell(Indx(6, 1)).ForeColor = QBColor(2)
  Let txtCell(Indx(8, 1)).Text = "Expenses"
  Let txtCell(Indx(8, 1)).ForeColor = QBColor(5)
  Let txtCell(Indx(14, 1)).Text = "Total"
  Let txtCell(Indx(14, 1)).ForeColor = QBColor(2)
  Let txtCell(Indx(16, 1)).Text = "Balance"
  Let txtCell(Indx(16, 1)).ForeColor = QBColor(2)
  Let incStartRow = 3
  Let incStopRow = 5
  Let incTotRow = 6
  Let expStartRow = 9
  Let expStopRow = 13
  Let expTotRow = 14
  Let balRow = 16
  Let startCol = 2
  Let stopCal = 5
  Let totCol = 6
End Sub
```

```
Sub ShowBalances (itot() As Single, etot() As Single)
  Dim col As Integer
  For col = startCol To stopCal
    Let txtCell(Indx(balRow, col)).Text = Format$(itot(col) - etot(col), "0")
  Next col
End Sub

Sub ShowGrandTotals (itot() As Single, etot() As Single)
  Dim col As Integer, iTotal As Single, eTotal As Single
  Rem Compute and display grand totals for income, expenses, and balance
  Let iTotal = 0
  Let eTotal = 0
  For col = startCol To stopCal
    Let iTotal = iTotal + itot(col)
    Let eTotal = eTotal + etot(col)
  Next col
  Let txtCell(Indx(incTotRow, totCol)) = Format$(iTotal, "0")
  Let txtCell(Indx(expTotRow, totCol)) = Format$(eTotal, "0")
  Let txtCell(Indx(balRow, totCol)) = Format$(iTotal - eTotal, "0")
End Sub

Sub TotalExpenses (etot() As Single)
  Dim row As Integer, col As Integer
  Rem Total expenses for each of four quarters
  For col = startCol To stopCal
    Let etot(col) = 0
    For row = expStartRow To expStopRow
      Let etot(col) = etot(col) + Val(txtCell(Indx(row, col)).Text)
    Next row
    Let txtCell(Indx(expTotRow, col)).Text = Format$(etot(col), "0")
  Next col
End Sub

Sub TotalIncome (itot() As Single)
  Dim row As Integer, col As Integer
  Rem Total income for each of four quarters
  For col = startCol To stopCal
    Let itot(col) = 0
    For row = incStartRow To incStopRow
      Let itot(col) = itot(col) + Val(txtCell(Indx(row, col)).Text)
    Next row
    Let txtCell(Indx(incTotRow, col)).Text = Format$(itot(col), "0")
  Next col
End Sub

Sub TotalRows ()
  Dim row As Integer, col As Integer, rowTot As Single
  Rem Total each income category
  For row = incStartRow To incStopRow
    Let rowTot = 0
    For col = startCol To stopCal
      Let rowTot = rowTot + Val(txtCell(Indx(row, col)).Text)
    Next col
    Let txtCell(Indx(row, totCol)).Text = Format$(rowTot, "0")
  Next row
```

```
    Rem Total each expense category
    For row = expStartRow To expStopRow
      Let rowTot = 0
      For col = startCol To stopCal
        Let rowTot = rowTot + Val(txtCell(Indx(row, col)).Text)
      Next col
      Let txtCell(Indx(row, totCol)).Text = Format$(rowTot, "0")
    Next row
End Sub

Sub txtCell_GotFocus (Index As Integer)
  Dim row As Integer, col As Integer
  Rem Force focus into a data txtCell for this application
  Let row = Int((Index - 1) / maxCol) + 1
  Let col = ((Index - 1) Mod maxCol) + 1
  If col > stopCol Then
      Let row = row + 1
      Let col = startCol
  End If
  If row < incStartRow Then
      Let row = incStartRow
    ElseIf (row > incStopRow) And (row < expStartRow) Then
      Let row = expStartRow
    ElseIf row > expStopRow Then
      Let row = incStartRow
  End If
  If Indx(row, col) <> Index Then
      txtCell(Indx(row, col)).SetFocus
  End If
End Sub

Sub txtCell_LostFocus (Indx As Integer)
  Call DisplayTotals
End Sub
```

Chapter 7
Summary

1. For programming purposes, tabular data are most efficiently processed if stored in an *array*. The *ranges* of variable arrays are specified by Dim or ReDim statements.

2. An array of labels, text boxes, or command buttons, referred to in general as a *control array*, can be created by assigning a value (usually zero) to the *Index* property of the control at design-time. Additional elements of the control array are created either at design-time by using Ctrl+C and Ctrl+V to copy the first element in the array or at run-time by using the Load statement. New elements created in either way inherit all the properties of the first element except the Index, Visible (if created with Load), Top (when copied at design-time), and Left (when copied at design-time) properties.

3. Two of the best known methods for ordering (or *sorting*) arrays are the *bubble sort* and the *Shell sort*.

4. Any array can be searched *sequentially* to find the subscript associated with a sought-after value. Ordered arrays can be searched most efficiently by a *binary search*.

5. A table can be effectively stored in a *two-dimensional array*.

Chapter 7
Programming Projects

1. Table 7.21 contains some lengths in terms of feet. Write a program that displays the nine different units of measure, requests the unit to convert from, the unit to convert to, and the quantity to be converted, and then displays the converted quantity. A typical outcome is shown in Figure 7.15.

1 inch = .0833 feet	1 rod = 16.5 feet
1 yard = 3 feet	1 furlong = 660 feet
1 meter = 3.2815 feet	1 kilometer = 3281.5 feet
1 fathom = 6 feet	1 mile = 5280 feet

Table 7.21 Equivalent lengths.

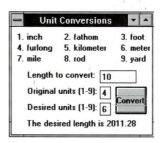

Figure 7.15 Possible outcome of Project 1.

2. Statisticians use the concepts of **mean** and **standard deviation** to describe a collection of data. The mean is the average value of the items, and the standard deviation measures the spread or dispersal of the numbers about the mean. Formally, if $x_1, x_2, x_3, ..., x_n$ is a collection of data, then

$$m = \text{mean} = \frac{x_1 + x_2 + x_3 + ... + x_n}{n}$$

$$s = \text{standard deviation} = \sqrt{\frac{(x_1 - m)^2 + (x_2 - m)^2 + (x_3 - m)^2 + ... + (x_n - m)^2}{n - 1}}$$

Write a computer program to

(a) Place the exam scores 59, 60, 65, 75, 56, 56, 66, 62, 98, 72, 95, 71, 63, 77, 65, 77, 65, 59, 85, and 62 into an array.

(b) Calculate the mean and standard deviation of the exam scores.

(c) Assign letter grades to each exam score, ES, as follows:

$ES \geq m + 1.5s$	A
$m + .5s \leq ES < m + 1.5s$	B
$m - .5s \leq ES < m + .5s$	C
$m - 1.5s \leq ES < m - .5s$	D
$ES < m - 1.5s$	F

For instance, if m were 70 and s were 12, then grades of 88 or above would receive A's, grades between 76 and 87 would receive B's, and so on. A process of this type is referred to as *curving grades*.

(d) Display a list of the exam scores along with their corresponding grades.

3. *Rudimentary Translator.* Table 7.22 gives English words and their French and German equivalents. Store these words in a data file and read them into three parallel arrays, one for each language. Write a program that sorts all three arrays according to the array of English words. The program should then request an English sentence as input from the keyboard and translate it into French and German. For example, if the English sentence given is MY PENCIL IS ON THE TABLE, then the French translation will be MON CRAYON EST SUR LA TABLE, and the German translation will be MEIN BLEISTIFT IST AUF DEM TISCH.

YES	OUI	JA	LARGE	GROS	GROSS
TABLE	TABLE	TISCH	NO	NON	NEIN
THE	LA	DEM	HAT	CHAPEAU	HUT
IS	EST	IST	PENCIL	CRAYON	BLEISTIFT
YELLOW	JAUNE	GELB	RED	ROUGE	ROT
FRIEND	AMI	FREUND	ON	SUR	AUF
SICK	MALADE	KRANK	AUTO	AUTO	AUTO
MY	MON	MEIN	OFTEN	SOUVENT	OFT

Table 7.22 English words and their French and German equivalents.

4. Write a program that allows a list of no more than 50 personal computer vendors and their percent changes in market share for a particular year to be input and displays the information in two lists titled *gainers* and *losers*. Each list should be sorted by the *magnitude* of the percent change. Try your program on the 1991 data for the top 10 U.S. vendors in Table 7.23. **Note:** You will need to store the data initially in an array to determine the number of gainers and losers.

Company	% Change	Company	% Change
Apple	2.8	Gateway 2000	1.4
AST	0.7	IBM	–1.5
Bull/ZDS	0.0	Packard Bell	0.3
Compaq	–0.5	Tandy	1.1
Everex	0.2	Toshiba	–0.02

Table 7.23 Changes in market share of personal computer and single-user workstation market.

Source: International Data Corp. (Industry Surveys, Dec. 31, 1992)

5. Each team in a six-team soccer league played each other team once. Table 7.24 shows the winners. Write a program to

   (a) Place the team names in a one-dimensional array.
   (b) Place the data from Table 7.24 in a two-dimensional array.
   (c) Place the number of games won by each team in a one-dimensional array.
   (d) Display a listing of the teams giving each team's name and number of games won. The list should be in decreasing order by the number of wins.

	Jazz	Jets	Owls	Rams	Cubs	Zips
Jazz	—	Jazz	Jazz	Rams	Cubs	Jazz
Jets	Jazz	—	Jets	Jets	Cubs	Zips
Owls	Jazz	Jets	—	Rams	Owls	Owls
Rams	Rams	Jets	Rams	—	Rams	Rams
Cubs	Cubs	Cubs	Owls	Rams	—	Cubs
Zips	Jazz	Zips	Owls	Rams	Cubs	—

Table 7.24 Soccer league winners.

6. A poker hand can be stored in a two-dimensional array. The statement

```
DIM hand(1 TO 4, 1 TO 13) As Integer
```

declares a 52-element array where the first dimension ranges over the four suits and the second dimension ranges over the thirteen denominations. A poker hand is specified by placing ones in the elements corresponding to the cards in the hand. See Figure 7.16.

Write a program that requests the five cards as input from the user, creates the related array, and passes the array to subprograms to determine the type of the hand: flush (all cards have the same suit), straight (cards have consecutive denominations—ace can come either before 2 or after King), straight flush, four-of-a-kind, full house (3 cards of one denomination, 2 cards of another denomination), three-of-a-kind, two pairs, one pair, or none of the above.

	A	2	3	4	5	6	7	8	9	10	J	Q	K
Club	0	0	0	0	0	0	0	0	1	0	0	0	0
Diamond	1	0	0	0	0	0	0	0	0	0	0	0	0
Heart	1	0	0	0	0	0	0	0	0	0	0	1	0
Spade	0	0	0	0	1	0	0	0	0	0	0	0	0

Figure 7.16 Array for the poker hand A A 5 9 Q.

7. *Airline Reservations.* Write a reservation system for an airline flight. Assume the airplane has ten rows with four seats in each row. Use a two-dimensional array of strings to maintain a seating chart. In addition, create an array to be used as a waiting list in case the plane is full. The waiting list should be "first come, first served"; that is, people who are added early to the list get priority over those added later. Allow the user the following three options:

(1) Add a passenger to the flight or waiting list.
   (a) Request the passenger's name.
   (b) Display a chart of the seats in the airplane in tabular form.
   (c) If seats are available, let the passenger choose a seat. Add the passenger to the seating chart.
   (d) If no seats are available, place the passenger on the waiting list.
(2) Remove a passenger from the flight.
   (a) Request the passenger's name.
   (b) Search the seating chart for the passenger's name and delete it.
   (c) If the waiting list is empty, update the array so the seat is available.
   (d) If the waiting list is not empty, remove the first person from the list, and give him or her the newly vacated seat.
(3) Quit.

8. The Game of Life was invented by John H. Conway to model some genetic laws for birth, death, and survival. Consider a checkerboard consisting of an *n*-by-*n* array of squares. Each square can contain one individual (denoted by 1) or be empty (denoted by –). Figure 7.17(a) shows a 6-by-6 board with four of the squares occupied. The future of each individual depends on the number of his neighbors. After each period of time, called a *generation*, certain individuals will survive, others will die due to either loneliness or overcrowding, and new individuals will be born. Each nonborder square has eight neighboring squares. After each generation, the status of the squares change as follows:

(a) An individual *survives* if there are two or three individuals in neighboring squares.
(b) An individual *dies* if he has more than three individuals or less than two in neighboring squares.
(c) A new individual is *born* into each empty square with exactly three individuals as neighbors.

Figure 7.17(b) shows the status after one generation. Write a program to do the following:

(a) Dimension an *n*-by-*n* array, where *n* is input by the user, to hold the status of each square in the current generation. To specify the initial configuration, have the user input each row as a string of length *n*, and break the row into 1s or dashes with Mid$.

(b) Dimension an *n*-by-*n* array to hold the status of each square in the next generation. Compute the status for each square and produce the display in Figure 7.17(b). **Note:** The generation changes all at once. Only current cells are used to determine which cells will contain individuals in the next generation.

(c) Assign the next generation values to the current generation and repeat as often as desired.

(d) Display the number of individuals in each generation.

Hint: The hardest part of the program is determining the number of neighbors a cell has. In general, you must check a 3-by-3 square around the cell in question. Exceptions must be made when the cell is on the edge of the array. Don't forget that a cell is not a neighbor of itself.

(Test the program with the initial configuration shown in Figure 7.18. It is known as the figure-eight configuration and repeats after eight generations.)

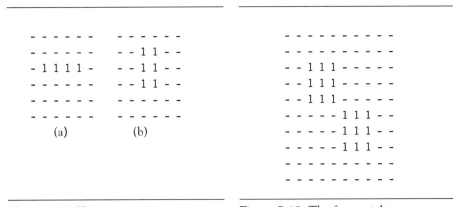

Figure 7.17 Two generations.   Figure 7.18 The figure eight.

9. Simulate the game Concentration. The Form_Load routine should create an array of 20 command buttons placed vertically on a form. A list of ten words should randomly be assigned as potential captions for the buttons, with each word assigned to two command buttons. Initially, none of the buttons should show their words. However, when a button is clicked on, its word is revealed as its caption. After two words have been revealed, either both of the command buttons should become invisible (if their words match) or their captions should again become blank (if the two words do not match). When all matches have been found, a message box should display the number of tries (pairs of words exposed) and an appropriate remark about the user's concentration ability. Possible remarks might be, "You must have ESP" (5 or 6 tries), "Amazing concentration" (7 or 8 tries), "Can't hide anything from you" (9 or 10 tries), "Perhaps a nap would recharge your concentration" (11 or 12 tries), "Better find a designated driver" (more than 12 tries).

8

Sequential Files

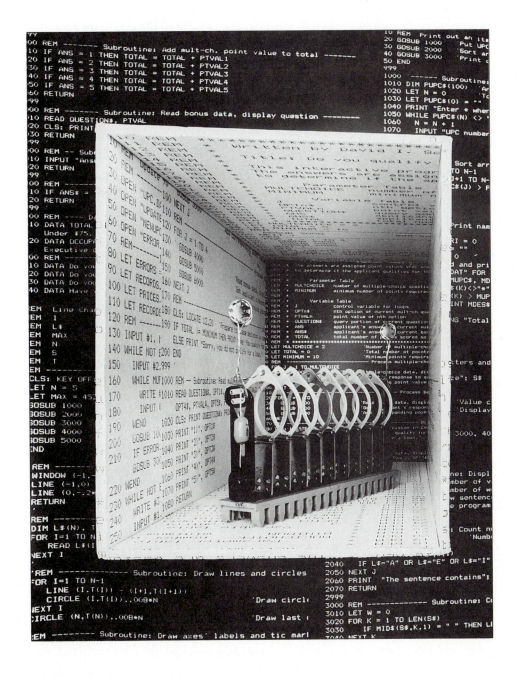

8.1 SEQUENTIAL FILES

Throughout this text we have processed data from files created with Windows' Notepad and saved on a disk. Such files are stored on disk as a sequence of characters. (Two characters, called the "carriage return" and "line feed" characters, are inserted at the end of each line to indicate where new lines should be started.) Such files are called **sequential files**. In this section, we create sequential files from Visual Basic programs and develop techniques for using sequential files.

Creating a Sequential File

There are many ways to organize data in a sequential file. The technique presented here is easy to implement. Other techniques are discussed in the comments. The following steps create a new sequential file and write data to it.

1. Choose a DOS **file name**. A DOS file name is a string consisting of a base name of at most eight characters followed by an optional extension consisting of a period and at most three characters. Letters, digits, and a few other assorted characters (see Comment 1) can be used in either the name or the extension. Blank spaces are not allowed. Some examples of file names are INCOME.86, CUSTOMER.TXT, and FORT500.

2. Choose a number from 1 through 255 to be the **reference number** of the file. While the file is in use, it will be identified by this number.

3. Execute the statement

   ```
   Open "filespec" For Output As #n
   ```

   where n is the reference number. This process is referred to as **opening a file for output**. It establishes a communications link between the computer and the disk drive for storing data *onto* the disk. It allows data to be output from the computer and recorded in the specified file.

4. Place data into the file with the Write# statement. If a is a string, then the statement

   ```
   Write #n, a
   ```

   writes the string a surrounded by quotation marks into the file. If c is a number, then the statement

   ```
   Write #n, c
   ```

   writes the number c, without any leading or trailing spaces, into file number n. The statement

   ```
   Write #n, a, c
   ```

   writes a and c as before, but with a comma separating them. Similarly, if the statement Write #n is followed by a list of several strings and/or numbers separated by commas, then all the strings and numbers appear as before, separated by commas. After each Write# statement is executed, the "carriage return" and "line feed" characters are placed into the file.

5. After all the data have been recorded in the file, execute

```
Close #n
```

where *n* is the reference number. This statement breaks the communications link with the file and dissociates the number *n* from the file.

EXAMPLE 1   The following program illustrates the different aspects of the Write# statement. Notice the absence of leading and trailing spaces for numbers and the presence of quotation marks surrounding strings.

```
Sub Command1_Click ()
  Dim name1 As String, name2 As String
  Rem Demonstrate use of Write # statement
  Open "PIONEER.TXT" For Output As #1
  Write #1, "ENIAC"
  Write #1, 1946
  Write #1, "ENIAC", 1946
  Let name1 = "Eckert"
  Let name2 = "Mauchly"
  Write #1, 14 * 139, "J.P. " + name1, name2, "John"
  Close #1
End Sub
```

[Run, click the command button, and then load the file PIONEER.TXT into Windows' Notepad. The following will appear on the screen.]

```
"ENIAC"
1946
"ENIAC",1946
1946,"J.P. Eckert","Mauchly","John"
```

Caution: If an existing sequential file is opened for output, the computer will erase the existing data and create a new empty file.

Write# allows us to create files just like the Notepad files that appear throughout this text. We already know how to read such files with Input#. The remaining major task is adding data to the end of sequential files.

Adding Items to a Sequential File

Data can be added to the end of an existing sequential file with the following steps.

1. Choose a number from 1 through 255 to be the reference number for the file. This number need not be the same number that was used when the file was created.

2. Execute the statement

```
Open "filespec" For Append As #n
```

where *n* is the reference number. This procedure is called **opening a file for append**. It allows data to be output from the computer and recorded at the end of the specified file.

3. Place data into the file with the Write# statement.

4. After all the data have been recorded into the file, close the file with the statement Close #*n*.

The Append option for opening a file is intended to add data to an already existing file. However, it also can be used to create a new file. If the file does not exist, then the Append option acts just like the Output option and creates the file.

A file should not be open in two modes at the same time. For instance, after a file has been opened for output and data have been written to the file, the file should be closed before being opened for input.

An attempt to open a nonexistent file for input results in the "File not found" error message. There is a function which tells us whether a certain file has already been created. If the value of

```
Dir$("filespec")
```

is the empty string "", then the specified file does not exist. Therefore, prudence often dictates that files be opened for input with code such as

```
If Dir$("filespec") <> "" Then
    Open "filespec" For Input As #1
  Else
    Let message = "Either no file has yet been created or "
    Let message = message + "the file is not where expected."
    MsgBox message, , "File Not Found"
End If
```

There is one file-management operation that we have yet to discuss—deleting an item of information from a file. An individual item of the file cannot be changed or deleted directly. A new file must be created by reading each item from the original file and recording it, with the single item changed or deleted, into the new file. The old file is then erased and the new file renamed with the name of the original file. Regarding these last two tasks, the Visual Basic statement

```
Kill "filespec"
```

removes the specified file from the disk and the statement

```
Name "filespec1" As "filespec2"
```

changes the name of the file identified by *filespec1* to the new name *filespec2*.

EXAMPLE 2   The following program creates and manages a file of names and years of birth.

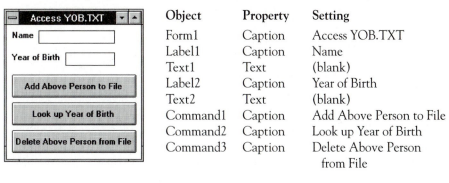

Object	Property	Setting
Form1	Caption	Access YOB.TXT
Label1	Caption	Name
Text1	Text	(blank)
Label2	Caption	Year of Birth
Text2	Text	(blank)
Command1	Caption	Add Above Person to File
Command2	Caption	Look up Year of Birth
Command3	Caption	Delete Above Person from File

```
Sub Command1_Click ()
  Dim msg As String
  Rem Add a person's name and year of birth to file
  If (Text1.Text <> "") And (Text2.Text <> "") Then
      Open "YOB.TXT" For Append As #1
      Write #1, Text1.Text, Val(Text2.Text)
      Close #1
      Let Text1.Text = ""
      Let Text2.Text = ""
      Text1.SetFocus
    Else
      Let msg = "You must enter a name and year of birth."
      MsgBox msg, , "Information Incomplete"
  End If
End Sub

Sub Command2_Click ()
  Dim message As String
  Rem Determine a person's year of birth
  If Text1.Text <> "" Then
      If Dir$("YOB.TXT") <> "" Then
          Call DisplayYearOfBirth
        Else
          Let message = "Either no file has yet been created or "
          Let message = message + "the file is not where expected."
          MsgBox message, , "File Not Found"
      End If
    Else
      MsgBox "You must enter a name.", , "Information Incomplete"
  End If
  Text1.SetFocus
End Sub

Sub Command3_Click ()
  Dim message As String
  Rem Remove a person from the file
  If Text1.Text <> "" Then
      If Dir$("YOB.TXT") <> "" Then
          Call DeletePerson
```

```
          Else
            Let message = "Either no file has yet been created or "
            Let message = message + "the file is not where expected."
            MsgBox message, , "File Not Found."
        End If
      Else
        MsgBox "You must enter a name.", , "Information Incomplete"
    End If
    Text1.SetFocus
End Sub


Sub DeletePerson ()
  Dim nom As String, yob As Integer, flag As String
  Let flag = "Not found"
  Open "YOB.TXT" For Input As #1
  Open "TEMP" For Output As #2
  Do While Not EOF(1)
    Input #1, nom, yob
    If nom <> Text1.Text Then
        Write #2, nom, yob
      Else
        Let flag = "Found"
    End If
  Loop
  Close #1
  Close #2
  Kill "YOB.TXT"
  Name "TEMP" As "YOB.TXT"
  If flag = "Not found" Then
      MsgBox "The name was not found.", , ""
    Else
      Let Text1.Text = ""
      Let Text2.Text = ""
  End If
End Sub


Sub DisplayYearOfBirth ()
  Dim nom As String, yob As Integer
  Rem Find the year of birth for the name in Text1
  Let Text2.Text = ""
  Open "YOB.TXT" For Input As #1
  Let nom = ""
  Do While (nom <> Text1.Text) And (Not EOF(1))
    Input #1, nom, yob
  Loop
  If nom = Text1.Text Then
      Let Text2.Text = Str$(yob)
    Else
      MsgBox "Person is not in file.", , ""
      Let Text1.Text = ""
  End If
  Close #1
End Sub
```

[Run. After several names have been added, the file might look as follows.]

```
"Barbra",1942
"Ringo",1940
"Sylvester",1946
```

Figure 8.1 Sample contents of YOB.TXT.

Comments:

1. Sequential files make efficient use of disk space and are easy to create and use. Their disadvantages are as follows:

   (a) Often a large portion of the file must be read in order to find one specific item.
   (b) An individual item of the file cannot be changed or deleted easily.

   Another type of file, known as a **random-access file**, has neither of the disadvantages of sequential files; however, random-access files typically use more disk space, require greater effort to program, and are not flexible in the variety and format of the stored data. Random-access files are discussed in Chapter 9.

2. Consider the sequential file shown in Figure 8.1 at the end of Example 2. This file is said to consist of three records of two fields each. A **record** holds all the data about a single individual. Each item of data is called a **field**. The three records are

   "Barbra", 1942
   "Ringo", 1940
   "Sylvester", 1946

   and the two fields are

   name field, year of birth field

PRACTICE PROBLEMS 8.1

1. Compose a subprogram RemoveDups that could be used in Example 2 to delete from YOB.TXT all repeated records except the first instance of a name matching the name in Text1. (Assume that the existence of YOB.TXT is checked prior to the execution of this subprogram.)

2. Compose a subprogram AddNoDuplicate to add a name and year of birth to the end of the file YOB.TXT only if the name to be added is not already present in the file. (Assume that the existence of YOB.TXT is checked prior to the execution of this subprogram.)

EXERCISES 8.1

In Exercises 1 through 4, determine the output displayed in the picture box when the command button is clicked.

1.
```
Sub Command1_Click ()
    Dim g As String
    Open "GREETING.TXT" For Output As #1
    Write #1, "Hello"
    Write #1, "Aloha"
    Close #1
    Open "GREETING.TXT" For Input As #1
    Input #1, g
    Picture1.Print g
    Close #1
End Sub
```

2.
```
Sub Command1_Click ()
    Dim g As String, h As String
    Open "GREETING.TXT" For Output As #2
    Write #2, "Hello", "Aloha"
    Close #2
    Open "GREETING.TXT" For Input As #1
    Input #1, g, h
    Picture1.Print h
    Close #1
End Sub
```

3.
```
Sub Command1_Click ()
    Dim g As String
    Open "GREETING.TXT" For Output As #2
    Write #2, "Hello"
    Write #2, "Aloha"
    Write #2, "Bon Jour"
    Close #2
    Open "GREETING.TXT" For Input As #1
    Do While Not EOF(1)
      Input #1, g
      Picture1.Print g
    Loop
    Close #1
End Sub
```

4. Assume the contents of the file GREETING.TXT are as shown in Figure 8.2.
```
Sub Command1_Click ()
    Dim file As String, salutation As Integer, g As String
    Let file = "GREETING.TXT"
    Open file For Append As #3
    Write #3, "Buenos Dias"
    Close #3
    Open file For Input As #3
    For salutation = 1 To 4
      Input #3, g
      Picture1.Print g
    Next salutation
    Close #3
End Sub
```

> "Hello"
> "Aloha"
> "Bon Jour"

Figure 8.2 Contents of the file GREETING.TXT.

5. Assume that the contents of the file GREETING.TXT are as shown in Figure 8.2. What is the effect of the following program?

```
Sub Command1_Click ()
  Dim g As String
  Open "GREETING.TXT" For Input As #1
  Open "WELCOME" For Output As #2
  Do While Not EOF(1)
    Input #1, g
    If g <> "Aloha" Then
        Write #2, g
    End If
  Loop
  Close
End Sub
```

6. Assume that the contents of the file YOB.TXT is as shown in Figure 8.1. What is the effect of the following program?

```
Sub Command1_Click ()
  Dim flag As Integer, nom As String, year As Integer
  Open "YOB.TXT" For Input As #1
  Open "YOB2.TXT" For Output As #2
  Let flag = 0
  Let nom = ""
  Do While (nom < "Clint") And (Not EOF(1))
    Input #1, nom, year
    If nom >= "Clint" Then
      Write #2, "Clint", 1930
      Let flag = 1
    End If
    Write #2, nom, year
  Loop
  Do While Not EOF(1)
    Input #1, nom, year
    Write #2, nom, year
  Loop
  If flag = 0 Then
      Write #2, "Clint", 1930
  End If
  Close
End Sub
```

In Exercises 7 through 12, identify the errors. Assume that the contents of the files YOB.TXT and GREETING.TXT are as shown in Figures 8.1 and 8.2.

7.
```
Sub Command1_Click ()
  Open YOB.TXT For Append As #1
  Write #1, "Michael"
  Close #1
End Sub
```

8. ```
   Sub Command1_Click ()
       Dim nom As String, yr As Integer
       Open "YOB.TXT" For Output As #2
       Input #2, nom, yr
       Picture1.Print yr
       Close #2
   End Sub
   ```

9. ```
   Sub Command1_Click ()
       Dim i As Integer, g As String
       Open "GREETING.TXT" For Input As #1
       For i = 1 To EOF(1)
         Input #1, g
         Picture1.Print g
       Next i
       Close #1
   End Sub
   ```

10. ```
    Sub Command1_Click ()
        Dim g As String
        Open "GREETING.TXT" For Input As #1
        Do While Not EOF
          Input #1, g
          Picture1.Print g
        Loop
        Close #1
    End Sub
    ```

11. ```
    Sub Command1_Click ()
        Dim nom As String, g As String
        Open "GREETING.TXT" For Input As #1
        Let nom = "NEW.GREET.TXT"
        Open nom For Output As #2
        Do While Not EOF(1)
          Input #1, g
          Write #2, g
        Loop
        Close
    End Sub
    ```

12. ```
    Sub Command1_Click ()
        Open "GREETING.TXT" For Input As #1
        Close "GREETING.TXT"
    End Sub
    ```

Exercises 13 through 20 are related and use the data in Table 8.1. The file created in Exercise 13 should be used in Exercises 14 through 20.

13. Write a program to create the sequential file COWBOY.TXT containing the information in Table 8.1.

Colt Peacemaker	12.20
Holster	2.00
Levi Strauss Jeans	1.35
Saddle	40.00
Stetson	10.00

Table 8.1 Prices paid by cowboys for certain items in Mid-1800s.
    ```

14. Write a program to display all items in the file COWBOY.TXT that cost more than $10.

15. Write a program to add the data *Winchester rifle, 20.50* to the end of the file COWBOY.TXT.

16. Suppose an order is placed for three Colt Peacemakers, two Holsters, ten pairs of Levi Strauss Jeans, one saddle, and four Stetsons. Write a program to

    (a) Create the sequential file ORDER.TXT to hold the numbers 3, 2, 10, 1, 4.
    (b) Use the files COWBOY.TXT and ORDER.TXT to display a sales receipt with three columns giving the name of each item, the quantity ordered, and the cost for that quantity.
    (c) Compute the total cost of the items and display it at the end of the sales receipt.

17. Write a program to request an additional item and price from the user. Then create a sequential file called COWBOY2.TXT containing all the information in the file COWBOY.TXT with the additional item (and price) inserted in its proper alphabetical sequence. Run the program for both of the following data items: *Boots, 20* and *Horse, 35*.

18. Suppose the price of saddles is reduced by 20 percent. Use the file COWBOY.TXT to create a sequential file, COWBOY3.TXT, containing the new price list.

19. Write a program to create a sequential file called COWBOY4.TXT, containing all the information in the file COWBOY.TXT except for the data *Holster, 2*.

20. Write a program to allow additional items and prices to be input by the user and added to the end of the file COWBOY.TXT. Include a method to terminate the process.

21. Suppose the file YOB.TXT contains many names and years, and that the names are in alphabetical order. Write a program that requests a name as input and either gives the person's age or reports that the person is not in the file. **Note:** Since the names are in alphabetical order, usually there is no need to search to the end of the file.

22. Suppose the file YOB.TXT contains many names and years. Write a program that creates two files, called SENIORS.TXT and JUNIORS.TXT, and copies all the data on people born before 1940 into the file SENIORS and the data on the others into the file JUNIORS.TXT.

23. A publisher maintains two sequential files, HARDBACK.INV and PAPERBCK.INV. Each record consists of the name of a book and the quantity in stock. Write a program to access these files. (The program should allow for the case where the book is not in the file.) A run of the program might look as follows:

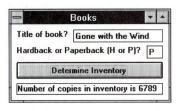

SOLUTIONS TO PRACTICE PROBLEMS 8.1

1. A record in YOB.TXT is kept if the name in the record does not match the search name, or if the name in the record matches the search name and a flag indicates that the search name has not been found previously.

```
Sub RemoveDups ()
  Dim nom As String, yob As Integer, flag As String
  Let flag = "Not found"
  Open "YOB.TXT" For Input As #1
  Open "TEMP" For Output As #2
  Do While Not EOF(1)
    Input #1, nom, yob
    If nom <> Text1.Text Then
        Write #2, nom, yob
      Else
        If flag = "Not Found" Then
            Write #2, nom, yob
        End If
        Let flag = "Found"
    End If
  Loop
  Close #1
  Close #2
  Kill "YOB.TXT"
  Name "TEMP" As "YOB.TXT"
  If flag = "Not found" Then
      MsgBox "The name was not found.", , ""
    Else
      Let Text1.Text = ""
      Let Text2.Text = ""
  End If
End Sub
```

2. The file YOB.TXT is first opened for Input and scanned for the new name. If the name is not found, YOB.TXT is reopened for Append and the name and year of birth are added to the end of the file.

```
Sub AddNoDuplicate ()
  Dim nom As String, yob As Integer, found As Integer
  Open "YOB.TXT" For Input As #1
  Let found = 0
  Do While (Not(EOF(1))) And (found = 0)
    Input #1, nom, yob
    If nom = Text1.Text Then
        Let found = 1
    End If
  Loop
  Close #1
  If found = 0 Then
      Open "YOB.TXT" For Append As #1
      Write #1, Text1.Text, Val(Text2.Text)
      Close #1
  End If
End Sub
```

8.2 USING SEQUENTIAL FILES

In addition to being accessed for information, sequential files are regularly updated by modifying certain pieces of data, removing some records, and adding new records. These tasks can be performed most efficiently if the files are first sorted.

Sorting Sequential Files

The records of a sequential file can be sorted on any field by first reading the data into parallel arrays and then sorting on a specific array.

EXAMPLE 1   Compose a program to sort the sequential file YOB.TXT of the previous section by year of birth.

SOLUTION

```
Sub Command1_Click ()
  Dim numPeople As Integer
  Rem Sort data from YOB.TXT file by year of birth
  Let numPeople = 4              'Number of people in file
  ReDim nom(1 To numPeople) As String
  ReDim yearBorn(1 To numPeople) As Integer
  Call ReadData(nom(), yearBorn(), numPeople)
  Call SortData(nom(), yearBorn(), numPeople)
  Call ShowData(nom(), yearBorn(), numPeople)
  Call WriteData(nom(), yearBorn(), numPeople)
End Sub

Sub ReadData (nom() As String, yearBorn() As Integer, numPeople As Integer)
  Dim index As Integer
  Rem Read data from file into arrays
  Open "YOB.TXT" For Input As #1
  For index = 1 To numPeople
    Input #1, nom(index), yearBorn(index)
  Next index
  Close #1
End Sub

Sub ShowData (nom() As String, yearBorn() As Integer, numPeople As Integer)
  Dim index As Integer
  Rem Display the sorted list
  Picture1.Cls
  For index = 1 To numPeople
    Picture1.Print nom(index), yearBorn(index)
  Next index
End Sub
```

```
Sub SortData (nom() As String, yearBorn() As Integer, numPeople As Integer)
  Dim passNum As Integer, index As Integer
  Rem Bubble sort arrays by year of birth
  For passNum = 1 To numPeople - 1
    For index = 1 To numPeople - passNum
      If yearBorn(index) > yearBorn(index + 1) Then
          Call SwapData(nom(), yearBorn(), index)
      End If
    Next index
  Next passNum
End Sub

Sub SwapData (nom() As String, yearBorn() As Integer, index As Integer)
  Dim stemp As String, ntemp As Integer
  Rem Swap names and years
  Let stemp = nom(index)
  Let nom(index) = nom(index + 1)
  Let nom(index + 1) = stemp
  Let ntemp = yearBorn(index)
  Let yearBorn(index) = yearBorn(index + 1)
  Let yearBorn(index + 1) = ntemp
End Sub

Sub WriteData (nom() As String, yearBorn() As Integer, numPeople As Integer)
  Dim index As Integer
  Rem Write data back into file
  Open "YOB.TXT" For Output As #1
  For index = 1 To numPeople
    Write #1, nom(index), yearBorn(index)
  Next index
  Close #1
End Sub
```

If the program is run, the command button pressed, and then YOB.TXT is examined using Windows' Notepad, the following will be seen:

"Ringo",1940
"Barbra",1942
"Sylvester",1946

Merging Sequential Files

In Section 7.2, we considered an algorithm for merging two arrays. This same algorithm can be applied to merging two ordered files.

Suppose you have two ordered files (possibly with certain items appearing in both files), and you want to merge them into a third ordered file (without duplications). The technique for creating the third file is as follows.

1. Open the two ordered files For Input and open a third file For Output.

2. Try to get an item of data from each file.

3. Repeat steps (a) and (b) below until an item of data is not available in one of the files.

    (a) If one item precedes the other, write it into the third file and try to get another item of data from its file.

    (b) If the two items are identical, write one into the third file and try to get another item of data from each of the two ordered files.

4. At this point, an item of data has most likely been retrieved from one of the files and not yet written to the third file. In this case, write that item and all remaining items in that file to the third file.

5. Close the three files.

EXAMPLE 2   The following program merges two ordered files of numbers into a third file.

Object	Property	Setting
Form1	Caption	Merge Two Files
Label1	Caption	Name of first file:
Text1	Text	(blank)
Label2	Caption	Name of second file:
Text2	Text	(blank)
Label3	Caption	Name for merged file:
Text3	Text	(blank)
Command1	Caption	Proceed to Merge
Picture1		

```
Sub Command1_Click ()
  Dim file1 As String, file2 As String, file3 As String
  Dim have1data As String, have2data As String
  Dim num1 As Single, num2 As Single
  Dim recCount As Integer
  Rem Merge two ordered files
  Picture1.Cls
  Let file1 = Text1.Text
  Let file2 = Text2.Text
  Let file3 = Text3.Text
  Open file1 For Input As #1
  Open file2 For Input As #2
  Open file3 For Output As #3
  Let have1data = Get1data(num1)
  Let have2data = Get2data(num2)
  Let recCount = 0
  Do While (have1data = "T") And (have2data = "T")
    Select Case num1
      Case Is < num2
        Write #3, num1
        Let have1data = Get1data(num1)
      Case Is > num2
        Write #3, num2
        Let have2data = Get2data(num2)
```

```
        Case num2
          Write #3, num1
          Let have1data = Get1data(num1)
          Let have2data = Get2data(num2)
      End Select
      Let recCount = recCount + 1
    Loop
    Do While (have1data = "T")
      Write #3, num1
      Let recCount = recCount + 1
      Let have1data = Get1data(num1)
    Loop
    Do While (have2data = "T")
      Write #3, num2
      Let recCount = recCount + 1
      Let have2data = Get2data(num2)
    Loop
    Close #1, #2, #3
    Picture1.Print recCount; "records written to "; file3
End Sub

Function Get1data (num1 As Single) As String
  Rem If possible, read next value from file 1
  Rem Return a value of "T" when new data is read; "F" if data not available
  If Not EOF(1) Then
      Input #1, num1
      Get1data = "T"
    Else
      Get1data = "F"
  End If
End Function

Function Get2data (num2 As Single) As String
  Rem If possible, read next value from file 2
  Rem Return a value of "T" when new data is read; "F" if data not available
  If Not EOF(2) Then
      Input #2, num2
      Get2data = "T"
    Else
      Get2data = "F"
  End If
End Function
```

Control Break Processing

Suppose a small real estate company stores its sales data for a year in a sequential file in which each record contains four fields: month of sale (1 through 12), day of sale (1 through 31), address, price. Typical data for the sales of the first quarter of a year are shown in Figure 8.3. The records are ordered by date of sale.

Month	Day	Address	Price
January	9	102 Elm Street	$203,000
January	20	1 Main Street	$315,200
January	25	5 Maple Street	$123,450
February	15	1 Center Street	$100,000
February	23	2 Vista Drive	$145,320
March	15	205 Rodeo Circle	$389,100

Figure 8.3 Real estate sales for first quarter of year.

Figure 8.4 shows the output of a program that displays the total sales for the quarter year, with a subtotal for each month.

```
January    9    102 Elm Street       $203,000.00
January    20   1 Main Street        $315,200.00
January    25   5 Maple Street       $123,450.00

           Subtotal for January:     $641,650.00

February   15   1 Center Street      $100,000.00
February   23   2 Vista Drive        $145,320.00

           Subtotal for February:    $245,320.00

March      15   205 Rodeo Circle     $389,100.00

           Subtotal for March:       $389,100.00

Total for First Quarter: $1,276,070.00
```

Figure 8.4 Output of Example 3.

A program to produce the output of Figure 8.4 must calculate a subtotal at the end of each month. The variable holding the month triggers a subtotal whenever its value changes. Such a variable is called a **control variable** and each change of its value is called a **break**.

EXAMPLE 3 Write a program to produce the output of Figure 8.4. Assume the data of Figure 8.3 are stored in the sequential file HOMESALE.TXT.

SOLUTION The following program allows for months with no sales. Since monthly subtotals will be printed, the month-of-sale field is an appropriate control variable.

```
Sub Command1_Click ()
  Dim currentMonth As String, newMonth As String
  Dim dayNum As Integer, address As String
  Dim price As Currency, monthTotal As Currency
  Dim yearTotal As Currency, done As Integer
  Rem Display home sales by month
  Picture1.Cls
  Open "HOMESALE.TXT" For Input As #1
```

```
      Let currentMonth = ""            'Name of month being subtotaled
      Let monthTotal = 0
      Let yearTotal = 0
      Let done = 0                     'Flag to indicate end of list
      Do While done = 0
        If Not EOF(1) Then
            Input #1, newMonth, dayNum, address, price
          Else
            Let done = 1              'End of list
        End If
        If (newMonth <> currentMonth) Or (done = 1) Then 'Control break processing
            If currentMonth <> "" Then      'Don't print subtotal before 1st month
                Picture1.Print
                Picture1.Print Tab(15); "Subtotal for " + currentMonth + ":";
                Picture1.Print Tab(38); Format$(monthTotal, "Currency")
                Picture1.Print
            End If
            Let currentMonth = newMonth
            Let monthTotal = 0
        End If
        If done = 0 Then
            Picture1.Print newMonth;
            Picture1.Print Tab(11); Format$(dayNum, "0");
            Picture1.Print Tab(18); address;
            Picture1.Print Tab(38); Format$(price, "Currency")
            Let yearTotal = yearTotal + price
        End If
        Let monthTotal = monthTotal + price
      Loop
      Close #1
      Picture1.Print "Total for First Quarter: "; Format$(yearTotal, "Currency")
    End Sub
```

Comments:

1. In the examples of this and the previous section, the files to be processed have been opened and closed within a single event procedure or subprogram. However, the solution to some programming problems requires that a file be opened just once the instant the program is run and stay open until the program is terminated. This is easily accomplished by placing the Open statement in the Form_Load event procedure and the Close and End statements in the click event procedure for a command button labeled "Quit."

2. DOS has a command called SORT that orders the records of a sequential file. The command

```
SORT <filename1 >filename2
```

sorts the records of the first file in ascending order by the first field and places them into a new file called *filename2*. The DOS command

```
SORT <filename1 >filename2  /R
```

produces a descending sort.

PRACTICE PROBLEMS 8.2

1. The program in Example 2 contains three Do loops. Explain why at most one of the last two loops will be executed. Under what circumstances will neither of the last two loops be executed?

2. Modify the program in Example 2 so that duplicate items will be repeated in the merged file.

EXERCISES 8.2

Exercises 1 through 4 are related. They create and maintain the sequential file AVERAGE.TXT to hold batting averages of baseball players.

1. Suppose the season is about to begin. Compose a program to create the sequential file containing the name of each player, his times at bat, and his number of hits. The program should allow the user to type a name into a text box and then click a command button to add a record to the file. The times at bat and number of hits initially should be set to 0. (**Hint:** Open the file for Input in the Form_Load event procedure and Close the file when a "Quit" command button is clicked.)

2. Each day, the statistics from the previous day's games should be used to update the file. Write a program to read the records one at a time and allow the user to enter the number of times at bat and the number of hits in yesterday's game for each player in appropriate text boxes on a form. When a command button is clicked, the program should update the file by adding these numbers to the previous figures. (**Hint:** Open files in the Form_Load event procedure. Close the files and end the program when all data have been processed.)

3. Several players are added to the league. Compose a program to update the file.

4. Compose a program to sort the file AVERAGE.TXT with respect to batting averages and display the players with the top ten batting averages. **Hint:** The file must be read once to determine the number of players and again to load the players into an array.

Exercises 5 and 6 refer to the ordered file BLOCK.TXT containing the names of people on your block and the ordered file TIMES.TXT containing the names of all people who subscribe to the NY Times.

5. Write a program that creates a file consisting of the names of all people on your block who subscribe to *The New York Times*.

6. Write a program that creates a file consisting of the names of all *New York Times* subscribers who do not live on your block.

7. Suppose a file of positive integers is in ascending order. Write a program to determine the maximum number of times any integer is repeated in the file. (For instance, if the entries in the file are 5, 5, 6, 6, 6, and 10, then the output is 3.)

8. Suppose each record of the file SALES.TXT contains a salesperson's name and the dollar amount of a sale, and the records are ordered by the names. Write a program to display the name, number of sales, and average sale amount for each salesperson. For instance, if the first four records of the file are

"Adams", 123.45
"Adams", 432.15
"Brown", 89.95
"Cook", 500.00

then the first two entries of the output would be

```
Salesperson    Number of Sales    Average Sale Amount
Adams          2                  $277.80
Brown          1                  $89.95
```

9. An elementary school holds a raffle to raise funds. Suppose each record of the file RAFFLE.TXT contains a student's grade (1 through 6), name, and the number of raffle tickets sold, and that the records are ordered by grade. Write a program using a control break to display the number of tickets sold by each grade and the total number of tickets sold.

10. *Multiple Control Breaks.* Suppose the sorted sequential file CENSUS.TXT contains names of all residents of a state, where each record has the form "lastName","firstName". Write a program to determine, in one pass through the file, the most common last name and most common full name. (**Note:** In the unlikely event of a tie, the program should display the first occurring name.) For instance, the output in the picture box might be as follows.

```
The most common last name is Brown
The most common full name is John Smith
```

In Exercises 11 and 12, suppose the file MASTER.TXT contains the names and phone numbers of all members of an organization, where the records are ordered by name.

11. Suppose the ordered file MOVED.TXT contains the names and new phone numbers of all members who have changed their phone numbers. Write a program to update the file MASTER.TXT.

12. Suppose the ordered file QUIT.TXT contains the names of all members who have left the organization. Write a program to update the file MASTER.TXT.

13. Suppose a file must be sorted by Visual Basic, but is too large to fit into an array. How can this be accomplished?

14. What are some advantages of files over arrays?

SOLUTIONS TO PRACTICE PROBLEMS 8.2

1. Execution proceeds beyond the first Do loop only when EOF becomes True for one of the input files. Since each of the last two Do loops executes only if EOF is not True, at most one loop can execute.

Neither of the last two loops will be executed if each input file is empty or if the last entries of the files are the same.

2. Change the SELECT CASE block to the following:

```
Select Case num1
  Case Is <= num2
    Write #3, num1
    Input #1, num1
  Case Is > num2
    Write #3, num2
    Input #2, num2
End Select
```

8.3 A CASE STUDY: RECORDING CHECKS AND DEPOSITS

The purpose of this section is to take you through the design and implementation of a quality program for personal checkbook management. Nothing in this chapter shows off the power of Visual Basic better than the program in this section. That a user-friendly checkbook management program can be written in only four pages of code clearly shows Visual Basic's ability to improve the productivity of programmers. It is easy to imagine an entire finance program, similar to programs that have generated millions of dollars of sales, being written in only a few weeks by using Visual Basic!

The Design of the Program

Though there are many commercial programs available for personal financial management, they include so many bells and whistles that their original purpose—keeping track of transactions and reporting balances—has become obscured. The program in this section was designed specifically as a checkbook program. It keeps track of expenditures and deposits and produces a printed report. Adding a reconciliation feature would be easy enough, although we did not include one.

The program is supposed to be user friendly. Therefore, it showcases many of the techniques and tools available in Visual Basic.

The general design goals for the program included the abilities to

- Automatically enter the user's name on each check and deposit slip.
- Automatically provide the next consecutive check or deposit slip number. (The user can override this feature if necessary.)
- Automatically provide the date. (Again, this feature can be overridden.)
- For each check, record the payee, the amount, and optionally a memo.
- For each deposit slip, record the source, the amount, and optionally a memo.
- Display the current balance at all times.
- Produce a printout detailing all transactions.

The User Interface

With Visual Basic we can place a replica of a check or deposit slip on the screen and let the user supply the information as if actually filling out a check or deposit slip. Figure 8.5 shows the form in its check mode. A picture box forms the boundary of the check. Below the picture box are two labels for the current balance and four command buttons.

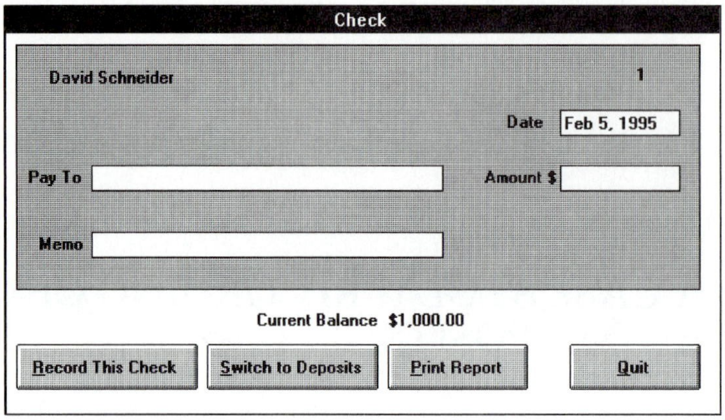

Figure 8.5 Template for entering a check.

The first time the user runs the program, the user is asked for his or her name, the starting balance, and the numbers of the first check and deposit slip. Suppose the user's name is David Schneider, the first check has number 1, the starting balance is $1000, and the first deposit slip is also number 1. Figure 8.5 shows the form after the three pieces of input. The upper part of the form looks like a check. The check has color light turquoise blue (or cyan). The Date box is automatically set to today's date, but can be altered by the user. The user fills in the payee, amount, and optionally a memo. When the user pushes the Record This Check button, the information is written to a file, the balance is updated, and check number 2 appears.

To record a deposit, the user pushes the Switch to Deposits button. The form then appears as in Figure 8.6. The form's title bar now says Deposit Slip, the words Pay To have changed to Source, and the color of the slip has changed to yellow. Also, in the buttons at the bottom of the form, the words Check and Deposit have been interchanged. A deposit is recorded in much the same way as a check. When the Print Report button is pushed, a printout similar to the one in Figure 8.7 is printed on the printer.

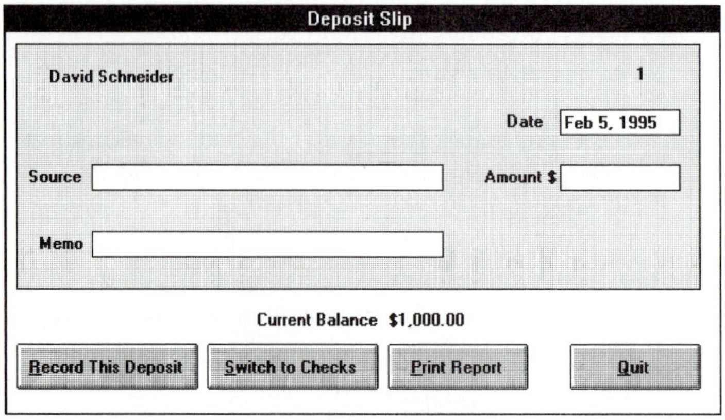

Figure 8.6 Template for entering a deposit slip.

			Feb 5, 1995
Name: David Schneider	Starting balance: $1,000.00		
Date	Transaction	Amount	Balance
Jan 21, 1995	Check #: 1 Paid to: Land's End Memo: shirts	$75.95	$924.05
Jan 29, 1995	Check #: 2 Paid to: Bethesda Coop Memo: groceries	$125.00	$799.05
Feb 5, 1995	Deposit #: 1 Source: Macmillan Memo: typing expenses	$245.00	$1,044.05
	Ending Balance: $1,044.05		

Figure 8.7 Sample printout of transactions.

The common design for the check and deposit slip allows one set of controls to be used for both items. Figure 8.8 shows the controls and their suggestive names. (The only control not named is the picture box, Picture1.) Each control name, except Picture1, begins with a three-letter prefix identifying the type of the object. The caption of the label lblToFrom will change back and forth between Pay To and Source.

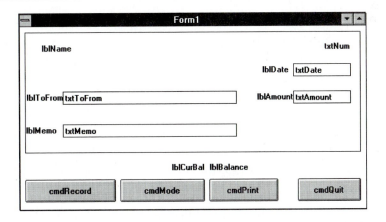

Figure 8.8 Control names for checkbook management program.

Table 8.2 lists the objects and their initial properties. Since the program will always begin by displaying the next check, the various captions and the Background property of the picture box could have been set at design-time. We chose instead to leave these assignments to the SetupCheck subprogram, which is normally used to switch from deposit entry to check entry, but also can be called by the Form_Load event procedure to prepare the initial mode (check or deposit) for the form. However, in order to write the setup subprograms, we do note the values that Visual Basic displays for the Background property if we select the light blue or yellow colors from the third row of the color palette. These values are &H00FFFF00& and &H0000FFFF&, respectively.

Object	Property	Setting
Form1		
Picture1		
lblName	BackStyle	0 – Transparent
txtNum	BorderStyle	0 – None
lblDate	BackStyle	0 – Transparent
	Caption	Date
txtDate		
lblToFrom	BackStyle	0 – Transparent
txtToFrom		
lblAmount	BackStyle	0 – Transparent
	Caption	Amount $
txtAmount		
lblMemo	BackStyle	0 – Transparent
	Caption	Memo
txtMemo		
lblCurBal	Caption	Current Balance
lblBalance		
cmdRecord		
cmdMode		
cmdPrint	Caption	&Print Report
cmdQuit	Caption	&Quit

Table 8.2 Objects and initial properties for the checkbook management program.

The transactions are stored in a data file named CHKBOOK.TXT. The first four entries of the file are the name to appear on the check or deposit slip, the starting balance, the number of the first check, and the number of the first deposit slip. After that, each transaction is recorded as a sequence of eight items—the type of transaction, the contents of txtToFrom, the current balance, the number of the last check, the number of the last deposit slip, the amount of money, the memo, and the date.

Coding the Program

The top row of Figure 8.9 shows the different events to which the program must respond. Table 8.3 identifies the corresponding event procedures and the general procedures they call.

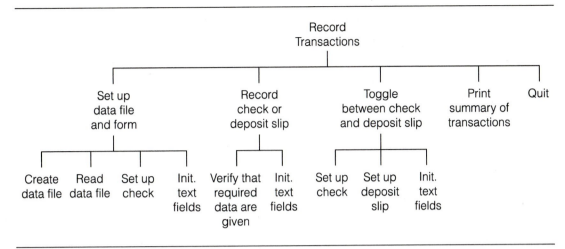

Figure 8.9 Hierarchy chart for checkbook management program.

Task	Procedure
1. Set up data file and form	Form_Load
1.1 Create data file	CreateDataFile
1.2 Read data file	ReadDataFile
1.3 Set up check	SetupCheck
1.4 Initialize text fields	InitializeFields
2. Record check or deposit slip	cmdRecord_Click
2.1 Verify that required data are given	AllDataGiven
2.2 Initialize text fields	InitializeFields
3. Toggle between check & deposit slip	cmdMode_Click
3.1 Set up check	SetupCheck
3.2 Set up deposit slip	SetupDeposit
3.3 Initialize text fields	InitializeFields
4. Print summary of transaction	cmdPrint_Click
5. Quit	cmdQuit_Click

Table 8.3 Tasks and their procedures.

Let's examine each event procedure.

1. **Form_Load** first looks to see if the file CHKBOOK.TXT has been created. The function Dir$ returns "CHKBOOK.TXT" if the file exists and otherwise returns the empty string. If CHKBOOK.TXT does not exist, the routine CreateDataFile is called. CreateDataFile prompts the user for the name to appear on the checks and deposit slips, the starting balance, and the numbers of the first check and deposit slip, and then writes these items to the data file. If CHKBOOK.TXT does exist, the routine ReadDataFile is called to read through the entire file to determine all information needed to proceed. The event procedure calls SetupCheck to set the transaction type to Check and set the appropriate captions and background colors for a check. The event procedure then calls InitializeFields, which initializes all the text boxes.

In the first Let statement of the procedure, the drive is specified as the A drive. Therefore, the data file will be written to and read from a diskette on the A drive. Feel free to change the letter A to whatever drive you prefer. You may even want to specify an entire path.

2. **cmdRecord_Click** first confirms that the required fields contain entries. This is accomplished by calling the function AllDataGiven. If the value returned is "YES," then cmdRecord_Click opens the data file for output as Append, sends eight pieces of data to the file, and then closes the file. When AllDataGiven returns "NO," the function itself pops up a message box to tell the user where information is needed. The user must type in the information and then press the Record button again.

3. **cmdMode_Click** toggles back and forth from a check to a deposit slip. It calls SetupCheck, or its analog SetupDeposit, and then calls InitializeFields.

4. **cmdPrint_Click** prints out a complete history of all transactions as shown in Figure 8.7.

5. **cmdQuit_Click** ends the program.

```
Rem Record Checks and Deposits
Rem
Rem **************************************************************************
Rem *                                                                      *
Rem *   fileName    Name of the file containing previous data, if any      *
Rem *   nameOnChk   Name to appear on checks                               *
Rem *   lastCkNum   Number of last check written                          *
Rem *   lastDpNum   Number of last deposit slip processed                 *
Rem *   curBal      Current balance in account                           *
Rem *   transType   Type of transaction, check or deposit                *
Rem *                                                                      *
Rem **************************************************************************

Dim fileName As String, nameOnChk As String
Dim lastCkNum As Integer, lastDpNum As Integer
Dim curBal As Single, transType As String

Function AllDataGiven () As String
  Dim message As String
  Rem If one of the four required pieces of information
  Rem is missing, assign its name to message
  Let message = ""
  If txtDate.Text = "" Then
      Let message = "Date"
      txtDate.SetFocus
    ElseIf txtToFrom.Text = "" Then
      If transType = "Check" Then
         Let message = "Pay To"
       Else
         Let message = "Source"
      End If
      txtToFrom.SetFocus
```

```
      ElseIf txtAmount.Text = "" Then
        Let message = "Amount"
        txtAmount.SetFocus
      ElseIf txtNum.Text = "" Then
        If transType = "Check" Then
            Let message = "Check Number"
          Else
            Let message = "Deposit Number"
        End If
        txtNum.SetFocus
    End If
    If message = "" Then
        Rem All required data fields have been filled; recording can proceed
        AllDataGiven = "YES"
      Else
        Rem Advise user of required data which is missing
        MsgBox "The '" + message + "' field must be filled", , "Error"
        AllDataGiven = "NO"
    End If
End Function


Sub cmdMode_Click ()
    Rem Toggle from Check to/from Deposit Slip
    If transType = "Check" Then
        Call SetupDeposit
      Else    'transType = "Deposit"
        Call SetupCheck
    End If
    Call InitializeFields
    txtToFrom.SetFocus
End Sub


Sub cmdPrint_Click ()
    Dim temp As String, lineNo As Integer
    Dim nameOnChk As String, balance As Single, ck As Integer, dp As Integer
    Dim toFrom As String, amount As String, memo As String, theDate As String
    Rem Print out a detailed list of all transactions.
    Let temp = Form1.Caption              'Save the current form caption
    Let Form1.Caption = "Printing..."     'Set form caption to indicate printing
    Let lineNo = 1                        'Line number being printed
    Open fileName For Input As #1         'Open the file
    Input #1, nameOnChk, balance, ck, dp 'Read in the file header
    Rem Print the details of the individual transactions.
    Do Until EOF(1)
      If lineNo >= 57 Then
          Rem 57 or more lines have been printed; start a new page
          Printer.NewPage
          Let lineNo = 1
      End If
      If lineNo = 1 Then
          Rem Print the report header
          Printer.Print
          Printer.Print "Name: ";nameOnChk;Tab(65);Format$(Date, "mmm d, yyyy")
          Printer.Print
```

```
            Printer.Print , "Starting balance: "; Format$(balance, "Currency")
            Printer.Print
            Printer.Print "Date", "Transaction"; Tab(50); "Amount";
            Printer.Print Tab(65); "Balance"
            Printer.Print "_____", "_____"; Tab(50); "_____";
            Printer.Print Tab(65); "_____"
            Printer.Print
            Printer.Print
            Let lineNo = 10
        End If
        Input #1, transType, toFrom, balance, ck, dp, amount, memo, theDate
        If transType = "Check" Then
            Printer.Print theDate, "Check #: "; ck; Tab(50); amount;
            Printer.Print Tab(65); Format$(balance, "Currency")
            Printer.Print , "Paid to: "; toFrom
          Else              'Transaction was a deposit
            Printer.Print theDate, "Deposit #: "; dp; Tab(50); amount;
            Printer.Print Tab(65); Format$(balance, "Currency")
            Printer.Print , "Source: "; toFrom
        End If
        Let lineNo = lineNo + 2
        Rem If there was a memo, then print it.
        If memo <> "" Then
            Printer.Print , "Memo: "; memo
            Let lineNo = lineNo + 1
        End If
        Printer.Print
        Let lineNo = lineNo + 1
    Loop
    Close #1                      'Close the file
    Rem Print the ending balance
    Printer.Print
    Printer.Print , "Ending Balance: "; Format$(balance, "Currency")
    Printer.EndDoc                'Send the output to the Printer
    Let Form1.Caption = temp      'Restore the form caption
    txtToFrom.SetFocus            'Set focus for the next entry
End Sub

Sub cmdQuit_Click ()
  Rem  Exit the program
  End
End Sub

Sub cmdRecord_Click ()
  Dim amt As String, amount As Single, itemNum As Integer
  Rem Check to ensure all required fields are filled
  If AllDataGiven() = "YES" Then
      Let amt = txtAmount.Text 'Amount of transaction as string
      Let amount = Val(amt)     'Amount of transaction as number
      Let amt = Format$(amt, "Currency")
      Let itemNum = Val(txtNum.Text)
      If transType = "Check" Then
          Let curBal = curBal - amount
          Let lastCkNum = itemNum
```

```
        Else              'transType = "Deposit"
          Let curBal = curBal + amount
          Let lastDpNum = itemNum
      End If
      Let lblBalance.Caption = Format$(curBal, "Currency")
      Open fileName For Append As #1
      Rem The following two lines must be entered as a single program line
      Write #1, transType, txtToFrom.Text, curBal, lastCkNum, lastDpNum, amt,
                                          txtMemo.Text, txtDate.Text

      Close #1
      Call InitializeFields
      txtToFrom.SetFocus
  End If
End Sub


Sub CreateDataFile ()
  Dim startBal As Single, ckNum As integer
  Rem The first time the program is run, create a data file
  Open fileName For Output As #1
  Let nameOnChk = InputBox$("Name to appear on checks:")
  Let startBal = Val(InputBox$("Starting balance:"))
  Let ckNum = Val(InputBox$("Number of the first check:"))
  Let lastCkNum = ckNum - 1    'Number of "last" check written
  Let ckNum = Val(InputBox$("Number of the first deposit slip:"))
  Let lastDpNum = ckNum - 1    'Number of "last" deposit slip processed
  Let curBal = startBal        'Set current balance
  Rem First record in data file records name to appear on checks
  Rem plus initial data for account
  Write #1, nameOnChk, startBal, lastCkNum, lastDpNum
  Close #1
End Sub


Sub Form_Load ()
  Dim drive As String
  Rem If no data file exists, create one. Otherwise, open the
  Rem data file and get the user's name, last used check and
  Rem deposit slip numbers, and current balance.
  Rem In next line adjust drive as necessary
  Let drive = "A:"                     'Drive (or path) for data file
  Let fileName = drive + "CHKBOOK.TXT"  'Program uses one data file
  If Dir$(fileName) = "" Then
      Rem Data file does not exist, so create it and obtain initial data
      Call CreateDataFile
    Else
      Call ReadDataFile
  End If
  Rem Set name and balance labels
  Let lblName.Caption = nameOnChk
  Let lblBalance.Caption = Format$(curBal, "Currency")
  Rem Set the date field to the current date
  Let txtDate.Text = Format$(Date, "mmm d, yyyy")
  Call SetupCheck                      'Always start session with checks
  Call InitializeFields
End Sub
```

```
Sub InitializeFields ()
  Rem Initialize all text entry fields except date
  Let txtToFrom.Text = ""
  Let txtAmount.Text = ""
  Let txtMemo.Text = ""
  If transType = "Check" Then
      Rem Make txtNum text box reflect next check number
      Let txtNum.Text = Format$(lastCkNum + 1, "#")
    Else              'transType = "Deposit"
      Rem Make txtNum text box reflect next deposit slip number
      Let txtNum.Text = Format$(lastDpNum + 1, "#")
  End If
End Sub


Sub ReadDataFile ()
  Dim t As String, s As String, n As String, m As String, d As String
  Rem Recover name to appear on checks, current balance,
  Rem number of last check written, and number of last deposit slip processed
  Open fileName For Input As #1
  Input #1, nameOnChk, curBal, lastCkNum, lastDpNum
  Do Until EOF(1)
    Rem Read to the end of the file to recover the current balance and the
    Rem last values recorded for ckNum and dpNum.
    Rem t, s, n, m and d are dummy variables and are not used at this point
    Input #1, t, s, curBal, lastCkNum, lastDpNum, n, m, d
  Loop
  Close #1
End Sub


Sub SetupCheck ()
  Rem Prepare form for the entry of a check
  Let transType = "Check"
  Let Form1.Caption = "Check"
  Let lblToFrom.Caption = "Pay To"
  Let cmdRecord.Caption = "&Record This Check"
  Let cmdMode.Caption = "&Switch to Deposits"
  Let Picture1.BackColor = &H00FFFF00&" ' color of check is light blue
  Let txtNum.BackColor = &H00FFFF00&
End Sub


Sub SetupDeposit ()
  Rem Prepare form for the entry of a deposit
  Let transType = "Deposit"
  Let Form1.Caption = "Deposit Slip"
  Let lblToFrom.Caption = "Source"
  Let cmdRecord.Caption = "&Record This Deposit"
  Let cmdMode.Caption = "&Switch to Checks"
  Let Picture1.BackColor = &H0000FFFF& ' color of deposit slip is yellow
  Let txtNum.BackColor = &H0000FFFF&
End Sub
```

Chapter 8
Summary

1. When sequential files are *opened*, we must specify whether they will be created and written to, added to, or read from by use of the terms Output, Append, or Input. The file must be *closed* before the operation is changed. Data are written to the file with Write# statements and retrieved with Input# statements. The EOF function tells if we have read to the end of the file.

2. A sequential file can be ordered by placing its data in arrays, sorting the arrays, and then writing the ordered data into a file. This process should precede adding, deleting, or altering items in a master file.

Chapter 8
Programming Projects

1. Table 8.3 gives the leading eight soft drinks and their percentage share of the market. Write and execute a program to place these data into a sequential file. Then write a second program to use the file to

   (a) display the eight brands and their gross sales in billions. (The entire soft drink industry grosses about $40 billion.)
   (b) calculate the total percentage market share of the leading eight soft drinks.

Coke Classic	19.3	Dr. Pepper	5.3
Pepsi	16.1	Mountain Dew	4.3
Diet Coke	9.8	Sprite	3.9
Diet Pepsi	6.2	7 Up	2.9

Table 8.3 Leading soft drinks and percentages of market share for 1993.
Source: Beverage Marketing Corp.

2. Suppose the sequential file ALE.TXT contains the information shown in Table 8.4. Write a program to use the file to produce Table 8.5 in which the baseball teams are in descending order by the percentage of games won.

Team	Won	Lost
Baltimore	82	70
Boston	78	73
Cleveland	73	80
Detroit	78	74
Milwaukee	65	88
New York	83	70
Toronto	87	64

Table 8.4 American League East games won and lost, 9/23/93.

	American League East		
	W	L	Pct
Toronto	87	64	.576
New York	83	70	.542
Baltimore	82	70	.539
Boston	78	73	.517
Detroit	78	74	.513
Cleveland	73	80	.477
Milwaukee	65	88	.425

Table 8.5 American League East standings on 9/23/93.

3. Write a rudimentary word processing program. The program should do the following:

(a) Use InputBox$ to request the name of the sequential file to hold the document being created.

(b) Set the label for a text box to "Enter Line 1" and allow the user to enter the first line of the document into a text box.

(c) When the Enter key is pressed or a "Record Line" command button is clicked, determine if the line is acceptable. Blank lines are acceptable input, but lines exceeding 60 characters in length should not be accepted. Advise the user of the problem with a message box, then set the focus back to the text box so that the user can edit the line to an acceptable length.

(c) When an acceptable line is entered, write this line to the file and display it in a picture box.

(d) Change the prompt to "Enter Line 2," clear the text box, allow the user to enter the second line of the document into the text box, and carry out (c) for this line using the same picture box. (Determine in advance how many lines the picture box can display and only clear the picture box when the lines already displayed do not leave room for a new line.)

(e) Continue as in (d) with appropriate labels for subsequent lines until the user clicks on a "Finished" command button.

(f) Clear the picture box and display the number of lines written and the name of the data file created.

4. Write a program that counts the number of times a word occurs in the sequential file created in Programming Project 3. The file name and word should be read from text boxes. The search should not be sensitive to the case of the letters. For instance, opening a file that contained the first three sentences of the directions to this problem and searching for "the" would produce the output: "the" occurs 6 times.

5. *Create and Maintain Telephone Directories.* Write a program to create and maintain telephone directories. Each directory will be a separate sequential file. The following command buttons should be available:

(a) Select a directory to access. A list of directories that have been created should be stored in a separate sequential file. When a request is made to open a directory, the list of available directories should be displayed as part of an InputBox$ prompt requesting the name of the directory to be accessed. If the user responds with a directory name not listed, the desire to create a new directory should be confirmed, and then the new directory created and added to the list of existing directories.

(b) Add name and phone number (as given in text boxes) to the end of the current directory.

(c) Delete name (as given in text box) from the current directory.

(d) Sort the current directory into name order.

(e) Print out the names and phone numbers contained in the current directory.

(f) Terminate the program.

6. Table 8.6 contains the statistics for a stock portfolio.

Stock	Number of Shares	Date Purchased	Purchase Price/Share	Current Price/Share
AT&T	200	12/4/84	18 3/4	64 1/2
GM	600	4/16/85	61 5/8	48 3/8
IBM	300	8/8/85	129 1/4	43 5/8
Xerox	400	11/16/85	56 5/8	73 1/4
Exxon	100	3/1/86	52 1/4	64 3/4

Table 8.6 Stock portfolio.

(a) Compose a program to create the sequential file STOCKS.TXT containing the information in Table 8.6.

(b) Compose a program to perform the following tasks. A possible form design is shown in Figure 8.10.

   (1) Display the information in the file STOCKS.TXT as in Table 8.6 when the user clicks on a "Display Stocks" command button.

   (2) Add an additional stock onto the end of the file STOCKS.TXT when the user clicks on an "Add Stock" command button. The data for the new stock should be read from appropriately labeled text boxes.

   (3) Update the Current Price/Share of a stock in the file STOCKS.TXT when the user clicks on an "Update Price" command button. The name of the stock to be updated and the new price should be read from the appropriate text boxes. The file STOCKS.TXT should then be copied to a temp file until the specified stock is found. The update record for this stock should then be written to the temp file, followed by all remaining records in STOCKS.TXT. Finally, the original STOCKS.TXT file should be erased and the temp file renamed to STOCKS.TXT.

   (4) Process the data in the file STOCKS.TXT and produce the display shown in Figure 8.11 when a "Show Profit/Loss" command button is clicked.

   (5) Quit.

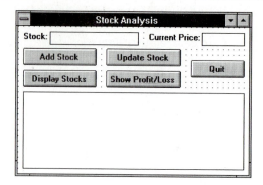

Figure 8.10 Possible form design for Programming Project 6.

Stock	Cost	Current Value	Profit (or Loss)
=====	==========	==========	==========
AT&T	$3,750.00	$12,900.00	$9,150.00
GM	$36,975.00	$29,025.00	($7,950.00)
IBM	$38,775.00	$13,087.50	($25,687.50)
Xerox	$22,650.00	$29,300.00	$6,650.00
Exxon	$5,225.00	$6,475.00	$1,250.00

Figure 8.11 Output of Project 6.

7. A department store has a file containing all sales transacted for a year. Each record contains a customer's name, zip code, and amount of the sale. The file is ordered first by zip code and then by name. Write a program to display the total sales for each customer, the total sales for each zip code, and the total sales for the store. For instance, if the first seven records of the file are

```
"Adams, John", 10023, 34.50
"Adams, John", 10023, 60.00
"Jones, Bob", 10023, 62.45
"Green, Mary", 12345, 54.00
"Howard, Sue", 12345, 79.25
"Smith, George", 20001, 25.10
```

then the output in the picture box will begin as shown if Figure 8.12.

Customer	Total Sales
Adams, John	$94.50
Jones, Bob	$62.45
Total sales of zip code 10023: $156.95	
Green, Mary	$54.00

Figure 8.12 Sample output for Programming Project 7.

8. *Savings Account.* FILE1.TXT is a sequential file containing the name, account number, and beginning-of-month balance for each depositor. FILE2.TXT is a sequential file containing all the transactions (deposits and withdrawals) for the month. Use FILE2.TXT to upgrade FILE1.TXT. For each customer, print a statement similar to the one received from banks that shows all transactions and the end-of-month balance. Also, record all overdrawn accounts in a file. (As an optional embellishment, deduct a penalty if the balance fell below a certain level any time during the month. The penalty could include a fixed fee of $10 plus a charge of $1 for each check and deposit.) **Hint:** Assume no more than 500 transactions have occurred.

9. A fuel economy study was carried out for five models of cars. Each car was driven for 100 miles of city driving, then the model of the car and the number of gallons used were placed in the sequential file MILEAGE.TXT with the statement

```
Write #1, modelName, gallons
```

Table 8.7 shows the first entries of the file. Write a program to display the models and their average miles per gallon in decreasing order with respect to mileage. The program should utilize three parallel arrays of range 1 to 5. The first array should record the name of each model of car. This array is initially empty; each car model name is added when first encountered in reading the file. The second array should record the number of test vehicles for each model. The third array should record the total number of gallons used by that model. **Note:** The first array must be searched each time a record is read to determine the appropriate index to use with the other two arrays.

Model	Gal	Model	Gal	Model	Gal
LeBaron	4.9	Cutlass	4.5	Cutlass	4.6
Escort	4.1	Escort	3.8	LeBaron	5.1
Beretta	4.3	Escort	3.9	Escort	3.8
Skylark	4.5	Skylark	4.6	Cutlass	4.4

Table 8.7 Gallons of gasoline used in 100 miles of city driving.

9

Random-Access Files

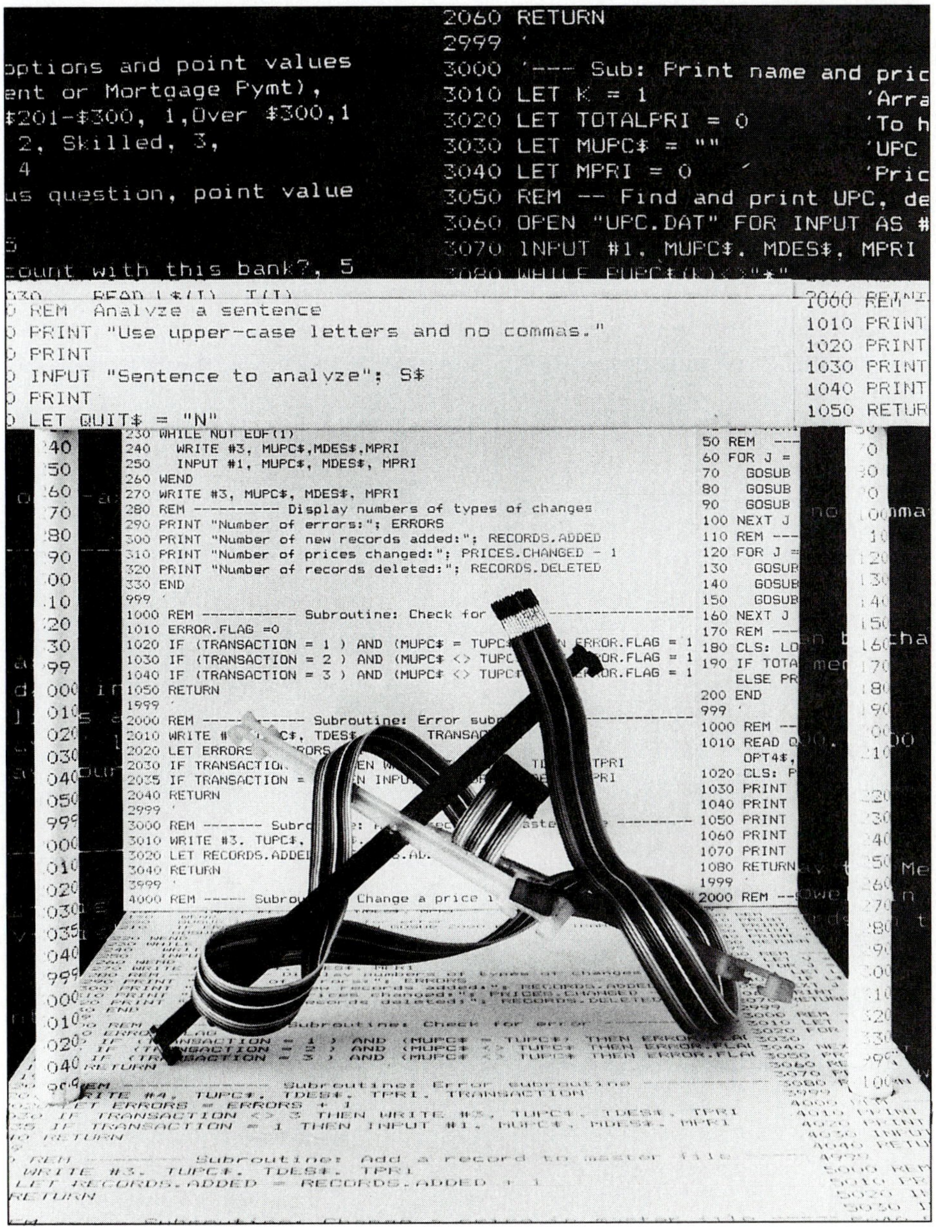

9.1 DATA TYPES

Records provide a convenient way of packaging as a single unit several related variables of different types. Before we can explore this powerful variable type, we must first explore a new category of variable, the fixed-length string.

Fixed-Length Strings

Fixed-length string variables are named following the same rules as other variable types. They are declared by statements of the form

```
Dim var As String * n
```

where n is a positive integer. After such a declaration, the value of *var* will always be a string of length n. Suppose *info* is an ordinary string and a statement of the form

```
Let var = info
```

is executed. If *info* has more than n characters, then only the first n characters will be assigned to *var*. If *info* has less than n characters, then spaces will be added to the end of the string to guarantee that *var* has length n.

EXAMPLE 1 The following program uses fixed-length strings. In the output, San Francisco is truncated to a string of length 9 and Detroit is padded on the right with two blank spaces.

```
Sub Command1_Click ()
  Dim city As String * 9
  Rem Illustrate fixed-length strings
  Picture1.Cls
  Picture1.Print "123456789"
  Let city = "San Francisco"
  Picture1.Print city
  Let city = "Detroit"
  Picture1.Print city; "MI"
  Picture1.Print Len(city)
End Sub
```

[Set Picture1's FontName property to Courier. Run and click the command button.]

Care must be taken when comparing an ordinary (variable-length) string with a fixed-length string or comparing two fixed-length strings of different lengths.

EXAMPLE 2   In the following program, the strings assigned to the variables *city*, *town*, and *municipality* have lengths 9, 7, and 12, respectively, and therefore are all different.

```
Sub Command1_Click ()
  Dim town As String
  Dim city As String * 9
  Dim municipality As String * 12
  Rem Illustrate fixed-length strings
  Let town = "Chicago"
  Let city = "Chicago"
  Let municipality = "Chicago"
  Picture1.Cls
  If (city = town) Or (city = municipality) Then
      Picture1.Print "same"
    Else
      Picture1.Print "different"
  End If
  Picture1.Print "123456789012345"
  Picture1.Print city + "***"
  Picture1.Print town + "***"
  Picture1.Print municipality + "***"
End Sub
```

[Set Picture1's FontName property to Courier. Run and click the command button.]

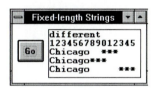

There are times when we want to consider the values assigned to variables of different types as being the same, such as *city* and *town* in Example 2. In this situation, the function RTrim$ comes to the rescue. If *info* is an ordinary string or a fixed-length string, then the value of

```
RTrim$(info)
```

is the (variable-length) string consisting of *info* with all right-hand spaces removed. For instance, the value of RTrim$("hello   ") is the string "hello". In Example 2, if the If block is changed to

```
If (RTrim$(city) = town) And (RTrim$(city) = RTrim$(municipality)) Then
    Picture1.Print "same"
  Else
    Picture1.Print "different"
End If
```

then the first line of the output will be "same".

Records

In this text, we have worked with numbers, strings, arrays, and now fixed-length strings. Strings and numbers are built-in data types that can be used without being declared, although we have always elected to declare numeric and string variable using Dim statements. On the other hand, arrays and fixed-length strings are user-defined data types that must be declared with a Dim statement before being used. A record is a user-defined data type that groups related variables of different types.

Figure 9.1 shows an index card that can be used to hold data about colleges. The three pieces of data—name, state, and year founded—are called fields. Each field functions like a variable in which information can be stored and retrieved. The length of a field is the number of spaces allocated to it. In the case of the index card, we see that there are three fields having lengths 30, 2, and 4, respectively. The layout of the index card can be identified by a name, such as collegeData, called a record type.

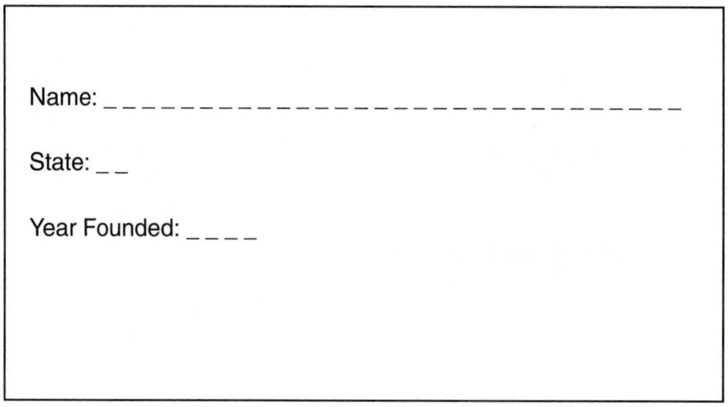

Name: _

State: _ _

Year Founded: _ _ _ _

Figure 9.1 An index card having three fields.

For programming purposes, the layout of the record is declared by the block of statements

```
Type collegeData
   nom As String * 30
   state As String * 2
   yearFounded As Integer
End Type
```

Each character of a string is stored in a piece of memory known as a byte. Therefore, a field of type String * n requires n bytes of memory. However, numbers (that is, the integer or single-precision numbers we use in this text) are stored in a different manner than strings. Integer numbers *always* use two bytes of memory while single-precision numbers *always* use four bytes of memory.

Visual Basic requires that Type declarations, such as the record structure *collegeData* above, be placed in a special file, referred to as a BAS Module. (In each of our previous programs, we have written the lines of the program into a single file that is sometimes referred to as a Form Module). To create a BAS Module for the program currently being designed, press Alt/F/M. A window like the one in Figure 9.2 will appear. This window is where Type declarations must be entered.

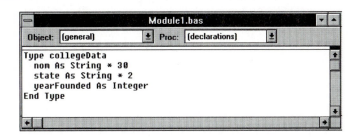

Figure 9.2 BAS module window for type declarations.

To move back and forth between this BAS Module window and the Form Module window with which we are familiar, press F2 to open the View Procedures window. Displayed in the top list box of this window are the names of the two files now associated with the current program. To access the Form Module window, select the name ending with ".frm" and then click on OK. Similarly, to access the BAS Module window, select the name ending with ".bas" and then click on OK. (You can also switch between the BAS Module and Form Module windows by clicking on any portion of the desired window that is sticking out from behind the currently active window.)

A record variable capable of holding the data for a specific college is declared in the Form Module by a statement such as

```
Dim college As collegeData
```

Each field is accessed by giving the name of the record variable and the field, separated by a period. For instance, the three fields of the record variable college are accessed as *college.nom*, *college.state*, and *college.yearFounded*. Figure 9.3 shows a representation of the way the record variable is organized.

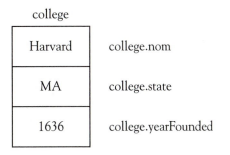

Figure 9.3 Record variable with values assigned to the fields.

In general, a record type is created in a BAS Module by a Type block of the form

```
Type recordType
  fieldName1 As fieldType1
  fieldname2 As fieldType2
    .
    .
    .
End Type
```

where *recordType* is the name of the user-defined data type, *fieldName1*, *field-Name2*, . . . are the names of the fields of the record variable, and *fieldType1*, *fieldType2*, . . . are the corresponding field types, either String ∗ *n*, for some *n*, Integer, or Single in this text. In the Form Module, a record variable *recordVar* is declared to be of the user-defined type by a statement of the form

```
Dim recordVar As recordType
```

EXAMPLE 3   The following program processes records.

```
Rem In BAS Module
Type collegeData
  nom As String * 30
  state As String * 2
  yearFounded As Integer
End Type

Rem In Form Module
Sub Command1_Click ()
  Dim century As Integer, when As String
  Rem Demonstrate use of records
  Picture1.Cls
  Dim college As collegeData
  Let college.nom = Text1.Text
  Let college.state = Text2.Text
  Let college.yearFounded = Val(Text3.Text)
  Let century = 1 + Int(college.yearFounded / 100)
  Picture1.Print RTrim$(college.nom); " was founded in the" + Str$(century);
  Picture1.Print "th century in "; college.state
  Dim university As collegeData
  Let university.nom = "M.I.T."
  Let university.state = "MA"
  Let university.yearFounded = 1878
  If college.yearFounded < university.yearFounded Then
      Let when = "before "
    Else
      Let when = "after "
  End If
  Picture1.Print RTrim$(college.nom); " was founded ";
  Picture1.Print when; RTrim$(university.nom)
End Sub
```

[Run, type data below into text boxes, and press the command button.]

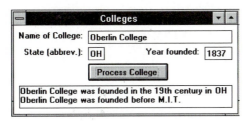

Type statements can only appear in the (declarations) section of a .BAS module, never in the (declarations) section or procedures of a .FRM file. However, Dim statements can be used in procedures to declare a local record variable. When records are passed to and from procedures, the parameter in the Sub or Function statement must have the form

parameter As *recordType*

EXAMPLE 4 The following program uses procedures to perform the same tasks as the program in Example 3.

```
Rem In BAS Module
Type collegeData
  nom As String * 30
  state As String * 2
  yearFounded As Integer
End Type

Rem In Form Module
Sub Command1_Click ()
  Rem Demonstrate use of records
  Picture1.Cls
  Dim college As collegeData
  Call GetDat(college)
  Call DisplayStatement(college)
End Sub

Sub DisplayStatement (school As collegeData)
  Dim century As Integer, when As String
  Let century = 1 + Int(school.yearFounded / 100)
  Picture1.Print RTrim$(school.nom); " was founded in the" + Str$(century);
  Picture1.Print "th century in "; school.state
  Dim university As collegeData
  Let university.nom = "M.I.T."
  Let university.state = "MA"
  Let university.yearFounded = 1878
  If school.yearFounded < university.yearFounded Then
      Let when = "before "
    Else
      Let when = "after "
  End If
  Picture1.Print RTrim$(school.nom); " was founded ";
  Picture1.Print when; RTrim$(university.nom)
End Sub
```

```
Sub GetDat (school As collegeData)
  Let school.nom = Text1.Text
  Let school.state = Text2.Text
  Let school.yearFounded = Val(Text3.Text)
End Sub
```

Comments:

1. Record variables are similar to arrays in that they both store and access data items using a common name. However, the elements in an array must be of the same data type, whereas the fields in a record variable can be a mixture of different data types. Also, the different elements of an array are identified by their indices, whereas the fields of a record are identified by a name following a period.

2. If the record variables *recVar1* and *recVar2* have the same type, then all the field values of *recVar2* can be assigned simultaneously to *recVar1* by the statement

   Let *recVar1* = *recVar2*

3. Statements of the form

   Picture1.Print *recVar*

   are invalid, where *recVar* is a record variable. Each field of a record must appear separately in a Picture1.Print statement. Also, comparisons involving records using the relational operators <, >, =, <>, <=, and >= are valid only with the record fields, and not with the records themselves.

4. In addition to being declared as numeric or fixed-length string data types, the elements of a user-defined variable type can also be declared as other types of records. However, we do not use such structures in this text.

5. An array of fixed-length strings is declared by a statement of the form

   Dim *arrayName (a* To *b)* As String * *n*

6. When fixed-length strings are passed to and from procedures, the corresponding parameter in the Sub or Function statement must be an ordinary (variable-length) string.

PRACTICE PROBLEMS 9.1

1. Find the errors in the following event procedure.

```
Sub Command1_Click ()
  Type Team
    school As String
    mascot As String
  End Type
  Dim squad As Team
  Let squad.school = "Rice"
  Let squad.mascot = "Owls"
  Picture1.Print squad.school + " " + squad.mascot
End Sub
```

2. Correct the code in Problem 1.

EXERCISES 9.1

In Exercises 1 through 4, determine the output displayed in the picture box when the command button is clicked.

1.
```
Sub Command1_Click ()
    Dim ocean As String * 10
    Dim river As String * 10
    Let ocean = "Pacific"
    Let river = "Mississippi"
    Picture1.Print ocean; river
End Sub
```

2.
```
Sub Command1_Click ()
    Dim color As String
    Dim colour as String * 6
    Let colour = "Blue"
    Let color = "Red"
    Picture1.Print colour; color; colour
End Sub
```

3.
```
Rem In BAS Module
Type appearance
    height As Single
    weight As Single
    eyeColor As String * 5
End Type

Rem In Form Module
Sub Command1_Click ()
    Dim person1 As appearance
    Dim person2 As appearance
    Let person1.height = 72
    Let person1.weight = 170
    Let person1.eyeColor = "brown"
    Let person2.height = 12 * 6
    Let person2.weight = person1.weight
    Let person2.eyeColor = "brownish green"
    If person1.height = person2.height Then
        Picture1.Print "heights are same"
    End If
    Picture1.Print person2.weight
    If person1.eyeColor = person2.eyeColor Then
        Picture1.Print "eye colors are same"
    End If
End Sub
```

4.
```
Rem In BAS Module
Type testData
    nom As String * 5
    score As Single
End Type
```

```
Rem In Form Module
Sub Command1_Click ()
  Dim i As Integer
  Dim student As testData
  Open "SCORES.TXT" For Input As #1
  Picture1.Cls
  For i = 1 to 3
    Call GetScore(student)
    Call PrintScore(student)
  Next i
  Close #1
End Sub

Sub GetScore (student As testData)
  Input #1, student.nom, student.score
End Sub

Sub PrintScore (student As testData)
  Picture1.Print student.nom; student.score
End Sub
```

(Assume that the file SCORES.TXT contains the following three lines.)

"Joe", 18
"Moe", 20
"Albert", 25

In Exercises 5 through 10, determine the errors.

5.
```
Rem In BAS Module
Type zodiac
  nom As String * 15
  sign As String * 11
End Type

Rem In Form Module
Sub Command1_Click ()
  Dim astrology As zodiac
  Let nom = "Michael"
  Let sign = "Sagittarius"
End Sub
```

6.
```
Sub Command1_Click ()
  Type address
    street As String * 30
    city As String * 20
    state As String * 2
    zip As String * 10
  End Type
  Dim whiteHouse As address
  Let whiteHouse.street = "1400 Pennsylvania Avenue"
  Let whiteHouse.city = "Washington"
  Let whiteHouse.state = "DC"
  Let whiteHouse.zip = "20500"
End Sub
```

7.
```
Rem In BAS Module
Type employee
  name As String * 15
   socSecNum As String * 11
  payRate As Single
  exemptions As Integer
  maritalStat As String * 1
```

```
Rem In Form Module
Sub Command1_Click ()
  Dim gabriel As employee
End Sub
```

8.
```
Type print
   firstWord As String * 5
   secondWord As String * 5
End Type
```

9.
```
Type values
   label As String * 5
   var2 As Number
End Type
```

10.
```
Rem In BAS Module
Type vitamins
   a As Single
   b As Single
End Type
```

```
Rem In Form Module
Sub Command1_Click ()
  Dim minimum As vitamins
  Let minimum.b = 200
  Let minimum.a = 500
  Picture1.Print minimum
End Sub
```

In Exercises 11 through 14, write a Type block to declare a user-defined data type of the given name and types of elements.

11. Name: planet; Elements: planetName, distanceFromSun

12. Name: taxData; Elements: SSN, grossIncome, taxableIncome

13. Name: car; Elements: make, model, year, mileage

14. Name: party; Elements: numberOfGuests, address

15. Write a program that reads words from three text boxes and then displays them in a picture box in the first three zones without using any commas in the Picture1.Print statement. Do this by declaring the variables used to hold the words as fixed-length strings of the appropriate length, and setting the FontName property of the picture box to Courier.

16. Write a program to look up data on notable tall buildings. The program should declare a user-defined data type named "building" with the elements "nom", "city", "height", and "stories". This interactive program should allow the user to type the name of a building into a text box and then search through a data file to determine the city, height, and number of stories of the building when a command button is pressed. If the building is not in the data file, then the program should so report. Use the information in Table 9.1 for the data file.

Building	City	Height (ft)	Stories
Empire State	New York	1250	102
Sears Tower	Chicago	1454	110
Texas Commerce Tower	Houston	1002	75
Transamerica Pyramid	San Francisco	853	48

Table 9.1 Tallest buildings.

SOLUTIONS TO PRACTICE PROBLEMS 9.1

1. The event procedures contains two errors, both related to the Type declaration. First, the Type declaration cannot be inside a procedure. Instead, we must enter the Type declaration in a BAS module that we open by pressing Alt/F/M and entering a file name. Second, strings in a Type declaration must be fixed length; an asterisk and a whole number must follow String in defining the elements *school* and *mascot*.

2. In addition to correcting the errors that Visual Basic notices, we also need to keep the output looking as intended, thus the addition of the RTrim$ functions below.

```
Rem In BAS Module
Type Team
  school As String * 20
  mascot As String * 20
End Type


Rem In Form Module
Sub Command1_Click ()
  Dim squad As Team
  Let squad.school = "Rice"
  Let squad.mascot = "Owls"
  Picture1.Print RTrim$(squad.school) + " " + RTrim$(squad.mascot)
End Sub
```

9.2 RANDOM-ACCESS FILES

A random-access file is like an array of records stored on a disk. The records are numbered 1, 2, 3, and so on, and can be referred to by their numbers. Therefore, a random-access file resembles a box of index cards, each having a numbered tab. Any card can be selected from the box without first reading every index card preceding it; similarly, any record of a random-access file can be read without having to read every record preceding it.

One statement suffices to open a random-access file for all purposes: creating, appending, writing, and reading. Suppose a record type has been defined with a Type block and a record variable, called *recVar*, has been declared with a Dim statement. Then after the statement

```
Open "filespec" For Random As #n Len = Len(recVar)
```

is executed, records may be written, read, added, and changed. The file is referred to by the number n. Each record will have as many characters as allotted to each value of *recVar*.

Suppose appropriate Type, Dim, and Open statements have been executed. The two-step procedure for entering a record into the file is as follows.

1. Assign a value to each field of a record variable.

2. Place the data into record *r* of file *#n* with the statement

```
Put #n, r, recVar
```

where *recVar* is the record variable from step 1.

EXAMPLE 1 The following program creates and writes records to the random-access file COLLEGES.TXT.

```
Rem In BAS Module
Type collegeData
  nom As String * 25      'Name of college
  state As String * 2     'State where college is located
  yrFounded As Integer    'Year college was founded
End Type

Rem In Form Module
Dim recordNum As Integer

Sub Command1_Click ()
  Rem Write a record into the file COLLEGES.TXT
  Dim college As collegeData
  Let college.nom = Text1.Text
  Let college.state = Text2.Text
  Let college.yrFounded = Val(Text3.Text)
  Let recordNum = recordNum + 1
  Put #1, recordNum, college
  Let Text1.Text = ""
  Let Text2.Text = ""
  Let Text3.Text = ""
  Text1.SetFocus
End Sub

Sub Command2_Click ()
  Close #1
  End
End Sub

Sub Form_Load ()
  Rem Create COLLEGES.TXT
  Dim college As collegeData
  Open "COLLEGES.TXT" For Random As #1 Len = Len(college)
  Let recordNum = 0
End Sub
```

[Run, type into the text boxes the data shown in the first window below. Click the "Add College to File" command button. Record number 1 is added to COLLEGES.TXT and the text boxes are cleared. Proceed to record the data shown for the other two colleges, then click the "Done" command button.]

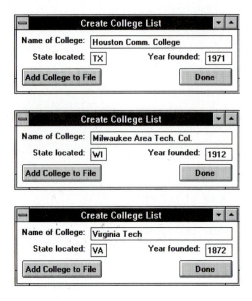

The two-step procedure for reading data from a record is as follows:

1. Execute the statement

```
Get #n, r, recVar
```

to assign record *r* of file #*n* to the record variable *recVar*.

2. Use the field variables of the record variable to either display values with Picture1.Print or to transfer values to other variables with Let.

EXAMPLE 2   Write a program to display the entire contents of the random-access file COLLEGES.TXT.

SOLUTION
```
Rem In BAS Module
Type collegeData
   nom As String * 25     'Name of college
   state As String * 2    'State where college is located
   yrFounded As Integer   'Year college was founded
End Type

Rem In Form Module
Sub Command1_Click ()
  Call DisplayFile
End Sub

Sub DisplayFile ()
  Dim recordNum As Integer
```

```
    Rem Access the random-access file COLLEGES.TXT
    Dim college As collegeData
    Open "COLLEGES.TXT" For Random As #1 Len = Len(college)
    Picture1.Cls
    Picture1.Print "College", , "State", "Year founded"
    For recordNum = 1 To 3
      Get #1, recordNum, college
      Picture1.Print college.nom, college.state, college.yrFounded
    Next recordNum
    Close #1
End Sub
```

[Run and click the command button.]

College	State	Year founded
Houston Comm. College	TX	1971
Milwaukee Area Tech. Col.	WI	1912
Virginia Tech	VA	1872

The total number of characters in the file with reference number n is given by the value of the function

```
    LOF(n)
```

The number of the last record in the file can be calculated by dividing this value by the record length. The LOF function, rather than the EOF function, should be used to determine when the end of the file has been reached. For instance, in Example 2 the For statement in the subprogram DisplayFile can be written as

```
    For recordNum = 1 To LOF(1) / Len(college)
```

Also, the pair of statements

```
    Let lastRecord = LOF(1) / Len(college)
    Put #1, lastRecord + 1, college
```

can be used to add a record to the end of the file.

Comments:

1. Random-access files are also known as **direct-access** or **relative** files. Since each record has the same number of characters, the computer can calculate where to find a specified record and, therefore, does not have to search for it sequentially.

2. Unlike sequential files, random-access files needn't be closed between placing information into them and reading from them.

3. Random-access files do not have to be filled in order. For instance, a file can be opened and the first Put statement can be Put #n, 9, recVar. In this case, space is allocated for the preceding eight records.

4. If the record number *r* is omitted from a Put or Get statement, then the record number used will be the one following the number most recently used in a Put or Get statement. For instance, if the line

```
Put #1, , college
```

is added to the program in Example 1 after the existing Put statement, then the information on Houston Comm. College will occupy records 1 and 2, Milwaukee Area Tech. Col. records 3 and 4, and Virginia Tech. records 5 and 6 of the file COLLEGES.TXT.

5. Users often enter records into a random-access file without keeping track of the record numbers. If file #*n* is open, then the value of the function

```
Loc(n)
```

is the number of the record most recently written to or read from file *n* with a Put or Get statement.

6. Each record in a random-access file has the same length. This length can be any number from 1 to 32767.

7. When the statement Open "COLLEGES.TXT" For Random As #1 Len = Len(college) is typed, the words "For Random" can be omitted. The smart editor will insert them automatically.

8. The decision of whether to store data in a sequential file or in a random-access file depends on how the data are to be processed. If processing requires a pass though all the data in the file, then sequential files are probably desirable. If processing involves seeking out one item of data, however, random-access files are the better choice.

PRACTICE PROBLEM 9.2

1. In Example 2, the first Picture1.Print statement clearly displays "State" in the 3rd print zone. Why will the second Picture1.Print statement also display the value of college.state in the 3rd print zone?

EXERCISES 9.2

In Exercises 1 through 8, determine the output displayed in the picture box when the command button is clicked. For each problem, assume that the file COLLEGES.TXT was just created by Example 1 and that the given code replaces the ????? in the following program.

```
Rem In BAS Module
Type collegeData
  nom As String * 25     'Name of college
  state As String * 2    'State where college is located
  yrFounded As Integer   'Year college was founded
End Type
```

```
Rem In Form Module
Sub Command1_Click ()
  Dim i As Integer
  Dim college As collegeData
  Picture1.Cls
  Open "COLLEGES.TXT" For Random As #1 Len = Len(college)
  ?????
  Close #1
End Sub
```

1. ```
   Get #1, 3, college
     Picture1.Print college.state
   ```

2. ```
   Get #1, 3, college
     Picture1.Print LOF(1); Loc(1)
   ```

3. ```
   For i = 1 To LOF(1) / Len(college)
       Get #1, i, college
         Picture1.Print college.state
     Next i
     Picture1.Print Loc(1)
   ```

4. ```
   Let college.yrFounded = 1876
     Put #1, 2, college
     Get #1, 2, college
     Picture1.Print college.nom; college.yrFounded
   ```

5. ```
   Let college.nom = "Harvard"
     Let college.state = "MA"
     Let college.yrFounded = 1636
     Put #1, 4, college
     For i = 3 To 4
       Get #1, i, college
       Picture1.Print college.nom, college.state, college.yrFounded
     Next i
   ```

6. ```
   Let college.nom = "Michigan State"
     Let college.state = "MI"
     Let college.yrFounded = 1855
     Put #1, 1, college
     For i = 1 To 3
       Get #1, i, college
       Picture1.Print college.nom
     Next i
   ```

7. ```
   Get #1, 1, college
     Get #1, , college
     Picture1.Print college.nom, college.state, college.yrFounded
   ```

8. ```
   Let lastRec = LOF(1) / Len(college)
     Get #1, lastRec, college
     Picture1.Print college.nom, college.state, college.yrFounded
   ```

In Exercises 9 through 12, identify the errors. Assume the given code replaces the ????? in the following program.

```
Rem In BAS Module
Type filmCredits
  nom As String * 25     'Name of actor or actress
  film As String * 35    'Name of film
End Type

Rem In Form Module
Sub Command1_Click ()
  Dim lastRec As Integer
  Dim actor As filmCredits
  ?????
End Sub
```

9.
```
Open "ACTORS.TXT" For Random As #2 Len = Len(filmCredits)
Let actor.nom = "Bogart"
Let actor.film = "Casablanca"
Put #2, 3, actor
Close #2
```

10.
```
Open ACTRESS.TXT For Random As #3 Len = Len(actor)
Let actor.nom = "Garland"
Let actor.film = "Wizard of Oz"
Let lastRec = LOF(3) / Len(actor)
Put #3, lastRec + 1, actor
Close #3
```

11.
```
Open "ACTORS.TXT" For Random As #1 Len = Len(actor)
Let actor.nom = "Stallone"
Let actor.film = "Rocky"
Put #1, 1, actor
Get #1, 1, actor
Close #1
Picture1.Print actor
```

12.
```
Open "ACTRESS.TXT" For Random As #3 Len = Len(actor)
Put #1, 1, actor
Close #1
```

13. Give an Open statement and Type block for a random-access file named NUMBERS.TXT in which each record consists of three numbers.

14. Give an Open statement and Type block for a random-access file named ACCOUNTS.TXT in which each record consists of a person's name (up to 25 characters) and the balance in their savings account.

15. Consider the sequential file YOB.TXT discussed in Section 8.1 and assume the file contains many names. Write a program to place all the information into a random-access file.

16. Write a program that uses the random-access file created in Exercise 15 and displays the names of all people born before 1970.

17. Write a program that uses the random-access file created in Exercise 15 to determine a person's year of birth. The program should request that the name be typed into a text box, then search for the proper record when the command button is pressed, and either give the year of birth or report that the person is not in the file.

18. Write a program that uses the random-access file created in Exercise 15 and adds the data *Joan, 1934* to the end of the file.

Exercises 19 through 22 refer to the file COLLEGES.TXT. Assume many colleges have been added to the file in no particular order.

19. Write a program to allow additional colleges to be added to the end of the file using the same user interface as shown in Example 1.

20. Modify the program in Exercise 19 to issue an error message rather than record the data if the name of the college input has more than 25 characters.

21. Write a program to find the two oldest colleges.

22. Write a program to display the data on any college whose name is typed into a text box by the user. The college should be identified by name and located by a sequential search of the records. **Note:** Remember to take into account the fact that each college name retrieved from the file will contain 25 characters.

23. Extend the program in Exercise 22 in the following way: After the information on a college is displayed, exchange its record with the previous record, unless, of course, the displayed record is the first record. (A familiar rule of thumb for office filing is, 80% of the action involves 20% of the records. After the program has been used many times, the most frequently requested records will tend to be near the top of the file and the average time required for searches should decrease.)

SOLUTION TO PRACTICE PROBLEM 9.2

1. The value of college.nom will have length 25 for each college. Therefore, it will extend into the second print zone and force the value of college.state into the third print zone.

Chapter 9
Summary

1. A *fixed-length string* is a variable declared with a statement of the form Dim *var* As String * n. The value of *var* is always a string of n characters.

2. A *record* is a composite user-defined data type with a fixed number of fields that either are of fixed-length string or numeric type. Type statements (appearing in the (declarations) section of a BAS Module) define record types and Dim statements are used to declare a variable to be of that type.

3. After a record type has been specified, the associated *random-access file* is an ordered collection of record values numbered 1, 2, 3, and so on. Record values are placed into the file with Put statements and read from the file with Get statements. At any time, the value of LOF(*n*) / Len(*recordVar*) is the number of the highest record value in the file and the value of Loc is the number of the record value most recently accessed by a Put or Get statement.

Chapter 9
Programming Projects

1. *Balance a Checkbook.* Write an interactive program to request information (payee, check number, amount, and whether or not the check has cleared) for each check written during a month and store this information in a random file. The program should then request the balance at the beginning of the month and display the current balance and the payee and amount for every check still outstanding.

2. A teacher maintains a random-access file containing the following information for each student: name, social security number, grades on each of two hourly exams, and the final exam grade. Assume the random-access file GRADES.TXT has been created with string fields of lengths 25 and 11 and three numeric fields, and all the names and social security numbers have been entered. The numeric fields have been initialized with zeros. Write a program with the five command buttons "Display First Student," "Record Grade(s) & Display Next Student," "Locate Student," "Print Grade List," and "Done" to allow the teacher to do the following.

(a) Enter all the grades for a specific exam.
(b) Locate and display the record for a specific student so that one or more grades may be changed.
(c) Print a list of final grades that can be posted. The list should show the last four digits of the social security number, the grade on the final exam, and the semester average of each student. The semester average is determined by the formula (exam1 + exam2 + 2 * finalExam) / 4.

10

The Graphical Display of Data

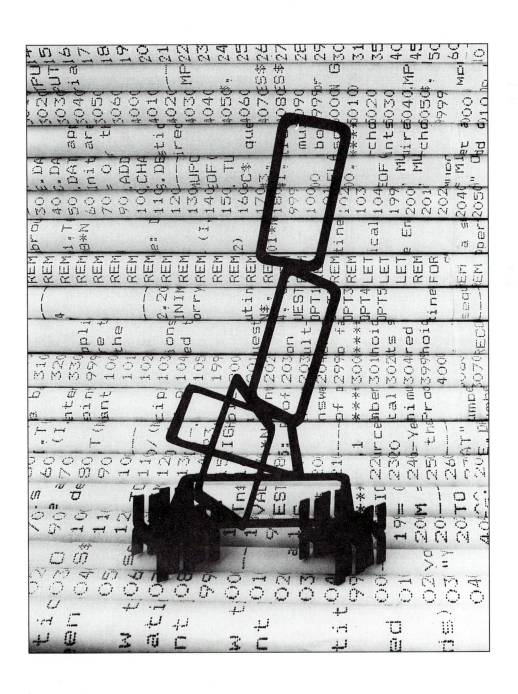

10.1 INTRODUCTION TO GRAPHICS

Visual Basic has impressive graphics capabilities. Figure 10.1 shows four types of charts that can be displayed in a picture box and printed by the printer.

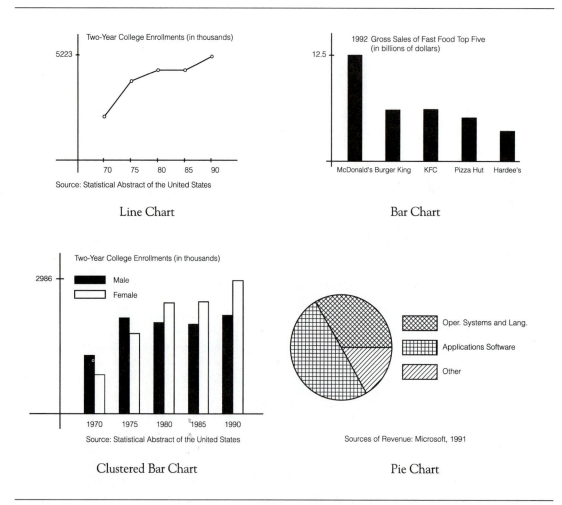

Figure 10.1 Four types of charts.

The construction of each of these charts involves three basic steps: (1) define a coordinate system, (2) use graphics methods to draw the appropriate lines, rectangles, and circles, and (3) place text at appropriate points on the chart. The basic tools for accomplishing each of these steps are presented below.

Specifying a Coordinate System

Suppose we have a piece of paper, a pencil, and a ruler and we want to graph a line extending from (2, 40) to (5, 60). We would most likely use the following three-step procedure:

1. Use the ruler to draw an x-axis and a y-axis. Focus on the first quadrant since both points are in that quadrant.

2. Select scales for the two axes. For instance, we might decide that the numbers on the x-axis range from –1 to 6 and that the numbers on the y-axis range from –10 to 80.

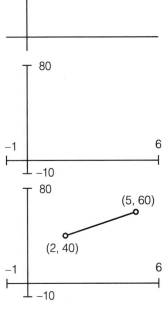

3. Plot the two points and use the ruler to draw the straight line segment joining them.

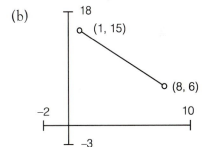

EXAMPLE 1   (a) Draw a coordinate system with the numbers on the x-axis ranging from –2 to 10, and the numbers on the y-axis ranging from –3 to 18.
(b) Draw the straight line from (1, 15) to (8, 6).
(c) Draw the straight line from (–2, 0) to (10, 0).

SOLUTION   (a)   (b)

(c) The point (–2, 0) is the left-hand endpoint of the x-axis and the point (10, 0) is the right-hand endpoint; therefore, the line joining them is just the portion of the x-axis we have pictured.

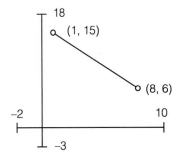

We draw these graphs on the screen with the same three steps we use with paper, pencil, and ruler. The only difference is that we first do step 2, and then steps 1 and 3. The Visual Basic method Scale is used to specify the range of values for the axes and the method Line serves as the ruler.

The statement

```
Picture1.Scale (a, d)-(b, c)
```

specifies that numbers on the *x*-axis range from *a* to *b* and that numbers on the *y*-axis range from *c* to *d*. (See Figure 10.2.) The ordered pair (*a*, *d*) gives the coordinates of the top left corner of the picture box, while the ordered pair (*b*, *c*) gives the coordinates of the bottom right corner of the picture box.

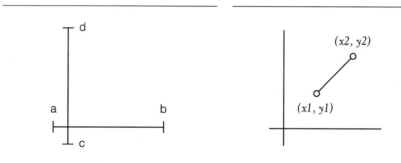

Figure 10.2 Result of scale method.   **Figure 10.3** Result of the line method.

Graphics Methods for Drawing Lines, Points, and Circles

After an appropriate coordinate system has been specified by a Picture1.Scale statement, graphics can be drawn in the picture box using the Line and Circle methods. The statement

```
Picture1.Line (x1, y1)-(x2, y2)
```

draws the line segment from the point with coordinates (*x1*, *y1*) to the point with coordinates (*x2*, *y2*) in the picture box (see Figure 10.3). In particular, the statement Picture1.Line (*a*, 0)–(*b*, 0) draws the *x*-axis and the statement Picture1.Line (0, *c*)–(0, *d*) draws the *y*-axis.

The following event procedure produces the graph of Example 1, part (b):

```
Sub Command1_Click ()
  Picture1.Cls
  Picture1.Scale (-2, 18)-(10, -3)  'Specify coordinate system
  Picture1.Line (-2, 0)-(10, 0)     'Draw x-axis
  Picture1.Line (0, -3)-(0, 18)     'Draw y-axis
  Picture1.Line (1, 15)-(8, 6)      'Draw the straight line
End Sub
```

EXAMPLE 2   Consider Figure 10.4.

(a) Give the statement that specifies the range for the numbers on the axes.
(b) Give the statements that will draw the axes.
(c) Give the statement that will draw the line.

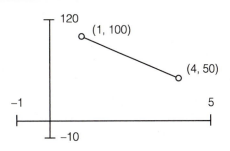

Figure 10.4 Graph for Example 2.

SOLUTION   (a) `Picture1.Scale (-1, 120)-(5, -10)`

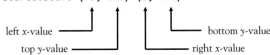

left *x*-value

top *y*-value

bottom *y*-value

right *x*-value

(b) *x*-axis: `Picture1.Line (-1, 0)-(5, 0)`

a

b

   y-axis: `Picture1.Line (0, -10)-(0, 120)`

c

d

(c) `Picture1.Line (1, 100)-(4, 50)`

There are two other graphics methods that are just as useful as the Line method. The statement

   `Picture1.PSet (x, y)`

plots the point with coordinates (*x*, *y*). The statement

   `Picture1.Circle (x, y), r`

draws the circle with center (*x*, *y*) and radius *r*.

EXAMPLE 3   Write an event procedure to plot the point (7, 6) in a picture box and draw a circle of radius 3 about the point.

SOLUTION   The rightmost point to be drawn will have *x*-coordinate 10; therefore the numbers on the *x*-axis must range beyond 10. In the following event procedure we allow the numbers to range from –2 to 12. (See Figure 10.5.)

```
Sub Command1_Click ()
   Rem Draw circle with center (7, 6) and radius 3
   Picture1.Cls                        'Clear picture box
   Picture1.Scale (-2, 12)-(12, -2)'Specify coordinate system
   Picture1.Line (-2, 0)-(12, 0)    'Draw x-axis
   Picture1.Line (0, -2)-(0, 12)    'Draw y-axis
   Picture1.PSet (7, 6)              'Draw center of circle
   Picture1.Circle (7, 6), 3        'Draw the circle
End Sub
```

[Run and then click the command button. The resulting picture box is shown below.]

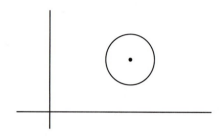

Figure 10.5 Graph for Example 3.

The numbers appearing in the Scale, Line, PSet, and Circle methods can be replaced by variables or expressions. The following example demonstrates this feature.

EXAMPLE 4   Write an event procedure to draw a graph of the square root function.

SOLUTION   We will graph the function for values of *x* from 0 to 100. (See Figure 10.6.)

```
Sub Command1_Click ()
  Dim r As Single, h As Single, x As Single
  Rem Graph the Square Root Function
  Let r = 100                          'Largest x-value used
  Let h = 10                           'Largest y-value used
  Picture1.Cls
  Picture1.Scale (-20, 12)-(120, -2)   'Specify coordinate system
  Picture1.Line (-5, 0)-(r, 0)         'Draw x-axis
  Picture1.Line (0, -1)-(0, h)         'Draw y-axis
  For x = 0 To r Step .2               'Plot about 500 points
    Picture1.PSet (x, Sqr(x))          'Plot point on graph
  Next x
End Sub
```

[Run and then click the command button. The resulting picture box is shown below.]

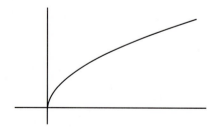

Figure 10.6 Graph of the square root function.

Positioning Text

There are times when text is placed on the screen in conjunction with graphics. This would be the case if a graph were to be titled or a tick mark needed a label. The ability to position such text appropriately in the picture box is essential to good-looking graphs. A picture box has two properties, CurrentX and CurrentY, and two methods, TextHeight and TextWidth, which allow us to precisely position text alongside graphics.

The properties CurrentX and CurrentY record the precise horizontal and vertical location at which the next character of text will be printed. By assigning appropriate values to these properties prior to executing a Print method, text can be positioned very precisely in the picture box. In the following event procedure, the coordinates of the right end of the tick mark are $(x, y) = (.1, 3)$. As a first attempt at labeling a tick mark on the y-axis, the CurrentX and CurrentY properties are set to these coordinates. The results are shown in Figure 10.7a.

```
Sub Command1_Click ()
  Picture1.Cls
  Picture1.Scale (-4, 4) - (4, -4)
  Picture1.Line (-4, 0) - (4, 0)     'Draw x-axis
  Picture1.Line (0, -4) - (0, 4)     'Draw y-axis
  Picture1.Line (-.1, 3) - (.1, 3)   'Draw tick mark
  Let Picture1.CurrentX = .1         'Right end of tick mark
  Let Picture1.CurrentY = 3          'Same vertical position as tick mark
  Picture1.Print "y=3"               'Label for tick mark
End Sub
```

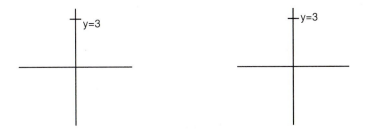

Figure 10.7a Placing labels, first attempt.   **Figure 10.7b** Placing labels, second attempt.

Note that the top of the text is even with the tick mark. This reflects the fact that the value of the CurrentY property used by Visual Basic is the location for the **top** of the character cursor. Ideally the text should be moved up so that the tick mark aligns with the middle of the text. To do this, the value of the CurrentY property needs to be increased by one half the height of the text. The following statement assigns a corrected value to the CurrentY property by using the TextHeight method to obtain the height of the text being used as the tick mark label.

```
Let Picture1.CurrentY = 3 + Picture1.TextHeight("y=3") / 2
```

The result of using this corrected value for CurrentY is shown in Figure 10.7b.

When using the TextHeight method, all characters have the same height. Thus the height of a string can be obtained by asking for the height of any single character. The following procedure uses the TextHeight method with a space character to center the text cursor at the requested graphic point.

```
Sub PositionText(x As Single, y As Single)
  Rem Center text cursor at the point (x, y)
  Let Picture1.CurrentX = x
  Let Picture1.CurrentY = y + Picture1.TextHeight(" ") / 2
End Sub
```

Another useful picture box method is TextWidth. Whereas the Len function returns the number of characters in a string, the TextWidth method takes into account the varying widths of characters and returns the physical width of the entire string in the units of the current scale for the picture box. The TextWidth method is essential when centering text, as illustrated in the following example.

EXAMPLE 5 Write an event procedure to display the phrase "Th-that's all folks!" centered and double underlined in a picture box with x values ranging from 0 to 6 and y values ranging from 0 to 4.

SOLUTION Centering text requires knowing the coordinates of the center of the picture box, which for the given ranges will be the point $(3, 2)$. Next, we need the width and height of the text being centered. These values are available using the TextWidth and TextHeight methods. The text cursor needs to start with a CurrentX that is half the text's width to the left of center and a CurrentY that is half the text's height above center. The first underline can be placed half the text's height below center. The additional distance down to the second underline should be in proportion to the height of the text. We decided after some experimenting to use a proportion of 1/6th.

```
Sub Command1_Click ()
  Rem Center and double underline a phrase
  Dim xCenter As Single, yCenter As Single, phrase as String
  Dim w As Single, h As Single, leftEdge As Single, rightEdge As Single
  Dim ul1Pos As Single, ul2Pos As Single
  Picture1.Scale (0, 4)-(6, 0)
  Picture1.Cls
  Let xCenter = 3
  Let yCenter = 2
  Let phrase = "Th-that's all Folks!"
  Let w = Picture1.TextWidth(phrase)
  Let h = Picture1.TextHeight(" ")
  Let Picture1.CurrentX = xCenter - w / 2
  Let Picture1.CurrentY = yCenter + h / 2
  Picture1.Print phrase
  Let leftEdge = xCenter - w / 2
  Let rightEdge = xCenter + w / 2
  Let ul1Pos = yCenter - h / 2
  Let ul2Pos = ul1Pos - h / 6
  Picture1.Line (leftEdge, ul1Pos)-(rightEdge, ul1Pos)
  Picture1.Line (leftEdge, ul2Pos)-(rightEdge, ul2Pos)
End Sub
```

[Run and then click the command button. The resulting picture box is shown below.]

```
Th-that's all Folks!
```

Comments:

1. In Examples 1 through 4, the examples that produce graphs, the range of numbers on the axes extended from a negative number to a positive number. Actually, any values of a, b, c, and d can be used in a Scale method. In certain cases, however, you will not be able to display one or both of the axes on the screen. (For instance, after Picture1.Scale (1, 10)–(10, –1) has been executed, the y-axis cannot be displayed.)

2. The following technique can be used to determine a good range of values for a Scale method when graphs with only positive values are to be drawn.

   (a) Let r be the x-coordinate of the rightmost point that will be drawn by any Line, PSet, or Circle method.
   (b) Let h be the y-coordinate of the highest point that will be drawn by any Line, PSet, or Circle method.
   (c) Let the numbers on the x-axis range from about –[20% of r] to about r + [20% of r]. Let the numbers on the y-axis range from about –[20% of h] to about h + [20% of h]. That is, use

   ```
   Picture1.Scale (-.2 * r, 1.2 * h)-(1.2 * r, -.2 * h)
   ```

3. The radius of a circle uses the scale specified for the x-axis.

4. If one or both of the points used in the Line method fall outside the picture box, the computer only draws the portion of the line that lies in the picture box. This behavior is referred to as **line clipping** and is used for the Circle method also.

5. A program can execute a Picture1.Scale statement more than once. Executing a new Picture1.Scale statement has no effect on the text and graphics already drawn; however, future graphics statements will use the new coordinate system. This technique can be used to produce the same graphics figure in different sizes and/or locations within the picture box. The output from the following event procedure in shown in Figure 10.8.

```
Sub Command1_Click ()
  Dim i As Integer
  Picture1.Cls
  For i = 0 To 3
    Picture1.Scale (0, 2 ^ i)-(2 ^ i, 0)
    Picture1.Line (0, 0)-(.5, 1)
    Picture1.Line (.5, 1)-(.8, 0)
    Picture1.Line (.8, 0)-(0, .8)
    Picture1.Line (0, .8)-(1, .5)
    Picture1.Line (1, .5)-(0, 0)
  Next i
End Sub
```

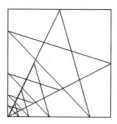

Figure 10.8 Output from Comment 5.

6. The programs in this section can be modified to produce colorful displays. The numbers 0 through 15 identify colors as shown in Table 10.1.

0 Black	4 Red	8 Gray	12 Light red
1 Blue	5 Magenta	9 Light blue	13 Light magenta
2 Green	6 Yellow	10 Light green	14 Light Yellow
3 Cyan	7 White	11 Light cyan	15 High-intensity white

Table 10.1 Values for colors from the QBColor function.

Lines, points, and circles can be drawn in these colors through use of the QBColor function. To use color *c*, place ", QBColor(c)" at the end of the corresponding graphics statement. For instance, the statement

```
Picture1.Line (x1, y1)-(x2, y2), QBColor(4)
```

draws a red line.

PRACTICE PROBLEMS 10.1

Suppose you want to write a program to draw a line from (3, 45) to (5, 80).

1. Use the technique of Comment 2 to select appropriate values for the Scale method.

2. Write an event procedure to draw the axes, the line, and a small circle around each end point of the line.

3. Write the statements that draw a tick mark on the y-axis at height 80 and label it with the number 80.

EXERCISES 10.1

1. Determine the Scale method corresponding to the coordinate system of Figure 10.9.

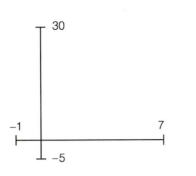

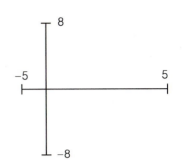

Figure 10.9 Coordinate system for Exercise 1.

Figure 10.10 Coordinate system for Exercise 2.

2. Determine the Scale method corresponding to the coordinate system of Figure 10.10.

3. Suppose the statement Picture1.Scale (–1, 40)–(4, –8) has been executed. Write down the statements that draw the x-axis and the y-axis.

4. Suppose the statement Picture1.Scale (–3, 1)–(18, –.2) has been executed. Write down the statements that draw the x-axis and the y-axis.

In Exercises 5 through 8, write an event procedure to draw a line between the given points. Select an appropriate Scale method, draw the axes, and draw a small circle around each end point of the line.

5. (3, 200), (10, 150)

6. (4, 4), (9, 9)

7. (2, .5), (4, .3)

8. (5, 30), (6, 30)

In Exercises 9 through 20, write an event procedure to draw the given figures in a picture box. Draw the axes only when necessary.

9. Draw a circle whose center is located at the center of the picture box.

10. Draw a tick mark on the x-axis at a distance of 5 from the origin.

11. Draw a tick mark on the y-axis at a distance of 70 from the origin.

12. Draw a circle whose leftmost point is at the center of the picture box.

13. Draw four small quarter-circles, one in each corner of the picture box.

14. Draw a triangle with two sides of the same length.

15. Draw a rectangle.

16. Draw a square.

17. Draw five concentric circles, that is, five circles with the same center.

18. Draw a point in the center of the picture box.

19. Draw a circle and a line that is tangent to the circle.

20. Draw two circles that touch at a single point.

In Exercises 21 through 24, consider the following event procedure. What would be the effect on the circle if the Picture1.Scale statement were replaced by the given Picture1.Scale statement?

```
Sub Command1_Click ()
  Picture1.Cls
  Picture1.Scale (-5, 5)-(5, -5)    'Specify coordinate system
  Picture1.Circle (0, 0), 3         'Draw circle centered at origin
End Sub
```

21. `Picture1.Scale (-8, 8)-(8,-8)`   **22.** `Picture1.Scale (-5, 8)-(5, -8)`

23. `Picture1.Scale (-8, 5)-(8, -5)`   **24.** `Picture1.Scale (-4, 4)-(4, -4)`

In Exercises 25 through 27, write an event procedure to perform the given task.

25. Draw a graph of the function $y = x^2$ for x between 0 and 10.

26. Draw a graph of the function $200 / (x + 5)^2$ for x between 0 and 20.

27. Draw displays such as the one in Figure 10.11. Let the user specify the maximum number (in this display, 8).

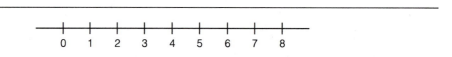

Figure 10.11 Display for Exercise 27.

In Exercises 28 through 30, use the statement Picture1.Scale (0, 50)–(100, 0).

28. Write a program to produce Figure 10.12. Let the maximum line number (in this display, 3) be specified by the user.

------------------- LINE 1

------------------- LINE 2

------------------- LINE 3

Figure 10.12 Display for Exercise 28.

29. Write a program to produce a sheet of graph paper.

30. Write a program to produce a form for a course schedule. (See Figure 10.13.)

COURSE SCHEDULE						
Time	Mon.	Tues.	Wed.	Thurs.	Fri.	Sat./Sun.

Figure 10.13 Course schedule.

SOLUTIONS TO PRACTICE PROBLEMS 10.1

1. The largest value of any x-coordinate is 5. Since 20% of 5 is 1, the numbers on the x-axis should range from –1 to 6 (= 5 + 1). Similarly, the numbers on the y-axis should range from –16 to 96 (= 80 + 16). Therefore, an appropriate scaling statement is

```
Picture1.Scale (-1, 96)-(6, -16)
```

2. ```
Sub Command1_Click()
   Picture1.Scale (-1, 96)-(6, -16) 'Specify coordinate system
   Picture1.Line (-1, 0)-(6, 0)   'Draw x-axis
   Picture1.Line (0, -16)-(0, 96)   'Draw y-axis
   Picture1.Line (3, 45)-(5, 80)   'Draw the line
   Picture1.Circle (3, 45), .1   'Draw small circle about left endpoint
   Picture1.Circle (5, 80), .1   'Draw small circle about right endpoint
End Sub
```

The radius for the small circles about the endpoints was determined by trial and error. As a rule of thumb, it should be about 2% of the length of the $x$-axis.

3. Add the following lines before the End Sub statement of the preceding event procedure. The length of the tick mark was taken to be the diameter of the circle. See Figure 10.14 for the output of the entire program.

```
Picture1.Line (-.1, 80)-(.1, 80) 'Draw tick mark
Let Picture1.CurrentX = .1   'Prepare cursor position for label
Let Picture1.CurrentY = 80 + Picture1.TextHeight(" ") / 2
Picture1.Print "80"   'Display label
```
```

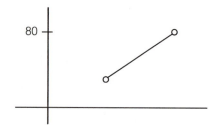

Figure 10.14 Final output from practice problems.

10.2 LINE CHARTS

A line chart displays the change in a certain quantity in relation to another quantity (often time). The following steps produce a line chart.

1. Look over the data to be displayed. A typical line chart displays between 5 and 20 items of data corresponding to evenly spaced units of time: years, months, or days. The positions on the x-axis will contain labels such as "Jan Feb Mar ..." or "91   92   93   94 ... ." These labels can be placed at the locations 1, 2, 3, ... on the x-axis.

2. Choose a coordinate system based on the number of data items and the size of the quantities. A convenient scale for the x-axis is from –1 to one more than the number of data items. The scale for the y-axis is determined by the largest quantity to be displayed.

3. Draw the line segments. It is a good idea to draw a small circle around the endpoints of the line segments.

4. Draw and label tick marks on the coordinate axes. The x-axis should have a tick mark for each time period. The y-axis should have at least one tick mark to indicate the magnitude of the quantities displayed.

5. Title the chart and give the source of the data.

EXAMPLE 1   Table 10.2 gives enrollment data for two-year colleges taken from the Statistical Abstract of the United States. Write a program to display the total enrollments for the given years in a line chart.

Year	1970	1975	1980	1985	1990
Male	1317	2165	2047	2002	2237
Female	906	1805	2479	2529	2986
Total	2223	3970	4526	4531	5223

Table 10.2 Two-year college enrollments (in thousands).

SOLUTION   Figure 10.15 shows the graph that results from executing the following program. The data in ENROLL.TXT are taken from the first and last lines of Table 10.2.

For example, the first line in the file is "1970", 2223. (Explanatory remarks follow the program.)

```
Rem In (declarations) section of (general)
Dim numYears As Integer, maxEnroll As Single

Sub Command1_Click ()
  Rem Line Chart of Total Two-Year College Enrollments
  Let numYears = 5
  ReDim label(1 To numYears) As String
  ReDim total(1 To numYears) As Single
  Call ReadData(label(), total())
  Call DrawAxes
  Call DrawData(total())
  Call ShowTitle
  Call ShowLabels(label())
End Sub


Sub DrawAxes ()
  Rem Draw axes
  Picture1.Scale (-1, 1.2 * maxEnroll) - (numYears + 1, -.2 * maxEnroll)
  Picture1.Line (-1, 0)-(numYears + 1, 0)
  Picture1.Line (0, -.1 * maxEnroll)-(0, 1.2 * maxEnroll)
End Sub

Sub DrawData (total() As Single)
  Dim i As Integer
  Rem Draw lines connecting data and circle data points
  For i = 1 To numYears
    If i < numYears Then
        Picture1.Line (i, total(i))-(i + 1, total(i + 1))
    End If
    Picture1.Circle (i, total(i)), .01 * numYears
  Next i
End Sub

Sub Locate (x As Single, y As Single)
  Let Picture1.CurrentX = x
  Let Picture1.CurrentY = y
End Sub

Sub ReadData (label() As String, total() As Single)
  Dim i As Integer
  Rem Assume the data has been placed in the file "ENROLL.TXT"
  Rem (First line of the file is "1970",2223)
  Rem Read data into arrays, find highest enrollment
  Let maxEnroll = 0
  Open "ENROLL.TXT" For Input As #1
  For i = 1 To numYears
    Input #1, label(i), total(i)
    If total(i) > maxEnroll Then
        Let maxEnroll = total(i)
    End If
  Next i
  Close #1
End Sub
```

```
Sub ShowLabels (label() As String)
   Dim i As Integer, lbl As String, lblWid As Single
   Dim lblHght As Single, tickFactor As Single
   Rem Draw tick marks and label them
   For i = 1 To numYears
      Let lbl = Right(label(i), 2)
      Let lblWid = Picture1.TextWidth(lbl)
      Let tickFactor = .02 * maxEnroll
      Picture1.Line (i, -tickFactor)-(i, tickFactor)
      Call Locate(i - lblWid / 2, -tickFactor)
      Picture1.Print lbl
   Next i
   Let lbl = Str$(maxEnroll)
   Let lblWid = Picture1.TextWidth(lbl)
   Let lblHght = Picture1.TextHeight(lbl)
   Let tickFactor = .02 * numYears
   Picture1.Line (-tickFactor, maxEnroll)-(tickFactor, maxEnroll)
   Call Locate(-tickFactor - lblWid, maxEnroll + lblHght / 2)
   Picture1.Print lbl
End Sub

Sub ShowTitle ()
   Rem Display source and title
   Call Locate(.5, -.1 * maxEnroll)
   Picture1.Print "Source: Statistical Abstract of the United States"
   Call Locate(.5, 1.2 * maxEnroll)
   Picture1.Print "Two-Year College Enrollments (in thousands)"
End Sub
```

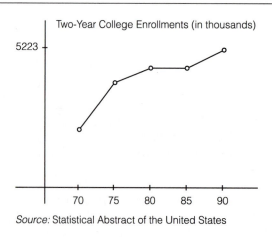

Figure 10.15 Chart for Example 1.

Remarks on the program in Example 1:

1. The value of *tickFactor* in the subprogram ShowLabels was set to 2% of the scale determiners (*numYears* and *maxEnroll*) for the *x* and *y* axes. This percentage is appropriate for picture boxes that occupy 1/4th to 1/3rd of the screen. Smaller picture boxes might require a factor of 3% or 4% for good-looking tick marks. Picture boxes that almost fill the screen might have good results with a factor as small as 1%.

2. In the subprogram ShowLabels, the TextWidth and TextHeight methods were used to obtain the width and height of each label. These values were used together with the coordinates of the appropriate end of the tick mark to assign values to CurrentX and CurrentY for proper placement of the label relative to the graphics.

3. In the event procedure Command1_Click, the number of data points (5) was assigned to the variable *numYears*, and then *numYears* was used as a parameter to all other subprograms. This feature makes it easy to add additional data to the line chart. For instance, if we decide to include the data for one additional year, we will only have to change the value of *numYears* and add one more line to the data file.

Line Styling

Patterned, or "styled" lines can be drawn between two points. The available line styles are shown in Figure 10.16. Each line has an associated number identifying its style. If *s* is one of the numbers in Figure 10.16, then the statements

```
Let Picture1.DrawStyle = s
Picture1.Line (a, b)-(c, d)
```

draw the line from (a, b) to (c, d) in the style corresponding to the number *s*.

Draw Style #	Line Pattern
0	————————————————————————
1	— — — — — — — — — — — — —
2	- - - - - - - - - - - - - - -
3	– — – — – — – — – — – — –
4	– — - – — - – — - – — - –

Figure 10.16 Line Patterns.

Styling is useful when displaying several line charts on the same coordinate system.

EXAMPLE 2 Alter the program in Example 1 so that it will draw line charts displaying the male, female, and total enrollments of two-year colleges.

SOLUTION The data file must be changed to contain the enrollment figures for males and females, and arrays must be created to hold this information. The totals can be computed from the other numbers. The styled lines for male and female enrollments must be drawn. Finally, legends must be given to identify the different line charts. Figure 10.17 shows the picture box that results from the modified program.

```
Rem In (declarations) section of (general)
Dim numYears As Integer, maxEnroll As Single

Sub Command1_Click ()
  Rem Line Chart of Total Two-Year College Enrollments
  Let numYears = 5
  ReDim label(1 To numYears) As String
  ReDim male(1 To numYears) As Single
  ReDim female(1 To numYears) As Single
  ReDim total(1 To numYears) As Single
  Call ReadData(label(),male(),female(),total())
  Call DrawAxes
  Call DrawData(male(), female(), total())
  Call ShowTitle
  Call ShowLabels(label())
  Call ShowLegend
End Sub

Sub DrawAxes ()
  Rem Draw axes
  Picture1.Scale (-1, 1.2 * maxEnroll) - (numYears + 1, -.2 * maxEnroll)
  Picture1.Line (-1, 0)-(numYears + 1, 0)
  Picture1.Line (0, -.1 * maxEnroll)-(0, 1.2 * maxEnroll)
End Sub

Sub DrawData (male() As Single, female() As Single, total() As Single)
  Dim i As Integer
  For i = 1 To numYears
    If i < numYears Then
        Rem Draw lines connecting data points
        Let Picture1.DrawStyle = 2
        Picture1.Line (i, male(i))-(i + 1, male(i + 1))
        Let Picture1.DrawStyle = 1
        Picture1.Line (i, female(i))-(i + 1, female(i + 1))
        Let Picture1.DrawStyle = 0
        Picture1.Line (i, total(i))-(i + 1, total(i + 1))
    End If
    Rem Draw small circles around data points
    Picture1.Circle (i, male(i)), .01 * numYears
    Picture1.Circle (i, female(i)), .01 * numYears
    Picture1.Circle (i, total(i)), .01 * numYears
  Next i
End Sub

Sub Locate (x As Single, y As Single)
  Let Picture1.CurrentX = x
  Let Picture1.CurrentY = y
End Sub

Sub ReadData (label() As String, male() As Single, female() As Single,
                                            total() As Single)
  Rem The two lines above should be enter as one line
  Dim i As Integer
  Rem Assume the data has been placed in the file "ENROLLMF.TXT"
  Rem (First line of file is "1970",1317,906)
  Rem Read data into arrays, find highest enrollment
```

```
        Open "ENROLLMF.TXT" For Input As #1
      Let maxEnroll = 0
      For i = 1 To numYears
        Input #1, label(i), male(i), female(i)
        Let total(i) = male(i) + female(i)
        If maxEnroll < total(i) Then
            Let maxEnroll = total(i)
        End If
      Next i
      Close #1
    End Sub

    Sub ShowLabels (label() As String)
      Dim i As Integer, lbl As String, lblWid As Single
      Dim lblHght As Single, tickFactor As Single
      Rem Draw tick marks and label them
      For i = 1 To numYears
        Let lbl = Right(label(i), 2)
        Let lblWid = Picture1.TextWidth(lbl)
        Let tickFactor = .02 * maxEnroll
        Picture1.Line (i, -tickFactor)-(i, tickFactor)
        Call Locate(i - lblWid / 2, -tickFactor)
        Picture1.Print lbl
      Next i
      Let lbl = Str$(maxEnroll)
      Let lblWid = Picture1.TextWidth(lbl)
      Let lblHght = Picture1.TextHeight(lbl)
      Let tickFactor = .02 * numYears
      Picture1.Line (-tickFactor, maxEnroll)-(tickFactor, maxEnroll)
      Call Locate(-tickFactor - lblWid, maxEnroll + lblHght / 2)
      Picture1.Print lbl
    End Sub

    Sub ShowLegend ()
      Rem Show legend
      Let Picture1.DrawStyle = 2
      Picture1.Line (.1, 1.05 * maxEnroll)-(.9, 1.05 * maxEnroll)
      Call Locate(1, 1.1 * maxEnroll)
      Picture1.Print "Male"
      Let Picture1.DrawStyle = 1
      Picture1.Line (.1, .95 * maxEnroll)-(.9, .95 * maxEnroll)
      Call Locate(1, maxEnroll)
      Picture1.Print "Female"
      Let Picture1.DrawStyle = 0
      Picture1.Line (.1, .85 * maxEnroll)-(.9, .85 * maxEnroll)
      Call Locate(1, .9 * maxEnroll)
      Picture1.Print "Total"
    End Sub

    Sub ShowTitle ()
      Rem Display source and title
      Call Locate(.5, -.1 * maxEnroll)
      Picture1.Print "Source: Statistical Abstract of the United States"
      Call Locate(.5, 1.2 * maxEnroll)
      Picture1.Print "Two-Year College Enrollments (in thousands)"
    End Sub
```

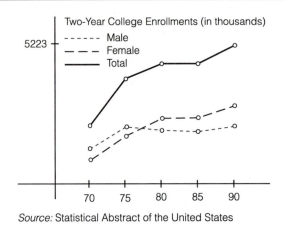

Source: Statistical Abstract of the United States

Figure 10.17 Chart for Example 2.

PRACTICE PROBLEMS 10.2

Consider the programs of Examples 1 and 2 that draw the three-line chart of two-year college enrollments.

1. The enrollments for 1965 were Males—734, Females—439, Total—1173. Change the program to include this data.

2. Suppose the enrollment data were given in units of millions instead of thousands. How would this affect the appearance of the three-line chart?

3. Why wasn't 1990 (or 90) used in the Picture1.Scale statement to determine the scale for the *x*-axis? It is the largest value of *x*.

EXERCISES 10.2

In Exercises 1 and 2, determine a Picture1.Scale statement that could have been used to obtain the chart.

1.

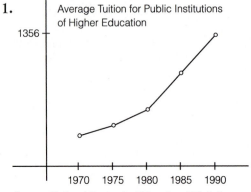

Source: National Center for Educational Statistics

2.

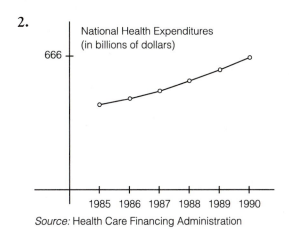

Source: Health Care Financing Administration

In Exercises 3 through 7, write a program to display the given information in a line chart.

3. The Consumer Price Index is a measure of living costs based on changes in retail prices, with 1967 taken as the base year.

Year	1967	1971	1975	1979	1983	1987	1991
CPI	100.0	121.3	161.2	217.7	297.4	335.0	399.9

Source: Bureau of Labor Statistics

4. Workers with Personal Computers (in millions)

Year	1981	1984	1987	1990
Workers	2	6	14	24

Source: Future Computing Incorporated

5. Freshman Life Goals (% of students committed to goal)

	1968	1976	1984	1992
Be very well off financially	45	57	70	73
Develop a meaningful philosophy of life	80	57	45	46

Source: Higher Education Research Institute

6. Normal Monthly Precipitation (in inches)

	Jan	Apr	July	Oct
Mobile, AL	4.6	5.35	7.7	2.6
Phoenix, AZ	.7	.3	.7	.6
Portland, OR	6.2	2.3	.5	3.0
Washington, DC	2.8	2.9	3.9	2.9

Source: Statistical Abstract of the United States

7. Age Distribution (%) of the Labor Force

	16–24	25–34	35–54	Over 54
1975	24	24	36	15
1990	17	29	42	12
2005	16	21	48	15

Source: The 1994 Information Please Business Almanac

SOLUTIONS TO PRACTICE PROBLEMS 10.2

1. Change *numYears* to 6 in the Command1_Click event procedure and add the following line to the beginning of the data file.

   `"1965", 734, 439`

2. Not at all. The value of *maxEnroll*, 5940, would change to 5.94 but the Picture1.Scale statement would scale the y-axis with respect to this new value of *maxEnroll* and the line charts would look exactly the same as before.

3. If 1990 (or 90) had been used, the line charts would have been unreadable. Line charts are used to illustrate from about 3 to 15 pieces of data. These are best placed at the numbers 1, 2, 3, ... on the x-axis. In many cases the classifications given below the tick marks will be words (such as Jan, Feb, ...) instead of numbers.

10.3 BAR CHARTS

Drawing bar charts requires a variation of the line statement. If $(x1, y1)$ and $(x2, y2)$ are two points on the screen, then the statement

```
Picture1.Line (x1, y1) - (x2, y2), , B
```

draws a rectangle with the two points as opposite corners. If B is replaced by BF, a solid rectangle will be drawn (see Figure 10.18).

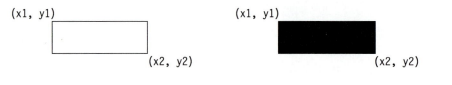

```
Picture.Line (x1, y1) - (x2, y2), , B    Picture.Line (x1, y1) - (x2, y2), , BF
```

Figure 10.18 Line method with B and BF options.

EXAMPLE 1   The populations of California and New York are 30 and 18 million, respectively. Draw a bar chart to compare the populations.

SOLUTION   The following program produces the chart shown in Figure 10.19. The first five lines are the same as those of a line chart with two pieces of data. The base of the rectangle for California is centered above the point $(1, 0)$ on the x-axis and extends .3 unit to the left and right. (The number .3 was chosen arbitrarily; it had to be less than .5 so that the rectangles would not touch.) Therefore, the upper left corner of the rectangle has coordinates (.7, 30) and the lower right corner has coordinates (1.3, 0). Figure 10.20 shows the coordinates of the principal points of the rectangles.

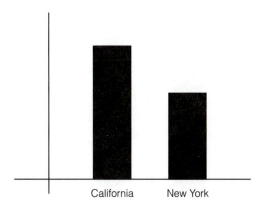

Figure 10.19 Bar chart for Example 1.

```
Sub Command1_Click ()
  Rem Populations of California and New York
  Picture1.Scale (-1, 40)-(3, -5)        'Specify coordinates
  Picture1.Line (-1, 0)-(3, 0)           'Draw x-axis
  Picture1.Line (0, -5)-(0, 40)          'Draw y-axis
  Picture1.Line (.7, 30)-(1.3, 0),,BF    'Draw solid rectangle for CA
  Picture1.Line (1.7, 18)-(2.3, 0),,BF   'Draw solid rectangle for NY
  Let Picture1.CurrentY = -1
  Let Picture1.CurrentX = .7
  Picture1.Print "California";
  Let Picture1.CurrentX = 1.7
  Picture1.Print "New York";
End Sub
```

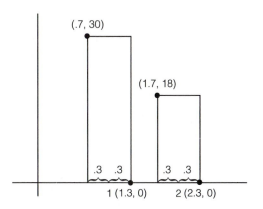

Figure 10.20 Coordinates of principal points of Example 1.

Any program that draws a line chart can be easily modified to produce a bar chart. Multiple line charts are converted into so-called **clustered bar charts**.

EXAMPLE 2 Display the two-year college enrollments for males and females in a clustered bar chart. Use the data in Table 10.2 of Section 10.2.

SOLUTION The output of the following program appears in Figure 10.21. This program is very similar to the program that produced Figure 10.17 of Section 10.2.

```
Sub Command1_Click ()
  Dim numYears As Integer, maxEnroll As Single
  Rem Bar Chart of Total Two-Year College Enrollments
  Let numYears = 5
  ReDim label(1 To numYears) As String
  ReDim male(1 To numYears) As Single
  ReDim female(1 To numYears) As Single
  Call ReadData(label(), male(), female(), numYears, maxEnroll)
  Call DrawAxes(numYears, maxEnroll)
  Call DrawData(male(), female(), numYears)
  Call ShowTitle(maxEnroll)
  Call ShowLabels(label(), numYears, maxEnroll)
  Call ShowLegend(maxEnroll)
End Sub

Sub DrawAxes (numYears As Integer, maxEnroll As Single)
  Rem Draw axes
  Picture1.Scale (-1, 1.2 * maxEnroll) - (numYears + 1, -.2 * maxEnroll)
  Picture1.Line (-1, 0)-(numYears + 1, 0)
  Picture1.Line (0, -.1 * maxEnroll)-(0, 1.2 * maxEnroll)
End Sub

Sub DrawData (male() As Single, female() As Single, numYears As Integer)
  Dim i As Integer
  Rem Draw rectangles
  For i = 1 To numYears
    Picture1.Line (i - .3, male(i))-(i, 0), , BF
    Picture1.Line (i, female(i))-(i + .3, 0), , B
  Next i
End Sub

Sub Locate (x As Single, y As Single)
  Let Picture1.CurrentX = x
  Let Picture1.CurrentY = y
End Sub

Sub ReadData (label() As String, male() As Single, female() As Single,
                         numYears As Integer, maxEnroll As Single)
  Rem The two lines above should be entered as one line
  Dim i As Integer
  Rem Assume the data has been placed in the file ENROLLMF.TXT
  Rem (First line is file is "1970",1317,906)
  Rem Read data into arrays, find highest enrollment
  Open "ENROLLMF.TXT" For Input As #1
  Let maxEnroll = 0
```

```
      For i = 1 To numYears
        Input #1, label(i), male(i), female(i)
        If male(i) > maxEnroll Then
            Let maxEnroll = male(i)
        End If
        If female(i) > maxEnroll Then
            Let maxEnroll = female(i)
        End If
      Next i
      Close #1
  End Sub

  Sub ShowLabels (label() As String, numYears As Integer, maxEnroll As Single)
    Dim i As Integer, lbl As String, lblWid As Single
    Dim lblHght As Single, tickFactor As Single
    Rem Draw tick marks and label them
    For i = 1 To numYears
      Let lbl = label(i)
      Let lblWid = Picture1.TextWidth(lbl)
      Let tickFactor = .02 * maxEnroll
      Picture1.Line (i, -tickFactor)-(i, tickFactor)
      Call Locate(i - lblWid / 2, -tickFactor)
      Picture1.Print lbl
    Next i
    Let lbl = Str$(maxEnroll)
    Let lblWid = Picture1.TextWidth(lbl)
    Let lblHght = Picture1.TextHeight(lbl)
    Let tickFactor = .01 * numYears
    Picture1.Line (-tickFactor, maxEnroll)-(tickFactor, maxEnroll)
    Call Locate(-tickFactor - lblWid, maxEnroll + lblHght / 2)
    Picture1.Print lbl
  End Sub

  Sub ShowLegend (maxEnroll As Single)
    Rem Show legend
    Picture1.Line (.1, 1.05 * maxEnroll)-(.9, .95 * maxEnroll), , BF
    Call Locate(1, 1.05 * maxEnroll)
    Picture1.Print "Male"
    Picture1.Line (.1, .9 * maxEnroll)-(.9, .8 * maxEnroll), , B
    Call Locate(1, .9 * maxEnroll)
    Picture1.Print "Female"
  End Sub

  Sub ShowTitle (maxEnroll As Single)
    Rem Display source and title
    Call Locate(.5, -.1 * maxEnroll)
    Picture1.Print "Source: Statistical Abstract of the United States"
    Call Locate(.5, 1.2 * maxEnroll)
    Picture1.Print "Two-Year College Enrollments (in thousands)"
  End Sub
```

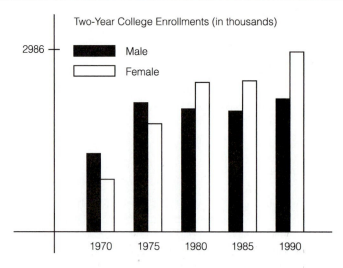

Source: Statistical Abstract of the United States

Figure 10.21 Chart for Example 2.

Comments:

1. Any line chart can be converted to a bar chart and vice versa. Line charts are best suited for displaying quantities that vary with time. The slopes of the individual line segments clearly portray the rates at which the quantity is changing. Bar charts excel in contrasting the magnitudes of different entities.

2. The Line method can produce colored rectangles. The statement Picture1.Line $(x1, y1)–(x2, y2)$, QBColor(c), B draws a rectangle in color c of Table 10.1 in Section 10.1. A solid rectangle of color c will be produced if B is replaced by BF. The use of color permits clustered bar charts with three bars per cluster.

3. In Section 10.4, we discuss a method to fill in rectangles using various patterns, such as horizontal lines and crosshatches. Using this technique, we can create black-and-white clustered bar charts having three or more bars per cluster.

PRACTICE PROBLEMS 10.3

Consider the bar chart in Figure 10.22.

1. How does this bar chart differ from the other charts considered so far?

2. Outline methods to achieve the effects referred to in the solution to Practice Problem 1.

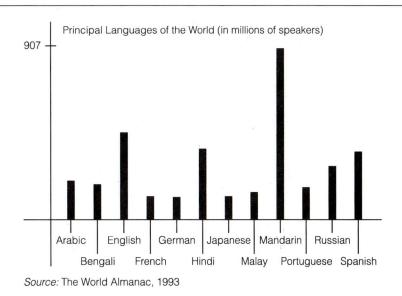

Principal Languages of the World (in millions of speakers)

Source: The World Almanac, 1993

Figure 10.22 Bar chart for practice problems.

EXERCISES 10.3

1. Suppose data for a few more years are added to the data of Example 2. What changes will have to be made in the program?

In Exercises 2 through 9, write a program to display the given information in a bar chart.

2. United States Minimum Wage

1951	.75
1961	1.00
1971	1.25
1981	3.35
1991	4.25

3. Number of Computers in U.S. Public Schools, K-12 (in millions)

1986	1.1
1987	1.4
1988	1.5
1989	1.7
1990	2.0

Source: 1992 Statistical Abstract of the U.S.

4. Largest Law Firms in Washington, D.C. (in number of lawyers)

Arnold & Porter	370
Covington & Burling	294
Hogan & Hartson	264
Shaw, Pittman, Potts, and Trowbridge	237
Arent, Fox, Kitner, Plotkin & Kahn	230

Source: Book of Lists 8th Annual 1992–1993 Reference Guide to the Washington Area's Leading Industries

5. Average Tuition and Required Fees at Four-Year Universities

	1970	1975	1980	1985	1990
Public	427	599	840	1388	2006
Private	1809	2614	3811	6826	10400

Source: Statistical Abstract of the United States, 1992

6. Educational Attainment of Persons 25 Years Old and Older (in %)

	1970	1980	1990
High School Graduate	52.3	66.5	77.6
College Graduate	10.7	16.2	21.3

Source: Statistical Abstract of the United States, 1992

7. New Automobile Retail Sales (in millions)

	1975	1980	1985	1990
Domestic	7.1	6.6	8.0	6.9
Imports	1.6	2.4	2.4	2.4

Source: Statistical Abstract of the United States, 1992

8. Principal Languages of the World (in millions of speakers)

Arabic	208	Japanese	126
Bengali	189	Malay	148
English	456	Mandarin	907
French	123	Portuguese	177
German	119	Russian	293
Hindi	383	Spanish	362

Source: The World Almanac, 1993

9. 1990 Federal Funding for Research and Development to Universities and Colleges (in millions of $)

Johns Hopkins Univ.	471	UC, Los Angeles	177
Stanford Univ.	248	Univ. of Michigan	177
MIT	218	UC, San Francisco	167
Univ. of Washington	217	UC, San Diego	165

Source: National Science Foundation

The program that follows draws a circle in the center of the picture box. In Exercises 10 through 12, rewrite the Picture1.Scale statement in order to achieve the stated result.

```
Sub Command1_Click ()
  Picture1.Cls
  Picture1.Scale (-5, 5)-(5, -5)
  Picture1.Circle (0, 0), 2
End Sub
```

10. Draw the circle in the left half of the picture box.

11. Draw the circle in the right half of the picture box.

12. Draw the circle in the upper left corner of the picture box.

13. Clustered bar charts are sometimes drawn with overlapping rectangles. (See Figure 10.23.) What changes would have to be made to do this in the program of Example 2?

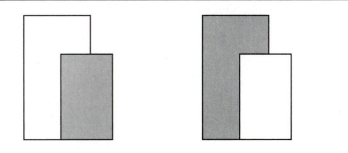

Figure 10.23 Clustered Bar Chart

SOLUTIONS TO PRACTICE PROBLEMS 10.3

1. (a) The number of characters in the labels is so large the labels must be placed in two rows.

   (b) Every other label had to be lowered.

   (c) Short vertical lines extend from the bars to the legends.

2. (a) A slight change in the Picture1.Scale statement will produce extra room at the bottom of the screen. The negative number that specifies the lower range of the y-axis should be increased in magnitude.

   (b) The For...Next loop that places the label should be replaced by two loops that increment by 2 and place the labels on two rows.

   (c) The For...Next loops in step (b) should each draw vertical lines at the same spots where tick marks usually appear. The lines should extend from the x-axis to the appropriate label. The length of these lines can be determined by experimentation.

10.4 PIE CHARTS

Drawing pie charts requires the Circle method and the FillStyle property. The Circle method draws not only circles, but also sectors (formed by an arc and two radius lines). The FillStyle property determines what pattern, if any, is used to fill a sector. The FillColor property can be used, if desired, to lend color to the fill patterns.

Figure 10.24 shows a circle with several radius lines drawn. The radius line extending to the right from the center of the circle is called the **horizontal radius line**. Every other radius line is assigned a number between 0 and 1 according to the percentage of the circle that must be swept out in the counterclockwise direction in order to reach that radius line. For instance, beginning at the horizontal radius line and rotating 1/4 of the way around the circle counterclockwise, we reach the radius line labeled .25.

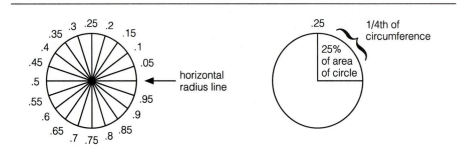

Figure 10.24 Numbers assigned to radius lines.

EXAMPLE 1 In Figure 10.25, what percentage of the area of the circle lies in the shaded sector?

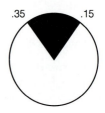

Figure 10.25 Circle for Example 1.

SOLUTION The percentage of the circle contained between the radius lines labeled .15 and .35 is 35% − 15%, or 20%.

The statement

```
Picture1.Circle (x, y), r
```

draws the circle with center (x, y) and radius r. More precisely, the length of the horizontal radius line will be r units in the scale for the x-axis determined by the Picture1.Scale statement. If $0 < a < b < 1$ and c is the circumference of the unit circle ($2*\pi$), then the statement

```
Picture1.Circle (x, y), r, , a * c, b * c
```

draws an arc from the end of radius line a to the end of radius line b (see Figure 10.26a). The statement

```
Picture1.Circle (x, y), r, , -a * c, -b * c
```

draws the sector corresponding to that arc (see Figure 10.26b).

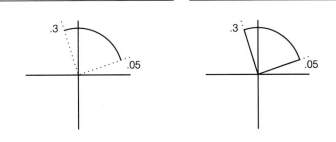

Figure 10.26(a) Arc of a circle.   **Figure 10.26(b)** Sector of a circle.

A special case occurs when a is 0. The expression $-a * c$ will be zero rather than a negative number. As a result, Visual Basic does not draw the horizontal radius line associated with $a = 0$. In order to create a sector that has the horizontal radius line as one of its edges, use a small number such as .0000001 for a.

EXAMPLE 2   Write a program to draw a sector whose sides are a horizontal radius line and the radius line that is 40% of the way around the circle.

SOLUTION   The following program draws the sector with its center at the center of the picture box. The radius was arbitrarily chosen to be 2 and the Picture1.Scale statement was chosen so that the circle would be fairly large. The output displayed in the picture box is shown in Figure 10.27.

```
Sub Command1_Click ()
  Dim c As Single
  Picture1.Cls
  Picture1.Scale (-3, 3)-(3, -3)     'Specify coordinate system
  Let c = 2 * 3.14159
  Let a = .0000001
  Let b = .4
  Rem Draw sector with radius lines corresponding to 0 and .4
  Picture1.Circle (0, 0), 2, , -a * c, -b * c
End Sub
```

Figure 10.27 Display from Example 2.

A sector can be "painted" using any of the patterns shown in Figure 10.28. Which pattern is used to fill a sector is determined by the value of the FillStyle property. The default value of this property is 1 for transparent. Thus by default, the interior of a sector is not painted.

Fill Style #	Fill Pattern	Fill Style #	Fill Pattern
0	■	4	▨
1	□	5	▨
2	▤	6	▦
3	▥	7	▨

Figure 10.28 Fill patterns.

EXAMPLE 3 Write a program to draw the sector consisting of the bottom half of a circle and fill it with vertical lines.

SOLUTION Vertical lines correspond to a FillStyle of 3. See Figure 10.29 for the output of the following program.

```
Sub Command1_Click ()
  Dim c As Single
  Rem Draw bottom half of circle filled with vertical lines
  Let c = 2 * 3.14159
  Picture1.Cls
  Picture1.Scale (-3, 3)-(3, -3)          'Specify coordinate system
  Let Picture1.FillStyle = 3              'Vertical lines
  Picture1.Circle (0, 0), 2, , -.5 * c, -1 * c
End Sub
```

Figure 10.29 Display from Example 3.

The color used to fill the interior of a sector is determined by the value of the FillColor property. If the FillStyle of a picture box is any value except 1, then the statement

```
Let Picture1.FillColor = QBColor(c)
```

will cause new circles and sectors drawn in the picture box to be filled with a pattern in color c of Table 10.1 in Section 10.1

EXAMPLE 4   Write a program to subdivide a circle into four quadrants and fill in the second quadrant, that is, the quadrant extending from radius line .25 to radius line .5, with magenta cross-hatched lines.

SOLUTION   Magenta corresponds to a FillColor of 5. Cross-hatched lines correspond to a FillStyle of 6. See Figure 10.30 for the output of the following program.

```
Sub Command1_Click ()
  Dim c As Single
  Rem Draw quarters of circle and paint upper-left quadrant
  Let c = 2 * 3.14159
  Picture1.Cls
  Picture1.Scale (-3, 3)-(3, -3)        'Specify coordinate system
  Picture1.Circle (0, 0), 2, , -.0000001 * c, -.25 * c
  Let Picture1.FillStyle = 6            'Cross-hatched
  Let Picture1.FillColor = QBColor(5)   'Magenta
  Picture1.Circle (0, 0), 2, , -.25 * c, -.5 * c
  Let Picture1.FillStyle = 1            'Transparent
  Picture1.Circle (0, 0), 2, , -.5 * c, -.75 * c
  Picture1.Circle (0, 0), 2, , -.75 * c, -1 * c
End Sub
```

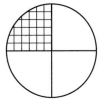

Figure 10.30 Display from Example 4.

The FillStyle and FillColor properties can be used when creating rectangles. The statements

```
Let Picture1.FillStyle = s
Let Picture1.FillColor = QBColor(c)
Picture1.Line (x1, y1)-(x2, y2), , B
```

draw a rectangle filled with the pattern specified by s in the color specified by c. This capability is often used when creating the legend to accompany a graph.

The procedure for drawing a pie chart is as follows:

1. Read the categories and the quantities into arrays, such as *category*( ) and *quantity*( ).

2. Determine the radius lines. The number associated with the ith radius line is *cumPercent*(i). This number is a total of *quantity*(i) and the preceding percentages.

3. Draw and fill each sector with a pattern. The first sector extends from the horizontal radius line to radius line 1, the second sector from radius line 1 to radius line 2, and so on.

4. Draw rectangular legends to associate each sector with its category.

EXAMPLE 5   Table 10.3 gives the distribution of the 1991 revenue of the Microsoft Corporation. Construct a pie chart that displays the sources of revenue.

	Revenue (in millions)	Percent of Total Revenue
Operating systems & languages	648	36%
Applications software	918	51%
Other	234	13%

Table 10.3 Sources of revenue: Microsoft Corp. 1991.

SOLUTION   Figure 10.31 shows the output displayed in Picture1 by the following program.

```
Sub Command1_Click ()
  Dim numItems As Integer, radius As Single
  Rem Draw pie chart of Microsoft Corporation's 1991 revenues
  Let numItems = 3
  ReDim category(1 To numItems) As String
  ReDim quantity(1 To numItems) As Single
  Call ReadData(category(), quantity(), numItems)
  Call DrawData(quantity(), numItems, radius)
  Call ShowLegend(category(), numItems, radius)
  Call ShowTitle(radius)
End Sub

Sub DrawData (quantity() As Single, numItems As Integer, radius As Single)
  Dim circumf As Single, leftEdge As Single, rightEdge As Single
  Dim topEdge As Single, bottomEdge As Single, i As Integer
  Dim startAngle As Single, stopAngle As Single
  Rem Draw and fill each sector of pie chart
  Rem All scaling & text positioning done as a percentage of radius
  Let radius = 1  'actual value used is not important
  Rem Make picture 4 radii wide to provide plenty of space for
  Rem circle and legends. Place origin 1.25 radii from left edge;
  Rem space of 1.75 radii will remain on right for legends.
  Let leftEdge = -1.25 * radius
  Let rightEdge = 2.75 * radius
  Rem Force vertical scale to match horizontal scale;
  Rem center origin vertically
  Let topEdge = 2 * radius * (Picture1.Height / Picture1.Width)
  Let bottomEdge = -topEdge
  Picture1.Cls
  Picture1.Scale (leftEdge, topEdge)-(rightEdge, bottomEdge)
  Let circumf = 2 * 3.14159
  ReDim cumPercent(0 To numItems)
```

```
      Let cumPercent(0) = .0000001 'a "zero" that can be made negative
      For i = 1 To numItems
        Let cumPercent(i) = cumPercent(i - 1) + quantity(i)
        Let startAngle = cumPercent(i - 1) * circumf
        Let stopAngle = cumPercent(i) * circumf
        Let Picture1.FillStyle = (8 - i) 'use fill patterns 7, 6, and 5
        Picture1.Circle (0, 0), radius, , -startAngle, -stopAngle
      Next i
    End Sub


  Sub Locate (x As Single, y As Single)
    Let Picture1.CurrentX = x
    Let Picture1.CurrentY = y
  End Sub


  Sub ReadData (category() As String,quantity() As Single,numItems As Integer)
    Dim i As Integer
    Rem Load categories and percentages of revenue
    Rem Assume the data has been placed in the file REVENUE.TXT
    Rem (First line in file is "Oper. Systems and Lang.",.36)
    Open "REVENUE.TXT" For Input As #1
    For i = 1 To numItems
      Input #1, category(i), quantity(i)
    Next i
    Close #1
  End Sub


  Sub ShowLegend (category() As String, numItems As Integer, radius As Single)
    Dim lblHght As Single, legendSize As Single
    Dim i As Integer, vertPos As Single
    Rem Place legend centered to right of pie chart
    Rem Make separation between items equal to one line of text
    Rem "Text lines" needed for legends is thus (2*numItems-1)
    Let lblHght = Picture1.TextHeight(" ")
    Let legendSize = lblHght * (2 * numItems - 1)
    For i = 1 To numItems
      Let Picture1.FillStyle = (8 - i)
      Let vertPos = (legendSize / 2) - (i - 1) * (2 * lblHght)
      Picture1.Line (1.1 * radius, vertPos)-(1.4 * radius, vertPos - lblHght),,B
      Call Locate(1.5 * radius, vertPos)
      Picture1.Print category(i)
    Next i
  End Sub

  Sub ShowTitle (radius As Single)
    Dim lbl As String, lblWid As Single
    Rem Display title right below circle
    Let lbl = "Sources of Revenue: Microsoft, 1991"
    Let lblWid = Picture1.TextWidth(lbl)
    Call Locate(-lblWid / 2, -radius)
    Picture1.Print lbl
  End Sub
```

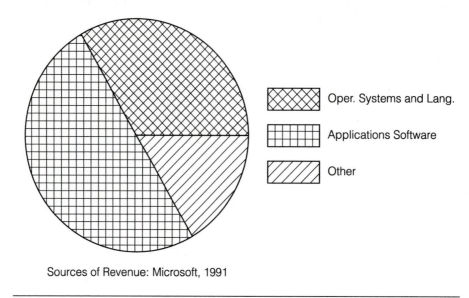

Sources of Revenue: Microsoft, 1991

Figure 10.31 Display from Example 5.

PRACTICE PROBLEMS 10.4

1. Label each of the radius lines in Figure 10.32 with a number from 0 to 1.

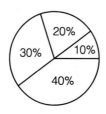

Figure 10.32 Circle for Practice Problem 1.

2. Write a program to draw the circle and radius lines in Problem 1 and to fill in the sector consisting of 30% of the area of the circle.

EXERCISES 10.4

1. Label each of the radius lines in Figure 10.33(a) with a number from 0 to 1.

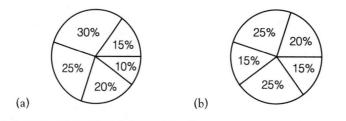

(a)   (b)

Figure 10.33 Circles for Exercises 1 and 2.

2. Label each of the radius lines in Figure 10.33(b) with a number from 0 to 1.

3. Write a program to draw the circle and radius lines of Figure 10.33(a) and to fill in the sector consisting of 10% of the circle.

4. Write a program to draw the circle and radius lines of Figure 10.33(b) and to fill in the sector consisting of 25% of the circle.

In Exercises 5 and 6, draw a pie chart to display the given data.

5. United States Beverage Consumption

Soft Drinks 51%
Beer 24%
Fruit Juices & Drinks 13%
Bottled Water 9%
Other 3%
Source: Beverage World, May 1993

6. Average Number of Miles from College to Home for College Freshmen, Fall 1992

5 or less	10%	51 to 100	15%
6 to 10	8%	101 to 500	28%
11 to 50	30%	more than 500	9%

Source: Higher Education Research Institute

7. Construct a general pie-chart program that prompts the user for the title, the number of sectors (2 through 8), and legends. Try the program with the following data.

Share of Pizza Delivery Market, 1991

Domino's 47%
Pizza Hut 20%
Other 33%

8. Modify the program in Exercise 7 to accept raw data and convert it to percentages. Try the program with the following data.

Fiscal Year 1994 Operating Budget for Montgomery County, Maryland (in millions of dollars)

Board of Education, 790	Montgomery College, 87
County Government, 662	Other, 50
Debt Service, 115	

Source: Montgomery County Government Department of Finance

9. Write a program that produces the drawing in Figure 10.34.

Figure 10.34 Drawing for Exercise 9.

10. Write a program that draws a smiling face. See Figure 10.35.

Figure 10.35 Drawing for Exercise 10.

SOLUTIONS TO PRACTICE PROBLEMS 10.4

1. Each number was obtained by summing the percentages for each of the sectors from the horizontal radius line to the radius line under consideration.

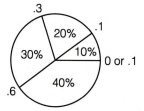

2. The 30% sector is the third sector, extending from radius line .3 to radius line .6.

```
Sub Command1_Click ()
  ReDim perc(4) As Single
  Let perc(0) = .0000001
  Let perc(1) = .1
  Let perc(2) = .3
  Let perc(3) = .6
  Let perc(4) = 1
  Picture1.Cls
  Picture1.Scale (-3, 3)-(3, -3)  'Specify coordinate system
  Let c = 2 * 3.14159
  For i = 1 To 4
    If i = 3 Then
        Picture1.FillStyle = 0    'Solid fill
      Else
        Picture1.FillStyle = 1    'Transparent fill
    End If
    Picture1.Circle (0, 0), 2,, -perc(i - 1)*c, -perc(i)*c   'Draw sector
  Next i
End Sub
```

Chapter 10
Summary

1. Data can be vividly displayed in *line*, *bar*, *clustered bar*, and *pie charts*. Screen dumps of these charts produce printed copy.

2. The programmer can select his or her own coordinate system with the Scale method.

3. The Line method draws lines, rectangles, solid rectangles. Styled lines can be drawn by assigning appropriate values to the DrawStyle property.

4. The Circle method statement is used to draw circles, radius lines, and sectors. Each radius line is specified by a number between 0 and 1. The number $2 * \pi$ (or 6.283185) is used by the Circle method when drawing radii and sectors.

5. The PSet method turns on a single point and is useful in graphing functions.

6. The FillStyle property allows circles, sectors, or rectangles to be filled with one of eight patterns, while the QBColor( ) function allows them to appear in assorted colors.

Chapter 10
Programming Projects

1. Look in magazines and newspapers for four sets of data, one suited to each type of chart discussed in this chapter. Write programs to display the data in chart form.

2. Figure 10.36 is called a *horizontal bar chart*. Write a program to produce this chart.

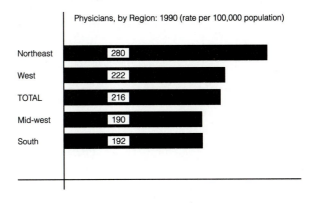

Figure 10.36 Horizontal bar chart.

3. Figure 10.37 is called a segmented bar chart. Write a program to construct this chart.

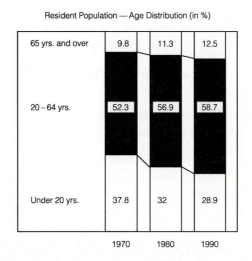

Figure 10.37 Segmented bar chart.

4. Figure 10.38 is called a *range chart*. Using the data in Table 10.4, write a program to produce this chart.

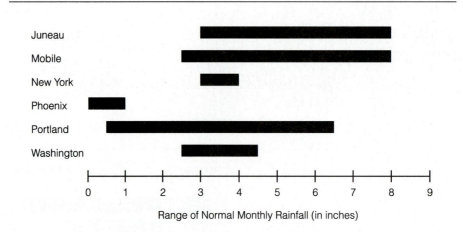

Figure 10.38 Range chart.

	Lowest NMR	Highest NMR
Mobile	2.6	7.7
Portland	.5	6.4
Phoenix	.1	1.0
Washington	2.6	4.4
Juneau	2.9	7.7
New York	3.1	4.2

Table 10.4 Range of normal monthly rainfall for selected cities (in inches).

11

Special Features of Visual Basic

11.1 LIST BOXES AND COMBO BOXES

The Open Project dialog box in Figure 11.1 contains one **list box** and three **combo boxes**. The Directories list box displays a list of directories. You click on a directory to highlight it and double-click on a directory to make it the current directory. A combo box combines the features of a text box and a list box. In the File Name combo box, you click on a file to have it duplicated in the associated text box and double-click on a file to open it. With the other two combo boxes (known as drop-down combo boxes), only the text box part is showing. The associated list drops down when you click on the arrow to the right of the text box part.

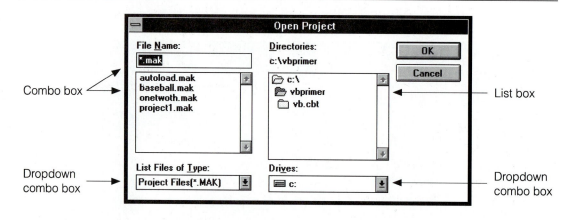

Figure 11.1 Open Project dialog box.

The List Box Control

The fifth row of the Toolbox contains the combo box icon on the left and the list box icon on the right. The entries (or **items**) of the list box are strings that can only be placed in the list during run-time.

The Sorted property is perhaps the most interesting list box property. When it is set to True, the items will automatically be displayed in alphabetical (that is, ANSI) order. The default value of the Sorted property is False.

If *str* is a string, then the statement

```
List1.AddItem str
```

adds *str* to the list. The item is added at the proper sorted position if the Sorted property is True, and otherwise is added to the end of the list. At any time, the value of

```
List1.ListCount
```

is the number of items in the list box.

Each item in the List1 list box is identified by an index number ranging from 0 through List1.ListCount – 1. The value of

```
List1.NewIndex
```

is the index number of the item most recently added to List1 by the AddItem method. During run-time you can highlight an item from a list by clicking on it with the mouse or by moving to it with the up- and down-arrow keys. (The second method triggers the Click event each time an arrow key causes the highlight to move.) The value of

```
List1.ListIndex
```

is the index number of the item currently highlighted in List1.

The string array List1.List( ) holds the list of items stored in the list box. In particular, the value of

```
List1.List(n)
```

is the item of List1 having index *n*. For instance, the statement Print List1.List(0) displays the first item of the list box List1. The value of

```
List1.List(List1.ListIndex)
```

is the item (string) currently highlighted in list box List1. Alternatively, the value of

```
List1.Text
```

is the currently highlighted item. Unlike the Text property of a text box, you may not assign a value to List1.Text.

The statement

```
List1.RemoveItem n
```

deletes the item of index *n* from List1, the statement

```
List1.RemoveItem List1.ListIndex
```

deletes the item currently highlighted in List1, and the statement

```
List1.Clear
```

deletes every item of List1.

EXAMPLE 1 An oxymoron is a pairing of contradictory or incongruous words. The following program displays a sorted list of oxymorons. When you click an item (or highlight it with the up- and down-arrow keys), it is displayed in a picture box. A command button allows you to add an additional item with an Input box. You can delete an item by double-clicking on it with the mouse. (**Note:** When you double-click the mouse, two events are processed—the Click event and the double-click event.) After running the program, click on different items, add an item or two (such as "same difference" or "liquid gas"), and delete an item.

Object	Property	Setting
frmOxyMor	Caption	OXYMORONS
lstOxys	Sorted	True
cmdAdd	Caption	Add an Item
lblDelete	Caption	[To delete an item, double-click on it.]
picSelected		

```
Sub cmdAdd_Click ()
  Dim item As String
  Let item = InputBox$("Item to Add:")
  lstOxys.AddItem item
End Sub

Sub Form_Load ()
  lstOxys.AddItem "jumbo shrimp"
  lstOxys.AddItem "definite maybe"
  lstOxys.AddItem "old news"
  lstOxys.AddItem "good grief"
End Sub

Sub lstOxys_Click ()
  picSelected.Cls
  picSelected.Print "The selected item is"
  picSelected.Print Chr$(34) + lstOxys.Text + Chr$(34) + "."
End Sub

Sub LstOxys_DblClick ()
  lstOxys.RemoveItem lstOxys.ListIndex
End Sub
```

[Run and then click on the second item of the list box.]

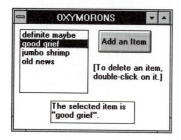

When the Sorted property of a list box is True, the index associated with an item will change when a "lesser" item is added to or removed from the list. In many applications it is important to have a fixed number associated with each item in a list box. Visual Basic makes this possible using the ItemData property. The statement

```
List1.ItemData(n) = m
```

associates the number m with the item of index n, and the statement

```
List1.ItemData(List1.NewIndex) = m
```

associates the number m with the item most recently added to the list box. Thus the List1 list box can be thought of as consisting of two arrays, List1.List( ) and List1.ItemData( ). The contents of List1.List( ) are displayed in the list box allowing the user to make a selection while the hidden contents of List1.ItemData( ) can be used by the programmer to index records or, as illustrated in Example 2 below, to set up parallel arrays that hold other data associated with each item displayed in the list box.

EXAMPLE 2   The following program uses NewIndex and ItemData to provide data about inventions. When an item is highlighted, its ItemData value is used to locate the appropriate entries in the inventor( ) and date( ) arrays. Assume the file INVENTOR.TXT contains the following three lines:

"Ball-point pen", "Lazlo and George Biro", 1938
"Frozen food", "Robert Birdseye", 1929
"Bifocal lenses", "Ben Franklin", 1784

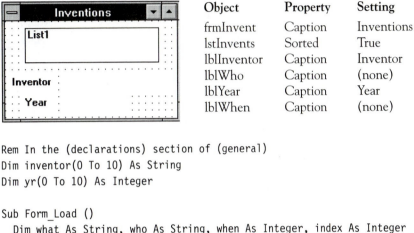

Object	Property	Setting
frmInvent	Caption	Inventions
lstInvents	Sorted	True
lblInventor	Caption	Inventor
lblWho	Caption	(none)
lblYear	Caption	Year
lblWhen	Caption	(none)

```
Rem In the (declarations) section of (general)
Dim inventor(0 To 10) As String
Dim yr(0 To 10) As Integer

Sub Form_Load ()
  Dim what As String, who As String, when As Integer, index As Integer
  Open "INVENTOR.TXT" For Input As #1
  Let index = 0
  Do While (index < UBound(inventor)) And (Not EOF(1))
    Input #1, what, who, when
    Let index = index + 1
    lstInvents.AddItem what
    Let lstInvents.ItemData(lstInvents.NewIndex) = index
    Let inventor(index) = who
    Let yr(index) = when
  Loop
End Sub

Sub lstInvents_Click ()
  Let lblWho.Caption = inventor(lstInvents.ItemData(lstInvents.ListIndex))
  Let lblWhen.Caption = Str$(yr(lstInvents.ItemData(lstInvents.ListIndex)))
End Sub
```

[Run and then highlight the second entry in the list.]

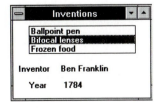

The Combo Box Control

A combo box is best thought of as a text box with a help list attached. With an ordinary text box, the user must type information into the box. With a combo box, the user has the option of either typing in information or just selecting the appropriate piece of information from a list. The two most useful types of combo box are denoted as style 0 and style 1 combo boxes. See Figure 11.2.

Style 0 Combo Box   Style 1 Combo Box

Figure 11.2 Styles of combo boxes.

With a style 1 combo box, the list is always visible. With a style 0 combo box, the list drops down when the user clicks on the arrow, and then disappears after a selection is made. In either case, when an item from the list is highlighted, the item automatically appears in the text box at the top and its value is assigned to the Text property of the combo box.

Combo boxes have essentially the same properties, events, and methods as list boxes. In particular, all the statements discussed above for list boxes also hold for combo boxes. The Style property of a combo box is usually specified at design-time.

EXAMPLE 3   The following program uses a style 1 combo box to obtain a person's title for the first line of the address of a letter. (**Note:** At design-time, first set the combo box's Style property to 1, and then lengthen the combo box.)

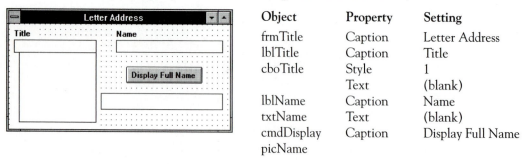

Object	Property	Setting
frmTitle	Caption	Letter Address
lblTitle	Caption	Title
cboTitle	Style	1
	Text	(blank)
lblName	Caption	Name
txtName	Text	(blank)
cmdDisplay	Caption	Display Full Name
picName		

```
Sub cmdDisplay_Click ()
  picName.Cls
  picName.Print cboTitle.Text + " " + txtName.Text
End Sub
```

```
Sub Form_Load ()
  cboTitle.AddItem "Mr."
  cboTitle.AddItem "Ms."
  cboTitle.AddItem "Dr."
  cboTitle.AddItem "Sir"
  cboTitle.AddItem "Lady"
  cboTitle.AddItem "The Honorable"
  cboTitle.AddItem "Her Excellency"
  cboTitle.AddItem "General"
End Sub
```

[Run, select an item from the combo box, type a name into the Name text box, and click the command button.]

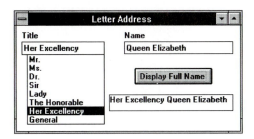

The same program with a style 0 combo box produces the output shown below.

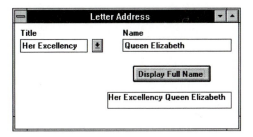

Drive ⌷, Directory ⌷, and File ⌷ List Box Controls

Boxes similar to those inside the Open Project dialog box of Figure 11.1 are available to any Visual Basic program via icons from the Toolbox. Visual Basic does much of the work of providing the appropriate lists for the three boxes. Windows determines the contents of the drive box. The programmer determines the contents of directory list boxes and file list boxes with Path properties.

Most of the properties, methods, and events of list boxes are also valid for the three file-related list boxes. For instance, in the file list box File1, File1.ListCount is the number of files and File1.List(n) is the name of the nth file, where counting begins with 0. The selected items for the three controls are identified by the Drive, Path, and Filename properties, respectively. For instance, in the drive list box Drive1, the selected drive is given by the string Drive1.Drive.

Suppose a form contains a drive list box named Drive1, a directory list box named Dir1, and a file list box named File1. (These names are the default names supplied by Visual Basic.) When the user selects a new drive from the Drive1 list box, the directories in Dir1 should reflect this change. The proper event procedure to effect the change is

```
Sub Drive1_Change ()
   Dir1.Path = Drive1.Drive
End Sub
```

This event is triggered by clicking on the drive name or using the arrow keys to highlight the drive name and then pressing Enter. When the user selects a new directory in Dir1, the files in File1 can be changed with the event procedure

```
Sub Dir1_Change ()
   File1.Path = Dir1.Path
End Sub
```

This event procedure is triggered by double-clicking on a directory name. If the two event procedures above are in place, a change of the drive will trigger a change of the directory, which in turn will trigger a change in the list of files.

EXAMPLE 4   The following program can be used to display the full name of any file on any drive.

Object	Property	Setting
frmFiles	Caption	Select a File
drvList		
dirList		
filList		
cmdDisplay	Caption	Display Complete Name of File
picFileSpec		

```
Sub cmdDisplay_Click ()
  picFileSpec.Cls
  picFileSpec.Print dirList.Path;
  If Right$(dirList.Path, 1) <> "\" Then
      picFileSpec.Print "\";
  End If
  picFileSpec.Print filList.FileName
End Sub

Sub dirList_Change ()
  Let filList.Path = dirList.Path
End Sub

Sub drvList_Change ()
  Let dirList.Path = drvList.Drive
End Sub
```

[Run, select a drive, double-click on a directory, select a file, and then click the command button.]

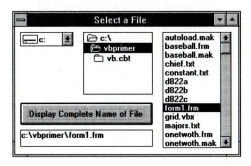

Comments:

1. If a list or combo box is too short to display all the items that have been added to it, Visual Basic automatically places a vertical scroll bar on the right side of the list box. The user can then scroll to see the remaining items of the list.

2. When the Style property of a combo box is set to 2, the combo box becomes a dropdown list box, which is much less useful that the other two styles of combo boxes.

3. The standard Windows convention for opening a file is to double-click on a name in a file list box. The program must contain code for a DblClick event procedure to carry out this task.

4. There is an important difference between the "selected drive" and the "current drive." The selected drive is the drive highlighted in a drive text box. The current drive is the default drive used by DOS. To make the current drive be the same as the selected drive, include the line

   ```
   ChDrive Drive1.Drive
   ```

   in the Drive1_Change ( ) event procedure. Similarly, to change the "current directory" to the "selected directory" include the line

   ```
   ChDir Dir1.Path
   ```

   in the Dir1_Change ( ) event procedure.

5. File list boxes can be made to display selective lists based on the DOS wildcard characters by setting the Pattern property. For instance, setting File1.Pattern equal to "*.TXT" dictates that only files with the extension TXT will be displayed.

PRACTICE PROBLEMS 11.1

1. Write code to record the contents of a list box into a file.

2. Give a statement that will display the last item in the combo box Combo1.

EXERCISES 11.1

For Exercises 1 through 10, suppose that the list box List1 is as shown below and determine the effect of the code. (Assume the Sorted property is set to True.)

1. ```
Picture1.Print List1.Text
```

2. ```
Picture1.Print List1.List(2)
```

3. ```
Picture1.Print List1.List(List1.ListCount - 1)
```

4. ```
List1.AddItem "Haydn"
```

5. ```
List1.AddItem "Brahms"
Picture1.Print List1.List(List1.NewIndex)
```

6. ```
List1.RemoveItem 0
```

7. ```
List1.RemoveItem List1.ListIndex
```

8. ```
List1.RemoveItem List1.ListCount - 1
```

9. ```
List1.Clear
```

10. ```
Open "COMPOSER.TXT" For Output As #1
For n = 1 To List1.ListCount - 1
  Write #1, List1.List(n)
Next n
Close #1
```

11. ```
For n = 0 To List1.ListCount - 1
    If Len(List1.List(n)) = 6 Then
        List1.RemoveItem n
    End If
Next n
```

12. ```
For n = 0 To List1.ListCount - 1
    Let Composer(n) = List1.List(n)   'Composer() is a string array
Next n
List1.Sorted = False
List1.Clear
For n = List1.ListCount - 1 To 0 Step -1
  List1.AddItem Composer(n)
Next n
```

In Exercises 13 through 24, assume that the combo box Combo1 appears as shown below and that the Sorted property is set to True. Give a statement or statements that will carry out the stated task.

13. Display the string "Dante".

14. Display the string "Goethe".

15. Display the first item of the list. (The statement should do the job even if additional items were added to the list.)

16. Delete the string "Shakespeare".

17. Delete the string "Goethe".

18. Delete the last item of the list. (The statement should do the job even if additional items were added to the list.)

19. Insert the string "Cervantes". Where will it be inserted?

20. Display every other item of the list in a picture box.

21. Delete every item beginning with the letter "M". (The code should do the job even if additional items were added to the list.)

22. Determine if "Cervantes" is in the list. (The statement should do the job even if additional items have been added to the list.)

23. Display the item most recently added to the list.

24. Store the items in the file AUTHOR.TXT.

In Exercises 25 through 30, suppose the form contains a list box containing positive numbers, a command button, and a picture box. Write a click event procedure for the command button that displays the requested information in the picture box.

25. The average of the numbers in the list.

26. The largest number in the list.

27. Every other number in the list.

28. All numbers greater than the average.

29. The *spread* of the list, that is, the difference between the largest and smallest numbers in the list.

30. The median of the numbers in the list.

31. Assume the data in Table 11.1 is contained in the sequential file STATEINF.TXT. Write a program that shows the states in a sorted list box and displays a state's nickname and motto when the state is double-clicked.

State	Nickname	Motto
Wisconsin	Badger State	Forward
Rhode Island	Ocean State	Hope
Texas	Lone Star State	Friendship
Utah	Beehive State	Industry

Table 11.1 State nicknames and mottos.

32. Table 11.2 contains the five U.S. Presidents rated highest by history professors. Create a form with a list box and two command buttons captioned "Order by Year Inaugurated" and "Order by Age at Inaugural." Write a program that shows the Presidents in the list box. When one of the command buttons is clicked, the list box should display the Presidents in the requested order.

President	Year Inaugurated	Age at Inaugural
Abraham Lincoln	1861	52
Franklin Roosevelt	1933	51
George Washington	1789	57
Thomas Jefferson	1801	58
Theodore Roosevelt	1901	42

Table 11.2 Highest rated U.S. presidents.

33. Table 11.3 contains wind-chill factors for several temperatures (in degrees Fahrenheit) and wind speeds (in miles per hour). Write a program containing the temperatures in one list box and the wind speeds in another. When the user selects an item from each list box and clicks on a command button, the program should display the corresponding wind-chill factor.

		Speed		
	5	10	15	20
0	−5	−22	−31	−39
5	0	−15	−25	−31
10	7	−9	−18	−24
15	12	−3	−11	−17

Temperature values in leftmost column: 0, 5, 10, 15.

Table 11.3 Wind-chill factors.

34. Suppose a form contains a list box (with Sorted = False), a label, and two command buttons captioned "Add an Item" and "Delete an Item". When the Add an Item button is clicked, the program should request an item with an input box and then insert the item above the currently highlighted item. When the Delete an Item button is clicked, the program should remove the highlighted item from the list. At all times, the label should display the number of items in the list.

35. Consider the Length Converter in Figure 11.3. Write a program to place the items in the list and carry out the conversion. (See the first programming project in Chapter 7 for a table of equivalent lengths.)

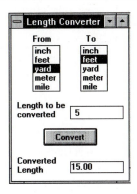

Figure 11.3 Form for Exercise 35.

36. Write a program to ask a person which Monopoly®space he or she has landed on and then display the result in a picture box. The response should be obtained with a combo box listing the squares most commonly landed on—Illinois Avenue, Go, B&O Railroad, and Free Parking. (One possible outcome to be displayed in the picture box is "You have landed on Park Place.")

37. Write a program to question a person about his or her IBM compatible computer and then display a descriptive sentence in a picture box. The form should contain combo boxes for brand, amount of memory, and size of screen. The lists should contain the most common responses for each category. The most common PCs are Compaq, Packard Bell, IBM, and Gateway 2000. The most common amounts of memory are 4K, 8K, and 16K. The most common screen sizes are 14 inch, 15 inch, and 17 inch. (One possible outcome to displayed in the picture box is "You have a Gateway 2000 computer with 32K of memory and a 17 inch monitor.")

38. Modify the program in Example 4 so that the names of all the files with extension .frm in the files list box are printed on the printer.

39. Write a program to display a picture (contained in a .bmp file in the Windows directory) in a picture box. A file should be selected with drive, directory, and file list boxes and the picture displayed with a statement of the form Let Picture1.Picture = LoadPicture(*full name of file*).

SOLUTIONS TO PRACTICE PROBLEMS 11.1

```
1. Sub SaveListBox ()
     Dim i As Integer
     Open "LISTDATA.TXT" For Output As #1
     For i = 0 to List1.ListCount - 1
       Write #1, List1.List(i)
     Next i
     Close #1
   End Sub
```

```
2. Picture1.Print Combo1.List(Combo1.ListCount - 1)
```

11.2 NINE ELEMENTARY CONTROLS

In this section, we discuss the nine controls indicated on the Toolbox in Figure 11.4.

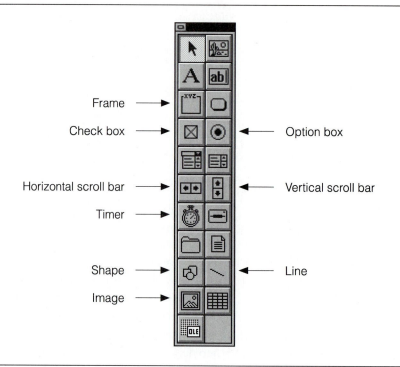

Figure 11.4 Nine elementary controls.

The Frame Control

```
┌─Frame1─────────┐
│ ┌────────────┐ │
│ │Text1       │ │
│ └────────────┘ │
│ ┌────────────┐ │
│ │Text2       │ │
│ └────────────┘ │
│ ┌────────────┐ │
│ │Text3       │ │
│ └────────────┘ │
└────────────────┘
```

Frames are passive objects used to group related sets of controls for visual effect. You rarely write event procedures for frames. The frame above has a group of three text boxes attached to it. When you drag the frame, the attached controls follow as a unit. If you hide the frame, the attached controls will be hidden as well.

A control must be attached to a frame in a special way. You cannot just double-click to create the control and then drag it into a frame. To attach a control to a frame, first create the frame. Next, single-click on the control icon to activate it, then move the mouse pointer inside the frame to the point where you want to place the upper-left corner of the control. Finally, drag the mouse to the right and down, and then release the mouse button when you are satisfied with the size of the control. This is referred to as the **single-click-draw technique**.

A group of controls also can be attached to a picture box. The advantages of using frames are that they have a title sunk into their borders that can be set with the Caption property and that they cannot receive the focus. As shown later in this section, the frame control is particularly important when working with groups of option button controls.

The Check Box Control ⊠

A check box, which consists of a small square and a caption, presents the user with a yes/no choice. The form in Example 1 uses four check box controls. The Value property of a check box is 0 when the square is empty and is 1 when the square is checked. At run-time, the user clicks on the square to toggle between the unchecked and checked states. So doing also triggers the Click event.

EXAMPLE 1 The following program allows an employee to compute the monthly cost of various benefit packages.

		Benefits Menu ▾ ▴
☐ Prescription Drug Plan ($12.51)		
☐ Dental Plan ($9.68)		
☐ Vision Plan ($1.50)		
☐ Medical Plan ($25.25)		
Total monthly payment: $0.00		

Object	Property	Setting
frmBenefits	Caption	Benefits Menu
chkDrugs	Caption	Prescription Drug Plan ($12.51)
	Value	0 – Unchecked
chkDental	Caption	Dental Plan ($9.68)
	Value	0 – Unchecked
chkVision	Caption	Vision Plan ($1.50)
	Value	0 – Unchecked
chkMedical	Caption	Medical Plan ($25.25)
	Value	0 – Unchecked
lblTotal	Caption	Total monthly payment:
lblAmount	Caption	$0.00

```
Sub chkDrugs_Click ()
  Call Tally
End Sub

Sub chkDental_Click ()
  Call Tally
End Sub

Sub chkVision_Click ()
  Call Tally
End Sub

Sub chkMedical_Click ()
  Call Tally
End Sub

Sub Tally ()
  Dim sum As Single
  If chkDrugs.Value = 1 Then
      Let sum = sum + 12.51
  End If
  If chkDental.Value = 1 Then
      Let sum = sum + 9.68
  End If
```

```
        If chkVision.Value = 1 Then
            Let sum = sum + 1.5
        End If
        If chkMedical.Value = 1 Then
            Let sum = sum + 25.25
        End If
        Let lblAmount.Caption = Format$(sum, "Currency")
End Sub
```

[Run and then click on the desired options.]

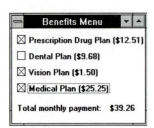

When a check box has the focus, the spacebar can be used to check (or uncheck) the box and invoke the click event. In addition, the state of a check box can be toggled from the keyboard without first setting the focus to the check box if you create an access key for the check box by including an ampersand in the Caption property. (Access keys appear underlined at run-time). For instance, if the Caption property for the Dental Plan in Example 1 is set as "&Dental Plan", then the user can check (or uncheck) the box by pressing Alt+D.

Notice that the program code for the solution to Example 1 involved four identical click event procedures. This is a good indication that a control array of check boxes will simplify the program as shown in Example 2.

EXAMPLE 2   The following program reworks Example 1 using a control array of check boxes, with an access key for each check box. The program has been made more general and easy to update by placing the name and cost of each benefit plan in the data file BENEFITS.TXT. Each line of the file consists of the name of the plan followed by the cost of the plan, as illustrated by the first line of the file:

"&Prescription Drug Plan", 12.51

Object	Property	Setting
frmBenefits	Caption	Benefits Menu
chkPlan( )	Index	0 through 3
lblTotal	Caption	Total monthly payment:
lblAmount	Caption	$0.00

```
Dim price(0 To 3) As Single 'In (declarations) section of (general)
Dim sum As Single

Sub Form_Load ()
    Dim i As Integer, plan As String, cost As Single
    Open "BENEFITS.TXT" For Input As #1
```

```
  For i = 0 To 3
    Input #1, plan, cost
    Let price(i) = cost
    Let chkPlan(i).Caption = plan + " (" + Format$(cost, "Currency") +")"
  Next i
  Close 1
  Let Sum = 0
End Sub

Sub chkPlan_Click (Index As Integer)
  If chkPlan(Index).Value = 1 Then
      Let sum = sum + price(Index)
    Else
      Let sum = sum - price(Index)
  End If
  Let lblAmount.Caption = Format$(sum, "Currency")
End Sub
```

The Value property of a check box also can be set to "2-Grayed". When a grayed square is clicked, it becomes unchecked. When clicked again, it becomes checked.

The Option Button Control

Option buttons are used to give the user a single choice from several options. Normally a group of several option buttons are attached to a frame or picture box with the single-click-draw technique. Each button consists of a small circle accompanied by text that is set with the Caption property. When a circle or its accompanying text is clicked, a solid dot appears in the circle and the button is said to be "on." At most one option button in a group can be on at the same time. Therefore, if one button is on and another button in the group is clicked, the first button will turn off.

The Value property of an option button tells if the button is on or off. The condition

```
Option1.Value
```

is True when Option1 is on and False when Option1 is off. The statement

```
Let Option1.Value = True
```

turns on Option1 and turns off all other buttons in its group. The statement

```
Let Option1.Value = False
```

turns off Option1 and has no effect on the other buttons in its group.

The Click event for an option button is triggered only when an off button is turned on with a mouse click or a statement. It is not triggered when an on button is clicked.

EXAMPLE 3   The following program tells which option button is on.

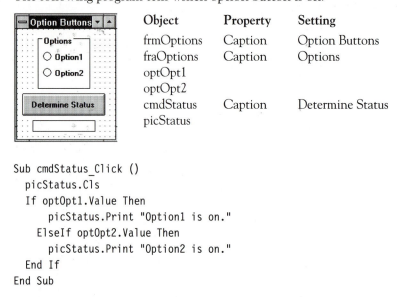

Object	Property	Setting
frmOptions	Caption	Option Buttons
fraOptions	Caption	Options
optOpt1		
optOpt2		
cmdStatus	Caption	Determine Status
picStatus		

```
Sub cmdStatus_Click ()
  picStatus.Cls
  If optOpt1.Value Then
      picStatus.Print "Option1 is on."
    ElseIf optOpt2.Value Then
      picStatus.Print "Option2 is on."
  End If
End Sub

Sub Form_Load ()
  Let optOpt1 = False    'Turn off optOpt1
  Let optOpt2 = False    'Turn off optOpt2
End Sub
```

[Run, click on one of the option buttons, and then click the command button.]

The text alongside an option button is specified with the Caption property. As with a command button and a check box, an ampersand can be used to create an access key for an option button.

EXAMPLE 4   The following program allows the user to select text size in a text box. The three option buttons have been attached to the frame with the single-click-draw technique.

Object	Property	Setting
fraFontSize	Caption	Font Size
opt12pt	Caption	&12
opt18pt	Caption	1&8
opt24pt	Caption	&24
txtInfo	Text	Hello

```
Sub opt12pt_Click ()
  Let txtInfo.FontSize = 12
End Sub

Sub opt18pt_Click ()
  Let txtInfo.FontSize = 18
End Sub

Sub opt24pt_Click ()
  Let txtInfo.FontSize = 24
End Sub
```

[Run and click on the last option button (or press Alt+2).]

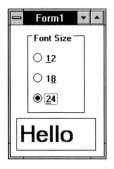

A single form can have several groups of option buttons. However, each group must be attached to its own frame or picture box.

The Horizontal and Vertical Scroll Bar Controls

Figure 11.5 shows the two types of scroll bars. When the user clicks on one of the arrow buttons, the thumb moves a small amount toward that arrow. When the user clicks between the thumb and one of the arrow buttons, the thumb moves a large amount toward that arrow. The user can also move the thumb by dragging it. The main properties of a scroll bar control are Min, Max, Value, SmallChange, and LargeChange, which are set to whole numbers. At any time, HScroll1.Value is a number between HScroll1.Min and HScroll1.Max determined by the position of the thumb. If the thumb is halfway between the two arrows, then HScroll1.Value is a number halfway between HScroll1.Min and HScroll1.Max. If the thumb is near the left arrow button, then HScroll1.Value is an appropriately proportioned value near HScroll1.Min, etc. When an arrow button is clicked, HScroll1.Value changes by HScroll1.SmallChange and the thumb moves accordingly. When the bar between the thumb and one of the arrows is clicked, HScroll1.Value changes by HScroll1.LargeChange and the thumb moves accordingly. When the thumb is dragged, HScroll1.Value changes accordingly. The default values of Min, Max, SmallChange, and LargeChange are 0, 32767, 1, and 1, respectively. However, these values are usually reset at design-time. **Note:** The setting for the Min property can be a number greater than the setting for the Max property. The Min property determines the values for the left and top arrows. The Max property determines the values for the right and bottom arrows.

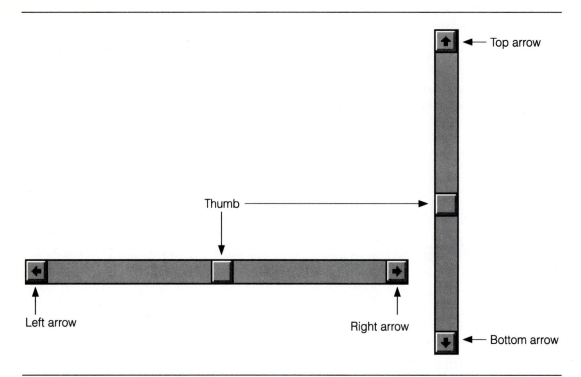

Figure 11.5 Horizontal and vertical scroll bars.

The Change event is triggered whenever an arrow or bar is clicked, or after the thumb has been dragged. The Scroll event is triggered whenever the thumb is being dragged.

EXAMPLE 5 The following program uses scroll bars to move a smiling face around the form. The face is a large Wingdings character J inside a label. The values Label1.Left and Label1.Top are the distances in twips of the label from the left side and top of the form. (When printing, 1440 twips equal one inch; on the screen, 1440 twips are more or less an inch.)

Object	Property	Setting
frmFace	Caption	Smiling Face
hsbXPos	Min	0
	Max	3000
	SmallChange	100
	LargeChange	500
	Value	0
vsbYPos	Min	500
	Max	3000
	SmallChange	100
	LargeChange	500
	Value	500
lblFace	Caption	J
	FontName	Wingdings
	FontSize	24
	Left	0
	Top	500

```
Sub hsbXPos_Change ()
  Let lblFace.Left = hsbXPos.Value
End Sub

Sub vsbYPos_Change ()
  Let lblFace.Top = vsbYPos.Value
End Sub
```

[Run and move the thumbs on the scroll bars.]

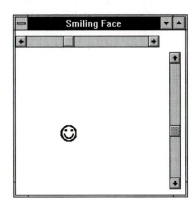

In Example 5, when you drag the thumb, the face does not move until the dragging is completed. This can be corrected by adding the following two event procedures.

```
Sub hsbXPos_Scroll ()
  Let lblFace.Left = hsbXPos.Value
End Sub

Sub vsbYPos_Scroll ()
  Let lblFace.Top = vsbYPos.Value
End Sub
```

The Timer Control

The timer control, which is invisible during run-time, triggers an event after a specified amount of time. The length of time, measured in milliseconds, is set with the Interval property to be any number from 0 to 65,535 (about one minute and five seconds). The event triggered each time Timer1.Interval milliseconds elapses is called Timer1_Timer ( ). In order to begin timing, a timer must first be turned on by setting its Enabled property to True. A timer is turned off either by setting its Enabled property to False or by setting its Interval property to 0.

EXAMPLE 6 The following program creates a stopwatch that updates the time every tenth of a second.

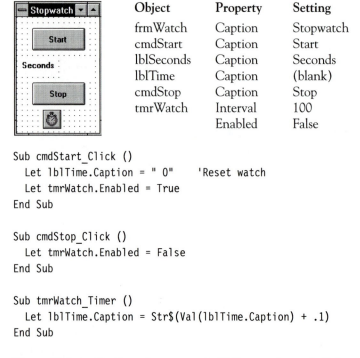

Object	Property	Setting
frmWatch	Caption	Stopwatch
cmdStart	Caption	Start
lblSeconds	Caption	Seconds
lblTime	Caption	(blank)
cmdStop	Caption	Stop
tmrWatch	Interval	100
	Enabled	False

```
Sub cmdStart_Click ()
  Let lblTime.Caption = " 0"       'Reset watch
  Let tmrWatch.Enabled = True
End Sub

Sub cmdStop_Click ()
  Let tmrWatch.Enabled = False
End Sub

Sub tmrWatch_Timer ()
  Let lblTime.Caption = Str$(Val(lblTime.Caption) + .1)
End Sub
```

[Run, click on the Start button, wait 10.8 seconds, and click on the Stop button.]

The Shape Control

The shape control assumes one of six possible predefined shapes depending on the value of its Shape property. Figure 11.6 shows the six shapes and the values of their corresponding Shape properties. Shapes are usually placed on a form at design time for decoration or to highlight certain parts of the form.

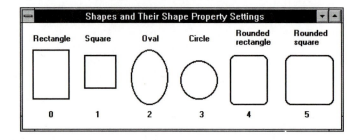

Figure 11.6 The six possible shapes for a shape control.

The most useful properties of shapes are BackStyle (transparent vs. opaque, see Figure 11.7), BorderWidth (thickness of border), BorderStyle (solid, dashed, dotted, etc.), BackColor (background color), FillStyle (fill-in pattern: horizontal lines, upward diagonal lines, etc., as in Figure 10.28), FillColor (color used by FillStyle), and Visible.

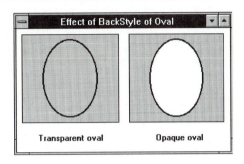

Figure 11.7 Effect of the value of the BackStyle property.

Figure 11.8 shows several effects that can be achieved with shapes. In the first effect, a command is set-off by placing it on top of a rounded rectangle shape whose BackStyle is opaque, BackColor is blue, FillStyle is downward diagonal, and FillColor is yellow. In the second effect, the TRFFC20.ICO icon (displayed in an appropriately sized, borderless picture box) is "framed" by placing it on top of an oval shape whose BackStyle is opaque and BackColor is the same as the background color of the icon. In the last effect, two command buttons are tied together by surrounding them with a circle shape whose FillStyle is transparent, BorderWidth is 8, and BorderColor is green, and by placing behind the command buttons an oval shape whose FillStyle is transparent, BorderWidth is 3, and BorderColor is blue.

Figure 11.8 Several effects achieved with shape controls.

The Line Control

The Line control, which produces lines of various thickness, styles, and colors, is primarily used to enhance the visual appearance of forms. The most useful properties of lines are BorderColor (color of the line), BorderWidth (thickness of the line), BorderStyle (solid, dashed, dotted, etc.), and Visible. Figure 11.9 shows several effects that can be achieved with lines.

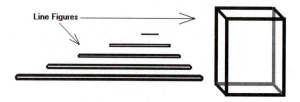

Figure 11.9 Several effects achieved with line controls.

The Image Control

The image control is designed to hold pictures stored in graphics files such as .BMP files created with Windows' Paintbrush or .ICO files of icons that come with Visual Basic. Pictures are placed in image controls with the Picture property. If you double-click on the Picture property during design time, a file selection dialog box appears and assists you in selecting an appropriate file. However, prior to setting the Picture property, you should set the Stretch property. If the Stretch property is set to False (the default value), the image control will be resized to fit the picture. If the Stretch property is set to True, the picture will be resized to fit the image control. Therefore, with Stretch property True, pictures can be reduced (by placing them into a small image control) or enlarged (by placing them into an image control bigger than the picture). Figure 11.10 shows a picture created with Paintbrush and reduced to several different sizes.

A picture can be assigned to an image control at run-time. However a statement such as

```
Let Image1.Picture = "filespec"
```

will not do the job. Instead, we must use the LoadPicture function in a statement such as

```
Let Image1.Picture = LoadPicture("filespec")
```

Image controls enhance the visual appeal of programs. Also, since image controls respond to the Click event and can receive the focus, they can serve as pictorial command buttons.

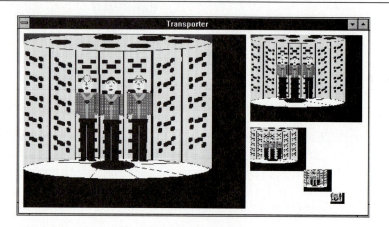

Figure 11.10 A picture created with Paintbrush and reduced several times.

Comment:

1. When placing Line and Shape controls on a form, greater precision can be achieved by first turning off the "Align to Grid" option in the Environment submenu of the Options menu.

PRACTICE PROBLEMS 11.2

1. Suppose you create a frame and then drag a preexisting text box into the frame? How will this text box differ from a text box that was attached to the frame by the single-click-draw method?

2. What is the difference between a group of check boxes attached to a frame and a group of option buttons attached to a frame?

EXERCISES 11.2

In Exercises 1 through 18, determine the effect of setting the property to the value shown.

1. `Frame1.Caption = "Income"`

2. `Check1.Value = 1`

3. `Check1.Value = 0`

4. `Check1.Caption = "&Vanilla"`

5. `Option1.Value = False`

6. `Option1.Caption = "Punt"`

7. `Let HScroll2.Value = HScroll2.Max`

8. `Let HScroll2.Value = (HScroll2.Max + HScroll2.Min) / 2`

9. `Let VScroll2.SmallChange = VScroll2.LargeChange`

10. `Timer1.Interval = 5000`

11. `Timer1.Interval = 0`

12. `Timer1.Enabled = False`

13. `Shape1.Shape = 2`

14. `Let Shape2.BackColor = Shape1.BackColor`

15. `Shape1.FillStyle = 6`

16. `Let Line1.Visible = False`

17. `Let Line1.BorderWidth = 2 * Line1.BorderWidth`

18. `Image1.Stretch = True`

In exercises 19 through 28, write one or more lines of code to carry out the task.

19. A frame has two option buttons attached to it. Move all three objects 100 twips to the right.

20. Clear the small rectangular box of Check1.

21. Turn off Option2.

22. Move the thumb of VScroll2 as high as possible.

23. Move the thumb of HScroll2 one-third of the way between the left arrow and the right arrow.

24. Specify that Timer1 trigger an event every half second.

25. Specify that Timer1 trigger an event every 2 minutes and ten seconds. **Hint:** Use a global variable called Flag.

26. Make Shape1 a circle.

27. Fill Shape1 with vertical lines.

28. Make Image1 vanish.

In Exercises 29 and 30, determine the state of the two option buttons after the command button is clicked.

29.
```
Sub Command1_Click ()
    Option1.Value = True
    Option2.Value = True
End Sub
```

30.
```
Sub Command1_Click ()
    Option1.Value = False
    Option2.Value = False
End Sub
```

31. Which of the controls presented in this section can receive the focus? Design a form containing all of the controls and repeatedly press the Tab key to confirm your answer.

32. Create a form with two frames, each having two option buttons attached to it. Run the program and confirm that the two pairs of option buttons operate independently of each other.

33. Suppose a frame has two option buttons attached to it. If the statement Let Frame1.Visible = False is executed, will the option buttons also vanish? Test your answer.

34. Why are option buttons also called "radio buttons"?

A form contains a command button, a small picture box, and a frame with three check boxes (Check1, Check2, and Check3) attached to it. In Exercises 35 and 36, write a click event for the command button that displays the stated information in the picture box when the command button is clicked.

35. The number of boxes checked.

36. The captions of the checked boxes.

37. A computer dealer offers two basic computers, the Deluxe ($1500) and the Super ($1700). In addition, the customer can order any of the following additional options: multimedia kit ($300), internal modem ($100), 4K of added memory ($150). Write a program that computes the cost of the computer system selected.

38. Item 33a of Form 1040 for the U.S. Individual Income Tax Return reads as follows:

33a Check if: ☐ **You** were 65 or older, ☐ Blind; ☐ **Spouse** was 65 or older, ☐ Blind
Add the number of boxes checked above and enter the total here   → 33a ☐

Write a program that looks at the checked boxes and displays the value for the large square.

39. Write a program for the Font Style form in Figure 11.11. The style of the words in the text box should be determined by the settings in the two frames.

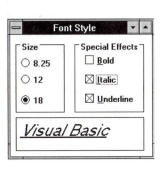

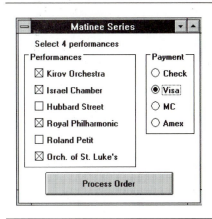

Figure 11.11 Form for Exercise 39.

Figure 11.12 Form for Exercise 40.

40. Subscribers to the Matinee Series for the 1994-1995 season at the Kennedy Center for the Performing Arts must select four performances out of the six shown in the Matinee Series form in Figure 11.12, and must indicate the method of payment. Write the click event procedure for the command button. The procedure should first determine whether exactly four performances have been checked. If not, the user should be so informed with a message box. Then the method of payment should be examined. If no method has been indicated, the user must be reminded to select one. Depending on the method of payment, the user should be told with a message box to either mail in the check with the order form, or to give the credit card number with an input box request. At the end of the process, the caption on the command box should change to "Thank You."

41. Create a form with a line, an oval, and a horizontal scroll box. Write a program that uses the scroll bar to alter the thickness of the line and the oval from 1 through 12. At any time, the number for the thickness should be displayed in a label.

42. *Simulation of Times Square Ball* Create a form with a vertical scroll bar and a timer control. When the program is run, the thumb should be at the top of the scroll bar. Each second the thumb should descend one-tenth of the way down. When the thumb reaches the bottom after ten seconds, a message box displaying HAPPY NEW YEAR should appear.

43. Write a program to synchronize the two thermometers shown in the Temperatures form in Figure 11.13. When the thumb of either thermometer is moved, the other thermometer moves to the corresponding temperature and each temperature is displayed above the thermometer.

Figure 11.13 Form for Exercise 43.   **Figure 11.14** Form for Exercise 44.

44. Write a program to create a decorative digital clock. The clock in the Digital Clock form in Figure 11.14 is inserted in an image control containing a .BMP picture found in the Windows directory. The values for hour, minute, and second can be obtained as Hour(Now), Minute(Now), and Second(Now) and can be formatted with the format string "00".

45. (This exercise requires an icon directory that is not contained in the Primer Edition of Visual Basic.) The Standard editions of Visual Basic contain icons named MOON01.ICO, MOON02.ICO, . . ., MOON08.ICO which show eight phases of the moon. Create a form consisting of an image control, a timer control, and a file list box. Set the Path property of the file list box to the directory containing the moon icons (such as "VB3\ICONS\ELEMENTS\", set the Pattern property to MOON??.ICO, and set the Visible property to False. Every two seconds assign another file from the file list box to the Picture property of the Image control to see the moon cycle through its phases every 16 seconds. One phase is shown in Figure 11.15.

Figure 11.15 Form for Exercise 45.

SOLUTIONS TO PRACTICE PROBLEMS 11.2

1. The text box attached by the single-click-draw method will move with the frame, whereas the other text box will not.

2. With option buttons, at most one button can be on at any given time, whereas several check boxes can be checked simultaneously.

11.3 FIVE ADDITIONAL OBJECTS

In this section we discuss three controls and two objects that are not controls. The three controls are the grid control, the menu control (not accessed through the toolbar), and the common dialog box control (available only in Visual Basic 3.0 and later versions). The two objects are the clipboard and the form. The discussion of the form deals with the use of multiple forms. Multiple forms are available with every version of Visual Basic except the Primer Edition.

The Grid Control

A grid is a rectangular array used to display tables or to create spreadsheet-like applications. The grid in Figure 11.16 has 6 rows and 7 columns. The number of rows and columns can be specified at design-time with the Rows and Columns properties or at run-time with statements such as Let Grid1.Rows = 6 and Let Grid1.Columns = 7. Rows and columns are numbered beginning with 0. For instance, the rows in Figure 11.16 are numbered (from top to bottom) as 0, 1, 2, 3, 4, and 5.

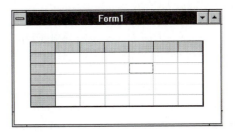

Figure 11.16 A simple grid control.

The width, measured in twips (there are about 1440 twips to an inch), of each column can be specified only at run-time with the ColWidth property. A typical statement is Let Grid1.ColWidth(3) = 1200, which sets the width of column 3 to 1200 twips. (The default column width is 555 twips.) Similarly, the RowHeight property specifies the height of each row. The width and height of the entire grid can be specified at design-time by dragging the mouse or by setting the Width and Height properties.

The grayed row and column in Figure 11.16 are referred to as **fixed**. Fixed rows and columns must be at the top and left sides of the grid. The number of fixed rows and columns is specified by the FixedRows and FixedCols properties. The grid in Figure 11.16 has the default settings FixedRows = 1 and Fixed-Cols = 1.

If the width of the grid is too small to show all the columns, a horizontal scroll bar will automatically appear across the bottom of the grid. Then, during run-time, the nonfixed columns can be scrolled to reveal the hidden columns. Similarly, a vertical scroll bar appears when the height of the grid is too small to show all the rows. Scroll bars can be suppressed by setting the ScrollBars property of the grid to 0 – None. (The default value of the ScrollBars property is 3 – Both.)

The individual small rectangles are called **cells.** Each cell is identified by its row and column numbers. At any time, one cell is singled out as the **active cell.** Initially, the cell in row 1, column 1 is the active cell. The pair of statements Let Grid1.Row = *m*, Let Grid1.Col = *n* set the active cell to the cell in the *m*th row and *n*th column. The active cell in a nonfixed row or column is identified by a dotted border. (In Figure 11.16, the cell in row 2, column 4 is the active cell.) Whenever the user clicks on a cell in a nonfixed row or column, that cell becomes the active cell. The horizontal and vertical lines forming the cells can be turned off by setting the GridLines property to 0.

When the user clicks on a grayed cell in the top row, the cell below the clicked-on cell becomes active, and the rest of the column is colored blue. We say that the column has been **selected.** Similarly, when the user clicks on a grayed cell in the left column, its row is selected. Also, a rectangular block of cells can be selected by dragging the cursor across them. When a cell is selected, its CellSelected property is True and otherwise is False.

Unfortunately, you can't just place text into a cell by clicking on the cell and typing, as you would with a text box. The statement Let Grid1.Text = *str* places text into the active cell and the statement Let *str* = Grid1.Text reads the contents of the active cell. The text inside all the nonfixed cells of column *n* can be displayed left-aligned, right-aligned, or centered with a statement of the form Let Grid1.ColAlignment(*n*) = *r*, where *r* is 0 for left-alignment, 1 for right-alignment, and 2 for centered. (The fixed cells of column *n* can be justified with a statement of the form Let Grid1.FixedAlignment(*n*) = *r*.)

EXAMPLE 1   The following program uses a grid to display an improved version of the table of student expenses from Example 5 of Section 3.5. The five expense categories and numeric data for the table are stored in the sequential file STCOSTS.TXT. Each record of the file consists of a string followed by four numbers.

Object	Property	Setting
frmCosts	Caption	Average Expenses of Commuter Students (1991–92)
grdCosts	BorderStyle	0 – None
	Cols	5
	FixedCols	0
	FixedRows	0
	GridLines	0 – False
	Rows	9
	ScrollBars	0 – None

```
Sub Form_Load ()
   Dim rowNum As Integer, colNum As Integer
   Dim strData As String, numData As Single
   Rem  Column headings
   Let grdCosts.Row = 0
   Let grdCosts.Col = 1
   Let grdCosts.Text = "Pb 2-yr"
   Let grdCosts.Col = 2
   Let grdCosts.Text = "Pr 2-yr"
   Let grdCosts.Col = 3
```

```
        Let grdCosts.Text = "Pb 4-yr"
        Let grdCosts.Col = 4
        Let grdCosts.Text = "Pr 4-yr"
        Rem  Read data from data file and obtain column totals
        ReDim total(1 To 4) As Single
        Open "STCOSTS.TXT" For Input As #1
        For rowNum = 2 To 6    'row 0 holds headings, row 1 is blank
          For colNum = 0 To 4
            Let grdCosts.Row = rowNum
            Let grdCosts.Col = colNum
            If colNum = 0 Then
                Input #1, strData
                Let grdCosts.Text = strData
              Else
                Input #1, numData
                Let grdCosts.Text = Format$(numData, "Currency")
                Let total(colNum) = total(colNum) + numData
            End If
          Next colNum
        Next rowNum
        Rem  Display totals
        Let grdCosts.Row = 8
        Let grdCosts.Col = 0
        Let grdCosts.Text = "Total"
        For colNum = 1 To 4
          Let grdCosts.Col = colNum
          Let grdCosts.Row = 7
          Let grdCosts.Text = "----------------"
          Let grdCosts.Row = 8
          Let grdCosts.Text = Format$(total(colNum), "Currency")
        Next colNum
        Rem  Set column widths to accommodate data; right-justify dollar amounts
        Let grdCosts.ColWidth(0) = 2000        'Space for category names
        Let grdCosts.ColAlignment(0) = 0       'Show data left-justified
        For colNum = 1 To 4
          Let grdCosts.ColWidth(colNum) = 1200   'Space for dollar amounts
          Let grdCosts.ColAlignment(colNum) = 1  'Show data right-justified
        Next colNum
        Rem  Set overall grid size to minimum needed for the data
        Let grdCosts.Width = 2000 + 4 * 1200
        Let grdCosts.Height = 9 * grdCosts.RowHeight(0)
      End Sub
```

[Run and then click on the cell in the lower left corner to remove the blue bar.]

Average Expenses of Commuter Students (1991-92)	Pb 2-yr	Pr 2-yr	Pb 4-yr	Pr 4-yr
Tuition & Fees	$1,022.00	$5,290.00	$2,137.00	$10,017.00
Books & Supplies	$480.00	$476.00	$485.00	$508.00
Board	$1,543.00	$1,529.00	$1,468.00	$1,634.00
Other Expenses	$966.00	$925.00	$1,153.00	$1,029.00
Transportation	$902.00	$786.00	$793.00	$795.00
	----------------	----------------	----------------	----------------
Total	$4,913.00	$9,006.00	$6,036.00	$13,983.00

EXAMPLE 2   The following program creates a simplified spreadsheet. The user places a number into the active cell by typing the number into an input box. The program keeps a running total of the sum of the numbers.

Object	Property	Setting
frmSprdSht	Caption	Spreadsheet
lblAdjust	Caption	Adjust
cmdRows	Caption	Rows
cmdCols	Caption	Columns
cmdQuit	Caption	Quit
lblMsg	Caption	Click on a cell to change its value
grdSprdSht	ScrollBars	False
	FixedRows	0
	FixedCols	0

```
Rem In (declarations) section of (general)
Dim numRows As Integer, numCols As Integer

Sub cmdRows_Click ()
  Dim temp As String
  Rem Adjust the number of rows in the spreadsheet
  Let temp = InputBox$("Enter new number of rows (4-24):")
  If Val(temp) >= 4 And Val(temp) <= 24 Then
      Let numRows = Val(temp)
      Call SetUpGrid
      Call ShowValues
      Call ShowTotals
  End If
End Sub

Sub cmdCols_Click ()
  Dim temp As String
  Rem Adjust number of columns in the spreadsheet
  Let temp = InputBox$("Enter new number of columns (2-7):")
  If Val(temp) >= 2 And Val(temp) <= 7 Then
      Let numCols = Val(temp)
      Call SetUpGrid
      Call ShowValues
      Call ShowTotals
  End If
End Sub

Sub cmdQuit_Click ()
  End
End Sub

Sub Form_Load ()
  Rem Set default number of rows and columns
  Let numRows = 8 'row 0 is for headings, last 2 rows are for totals
  Let numCols = 2 'column 0 is for category names
  Call SetUpGrid
  Call ShowValues
  Call ShowTotals
End Sub
```

```
Sub grdSprdSht_Click ()
  Dim temp As String, msg As String
  Rem Obtain new value for cell if it is not in the "total" rows
  If grdSprdSht.Row < numRows - 2 Then
      Let msg = "Enter new value for the row "
      Let msg = msg + Format$(grdSprdSht.Row + 1, "#") + " column "
      Let msg = msg + Format$(grdSprdSht.Col + 1, "#") + " cell:"
      Let temp = InputBox$(msg,,grdSprdSht.Text) 'Propose old value as default
      If grdSprdSht.Col = 0 Or grdSprdSht.Row = 0 Then
          Let grdSprdSht.Text = temp
        Else
          Let grdSprdSht.Text = Format$(Val(temp), "0.00")
          Call ShowTotals
      End If
  End If
End Sub

Sub SetUpGrid ()
  Dim colNum As Integer
  Rem Set up grid
  Let grdSprdSht.Col = 0
  Let grdSprdSht.Row = grdSprdSht.Rows - 1
  Let grdSprdSht.Text = "" 'erase "Total" in case increasing rows
  Let grdSprdSht.Rows = numRows
  Let grdSprdSht.Cols = numCols
  Rem Set column widths; right-justify columns with numeric data
  Let grdSprdSht.ColWidth(0) = 2000    ' space for category names
  Let grdSprdSht.ColAlignment(0) = 0  ' show data left-justified
  For colNum = 1 To numCols - 1
    Let grdSprdSht.ColWidth(colNum) = 1200  ' space for dollar amounts
    Let grdSprdSht.ColAlignment(colNum) = 1 ' show data right-justified
  Next colNum
  Rem Set overall grid size to minimum needed for the data
  Let grdSprdSht.Width = 2000 + (numCols - 1) * 1200 + 15 * (numCols + 1) + 8
  Let grdSprdSht.Height = numRows*grdSprdSht.RowHeight(0)+15*(numRows + 1)+8
  Rem Adjust form to accommodate grid and other controls
  Let frmSprdSht.Width = grdSprdSht.Left + grdSprdSht.Width + 200
  Let frmSprdSht.Height = grdSprdSht.Top + grdSprdSht.Height + 500
  Let frmSprdSht.Top = 0
  Let frmSprdSht.Left = 0
End Sub

Sub ShowTotals ()
  Dim colNum As Integer, rowNum As Integer, total As Single
  Rem Compute and display total of each numeric column
  Let grdSprdSht.Row = numRows - 1
  Let grdSprdSht.Col = 0
  Let grdSprdSht.Text = "Total"
  For colNum = 1 To numCols - 1
    Let total = 0
    For rowNum = 1 To numRows - 3
      Let grdSprdSht.Row = rowNum
      Let grdSprdSht.Col = colNum
      Let total = total + Val(grdSprdSht.Text)
    Next rowNum
```

```
        Let grdSprdSht.Row = numRows - 2
        Let grdSprdSht.Text = "----------------"
        Let grdSprdSht.Row = numRows - 1
        Let grdSprdSht.Text = Format$(total, "Currency")
    Next colNum
End Sub

Sub ShowValues ()
    Dim rowNum As Integer, colNum As Integer
    Rem Refresh values displayed in cells
    For rowNum = 1 To numRows - 1
        For colNum = 1 To numCols - 1
            Let grdSprdSht.Row = rowNum
            Let grdSprdSht.Col = colNum
            Let grdSprdSht.Text = Format$(Val(grdSprdSht.Text), "0.00")
        Next colNum
    Next rowNum
End Sub
```

[A possible run of the program is shown below.]

```
┌───────────────────────────────────┐
│ ─  │     Spreadsheet      │ ▼ │ ▲ │
├───────────────────────────────────┤
│ Adjust │ Rows │ Columns │ Quit │   │
│ Click on a cell to change its value │
│ ┌─────────────────┬─────────────┐ │
│ │                 │  Fall Term  │ │
│ │ Tuition & Fees  │    3500.00  │ │
│ │ Books & Supplies│     438.00  │ │
│ │ Board           │    1750.00  │ │
│ │ Other Expenses  │    1200.00  │ │
│ │ Transportation  │     825.00  │ │
│ │                 │ ----------- │ │
│ │ Total           │  $7,713.00  │ │
│ └─────────────────┴─────────────┘ │
└───────────────────────────────────┘
```

So far we have used the Text property of grids to place strings into cells. Grids also have a Picture property. A picture (such as a .BMP file created with Paintbrush or an .ICO file from Visual Basic's icon directory) is placed into the active cell with a statement of the form

```
Let Grid1.Picture = LoadPicture("filespec")
```

If both text and a picture are assigned to a cell, then the picture appears in the upper left portion of the cell, and the text appears to the right of the picture.

The Menu Control

Visual Basic forms can have menu bars similar to the menu bar in the Visual Basic environment. Figure 11.17 shows a typical menu, with the submenu for the Font menu item dropped down. Here, the menu bar contains two menu items (Font and Size), referred to as **top-level** menu items. When the Font menu item is clicked, a dropdown list of two second-level menu items (Courier and TimesRm) appears. Although not visible here, the dropdown list under Size contains the two second-level menu items "12" and "24". Each menu item is treated as a distinct control that responds to only one event—the click event. The click event is triggered not only by the click of the mouse button, but also for top-level items by pressing Alt+*accessKey* and for second-level items by just pressing the access key. The click event for the Courier menu item in Figure 11.17 can be activated directly by pressing the shortcut key F1.

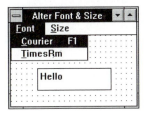

Figure 11.17 A simple menu.

Menus are created with the Menu Design window available from the Window menu on the Visual Basic main menu bar. Figure 11.18 shows the Menu Design window used to create the menu in Figure 11.17. Each menu item has a Caption property (what the user sees) and a Name property (used to refer to the item in the program.) For instance, the last menu item in Figure 11.18 has Caption property "24" and Name property "mnu24". The following steps are used to create the Font-Size menu:

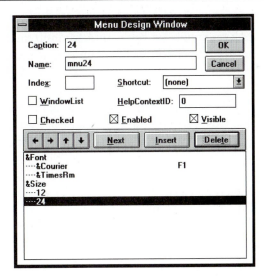

Figure 11.18 The Menu Design window used to create the menu in Figure 11.17.

1. Type &Font into the Caption box and type mnuFont into the Name box.

2. Click on the Next button.

3. Click on the Right Arrow button. (This creates the ellipses and indents the next menu item which will be a second-level item.)

4. Type &Courier into the Caption box and type mnuCourier into the Name box.

5. Click on the arrow to the right of the Shortcut box and select F1 from the dropdown list.

6. Click on the Next button.

7. Type &TimesRm into the Caption box and type mnuTimesRm into the Name box.

8. Click on the Next button

9. Click on the Left Arrow button. (This causes the next item to appear flush left to indicate that it is a top-level menu item.

10. Type &Size into the Caption box and type mnuSize into the Name box.

11. Click on the Next button and then click on the Right Arrow button.

12. Type 12 into the Caption box and type mnu12 into the Name box.

13. Click on the Next button.

14. Type 24 into the Caption box and type mnu24 into the Name box. Your Menu Design window should now appear as in Figure 11.18.

15. Click the OK button to close the Menu Design window.

Three of the check boxes on the Menu Design window are especially useful. When the Checked box is checked, a checkmark appears in front of the menu item. This checkmark can be altered in code with statements such as Let mnuItem.Checked = False and Let mnuItem.Checked = True. When the Enable box is unchecked, the menu item appears gray and does not respond to the click event. The enabled state can be altered in code with statements such as Let mnuItem.Enabled = False and Let mnuItem.Enabled = True. When the Visible property is unchecked, the menu item is invisible.

EXAMPLE 3   The following program creates the application in Figure 11.17, in which the menu is used to alter the appearance of the contents of a text box. The form has caption "Alter Font & Size" and the properties of the menu items are as created above.

```
Sub mnu12_Click ()
  Let txtInfo.FontSize = 12
End Sub

Sub mnu24_Click ()
  Let txtInfo.FontSize = 24
End Sub

Sub mnuCourier_Click ()
  Let txtInfo.FontName = "Courier"
End Sub

Sub mnuTimesRm_Click ()
  Let txtInfo.FontName = "Times New Roman"
End Sub
```

The Clipboard Object

The clipboard object is used to copy or move text from one location to another. It is maintained by Windows and therefore can even be used to transfer information from one Windows application to another. It is actually a portion of memory that holds text and has no properties or events.

If *str* is a string, then the statement

```
Clipboard.SetText str
```

replaces any text currently in the clipboard with *str*. The statement

```
Let str = Clipboard.GetText()
```

assigns the text in the clipboard to the string variable *str*.

The statement

```
Clipboard.Clear
```

deletes the contents of the clipboard.

A portion of the text in a text box or combo box can be **selected** by dragging the mouse across it or by moving the cursor across it while holding down the Shift key. After you select text, you can place it into the clipboard by pressing Ctrl+Ins. Also, if the cursor is in a text box and you press Shift+Ins, the contents of the clipboard will be inserted at the cursor position. These tasks also can be carried out in code. The SelText property of a text box holds the selected string from the text box and a statement such as

```
Clipboard.SetText Text1.SelText
```

copies this selected string into the clipboard. The statement

```
Let Text1.SelText = Clipboard.GetText()
```

replaces the selected portion of Text1 with the contents of the clipboard. If nothing has been selected, the statement inserts the contents of the clipboard into Text1 at the cursor position.

Multiple Forms
(Not available with the Primer Edition of Visual Basic)

A Visual Basic program can contain more than one form. Additional forms are created from the File menu with New Form (Alt/F/F). The name of each form appears in the project window, and any form can be made the active form by double-clicking on its name in the project window. (**Hint:** After creating a new form, move it down slightly so that you can see at least the title bars of the other forms. Then you can activate any form by just clicking on its title bar.) The second form has default name Form2, the third form has default name Form3, and so on. Forms are hidden or activated with statements such as

```
Form1.Hide
```

or

```
Form2.Show
```

When a program is run, the first form created is the only one visible. After that, the Hide and Show methods can be used to determine what forms appear. Two or more forms can be visible at the same time.

Often, additional forms, such as message and dialog boxes, are displayed to present a special message or request specific information. When a message or dialog box appears, the user cannot shift the focus to another form without first hiding the message or dialog box by clicking an OK or Cancel command button. If a form is displayed with a statement of the type

```
formName.Show 1
```

then the form will exhibit this same behavior. The user will not be allowed to shift the focus to any other form until *formName* is hidden. Such a form is said to be **modal**. It is customary to set the BorderStyle property of modal forms to "3-Fixed Double."

Each form has its own controls and code. However, code from one form can refer to a control in another form. If so, the control must be prefixed with the name of the other form, followed by a period. For instance, the statement

```
Let Form2.Text1.Text = "Hello"
```

in Form1 causes text to be displayed in a text box on Form2. (**Note:** Two forms can have a text box named Text1. Code using the name Text1 refers to the text box in its own form unless prefixed with the name of another form.)

EXAMPLE 4   The following program uses a second form as a dialog box to total the different sources of income. Initially only frmIncome is visible. The user types in his or her name and then can either type in the income or click on the command button for assistance in totaling the different sources of income. Clicking on the command button from frmIncome causes frmSources to appear and be active. The user fills in the three text boxes and then clicks on the command button to have the amounts totaled and displayed in the income text box of the first form.

Object	Property	Setting
frmIncome	Caption	Income
lblName	Caption	Name
txtName	Text	(blank)
lblTotal	Caption	Total Income
txtTotal	Text	(blank)
cmdShowTot	Caption	Determine Total Income

Object	Property	Setting
frmSources	Caption	Sources of Income
	BorderStyle	3 – Fixed Double
lblWages	Caption	Wages
txtWages	Text	(blank)
lblInterest	Caption	Interest Income
txtInterest	Text	(blank)
lblDividend	Caption	Dividend Income
txtDividend	Text	(blank)
cmdCompute	Caption	Calculate Total Income

```
Sub cmdShowTot_Click ()
  frmSources.Show 1
End Sub

Sub cmdCompute_Click ()
  Dim sum As Single
  Let sum = Val(txtWages.Text) + Val(txtInterest.Text) + Val(txtDividend.Text)
  Let frmIncome.txtTotal.Text = Format$(Str$(sum), "Currency")
  frmSources.Hide
End Sub
```

[Run, enter name, click the command button, and fill in the sources of income.]

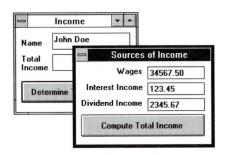

All variables declared and procedures created in a form are local to that form; that is, they are not available to any other form. Such variables and procedures are said to be **form level**. However, you can declare global variables and procedures that are available to all forms. To do so, select New Module from the File menu. A code window will appear with Module1.bas in the title bar. Procedures created in this window will be available to all forms. To declare a variable that is available to all forms, declare it in the Module1.bas window, but use the word Global instead of Dim. For instance, if the statement

```
Global person As String
```

appears in the Module1.bas code window, the variable *person* can be accessed anywhere in the program.

The Common Dialog Box Control
(Available only in Visual Basic 3.0 and later versions)

The common dialog box control can produce each of the useful dialog boxes in Figures 11.19 through 11.23, thereby saving the programmer the trouble of designing custom dialog boxes for these purposes. The common dialog box control has no events or methods, only properties. Actually, like the Timer control, the common dialog box control is invisible. However, when the Action property is set to a number from 1 through 5, one of the five custom dialog boxes pops up on the screen. The type of dialog box produced by the statement

```
Let CMDialog1.Action = n
```

is determined by the value of *n* as shown in Table 11.4.

n	Type of Dialog box	Purpose of Dialog Box
1	Open	Determine what disk file to open
2	Save As	Determine where and with what name to save a disk file
3	Color	Select one color from about 1.6 million colors
4	Font	Select a font for the screen or printer
5	Print	Help control the printer

Table 11.4 Result of setting the Action property to various values of n.

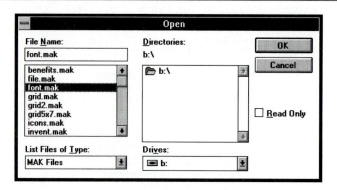

Figure 11.19 The Open common dialog box.

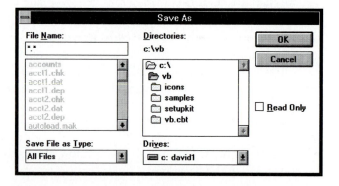

Figure 11.20 The Save As common dialog box.

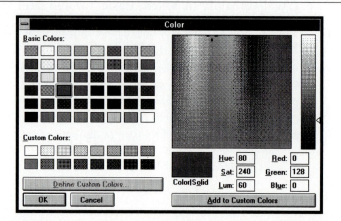

Figure 11.21 The Color common dialog box.

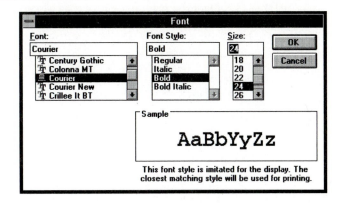

Figure 11.22 The Font common dialog box.

Figure 11.23 The Print common dialog box.

The Flags property influences certain features of the dialog box and should be set prior to setting the Action property. A complete discussion of the Flags property would be too great a digression. For our purposes, we will be well served by always setting the Flags property to 3 with the statement

```
Let CMDialog1.Flags = 3
```

After selections are made from a common dialog box and the OK button is clicked, the values of the selections are stored in properties such as FileName, Color, FontName, and Copies. For instance, the following event procedure specifies the font for the contents of a text box.

```
Sub Command1_Click ()
  Let CMDialog1.Flags = 3
  Let CMDialog1.Action = 3  'Invoke Font common dialog box
  Rem  Select Font, Font Style, and Size and then click on OK
  Let Text1.FontName = CMDialog1.FontName
  Let Text1.FontBold= CMDialog1.FontBold
  Let Text1.FontItalic = CMDialog1.FontItalic
  Let Text1.FontSize = CMDialog1.FontSize
End Sub
```

Table 11.5 gives the principal properties whose setting are garnered from the common dialog boxes.

Type of Common Dialog Box	Principal Properties
Open	FileName
Save As	FileName
Color	Color
Font	FontName, FontSize, FontBold, FontItalic
Print	Copies, FromPage, ToPage

Table 11.5 Principal properties of the common dialog boxes.

With Open and Save As common dialog boxes, a property is needed to specify what types of files should be displayed. A statement of the form

```
Let CMDialog1.Filter ="dscrpt1|filter1|dscrpt2|filter2|dscrpt3|filter3"
```

provides verbal descriptions for the Type box and DOS strings using wildcard characters (filters) to identify the files. A specific statement might be

```
Let CMDialog1.Filter = "Text Files|*.TXT|MAK Files|*.MAK|All Files|*.*"
```

After the filter property is set, the FilterIndex property can be used to set the default filter. For instance, if the statement above is followed with

```
Let CMDialog1.FilterIndex = 1
```

the default will be the first pair of filter items. That is, when the dialog box pops up, the Type box will display Text Files, and the File Name box will show only files with the extension TXT.

Comment:

1. There is another Common Dialog Box—the Help dialog box specified by Action property = 6.

PRACTICE PROBLEMS 11.3

1. What is the difference between the Row property and the Rows property of a grid?

2. What is the effect of the statement Let Text1.SelText = ""?

EXERCISES 11.3

In Exercises 1 through 32, describe the effect of executing the statement.

1. `Let Grid1.Columns = 5`   2. `Let Grid1.Rows = 3`

3. `Let Grid1.RowHeight(3) = 400` **4.** `Let Grid1.ColWidth(2) = 2000`

5. `Let Grid1.FixedCols = 1` **6.** `Let Grid1.FixedRows = 2`

7. `Let Grid1.Row = 3` **8.** `Let Grid1.Col = 4`

9. `Let Grid1.Text = "Income"` **10.** `Let amount = Val(Grid1.Text)`

11. `Let Grid1.ColAlignment(3) = 2` **12.** `Let Grid1.ColAlignment(2) = 1`

13. `Let Grid1.GridLines = False` **14.** `Let Grid1.GridLines = True`

15. `Let Grid1.ScrollBars = 0` **16.** `Let mnuCopy.Enabled = False`

17. `Let mnuCut.Enabled = True` **18.** `Let mnuPaste.Checked = True`

19. `Let mnuSave.Checked = False` **20.** `Let phrase = Clipboard.GetText()`

21. `Clipboard.Clear` **22.** `Clipboard.SetText "Hello"`

23. `Clipboard.SetText Text1.SelText`

24. `Let Text1.SelText = Clipboard.GetText()`

25. `Form2.Show` **26.** `Form2.Show 1`

27. `Form1.Hide` **28.** `Global amount As Single`

29. `Let CMDialog1.Action = 3` **30.** `Let CMDialog1.Action = 4`

31. `Let CMDialog1.Filter = "All Files|*.*|Notepad Files|*.TXT|"`

32. `Let CMDialog1.FilterItem = 2`

In Exercises 33 through 58, write one or more lines of code to carry out the task.

33. Set the number of rows in Grid1 to 7.

34. Set the number of columns in Grid1 to 5.

35. Set the width of the first column of Grid1 to 3000 twips.

36. Set the height of the first row of Grid1 to 300 twips.

37. Fix the top two rows of Grid1.

38. Fix the leftmost column of Grid 1.

39. Specify that the active cell of Grid1 be in the third column (that is, column number 2).

40. Specify that the active cell of Grid1 be in the fourth row (that is, row number 3).

41. Display the contents of the active cell of Grid1 in Picture1.

42. Place the number 76 into the active cell of Grid1.

43. Right-align the contents of the nonfixed cells in the second column of Grid1.

44. Center the contents of the nonfixed cells in the third row of Grid1.

45. Show grid lines in Grid1.

46. Delete grid lines from Grid1.

47. Disable the menu item mnuExit and make it appear gray.

48. Ungray the menu item mnuExit.

49. Place a check mark to the left of the menu item mnuNormal.

50. Remove a check mark from the left of the menu item mnuBold.

51. Assign the contents of the clipboard to the variable *street*.

52. Clear out the contents of the clipboard.

53. Place the word "Happy" into the clipboard.

54. Copy the selected text in Text2 into the clipboard.

55. Insert the contents of the clipboard at the cursor position in Text2.

56. Replace the selected portion of Text1 by the contents of the clipboard.

57. Delete the selected portion of Text1.

58. Display Form2 as a nonmodal form.

59. Display Form2 as a modal form.

60. Declare the variable *wholeNumber* as an Integer variable recognized by every form.

61. Remove Form2 from the screen.

62. Specify that a Save As dialog box be displayed in a common dialog box.

63. Specify that an Open dialog box be displayed in a common dialog box.

64. Specify that the types of files listed in a Save As or Open dialog box's Type list box be of the types "*.MAK" or "*.FRM".

In Exercises 65 and 66, determine what happens to Grid1 when the command button is clicked.

65.
```
Sub Command1_Click ()
    Grid1.Row = 4
    Grid1.Col = 5
    Grid1.Text = Str$(32)
End Sub
```

66.
```
Sub Command1_Click ()
    Dim i As Integer, j As Integer
    For i = 0 To 5
      Grid1.Row = i
      For j = 0 To 5
        Grid1.Col = j
        Grid1.Text = Str$(i) + "," + Str$(j)
      Next j
    Next i
End Sub
```

67. Write a program to create the powers of two table shown in Figure 11.24.

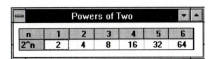

Figure 11.24 Table for Exercise 67. 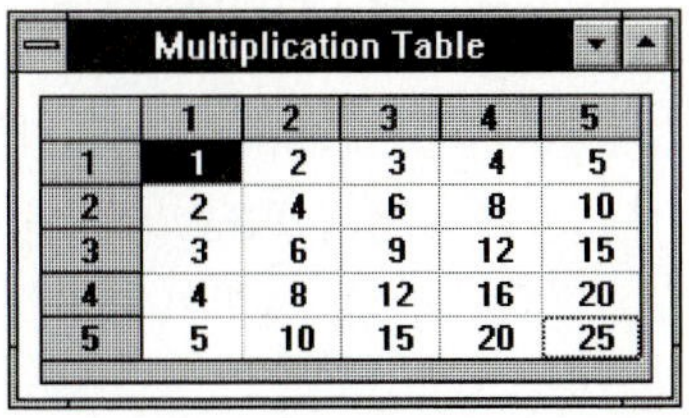   **Figure 11.25** Table for Exercise 68.

68. Write a program to create the multiplication table shown in Figure 11.25.

69. Write a program to produce a spreadsheet that serves as an order form. The grid should have three columns headed "Description," "Qty.," and "Price Each." The user should be able to fill in an entry by clicking on it and then responding to an input box. When the command button is clicked, the total cost of the order should appear in a picture box. A sample run is shown in Figure 11.26.

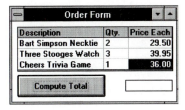

Figure 11.26 Sample run of Exercise 69.

70. The Colleges form in Figure 11.27 contains information about five colleges where the author of this book either attended or taught. Write a program to place the data into a grid as shown. When the heading of a column is clicked, the program should sort the entire grid by that column. For instance, if "Yr. Founded" is clicked, the colleges should reappear in order of their age.

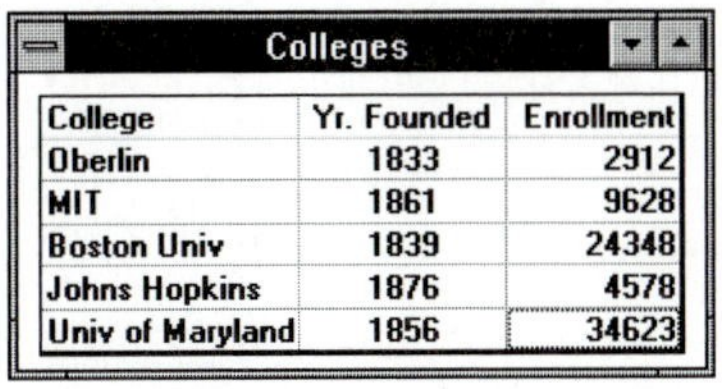

Figure 11.27 Form with data in grid for Exercise 70.

71. Redo Exercise 70 with a menu and include a search capability. The top level items should be Sort (with second-level items College, Year, Enrollment) and Search (with second-level items College and Year). The sort should be the same as in Exercise 70. The search options should allow the user to enter a college or a year into an input box and should display the relevant information about the row containing the college or year. If the college or year cannot be found, the user should be so informed.

72. Modify the spreadsheet program in Example 2 to add an additional column on the right to hold the sums of the rows. Also, a thin column should be added before the final sums column to set it off.

73. Modify the spreadsheet program in Example 2 to sum only the changed column when the Grid1_Click event is called.

74. Write a program with a single text box and a menu with the single top-level item Edit and the four second-level items Copy, Paste, Cut, and Exit. Copy should place a copy of the selected portion of Text1 into the clipboard, Paste should duplicate the contents of the clipboard at the cursor position, Cut should delete a selected portion of the text box and place it in the clipboard, and Exit should terminate the program.

Exercises 75 and 76 require Visual Basic 3.0 or a later version.

75. Write a program containing the two forms shown in Figure 11.28. Initially the Number to Dial form appears. When the Show Push Buttons command button is clicked, the Push Button form appears. The user enters a number by clicking on successive push buttons and then clicks on Enter to have the number transferred to the label at the bottom of the first form.

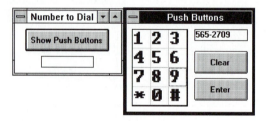

Figure 11.28 Sample run of Exercise 75.

76. Consider the Select Style form shown in Figure 11.29. Write a program to select the color and the font for the text box. When the user clicks on a command button, the corresponding custom dialog box should appear to expedite the choice.

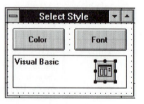

Figure 11.29 Form for Exercise 76.

SOLUTIONS TO PRACTICE PROBLEMS 11.3

1. The Rows property determines how many rows a grid contains, and the Row property specifies which row in the grid contains the active cell.

2. If part of the contents of Text1 has been selected, the selected text will be deleted. Otherwise, nothing happens.

11.4 COMMUNICATING WITH OTHER WINDOWS APPLICATIONS

This section pertains to Visual Basic 3.0 or later versions.

The most used Windows applications are word processors (such as Word, WordPerfect, and AmiPro), spreadsheets (such as Lotus 1-2-3, Excel, and Quattro Pro), and database managers (such as dBase, FoxPro, Paradox, and Access). This section considers the **Data control**, which lets you access the sophisticated database files created by most powerful database managers, and the **OLE control**, which allows Visual Basic programs to utilize other Windows applications.

The Data Control

A random access file is an elementary device for storing and accessing data. It contains many records, each composed of the same set of fields. The file itself does not contain any information about the number and types of the fields. This information is known only to the programmer who created the file. A database file contains not only records, but usually a header giving a name, type, and length for each field, and possibly a great deal more information. The header also can be used to identify the software application (such as Access, dBase, or FoxPro) that created the file. Databases created with Access can contain several sets of records, called tables, along with a header giving all the field information. FoxPro and dBase databases consist of a single table and its header.

Data controls are used to read, modify, delete, and add new records to databases. The following walkthrough uses a data control to look at information from a FoxPro database.

1. Press Alt/**F**ile/**N**ew Project.

2. Double-click on the data control.

3. Stretch it horizontally to see the caption Data1.

4. Go to the properties window, select the Connect property, and set it to "FoxPro 2.5;".

5. We will examine a file called CITIES.DBF in the EXAMPLES subdirectory of the diskette accompanying this book. Select the DatabaseName property and set it to the path for this file, such as A:\EXAMPLES\. (Be sure to include a backslash at the end of the path.)

6. Select the RecordSource property and set it to CITIES.

7. Place a text box on the form. (Text boxes are said to be **data-aware** since they can be bound to a data control and access its data.)

8. Select the text box's DataSource property.

9. Click on the down arrow to the right of the settings box and select Data1.

10. Select the DataField property and click on the down arrow to the right of the settings box. You will see the names of the different fields in the table.

11. Select the field "city". (The text box now is said to be **bound** to the data control.)

12. Run the program. The form will appear as in Figure 11.30. The arrows on the data control look like VCR buttons. The buttons have been identified by the tasks they perform.

13. Click on the various arrows on the data control to see the different cities in the Population table.

Figure 11.30 A Data Control with a text box bound to it.

Only one record can be accessed at any one time; this is called the **current record**. In the walkthrough, the text box bound to the data control showed the contents of the City field of the current record. The user can click on the arrows of the data control to select a new current record. The methods MoveNext, MovePrevious, MoveLast, and MoveFirst also select a new current record. For instance, the statement

```
Data1.RecordSet.MoveLast
```

specifies the last record of the table to be the current record. (The word Recordset is inserted in most data control statements that manipulate records for reasons that needn't concern us.)

The contents of the field *fieldName* of the current record is

```
Data1.RecordSet.Fields("fieldName").Value
```

For instance, with the status as in Figure 11.30, the statement

```
Let strVar = Data1.RecordSet.Fields("city").Value
```

assigns "New York" to the variable *strVar*. and the statements

```
Data1.RecordSet.Edit
Let Data1.RecordSet.Fields("city").Value = "Big Apple"
Data1.RecordSet.Update
```

change the "city" field of the current record to "Big Apple".

The EOF (End Of File) and BOF (Beginning Of File) run-time properties indicate whether the end or beginning of the file has been reached. For instance, the following statements place the cities into a list box:

```
Data1.RecordSet.MoveFirst
Do While Not Data1.RecordSet.EOF
  List1.AddItem Data1.RecordSet.Fields("city").Value
  Data1.RecordSet.MoveNext
Loop
```

The current record can be marked for removal with the statement

```
Data1.RecordSet.Delete
```

The record will be removed when a data control arrow is clicked or a Move method is executed. A new record can be added to the end of the file with the statement

```
Data1.RecordSet.AddNew
```

followed by Let Data1.RecordSet.Fields(*"fieldName"*).Value statements and a Data1.RecordSet.Update statement. Alternatively, the AddNew method can be followed by the user typing the information into text boxes bound to the data control and then moving to another record. (**Note:** When you add a record and then click on the MovePrevious button, you will not see the next to last record, but will see the record preceding the record that was current when AddNew was executed.)

EXAMPLE 1 The following program is a general database manager for the Population table in the Cities database. It allows the user to edit the Population table as needed and to locate information based on the city name.

Object	Property	Setting
frmDBMan	Caption	Database Management
cmdAdd	Caption	Add
cmdDelete	Caption	Delete
cmdSearch	Caption	Search
cmdQuit	Caption	Exit
datCities	Caption	Large World Cities
	Connect	FoxPro 2.5;
	Database	A:\EXAMPLES\
	RecordSource	CITIES
lblCity	Caption	City:
txtCity	Text	(blank)
	DataSource	Data1
	DataField	City
lblPopulation	Caption	Population (1000s):
txtPopulation	Text	(blank)
	DataSource	Data1
	DataField	Population
lblDensity	Caption	Population per square mile:
	Alignment	1 – Right Justify
txtDensity	Text	(blank)
	DataSource	Data1
	DataField	Density

```
Sub cmdAdd_Click ()
  Rem Add a new record
  datCities.Recordset.AddNew
    txtCity.SetFocus    'Data must be entered before moving or no record is added
End Sub
```

```
Sub cmdDelete_Click ()
  Rem Delete the currently displayed record
  datCities.Recordset.Delete
  Rem Move so that user sees deleted record disappear
  datCities.Recordset.MoveNext
  If datCities.Recordset.EOF Then
      datCities.Recordset.MovePrevious
  End If
End Sub

Sub cmdSearch_Click ()
  Dim searchFor As String, found As Integer
  Rem Search for the city specified by the user
  Let searchFor = UCase$(InputBox$("Name of city to find:"))
  If Len(searchFor) > 0 Then
      datCities.Recordset.MoveFirst
      Let found = 0
      Do While found = 0 And Not datCities.Recordset.EOF
        If UCase$(datCities.RecordSet.Fields("City").Value) = searchFor Then
            Let found = 1
        Else
            datCities.Recordset.MoveNext
        End If
      Loop
      If found = 0 Then
          MsgBox "Unable to locate requested city"
          datCities.RecordSet.MoveLast  'move so that EOF is no longer true
      End If
  End If
End Sub

Sub cmdQuit_Click ()
  datCities.Recordset.Update
  End
End Sub
```

[Run, click Search, and enter Bombay.]

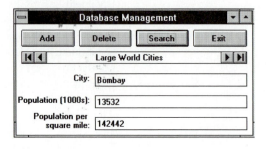

The above discussion showed how to work with a database created with FoxPro. If the database had been created with dBase IV, then the only change required in the walkthrough occurs in Step 4 where the setting "FoxPro 2.5;" for the Connect property would be changed to "dbase IV;". If Access had been used to create the database (assume it is named CITIES.MDB and contains the single table Population), then steps 4 through 6 of the walkthrough would be replaced with the following steps.

4. Go to the properties window and double-click on the DatabaseName property.

5. An Open dialog box appears with the title DatabaseName. Use this dialog box to select the desired database (CITIES.MDB in this example).

6. Select the RecordSource property and click on the down arrow to the right of the settings box. The names of the tables in the database are displayed. Select the desired table. (Population is the only table available in this example.)

Note: In the standard edition of Visual Basic, text boxes, labels, check boxes, image controls, and picture boxes are the only data-aware controls. Unfortunately, neither the grid control nor list and combo boxes are data-aware.

The OLE Control

An OLE (Object Linking and Embedding) control provides a bridge to another Windows application, such as a spreadsheet or word-processor. Below are walkthroughs that demonstrate two types of OLE. (A third type of OLE, called OLE Automation, allows you to write Visual Basic code to access and manipulate OLE objects residing in other applications. We do not cover OLE Automation in this text.) The first walkthrough illustrates **linking** a Windows' Paintbrush picture into a Visual Basic project. The second walkthrough illustrates **embedding** a Lotus 1-2-3 for Windows spreadsheet in a Visual Basic project. (You can carry out the second walkthrough only if Lotus 1-2-3 for Windows is installed on your computer and you have an elementary understanding of its use.)

A Linking Walkthrough

1. Before starting Visual Basic, make a copy of an existing picture that can be edited by Windows' Paintbrush application or use Paintbrush to create a new picture. In this walkthrough we assume that the picture you have copied or created now resides on drive A and is named MYPICTUR.BMP.

2. Invoke Visual Basic.

3. Click the OLE icon in the Toolbox and use the single-click-draw technique to create a large rectangle on the form.

4. An Insert Object dialog box appears (see Figure 11.31). Select Paintbrush Picture from the Object Type list and then click on the "Create from File" option button. The Object Type list box is replaced by a File name text box and a Browse command button (see Figure 11.32).

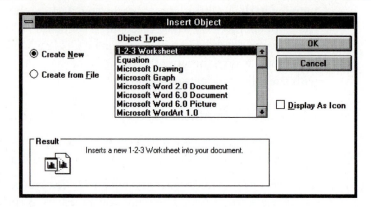

Figure 11.31 An OLE Insert Object dialog box.

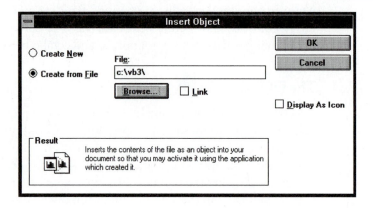

Figure 11.32 Dialog box when creating OLE link from a file.

5. Type A:\MYPICTUR.BMP into the File name text box (you could also click Browse to select the name from an Open file dialog box), click the Link check box, and then click OK. The picture saved in MYPICTUR.BMP is displayed in the OLE rectangle.

6. Run the program and double-click the OLE rectangle. Paintbrush is invoked and the MYPICTUR.BMP picture is displayed. (Your view in Paintbrush will be the lower-right portion of the picture. If your picture appears blank, use the scroll bars to move back to the upper-left corner.)

7. Make some changes to the picture; then press Alt/**F**ile/**S**ave and Alt/**F**ile/**Ex**it to save your changes and exit from Paintbrush. The modified picture is displayed in the OLE rectangle on the Visual Basic form.

8. End the program and display the form if it is hidden. Notice that the picture in the OLE rectangle is the original picture, not the modified version. Visual Basic maintains an image of this original picture in the program to display at run-time if it is unable to display the latest version of the data (picture).

9. Run the program. The picture is still the original version.

10. Double-click on the OLE rectangle to invoke Paintbrush and notice that the picture displayed is the modified version. Exit back to Visual Basic .

11. Double-click on the form and add the code

```
Let Ole1.Action = 6   'Update OLE image
```

to the Form_Load event procedure.

12. Run the program. Notice that Visual Basic has updated the picture to the last version saved while in Paintbrush even though you have not yet accessed Paintbrush by double-clicking.

An Embedding Walkthrough

1. Press Alt/**F**ile/**N**ew Project.

2. Click the OLE icon in the Toolbox and use the single-click-draw technique to create a large rectangle on the form.

3. The Insert Object dialog box appears. Double-click on "1-2-3 Worksheet" in the Object Type list. Lotus 1-2-3 will be invoked and you will be able to create a spreadsheet.

4. Enter the following data into cells A1 through F1: 12, 14, 11, 18, 21, 15.

5. Drag to select cells A1 through F1, click on the Graph icon 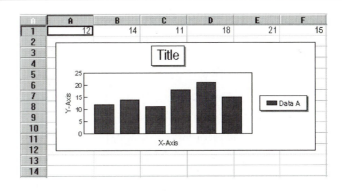, move the mouse pointer to cell A2, and drag to cell F12. Your spreadsheet should appear as in Figure 11.33.

Figure 11.33 A Lotus 1-2-3 spreadsheet.

6. Press Alt/**F**ile/**U**pdate.

7. Press Alt/**F**ile/**Ex**it to exit Lotus 1-2-3 and return to Visual Basic. The values you entered and the graph you created in Lotus are now displayed in the OLE rectangle in Visual Basic form. If needed, you can resize the OLE rectangle to show any hidden material.

8. Double-click on the OLE rectangle to reinvoke Lotus 1-2-3.

9. Change the value in cell C3 to 21.

10. Press Alt/**F**ile/**U**pdate and then Alt/**F**ile/**Ex**it to exit Lotus 1-2-3.

11. Note that the changes made in Lotus 1-2-3 are reflected in the OLE control.

12. Click the End icon to end the program.

13. Click the Run icon to restart the program. Notice that the changes made to the data and graph have been lost.

14. Click the End icon to end the program.

15. Add a command button to the form and caption it Save Changes.

16. Add a second command button to the form and caption it Load Data.

17. Double-click on the first command button to open the Command1_Click event procedure code window. Enter the following program lines into this window:

```
Open "LOTUSOLE.TXT" For Binary As #1
Let Ole1.FileNumber = 1
Let Ole1.Action = 11    'Save data
Close #1
```

18. Double-click on the second command button to open the Command2_Click event procedure code window. Enter the following program lines into this window:

```
Open "LOTUSOLE.TXT" For Binary As 1
Let Ole1.FileNumber = 1
Let Ole1.Action = 12    'Read data
Close #1
```

19. Run the program. Double-click on the OLE rectangle to invoke Lotus 1-2-3.

20. Again change cell C3 to 21, issue the update command, and exit back to Visual Basic.

21. Click on the Save Changes command button.

22. Click the End icon to end the program.

23. Click on the Run icon to restart the program.

24. Note again that the changes made in Lotus are not reflected in the OLE rectangle.

25. Click the Load Data command button. Notice that the changes have been recovered. A program containing OLE controls should save the OLE data whenever the data changes and reload the OLE data in the Form_Load event procedure.

EXERCISES 11.4

Exercises 1 through 4 refer to the data control used in Example 1. Write code to carry out the stated task.

1. Place the cities in a list box in alphabetical order.

2. Place the cities in a list box in the reverse order that the cities appear in the file.

3. Place the cities with population density greater than 50000 in a list box.

4. Count the number of cities in the table and display it in Picture1.

5. Assume the sequential file LARGE.TXT contains an updated list of large world cities. Each record in LARGE.TXT consists of a city name, population

(in 1000s), and population density. Write a program to use the information in LARGE.TXT to update the CITIES database. If a record in LARGE.TXT corresponds to a record in CITIES, then the population and population density of CITIES should be replaced with the corresponding values from LARGE.TXT. If a record in LARGE.TXT is not found in CITIES, a new record should be added.

6. The diskette accompanying this book contains the FoxPro 2.5 file CITIES2.DBF involving the same cities as the file CITIES.DBF. Each record of CITIES2.DBF contains two fields, city and pop2000, where the second field gives the projected population in the year 2000, and the cities are ordered alphabetically. (The file CITIES.DBF gives populations for 1995.) Write a program with two data controls, one for each table, and four text boxes, labeled City, Pop1995, Pop2000, and Percentage Growth. (The data control for the CITIES2 file should be invisible.) When the visible data control is clicked, the program should update all the text boxes.

Exercises 7 and 8 assume your system has a word processor for Windows, such as Word for Windows.

7. Create a small document in your word processor, then exit the word processor and write a Visual Basic program that includes an OLE control displaying the latest version of the document whenever the program is run.

8. Write a program that uses your word processor to check the spelling of the contents of a text box. Create a form with an OLE control bridged to your word processor. When establishing the bridge, check the "Display As Icon" check box and embed a new file. Add a text box to your form and label it "Enter word or phrase to spell-check." Write code in the Ole1_Click event procedure to carry out the following:

(a) Place the contents of the text box into the Clipboard.
(b) Display a message explaining that a word processor is being invoked and that the user should do the following when a blank document appears: Press Shift+Ins to place the text in the document. Run the spell checker and then delete the text. Exit the word processor.
(c) Activate the OLE. (**Hint:** To activate Ole1, use the statement Let Ole1.Action = 7.)

Chapter 11
Summary

1. *List boxes* provide easy access to lists of strings. The lists can be automatically sorted (Sorted property = True), altered (AddItem, RemoveItem, and Clear methods), the currently highlighted item identified (Text property), and the number of items determined (ListCount property). The array List() holds the items stored in the list. Each item is identified by an index number (0, 1, 2, . . .). The most recently inserted item can be determined with the NewIndex property.

2. *Combo boxes* are enhanced text boxes. They not only allow the user to enter information by typing it into a text box (read with the Text property), but allow the user to select the information from a list of items.

3. *Drive, directory,* and *file list boxes* are specialized list boxes managed largely by Windows. The selected items are identified by the Drive, Path, and Filename properties, respectively. A directory list box always displays the subdirectories of the directory identified by its Path property, and a files list box displays the files in the directory identified by its Path property.

4. Selections are made with *check boxes* (allow several) and *option buttons* (allow at most one). The state of the control (*checked* vs. *unchecked* or *on* vs. *off*) is stored in the Value property. Clicking on a check box toggles its state. Clicking on an option button gives it the *on* state and turns *off* the other option buttons in its group.

5. Frames are used to group controls, especially option buttons, as a unit.

6. *Horizontal* and *vertical scroll bars* permit the user to select from among a range of numbers by clicking or dragging the mouse. The range is specified by the Min and Max properties, and new settings trigger the Click and Change events.

7. The *timer control* triggers an event after a specified amount of time.

8. The *shape* and *line controls* enhance the visual look of a form with rectangles, ovals, circles, and lines of different size, thickness, and color.

9. The *image control*, which displays pictures or icons, can either expand to accommodate the size of the drawing or have the drawing alter its size to fit the image control.

10. A *grid* is a rectangular array of cells, each identified by a row and column number. The numbers of rows and columns are specified by the Rows and Cols properties. If the size of the grid is larger than provided by the control, scroll bars can be used to look at different parts of the grid. The FixedRows and FixedCols properties fix a certain number of the top rows and leftmost columns so that they will not scroll. The Row and Col properties are used to designate one cell as *active*. The Text property is used to read or place text into the active cell.

11. *Menus,* similar to the menus of Visual Basic itself, can be created with the Menu Design window.

12. The *clipboard* is filled with the SetText method or by pressing Ctrl+Ins, and is copied with the GetText function or with Shift+Ins.

13. *Additional forms* serve as new windows or dialog boxes. They are revealed with the Show method and concealed with the Hide method.

14. *Common dialog boxes* provide an effortless way of specifying files, colors, and fonts, and of communicating with the printer.

15. The *data control* allows Visual Basic programs to read and modify databases created with sophisticated software packages.

16. *OLE, Object Linking and Embedding,* allows Visual Basic programs to utilize other Windows applications.

Chapter 11
Programming Projects

1. *Membership List* Write a menu-driven program to manage a membership list. (See the Membership List form below.) Assume that the names and phone numbers of all members are stored in the sequential file MEMBERS.TXT. The names should be read into the list box when the form is loaded and the phone numbers should be read into an array. When a name is highlighted, both the name and phone number of the person should appear in the text boxes at the bottom of the screen. To delete a person, highlight his or her name and click on the Delete menu item. To change either the phone number or the spelling of the person's name, make the corrections in the text boxes and click on the menu item Modify. To add a new member, type his or her name and phone number into the text boxes and click on the menu item Add. When Exit is clicked, the new membership list should be written to a file and the program should terminate.

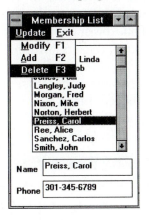

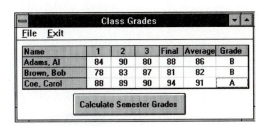

2. *Grade Book* Write a comprehensive program that a professor could use to record student grades for several classes and save the records in sequential files. (See the Class Grades form above.) Each class has three hourly exams and a final exam. The file for a single class should consist of the number of students in the class, call it *n*, and a record of five fields (name, grade1, grade2, grade3, final) for each student, with the records ordered alphabetical by the student's name. (A typical name might appear as "Doe, John".) Initially, the four grade fields should contain zeros. The program should contain a top-level menu item, File, with second-level subitems for Open, Save, Add Student, Remove Student. When a file is opened (via a file list directory or common dialog box), the data for the students should be loaded into a grid of *n*+1 rows and 7 columns. (The last two columns should remain blank.) The professor should be able to enter (or alter) exam data by clicking on the cell and responding to an input box. When a student is added, the grid should be enlarged by one row and the student inserted in proper alphabetical position. When a student is deleted, the grid should be reduced by one row. When the Calculate Semester Grades button is clicked, the last two columns should be filled in by the program. (Assume that the final exam counts as two hour exams.) If a grade is changed after the last two columns have been filled in, the corresponding average and grade should be recomputed.

3. *Tic-Tac-Toe*. Write a program that "officiates" a game of tic-tac-toe. That is, the program should allow two players to alternate entering X's and O's into a tic-tac-toe board until either someone wins or a draw is reached. If one of the players wins, the program should announce the winner immediately; in case of a draw, the program should display "Cat's game." The players should enter their plays by clicking on the desired cell in the tic-tac-toe grid, and the program should check that each play is valid. **Optional Enhancement:** Allow the players to enter a number *n*. The program should officiate a best-of-*n* tournament, keeping track of the number of games won by each player until one of them wins more than half of the games. Ignore draws.

4. *Hangman*. Write a program to play Hangman. (See the Hangman form below.) A list of 20 words should be placed in a sequential file and one selected at random with Rnd. The program should

(a) Draw a gallows on the screen with three line controls.
(b) Create a grid having 1 row and 26 columns, and fill the grid with the 26 letters of the alphabet. (If you are using the Visual Basic Primer, use two rows, make the first row a Fixed row and use the second row.)
(c) Create a second grid of one row and the number of columns equal to the length of the word selected. (Again, with the Visual Basic Primer, use two rows as in (b).)
(d) Each time the user clicks on one of the letters of the alphabet, that letter should be removed. If the letter is in the selected word, its location(s) should be revealed in the second grid. If the letter is not in the word, another piece of the man should be drawn with a shape control.

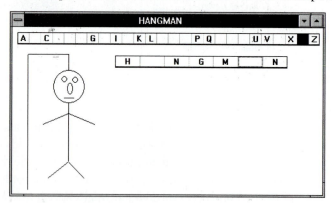

5. *Inventory Control* Write an inventory program for a book store and save the information in a sequential file. Each record should consist of five fields—title, author, category, wholesale price, and number in stock. (The two categories are fiction and nonfiction.) At any time, the program should display the titles of the books in stock in a list box, for which the user should have the option of displaying either all titles or just those in one of the two categories. When a book is selected from the list, its title, author, category, wholesale price, and number in stock should be displayed in a picture box. The user should be able to add a new book, delete a book, or change the inventory level of a book in stock. At any time, the user should be able to calculate the total value of all books, or the total value of the books in either category.

6. *Voting Machine* The members of the local Gilligan's Island fan club bring a computer to their annual meeting to use in the election of a new president. Write a program to handle the election. The program should add each candidate to a list box as he or she is nominated. After the nomination process is complete, club members should be able to approach the computer one at a time and double-click on the candidate of their choice. When a "Tally Votes" command button is clicked, a second list box, showing the number of votes received by each candidate, should appear alongside the first list box. Also, the name(s) of the candidate(s) with the highest number of votes should be displayed in a picture box.

7. *Airplane Seating Chart* An airplane has thirty rows (numbered 1 through 30), with six seats (labeled A, B, C, D, E, and F) in each row. Write a program to display a 7 by 31 grid with a cell for each seat. As each passenger selects a seat and a meal (regular, low calorie, or vegetarian), the ticket agent clicks on the cell corresponding to the seat. A dialog box requests the type of meal and then one of the letters R, L, or V is placed in the cell clicked. At any time, the agent can request the number of seats filled, the number of window seats vacant, and the numbers of each type of meal ordered.

Appendix A

ANSI Values

ANSI Value	Character	ANSI Value	Character	ANSI Value	Character
000	(null)	040	(	080	P
001	□	041	)	081	Q
002	□	042	*	082	R
003	□	043	+	083	S
004	□	044	,	084	T
005	□	045	–	085	U
006	□	046	.	086	V
007	□	047	/	087	W
008	□	048	0	088	X
009	(tab)	049	1	089	Y
010	(line feed)	050	2	090	Z
011	□	051	3	091	[
012	□	052	4	092	\
013	(carriage return)	053	5	093	]
014	□	054	6	094	^
015	□	055	7	095	_
016	□	056	8	096	'
017	□	057	9	097	a
018	□	058	:	098	b
019	□	059	;	099	c
020	□	060	<	100	d
021	□	061	=	101	e
022	□	062	>	102	f
023	□	063	?	103	g
024	□	064	@	104	h
025	□	065	A	105	i
026	□	066	B	106	j
027	□	067	C	107	k
028	□	068	D	108	l
029	□	069	E	109	m
030	□	070	F	110	n
031	□	071	G	111	o
032		072	H	112	p
033	!	073	I	113	q
034	"	074	J	114	r
035	#	075	K	115	s
036	$	076	L	116	t
037	%	077	M	117	u
038	&	078	N	118	v
039	'	079	O	119	w

ANSI Value	Character	ANSI Value	Character	ANSI Value	Character
120	x	166	¦	212	Ô
121	y	167	§	213	Õ
122	z	168	¨	214	Ö
123	{	169	©	215	×
124	|	170	ª	216	Ø
125	}	171	«	217	Ù
126	~	172	¬	218	Ú
127	□	173	-	219	Û
128	□	174	®	220	Ü
129	□	175	¯	221	Ý
130	,	176	°	222	þ
131	ƒ	177	±	223	ß
132	„	178	²	224	à
133	…	179	³	225	á
134	†	180	´	226	â
135	‡	181	µ	227	ã
136	^	182	¶	228	ä
137	‰	183	·	229	å
138	Š	184	¸	230	æ
139	‹	185	¹	231	ç
140	Œ	186	º	232	è
141	□	187	»	233	é
142	□	188	¼	234	ê
143	□	189	½	235	ë
144	□	190	¾	236	ì
145	'	191	¿	237	í
146	'	192	À	238	î
147	"	193	Á	239	ï
148	"	194	Â	240	õ
149	•	195	Ã	241	ñ
150	–	196	Ä	242	ò
151	—	197	Å	243	ó
152	~	198	Æ	244	ô
153	™	199	Ç	245	õ
154	š	200	È	246	ö
155	›	201	É	247	÷
156	œ	202	Ê	248	ø
157	□	203	Ë	249	ù
158	□	204	Ì	250	ú
159	Ÿ	205	Í	251	û
160		206	Î	252	ü
161	¡	207	Ï	253	ý
162	¢	208	Ð	254	þ
163	£	209	Ñ	255	ÿ
164	¤	210	Ò		
165	¥	211	Ó		

Appendix B

How To

How to Install, Invoke, and Exit Visual Basic

A. Install the Primer Edition of Visual Basic.

1. Invoke Windows.
2. Insert the Primer Edition diskette into one of the drives, say the A drive.
3. Invoke Windows' Program Manager if it is not already invoked.
4. Press Alt/F/R to execute the Run command from the File menu.
5. Type A:\VBPRIMER\SETUP into the Command Line box.
6. Press the Enter key or click on the OK button. After a few seconds a Welcome screen will appear.
7. Press the Enter key to continue. A Location screen will appear.
8. Press the Enter key to use the default directory as displayed.
9. When you are advised that the directory does not yet exist, press the Enter key to allow the creation of the directory.
10. When the Installation Complete screen appears, press the Enter key to proceed and invoke Visual Basic.

B. Install the Standard or Professional edition of Visual Basic onto a hard disk.

1. Invoke Windows.
2. Place the first (Setup) Visual Basic diskette into one of the diskette drives, say the A drive.
3. Invoke Windows' Program Manager if it is not already invoked.
4. Press Alt/F/R to execute the Run command from the File menu.
5. Type A:\SETUP and press the Enter key.
6. Follow the directions given by SETUP.

C. Invoke Visual Basic (with icon) after installation.

1. Invoke Windows.
2. Invoke Windows' Program Manager if it is not already invoked.
3. Double click on the Visual Basic icon.

Note: The first time you invoke Visual Basic, the ToolBox may not be visible. If so, press Alt/W/T to display it.

D. Invoke Visual Basic (without icon) after installation.

1. Invoke Windows.
2. Invoke Windows' Program Manager if it is not already invoked.
3. Press Alt/**File**/**R**un.
4. Enter VB, preceded by path. (One possibility is C:\VBPRIMER\VB.)

E. Exit Visual Basic.

1. Press the Esc key.
2. Press Alt/F/X.
3. If an unsaved program is present, Visual Basic will prompt you about saving it.

Note: In many situations, Step 1 is not needed.

How to Manage Programs

A. Run a program from Visual Basic.

1. Click on the Run icon (right arrowhead).

   or

1. Press Alt/R and make a selection from the Run menu.

B. Save the current program on a disk.

1. Press Alt/F/V.
2. Fill in the requested information. Do not give an extension as part of the project name or the file name. Two files will be created—one with extension .MAK and the other with extension .FRM. The .MAK file holds a list of files related to the project. The .FRM file actually holds the program.

Note: After a program has been saved once, updated versions can be saved under the same name by pressing Alt/F/V. Alt/F/E is used to save the program under a new name.

C. Begin a new program.

1. Press Alt/F/N.
2. If an unsaved program is present, Visual Basic will prompt you about saving it.

D. Open a program stored on a disk.

1. Press Alt/F/O.
2. Type a filespec into the top rectangle of the dialog box and press the Enter key. Alternatively, press the Tab key to penetrate the region containing the names of the files on the disk, and then use the direction keys and the Enter key to select one of the listed files. (If an unsaved program is present, Visual Basic will prompt you about saving it.)

Note: The form for the project does not appear, but the title of the Project window shows that the project has been opened.

E. Display the form associated with a program.

1. Press Alt/W/R to activate the Project window.
2. Click on View Form.

F. Name a program.

1. Save it.

G. Save a program as a text file readable by other word processors.

    1. Press Alt/F/A.

    2. If the box preceding the phrase Save as Text is not marked with an X, click in the box or press Alt+S.

    3. Make any other desired changes to the information displayed regarding the saving of this program.

    4. Click on OK. The .FRM file for the program is now a text file.

How to Use the Editor

A. Mark a section of text as a block.

    1. Move the cursor to the beginning or end of the block.

    2. Hold down a Shift key and use the direction keys to highlight a block of text.

    3. Release the Shift key.

    or

    1. Move the mouse to the beginning or end of the block.

    2. Hold down the left mouse button and move the mouse to the other end of the block.

    3. Release the left mouse button.

Note: To unblock text, press a direction key or click outside the block.

B. Delete a line of a program.

    1. Move the cursor to the line.

    2. Press Ctrl+Y.

    or

    1. Mark the line as a block. (See item A of this section.)

    2. Press Shift+Del.

Note: In the maneuvers above, the line is placed in the clipboard and can be retrieved by pressing Shift+Ins. To delete the line without placing it in the clipboard, mark it as a block and press Del.

C. Move a line within the Code window.

    1. Move the cursor to the line and press Ctrl+Y.

    2. Move the cursor to the target location.

    3. Press Shift+Ins.

D. Use the clipboard to move or duplicate statements.

    1. Mark the statements as a block.

    2. Press Shift+Del to delete the block and place it into the clipboard. Or, press Ctrl+Ins to place a copy of the block into the clipboard.

    3. Move the cursor to the location where you desire to place the block.

    4. Press Shift+Ins to place a copy of the text from the clipboard at the cursor.

E. Search for specific text in program.

1. Press Alt/E/F.
2. Type sought-after text into rectangle.
3. Select desired options if different from the defaults.
4. Press the Enter key.
5. To repeat the search, press F3.

F. Search and change.

1. Press Alt/E/R.
2. Type sought-after text into first rectangle.
3. Press Tab.
4. Type replacement text into second rectangle.
5. Select desired options if different from the defaults.
6. Press the Enter key.

G. Check the syntax of a line.

1. Move the cursor to the line.
2. Edit the line in some way. For example, type = and then press Backspace.
3. Press the Down Arrow key.

Note: The syntax of a line is automatically checked whenever the cursor is moved off an edited line by pressing either the Enter key or a direction key.

H. Cancel changes made to a line.

1. Press Alt/E/U to undo the last set of changes made to the most recently edited line.

Note: A *set* of changes is all changes made to a line without moving the cursor off the line. Moving the cursor off a line ends the current set of changes and causes the syntax of the line to be checked.

How to Get Help (Standard and Professional Editions only)

A. View the syntax and purpose of a Visual Basic keyword.

1. Type the word into the Code window.
2. Place the cursor on, or just following, the keyword.
3. Press F1.

or

1. Press Alt/H/S
2. Type in the keyword or term of interest and press the Enter key.
3. Double click on the topic of interest in the second list.

B. Display an ANSI table.

1. Press Alt/H/S.
2. Type ANSI and press the Enter key twice.
3. Press the Tab key followed by the Enter key to move between the displays for ANSI characters 0–127 and 128–255.

C. Obtain general help on designing a form.

    1. Press Alt/H/C.
    2. Click on Creating the Interface.
    3. Click on the topic of interest in the window that appears.

D. Obtain general help on setting properties.

    1. Press Alt/H/C.
    2. Click on Setting Properties.
    3. Click on the topic of interest in the window that appears.

E. Obtain general help on writing and debugging code.

    1. Press Alt/H/C.
    2. Click on Writing and Debugging Code.
    3. Click on the topic of interest in the window that appears.

F. Obtain other useful reference information.

    1. Press Alt/H/C.
    2. Click on the topic of interest.

G. Obtain general information about using the Help menu.

    1. Press Alt/H/C and then press Alt/H/H.
    2. Click on the topic of interest.

H. Obtain information about the selections in a pull-down menu.

    1. See item D in How to Manage Menus.

I. Obtain a list of Visual Basic's reserved words.

    1. Press Alt/H.
    2. Click on Programming Language in the Reference list.
    3. Click on the first letter of the keyword(s) of interest, or use the mouse with the vertical elevator to scroll through the list.

    or

    1. Place the cursor on a blank line in the Code window and press F1.
    2. Proceed as in Step 2 above.

Note: To obtain information about a keyword, click on it. When finished, close this window by pressing Alt/F/X

J. Exit Help.

    1. Press Alt/F/X.

How to Manipulate a Dialog Box

A. Use a dialog box.

A dialog box contains three types of items: rectangles (text boxes), option lists, and command buttons. An option list is a sequence of option buttons of the form ◯ *option* or ▢ *option*.

1. Move from item to item with the Tab key. (The movement is from left to right and top to bottom. Use Shift+Tab to reverse the direction.)
2. Inside a rectangle, either type in the requested information or use the direction keys to make a selection.
3. In an option list, an option button of the form ○ *option* can be activated with the direction keys. A dot inside the circle indicates that the option has been activated.
4. In an option list, an option button of the form ☐ *option* can be activated or deactivated by pressing the space bar. An ✕ inside the square indicates that the option has been activated.
5. A highlighted command button is invoked by pressing the Enter key.

B. Cancel a dialog box

1. Press the Esc key.

or

1. Press the Tab key until the command button captioned "Cancel" is highlighted; press the Enter key.

How to Manage Menus

A. Open a pull-down menu.

1. Click on the menu name.

or

1. Press Alt.
2. Press the first letter of the name of the menu. Alternatively, use the Right Arrow key to move the highlighted cursor bar to the menu name, then press the Down Arrow key.

B. Make a selection from a pull-down menu.

1. Open the pull-down menu.
2. Click on the desired item.

or

1. Open the pull-down menu. One letter in each item that is eligible to be used will be underlined.
2. Press the underlined letter. Alternatively, use the Down Arrow key to move the cursor bar to the desired item and then press the Enter key.

C. Obtain information about the selections in the pull-down menu currently displayed. (Not available with the Primer Edition.)

1. Press F1.
2. Click on name of the menu of interest.
3. Click on selection of interest.

D. Look at all the menus in the menu bar.

1. Press Alt/F.
2. Press the Right Arrow key each time you want to see a new menu.

E. Close a pull-down menu.

    1. Press the Esc key or click anywhere outside the menu.

How to Utilize the Windows Environment

A. Place a section of code in the Windows clipboard.

    1. Mark the section of code as a block as described in the How to Use the Editor section.

    2. Press Ctrl+Ins.

B. Access Windows' Notepad.

    1. Hold down the Alt key and repeatedly press the Tab key until Program Manager appears; then release the Alt key.

    2. Double-click on the Accessories icon.

    3. Double-click on the Notepad icon.

C. Display all characters in a font.

    1. Hold down the Alt key and repeatedly press the Tab key until Program Manager appears, then release the Alt key.

    2. Double-click on the Accessories icon.

    3. Double-click on the Character Map icon.

    4. Click on the underlined down arrow at the right end of the Font box.

    5. Highlight the desired font and press the Enter key, or double-click on the desired font.

D. Display an ANSI or ASCII code for a character with a code above 128.

    1. Proceed as described in item C of this section to display the font containing the character of interest.

    2. Click on the character of interest. Displayed at the right end of the bottom line of the font table is Alt+0xxx, where xxx is the code for the character.

E. Temporarily go to DOS.

    1. Hold the Alt key down and repeatedly press the Tab key until Program Manager appears. Then release the Alt key.

    2. Double-click on the Main icon.

    3. Double-click on the MS-DOS Prompt icon.

    4. Enter one or more desired commands at the DOS prompt.

    5. Enter EXIT to return to Windows.

    6. Hold the Alt key down and repeatedly press the Tab key until Microsoft Visual Basic appears. Then release the Alt key.

How to Design a Form

A. Display the ToolBox.

    1. Press Alt/W/T.

B. Place a new control on the form.

Option I: (new control with default size and position)

1. Double click on the control's icon in the ToolBox. The new control appears at the center of the form.
2. Size and position the control as described in item H below.

Option II: (a single new control sized and positioned as it is created)

1. Click on the control's icon in the ToolBox.
2. Move the mouse to the approximate position on the form desired for the upper-left corner of the control.
3. Press and hold the left mouse button.
4. Move the mouse to the position on the form desired for the lower-right corner of the control. A dashed box will indicate the overall shape of the new control.
5. Release the left mouse button.
6. The control can be resized and repositioned as described below.

Option III: (multiple instances of the same control)

1. Click on the control's icon in the ToolBox while holding down the Ctrl key.
2. Repeatedly use Steps 2 through 5 of Option II to create instances of the control.
3. When finished creating instances of this control, click on the arrow icon in the ToolBox

C. Create a related group of controls.

1. To hold the related group of controls, place a PictureBox control (top right in ToolBox) on the form.
2. Use Option II or III in Item B of this section to place controls on the PictureBox.

D. Set the focus to a particular control.

1. Click on the control.

   or

2. Press the Tab key until the control receives the focus.

E. Delete a control.

1. Set the focus to the control to be deleted.
2. Press the Del key.

F. Delete a related group controls.

1. Set the focus to the PictureBox holding the related group of controls.
2. Press the Del key.

G. Move a control, related group of controls, or form to a new location.

1. Move the mouse onto the control, the PictureBox containing the related group of controls, or the title of the form.
2. Drag the object to the new location.

H. Change the size of a control.

    1. Set the focus to the desired control.

    2. Move the mouse to one of the eight sizing handles located around the edge of the control. The mouse pointer will change to a double arrow that points in the direction that resizing can occur.

    3. Drag to the desired size.

I. Change the size of a form.

    1. Set the focus to the form.

    2. Move the mouse to the edge or corner of the form that is to be stretched or shrunk. The mouse pointer will change to a double arrow that points in the direction that resizing can occur.

    3. Drag to the desired size.

J. Use the color palette to set foreground and background colors.

    1. Set the focus to the desired control or the form.

    2. Press Alt/W/C to activate the Color Palette.

    3. If the Color Palette obscures the object you are working with, you may want to use the mouse to grab the Color Palette by its title bar and move it so that at least some of the object shows.

    4. To set the foreground color, click on the square within a square at the far left in the Color Palette. To set the background color, click on the region within the outer square but outside the inner square.

    5. Click on the desired color from the palette.

How to Work with the Properties of an Object

A. Activate the Properties window.

    1. Press Alt/W/O.

    or

    1. Press F4.

B. Highlight a property in the Properties window.

    1. Activate the Properties window and press the Enter key.

    2. Use the up or down arrow keys to move the highlight bar to the desired property.

    or

    1. Activate the Properties window.

    2. Click on the up or down arrow located at either end of the vertical scroll bar at the right side of the Properties window until the desired property is visible.

    3. Click on the desired property.

C. Select or specify a setting for a property.

    1. Highlight the property whose setting is to be changed.

    2. Click on the settings box or press Tab to place the cursor in the settings box.

    a. If a black, underlined down arrow appears at the right end of the settings box, use the up or down arrow keys to display the allowed settings for the property. When the desired setting is displayed, press the Enter key. Alternatively, click on the down arrow at the end of the settings box to display a list of all allowed settings, then click on the desired setting.

    b. If an ellipsis (. . .) appears at the right end of the settings box, press F4 or click on the ellipsis to display a dialog box or a color palette. Answer the questions in the dialog box and click on OK, or click on the desired color in the color palette.

    c. If a gray, underlined down arrow appears at the right end of the settings box, type in the new setting for the property.

Note: The settings box refers to the second box below the title "Properties." It is preceded by X and √ icons.

D. Change a property setting of an object.

    1. Set the focus to the desired object.
    2. Activate the Properties window .
    3. Highlight the property whose setting is to be changed.
    4. Select or specify the new setting for the property.

E. Let a label change size to accommodate its caption.

    1. Set the label's AutoSize property to True. (The label will shrink to the smallest size needed to hold the current caption. If the caption is changed, the label will automatically grow or shrink to accommodate the new caption.)

F. Let a label caption use more than one line.

    1. Set the label's WordWrap property to True. (If the label is not wide enough to accommodate the entire caption on one line, part of the caption will wrap to additional lines. If the label height is too small, then part or all of these wrapped lines will not be visible.)

G. Let a text box display more than one line.

    1. Set the text box's MultiLine property to True. (If the text box is not wide enough to accommodate the text entered by the user, the text will scroll down to new lines. If the text box is not tall enough, lines will scroll up out of view, but can be redisplayed by cursoring up.)

H. Assign a hot key to a label or command button.

    1. When assigning a value to the Caption property, precede the desired hot key character with an ampersand (&).

I. Place the initial focus on a particular command button.

    1. Set the command button's Default property to True.

J. Adjust the order in which the Tab key moves the focus.

1. Set the focus to the first object in the tabbing sequence.
2. Change the setting of the TabIndex property for this object to 1.
3. Set the focus to the next object in the tabbing sequence.
4. Change the setting of the TabIndex property for this object to 2.
5. Repeat Steps 3 and 4 until all objects on the form have been assigned a new TabIndex setting.

K. Allow the pressing of Esc to activate a particular command button.

1. Set the command button's Cancel property to True. (Setting the Cancel property True for one command button automatically sets it False for all other command buttons.)

How to Manage Procedures

A. Access the Code Window.

1. Press the Esc key followed by F7. (It is not always necessary to press the Esc key.)

B. Look at an existing procedure.

1. Access the Code Window.
2. Press Ctrl+Down Arrow or Ctrl+Up Arrow repeatedly to cycle through all the procedures.

   or

1. Access the Code Window.
2. Press F2. The top entry is the declarations section of the program and the remaining entries are procedures.
3. Use the direction keys and the Enter key to select the desired procedure.

C. Create a procedure.

1. Access the Code Window.
2. Move to a blank line.
3. Type Sub (for a subprogram) or Function (for a function) followed by the name of the procedure and any parameters.
4. Press the Enter key. (The Code Window will now display the new procedure heading and an End statement.)
5. Type the procedure into the Code Window.

   or

1. Access the Code Window.
2. Press Alt/V/N. (A dialog box will appear.)
3. Type the name of the procedure into the *Name* rectangle.
4. Select the type of procedure (subprogram or function) by clicking on the procedure type or pressing Alt+S for a subprogram or Alt+F for a function.
5. Press the Enter key. (The Code window will now display the new procedure heading and an End statement.)
6. Type the procedure into the Code Window.

D. Alter a procedure.

    1. Bring the procedure into the Code Window as described in item B of this section.

    2. Make changes as needed.

E. Remove a procedure.

    1. Bring the procedure into the Code Window as described in item B of this section.

    2. Mark the entire procedure as a block. That is, press Ctrl+Home to move the cursor to the beginning of the procedure, then hold down a Shift key and press Ctrl+End to move the cursor to the end of the procedure.

    3. Press the Del key.

F. Insert an existing procedure into a program.

    1. Open the program containing the procedure.

    2. Bring the procedure into the Code Window as described in item B of this section.

    3. Mark the entire procedure as a block.

    4. Press Ctrl+Ins to place the procedure into the clipboard.

    5. Open the program in which the procedure is to be inserted and access the Code Window.

    6. Move the cursor to a blank line.

    7. Press Shift+Ins to place the contents of the clipboard into the program.

How to Manage Windows

A. Zoom the active window to fill the entire screen.

    1. Click on the maximize (up arrow) button in the upper-right corner of the active window.

    2. To return the window to its original size, click on the restore (double arrow) button that has replaced the maximize button.

B. Move a window.

    1. Move the mouse to the title bar of the window.

    2. Drag the window to the desired location.

C. Change the size of a window.

    1. Move the mouse to the edge of the window that is to be adjusted or to the corner joining the two edges to be adjusted.

    2. When the mouse becomes a double arrow, drag the edge or corner until the window has the desired size.

How to Use the Printer

A. Obtain a printout of a program when using the Primer Edition of Visual Basic.

    1. Save the program in a form readable by other word processors (i.e., in a text file).

2. Access Windows' Notepad.
3. Press Alt/F/O to specify a file to open.
4. If desired, enter *.FRM to see a list of form files saved in the current directory.
5. Type in the name under which the program is saved, or press the Tab key to penetrate the displayed list of files. Then highlight the desired file name. In either case, press the Enter key to open the file.
6. Press Alt/F/P to print the program.
7. Press Alt/F/X to close Notepad. Hold down the Alt key and press the Tab key repeatedly until Microsoft Visual Basic appears. Then release the Alt key.

B. Obtain a printout of a program when using the Standard or Professional Edition of Visual Basic.

1. Press Alt/F/P.
2. Press the Enter key.

Note: To print just the text selected as a block or the active (current) window, use the direction keys to select the desired option.

C. Obtain a printout of the form during run-time.

1. Place the statement PrintForm in the Form_Click( ) or other appropriate procedure of the program at the point when the desired output will be on the form.

How to Use the Debugger

A. Stop a program at a specified line.

1. Place the cursor at the beginning of the desired line.
2. Press F9. (This highlighted line is called a *breakpoint*. When the program is run, it will stop at the breakpoint before executing the statement.)

Note: To remove this breakpoint, repeat steps 1 and 2.

B. Remove all breakpoints.

1. Press Alt/D/L.

C. Run a program one statement at a time.

1. Press F8. The first executable statement will be highlighted. (An event must first occur for which an event procedure has been written.)
2. Press F8 each time you want to execute the currently highlighted statement.

Note: The Code Window may need to be reduced and/or moved in order to see the output appearing on the form. Also, to guarantee that output is retained while stepping through the program, the AutoRedraw property of the form and any picture boxes may need to be set to True.

D. Run the program one statement at a time, but execute each procedure call without stepping through the statements in the procedure one at a time.

1. Press Shift+F8. The first executable statement will be highlighted.

2. Press Shift+F8 each time you want to execute the currently highlighted statement.

E.   Continue execution of a program that has been suspended.

1. Press F5.

Note: Each time an attempt is made to change a suspended program in a way that would prevent the program from continuing, Visual Basic displays a dialog box warning that the program will have to be restarted from the beginning and gives the option to cancel the attempted change.

F.   Have further stepping begin at the line containing the cursor (no variables are cleared).

1. Press Alt/D/N.

Appendix C

Visual Basic Statements, Functions, Methods, Properties, Events, Data Types, and Operators

This appendix applies to the following objects: form, printer, text box, command button, label, and picture box. The last four are also called *controls*. Terms in brackets follow some of the discussions. These terms refer to supporting topics presented at the end of this appendix.

Abs The function Abs strips the minus signs from negative numbers while leaving other numbers unchanged. If x is any number, then the value of Abs(x) is the absolute value of x.

Action The type of a common dialog box is determined by the setting of the Action property (1-Open, 2-Save As, 3-Color, 4-Font, 5-Print). For an OLE control, the setting of the Action property during run-time determines the action to take.

AddItem The AddItem method adds an additional item to a list box or combo box and adds an additional row to a grid. A statement of the form List1.AddItem *str* inserts the string either at the end of the list (if Sorted = False) or in its proper alphabetical position (if Sorted = True). The statement List1.AddItem *str*, *n* inserts the item at the position with index *n*. The use of an index is not recommended when Sorted = True. The statement Grid1.AddItem "", *n* inserts a new row into the grid at position *n*.

AddNew The AddNew method is used with a data control to set the stage for the addition of a new record to the end of a file. It clears any controls bound to the data control. The actual addition takes place after Value and Update statements are executed.

Alignment The Alignment property of a text box or label affects how the text assigned to the Text property is displayed. If the Alignment property is set to 0 (the default), text is displayed left justified; if set to 1, text is right justified; and if set to 2, text is centered.

And (Logical Operator) The logical expression *condition1* And *condition2* is true only if both *condition1* and *condition2* are true. For example, (3<7) And ("abc">"a") is true since 3<7 is true as is "abc">"a", while ("apple">"ape") And ("earth">"moon") is false since "earth">"moon" is false.

And (Bitwise Operator) The expression *byte1* And *byte2* is evaluated by expressing each byte as an 8-tuple binary number and then Anding together corresponding digits, where 1 And 1 equals 1, 1 And 0, 0 And 1, and 0 And 0 all equal 0. For example, the expression 37 And 157 translated to binary 8-tuples becomes 00100101 And 10011101. Anding together corresponding digits gives the binary 8-tuple 00000101 or decimal 5. Thus 37 And 157 is 5.

Asc Characters are stored as numbers from 0 to 255. If *str* is a string of characters, then Asc(*str*) is the number corresponding to the first character of *str*. For any *n* from 0 to 255, Asc(Chr$(*n*)) is *n*.

Atn The trigonometric function Atn, or *arctangent*, is the inverse of the tangent function. For any number *x*, Atn(*x*) is an angle in radians between –pi/2 and pi/2 whose tangent is *x*. [radians]

AutoRedraw The AutoRedraw property determines what happens to graphics and Printed material on a form or picture box after another object (for example, another picture box) temporarily obscures part of the form or picture box. If AutoRedraw is True, then Visual Basic will restore the graphics and Printed material from a copy that it has saved in memory. If AutoRedraw is False, then Visual Basic does not keep track of graphics and Printed material that have been obscured, but does invoke the Paint event of the form or picture box when the obstruction is removed. Thus only graphics and Printed material generated by the Paint event will be restored when AutoRedraw is False.

AutoSize If the AutoSize property of a label is True, Visual Basic automatically sets the width and height of the label so that the entire caption can be accommodated. If the AutoSize property is False, the size of the label is not adjusted by Visual Basic, and captions are clipped if they do not fit.

BackColor The BackColor property determines the background color of an object. For a Command Button, the background color is the color of the dotted rounded rectangle that surrounds the caption when the command button has the focus. If the BackColor of a form or picture box is changed while a program is running, all graphics and Printed text directly on the form or picture box are erased. [color]

BackStyle The BackStyle property of a label or shape is opaque (1) by default. The rectangular, square, circular, or oval region associated with the control is filled with the control's background color and possibly caption. If the BackStyle is set to transparent (0), whatever is behind the control remains visible; the background color of the control essentially becomes "see through."

Beep The statement Beep produces a sound of frequency 800 Hz that lasts a fraction of a second.

BOF When the BOF property of a data control is True, the current record position in the file is before the first record.

BorderColor The BorderColor property determines the color of a line or shape control. [color]

BorderStyle The BorderStyle property determines the border style for a form [0-none, 1-fixed single, 2-sizeable (default), 3-fixed double], line or shape [0-transparent, 1-solid, 2-dash, 3-dot, 4-dash-dot, 5-dash-dot-dot, 6-inside solid], grid image, label, picture box, and text box [0-none, 1-fixed single (default)]. You cannot change the borders of forms and text boxes during run time.

BorderWidth The BorderWidth property (with settings from 1 through 8192) determines the thickness of a line or shape control.

Call A statement of the form Call *SubprogramName*(*argList*) is used to execute the named subprogram, passing to it the variables and values in the list of arguments. Arrays appearing in the list of arguments should be specified by the array name followed by empty parentheses. The value of a variable argument may be altered by the subprogram unless the variable is surrounded by parentheses. After the statements in the subprogram have been executed, program execution continues with the statement following Call. **Note:** The keyword Call may be omitted. In this case, the parentheses are omitted and the statement is written *SubprogramName argList*.

Cancel The Cancel property provides a means of responding when the user presses the Esc key. At most one command button on a form may have its Cancel property set to True. If the Esc key is pressed while the program is running, Visual Basic will execute the click event procedure of the command button whose Cancel property is True.

Caption The Caption property holds the text that is to appear as the caption for a form, command button, or label. If an ampersand (&) is placed in the caption of a command button or label, the ampersand will not be displayed, but the character following the ampersand will become a hot key. Hot keys provide a quick way to access a command button or the control (usually a text box) following (in tab index order) a label. Hot keys are activated by holding down the Alt key and pressing the hot key character.

CCur The function CCur converts integer, long integer, single-precision, and double-precision numbers to currency numbers. If x is any number, then the value of CCur(x) is the currency number determined by x.

CDbl The function CDbl converts integer, long integer, single-precision, and currency numbers to double-precision numbers. If x is any number, then the value of CDbl(x) is the double-precision number determined by x.

Change The Change event occurs when the contents of a combo box, directory list box, drive list box, label, picture box, scroll bar, or text box is altered in a specific way. The alterations are: (a) change of text (combo box or text box), (b) user selects a new directory or drive (directory and drive list boxes), (c) thumb moves (scroll bar), (d) change of Caption property (label), (e) change of Picture property (picture box).

ChDir The statement ChDir *path* changes the current directory on the specified disk drive to the subdirectory specified by *path*. For example, ChDir "C:\" specifies the root directory of the C drive as the current directory. Omitting a drive letter in *path* causes the default drive to be used. [directories]

ChDrive The statement ChDrive *drive* changes the default drive to the drive specified by *drive*. For example, ChDrive "A" specifies the A drive as the new default drive.

Chr$ If n is a number from 0 to 255, then a statement of the form *objectName*.Print Chr$($n$) displays the nth character of the current font.

CInt The function CInt converts long integer, single-precision, double-precision, and currency numbers to integer numbers. If x is any number from -32768 to 32767, the value of CInt(x) is the (possibly rounded) integer constant that x determines.

Circle The graphics method *objectName*.Circle (x, y), r, c, $r1$, $r2$, a draws on *objectName* a portion, or all, of an ellipse. The center of the ellipse is the point (x, y) and the longer radius is r. The color of the ellipse is determined by c. If $r1$ and $r2$ are present, then the computer draws only the portion of the ellipse that extends from the radius line at an angle of Abs($r1$) radians with the horizontal radius line to the radius line at an angle of Abs($r2$) radians with the horizontal radius line in a counterclockwise direction. If either $r1$ or $r2$ is negative, the computer also draws its radius line. The ratio of the length of the vertical diameter to the length of the horizontal diameter will be a. After the Circle method is executed, the value of *objectName*.CurrentX becomes x and the value of *objectName*.CurrentY becomes y. [color] [coordinate systems] [radians]

Clear The method ClipBoard.Clear clears the clipboard, setting its contents to the null string. The statements List1.Clear and Combo1.Clear remove all items from the control's list.

Click The Click event applies to check boxes, combo boxes, command buttons, directory list boxes, file list boxes, forms, frames, grids, images, labels, list boxes, menu items, OLE controls, option buttons, picture boxes, and text boxes. A Click event occurs whenever the left mouse button is pressed and released while the mouse cursor is over the control or over a blank area on the form. In the case of a command button, the Click event is also called if the spacebar is pressed while the command button has the focus, or if the button's access key is used.

CLng The function CLng converts integer, single-precision, double-precision, and currency numbers to long integer numbers. If x is any number from $-2,147,483,648$ to $2,147,483,647$, the value of CLng(x) is the (possibly rounded) long integer constant that x determines.

Close The statement Close #n closes the file that has been opened with reference number n. By itself, Close closes all open files. The Close method for a data control closes the database.

Cls The method *formName*.Cls clears the form *formName* of all text and graphics that have been placed directly on the form with methods like *formName*.Print, *formName*.Circle, and so on. The method *pictureBox*.Cls clears the named picture box. The Cls method resets the CurrentX and CurrentY properties of the cleared object to the coordinates of the upper left corner (usually $(0, 0)$).

Col and Row The Col and Row properties specify the active cell of a grid. The statements Let Grid1.Col = m and Let Grid1.Row = n specify the cell in column m and row n to be the active cell. The statement Grid1.Text = *str* places the string into the active cell.

ColAlignment The statement Grid1.ColAlignment(m) = n, where $n = 0$ (left-align (default)), 1 (right-align), or 2 (centered), aligns the text in the nonfixed cells of the mth column of the grid.

Color The value of the Color property of a Color common dialog box identifies the selected color.

Cols and Rows The Rows and Cols properties of a grid specify the numbers of rows and columns.

ColWidth The statement Let Grid1.Colwidth(*m*) = *n* specifies that column *m* of the grid be *n* twips wide. (There are about 1440 twips in an inch.)

Const The statement Const *constantName* = *expression* causes Visual Basic to replace every occurrence of *constantName* with the value of the expression. This replacement takes place before any lines of the program are executed. Unlike Let, Const does not set up a location in the program's memory for a variable. A *constantName* may appear in only one Const statement and may not appear on the left side of a Let statement. We call *constantName* a "symbolic constant" or "named constant."

Control The Control data type may be used in the parameter lists of Sub and Function definitions to allow the passing of control names to the procedure.

ControlBox The ControlBox property determines whether or not a form has a ControlBox button in the upper left corner. If the ControlBox property is set to True (the default), the ControlBox button is displayed. Among the operations available from the ControlBox menu is the ability to close the form and thereby end the program. If the ControlBox property of a form is set to False, the ControlBox button is not displayed. Since, in this case, the user cannot end the program using the ControlBox or by pressing Alt+F4, it is important to provide a command button for this purpose.

Cos The value of the trigonometric function Cos(*x*) is the cosine of an angle of *x* radians. [radians]

CSng The function CSng converts integer, long integer, and double-precision numbers to single-precision numbers. If *x* is any number, the value of CSng(*x*) is the single-precision number that *x* determines.

CStr The function CStr converts integer, long integer, single-precision, double-precision, currency, and variant numbers to strings. If *x* is any number, the value of CStr(*x*) is the string determined by *x*. Unlike the Str$ function, CStr does not place a space in front of positive numbers. [variant]

**CurDir$** The value of the function CurDir$(*drive*) is a string specifying the current directory on the drive specified by *drive*. The value of CurDir$("") or CurDir$ is a string specifying the current directory on the default drive. [directories]

Currency The currency data type is extremely useful for calculations involving money. A variable of type Currency requires 8 bytes of memory and can hold any number from –922,337,203,685,477.5808 to 922,337,203,685,477.5807 with at most four decimal places. Currency values and variables may be indicated by the type tag @: 21436587.01@, Balance@.

CurrentX, CurrentY The properties CurrentX and CurrentY give the horizontal and vertical coordinates of the point on a form, picture box, or the printer at which the next Print or graphics method will begin. Initially, CurrentX and CurrentY are the coordinates of the upper left corner of the form or picture box. [coordinate systems]

CVar The function CVar converts strings and integer, long integer, single-precision, double-precision, and currency numbers to variants. If *x* is any string or number, the value of CVar(*x*) is the variant determined by *x*. [variant]

CVDate The function CVDate converts a numeric or string expression to an equivalent serial date. If *x* is any expression representing a valid date, the value of CVDate(*x*) is the serial date determined by *x*. Valid numeric values are –657434 (January 1, 100 AD.) to 2958465 (December 31, 9999). Valid string expressions either look like one of these valid numeric values (e.g., "19497" corresponding to May 18, 1953) or look like a date (e.g., "10 Feb 1955", "August 13, 1958", etc.) [date]

**Date$** The value of the function Date$ is the current date returned as a string of the form mm-dd-yyyy. If *dateStr* is a string of this form, the statement Date$ = *dateStr* resets the date as specified by *dateStr*.

DateSerial The value of the function DateSerial(*year, month, day*) is the serial date corresponding to the given year, month, and day. Values from 0 to 9999 are acceptable for *year*, with 0 to 99 interpreted as 1900 to 1999. Values of 1 to 12 for *month*, and 1 to 31 for *day* are normal, but any integer value is acceptable. Often, numeric expressions are used for *month* or *day*, which evaluate to numbers outside these ranges. For example, DateSerial(1993, 2, 10 + 90) is the date 90 days after Feb. 10, 1993. [date]

DateValue The value of the function DateValue(*str*) is the serial date corresponding to the date given in *str*. DateValue recognizes the following date formats: "2-10-1955", "2/10/1955", "February 10, 1955", "Feb 10, 1955", "10-Feb-1955", and "10 February 1955". For the years 1900 through 1999, the initial "19" is optional. [date]

Day The function Day extracts the day of the month from a serial date. If *d* is any valid serial date, the value of Day(*d*) is an integer from 1 to 31 giving the day of the month recorded as part of the date and time stored in *d*. [date]

DblClick The DblClick event applies to combo boxes, file list boxes, forms, frames, grids, images, labels, list boxes, OLE controls, option buttons, picture boxes, and text boxes. A DblClick event occurs whenever the left mouse button is pressed and released twice, in quick succession, while the mouse cursor is over the control or over a blank area on the form. Double-clicking on an object will first cause that object's Click event to occur, followed by its DblClick event. **Note:** When you double-click on an item in a drive list box, the item is automatically assigned to the Path property. When you double-click on an item in a file list box, the item is automatically assigned to the FileName property.

Default When the Default property of a command button is set to True and the focus is on an object that is not another command button, pressing the enter key has the same effect as clicking on the button. At most one command button on a form can have True as the value of its Default property.

DefInt, DefLng, DefSng, DefDbl, DefStr, DefCur, DefVar A variable can be assigned a type by either a type-declaration tag or an As clause. A statement of the form DefInt *letter* specifies that any "untyped" variable whose name begins with the specified letter will have integer type. A statement of the form DefInt *letter1-letter2* specifies that all "untyped" variables whose names begin with a letter in the range *letter1* through *letter2* will have integer type. The statements DefLng, DefSng, DefDbl, and DefStr specify the corresponding types for long integer, single-precision, double-precision, and string variables, respectively. The statements DefCur and DefVar specify which starting letters for the names of variables are to identify the default variable types currency and variant respectively. Def*Type* statements are placed in the (declarations) section of (general). [variant]

Delete The Delete method for a data control deletes the current record.

Dim The statement Dim *arrayName*(m To n) As *variableType* declares an array with subscripts ranging from m to n, inclusive, where m and n are in the normal integer range of –32768 to 32767. The *variableType* must be Integer, Long, Single, Double, Currency, String, String*n, Variant, or a user-defined type, and the statement must be placed in the (declarations) section of (general). A statement of the form Dim *arrayName*(m To n, p To q) As *variableType* declares a doubly subscripted, or two-dimensional, array. Three and higher dimensional arrays are declared similarly. If m and p are zero, the Dim statements above may be changed to Dim *arrayName*(n) As *variableType* and Dim *arrayName*(n, q) As *variableType*. The statement Dim *arrayName*( ) As *variableType* defines an array whose size is initially unknown but must be established by a ReDim statement before the array can be accessed. The statement Dim *variableName* As *variableType*, specifies the type of data that will be stored in *variableName*. Variables and arrays Dimmed in the (declarations) section of (general) are available to all procedures. In procedures, Dim is used to declare variables, but ReDim must be used to dimension arrays. [dynamic vs. static] [variant]

Dir$ If *fileTemplate* specifies a file (or a collection of files by including ? or *), then the value of the function Dir$(*fileTemplate*) is the filespec of the first file matching the pattern specified by *fileTemplate*. If this value is not the null string, the value of the function Dir$ is the next file that matches the previously specified pattern. For example, the value of Dir$("*.MAK") will be a string specifying the first file in the current directory of the default drive whose name has the .MAK extension. [directories] [filespec]

Do/Loop A statement of the form Do, Do While *cond*, or Do Until *cond* is used to mark the beginning of a block of statements that will be repeated. A statement of the form Loop, Loop While *cond*, or Loop Until *cond* is used to mark the end of the block. Each time a statement containing While or Until followed by a condition is encountered, the truth value of the condition determines whether the block should be repeated or whether the program should jump to the statement immediately following the block. A Do loop may also be exited at any point with an Exit Do statement.

DoEvents Executing the statement DoEvents permits Visual Basic to act upon any events may have occurred while the current event procedure has been executing.

Double A variable of type Double requires 8 bytes of memory and can hold 0, the numbers from 4.94065×10^{-324} to $1.797693134862316 \times 10^{308}$ with at most 17 significant digits and the negatives of these numbers. Double values and variables may be indicated by the type tag #: 2.718281828459045#, Pi#.

DrawMode The property DrawMode determines whether graphics are drawn in black, white, foreground color, or some interaction of these colors with the current contents of the form or picture box. The following table lists the allowed values for the DrawMode property and the rules for what RGB color number will be assigned at a given point when the RGB color number for the color currently displayed at that point is *display* and the RGB color number for the draw color is *draw*. [color]

DrawMode	Color Produced	
1	&H00000000& (Black)	
2	Not draw And Not display	(inverse of #15)
3	display And Not draw	(inverse of #14)
4	Not draw	(inverse of #13)
5	draw And Not display	(inverse of #12)
6	Not display	(inverse of #11)
7	draw Xor display	
8	Not draw Or Not display	(inverse of #9)
9	draw And display	
10	Not (draw Xor display)	(inverse of #7)
11	display	(transparent)
12	display Or Not draw	
13	draw (draw color)	
14	draw Or Not display	
15	draw Or display	
16	&H00FFFFFF& (White)	

DrawStyle When DrawWidth is 1 for a form or picture box (the default), the property DrawStyle determines whether graphics are drawn using a solid line or some combinations of dots and dashes. Use a DrawStyle of 0 (the default) for solid lines, 1 for dashed lines, 2 for dotted lines, 3 for dash-dot lines, or 4 for dash-dot-dot lines. A DrawStyle of 5 produces "invisible" graphics.

When thick lines are drawn as a result of setting DrawWidth to values greater than 1, graphics are always drawn using solid lines. In this case, DrawStyle can be used to either center the thick line over where line with a DrawWidth of 1 would be drawn or, when drawing closed figures like ellipses and rectangles, to place the thick line just inside where the line with a DrawWidth of 1 would be drawn. To draw thick graphics inside the normal closed figure, use a DrawStyle of 6. DrawStyles 1 through 4 will center thick graphics over the normal location.

DrawWidth The property DrawWidth determines the width in pixels of the lines that are drawn by graphics methods. The default is 1 pixel. Values from 1 to 32,767 are permitted.

Drive The Drive property of a drive list box gives the contents of the currently selected item.

Enabled The property Enabled determines whether or not a form or control responds to events. If the Enabled property of a form or control is set to True (the default), and if an event occurs for which an event procedure has been written, the event procedure will be executed. When the Enabled property of a form or control is set to False, all events relating to that control are ignored; no event procedures are executed.

End The statement End terminates the execution of the program and closes all files. Also, the statements End Def, End Function, End If, End Select, End Sub, and End Type are used to denote the conclusion of multiline function definitions, function blocks, If blocks, Select Case blocks, subprograms, and user-defined record type declarations.

EndDoc The method Printer.EndDoc is used to indicate that the document currently being printed is complete and should be released to the printer.

Environ$ Visual Basic has an environment table consisting of equations of the form "*name=value*" that is inherited from DOS when Windows is invoked. If *name* is the left side of an equation in Visual Basic's environment table, then the value of the function Environ$("*name*") will be the string consisting of the right side of the equation. The value of Environ$(*n*) is the *n*th equation in Visual Basic's environment table.

EOF Suppose a file has been opened for input with reference number *n*. The value of the function EOF(*n*) will be True (–1) if the end of the file has been reached and False (0) otherwise. (**Note:** The logical condition Not EOF(*n*) is true until the end of the file is reached.) When used with a communications file, EOF(*n*) will be true if the communications buffer is empty and false if the buffer contains data.

Eqv The logical expression *condition1* Eqv *condition2* is true if *condition1* and *condition2* are both true or both false. For example, (1>2) Eqv ("xyz"<"a") is true since both 1>2 and "xyz"<"a" are false, whereas ("apple">"ape") Eqv ("earth"> "moon") is false since "apple">"ape" is true but "earth">"moon" is false.

Erase For static arrays, the statement Erase *arrayName* resets each array element to its default value. For dynamic arrays, the statement Erase *arrayName* deletes the array from memory. **Note:** After a dynamic array has been Erased, it may be ReDimensioned. However, the number of dimensions must be the same as before. [dynamic vs. static]

Err and Erl (Functions) After an error occurs during the execution of a program, the value of the function Err will be a number identifying the type of error, and the value of the function Erl will be the line number of the program statement in which the error occurred. (If the statement containing the error has no line number, the nearest line number preceding it is returned. If no line number precedes it, a value of 0 is returned.) These functions are used in conjunction with the On Error statement.

Err (Statement) If *n* is a whole number from 0 to 32,767, the statement Err = *n* assigns a value to the Visual Basic's Err function. When run-time errors occur, Visual Basic assigns a value to Err. You can read Visual Basic's value and assign a new value to Err before invoking additional error-handlers.

Error The statement Error *n* simulates the occurrence of the run-time error identified by the number *n*, where *n* may range from 1 to 32,767. It is a useful debugging tool.

**Error$** The value of the function Error$ is the error message corresponding to the run-time error that has most recently occurred. The value of the function Error$(*errNum*) is the error message corresponding to the run-time error designated by *errNum*.

Exit The Exit statement may be used in any of five forms: Exit For, Exit Sub, Exit Function, Exit Def, and Exit Do. The Exit statement causes program execution to jump out of the specified structure prematurely: Exit For jumps out of a For/Next loop to the statement following Next, Exit Sub jumps out of a subprogram to the statement following the Call statement, and so on.

Exp The value of the function Exp(*x*) is e^x, where e (about 2.71828) is the base of the natural logarithm function.

False A predefined constant whose value is 0. False is used when setting the value of properties that are either True or False. For example, Picture1.FontItalic = False.

FileAttr After a file has been opened with reference number *n*, the value of the function FileAttr (*n*, 1) is 1, 2, 4, 8, or 32 depending upon whether the file was opened for Input, Output, Append, Random, or Binary, respectively. The value of the function FileAttr (*n*, 2) is the file's DOS file handle, a number that uniquely identifies the file and is used in assembly language programming.

FileCopy The statement FileCopy *source, destination* creates the file specified by *destination* by making a copy of the file specified by *source*. Both *source* and *destination* may specify drive and path information. If the file specified by *destination* already exists, it will be overwritten without a warning being issued.

FileDateTime The value of the function FileDateTime(*filename*) is a string giving the date and time that the file specified by the *filename* was created or last modified.

FileLen The value of the function FileLen(*filename*) is the length in characters (bytes) of the file specified by *filename*.

FileName The FileName property of a file list box is the contents of the currently selected item.

FillColor When the FillStyle property of a form or picture box is set to a value other than the default of 1, the property FillColor determines what color is used to paint the interior of ellipses and rectangles drawn with the Circle and Line graphics methods. The FillColor property may be assigned any valid RGB color number. The default value for FillColor is black (0). [color]

FillStyle The property FillStyle determines what pattern is used to paint the interior of ellipses and rectangles drawn on forms or picture boxes with the Circle and Line methods. The default value for FillStyle is transparent (1), which means that interiors are not painted. Other values available for FillStyle are solid (0), horizontal lines (2), vertical lines (3), diagonals running upward to the right (4), diagonals running downward to the right (5), vertical and horizontal lines [cross hatched] (6), and diagonal cross hatched (7). **Note:** Using BF in a Line method has the same effect as setting the FillStyle to 0 and the FillColor to the color of the bordering line.

Fix The value of the function Fix(*x*) is the whole number obtained by discarding the decimal part of the number *x*.

FixedAlignment The statement Grid1.FixedAlignment(*m*) = *n*, where *n* = 0 (left-align (default)), 1 (right-align), or 2 (centered), aligns the text in the fixed cells of the *m*th column of the grid.

FixedCols and FixedRows The FixedCols and FixedRows properties of a grid specify the number of fixed rows and fixed columns of a grid. Fixed rows and columns are used for headings and never disappear due to scrolling.

Flags The Flags property of a common dialog box sets a variety of options.

FontBold The property FontBold determines whether or not the characters Printed on a form, picture box, or printer, or assigned to a text box, command button, or label appear in bold or normal type. If the FontBold property is set to True (the default), then for a form, picture box, or printer, subsequent Printed characters appear bold. For a text box, command button, or label, the text or caption is immediately changed to bold. If the FontBold property is set to False, subsequent characters are Printed in normal type and characters assigned to the text or caption property change immediately to normal type.

FontCount   The value of the property Screen.FontCount is the number of fonts available for use on the screen. Similarly, the value of the property Printer.FontCount is the number of fonts available on the printer. The FontCount property is set according to your Windows environment and generally used to determine the limit on the index for the Fonts property.

FontItalic   The property FontItalic determines whether or not the characters Printed on a form, picture box, or printer, or assigned to a text box, command button, or label appear in italic or upright type. If the FontItalic property is set to True, then for a form, picture box, or printer, subsequent characters appear in italic. For a text box, command button, or label, the text or caption is immediately changed to italic. If the FontItalic property is set to False (the default), subsequent characters are Printed in upright type and characters assigned to the text or caption property change immediately to upright type.

FontName   The property FontName determines what type face is used when characters are Printed on a form, picture box, or printer, or assigned to a text box, command button, or label. If the FontName property of a form, picture box, or printer is set to a font obtained from the Fonts property, all subsequently Printed characters will appear in the new type face. When the FontName property of a text box, command button, or label is set to a new font, characters assigned to the text or caption property change immediately to the new type face.

Fonts   The value of the property Screen.Fonts(*fontNum*) is the name of a screen font available in the current Windows environment. The index *fontNum* can range from 0 to Screen.FontCount–1. Similarly, the value of the property Printer.Fonts(*fontNum*) is the name of an available printer font. The values in the Fonts property are set by your Windows environment and are generally used to determine which fonts are available for setting the FontName property.

FontSize   The property FontSize determines the size, in points, of characters Printed on forms, picture boxes, and the printer or displayed in text boxes and on command buttons and labels. Available font sizes depend on your Windows environment, but will always be between 1 and 2048. Default font sizes are usually between 8 and 12 point. **Note:** One point equals 1/72nd of an inch.

FontStrikeThru   The property FontStrikeThru determines whether or not the characters Printed on a form, picture box, or printer, or assigned to a text box, command button, or label appear in a strikethru or standard font. If the Font-StrikeThru property is set to True, then for a form, picture box, or printer, subsequent Printed characters appear with a horizontal line through the middle of each character. For a text box, command button, or label, the text or caption is immediately changed so that a horizontal line goes through the middle of each character. If the FontStrikeThru property is set to False (the default), subsequent characters are Printed in standard type and characters assigned to text or caption property change immediately to standard type.

FontTransparent   The property FontTransparent determines the degree to which characters Printed to forms and picture boxes obscure existing text and graphics.

If the FontTransparent property is set to True (the default), the existing text and graphics are obscured only by the dots (pixels) needed to actually form the new character. If the FontTransparent property is set to False, then all text and graphics are obscured within the character box (small rectangle surrounding a character) associated with the new character. Those dots (pixels) not needed to form the character are changed to the background color.

FontUnderline The property FontUnderline determines whether or not the characters printed on a form, picture box, or printer, or assigned to a text box, command button, or label appear with an underline. If the FontUnderline property is set to True, then for a form, picture box, or printer, subsequent characters Printed appear underlined. For a text box, command button, or label, the text or caption is immediately changed to underlined. If the FontUnderline property is set to False (the default), subsequent characters are Printed without underlines characters assigned to the text or caption property change immediately to nonunderlined.

For/Next The statement For *index* = *a* To *b* Step *s* sets the value of the variable *index* to *a* and repeatedly executes the statements between itself and the statement Next *index*. Each time the Next statement is reached, *s* is added to the value of *index*. This process continues until the value of *index* passes *b*. Although the numbers *a*, *b*, and *s* may have any numeric type, the lower the precision of the type, the faster the loop executes. The statement For *index* = *a* To *b* is equivalent to the statement For *index* = *a* To *b* Step 1. The index following the word Next is optional.

ForeColor The property ForeColor determines the color used to display text, captions, graphics, and Printed characters. If the ForeColor property of a form or picture box is changed, subsequent characters will appear in the new color. For a text box, command button, or label, text or caption is immediately changed to the new color. [color]

**Format$** The value of the function Format$(*expression*, *str*) is a string representing *expression* (a number, date, time, or string) formatted according to the rules given by *str*. Format$ is useful when assigning values to the Text property and when Printing to a form, picture box, or the printer.

Numeric output can be formatted with commas, leading and trailing zeros, preceding or trailing signs (+ or –), and exponential notation. This is accomplished either by using for *str* the name of one of several predefined numeric formats or by combining in *str* one or more of the following special numeric formatting characters: #, 0, decimal point (period), comma, %, E–, and E+. The expression to be formatted can evaluate to one of the numeric types or a string representing a number.

Predefined numeric formats include "General Number," which displays a number as is; "Currency," which displays a number with a leading dollar sign, commas every three digits to the left of the decimal, displays two decimal places, and encloses negative numbers in parentheses; "Fixed," which displays two digits to the right and at least one digit to the left of the decimal point; "Standard," which displays a number with commas and two decimal places but does not use parentheses for negative numbers; "Percent," which multiplies the value by 100 and displays a percent sign after two decimal places; and "Scientific," which displays numbers in standard scientific notation. For example, Format$(–5432.352, "Currency") gives the string "($5,432.35)".

The symbol # designates a place for a digit. If the number being formatted does not need all the places provided by the #'s given in *str*, the extra #'s are ignored. The symbol 0, like #, designates a place for a digit. However, if the number being formatted does not need all the places provided by the 0's given in *str*, the character 0 is displayed in the extra places. If the number being converted has more whole part digits than there is space reserved by #'s and 0's, additional space is used as if the format string had more #'s at its beginning. For example, Format$(56, "####") yields "56", Format$(56, "#") yields "56", Format$(0, "#") yields "", Format$(56, "0000") yields "0056", Format$(56, "0") yields "56", and Format$(0, "0") yields "0".

The decimal point symbol (.) marks the location of the decimal place. It separates the format rules into two sections, one applying to the whole part of the number and the other to the decimal part. When included in the format string, a decimal point will always appear in the resulting string. For example, Format$(56.246, "#.##") yields "56.25", Format$(.246, "#.##") yields ".25", Format$(.246, "0.##") yields "0.25", and Format$(56.2, "0.00") yields "52.20".

The comma symbol (,) placed to the left of the decimal point between #'s and/or 0's causes commas to be displayed to the left of every third digit to the left of the decimal point, as appropriate. If commas are placed to the immediate left of the decimal point (or to the right of all #'s and 0's when the decimal point symbol is not used), then before the number is formatted, it is divided by 1000 for each comma, but commas will not appear in the result. In order to divide by 1000s and display commas in the result, use format strings like "#,#,.00", which displays the number with commas in units of thousands, and "#,#,,.00", which displays the number with commas in units of millions. For example, Format$(1234000, "#,#") yields "1,234,000", Format$(1234000, "#,") yields "1234", Format$(1234000, "#,.") yields "1234.", Format$(1234000, "#,,.0") yields "1.2", and Format$(1234000, "#,0,.0") yields "1,234.0".

The percent symbol (%) placed to the right of all #'s, 0's, and any decimal point causes the number to be converted to a percentage (multiplied by 100) before formatting and the symbol % to be displayed. For example, Format$(.05624, "#.##%") yields "5.62%", and Format$(1.23, "#%") yields "123%".

The symbols E+ and E− placed to the right of all #'s, 0's, and any decimal point cause the number to be displayed in scientific notation. Places for the digits in the exponent must be reserved to the right of E+ or E− with #'s or 0's. When E+ is used and the exponent is positive, a plus sign appears in front of the exponent in the result. When E− is used and the exponent is positive, no sign or space precedes the exponent. When scientific notation is used, each position reserved by #'s to the left of the decimal point is used whenever possible. For example, Format$(1234.56, "#.##E+##") yields "1.23E+3", Format$(1234.56, "##.##E−##") yields "12.34E2", Format$(1234, "###.00E+##") yields "123.40E+1", and Format$(123, "###E+00") yields "123E+00".

Date and time output can be formatted using numbers or names for months, putting the day, month, and year in any order desired, using 12-hour or 24-hour notation, and so on. This is accomplished either by letting *str* be the name of one of several predefined date/time formats or by combining in *str* one or more special date/time formatting characters. The expression to be formatted can evaluate to a number that falls within the range of valid serial dates or to a string representing a date/time.

Predefined date/time formats include "General Date," which displays a date in mm/dd/yyyy format and, if appropriate, a time in hh:mm:ss PM format; "Long

Date," which displays the day of week, the full name of month, the day, and a four digit year; "Medium Date," which displays the day, abbreviated month name, and two digit year; "Short Date," which displays "mm/dd/yy"; "Long Time," which displays the time in hh:mm:ss PM format; "Medium Time," which displays time in hh:mm PM format; and "Short Time," which display time in 24-hour format as hh:mm. For example, let dt = DateSerial(55,2,10) + TimeSerial(21,45,30). Then Format$(dt, "General Date") yields "2/10/55 9:45:30 PM", Format$(dt, "Medium Date") yields "10-Feb-55", and Format$(dt, "Short Time") yields "21:45".

Format symbols for the day, month, and year include d (day as number but no leading zero), dd (day as number with leading zero), ddd (day as three-letter name), dddd (day as full name), m (month as number but no leading zero), mm (month as number with leading zero), mmm (month as three-letter name), mmmm (month as full name), yy (year as two-digit number), and yyyy (year as four-digit number). Separators such as slash, dash, and period may be used as desired to connect day, month, and year symbols into a final format. For example, Format$("August 13, 1958", "dddd, d.mmm.yy") yields "Wednesday, 13.Aug.58" and Format$("July 4, 1776", "ddd: mmmm dd, yyyy") yields "Thu: July 04, 1776". Additional format symbols for dates include w (day-of-week as number 1–7), ww (week-of-year as number 1–53), q (quarter-of-year as number 1–4), y (day-of-year as number 1–366), ddddd (same as short date), and dddddd (same as long date).

Format symbols for the second, minute, and hour include s (seconds with no leading zero), ss (seconds as two-digit number), n (minutes with no leading zero), nn (minutes as two-digit number), h (hours with no leading zero), hh (hours as two-digit number), AM/PM (use 12-hour clock and uppercase), am/pm (use 12-hour clock and lowercase), A/P (use 12-hour clock and single uppercase letter), a/p (use 12-hour clock and single lowercase letter), and ttttt (same as general date). Separators such as colons and periods may be used as desired to connect hour, minute, and second symbols into a final format. For example, Format$("14:04:01", "h:nn AM/PM") yields "2:04 PM", Format$("14:04:01", "h.n.s") yields "14.4.1", and Format$(0.75, "h:nna/p") yields "6:00p".

String output can be formatted as all uppercase, all lowercase, left justified or right justified. Symbols used to format strings are @ (define a field for at least as many characters as there are @ symbols; if less characters than @ symbols, fill remainder of field with spaces; if more characters than @ symbols, display the extra characters—don't clip), & (reserve space for entire output string), < (convert all characters to lowercase before displaying), > (convert all characters to uppercase before displaying), ! (left justify within field defined by @ symbols; default is to right justify). For example, Format$("Red", "@") yields "Red", Format$("Red", "@@@@@@") yields " Red" (3 leading spaces), Format$("Red", "!>@@@@@@") yields "RED " (3 trailing spaces), and Format$("Red", "<&") yields "red".

FreeFile   When files are opened, they are assigned a reference number from 1 to 255. At any time, the value of the function FreeFile is the next available reference number.

FromPage, ToPage   The FromPage and ToPage properties of a Print common dialog box identify the values selected for the From and To text boxes.

Function   A function is a multistatement block beginning with a statement of the form Function *FunctionName*(*parList*), followed on subsequent lines by one or more statements for carrying out the task of the function, and ending with the statement End Function. The parameter list, *parList*, is a list of variables through which values will be passed to the function when the function is called. Parameter types may be numeric, (variable-length) string, variant, user-defined record type, or array. The types of the parameters may be specified with type-declaration tags, Def*Type* statements, or As clauses. Array names appearing in the parameter list should be followed by an empty pair of parentheses. Functions are named with the same conventions as variables. The value of a variable argument used in calling a function may be altered by the function unless the variable is surrounded by parentheses. Variables appearing in a function are local to the function unless they have been declared in the (declarations) section of (general) and are not redeclared in Dim or Static statements within the function. A statement of the form Function *FunctionName*(*parList*) Static specifies that all variables local to the function be treated as static by default; that is, they are invisible outside of the function but retain their values between function calls. Functions may invoke themselves (called *recursion*) or other procedures. However, no procedure may be defined inside of a function.

Get User-defined record types provide an efficient means of working with random-access files. After a user-defined record type is defined and a variable of that type, call it *recVar*, is declared, the file is opened with a length equal to Len (*recVar*). The *r*th record of the random-access file is retrieved and assigned to *recVar* with the statement Get #*n*, *r*, *recVar*.

The Get statement is also used to retrieve data from a binary file and assign it to any type of variable. Suppose *var* is a variable that holds a value consisting of *b* bytes. (For instance, if *var* is an integer variable, then *b* is 2. If *var* is an ordinary string variable, then *b* will equal the length of the string currently assigned to it.) The statement Get #*n*, *p*, *var* assigns to the variable *var*, the *b* consecutive bytes beginning with the byte in position *p* of the binary file having reference number *n*. (**Note:** The positions are numbered 1, 2, 3, ...) If *p* is omitted, then the current file position is used as the beginning position. [binary file]

GetAttr The value of the function GetAttr(*filename*) is a number indicating the file attributes associated with the file specified by *filename*. Let *attrib* be a variable holding the value returned by GetAttr. Then the file specified by *filename* is a read-only file if *attrib* And 1 = 1, is a hidden file if *attrib* And 2 = 2, is a system file if *attrib* And 4 = 4, is a volume label if *attrib* And 8 = 8, is a directory name if *attrib* And 16 = 16, or has been modified since the last back-up if *attrib* And 32 = 32.

GetText The value of the method ClipBoard.GetText is a string containing a copy of the data currently stored in the clipboard.

Global The Global statement is used to create variables, including arrays, that are available to all procedures in all forms and BAS modules associated with a project. The Global statement must be placed in the (declarations) section of a BAS module, and has the same structure as a Dim statement. For example, the statement Global classList(1 to 30) As String, numStudents As Integer creates an array and a variable for use in all procedures of the project.

GoSub A statement of the form GoSub *lineLabel* causes a jump to the first statement following the specified line label. When the statement Return is reached, the program jumps back to the statement following the GoSub statement. The GoSub statement and its target must be in the same procedure. [line label] [subroutine]

GotFocus The GotFocus event applies to command buttons, text boxes, and picture boxes. A GotFocus event occurs when an object receives the focus, either through a user action or through code, via the SetFocus method.

GoTo The statement GoTo *lineLabel* causes an unconditional jump to the first statement after the specified line label. The GoTo statement and its target must be in the same procedure. [line label]

GridLines Grid lines are the light gray lines in a grid that separate columns and rows. The GridLines property determines whether the grid lines are visible (GridLines = True) or not (GridLines = False.)

Height The property Height determines the vertical size of an object. Height is measured in units of twips. For the Printer object, Height may be read (ph = Printer.Height is OK) but not assigned (Printer.Height = 100 causes an error).

Hex$ If *n* is a whole number from 0 to 2,147,483,647, then the value of the function Hex$(*n*) is the string consisting of the hexadecimal representation of *n*.

Hide The Hide method removes a form from the screen.

Hour The function Hour extracts the hours from a serial date. If *d* is any valid serial date, then the value of Hour(*d*) is a whole number from 0 to 23 indicating the hours recorded as part of the date and time store in *d*. [date]

If (single line) A statement of the form If *condition* Then *action* causes the program to take the specified action if *condition* is true. Otherwise, execution continues at the next line. A statement of the form If *condition* Then *action1* Else *action2* causes the program to take *action1* if *condition* is true and *action2* if *condition* is false.

If (block) A block of statements beginning with a statement of the form If *condition* Then and ending with the statement End If, indicates that the group of statements between If and End If are to be executed only when *condition* is true. If the group of statements is separated into two parts by an Else statement, then the first part will be executed when *condition* is true and the second part when *condition* is false. Statements of the form ElseIf *condition* may also appear and define groups of statements to be executed when alternate conditions are true.

If TypeOf To test for the type of a control when the control name is passed to a procedure, use If TypeOf *controlName* Is *controlType* Then *action1* Else *action2* in either the single line or block form of the If statement. ElseIf TypeOf is also permitted. For *controlType*, use one of the control names that appear in the Form Design ToolBox (CommandButton, Label, TextBox, etc.) For example, If TypeOf objectPassed Is Label Then . . . .

Imp The logical expression *condition1* Imp *condition2* is true except when *condition1* is true and *condition2* is false. For example, (3<7) Imp ("abc">"a") is true since both 3<7 and "abc">"a" are true, while ("apple">"ape") Imp ("earth"> "moon") is false since "apple">"ape" is true but "earth">"moon" is false.

Index Property When a control is part of a Control array, it is identified by the number specified by its Index Property.

Input# The statement Input #n, *var* reads the next item of data from a sequential file that has been opened for Input with reference number n and assigns the item to the variable *var*. The statement Input #n, *var1*, *var2*, . . . reads a sequence of values and assigns them to the variables.

Input$ The statement *str* = Input$(n, m) assigns the next n characters from the file with reference number m to *str*.

**InputBox$** The value of the function InputBox$(*prompt*) is the string entered by the user in response to the prompt given by *prompt*. The InputBox$ function automatically displays the prompt, a text box for user input, an OK button, and a Cancel button in a dialog box in the center of the screen. If the user selects Cancel, the value of the function is the null string (""). For greater control, use the function InputBox$(*prompt*, *title*, *defaultStr*, *xpos*, *ypos*) which titles the dialog box with *title*, displays *defaultStr* as the default value in the text box, and positions the upper left corner of the dialog box at coordinates (*xpos*, *ypos*) on the screen. [coordinate systems]

InStr The value of the function InStr(*str1*, *str2*) is the position of the string *str2* in the string *str1*. The value of InStr(n, *str1*, *str2*) is the first position at or after the nth character of *str1* that the string *str2* occurs. If *str2* does not appear as a substring of *str1*, the value is 0.

Int The value of the function Int(x) is the greatest whole number that is less than or equal to x.

Integer A variable of type Integer requires 2 bytes of memory and can hold the whole numbers from −32,768 to 32,767. Integer values and variables may be indicated by the type tag %: 345%, Count%.

Interval The Interval property of a Timer control is set to the number of milliseconds (1 to 65535) required to trigger a Timer event.

IsDate The value of the function IsDate(*str*) is True (−1) if the string *str* represents a date between January 1, 100 and December 31, 9999. Otherwise, the value is False (0). [date]

IsEmpty The value of the function IsEmpty(v) is True (−1) if v is a variable of unspecified type (i.e., is a variant) that has not yet been assigned a value. In all other cases the value of IsEmpty is False (0). [variant]

IsNull The value of the function IsNull(v) is True (−1) if v is a variant variable that has been assigned the special value Null. In all other cases the value of IsNull is False (0). [variant]

IsNumeric The value of the function IsNumeric(v) is True (−1) if v is a number, numeric variable, or a variant variable that has been assigned a number or a string that could be obtained by Formatting a number. In all other cases the value of IsNumeric is False (0). [variant]

ItemData When you create a list or combo box, Visual Basic automatically creates a long integer array referred to as ItemData. The statement Let List1.ItemData(m) = n assigns the value n to the mth subscripted variable of the array. It is commonly used with the NewIndex property to associate a number with each item in a list, and thereby create a mini-database. The ItemData property is especially useful for lists in which Sorted = True.

KeyPress The KeyPress event applies to command buttons, text boxes, and picture boxes. A KeyPress event occurs whenever the user presses a key while one of the above controls has the focus. A code identifying which key was pressed will be passed to the event procedure in the KeyAscii parameter. This information can then be used to determine what action should be taken when a given key is pressed.

Kill The statement Kill "*filespec*" erases the specified disk file. [filespec]

LargeChange When a scroll bar is clicked between the thumb and one of the arrow buttons, the Value property of the scroll bar changes by the value of the LargeChange property and the thumb moves accordingly.

LBound For a one-dimensional array *arrayName*, the value of the function LBound(*arrayName*) is the smallest subscript value that may be used. For any array *arrayName*, the value of the function LBound(*arrayName*, *n*) is the smallest subscript value that may be used for the *n*th subscript of the array. For example, after the statement Dim example(1 To 31, 1 To 12, 1990 To 1999) is executed, the value of LBound(example, 3) is the smallest value allowed for the third subscript of example( ), which is 1990.

**LCase$** The value of the string function LCase$(*str*) is a string identical to *str* except that all uppercase letters are changed to lowercase.

Left The property Left determines the position of the left edge of a form or control. The units of measure are twips for forms. The units of measure for a control are determined by the ScaleMode property of the container (form, picture box, etc.) upon which the control has been placed, with the position of the control measured from the edge of its container using the coordinate system established by the various Scale. . . properties for the container. By default, the unit of measure for a container is twips, with a value of 0 for the Left property placing the control against the left edge of the container.

**Left$** The value of the function Left$(*str*, *n*) is the string consisting of the leftmost *n* characters of *str*. If *n* is greater than the number of characters in *str*, the value of the function is *str*.

Len The value of Len(*str*) is the number of characters in the string *str*. If *var* is not a variable-length string variable, the value of Len(*var*) is the number of bytes needed to hold the value of the variable in memory. That is, Len(*var*) is 2, 4, 4, or 8 for integer, long integer, single-precision, and double-precision variables. Len(*var*), when *var* is a variable with a user-defined record type, is the number of bytes of memory needed to store the value of the variable. If *var* is a variant variable, Len(*var*) is the number of bytes needed to store *var* as a string. [variant]

Let The statement Let *var* = *expr* assigns the value of the expression to the variable. If *var* is a fixed-length string variable with length *n* and Len(*expr*) is greater than *n*, then just the first *n* characters of *expr* are assigned to *var*. If Len(*expr*) < n, then *expr* is padded on the right with spaces and assigned to *var*. If *var* has a user-defined type, then *expr* must be of the same type. The statement *var* = *expr* is equivalent to Let *var* = *expr*.

Line The graphics method *objectName*.Line (*x1*, *y1*)–(*x2*, *y2*) draws a line connecting the two points. The graphics method *objectName*.Line –(*x2*, *y2*) draws a line from the point (*objectName*.CurrentX, *objectName*.CurrentY) to the specified point. The object *objectName* can be a form, picture box, or the Printer. The line is in color *c* if *objectName*.Line (*x1, y1*)–(*x2, y2*), *c* is executed. The statement *objectName*.Line (*x1, y1*)–(*x2, y2*), ,B draws a rectangle with the two points as opposite vertices. (If B is replaced by BF, a solid rectangle is drawn.) After a Line method is executed, the value of *objectName*.CurrentX becomes *x2* and the value of *objectName*.CurrentY becomes *y2*. [color] [coordinate systems]

Line Input# After a file has been opened as a sequential file for Input with reference number *n*, the statement Line Input #*n*, *str* assigns to the string variable *str* the string of characters from the current location in the file up to the next pair of carriage return/line feed characters.

List The List property of a combo box, directory list box, drive list box, file list box, or list box is used to access items in the list. When one of these controls is created, Visual Basic automatically creates the string array List to hold the list of items stored in the control. The value of List1.List(*n*) is the item of List1 having index *n*. The value of List1.List (List1.ListIndex) is the item (string) currently highlighted in list box List1.

ListCount For a list or combo box, the value of List1.ListCount or Combo1.List-Count is the number of items currently in the list. For a directory list box, drive list box, or file list box the value of *control*.ListCount is the number of subdirectories in the current directory, the number of drives on the computer, or the number of files in the current directory that match the Pattern property, respectively.

ListIndex The ListIndex property gives the index of the currently selected item is a combo box, directory list box, drive list box, file list box, or list box.

Load The Load event applies only to forms and occurs only once, immediately when a program starts. This is the appropriate place to put code that should be executed every time a program is run, regardless of the user's actions.

Load If *controlName* is the name of a control in a control array whose Index property was assigned a value during form design and *num* is a whole number that has not yet been used as an index for the *controlName*() array, then the statement Load *controlName*(*num*) copies properties of *controlName*(0) and creates the element *controlName*(*num*) of the *controlName*() array.

LoadPicture The statement *objectName*.Picture = LoadPicture(*pictureFile*), where *objectName* is a form or picture box, places the picture defined in the file specified by *pictureFile* on *objectName*

Loc This function gives the current location in a sequential, random-access, or binary file. For a sequential file with reference number *n*, Loc(*n*) is the number of blocks of 128 characters read from or written to the file since it was opened. For a random-access file, Loc(*n*) is the current record (either the last record read or written, or the record identified in a Seek statement). For a binary file, Loc(*n*) is the number of bytes from the beginning of the file to the last byte read or written. For communications, the value of Loc(*n*) is the number of bytes waiting in the communications buffer with reference number *n*. [binary file]

Lock The Lock command is intended for use in programs that operate on a network. The DOS command Share enables file sharing and should be executed from DOS prior to using the Lock statement. After a file has been opened with reference number n, the statement Lock #n denies access to the file by any other process. For a random-access file, the statement Lock #n, $r1$ To $r2$ denies access to records $r1$ through $r2$ by any other process. For a binary file, this statement denies access to bytes $r1$ through $r2$. The statement Lock #n, $r1$ locks only record (or byte) $r1$. For a sequential file, all forms of the Lock statement have the same effect as Lock #n. The Unlock statement is used to remove locks from files. All locks should be removed before a file is closed or the program is terminated. [binary file]

LOF After a file has been opened with reference number n, the number of characters in the file (that is, the length of the file) is given by LOF(n). For communications, the value of LOF(n) equals the number of bytes waiting in the communications buffer with reference number n.

Log If x is a positive number, the value of Log(x) is the natural logarithm (base e) of x.

Long A variable of type Long requires 4 bytes of memory and can hold the whole numbers from $-2,147,483,648$ to $2,147,483,647$. Long values and variables may be indicated by the type tag &: 12345678&, Population&.

LostFocus The LostFocus event applies to command buttons, text boxes, and picture boxes. A LostFocus event occurs when an object loses the focus, either through a user action or through code, via the SetFocus method.

LSet If str is a string variable, then the statement LSet $str1$ = $str2$ replaces the value of $str1$ with a string of the same length consisting of $str2$ truncated or padded on the right with spaces. LSet also can be used to assign a record of one user-defined type to a record of a different user-defined type.

**LTrim$** The value of the function LTrim$($str$) is the string obtained by removing all the spaces from the beginning of the string str. The string str may be either of fixed or variable length.

Max and Min The Max and Min properties of scroll bars give the values of horizontal (vertical) scroll bars when the thumb is at the right (bottom) and left (top) arrows, respectively.

MaxButton The MaxButton property determines whether or not a form has a maximize button in the upper-right corner. If the value of the MaxButton property is set to True (the default), a maximize button is displayed when the program is run. The user then has the option to click on the maximize button to cause the form to enlarge and fill the entire screen. If the value of the MaxButton property is set to False, the maximize button is not displayed when the program is run, and the user is thus unable to "maximize" the form.

MaxLength The property MaxLength determines the maximum number of characters that a text box will accept. If the MaxLength property for a text box is set to 0 (the default), an unlimited number of characters may be entered in the text box.

**Mid$** The value of the function Mid$($str$, m, n) is the substring of str beginning with the mth character of str and containing up to n characters. If the parameter n is omitted, Mid$($str$, m) is all the characters of str from the mth character on. The statement Mid$($str$, m, n) = $str2$ replaces the characters of str, beginning with the mth character, by the first n characters of the string $str2$.

MinButton The MinButton property determines whether or not a form has a minimize button in the upper-right corner. If the value of the MinButton property is set to True (the default), a minimize button is displayed when the program is run. The user then has the option to click on the minimize button to cause the form to be replaced by a small icon at the bottom of the screen. If the value of the MinButton property is set to False, the minimize button is not displayed when the program is run, and the user is thus unable to "minimize" the form.

Minute The function Minute extracts the minutes from a serial date. If *d* is any valid serial date, the value of Minute(*d*) is a whole number from 0 to 59 giving the minutes recorded as part of the date and time stored in *d*. [date]

MkDir The statement MkDir *path\dirName* creates a subdirectory named *dirName* in the directory specified by *path*. [directories]

Mod The value of the expression *num1* Mod *num2* is the whole number remainder when *num1* is divided by *num2*. If either *num1* or *num2* is not a whole number, it is rounded to a whole number before the Mod operation is performed. If one or both of *num1* and *num2* are negative, the result of the Mod operation will have the same sign as *num1*. For example, 25 Mod 7 is 4, 18.7 Mod 3.2 is 1, –35 Mod –4 is –3, and 27 Mod –6 is 3.

Month The function Month extracts the month from a serial date. If *d* is any valid serial date, the value of Month(*d*) is a whole number from 1 to 12 giving the month recorded as part of the date and time stored in *d*. [date]

MousePointer The property MousePointer determines what shape the mouse pointer takes when the mouse is over a particular form or control. Valid values for the MousePointer property are whole numbers from 0 to 12. A value of 0 (the default) indicates that the mouse pointer should take on the normal shape for the control it is over. (The normal shape over text boxes is an I-beam, while for a form, picture box, label, or command button it is an arrow.) Use a MousePointer value of 1 for an arrow, 2 for cross-hairs, 3 for an I-beam, 4 for a small square within a square, 5 for a four-pointed arrow, 6 for a double arrow pointing up to the right and down to the left, 7 for a double arrow pointing up and down, 8 for a double arrow pointing up to the left and down to the right, 9 for a double arrow pointing left and right, 10 for an up arrow, 11 for an hourglass, and 12 for a "do not" symbol (circle with diagonal line).

Move The method *objectName*.Move *xpos, ypos* moves the named form or control so that its upper left corner has coordinates (*xpos, ypos*). For forms, positioning is relative to the upper left corner of the screen. For controls, positioning is relative to the upper left corner of the form, frame, or picture box to which the control is attached. The method *objectName*.Move *xpos, ypos, width, height* also resizes the named form or control to be *width* units wide and *height* units high. The Move method may be used whether or not a form or control is visible. If you wish to specify just a new width for an object, you CANNOT use *objectName*.Move ,,*width*. Instead, use *objectName*.Move *objectName*.Left, *object-Name*.Top, *width*. Similar considerations apply for changing just *ypos, height, width* and *height*, and so on.

MoveFirst, MoveLast, MoveNext, MovePrevious The data control methods MoveNext, MovePrevious, MoveLast, and MoveFirst select new current records in the expected way.

MsgBox (Statement and Function) The statement MsgBox *message* displays *message* in a dialog box with an OK button. The more general statement MsgBox *message, buttons, title* displays *message* in a dialog box titled with *title* and containing from one to three buttons as determined by the value of *buttons*. The value of *buttons* also determines which button is the default (has the focus) and which, if any, of four icons is displayed. The value to use for *buttons* can be computed as follows:

$$buttons = \text{set number} + \text{default number} + \text{icon number}$$

where set number, default number, and icon number are determined from the following tables:

Buttons Set	Set Number
OK	0
OK, Cancel	1
Abort, Retry, Ignore	2
Yes, No, Cancel	3
Yes, No	4
Retry, Cancel	5

Focus Default	Default Number
First Button	0
Second Button	256
Third Button	512

Icon	Icon Number
Stop sign	16
Question mark	32
Exclamation mark	48
Information	64

The value of the function MsgBox(*message, buttons, title*) indicates which of the displayed buttons the user pushed; in all other aspects the MsgBox statement and function act in the same manner. The values returned for each of the possible buttons pressed are 1 for OK, 2 for Cancel (or Esc), 3 for Abort, 4 for Retry, 5 for Ignore, 6 for Yes, and 7 for No.

MultiLine The property MultiLine determines whether or not a text box can accept and display multiple lines. If the MultiLine property of a text box is set to True, then text entered in the text box will wrap to a new line when the right side of the text box is reached. Pressing the Enter key will also start a new line. If the MultiLine property of a text box is set to False (the default), input is restricted to a single line that scrolls if more input is entered than can be displayed within the width of the text box.

Name (Property) The property Name is used at design time to give a meaningful name to a form or control. This new name will then be used by Visual Basic in naming all event procedures for the form or control.

Name (Statement) The statement Name "*filespec1*" As "*filespec2*" is used to change the name and/or the directory of *filespec1* to the name and/or directory specified by *filespec2*. The two filespecs must refer to the same drive. [filespec]

NewIndex The NewIndex property of a combo box or list box gives the index number of the item most recently added to the list.

NewPage The method Printer.NewPage indicates that the current page of output is complete and should be sent to the printer. A form feed (Chr$(12)) will also be sent to the printer to cause the paper to advance to the top of a new page.

Not (Logical Operator) The logical expression Not *condition1* is true if *condition1* is false and false if *condition1* is true. For example, Not (3<7) is false since 3<7 is true, while Not ("earth">"moon") is true since "earth">"moon" is false.

Not (Bitwise Operator) The expression Not *byte1* is evaluated by expressing the byte as an 8-tuple binary number and then Notting each individual digit, where Not 1 is equal to 0, while Not 0 is equal to 1. For example, the expression Not 37 translated to binary 8-tuples becomes Not 00100101. Notting each digit gives the binary 8-tuple 11011010 or decimal 218; thus Not 37 is 218.

Now The value of the function Now( ) is the serial date for the current date and time as recorded on the computer's internal clock. [date]

Oct$ If *n* is a whole number between 0 and 2,147,483,647, Oct$(*n*) is the octal (that is, base 8) representation of *n*.

On Error The statement On Error GoTo *lineLabel* sets up error trapping. An error then causes a jump to the error-handling routine beginning with the first statement following the specified line label. The On Error statement and its target must be in the same procedure. [line label]

On...GoSub and On...GoTo The statement On *expression* GoSub *lineLabel1*, *lineLabel2*, . . . causes a GoSub to *lineLabel1*, *lineLabel2*, . . . depending upon whether the value of the expression is 1, 2, ... Similarly, the GoTo variation causes an unconditional jump to the appropriate line label. The GoSub or GoTo statement and its target must be in the same procedure. [line label]

Open The statement Open "*filespec*" For *mode* As #*n* allows access to the file *filespec* in one of the following modes: Input (information can be read sequentially from the file), Output (a new file is created and information can be written sequentially to it), Append (information can be added sequentially to the end of a file), or Binary (information can be read or written in an arbitrary fashion). The statement Open "*filespec*" For Random As #*n* Len = *g* allows random-access to the file *filespec* in which each record has length *g*. Throughout the program, the file is referred to by the reference number *n* (from 1 through 255). Another variation of the Open statement is Open "LPT1" For Output As #*n*, which allows access to the printer as if it were a sequential file.

In a network environment, two enhancements to the Open statement are available. (The DOS command Share enables file sharing and should be executed from DOS prior to the use of the enhanced variations of the Open statement.) Visual Basic accesses data files in two ways: it reads from them or writes to them. When several processes may utilize a file at the same time, accurate file handling requires that certain types of access be denied to anyone but the person who has opened the file. The statement Open "*filespec*" For *mode* Lock Read As #*n* or Open "*filespec*" For Random Lock Read As #*n* Len = *g* opens the specified file and forbids any other process from reading the file as long as the file is open. Lock Write forbids any other process from writing to the file as long as the file is open. Lock Read Write forbids any other process from reading or writing to the file as long as the file is open. Lock Shared grants full access to any other process, except when a file is currently opened and locked by a process for a certain access mode, then another process attempting to open the file for the same mode will receive the message "Permission denied" and be denied access. [filespec] [binary file]

Option Base   After the statement Option Base *m* is executed, where *m* is 0 or 1, a statement of the form Dim *arrayName*(*n*) defines an array with subscripts ranging from *m* to *n*. Visual Basic's extended Dim statement, which permits both lower and upper subscript bounds to be specified for each array, achieves a wider range of results, making its use preferable to Option Base.

Option Compare   The statement Option Compare Text, placed in the (declarations) section of (general), causes string comparisons to be case insensitive. Thus, if Option Compare Text is in effect, the comparison "make" = "MaKe" will be true. The statement Option Compare Binary placed in the (declarations) section produces the default comparison rules, which are case sensitive and use the character order given in the ANSI/ASCII character tables.

Option Explicit   If the statement Option Explicit appears in the (declarations) section of (general), each variable must be declared before it is used. A variable is declared by appearing in a Const, Dim, Global, ReDim, or Static statement, or by appearing as a parameter in a Sub or Function definition.

Or   (Logical Operator) The logical expression *condition1* Or *condition2* is true except when both *condition1* and *condition2* are false. For example, ("apple">"ape") Or ("earth">"moon") is true since "apple">"ape" is true, while (1>2) Or ("moon"< "earth") is false since both (1>2) and ("moon"<"earth") are false.

Or   (Bitwise Operator) The expression *byte1* Or *byte2* is evaluated by expressing each byte as an 8-tuple binary number and then Oring together corresponding digits, where 1 Or 1, 1 Or 0, and 0 Or 1 are all equal to 1, while 0 And 0 is equal to 0. For example, the expression 37 Or 157 translated to binary 8-tuples becomes 00100101 Or 10011101. Oring together corresponding digits gives the binary 8-tuple 10111101 or decimal 189. Thus 37 Or 157 is 189.

Path   The Path property of a directory list box is the contents of the currently selected item, and for a files list box is the path identifying the directory whose files are displayed.

PathChange   For a files list box, the PathChange event is triggered by a change in the value of the Path property.

Pattern   The Pattern property of a files list box uses wildcard characters to determine which file names are displayed. A typical statement is Let File1.Pattern = "*.TXT."

PatternChange   For a files list box, the PatternChange event is triggered by a change in the value of the Pattern property.

Picture   The property Picture allows a form or picture box to be assigned a picture or icon for display. If *iconOrPicture* is a file defining an icon or bitmapped picture, then *objectName*.Picture = LoadPicture(*iconOrPicture*) places the icon or picture on the form or picture box identified by *objectName*.

Point   The value of the method *objectName*.Point(*x*, *y*) is the RGB number of the color of the point with coordinates (*x*, *y*) on the form or picture box identified by *objectName*. Thus if the point with coordinates (x, y) has been painted using color RGB(r, g, b), then the value of Point(x, y) will be $r+256*g+65536*b$. If the coordinates (x, y) identify a point that is not on *objectName*, the value of Point(x, y) will be -1. [color] [coordinate systems]

Print The print method is used to display data on the screen or printer. The statement *objectName*.Print *expression* displays the value of the expression at the current position of the cursor in the named object (form, picture box, or Printer) and moves the cursor to the beginning of the next line. (Numbers are displayed with a trailing space and positive numbers with a leading space.) If the statement is followed by a semicolon or comma, the cursor will not move to the next line after the display, but will move to the next position or print zone, respectively. Several expressions may be placed in the same Print method if separated by semicolons (to display them adjacent to one another) or by commas (to display them in successive zones.)

Print# After a file has been opened as a sequential file for output or append with reference number n, the statement Print #n, *expression* places the value of the expression into the file in the same way the Print method displays it in a picture box.

Printer The Printer object provides access to the printer. Methods available are Print to send text to the printer, NewPage to execute a form feed to begin a new page, EndDoc to terminate the printing process, and the graphics methods. Many properties available for forms and picture boxes, such as fonts and scaling, are also available for the printer.

PrintForm The method *formName*.PrintForm prints on the printer an image of the named form and all its contents.

PSet The graphics method *objectName*.PSet(x, y) displays the point with coordinates (x, y) in the foreground color. The method *objectName*.PSet(x, y), c causes the point (x, y) to be displayed in the RGB color specified by c. The size of the point is determined by the value of the DrawWidth property. The actual color(s) displayed depend on the values of the DrawMode and DrawStyle properties. After a PSet method is executed, the value of *objectName*.CurrentX becomes x and the value of *objectName*.CurrentY becomes y. [color] [coordinate systems]

Put The Put statement is used to place data into a random-access file. Suppose *recVar* is a variable of a user-defined record type and that a file has been opened with a statement of the form Open *fileName* For Random As #n Len = Len(*recVar*). The statement Put #n, r, *recVar* places the value of *recVar* in the rth record of the file.

The Put statement is also used to place data into a file opened as a binary file. Suppose *var* is a variable that holds a value consisting of b bytes. (For instance, if *var* is an integer variable, then b is 2. If *var* is an ordinary string variable, then b will equal the length of the string currently assigned to it.) The statement Put #n, p, *var* writes the successive bytes of *var* into the b consecutive locations beginning with position p in the binary file with reference number n. (**Note:** The positions are numbered 1, 2, 3, ...) If p is omitted, the current file position is used as the beginning position. [binary file]

QBColor The function QBColor provides easy access to 16 standard colors. If *colorAttrib* is a whole number from 0 to 15, the value of the functions QBColor (*colorAttrib*) is the RGB color number associated with *colorAttrib*. The table below names the colors produced by each of the possible values of *colorAttrib*.

0	Black	4	Red	8	Gray	12	Light Red
1	Blue	5	Magenta	9	Light Blue	13	Light Magenta
2	Green	6	Brown	10	Light Green	14	Yellow
3	Cyan	7	White	11	Light Cyan	15	Intense White

Randomize The statement Randomize automatically uses the computer's clock to seed the random number generator. If a program includes a Randomize statement in the Form_Load event procedure, the list of numbers generated by Rnd will vary each time the program is executed. Randomize *n* seeds the generator with a number determined by *n*. If a program does not seed the random number generator or seeds it with a set number, the list of numbers generated by Rnd will be the same each time the program is executed.

ReDim The statement ReDim *arrayName*(...) erases the array from memory and recreates it. The information inside the parentheses has the same form and produces the same results as that in a Dim statement. After the ReDimensioning, all elements have their default values. Although the ranges of the subscripts may be changed, the number of dimensions must be the same as in the original Dimensioning of the array. ReDim may be used only within procedures; it may not be used in the (declarations) section of (general). To establish an array that is available to all procedures and also can be resized, Dim it with empty parentheses in the (declarations) section of (general) and then ReDim it as needed within appropriate procedures.

Refresh The method *objectName*.Refresh causes the named form or control to be refreshed, that is, redrawn reflecting any changes made to its properties. Generally, refreshing occurs automatically, but if not, it may be forced with the Refresh method.

Rem The statement Rem allows documentation to be placed in a program. A line of the form Rem *comment* is ignored during execution. The Rem statement may be abbreviated as an apostrophe.

RemoveItem The RemoveItem method deletes items from list and combo boxes and deletes rows from grids. The statement List1.RemoveItem *n* (where *n* is 0, 1, „,) deletes the item with index *n*. For instance, List1.RemoveItem 0 deletes the top item and List1.RemoveItem ListCount − 1 deletes the bottom item in the list. The statement Grid1.RemoveItem *n* deletes row *n* from the grid.

Reset The statement Reset closes all open files. Using Reset is equivalent to using Close with no file reference numbers.

Resume When the statement Resume is encountered at the end of an error-handling routine, the program branches back to the statement in which the error was encountered. The variations Resume *lineLabel* and Resume Next cause the program to branch to the first statement following the indicated line label or to the statement following the statement in which the error occurred, respectively. (The combination of On Error and Resume Next is similar to the combination GoSub and Return.) [line label]

Return When the statement Return is encountered at the end of a subroutine, the program branches back to the statement following the one containing the most recently executed GoSub. The variation Return *lineLabel* causes the program to branch back to the first statement following the indicated line label. [line label] [subroutine]

RGB The value of the function RGB(*red*, *green*, *blue*) is the color number corresponding to a mixture of *red* red, *green* green, and *blue* blue. This color number is assigned to color properties or used in graphics methods to produce text or graphics in a particular color. Each of the three color components may have a value from 0 to 255. The color produced using RGB(0, 0, 0) is black, RGB(255, 255, 255) is white, RGB(255, 0, 0) is bright red, RGB(10, 0, 0) is a dark red, and so on. (The value of the function RGB(*r*, *g*, *b*) is the long integer $r+256*g+65536*b$.) [color]

**Right$** The value of the function Right$(*str*, *n*) is the string consisting of the rightmost *n* characters of *str*. If *n* is greater than the number of characters of *str*, then the value of the function is *str*.

RmDir If *path* specifies a directory containing no files or subdirectories, then the statement RmDir *path* removes the directory. [directories]

Rnd The value of the function Rnd is a randomly selected number from 0 to 1, not including 1. The value of Int(*n*∗Rnd)+1 is a random whole number from 1 to *n*.

RowHeight The statement Let Grid1.RowHeight(*m*) = *n* specifies that row *m* of the grid be *n* twips high. (There are about 1440 twips in an inch.)

RSet If *str1* is a string variable, the statement RSet *str1* = *str2* replaces the value of *str1* with a string of the same length consisting of *str2* truncated or padded on the left with spaces.

**RTrim$** The value of the function RTrim$(*str*) is the string obtained by removing all the spaces from the end of the string *str*. The string *str* may be either fixed-length or variable-length.

Scale The method *objectName*.Scale (*x1*, *y1*)–(*x2*, *y2*) defines a coordinate system for the form or picture box identified by *objectName*. This coordinate system has horizontal values ranging from *x1* at the left edge of *objectName* to *x2* at the right edge and vertical values ranging from *y1* at the top edge of *objectName* to *y2* at the bottom edge. Subsequent graphics methods and control positioning place figures and controls in accordance with this new coordinate system. As a result of using the Scale method, the ScaleMode property of *objectName* is set to 0, the ScaleLeft property to *x1*, the ScaleTop property to *y1*, the ScaleHeight property to *y2*–*y1*, and the ScaleWidth property to *x2*–*x1*. The method *objectName*.Scale without arguments resets the coordinate system of *objectName* to the default coordinate system where the unit of measure is twips and the upper-left corner of *objectName* has coordinates (0, 0).

ScaleHeight The property ScaleHeight determines the vertical scale on a form or picture box. After the statement *objectName*.ScaleHeight = *hght* is executed, the vertical coordinates range from *objectName*.ScaleTop at the top edge of *objectName* to *objectName*.ScaleTop + *hght* at the bottom edge. The default value of the ScaleHeight property is the height of *objectName* when measured in the units specified by *objectName's* ScaleMode property.

ScaleLeft The property ScaleLeft determines the horizontal coordinate of the left edge of a form or picture box. After the statement *objectName*.ScaleLeft = *left* is executed, the horizontal coordinates will range from *left* at the left edge of *objectName* to *left* + *objectName*.ScaleWidth at the right edge. The default value of the ScaleLeft property is 0.

ScaleMode The property ScaleMode determines the horizontal and vertical unit of measure for the coordinate system on a form or picture box. If the ScaleMode property of a form or picture box is set to 1 (the default), the unit of measure becomes twips. Other possible values for ScaleMode are 2 for points (72 points = 1 inch), 3 for pixels, 4 for characters (1 horizontal unit = 120 twips; 1 vertical unit = 240 twips), 5 for inches, 6 for millimeters, and 7 for centimeters. A value of 0 for the ScaleMode property indicates that units of measure are to be determined from the current settings of the ScaleHeight and ScaleWidth properties. Visual Basic automatically sets the ScaleMode property of an object to 0 when any of the object's Scale... properties are assigned values.

ScaleTop The property ScaleTop determines the vertical coordinate of the top edge of a form or picture box. After the statement *objectName*.ScaleTop = *top* is executed, the vertical coordinates range from *top* at the top edge of *objectName* to *top* + *objectName*.ScaleHeight at the bottom edge. The default value for the ScaleTop property is 0.

ScaleWidth The property ScaleWidth determines the horizontal scale on a form or picture box. After the statement *objectName*.ScaleWidth = *wdth* is executed, the horizontal coordinates range from *objectName*.ScaleLeft at the left edge of *objectName* to *objectName*.ScaleLeft + *wdth* at the right edge. The default value of the ScaleWidth property is the width of *objectName* when measured in the units specified by *objectName's* ScaleMode property.

ScrollBars The ScrollBars property of a grid or text box specifies whether the control has horizontal (setting = 1), vertical (setting = 2), both (setting = 3), or no (setting = 0) scroll bars. In order for a text box to have scroll bars, the MultiLine property must be set to True.

Second The function Second extracts the seconds from a serial date. If *d* is any valid serial date, the value of Second(*d*) is a whole number from 0 to 59 giving the seconds recorded as part of the date and time stored in *d*. [date]

Seek The statement Seek #*n*, *p* sets the current file position in the binary or random-access file referenced by *n* to the *p*th byte or record of the file, respectively. After the statement is executed, the next Get or Put statement will read or write bytes, respectively, beginning with the *p*th byte or record. The value of the function Seek(*n*) is the current file position either in bytes or by record number. After a Put or Get statement is executed, the value of Seek(*n*) is the number of the next byte or record. [binary file]

Select Case The Select Case statement provides a compact method of selecting for execution one of several blocks of statements based on the value of an expression. The Select Case block begins with a line of the form Select Case *expression* and ends with the statement End Select. In between are statements of the form Case *valueList* and perhaps the statement Case Else. The items in the *valueList* may be individual values, or ranges of values such as "*a* To *b*" or "Is < *a*". Each of these Case statements is followed by a block of one or more statements. The block of statements following the first Case *valueList* statement for which *valueList* includes the value of *expression* is the only block of statements executed. If none of the value lists include the value of *expression* and a Case Else statement is present, then the block of statements following the Case Else statement is executed.

SendKeys The statement SendKeys *str* places in the keyboard buffer the characters and keystrokes specified by *str*. The effect is exactly the same as if the user had typed the series of characters/keystrokes at the keyboard. The statement SendKeys str, True places keystrokes in the keyboard buffer and waits until these keystrokes are processed (used) before allowing program execution to continue with the next statement in the procedure containing the SendKeys statement. Keystrokes can be specified that do not have a displayable character or that result from using the Shift, Ctrl, or Alt keys. See the Visual Basic reference manual or Help for further details.

Set The statement Set *objectVar* = *objectExpression* associates the name *objectVar* with the object identified by *objectExpression*. For example, if the statements Dim Scenery As PictureBox and Set Scenery = Picture1 are executed, then Scenery becomes another name for Picture1, and references like Scenery.Print *message* are equivalent to Picture1.Print *message*.

SetAttr The statement SetAttr *fileName*, *attribute* sets the file attribute of the file specified by *fileName*. A file's attribute can be 0 for "Normal" or a combination of 1, 2, or 4 for "Read-only", "Hidden", and "System." In addition, a file can be marked as "changed since last backup" by adding 32 to its attribute. Thus, for example, if a file's attribute is set to 35 (1+2+32), the file is classified as a Read-only Hidden file that has been changed since the last backup.

SetFocus The method *objectName*.SetFocus moves the focus to the named form or control. Only the object with the focus can receive user input from the keyboard or the mouse. If *objectName* is a form, the form's default control, if any, receives the focus. Disabled and invisible objects cannot receive the focus. If an attempt is made to set focus to a control that cannot receive the focus, the next control in tab order receives the focus.

SetText The method ClipBoard.SetText *info* replaces the contents of the clipboard with the string *info*.

Sgn The value of the function Sgn(x) is 1, 0, or –1, depending upon whether x is positive, zero, or negative, respectively.

Shell If *command* is a DOS command, the function Shell(*command*) causes *command* to be executed. If the DOS command requires user input, execution of the Visual Basic program will be suspended until the user input is supplied. Using the function Shell with no arguments suspends program execution and invokes a copy of DOS. Entering the command Exit resumes execution of the Visual Basic program. The value returned by the Shell function is a number used by Windows to identify the new task being performed.

Show The Show method makes an invisible form visible. The statement Form1.Show 1 also makes a form modal. No user input to any other form will be accepted until the modal form is hidden.

Sin For any number x, the value of the trigonometric function $\text{Sin}(x)$ is the sine of the angle of x radians. [radians]

Single A variable of type Single requires 4 bytes of memory and can hold 0, the numbers from 1.40129×10^{-45} to 3.40283×10^{38} with at most seven significant digits, and the negatives of these numbers. Single values and variables may be indicated by the type tag !: 32.156!, Meters!.

SmallChange When a scroll bar arrow button is clicked, the Value property of the scroll bar changes by the value of the SmallChange property and the thumb moves accordingly.

Sorted When the Sorted property of a list or combo box is set to True, the items are automatically presented in alphabetical order.

Space$ If n is an integer from 0 to 32767, the value of the function $\text{Space\$}(n)$ is the string consisting of n spaces.

Spc The function Spc is used in Print and Print# statements to generate spaces. For instance, the statement Print *str1*; Spc(n); *str2* skips n spaces between the displays of the two strings.

Sqr For any non-negative number x, the value of the square root function $\text{Sqr}(x)$ is the non-negative number whose square is x.

Static A statement of the form Static *var1*, *var2*, . . . can be used at the beginning of the definition of a procedure to specify that the variables *var1*, *var2*, . . . are static local variables in the procedure. Memory for static variables is permanently set aside by Visual Basic, allowing static variables to retain their values between successive calls of the procedure. The type of each variable is either determined by a Def*Type* statement, a type-declaration tag, or an As clause. Static variables have no connection to variables of the same name outside the procedure, and so may be named without regard to "outside" variables. Arrays created in a procedure by ReDim are lost when the procedure is exited. Arrays which are local to a procedure yet retained from one invocation of the procedure to the next can be created by dimensioning the array in the procedure with a Static statement rather than a ReDim statement. Dimensions for static arrays must be numeric constants. A local static array whose size is to be determined at run-time is declared by listing its name followed by empty parentheses in a Static statement, and then dimensioning the array in a subsequent ReDim statement.

Stop The statement Stop suspends the execution of a program. Execution can be resumed beginning with the first statement after the Stop statement by pressing F5.

**Str$** The Str$ function converts numbers to strings. The value of the function $\text{Str\$}(n)$ is the string consisting of the number n in the form normally displayed by a print statement.

StrComp The value of the function StrComp(*str1*, *str2*, *compMode*) is –1, 0, 1, or Null depending on whether *str1* < *str2*, *str1* = *str2*, *str1* > *str2*, or either of *str1* and *str2* is Null. The comparison will be case sensitive if *compMode* is 0 and case insensitive if *compMode* is 1.

Stretch When the Stretch property of an image control is set to False (the default value), the image control will be resized to fit the picture If the Stretch property is set to True, the picture will be resized to fit the image control

String A variable of type String can hold a string of up to 32,767 characters. String values are enclosed in quotes: "January 1, 2001". String variables can be indicated by the type tag $: FirstName$. A variable of type String*n holds a string of n characters, where n is a whole number from 1 to 32,767. Variables of this type have no type tag and must be declared in a Dim, Global, or Static statement. Until assigned a value, these variables contain a string of n Chr$(0)'s.

**String$** If n is a whole number from 0 to 32767, the value of String$(n, str) is the string consisting of the first character of str repeated n times. If m is a whole number from 0 to 255, the value of the function String$(n, m) is the string consisting of the character with ANSI value m repeated n times.

Style The Style property of a combo box determine whether the list is always visible (Style = 1) or whether the list drops down when the user clicks on the arrow and then disappears after a selection is made (Style = 0).

Sub/End Sub A subprogram is a multistatement block beginning with a statement of the form Sub SubprogramName(parList), followed on subsequent lines by one or more statements for carrying out the task of the subprogram, and ending with the statement End Sub. The parameter list parList is a list of variables through which values will be passed to the subprogram whenever the function is called. (See the discussion of Call.) Parameters may be numeric or (variable-length) string variables as well as arrays.

Tab The function Tab(n) is used in Print and Print# statements to move the cursor to position n and place spaces in all skipped-over positions. If n is less than the cursor position, the cursor is moved to the nth position of the next line.

TabIndex The property TabIndex determines the order in which the tab key moves the focus about the objects on a form. Visual Basic automatically assigns successive tab indexes as new controls are created at design time. Visual Basic also automatically prevents two controls on the same form from having the same tab index by renumbering controls with higher tab indexes when the designer or program directly assigns a new tab index to a control.

Tan For any number x (except for $x = \pi/2$, $-\pi/2$, $3*\pi/2$, $-3*\pi/2$, and so on), the value of the trigonometric function $\text{Tan}(x)$ is the tangent of the angle of x radians. [radians]

Text For a text box, the Text property holds the information assigned to a text box. A statement of the form Let textBoxName.Text = str changes the contents of textBoxName to the string specified by str. A statement of the form str = textBoxName.Text assigns the contents of textBoxName to str. For a list or combo box, control.Text is the contents of the currently highlighted item or the item in the text box, respectively. For a grid, Grid1.Text is the contents of the active cell.

TextHeight The value of the method objectName.TextHeight(strVar) is the amount of vertical space required to display the contents of strVar using the font currently assigned for objectName. These contents may include multiple lines of text resulting from the use of carriage return/line feed pairs (Chr$(13) + Chr$(10)) in strVar. The units of height are those specified by the ScaleMode and Scale-Height properties of objectName. (The default is twips.)

TextWidth The value of the method objectName.TextWidth(strVar) is the amount of horizontal space required to display the contents of strVar using the font currently assigned for objectName. When carriage return/line feed pairs

(Chr$(13) + Chr$(10)) create multiple lines in *strVar*, this will be the space required for the longest line.

**Time$** The value of the function Time$ is the current time expressed as a string of the form hh:mm:ss. (The hours range from 0 to 23, as in military time.) If *timeStr* is such a string, the statement Time$ = *timeStr* sets the computer's internal clock to the corresponding time.

Timer The value of the function Timer is the number of seconds from midnight to the time currently stored in the computer's internal clock.

Timer The Timer event is triggered by the passage of the amount of time specified by the Interval property of a timer control whose Enabled property is set to True.

TimeSerial The value of the function TimeSerial(*hour*, *minute*, *second*) is the serial date corresponding to the given hour, minute, and second. Values from 0 (midnight) to 23 (11 P.M.) for *hour*, and 0 to 59 for both *minute* and *second* are normal, but any Integer value may be used. Often, numeric expressions are used for *hour*, *minute*, or *second* that evaluate to numbers outside these ranges. For example, TimeSerial(15–5, 20–30, 0) is the serial time 5 hours and 30 minutes before 3:20 P.M.

TimeValue The value of the function TimeValue(*str*) is the serial date corresponding to the time given in *str*. TimeValue recognizes both the 24-hour and 12-hour time formats: "13:45:24" or "1:45:24PM".

Top The property Top determines the position of the top edge of a form or control. The units of measure are twips for forms. The units of measure for a control are determined by the ScaleMode property of the container (form, picture box, etc.) upon which the control has been placed, with the position of the control measure from the edge of its container using the coordinate system established by the various Scale... properties for the container. By default, the unit of measure for a container is twips, with a value of 0 for the Top property placing the control against the top edge of the container.

**Trim$** The value of the function Trim$(*str*) is the string obtained by removing all the spaces from the beginning and end of the string *str*. The string *str* may be either fixed-length or variable-length.

True A predefined constant whose value is –1. True is used when setting the value of properties that are either True or False. For example, Picture1.FontItalic = True.

Type/End Type A multistatement block beginning the Type *typeName* and ending with End Type creates a user-defined record type. Each statement inside the block has the form *elt* As *type*, where *elt* is a variable and *type* is either Integer, Long, Single, Double, Currency, Variant, String*n (that is, fixed-length string), or another user-defined record type. After a statement of the form Dim *var* As *typeName* appears, the element corresponding to the statement *elt* As *type* is referred to as *var.elt*. Type declaration blocks must be placed in the (declarations) section of a BAS module. [variant]

UBound For a one-dimensional array *arrayName*, the value of the function UBound(*arrayName*) is the largest subscript value that may be used. For any array *arrayName*, the value of the function UBound(*arrayName*, *n*) is the largest subscript value that may be used for the *n*th subscript of the array. For example, after the statement Dim example(1 To 31, 1 To 12, 1990 To 1999) is executed, the value of UBound(example, 3) is the largest value allowed for the third subscript of example( ), which is 1999.

**UCase$** The value of the string function UCase$(*str*) is a string identical to *str* except that all lowercase letters are changed to uppercase.

Unlock The Unlock command is intended for use in programs that operate on a network. The DOS command Share enables file sharing and should be executed from DOS prior to using the Lock and Unlock statements. After a Lock statement has been used to deny access to all or part of a file (see the discussion of Lock for details), a corresponding Unlock statement can be used to restore access. Suppose a data file has been opened as reference number *n*. The locks established by the statements Lock #n; Lock #n, *r1*; and Lock #n, *r1* To *r2* are undone by the statements Unlock #n; Unlock #n, *r1*; and Unlock #n, *r1* To *r2*, respectively. There must be an exact correspondence between the locking and the unlocking statements used in a program; that is, each set of paired statements must refer to the same range of record numbers or bytes.

Update The Update method of a data control is used to save changes made to the database.

Val The Val function is used to convert strings to numbers. If the leading characters of the string *str* corresponds to a number, then Val(*str*) will be the number represented by these characters. For any number *n*, Val(Str$(*n*)) is *n*.

Value The Value property of a scroll bar is a number between the values of the Min and Max properties of the scroll bar that is related to the position of the thumb. The Value property of an option button is True when the button is on and False when the button is off. The Value property of a check box is 0 (unchecked), 1 (checked), or 2 (grayed).

Variant A variable of type variant can be assigned numbers, strings, and several other types of data. Variant variables are written without type declaration tags. [variant]

VarType The value of the function VarType(var) is a number indicating the type of value stored in var. This function is primarily used to check the type of data stored in a variant variable. The values returned by VarType are 0 for "Empty," 1 for "Null," 2 for Integer, 3 for Long Integer, 4 for Single Precision, 5 for Double Precision, 6 for Currency, 7 for Date, and 8 for String. [variant]

Visible The property Visible determines whether or not a form or control is displayed. If the Visible property of an object is True, the object will be displayed (if not covered by other objects) and respond to events if its Enabled property is True. If the Visible property of an object is set to False, the object will not be displayed and cannot respond to events.

WeekDay The value of the function WeekDay(*d*) is a number giving the day of the week for the date store in *d*. These values will range from 1 for Sunday to 7 for Saturday.

While/Wend A While ... Wend loop is a sequence of statements beginning with a statement of the form While *condition* and ending with the statement Wend. After the While statement is executed, the computer repeatedly executes the entire sequence of statements inside the loop as long as the condition is true.

Width (Property) The property Width determines the horizontal size of an object. Width is measured in units of twips. For the Printer object, Width may be read (pw = Printer.Width is ok) but not assigned (Printer.Width = 100 causes an error).

Width (Statement) If *s* is an integer less than 255 and *n* is the reference number of a file opened in sequential mode, the statement Width #n, *s* causes Visual Basic to permit at most *s* characters to be printed on a single line in the file. Visual Basic will send a carriage return/line feed pair to the file after *s* characters have been printed on a line, even if the Print# or Write# statement would not otherwise start a new line at that point. The statement Width #n, 0 specifies infinite width; that is, a carriage return/line feed pair will be sent to the printer only when requested by Print# or Write#.

WordWrap The WordWrap property of a label with AutoSize property set to True determines whether or not long captions will wrap. (When a label's AutoSize property is False, word wrap always occurs, but the additional lines will not be visible if the label is not tall enough.) Assume a label's AutoSize property is True. If its WordWrap property is set to True, long captions will wrap to multiple lines; if its WordWrap property is False (the default), the caption will always occupy a single line. If a label has its WordWrap and AutoSize property set to True, the label's horizontal length is determined by its Width property, with long captions being accommodated by having the label expand vertically so that word wrap can spread the caption over several lines. If a label's WordWrap property is set to False while its AutoSize property is True, the label will be one line high and will expand or shrink horizontally to exactly accommodate its caption.

Write# After a sequential file is opened for output or append with reference number *n*, the statement Write #n, *exp1*, *exp2*, . . . records the values of the expressions one after the other into the file. Strings appear surrounded by quotation marks, numbers do not have leading or trailing spaces, all commas in the expressions are recorded, and the characters for carriage return and line feed are placed following the data.

Xor (Logical Operator) The logical expression *condition1* Xor *condition2* is true if *condition1* is true or *condition2* is true, but not if both are true. For example, (3<7) Xor ("abc">"a") is false since both 3<7 and "abc">"a" are true, while ("apple">"ape") Xor ("earth">"moon") is true since "apple">"ape" is true and "earth">"moon" is false.

Xor (Bitwise Operator) The expression *byte1* Xor *byte2* is evaluated by expressing each byte as an 8-tuple binary number and then Xoring together corresponding digits, where 1 Xor 0 and 0 Xor 1 both equal 1, while 1 Xor 1 and 0 Xor 0 both equal 0. For example, the expression 37 Xor 157 translated to binary 8-tuples becomes 00100101 Xor 10011101. Xoring together corresponding digits gives the binary 8-tuple 10111000 or decimal 184. Thus 37 Xor 157 is 184.

Year The function Year extracts the year from a serial date. If *d* is any valid serial date, then the value of Year(*d*) is a whole number from 100 to 9999 giving the year recorded as part of the date and time stored in *d*. [date]

Supporting Topics

[binary file]: A file that has been opened with a statement of the form Open *"filespec"* For Binary As *#n* is regarded simply as a sequence of characters occupying positions 1, 2, 3, ... At any time, a specific location in the file is designated as the "current position." The Seek statement can be is used to set the current position. Collections of consecutive characters are written to and read from the file beginning at the current position with Put and Get statements, respectively. After a Put or Get statement is executed, the position following the last position accessed becomes the new current position.

[color]: Numbers written in base 16 are referred to as hexadecimal numbers. They are written with the digits 0, 1, 2, 3, 4, 5, 6, 7, 8, 9, A (=10), B (=11), C (=12), D (=13), E (=14), and F (=15). A hexadecimal number such as *rst* corresponds to the decimal integer $t + 16*s + 16^2*r$. Each color in Visual Basic is identified by a long integer (usually expressed as a hexadecimal number of the form &H...&) and referred to as an RGB color number. This number specifies the amounts of red, green, and blue combined to produce the color. The amount of any color is a relative quantity, with 0 representing none of the color and 255 representing the maximum available. Thus black corresponds to 0 units each of red, green, and blue, while white corresponds to 255 units each of red, green, and blue. The RGB color number corresponding to *r* units of red, *g* units of green, and *b* units of blue is $r+256*g+65536*b$, which is the value returned by the function RGB(*r*, *g*, *b*). Hexadecimal notation provides a fairly easy means of specifying RGB color numbers. If the amount of red desired is expressed as a two-digit hexadecimal number, *rr*, the amount of green in hexadecimal as *gg*, and the amount of blue in hexadecimal as *bb*, then the RGB color number for this color is &H00*bbggrr*&. For example, the RGB color number for a bright green would come from 255 (FF in hexadecimal) units of green, so the RGB color number in hexadecimal is &H0000FF00&.

[coordinate systems]: The default coordinate system for a form, picture box, or the printer defines the upper-left corner as the point (0, 0). In this coordinate system, the point (*x*, *y*) lies *x* units to the right of and *y* units below the upper-left corner. The unit of measure in the default coordinate system is a twip. A twip is defined as 1/1440 of an inch (though varying screen sizes may result in 1440 twips not appearing as exactly an inch on the screen). Custom coordinate systems can be created using the Scale method and ScaleMode property.

[date]: Functions dealing with dates and times use the type 7 variant data type. Dates and times are stored as serial dates, double-precision numbers, with the whole part recording the date and the decimal part recording the time. Valid whole parts range from –657434 to 2958465, which correspond to all days from January 1, 100 to December, 31, 9999. A whole part of 0 corresponds to December 30, 1899. All decimal parts are valid, with .0 corresponding to midnight, .25 corresponding to 6 a.m., .5 corresponding to noon, and so on. In general, the decimal equivalent of *sec*/86400 corresponds to *sec* seconds past midnight. If a given date corresponds to a negative whole part, then times on that day are obtained by adding a negative decimal part to the negative whole part. For example, October, 24, 1898, corresponds to a whole part of –432. A time of 6 p.m. corresponds to .75, so a time of 6 p.m. on 10/24/1898 corresponds to –432 +–.75 = –432.75.

[directories]: Think of a disk as a master folder holding other folders, each of which might hold yet other folders. Each folder, other than the master folder, has a name. Each folder is identified by a *path:* a string beginning with a drive letter, a colon, and a backslash character, ending with the name of the folder to be identified, and listing the names of the intermediate folders (in order) separated by backslashes. For instance the path "C:\DAVID\GAMES" identifies the folder GAMES which is contained in the folder DAVID, which in turn is contained in the master folder of drive C.

Each folder is called a *directory* and the master folder is called the *root directory*. When a folder is opened, the revealed folders are referred to as its *subdirectories*. Think of a file as a piece of paper inside one of the folders. Thus, each directory contains files and subdirectories.

At any time, one of the directories is said to be the *current directory*. Initially the root directory is the current directory. The current directory can be changed from DOS with the CD command or from Visual Basic with the ChDir command. DOS and Visual Basic statements that access files, such as Dir$, act on the files in the current directory unless otherwise directed.

The *default drive* is the drive whose letter appeared in the DOS prompt when Windows was invoked. If a drive is missing from a path, the drive is assumed to be the default drive.

[dynamic vs. static]: Visual Basic uses two methods of storing arrays: dynamic and static. The memory locations for a static array are set aside the instant the program is executed and this portion of memory may not be freed for any other purpose. The memory locations for a dynamic array are assigned when a particular procedure requests that an array be created (a ReDim statement is encountered) and *can* be freed for other purposes. Although dynamic arrays are more flexible, static arrays can be accessed faster. Arrays Dimensioned in the (declarations) section of (general) use static allocation, except for arrays declared using empty parentheses. Arrays created by using the ReDim statement in procedures use dynamic allocation.

[filespec]: The filespec of a file on disk is a string consisting of the letter of the drive, a colon, and the name of the file. If directories are being used, the file name is preceded by the identifying path.

[line label]: Program lines that are the destinations of statements such as GoTo and GoSub are identified by placing a line label at the beginning of the program line or alone on the line proceeding the program line. Line labels may be placed only at the beginning of a line, are named using the same rules as variable, and are followed by a colon. Line numbers may be used in place of line labels, but program readability is greatly improved by using descriptive line labels.

[radians]: The radian system of measurement measures angles in terms of a distance around the circumference of the circle of radius 1. If the vertex of an angle between 0 and 360 degrees is placed at the center of the circle, the length of the arc of the circle contained between the two sides of the angle is the radian measure of the angle. An angle of d degrees has a radian measure of $(pi/180)*d$ radians.

[subroutine]: A subroutine is a sequence of statements beginning with a line label and ending with a Return statement. A subroutine is meant to be branched to by a GoSub statement and is usually placed after an Exit Sub or Exit Function statement at the bottom of a procedure so that it cannot be entered inadvertently.

[**variant**]: Variant is a generic variable type. Any variable that is used without a type declaration tag ($, %, &, !, #, @) or without being declared as a specific type using an As clause or a Def*Type* statement is treated as a variant variable. A variable of type Variant can hold any type of data. When values are assigned to a variant variable, Visual Basic keeps track of the "type" of data that has been stored. Visual Basic recognizes eight types of data: type 0 for "Empty" (nothing yet has been stored in the variable; the default), type 1 for "Null" (the special value Null has been assigned to the variable), type 2 for Integer, type 3 for Long integer, type 4 for Single precision, type 5 for Double precision, type 6 for Currency, type 7 for Date/time, and type 8 for String. A single variant variable may be assigned different data types at different points in a program, although this is usually not a good programming technique. The data assigned to a variant array need not all be of the same type. As a result, a variant array can be used in much the same way as a user-defined type to store related data.

Appendix D

Visual Basic Debugging Tools

Errors in programs are called *bugs* and the process of finding and correcting them is called *debugging*. Since Visual Basic does not discover errors due to faulty logic, they present the most difficulties in debugging. One method of discovering a logical error is by **desk checking**, that is, tracing the values of variables on paper by writing down their expected value after "mentally executing" each line in the program. Desk checking is rudimentary and highly impractical except for small programs.

Another method of debugging involves placing Print methods at strategic points in the program and displaying the values of selected variables or expressions until the error is detected. After correcting the error, the Print methods are removed. For many programming environments, desk checking and Print methods are the only debugging methods available to the programmer.

The Visual Basic debugger, used in conjunction with the Debug window, offers an alternative to desk checking and Print methods. The debugging tools are invoked from the Debug menu.

Using the Visual Basic Debugger

The three main features of the Visual Basic debugger are stepping, breakpoints, and printing in the Debug window.

The program can be executed one statement at a time, with each press of an appropriate function key executing a statement. This process is called **stepping**. After each step, values of variables, expressions, and conditions can be displayed in the Debug window, and the values of variables can be changed.

When a procedure is called, the lines of the procedure can be executed one at a time, referred to as "stepping through the procedure," or the entire procedure can be executed at once, referred to as "stepping over a procedure." A step over a procedure is called a **procedure step**.

Stepping begins with the first statement of the first event procedure invoked by the user. Program execution normally proceeds in order through the statements in the event procedure. However, at any time the programmer can specify the next statement to be executed.

As another debugging tool, Visual Basic allows the programmer to specify certain lines as **breakpoints**. Then, when the program is run, execution will stop at the first breakpoint reached. The programmer can then either step through the program or continue execution to the next breakpoint.

The tasks discussed above are summarized below, along with a means to carry out each task. The tasks invoked with function keys can also be produced from the menu bar.

Step (ordinary):	Press F8
Procedure step:	Press Shift+F8
Set a breakpoint:	Move cursor to line, press F9
Remove a breakpoint:	Move cursor to line containing breakpoint, press F9
Clear all breakpoints:	Press Alt/D/L
Set next statement:	Press Alt/D/N
Continue execution to next breakpoint or the end of the program:	Press F5
Open Debug window to display or change values:	Ctrl+B
Return to the code window from the Debug Window:	Press F7

Six Walkthroughs

The following walkthroughs use the debugging tools with the programming structures covered in Chapters 3, 4, 5, and 6.

Stepping Through an Elementary Program: Chapter 3

The following walkthrough demonstrates several capabilities of the debugger.

1. Create a form with a command button and a picture box. Then open the Code window and enter the following procedure:

```
Sub Command1_Click()
  Dim num As Single
  Picture1.Cls
  Let num = Val(InputBox$("Enter a number:"))
  Let num = num + 1
  Let num = num + 2
  Picture1.Print num
End Sub
```

2. Press F8 and click the command button. The Picture1.Cls statement is highlighted by being enclosed in a gray box. This indicates that the Picture1.Cls statement is the next statement to be executed.

3. Press F8. The Picture1.Cls statement is executed and the statement involving InputBox$ is highlighted to indicate that it is the next statement to be executed.

4. Press F8 to execute the statement containing InputBox$ and respond to the request by entering 5.

5. Press Alt+F4 to end the program.

6. Move the cursor to the line Let num = num + 2. Press F9 to highlight the line and set it as a breakpoint. (Pressing F9 has the same consequence as invoking the "Toggle Breakpoint" option from the Debug menu by pressing Alt/D/T.)

7. Press F5 and click on the command button. Respond to the request by entering 5. The program executes the first three lines and stops at the breakpoint. The breakpoint line is not executed.

8. Open the Debug window by pressing Ctrl+B. Type the statement

```
Print "num ="; num
```

into the Debug window and then press Enter to execute the statement. The appearance of "num = 6" on the next line of the Debug window confirms that the breakpoint line was not executed.

9. Press F7 to return to the Code window.

10. Move the cursor to the line Let num = num + 1 and then press Alt/D/N to specify that line as the next line to be executed.

11. Press F8 to execute the selected line.

12. Press Ctrl+B to return to the Debug window. Move the cursor to the line containing the print statement and press Enter to confirm that the value of *num* is now 7. Return to the Code window.

13. Move the cursor to the breakpoint line and press F9 to deselect the line as a breakpoint.

14. Press F5 to execute the remaining lines of the program. The value displayed is 9.

Stepping Through a Program Containing an Ordinary Procedure: Chapter 4

The following walkthrough uses the single-stepping feature of the debugger to trace the flow through a program and a subprogram Call.

1. Create a form with a command button and a picture box. Then open the Code window and enter the following two procedures:

```
Sub Command1_Click()
  Dim p As Single, b As Single
  Picture1.Cls
  Let p = 1000    'Principal
  Call GetBalance(p, b)
  Picture1.Print "The balance is"; b
End Sub

Sub GetBalance (prin As Single, bal As Single)
  Dim interest As Single
  Rem Calculate the balance at 5% interest rate
  Let interest = .05 * prin
  Let bal = prin + interest
End Sub
```

2. Press F8 and click the command button. The Picture1.Cls statement is highlighted to indicate that it is the next statement to be executed.

3. Press F8 two more times. The Call statement is highlighted.

4. Press F8 once and observe that the subprogram GetBalance is now displayed on the screen with its first executable statement highlighted. (The subprogram heading and Rem statement have been skipped.)

5. Press F8 twice to execute the Let statements and to highlight the End Sub statement.

6. Press F8 and notice that the Command1_Click event procedure is again displayed in the Code window with the highlight on the statement immediately following the Call statement.

7. Press Alt+F4 to end the program.

Communication Between Arguments and Parameters

The following walkthrough uses the Debug window to monitor the values of arguments and parameters during the execution of a program.

1. If you have not already done so, type the preceding program into the Code window.

2. Press F8, click the command button, then press F8 two more times to highlight the Call statement.

3. Press Ctrl+B to activate the Debug window. Enter the following statement to display the values of p and b:

```
Print "p ="; p, "b ="; b
```

4. Press F8 to call the subprogram

5. Press Ctrl+B to return to the Debug Window. Enter the following statement to display the values of $prin$ and bal. The variables $prin$ and bal have inherited the values of p and b.

```
Print "prin ="; prin, "bal ="; bal
```

6. Press F8 twice to execute the subprogram.

7. Press Ctrl+B to return to the Debug window, then display the values of $prin$ and bal.

8. Press F8 to return to Command1_Click event procedure.

9. Activate the Debug window and display the values of p and b. The variable b now has the same value as the variable bal.

10. Press Alt+F4 to end the program.

Stepping Through Programs Containing Selection Structures: Chapter 5

If Blocks

The following walkthrough demonstrates how an If statement evaluates a condition to determine whether to take an action.

1. Create a form with a command button and a picture box. Then open the Code window and enter the following procedure:

```
Sub Command1_Click()
   Dim wage As Single
   Picture1.Cls
   Let wage = Val(InputBox$("wage:"))
   If wage < 4.25 Then
       Picture1.Print "Below minimum wage."
     Else
       Picture1.Print "Wage Ok."
   End If
End Sub
```

2. Press F8, click the command button, and press F8 again. The Picture1.Cls statement will be highlighted and executed. Then the statement containing InputBox$ will be highlighted.

3. Press F8 once to execute the statement containing InputBox$. Type a wage of 3.25 and press the Enter key. The If statement is highlighted, but has not been executed.

4. Press F8 once and notice that the highlight for the current statement has jumped to the statement Picture1.Print "Below minimum wage." Since the condition "wage < 4.25" is true, the action associated with Then was selected.

5. Press F8 to execute the Picture1.Print statement. Notice that Else, the statement immediately following the Picture1.Print statement, is highlighted.

6. Press F8 again. Since the Else action is bypassed, we are through with the If block, and the statement following the If block, End Sub, is highlighted.

7. Press Alt+F4 to end the program.

8. If desired, try stepping through the program again with 5.75 entered as the wage. Since the condition "wage < 4.25" will be false, the Else action will be executed instead of the Then action.

Select Case Blocks

The following walkthrough illustrates how a Select Case block uses the selector to choose from among several actions.

1. Create a form with a command button and a picture box. Then open the Code window and enter the following procedure:

```
Sub Command1_Click()
   Dim age As Single, price As Single
   Picture1.Cls
   Let age = Val(InputBox$("age:"))
   Select Case age
     Case Is < 12
       Let price = 0
```

```
              Case Is < 18
                Let price = 3.5
              Case Is >= 65
                Let price = 4
              Case Else
                Let price = 5.5
           End Select
           Picture1.Print "Your ticket price is "; Format$(price, "Currency")
        End Sub
```

2. Press F8, click on the command button, and press F8 again. The Picture1.Cls statement will be highlighted and executed, and then the statement containing InputBox$ will be highlighted.

3. Press F8 once to execute the statement containing InputBox$. Type an age of 8 and press the Enter key. The Select Case statement is highlighted, but has not been executed.

4. Press F8 once and observe that the action associated with Case Is < 12 is highlighted.

5. Press F8 once to execute the Let statement. Notice that the clause following the Let statement, "Case Is < 18," is highlighted.

6. Press F8 once. Observe that although the selector, *age*, is less than 18, the action associated with that Case clause was ignored and the highlight jumped outside the Select Case block to the Picture1.Print statement. This demonstrates that when more than one Case clause is true, only the first is acted upon.

7. Press Alt+F4 to end the program.

8. If desired, step through the program again, entering a different age and predicting which Case clause will be acted upon.

Stepping Through a Program Containing a Do Loop: Chapter 6

Do Loops

The following walkthrough demonstrates use of the Debug window to monitor the value of a condition in a Do loop that searches for a name.

1. Access Windows' Notepad, enter the following line of data, and save the file on the A drive with the name DATA.TXT

```
Bert, Ernie, Grover, Oscar
```

2. Return to Visual Basic. Create a form with a command button and a picture box. Then open the Code window and enter the following procedure:

```
Sub Command1_Click()
   Dim searchName As String, nom As String
   Rem Look for a specific name
   Picture1.Cls
```

```
      Let searchName = InputBox$("Name:") 'Name to search for in list
      Open "A:DATA.TXT" For Input As #1
      Let nom = ""
      Do While (nom <> searchName) And Not EOF(1)
        Input #1, nom
      Loop
      If nom = searchName Then
          Picture1.Print nom
        Else
          Picture1.Print "Name not found"
      End If
End Sub
```

3. Press F8, click on the command button, then press F8 two more times to execute the Picture1.Cls statement and the statement containing Input-Box$. Enter the name "Ernie" at the prompt.

4. Press F8 twice to execute the Open statement and initialize the variable *nom*.

5. Press Ctrl+B to activate the Debug window.

6. Enter the following line,

```
Print searchName, nom, (searchName <> nom) And Not EOF(1)
```

7. As expected, the search name displays as "Ernie" and the zone for the variable *nom* is blank since *nom* is currently the empty string. The value of the While condition is displayed as –1. (True conditions are displayed as –1; false conditions are displayed as 0.) Since both the condition (nom <> searchName) and the condition Not EOF(1) are true, the compound condition is true.

8. Press F8 once. Since the While condition is true, the Do loop is entered.

9. Press F8 once to input the first item from the DATA.TXT file.

10. Press Ctrl+B to activate the Debug window. Move the cursor to the Print statement and press Enter. The value of *nom* is now "Bert." Although the highlight is on the word Loop, Visual Basic is really preparing to evaluate the While condition to see if the loop should be executed again.

11. Press F8. Since the While condition is true, the statement inside the loop is highlighted.

12. Press F8 to input the next item from the DATA.TXT file.

13. Execute the Print statement in the Debug window. Since *searchName* and *nom* have the value "Ernie", the condition (nom <> searchName) is false. Hence the entire While condition is false, and is displayed with the value 0.

14. Press F8 once. Since the While condition has become false, the highlight will move from the Loop statement to the statement immediately following the Do loop, that is, to the statement If nom = searchName Then.

15. Press Alt+F4 to end the program.

Answers

To Selected Odd-Numbered Exercises

CHAPTER 1

Exercises 1.2

1. COPY
3. RENAME
5. DIR
7. MD
9. RD

11. **a)** File name has 9 characters before the period; only 8 are allowed.
    b) Slashes are forward slashes; should be backwards slashes (\ ).
    c) The symbols < and > cannot be used as part of a filespec.
    d) File name has 4 characters after the period; only 3 are allowed.
    e) The symbol * cannot be used as part of a filespec.
    f) The symbol : can be used only after a drive letter at the beggining of a filespec.

Exercises 1.3

1. The program is busy carrying out a task, please wait.
5. Type WIN and press the Enter key. If this fails, enter CD \WINDOWS and then enter WIN.
7. Starting with an uppercase W, Windows refers to Microsoft's Windows program. Starting with a lowercase w, windows refers to the rectangular regions of the screen in which different programs are displayed.
9. Double-click on the Notepad icon.
11. (Untitled)
13. A toggle is a key like the Ins, NumLock and CapsLock keys that changes keyboard operations back and forth between two different typing modes.
15. Backspace

17. NumLock
19. CapsLock
21. End
23. Shift
25. Alt/F/P
27. Ctrl+Home
29. Alt
31. Alt
33. Alt/F/N
35. End/Enter
37. PgUp

CHAPTER 3

Exercises 3.1

1. Command buttons appear to be pushed down and then let up when they are clicked.

3. After a command button is clicked, its border becomes boldfaced and a rounded rectangle of small dots surrounds the caption.

(In Exercises 7 through 27, begin by pressing Alt/F/N to create a new form.)

7. Click on the Properties window or Press F4 to activate the Properties window.
   Press Shift+Ctrl+C to highlight the Caption property.
   Type in "CHECKING ACCOUNT".
9. Double-click the text box icon in the toolbox.
   Activate the Properties window and highlight the BackColor property.

Click on the ". . ." icon to the right of the Settings box.

Click on the desired yellow in the palette.

Press Shift+Ctrl+T followed by three down-arrows to highlight the Text property.

Click on the settings box and delete "Text1".

Click on the form to see the empty, yellow text box.

11. Double-click on the text box icon in the toolbox.

Activate the Properties window and highlight the Text property.

Type the requested sentence.

Highlight the MultiLine property.

Double-click on the highlighted MultiLine property to change its value to True.

Highlight the Alignment property.

Double-click twice on the highlighted Alignment property to change its value to 2-Center.

Click on the form.

Use the mouse to resize the text box so that the sentence occupies three lines.

13. Double-click on the text box icon in the toolbox.

Activate the Properties window and highlight the Text property.

Type "VISUAL BASIC".

Highlight the FontName property.

Click on the underlined down-arrow icon to the right of the Settings box.

Click on "Courier".

Click on the form to see the resulting text box.

15. Double-click on the command button icon in the toolbox.

Activate the Properties window and highlight the Caption property.

Type "PUSH".

Highlight the FontItalic property.

Type T and press Enter to change the property to True.

Change the FontSize property to the largest font size available (24 point).

Click on the form to see the resulting command button.

Resize the command button to properly accommodate its caption.

17. Double-click on the command button icon in the toolbox.

Activate the Properties window and highlight the Caption property.

Type "PUS&H".

Click on the form to see the resulting command button.

19. Double-click on the label icon in the toolbox.

Activate the Properties window and highlight the Caption property.

Type "ALIAS".

Click on the form to see the resulting label.

21. Double-click on the label icon in the toolbox.

Activate the Properties window and highlight the Alignment property.

Double-click twice on the highlighted Alignment property to change its value to "2-Center".

Highlight the Caption property.

Type "ALIAS".

Double-click on the BorderStyle property to change its value to "1–Fixed Single".

Highlight the FontItalic property.

Type T and press Enter to change the property to True.

Click on the form to see the resulting label.

23. Double-click on the label icon in the toolbox.

Activate the Properties window and highlight the FontName property.

Click on the underlined down-arrow icon to the right of the Settings box.

Type W and press Enter to select the Wingdings font.

Highlight the FontSize property.

Click on the underlined down-arrow icon to the right of the Settings box.

Click on largest font size available (24 point).

As one means of determining which keystroke in the Wingdings font corresponds to a diskette, follow these steps:

a) Press Alt+Esc until Window's Program Manager appears.
b) Double-click on the Accessories icon.
c) Double-click on the Character Map icon.
d) Click in the font box and press W to view the Wingdings font.
e) Click on the diskette character (4th from the end of the first row).
f) Note at the bottom of the font map window that the keystroke for the diskette character is a less than sign.
g) Close the Character Map and Accessories windows and use Alt+Esc to return to Visual Basic.

Highlight the Caption property.

Change the caption to a less than sign by pressing <.

Click on the form to see the resulting label.

25. Double-click on the picture box icon in the toolbox.

Activate the Properties window and highlight the BackColor property.

Click on the ". . ." icon to the right of the Settings box.

Click on the desired yellow in the palette.

Click on the form to see the yellow picture box.

27. Double-click on the picture box icon in the toolbox.

Increase the size of the picture box so that it can easily hold two standard size command buttons.

Click (do Not double-click) on the command button icon in the toolbox.

Move the mouse to the desired location in the picture box of the upper left corner of the first command button.

Press and hold the left mouse button and drag the mouse down and to the right until the rectangle attains the size desired for the first command button

Release the left mouse button.

Repeat the above four steps (starting with clicking on the command button icon in the toolbox) to place the second command button on the picture box.

29. Create a new project. Change its caption to "Dynamic Duo". Place two command buttons on the form. Enter as the caption of the first "&Batman" and of the second "&Robin". Increase the font size for both command buttons to 13.5.

31. Create a new project. Change its caption to "Fill in the Blank". Place a label, a text box, and another label on the form at appropriate locations. Change the caption of the first label to "Toto, I don't think we're in" and of the second label to "A Quote from the Wizard of Oz". Delete "Text1" from the text property of the text box. Resize and position the labels as needed.

33. Create a new project. Change its caption to "An Uncle's Advice". Place a picture box on the form and increase its size to provide plenty of space. Place on the picture box five labels and three command buttons. Change the captions of each label to the appropriate text. Change the BorderStyle property of the last label to "1–Fixed Single". Change the captions of the command buttons to "1", "2", and "3". Resize and position the labels and command buttons as is appropriate. Finally, the size of the picture box can be adjusted down as appropriate.

Exercises 3.2

1. The word Hello.

3. The word Hello in italic letters.

5. The text box vanishes; nothing is visible.

7. The word Hello in green letters.

9. The word Hello in big, fixed-spaced letters.

11. The name of the control has been given but not the property being assigned; Let Text1 ="Hello" needs to be changed to Let Text1.Text = "Hello".

13. Text boxes do not have a Caption property. Information to be displayed in a text box must be assigned to the Text property.

15. Only 0 and 1 are valid values for the BorderStyle property of a label.

17. `Let Label2.Caption = "E.T. phone home."`

19. `Let Text1.ForeColor = &HFF&`
    `Let Text1.Text = "The stuff that dreams are made of."`

21. `Let Text1.Text = ""`

23. `Let Label2.Visible = False`

25. `Let Picture1.BackColor = &HFF0000&`

27. `Let Text1.FontBold = True`
    `Let Text1.FontItalic = True`
    `Let Text1.Text = "Hello"`

29. `Command1.SetFocus`

31. `Let Label2.BorderStyle = 1`
    `Let Label2.Alignment = 2`

37.
```
Sub Command1_Click ()
   Let Label1.Alignment = 0
   Let Label1.Caption = "Left Justify"
End Sub

Sub Command2_Click ()
   Let Label1.Alignment = 2
   Let Label1.Caption = "Center"
End Sub

Sub Command3_Click ()
   Let Label1.Alignment = 1
   Let Label1.Caption = "Right Justify"
End Sub
```

35. Create a new project. Change its caption to "A Picture". Place a picture box and a label on the form. Change the label's caption to "LEAVES.BMP" or some other .BMP file and its BorderStyle property to "1–Fixed Single". Access the picture box's Picture property and select the LEAVES.BMP, or other, picture from the WINDOWS directory.

39.
```
Sub Command1_Click ()
   Let Text1.BackColor = &HFF&
End Sub

Sub Command2_Click ()
   Let Text1.BackColor = &HFF0000&
End Sub

Sub Command3_Click ()
   Let Text1.ForeColor = &HFFFFFF&
End Sub

Sub Command4_Click ()
   Let Text1.ForeColor = &HFFFF&
End Sub
```

41.
```
Sub Text2.GotFocus ()
   Let Text1.Text = "I like life, it's something to do."
End Sub

Sub Text3.GotFocus ()
   Let Text1.Text = "The future isn't what it used to be."
End Sub

Sub Text4.GotFocus ()
   Let Text1.Text = "Tell the truth and run."
End Sub
```

43.

Object	Property	Setting
Command1	Caption	Large
Command2	Caption	Small
Command3	Caption	Bold
Command4	Caption	Italic
Text1	Text	(blank)

```
Sub Command1_Click ()
   Let Text1.FontSize = 18
End Sub

Sub Command2_Click ()
   Let Text1.FontSize = 8.25
End Sub

Sub Command3_Click ()
   Let Text1.FontBold = True
   Let Text1.FontItalic = False
End Sub

Sub Command4_Click ()
   Let Text1.FontItalic = True
   Let Text1.FontBold = False
End Sub
```

45.

Object	Property	Setting
Form1	Caption	Face
Label1	FontName	Wingdings
	Caption	K
	FontSize	24
Command1	Caption	Vanish
Command2	Caption	Reappear

```
Sub Command1_Click ()
  Let Label1.Visible = False
End Sub

Sub Command2_Click ()
  Let Label1.Visible = True
End Sub
```

47.

Object	Property	Setting
Command1	Caption	Push Me
Command2	Caption	Push Me
Command3	Caption	Push Me
Command4	Caption	Push Me

```
Sub Command1_Click ()
  Let Command1.Visible = False
  Let Command2.Visible = True
  Let Command3.Visible = True
  Let Command4.Visible = True
End Sub

Sub Command2_Click ()
  Let Command1.Visible = True
  Let Command2.Visible = False
  Let Command3.Visible = True
  Let Command4.Visible = True
End Sub

Sub Command3_Click ()
  Let Command1.Visible = True
  Let Command2.Visible = True
  Let Command3.Visible = False
  Let Command4.Visible = True
End Sub

Sub Command4_Click ()
  Let Command1.Visible = True
  Let Command2.Visible = True
  Let Command3.Visible = True
  Let Command4.Visible = False
End Sub
```

Exercises 3.3

1. 12

3. .03125

5. 8

7. 3E+09

9. 4E-08

11. Valid

13. Valid

15. Not valid

17. 10

19. 16

21. 9

23.
```
Sub Command1_Click ()
  Picture1.Cls
  Picture1.Print 7 * 8 + 5
End Sub
```

25.
```
Sub Command1_Click ()
  Picture1.Cls
  Picture1.Print .055 * 20
End Sub
```

27.
```
Sub Command1_Click ()
  Picture1.Cls
  Picture1.Print 17 * (3 + 162)
End Sub
```

29.

x	y
2	0
2	6
11	6
11	6
11	6
11	7

31. 6

33. 1 2 3 4
11

35. 0
64

37. 27 12

39. The third line should read Let c = a + b

41. The first line should not contain a comma. The second line should not contain a dollar sign.

43.
```
Sub Command1_Click ()
  Picture1.Cls
  Picture1.Print 1; 2; 1 + 2
End Sub
```

45.
```
Sub Command1_Click ()
  Picture1.Cls
  Let revenue = 98456
  Let costs = 45000
  Let profit = revenue - costs
  Picture1.Print profit
End Sub
```

47.
```
Sub Command1_Click ()
    Picture1.Cls
    Let price = 19.95
    Let discountPercent = 30
    Let markDown = (discountPercent / 100) * price
    Let price = price - markDown
    Picture1.Print price
End Sub
```

49.
```
Sub Command1_Click ()
    Picture1.Cls
    Let balance = 100
    Let balance = balance + balance * .05
    Let balance = balance + balance * .05
    Let balance = balance + balance * .05
    Picture1.Print balance
End Sub
```

51.
```
Sub Command1_Click ()
    Picture1.Cls
    Let balance = 100
    Let balance = balance * (1.05 ^ 10)
    Picture1.Print balance
End Sub
```

53.
```
Sub Command1_Click ()
    Picture1.Cls
    Let acres = 30
    Let yieldPerAcre = 18
    Let corn = yieldPerAcre * acres
    Picture1.Print corn
End Sub
```

55.
```
Sub Command1_Click ()
    Picture1.Cls
    Let distance = 233
    Let elapsedTime = 7 - 2
    Let averageSpeed = distance / elapsedTime
    Picture1.Print averageSpeed
End Sub
```

57.
```
Sub Command1_Click ()
    Picture1.Cls
    Let waterPerPersonPerDay = 1600
    Let people = 260000000
    Let days = 365
    Let waterUsed = waterPerPersonPerDay * people * days
    Picture1.Print waterUsed
End Sub
```

Exercises 3.4

1.
```
Hello
1234
```

3. `12 12 TWELVE`

5. `A ROSE IS A ROSE IS A ROSE`

7. `  1234 Main Street`

9. `"We're all in this alone."  Lily Tomlin`

11.
```
17 2
-20 0
```

23.
```
Sub Command1_Click ()
    Dim firstName As String, middleName As String
    Dim lastName As String, yearOfBirth As Single
    Picture1.Cls
    Let firstName = "Thomas"
    Let middleName = "Alva"
    Let lastName = "Edison"
    Let yearOfBirth = 1847
    Picture1.Print firstName; " "; middleName; " "; lastName; ","; yearOfBirth
End Sub
```

25.
```
Sub Command1_Click ()
    Dim publisher As String
    Picture1.Cls
    Let publisher = "Prentice-Hall, Inc."
    Picture1.Print Chr$(169) + " " + publisher
End Sub
```

27.
```
Sub Command3_Click ()
    Picture1.Print Val(Text1.Text) + Val(Text2.Text)
End Sub
```

29.
```
Sub Command1_Click ()
    Let Label3.Caption = Str$(Val(Text1.Text) / 5)
End Sub
```

31.
```
Sub Command1_Click ()
    Dim cycling As Single, running As Single, swimming As Single, pounds As Single
    Picture1.Cls
    Let cycling = Val(Text1.Text)
    Let running = Val(Text2.Text)
    Let swimming = Val(Text3.Text)
    Let pounds = (200 * cycling + 475 * running + 275 * swimming) / 3500
    Picture1.Print pounds; "pounds were lost."
End Sub
```

13. The number of digits in 3567 is 4

15. The variable phone should be delcared as type String, not Single.

17. The sentence in the second line should be enclosed by quotation marks.

19. End is a keyword and cannot be used as a variable name.

33.

Object	Property	Setting
Form1	Caption	Net Income
Label1	Caption	Revenue
Text1	Text	(blank)
Label2	Caption	Expenses
Text2	Text	(blank)
Command1	Caption	Display Net Income
Picture1		

```
Sub Command1_Click ()
    Dim income As Single
    Rem Compute Net Income based on revenue and expenses
    Picture1.Cls
    Let income = Val(Text1.Text) - Val(Text2.Text)
    Picture1.Print "The company's net income is"; income
End Sub
```

35.

Object	Property	Setting
Form1	Caption	Price to Earnings Ratio
Label1	Caption	Price
Text1	Text	(blank)
Label2	Caption	Earnings
Text2	Text	(blank)
Command1	Caption	Display PER
Picture1		

```
Sub Command1_Click ()
    Dim per As Single
    Rem Compute Price to Earnings Ratio
    Picture1.Cls
    Let per = Val(Text1.Text) / Val(Text2.Text)
    Picture1.Print "The price to earnings ratio is"; per
End Sub
```

37.

Object	Property	Setting
Form1	Caption	Grass Seed
Label1	Caption	Ounces of seed recommended for 2000 square feet of lawn
Text1	Text	(blank)
Label2	Caption	Width of lawn in feet
Text2	Text	(blank)
Label3	Caption	Length of lawn in feet
Text3	Text	(blank)
Command1	Caption	Display Seed Needed
Picture1		

```
Sub Command1_Click ()
    Dim lbSeedPerFt As Single,area As Single, grassSeed As Single
    Rem Compute amount of grass seed needed for a given lawn.
    Picture1.Cls
    Let lbSeedPerFt = (Val(Text1.Text) / 16) / 2000
    Let area = Val(Text2.Text) * Val(Text3.Text)
    Let grassSeed = lbSeedPerFt * area
    Picture1.Print grassSeed; "pounds of grass seed are needed."
End Sub
```

39.

Object	Property	Setting
Command1	Caption	Increment
Label1	Caption	0

```
Sub Command1_Click ()
    Let Label1.Caption = Str$(Val(Label1.Caption) + 1)
End Sub
```

41.

Object	Property	Setting
Form1	Caption	Tipping
Label1	Caption	Amount of bill:
Text1	Text	(blank)
Label2	Caption	Percentage Tip
Text2	Text	(blank)
Command1	Caption	Compute Tip
Picture1		

```
Sub Command1_Click ()
    Picture1.Cls
    Picture1.Print "The tip is"; Val(Text1.Text) * Val(Text2.Text) / 100
End Sub
```

Exercises 3.5

1. 16

3. baseball

5. Age: 20

7. setup

9. The White House has 132 rooms.

11. 1 OneTwo 2
2
1

13. Harvard University is 360 years old.

15. You might win 180 dollars.

17. Hello John Jones

19. 1 one   won

21. one   two

23. 1234567890
           5

25. 1234567890
         one
                  two

27. 1234567890
           one two

29. The Input#1 statement will assign "John Smith" to str1, leaving nothing left to assign to str2. An "Input past end of file" error will occur.

31. Each line in the file consists of three items, but the Input#1 statements are reading just two. As a result, the second Input#1 statement will try to assign the numeric data 110 to the string variable *building* causing a "Data type mismatch" error.

33. The response is to be used as a number, so the input from the user should not contain commas. With the given user response, the value in the variable statePop will be 8.

35. No "Font" property exists; should be "FontName". Also, the name of the font to the right of the equal sign must be surrounded by quotes.

37. The caption information to the right of the equal sign must be surrounded by quotes.

39. When assigning properties of the form, the correct object name is Form1, not Form. Also, Spc(5) can only be used with a Print method.

41.

category	amount	total
(undefined)	(undefined)	(undefined)
""	(undefined)	(undefined)
""	0	(undefined)
""	0	0
""	0	0
"phone"	35.25	0
"phone"	35.25	35.25
"postage"	14.75	35.25
"postage"	14.75	50
"postage"	14.75	50
"postage	14.75	50
(undefined)	(undefined)	(undefinded)

43.
```
Sub Command1_Click ()
    Dim course As String, percent1982 As Single, percent1987 As Single
    Rem Compute course enrollment percentage change
    Picture1.Cls
    Open "DATA.TXT" For Input As #1
    Input #1, course, percent1982, percent1987
    Picture1.Print "The percentage change for "; course; " was"; percent1987 - percent1982
    Input #1, course, percent1982, percent1987
    Picture1.Print "The percentage change for "; course; " was"; percent1987 - percent1982
    Close #1
End Sub
```

45.
```
Sub Command1_Click ()
    Dim begOfYearPrice As Single, endOfYearPrice As Single, percentIncrease As Single
    Rem Report percent increase for a basket of goods
    Picture1.Cls
    Let begOfYearPrice = 200
    Let endOfYearPrice = Val(InputBox$("Enter price at the end of the year:"))
    Let percentIncrease = 100 * (endOfYearPrice - begOfYearPrice) / begOfYearPrice
    Picture1.Print "The percent increase for the year is"; percentIncrease
End Sub
```

47. `MsgBox "The future isn't what it used to be.", , ""`

49.
```
Sub Command1_Click ()
    Dim account As String, beginningBalance As Single
    Dim deposits As Single, withdrawals As Single
    Dim endOfMonth As Single, total As Single
    Rem Report checking account activity
    Picture1.Cls
    Open "DATA.TXT" For Input As #1
    Rem 1st account
    Input #1, account, beginningBalance, deposits, withdrawals
    Let endOfMonth = beginningBalance + deposits - withdrawals
    Let total = endOfMonth
    Picture1.Print "Monthly balance for account "; account " is"; endOfMonth
    Rem 2nd account
    Input #1, account, beginningBalance, deposits, withdrawals
    Let endOfMonth = beginningBalance + deposits - withdrawals
```

```
        Let total = total + endOfMonth
        Picture1.Print "Monthly balance for account "; account " is"; endOfMonth
        Rem 3rd account
        Input #1, account, beginningBalance, deposits, withdrawals
        Let endOfMonth = beginningBalance + deposits - withdrawals
        Let total = total + endOfMonth
        Picture1.Print "Monthly balance for account "; account " is"; endOfMonth
        Picture1.Print "Total for all accounts ="; total
        Close #1
    End Sub
```

51.
```
    Sub Command1_Click ()
        Dim socNmb As String, exam1 As Single, exam2 As Single, exam3 As Single
        Dim final As Single, average As Single, total As Single
        Rem Compute semester averages
        Picture1.Cls
        Open "DATA.TXT" For Input As #1
        Rem 1st student
        Input #1, socNmb, exam1, exam2, exam3, final
        Let average = (exam1 + exam2 + exam3 + final * 2) / 5
        Let total = average
        Picture1.Print "Semester average for "; socNmb; " is"; average
        Rem 2nd student
        Input #1, socNmb, exam1, exam2, exam3, final
        Let average = (exam1 + exam2 + exam3 + final * 2) / 5
        Let total = total + average
        Picture1.Print "Semester average for "; socNmb; " is"; average
        Rem 3rd student
        Input #1, socNmb, exam1, exam2, exam3, final
        Let average = (exam1 + exam2 + exam3 + final * 2) / 5
        Let total = total + average
        Picture1.Print "Semester average for "; socNmb; " is"; average
        Picture1.Print "Class average is"; total / 3
        Close #1
    End Sub
```

53.
```
    Sub Command1_Click ()
        Dim athlete As String, sport As String
        Dim winnings As Single, income As Single
        Rem Display a table of sports salaries
        Picture1.Cls
        Picture1.Print , , "Salary or", "Other"
        Picture1.Print "Athlete", "Sport", "Winnings", "Income", "Total"
        Open "DATA.TXT" For Input As #1
        Input #1, athlete, sport, winnings, income
        Picture1.Print athlete, sport, winnings, income, winnings + income
        Input #1, athlete, sport, winnings, income
        Picture1.Print athlete, sport, winnings, income, winnings + income
        Input #1, athlete, sport, winnings, income
        Picture1.Print athlete, sport, winnings, income, winnings + income
        Close #1
    End Sub
```

55.
```
    Sub Text2_GotFocus ()
        MsgBox "Be sure to include the area code!", , ""
    End Sub
```

57.
```
    Sub Command1_Click ()
        Dim price As Single, quantity As Single, revenue As Single
        Picture1.Cls
        Open "DATA.TXT" For Input As #1
        Input #1, price
        Input #1, quantity
        Let revenue = price * quantity
        Picture1.Print "The revenue is"; revenue
        Close #1
    End Sub
```

Exercises 3.6

1. MCD'S
3. 10
5. 6
7. AB
9. e
11. 4
13. 0
15. now
17. 2
19. 3
21. -3
23. 0
25. Lul
27. ullaby
29. LULLABY
31. 0
33. by
35. 8lab
37. Today is Thu
39. o
41. I guess your answer is yes
43. 1937 YANKEES
45. 320,000.00
47. 32.00
49. 0.03
51. ($23.00)

53. $0.75
55. $10.50
57. 0
59. 2345
61. -1
63. 6.25%
65. 100.00%
67. 2.50%
69. 2.00E-04
71. 1.00E+02
73. -1.41E+00
75. Saturday, January 01, 2000
77. 02-Jan-00
79. Manhattan $24.00
81. Name   Salary
   Bill $123,000.00
83. "Currency"
85. "@@@@@"
87. "Scientific"
89. "Standard"
91. 1234567890
       abcd
93. 1234567890
      1234.559
95. 1234567890
       $25.00

97. Mid$ requires a string as its first argument; 1980 should be "1980".

99. Cannot take the square root of a negative number.

101. The second argument of Format$ must be a string; Standard should be "Standard".

103. The function name Format$ is missing in front of the parenthesis.

105. yes

107. Integers from 10 through 19

109. Integers from 1 through 52

111. The 26 lowercase letters a through z

113. `2 * Rnd + 2`

115. `Int(2 * Rnd)`

117. `Chr$(Int(7 * Rnd) + 65)`

119.
```
Rem Display an area code from a phone number entered in the form xxx-xxx-xxxx
Picture1.Print Left$(Text1.Text, 3)
```

121.
```
Sub Command1_Click ()
    Dim grad As Integer
    Rem Display number of graduation tickets
    Picture1.Cls
    Let grad = Val(InputBox$("Enter number of graduates:"))
    Picture1.Print Int(2000 / grad); "tickets will be distributed to each student"
End Sub
```

123.
```
Sub Command1_Click ()
    Dim q As Single, h As Single, c As Single
    Rem Compute optimal inventory size
    Let q = Val(InputBox$("Enter quantity:"))
    Let h = Val(InputBox$("Enter ordering cost:"))
    Let c = Val(InputBox$("Enter storage cost:"))
    Picture1.Print "The optimum inventory size is"; Int(Sqr(2 * q * h / c))
End Sub
```

125.
```
Sub Command1_Click ()
    Dim number As Single, decPlaces As Integer
    Rem Round a number
    Let number = Val(InputBox$("Number to round:"))
    Let decPlaces = Val(InputBox$("Decimal places to which number should be rounded:"))
    Let number = Int(number * 10 ^ decPlaces + .5) / 10 ^ decPlaces
    Picture1.Cls
    Picture1.Print "The rounded number is"; number
End Sub
```

127.
```
Sub Command1_Click ()
    Dim cents As Integer, quarters As Integer
    Rem Quarters in change
    Let cents = Val(InputBox$("Number of cents (between 1 and 99):"))
    Let quarters = Int(cents / 25)
    Picture1.Cls
    Picture1.Print "The change will contain"; quarters; "quarters."
End Sub
```

129.
```
Sub Command1_Click ()
    Dim nautHour As Integer
    Rem Convert hours
    Let nautHour = Val(InputBox$("Nautical hour (0 to 23):"))
    Picture1.Cls
    Picture1.Print "The standard hour is"; nautHour Mod 12
End Sub
```

131.
```
Sub Command1_Click ()
    Dim num As String, ptPos As Integer
    Rem Determine number of digits before and after the decimal point
    Let num = InputBox$("Enter a number containing a decimal point:")
    Let ptPos = Instr(num, ".")
    Picture1.Cls
    Picture1.Print "There are"; ptPos - 1; "digits before the decimal point"
    Picture1.Print "and"; Len(num) - ptPos; "digits after the decimal point."
End Sub
```

133.

Object	Property	Setting
Form1	Caption	Compound Interest
Label1	Caption	Principal
Text1	Text	(blank)
Label2	Caption	Interest Rate
	Alignment	2 – Center
Text2	Text	(blank)
Command1	Caption	Compute Balance
Label3	Caption	Balance after 10 years
	Alignment	2 – Center
Label4	Caption	(blank)

```
Sub Command1_Click ()
    Dim principal As Single, intRate As Single, balance As Single
    Rem Show growth of money in a savings account
    Let principal = Val(Text1.Text)
    Let Text1.Text = Format$(principal, "Currency")
    Let intRate = Val(Text2.Text)
    Let Text2.Text = Format$(intRate, "Percent")
    Let balance = principal * (1 + intRate) ^ 10
    Let Label4.Caption = Format$(balance, "Currency")
End Sub

Sub Text1_GotFocus ()
    Let Text1.Text = ""
End Sub

Sub Text2_GotFocus ()
    Let Text2.Text = ""
End Sub
```

135.
```
Sub Command1_Click ()
    Dim state As String, capital As String, population As Single, Area As Single
    Dim nicePop As String, niceArea As String, niceDens As String
    Rem State data
    Open "STATEDAT.TXT" For Input As #1
    Printer.FontName = "Courier"
    Printer.FontBold = True
    Printer.Print "State"; Tab(12); "Capital"; Tab(24); "Population";
    Printer.Print Tab(38); "Area"; Tab(48); "Density"
    Printer.FontBold = False
    Input #1, state, capital, population, area
    Let nicePop = Format$(population, "#,#")
    Let niceArea = Format$(area, "#,#")
    Let niceDens = Format$(population / area, "Standard")
    Printer.Print state; Tab(12); capital; Tab(24); Format$(nicePop, "@@@@@@@@@@");
    Printer.Print Tab(38);Format$(niceArea,"@@@@@@@");Tab(48);Format$(niceDens,"@@@@@")
    Input #1, state, capital, population, area
    Let nicePop = Format$(population, "#,#")
    Let niceArea = Format$(area, "#,#")
    Let niceDens = Format$(population / area, "Standard")
    Printer.Print state; Tab(12); capital; Tab(24); Format$(nicePop, "@@@@@@@@@@");
    Printer.Print Tab(38);Format$(niceArea,"@@@@@@@");Tab(48);Format$(niceDens,"@@@@@")
    Input #1, state, capital, population, area
    Let nicePop = Format$(population, "#,#")
    Let niceArea = Format$(area, "#,#")
    Let niceDens = Format$(population / area, "Standard")
    Printer.Print state; Tab(12); capital; Tab(24); Format$(nicePop, "@@@@@@@@@@");
    Printer.Print Tab(38);Format$(niceArea,"@@@@@@@");Tab(48);Format$(niceDens,"@@@@@")
    Printer.EndDoc
    Close #1
End Sub
```

137.
```
Sub Command1_Click ()
    Dim m As Integer, y As Integer
    Rem Select a random month and year during the 1990's
    Randomize Timer
    Let m = Int(12 * Rnd) + 1
    Let y = Int(10 * Rnd) + 1990
    Picture1.Cls
    Picture1.Print m; "/"; y
End Sub
```

139.
```
Sub Text1_KeyPress (KeyAscii As Integer)
    Rem Replace the users keystroke with a random letter from A to Z
    Let KeyAscii = Int(26 * Rnd) + 65
End Sub
```

CHAPTER 4

Exercises 4.1

1. It isn't easy being green.
    Kermit the frog

3. Why do clocks run clockwise?
    Because they were invented in the northern
    hemisphere where sundials move clockwise.

5. Divorced, beheaded, died;
    Divorced, beheaded, survived.

7. Keep cool, but don't freeze.
    Source: A jar of mayonnaise.

9. 88 keys on a piano

11. It was the best of times.
    It was the worst of times.

13. Your name has 7 letters.
    The first letter is G

15. abcde

17. 144 items in a gross

19. 30% of M&M's Plain Chocolate Candies are brown.

21. 1440 minutes in a day

23. t is the 6 th letter of the word.

25. According to a poll in the May 31, 1988
    issue of PC Magazine, 75% of the people polled
    write programs for their companies.
    The four most popular languages used are as follows.
    22 percent of the respondents use BASIC
    16 percent of the respondents use Assembler
    15 percent of the respondents use C
    13 percent of the respondents use Pascal

27. President Bush is a graduate of Yale University
President Clinton is a graduate of Georgetown University

29. The first 6 letters are Visual

31. The negative of worldly is unworldly

33. 24 blackbirds baked in a pie.

35. There is a parameter in the subprogram, but no argument in the statement calling the subprogram.

37. Since *Print* is a keyword, it cannot be used as the name of a subprogram.

39.
```
Sub Command1_Click ()
  Dim num As Integer
  Rem Display a lucky number
  Picture1.Cls
  Let num = 7
  Call Lucky(num)
End Sub

Sub Lucky (num As Integer)
  Rem Display message
  Picture1.Print num; "is a lucky number."
End Sub
```

41.
```
Sub Command1_Click ()
  Dim tree As String, ht As Single
  Rem Information about trees
  Picture1.Cls
  Open "TREES.TXT" For Input As #1
  Input #1, tree, ht
  Call Tallest(tree, ht)
  Input #1, tree, ht
  Call Tallest(tree, ht)
  Close #1
End Sub

Sub Tallest (tree As String, ht As Single)
  Rem Display information about tree
  Picture1.Print "The tallest "; tree; " in the U.S. is"; ht; "feet."
End Sub
```

43.
```
Sub Command1_Click ()
  Dim num As Single
  Rem Given a number, display its triple
  Picture1.Cls
  Let num = Val(InputBox$("Enter a number:"))
  Call Triple(num)
End Sub

Sub Triple (num As Single)
  Rem Multiply the value of the number by 3
  Picture1.Print "The number's triple is"; 3 * num
End Sub
```

45.
```
Sub Command1_Click ()
  Dim word As String, col As Integer
  Rem Enter a word and column number to display
  Picture1.Cls
  Let word = InputBox$("Enter a word:")
  Let col = Val(InputBox$("Enter a column number between 1 and 10:"))
  Call PlaceNShow(word, col)
End Sub

Sub PlaceNShow (word As String, col As Integer)
  Rem Display the word at the given column number
  Picture1.Print Tab(col); word
End Sub
```

47.
```
Sub Command1_Click ()
   Rem Intended college majors
   Picture1.Cls
   Call DisplaySource
   Call Majors(18, "business")
   Call Majors(2, "computer science")
End Sub

Sub DisplaySource
   Rem Display the source of the information
   Picture1.Print "According to a 1991 survey of college freshmen"
   Picture1.Print "taken by the Higher Educational Research Institute:"
   Picture1.Print
End Sub

Sub Majors (students As Single, field As String)
   Rem Display the information about major
   Picture1.Print students; "percent said they intend to major in "; field
End Sub
```

49.
```
Sub Command1_Click ()
   Dim num As Single
   Rem Favorite number
   Picture1.Cls
   Let num = Val(Text1.Text)
   Call Sum (num)
   Call Product(num)
End Sub

Sub Product (num As Single)
   Picture1.Print "The product of your favorite number with itself is"; num * num
End Sub

Sub Sum (num As Single)
   Picture1.Print "The sum of your favorite number with itself is"; num + num
End Sub
```

51.
```
Sub Command1_Click ()
   Dim animal As String, sound As String
   Rem Old McDonald Had a Farm
   Picture1.Cls
   Open "FARM.TXT" For Input As #1
   Input #1, animal, sound
   Call ShowVerse(animal, sound)
   Picture1.Print
   Input #1, animal, sound
   Call ShowVerse(animal, sound)
   Picture1.Print
   Input #1, animal, sound
   Call ShowVerse(animal, sound)
   Picture1.Print
   Input #1, animal, sound
   Call ShowVerse(animal, sound)
   Close #1
End Sub

Sub ShowVerse (animal As String, sound As String)
   Rem Display a verse from Old McDonald Had a Farm
   Picture1.Print "Old McDonald had a farm. Eyi eyi oh."
   Picture1.Print "And on his farm he had a "; animal; ".  Eyi eyi oh."
   Picture1.Print "With a "; sound; " "; sound; " here, ";
   Picture1.Print "and a "; sound; " "; sound; " there."
   Picture1.Print "Here a "; sound; ", there a "; sound;
   Picture1.Print ", everywhere a "; sound; " "; sound; "."
   Picture1.Print "Old McDonald had a farm. Eyi eyi oh."
End Sub
```

53.
```
Sub Command1_Click ()
    Rem Display a table for occupation growth
    Picture1.Cls
    Open "DATA.TXT" For Input As #1
    Picture1.Print Tab(56); "Percent"
    Picture1.Print "Occupation"; Tab(40); "1982"; Tab(48); "1991"; Tab(56);"Change"
    Picture1.Print
    Call ComputeChange
    Call ComputeChange
    Call ComputeChange
    Close #1
End Sub

Sub ComputeChange
    Dim occupation As String, num82 As Single, num91 As Single, perChange As Single
    Rem Read data and compute percent change, display all data
    Input #1, occupation, num82, num91
    Let perChange = 100 * (num91 - num82) / num82
    Picture1.Print occupation; Tab(40); num82; Tab(48); num91; Tab(56); Format$(perChange, "0"); "%"
End Sub
```

Exercises 4.2

1. 9

3. Can Can

5. 25

7. Less is more

9. Gabriel was born in the year 1980

11. Buckeyes

13. 0

15. 1 1

17. discovered Florida

19. The variable c should be a parameter in the subprogram. That is, the Sub statement should be Sub Sum (x As Single, y As Single, c As Single).

21.
```
Sub Command1_Click ()
    Dim price As Single, tax As Single, cost As Single
    Rem Calculate sales tax
    Picture1.Cls
    Call InputPrice(price)
    Call Compute(price, tax, cost)
    Call ShowData(price, tax, cost)
End Sub

Sub Compute (price As Single, tax As Single, cost As Single)
    Rem Calculate the cost
    Let tax = .05 * price
    Let cost = price + tax
End Sub

Sub InputPrice (price As Single)
    Rem Get the price of the item
    Let price = Val(InputBox$("Enter the price of the item:"))
End Sub

Sub ShowData (price As Single, tax As Single, cost As Single)
    Rem Display bill
    Picture1.Print "Price: "; price
    Picture1.Print "Tax: "; tax
    Picture1.Print "--------------"
    Picture1.Print "Cost: "; cost
End Sub
```

23.
```
Sub Command1_Click ()
    Dim length As Single, wdth As Single, area As Single
    Rem Compute area of rectangle
    Picture1.Cls
    Call InputSize(length, wdth)
    Call ComputeArea(length, wdth, area)
    Call ShowArea(area)
End Sub

Sub ComputeArea (length As Single, wdth As Single, area As Single)
    Rem Calculate the area
    Let area = length * wdth
End Sub
```

```
   Sub InputSize (length As Single, wdth As Single)
     Rem Get the dimensions of the rectangle
     Let length = Val(Text1.Text)
     Let wdth = Val(Text2.Text)
   End Sub

   Sub ShowArea (area As Single)
     Rem Display the area of the rectangle
     Picture1.Print "The area of the rectangle is"; area
   End Sub
```

25. `Dim nom As String   'place in the (declarations) section of (general)`

27.
```
   Sub Command1_Click ()
     Dim first As String, last As String, fInit As String, lInit As String
     Rem Display initials
     Picture1.Cls
     Call InputNames (first, last)
     Call ExtractInitials(first, last, fInit, lInit)
     Call DisplayInitials(fInit, lInit)
   End Sub

   Sub DisplayInitials (fInit As String, lInit As String)
     Rem Display the initials
     Picture1.Print "The initials are "; fInit; "."; lInit; "."
   End Sub

   Sub ExtractInitials (first As String, last As String, fInit As String, lInit As String)
     Rem Determine the initials of the first and last names
     Let fInit = Left$(first,1)
     Let lInit = Left$(last,1)
   End Sub

   Sub InputNames (first As String, last As String)
     Rem Get the persons first and last name
     Let first = InputBox$("Enter your first name:")
     Let last = InputBox$("Enter your last name:")
   End Sub
```

29.
```
   Sub Command1_Click ()
     Dim cost As Single, price As Single, markup As Single
     Rem Calculate percentage markup
     Picture1.Cls
     Call InputAmounts(cost, price)
     Call ComputeMarkup(cost, price, markup)
     Call DisplayMarkup(markup)
   End Sub

   Sub ComputeMarkup (cost As Single, price As Single, markup As Single)
     Let markup = 100 * ((price - cost) / cost)
   End Sub

   Sub DisplayMarkup (markup As Single)
     Picture1.Print "The markup is "; Format$(markup, "0"); " percent."
   End Sub

   Sub InputAmounts (cost As Single, price As Single)
     Let cost = Val(InputBox$("Enter the cost:"))
     Let price = Val(InputBox$("Enter the selling price:"))
   End Sub
```

31.
```
   Sub Command1_Click ()
     Dim nom As String, atBats As Integer, hits As Integer, ave As Single
     Rem Calculate batting average
     Picture1.Cls
     Open "DATA.TXT" For Input As #1
     Call ReadStats(nom, atBats, hits)
     Call ComputeAverage(atBats, hits, ave)
     Call DisplayInfo(nom, ave)
     Close #1
   End Sub
```

```
Sub ComputeAverage (atBats As Integer, hits As Integer, ave As Single)
  Let ave = hits / atBats
End Sub


Sub DisplayInfo (nom As String, ave As Single)
  Picture1.Print "Name", "Batting Average"
  Picture1.Print nom,
  Picture1.Print Format$(ave,"Standard")
End Sub


Sub ReadStats (nom As String, atBats As Integer, hits As Integer)
  Input #1, nom, atBats, hits
End Sub
```

33.
```
Sub Command1_Click ()
  Rem Display Hat Rack mall comparison table
  Picture1.Cls
  Picture1.Print Tab(15); "Rent per"
  Picture1.Print Tab(15); "Square"; Tab(25); "Total"; Tab(35); "Monthly"
  Picture1.Print "Mall Name"; Tab(15); "Foot"; Tab(25); "Feet"; Tab(35); "Rent"
  Picture1.Print
  Open MALLS.TXT For Input As #1
  Call DisplayInfo
  Call DisplayInfo
  Call DisplayInfo
  Close #1
End Sub


Sub ComputeRent (rent As Single, feet As Single, total As Single)
  Rem Compute monthly rent given rent/foot and number of feet
  Let total = rent * feet
End Sub


Sub DisplayInfo ()
  Dim mall As String, rentPerFoot As Single, squareFeet As Single, rent As Single
  Rem Display the information for a single mall
  Input #1, mall, rentPerFoot, squareFeet
  Call ComputeRent(rentPerFoot, squareFeet, rent)
  Picture1.Print mall; Tab(15); rentPerFoot; Tab(25); squareFeet; Tab(35); rent
End Sub
```

35.
```
Dim total As Single   'In (declarations) section of (general)


Sub Command1_Click ()
  Dim item As String, price As Single
  Rem Produce a sales receipt
  Call InputData(item, price)
  Let total = total + price
  Call ShowData(item, price)
  Let Text1.Text = ""
  Let Text2.Text = ""
  Text1.SetFocus
End Sub


Sub Command2_Click ()
  Dim tax As Single
  Rem Display sum, tax, and total
  Let tax = total * .05
  Let tax = Int(100 * tax + .5) / 100
  Picture1.Print Tab(15); "-------"
  Call ShowData("Sum", total)
  Call ShowData("Tax", tax)
  Call ShowData("Total", total + tax)
End Sub


Sub InputData (item As String, price As Single)
  Rem Input item name and price
  Let item = Text1.Text
  Let price = Val(Text2.Text)
End Sub
```

```
Sub ShowData (strItem As String, numItem As Single)
   Rem Display data on specified line
   Picture1.Print strItem; Tab(15); Format$(numItem,"Standard")
End Sub
```

Exercises 4.3

1. 203

3. The population will double in 24 years.

5. Volume of cylinder having base area 3.14159
and height 2 is 6.28318
Volume of cylinder having base area 28.27431
and height 4 is 113.0972

7. train

9. moral has the negative amoral
political has the negative apolitical

11. The first line of the function definition should end with
As String, not *As Single.*

13.
```
Sub Command1_Click ()
   Dim radius As Single, height As Single
   Rem Tin Needed for a Tin Can
   Picture1.Cls
   Call InputDims(radius, height)
   Call ShowAmount(radius, height)
End Sub

Function CanArea (radius As Single, height As Single) As Single
   Rem Calculate surface area of a cylindrical can
   CanArea = 6.28 * (radius * radius + radius * height)
End Function

Sub InputDims (radius As Single, height As Single)
   Let radius = Val(InputBox$("Enter radius of can:"))
   Let height = Val(InputBox$("Enter height of can:"))
End Sub

Sub ShowAmount (radius As Single, height As Single)
   Picture1.Print "A can of radius"; radius; "and height"; height
   Picture1.Print "requires"; CanArea(radius, height); "square units to make."
End Sub
```

15.
```
Sub Command1_Click ()
   Dim m As Single, n As Integer
   Rem Round a positive number m to n decimal places
   Picture1.Cls
   Call InputData(m, n)
   Call RoundIt(m, n)
End Sub

Sub InputData (m As Single, n As Integer)
   Let m = Val(InputBox$("Enter a number to round:"))
   Let n = Val(InputBox$("Round it to how many decimal places?"))
End Sub

Function Rounded (m As Single, n As Integer) As Single
   Rem Round a number to a given number of decimal places
   Rounded = Int(m * 10 ^ n  + .5) / (10 ^ n)
End Function

Sub RoundIt (m As Single, n As Integer)
   Picture1.Print m; "rounded to"; n; "places is"; Rounded(m, n)
End Sub
```

17.
```
Sub Command1_Click ()
   Dim popcorn As Single, butter As Single, bucket As Single, price As Single
   Rem Popcorn Profits
   Picture1.Cls
   Call InputAmounts(popcorn, butter, bucket, price)
   Call ShowProfit(popcorn, butter, bucket, price)
End Sub
```

```
Sub InputAmounts (popcorn As Single,butter As Single,bucket As Single,price As Single)
  Let popcorn = Val(InputBox$("What is the cost of the popcorn kernels?"))
  Let butter = Val(InputBox$("What is the cost of the butter?"))
  Let bucket = Val(InputBox$("What is the cost of the bucket?"))
  Let price = Val(InputBox$("What is the sale price?"))
End Sub

Function Profit (popcorn As Single,butter As Single,bucket As Single,price As Single)
  Rem Calculate the profit on a bucket of popcorn
  Profit = price - (popcorn + butter + bucket)
End Function

Sub ShowProfit (popcorn As Single,butter As Single,bucket As Single,price As Single)
  Picture1.Print "The profit is";
  Picture1.Print Profit(popcorn, butter, bucket, price)
End Sub
```

19.
```
Sub Command1_Click ()
  Dim weight As Single
  Rem Original Cost of Airmail
  Picture1.Cls
  Call InputWeight(weight)
  Call ShowCost(weight)
End Sub

Function Ceil (x As Single) As Single
  Ceil = -Int(-x)
End Function

Function Cost (weight As Single) As Single
  Rem Calculate the cost of an airmail letter
  Cost = .05 + .10 * Ceil(weight - 1)
End Function

Sub InputWeight (weight As Single)
  Let weight = Val(Text1.Text)
End Sub

Sub ShowCost (weight As Single)
  Picture1.Print "The cost of mailing the letter is $"; Cost(weight)
End Sub
```

21.
```
Sub Command1_Click ()
  Dim nom As String
  Rem Display a greeting for a senator
  Picture1.Cls
  Let nom = InputBox$("Enter the senator's name:")
  Picture1.Print
  Picture1.Print "The Honorable "; nom
  Picture1.Print "United States Senate"
  Picture1.Print "Washington, DC 20001"
  Picture1.Print
  Picture1.Print "Dear Senator "; LastName$(nom); ","
End Sub

Function LastName$ (nom As String)
  Rem Determine the last name of a two part name
  Let spaceNmb = Instr(nom, " ")
  LastName$ = Mid$(nom, spaceNmb + 1, Len(nom) - spaceNmb)
End Function
```

CHAPTER 5

Exercises 5.1

1. True
3. True
5. True
7. True
9. False
11. False
13. True
15. True
17. False
19. False

21. False
23. True
25. Equivalent
27. Not Equivalent
29. Equivalent
31. Not Equivalent
33. Equivalent
35. a <= b
37. (a >= b) Or (c = d)
39. (a = "") Or (a >= b) Or (Len(a) >= 5)

Exercises 5.2

1. Less than ten
3. Tomorrow is another day.
5.   10
7. Cost of call: $11.26
9. The number of vowels is 2
11. positive
13. Incorrect conditional. Should be If (1 < num) And (num < 3) Then

15. no Then
17. Comparing numeric and string data
19. Incorrect conditional. Should be If (j = 4) Or (k = 4) Then
21. Let a = 5
23.
```
If j = 7 Then
    Let b = 1
  Else
    Let b = 2
End If
```

25.
```
Let message = "Is Alaska bigger than Texas and California combined?"
Let answer = InputBox$(message)
If UCase$(Left$(answer, 1)) = "Y" Then
    Picture1.Print "Correct"
  Else
    Picture1.Print "Wrong"
End If
```

27.
```
Sub Command1_Click ()
    Dim cost As Single, tip As Single
    Rem Give waiter a tip
    Picture1.Cls
    Let cost = Val(InputBox$("Enter cost of meal:"))
    Let tip = cost * .15
    If tip < 1 Then
        Let tip = 1
    End If
    Picture1.Print "Leave "; Format$(tip, "Currency"); " for the tip."
End Sub
```

29.
```
Sub Command1_Click ()
    Dim num As Single, cost As Single
    Rem Order diskettes
    Picture1.Cls
    Let num = Val(InputBox$("Number of diskettes:"))
    If num < 25 Then
        Let cost = num
      Else
        Let cost = .7 * num
    End If
    Picture1.Print "The cost is "; Format$(cost, "Currency")
End Sub
```

31.
```
Sub Text1_KeyPress (KeyAscii As Integer)
    If KeyAscii > 31 And KeyAscii < Asc("0") Or KeyAscii > Asc("9") Then
        Rem Ignore all regular keystrokes except the digits 0 through 9
        Let KeyAscii = 0
    End If
End Sub
```

33.
```
Sub Command1_Click ()
    Dim balance As Single, amount As Single
    Rem Savings account withdrawal
    Picture1.Cls
    Let balance = Val(InputBox$("Current balance:"))
    Let amount = Val(InputBox$("Amount of withdrawal:"))
    If (balance >= amount) Then
        Let balance = balance - amount
        Picture1.Print "New balance is "; balance
        If balance < 150 Then
            Picture1.Print "Balance below $150"
        End If
      Else
        Picture1.Print "Withdrawal denied."
    End If
End Sub
```

35.
```
Sub Command1_Click ()
    Dim d1 As Integer, d2 As Integer, d3 As Integer, lucky As String
    Rem Lottery
    Picture1.Cls
    Randomize Timer
    Let d1 = Int(7 * Rnd) + 1
    Let d2 = Int(7 * Rnd) + 1
    Let d3 = Int(7 * Rnd) + 1
    Let lucky = "Lucky seven"
    If d1 = 7 Then
        If (d2 = 7) Or (d3 = 7) Then
            Picture1.Print lucky
        End If
      Else
        If (d2 = 7) And (d3 = 7) Then
            Picture1.Print lucky
        End If
    End If
End Sub
```

37.
```
Sub Command1_Click ()
    Dim word As String, first As String
    Rem Convert to Pig Latin
    Picture1.Cls
    Let word = InputBox$("Enter a word (use all lowercase):")
    Let first = Left$(word, 1)
    If Instr("aeiou", first) <> 0 Then
        Let word = word + "way"
      Else
        Let word = Mid$(word, 2, Len(word) - 1) + first + "ay"
    End If
    Picture1.Print "The word in pig latin is "; word
End Sub
```

39.
```
Dim status As Integer   'In (declarations) section of (general)

Sub Command1_Click ()
  If status = 0 Then
      Picture1.Print "I came to Casablanca for the waters."
      Let status = 1
    ElseIf status = 2 Then
      Picture1.Print "I was misinformed."
      Let status = 0
  End If
End Sub


Sub Command2_Click ()
  If status = 1 Then
      Picture1.Print "But we're in the middle of the desert."
      Let status = 2
  End If
End Sub
```

41.

Object	Property	Setting
Form1	Caption	Yankee Doodle President
Label1	Caption	Which U.S. President was born on July 4?
Text1	Text	(blank)
Command1	Caption	Check Answer
Label2	Caption	0
Label3	Caption	guesses so far.

```
Sub Command1_Click ()
  Dim msg As String
  Rem Label2 keeps track of the number of guesses; increase number of guesses by 1
  Let Label2.Caption = Format$(Val(Label2.Caption) + 1 ,"#")
  If Instr(UCase$(Text1.Text), "COOLIDGE") > 0 Then
      MsgBox "Calvin Coolidge was born on July 4, 1872.", , "Correct"
    ElseIf Val(Label2.Caption) = 3 Then
      Let msg = "He once said, 'If you don't say anything,"
      Let msg = msg + " you won't be called upon to repeat it.'"
      MsgBox msg, , "Hint"
    ElseIf Val(Label2.Caption) = 7 Then
      MsgBox "His nickname was 'Silent Cal.'", , "Hint"
    ElseIf Val(Label2.Caption) = 10 Then
      MsgBox "Calvin Coolidge was born on July 4, 1872.", , "You've run out of guesses"
  End If
End Sub
```

43.
```
Sub Command1_Click ()
  Dim income As Single, tax As Single
  Rem Calculate New Jersey state income tax
  Picture1.Cls
  Let income = Val(InputBox$("Taxable income:"))
  If income <= 20000 Then
      Let tax = .02 * income
    Else
      If income <= 50000 Then
          Let tax = 400 + .025 * (income - 20000)
        Else
          Let tax = 1150 + .035 * (income - 50000)
      End If
  End If
  Picture1.Print "Tax is "; Format$(tax, "Currency")
End Sub
```

Exercises 5.3

1.
```
The price is $3.75
The price is $3.75
```

3.
```
Mesozoic Era
Paleozoic Era
?
```

5.
```
Nope.
He worked with the developer, von Neumann, on the ENIAC.
Correct
```

7.
```
The less things change, the more they remain the same.
Less is more.
Time keeps everything from happening at once.
```

9. Should have a Case clause.

11. Comparing numeric (0 To 9) and string data (string variable *a*).

13. Error in second Case.

15. Selector is a condition.

17. Valid

19. Invalid

21. Valid

23.
```
Select Case a
  Case 1
     Picture1.Print "one"
  Case Is > 5
     Picture1.Print "two"
End Select
```

25.
```
Select Case a
  Case 2
     Picture1.Print "yes"
  Case Is < 5
     Picture1.Print "no"
End Select
```

27.
```
Sub Command1_Click ()
    Dim percent As Single
    Rem Determine degree of cloudiness
    Picture1.Cls
    Let percent = Val(InputBox$("Percentage of cloud cover:"))
    Select Case percent
      Case 0 To 30
        Picture1.Print "Clear"
      Case 31 To 70
        Picture1.Print "Partly cloudy"
      Case 71 To 99
        Picture1.Print "Cloudy"
      Case 100
        Picture1.Print "Overcast"
      Case Else
        Picture1.Print "Percentage must be between 0 And 100."
    End Select
End Sub
```

29.
```
Sub Command1_Click ()
    Dim monthName As String, days As Integer
    Rem Give number of days in month
    Picture1.Cls
    Call InputMonth(monthName)
    Call GetDays(monthName, days)
    Call ShowDays(days, monthName)
End Sub

Sub GetDays (monthName As String, days As Integer)
  Dim answer As String
  Rem Compute number of days in the month
  Select Case UCase$(monthName)
    Case "FEBRUARY"
      Let answer= InputBox$("Is it a leap year?")
      If UCase$(Left$(answer, 1)) = "Y" Then
          Let days = 29
        Else
          Let days = 28
      End If
    Case "APRIL", "JUNE", "SEPTEMBER", "NOVEMBER"
      Let days = 30
    Case "JANUARY","MARCH","MAY","JULY","AUGUST","OCTOBER","DECEMBER"
      Let days = 31
  End Select
End Sub

Sub InputMonth (monthName As String)
  Rem Input a month of the year
  Let monthName = InputBox$("Enter a month (do not abbreviate):")
End Sub

Sub ShowDays (days As Integer, monthName As String)
  Rem Report number of days in month
  Picture1.Print monthName; " has"; days; "days."
End Sub
```

31.
```
Sub Command1_Click ()
    Dim score As Integer
    Rem Give letter grade for number score
    Picture1.Cls
    Call InputScore(score)
    Call ShowGrade(score)
End Sub

Function Grade$ (score As Integer)
  Rem Return letter grade for score
  Select Case score
    Case 90 To 100
      Grade$ = "A"
    Case 80 To 89
      Grade$ = "B"
    Case 70 To 79
      Grade$ = "C"
    Case 60 To 69
      Grade$ = "D"
    Case 0 To 59
      Grade$ = "F"
    Case Else
      Grade$ = "Invalid"
  End Select
End Function

Sub InputScore (score As Integer)
  Rem Input a number score
  Let score = Val(InputBox$("What is the score?"))
End Sub

Sub ShowGrade (score As Integer)
  Rem Show letter grade for score
  Picture1.Print "The letter grade is "; Grade$(score)
End Sub
```

33.
```
Sub Command1_Click ()
    Dim amount As Single
    Rem Determine cash award
    Picture1.Cls
    Let amount = Val(InputBox$("How much was recovered?"))
    Select Case amount
      Case Is <= 75000
        Let amount = .1 * amount
      Case Is <= 100000
        Let amount = 7500 + .05 * (amount - 75000)
      Case Is > 100000
        Let amount = 8750 + .01 * (amount - 100000)
        If amount > 50000 Then
            Let amount = 50000
        End If
    End Select
    Picture1.Print "The amount given as reward is ";
                    Format$(amount, "Currency")
End Sub
```

35.

Object	Property	Setting
Form1	Caption	Presidential Trivia
Label1	Caption	Last name of one of the four most recent Presidents
	Alignment	1 – Right Justify
Text1	Text	(blank)
Command1	Caption	OK
Picture1		

```
Sub Command1_Click ()
  Dim pres As String, state As String, trivia As String
  Let pres = Text1.Text
  Select Case UCase$(pres)
    Case Is = "CARTER"
      Let state = "Georgia"
      Let trivia = "The only soft drink served in the Carter "
      Let trivia = trivia + "White House was Coca-Cola."
    Case Is = "REAGAN"
      Let state = "California"
      Let trivia = "His secret service code name was Rawhide."
    Case Is = "BUSH"
      Let state = "Texas"
      Let trivia = "He was the third left-handed president."
    Case Is = "CLINTON"
      Let state = "Arkansas"
      Let trivia = "In college he did a good imitation of Elvis Presley."
    Case Else
      Let state = ""
      Let trivia = ""
  End Select
```

```
        If Not state = "" Then
            Picture1.Cls
            Picture1.Print "President " + pres + "'s ";
            Picture1.Print "home state was " + state + "."
            Picture1.Print trivia
        End If
        Let Text1.Text = ""
        Text1.SetFocus
    End Sub
37. Sub Command1_Click ()
        Let Label2.Caption = HumorMsg$(Val(Text1.Text))
    End Sub

    Sub Command2_Click ()
        Let Label2.Caption = InsultMsg$(Val(Text1.Text))
    End Sub

    Function HumorMsg$ (num As Integer)
      Dim temp As String
      Select Case num
        Case Is = 1
          HumorMsg$ = "I can resist everything except temptation"
        Case Is = 2
          HumorMsg$ = "I just heard from Bill Bailey. He's not coming home."
        Case Is = 3
          Let temp = "I have enough money to last the rest of my life,"
          HumorMsg$ = temp + " unless I buy something."
        Case Else
          HumorMsg$ = ""
          Text1.Text = ""
      End Select
    End Function

    Function InsultMsg$ (num As Integer)
      Select Case num
        Case Is = 1
          InsultMsg$ = "How much would you charge to haunt a house?"
        Case Is = 2
          InsultMsg$ = "I bet you have no more friends than an alarm clock."
        Case Is = 3
          InsultMsg$ = "When your IQ rises to 30, sell."
        Case Else
          InsultMsg$ = ""
          Text1.Text = ""
      End Select
    End Function
```

CHAPTER 6

Exercises 6.1

1. `17`

3. You are a super programmer!

5. `2`

7. Program never stops

9. Do and Loop interchanged.

11. `While num >= 7`

13. `Until response <> "Y"`

15. `Until nom = ""`

17. `Until (a <= 1) Or (a >= 3)`

19. `While n = 0`

21.
```
Sub Command1_Click ()
    Dim num As String, num As Integer
    Rem Request and display three names
    Picture1.Cls
    Let num = 0
    Do While num < 3
        Let nom = InputBox$("Enter a name:")
        Picture1.Print nom
        Let num = num + 1
    Loop
End Sub
```

23.
```
Sub Command1_Click ()
    Dim celsius As Single
    Rem Convert Celsius to Fahrenheit
    Picture1.Cls
    Picture1.Print "Celsius"; Tab(10); "Fahrenheit"
    Let celsius = -40
    Do While celsius <= 40
        Call ShowFahrenheit(celsius)
        Let celsius = celsius + 5
    Loop
End Sub

Function Fahrenheit (celsius As Single) As Single
    Rem Convert Celsius to Fahrenheit
    Fahrenheit = (9 / 5) * celsius + 32
End Function

Sub ShowFahrenheit (celsius As Single)
    Rem Give Fahrenheit equivalent
    Picture1.Print celsius; Tab(10); Fahrenheit(celsius)
End Sub
```

25.
```
Sub Command1_Click ()
    Dim counter As Integer, sevens As Integer, dieOne As Integer, dieTwo As Integer
    Randomize Timer
    Let counter = 0
    Let sevens = 0
    Do While Sevens < 10
        Let dieOne = Int(6 * Rnd) + 1
        Let dieTwo = Int(6 * Rnd) + 1
        Let counter = counter + 1
        If dieOne + dieTwo = 7 Then
            Let sevens = sevens + 1
        End If
    Loop
    Picture1.Cls
    Picture1.Print "The approximate odds of two die totaling seven is 1 in ";
    Picture1.Print Format$(counter / sevens, "Standard")
End Sub
```

27.
```
Sub Command1_Click ()
    Dim x As Integer, y As Integer, temp As Integer
    Rem First terms in the Fibonaci sequence
    Let x = 1
    Let y = 1
    Picture1.Print "Terms in the Fibonaci sequence between 1 and 100 are"
    Picture1.Print x;
    Do While y <= 100
        Picture1.Print y;
        Let temp = x + y
        Let x = y
        Let y = temp
    Loop
End Sub
```

29.
```
Sub Command1_Click ()
    Dim minuteHandPos As Single, hourHandPos As Single, difference As Single
    Rem When after 6:30 do clock hands exactly overlap?
    Let minuteHandPos = 0
    Let hourHandPos = 30
    Do While hourHandPos - minuteHandPos >= .0001
        Let difference = hourHandPos - minuteHandPos
        Let minuteHandPos = minuteHandPos + difference
        Let hourHandPos = hourHandPos + difference / 12
    Loop
    Picture1.Print "The hands overlap at"; minuteHandPos; "minutes after six."
End Sub
```

31.
```
Sub Command1_Click ()
    Dim height As Single, bounceFactor As Single, bounces As Integer, distance As Single
    Rem Bounce a ball and find total distance traveled
    Picture1.Cls
    Call InputData(height, bounceFactor)
    Call BounceBall(height, bounceFactor, bounces, distance)
    Call ShowData(bounces, distance)
End Sub

Sub BounceBall (hght As Single, bFactor As Single, bounces As Integer, dist As Single)
  Let bounces = 1            ' first bounce
  Let dist = hght
  Do While hght * bFactor >= 10
    Let bounces = bounces + 1
    Let hght = hght * bFactor
    Let dist = dist + 2 * hght       ' up then down again
  Loop
End Sub

Sub InputData (height As Single, bounceFactor As Single)
  Rem Input height and coefficient of restitution
  Let msg = "What is the cooefficient of restitution of the ball (0 to 1)?  "
  Let msg = msg + "Examples are .7 for a tennis ball, .75 for a basketball, "
  Let msg = msg + ".9 for a super ball, and .3 for a softball."
  Let bounceFactor = Val(InputBox$(msg))
  Let height = Val(InputBox$("From how many meters will the ball be dropped?"))
  Let height = height * 100      ' convert to centimeters
End Sub

Sub ShowData (bounces As Integer, distance As Single)
  Picture1.Print "The ball bounced"; bounces; "times and traveled about ";
  Picture1.Print Format$(distance / 100,"Standard"); " meters."
End Sub
```

33.
```
Sub Command1_Click ()
    Dim amt As Single, yrs As Integer
    Rem Years to deplete savings account
    Picture1.Cls
    Let amt = Val(InputBox$("Enter initial amount in account:"))
    Let yrs = 0
    If amt * 1.05 - 1000 >= amt Then
        Picture1.Print "Account will never be depleted."
      Else
        Do
          Let amt = amt * 1.05 - 1000
          Let yrs = yrs + 1
        Loop Until amt <= 0
        Picture1.Print "It takes"; yrs; "years to deplete the account."
    End If
End Sub
```

35.
```
Sub Command1_Click ()
    Dim age As Integer
    Rem Solution to age problem
    Picture1.Cls
    Let age = 1
    Do While 1980 + age <> age * age
      Let age = age + 1
    Loop
    Picture1.Print "The solution is"; age; "years old."
End Sub
```

37.
```
Sub Command1_Click ()
    Rem Capitalize entire sentence
    Picture1.Cls
    Picture1.Print Ucase$(Text1.Text)
End Sub
```

```
Sub Command2_Click ()
  Dim info As String, word As String
  Rem Capitalize first letter of each word
  Picture1.Cls
  Let info = LTrim$(Text1.Text)  'discard any leading spaces
  Do While info<>""
    Let word = NextWord$(info)
    Picture1.Print UCase$(Left$(word, 1)) + Mid$(word, 2) + " ";
  Loop
End Sub

Function NextWord$ (info As String)
  Dim spacePos As Integer
  Rem Take word from beginning of info; space assumed to be the word separator
  Let spacePos = Instr(info, " ")
  If spacePos = 0 Then
      Let NextWord$ = info
      Let info = ""
    Else
      Let NextWord$ = Left$(info, spacePos - 1)
      Let info = LTrim$(Mid$(info, spacePos))
  End If
End Function
```

39.
```
Sub Command1_Click ()
  Dim m As Single, n As Single, t As Single, q As Single
  Rem Greatest common divisor
  Picture1.Cls
  Call InputIntegers(m, n)
  Do While n <> 0
    Let t = n
    Let q = Int(m / n)
    Let n = m - q * n
    Let m = t
  Loop
  Picture1.Print "The greatest common divisor is"; m
End Sub

Sub InputIntegers (m As Single, n As Single)
  Rem Input two integers
  Let m = Val(InputBox$("Enter first integer:"))
  Let n = Val(InputBox$("Enter second integer:"))
End Sub
```

Exercises 6.2

1. 13

3. pie
    cake
    melon

5.   A
    Apple
    Apricot
    Avocado

      B
    Banana
    Blueberry

      G
    Grape

      L
    Lemon
    Lime

7. A group of ducks is called a brace

9. counters

11. Loop missing

13. Last president in file will not be printed.

15.
```
Sub Command1_Click ()
    Dim largest As Single, num as Single
    Rem Find largest of a collection of numbers
    Picture1.Cls
    Let largest = 0
    Do
      Let num = Val(InputBox$("Enter a number: (Enter -1 when finished)"))
      If num > largest Then
          Let largest = num
      End If
    Loop Until num = -1
    Picture1.Print "The largest number is"; largest
End Sub
```

17.
```
Sub Command1_Click ()
    Dim total As Single, numAboveAvg As Integer, grade As Single
    Dim average As Single, aaCount As Integer
    Rem Display percentage of grades that are above average
    Picture1.Cls
    Open "GRADES.TXT" For Input As #1
    Let total = 0
    Let numAboveAvg = 0
    Do While Not EOF(1)
      Input #1, grade
      Let total = total + grade
      Let numAboveAvg = numAboveAvg + 1
    Loop
    Close #1
    If numAboveAvg > 0 Then
        Let average = total / numAboveAvg
        Let aaCount = 0
        Open "GRADES.TXT" For Input As #1
        Do While Not EOF(1)
          Input #1, grade
          If grade > average Then
              Let aaCount = aaCount + 1
          End If
        Loop
        Close #1
        Picture1.Print Format$(aaCount / numAboveAvg, "Percent"); "of grades are above the average of";
        Picture1.Print Format$(average, "Standard")
    End If
End Sub
```

19.
```
Sub Command1_Click ()
    Dim n As Integer, num As Integer, nom As String
    Rem Display the name of the nth president
    Let n = Val(Text1.Text)
    If (1 <= n) And (n <= 42) Then
        Open "USPRES.TXT" For Input As #1
        Let num = 0
        Do
          Input #1, nom
          Let num = num + 1
        Loop Until num = n
        Picture1.Print nom; " was President number"; n
        Close #1
    End If
End Sub
```

21.
```
Sub Command1_Click ()
    Dim n As Single, numSteps As Single
    Rem Half problem
    Picture1.Cls
    Let n = Val(InputBox$("Enter an integer:"))
    Let numSteps = 0
    Do While n <> 1
      Let numSteps = numSteps + 1
      If (n / 2) = Int(n / 2) Then
          Let n = n / 2
          Picture1.Print n;
        Else
          Let n = 3 * n + 1
          Picture1.Print n;
      End If
    Loop
    Picture1.Print
    Picture1.Print "It took"; numSteps; "steps to reach 1."
End Sub
```

23.
```
Sub Command1_Click ()
     Dim totalWords As Integer, lineCount As Integer, sonnetLine As String
     Dim wordCount As Integer, word As String
     Rem Analyze a Shakespeare sonnet
     Picture1.Cls
     Let totalWords = 0
     Let lineCount = 0
     Open "SONNET.TXT" For Input As #1
     Do While Not EOF(1)
       Input #1, sonnetLine
       Let lineCount = lineCount + 1
       Let wordCount = 0
       Do While sonnetLine<>""
         Let word = nextWord$(sonnetLine)
         Let wordCount = wordCount + 1
       Loop
       Let totalWords = totalWords + wordCount
     Loop
     Picture1.Print "The sonnet contains and average of" totalWords / lineCount
     Picture1.Print "words per line and a total of "; totalWords; "words."
     Close #1
End Sub


Function NextWord$ (info As String)
   Dim spacePos As Integer
   Rem Take word from beginning of info; space assumed to be the word separator
   Let spacePos = Instr(info, " ")
   If spacePos = 0 Then
       Let NextWord$ = info
       Let info = ""
     Else
       Let NextWord$ = Left$(info, spacePos - 1)
       Let info = LTrim$(Mid$(info, spacePos))
   End If
End Function
```

25.
```
Sub Command1_Click ()
     Dim sentence As String, parensFlag As Integer, position As Integer, letter As String
     Rem Remove parentheses and their contents from a sentence
     Picture1.Cls
     Let sentence = Text1.Text
     Let parensFlag = 0
     Let position = 1
     Do Until position > Len(sentence)
       Let letter = Mid$(sentence, position, 1)
       Select Case letter
         Case "("
           Let parensFlag = 1
         Case ")"
           Let parensFlag = 0
         Case Else
           If parensFlag = 0 Then
               Picture1.Print letter;
           End If
       End Select
       Let position = position + 1
     Loop
End Sub
```

```
27. Sub Command1_Click ()
        Dim money As Single, liquid As String, price As Single
        Rem Display liquids available given an amount of money
        Picture1.Cls
        Let money = Val(Text1.Text)
        Picture1.Print "You can purchase one gallon of any of the following liquids."
        Open "DATA.TXT" For Input As #1
        Do While Not EOF(1)
          Input #1, liquid, price
          If price <= money Then
              Picture1.Print liquid
          End If
        Loop
        Close #1
    End Sub
```

Exercises 6.3

```
1.  Pass # 1
    Pass # 2
    Pass # 3
    Pass # 4
```

3. 2 4 6 8 Who do we appreciate?

5. 5 6 7 8 9 10 11 12 13

```
7.  Steve Cram      3:46.31
    Steve Scott     3:51.6
    Mary Slaney     4:20.5
```

```
9.  1    4    7    10
    2    5    8    11
    3    6    9    12
```

11. *******Hooray*******

13. Loop is never executed since 1 is less than 25.5 and the step is negative.

15. A For statement can only have one Next statement.

```
17. For num = 1 To 10 Step 2
        Picture1.Print num
    Next num
```

```
19. Sub Command1_Click ()
        Dim i As Integer
        Rem Display a row of ten stars
        Picture1.Cls
        For i = 1 To 10
          Picture1.Print "*";
        Next i
    End Sub
```

```
21. Sub Command1_Click ()
        Dim i As Integer, j As Integer
        Rem Display 10 x 10 array of stars
        Picture1.Cls
        For i = 1 To 10
          For j = 1 To 10
            Picture1.Print "*";
          Next j
          Picture1.Print
        Next i
    End Sub
```

```
23. Sub Command1_Click ()
        Dim sum As Single, denominator As Integer
        Rem Compute the sum 1 + 1/2 + 1/3 + 1/4 + ... + 1/100
        Picture1.Cls
        Let sum = 0
        For denominator = 1 To 100
          Let sum = sum + 1 / denominator
        Next denominator
        Picture1.Print "The sum is"; sum
    End Sub
```

```
25. Sub Command1_Click ()
        Dim result1 As Single, result2 As Single
        Rem Compare salaries
        Picture1.Cls
        Call Option1(result1)
        Call Option2(result2)
        If result1 > result2 Then
            Picture1.Print "Option 1";
          Else
            Picture1.Print "Option 2";
        End If
        Picture1.Print " pays better"
    End Sub

    Sub Option1 (result1 As Single)
        Dim i As Integer
        Rem Compute $100 per day
        Let result1 = 0
        For i = 1 To 10
          Let result1 = result1 + 100
        Next i
        Picture1.Print "Option 1 = "; Format$(result1, "Currency")
    End Sub

    Sub Option2 (result2 As Single)
        Dim i As Integer, daySalary As Single
        Rem Compute $1 then $2 ...
        Let result2 = 0
        Let daySalary = 1
        For i = 1 To 10
          Let result2 = result2 + daySalary
          Let daySalary = daySalary * 2
        Next i
        Picture1.Print "Option 2 = "; Format$(result2, "Currency")
    End Sub
```

27.
```
Sub Command1_Click ()
    Dim lower As Integer, upper As Integer
    Rem Ideal weights for men and women
    Picture1.Cls
    Call InputBounds(lower, upper)
    Call ShowWeights(lower, upper)
End Sub

Function IdealMan (height As Integer) As Single
    Rem Compute the ideal weight of a man given the height
    IdealMan = 4 * height - 128
End Function

Function IdealWoman (height As Integer) As Single
    Rem Compute the ideal weight of a woman given the height
    IdealWoman = 3.5 * height - 108
End Function

Sub InputBounds (lower As Integer, upper As Integer)
    Rem Input the lower and upper bounds on height
    Let lower = Val(InputBox$("Enter lower bound on height in inches:"))
    Let upper = Val(InputBox$("Enter upper bound on height in inches:"))
End Sub

Sub ShowWeights (lower As Integer, upper As Integer)
    Dim height As Integer
    Rem Display table of weights
    Picture1.Print
    Picture1.Print "Height", "Wt - Women", "Wt - Men"
    Picture1.Print
    For height = lower To upper
        Picture1.Print height, IdealWoman(height), IdealMan(height)
    Next height
End Sub
```

29.
```
Sub Command1_Click ()
    Dim sentence As String
    Rem Number of sibilants in sentence
    Picture1.Cls
    Let sentence = InputBox$("Enter a sentence:")
    Picture1.Print "There are"; Sibilants(sentence); "sibilants."
End Sub

Function Sibilants (sentence As String)
    Dim numSibs As Integer, i As Integer, letter As String
    Rem Count number of sibilants
    Let numSibs = 0
    For i = 1 To Len(sentence)
        Let letter = UCase$(Mid$(sentence, i, 1))
        If (letter = "S") Or (letter = "Z") Then
            Let numSibs = numSibs + 1
        End If
    Next i
    Sibilants = numSibs
End Function
```

31.
```
Sub Command1_Click ()
    Dim amt As Single, yearNum As Integer
    Rem Bank interest for ten years
    Picture1.Cls
    Let amt = 800
    For yearNum = 1 To 10
        Let amt = amt * 1.04 + 100
    Next yearNum
    Picture1.Print "The final amount is "; Format$(amt, "Currency")
End Sub
```

33.
```
Sub Command1_Click ()
    Dim grams As Single, yearNum As Integer
    Rem Radioactive decay
    Picture1.Cls
    Let grams = 10
    For yearNum = 1 To 5
      Let grams = .88 * grams
    Next yearNum
    Picture1.Print Format$(grams, "Standard"); " grams remain after 5 years."
End Sub
```

35.
```
Sub Command1_Click ()
    Dim stars As Integer, i As Integer
    Rem Draw a hollow box
    Picture1.Cls
    Picture1.FontName = "Courier"
    Let stars = Val(InputBox$("Number of stars?"))
    Call DrawSide(stars)
    For i = 1 To stars - 2
      Call DrawRow(stars)
    Next i
    Call DrawSide(stars)
End Sub

Sub DrawRow (stars As Integer)
  Dim i As Integer
  Rem Draw a row (put spaces between the two stars)
  Picture1.Print "*";
  For i = 1 To stars - 2
    Picture1.Print " ";
  Next i
  Picture1.Print "*"
End Sub

Sub DrawSide (stars As Integer)
  Dim i As Integer
  Rem Draw a solid side of stars
  For i = 1 To stars
    Picture1.Print "*";
  Next i
  Picture1.Print
End Sub
```

37.
```
Sub Command1_Click ()
    Dim m As Integer, n As Integer, row As Integer, col As Integer
    Rem Create a multiplication table
    Picture1.Cls
    Picture1.FontName = "Courier"
    Let m = Val(InputBox$("Enter number of rows:"))
    Let n = Val(InputBox$("Enter number of columns:"))
    For row = 1 To m
      For col = 1 To n
        Picture1.Print RightJustify6$(row * col);
      Next col
      Picture1.Print
    Next row
End Sub

Function RightJustify6$ (what As Integer)
  Dim s As String
  Let s = Format$(what, "#")
  RightJustify6$ = Format$(s, "@@@@@@")
End Function
```

39.
```
Sub Command1_Click ()
    Dim testValue As Single, amount As Single, i As Integer
    Rem Gambling casino problem
    Picture1.Cls
    Let testValue = 4
    Do
      Let testValue = testValue + 1    'Start test with $5
      Let amount = testValue
      For i = 1 To 3      'One iteration for each casino
        Let amount = amount - 1    'Entrance fee
        Let amount = amount / 2    'Funds lost
        Let amount = amount - 1    'Exit fee
      Next i
    Loop Until amount = 0
    Picture1.Print "Starting amount = "; Format$(testValue, "Currency")
End Sub
```

41.
```
Sub Command1_Click ()
    Dim which As Integer, i As Integer, word As String
    Rem Select random word from file of 20 words
    Randomize Timer
    Picture1.Cls
    Let which = Int(20 * Rnd) + 1
    Open "DATA.TXT" For Input As #1
    For i = 1 To which
      Input #1, word
    Next i
    Picture1.Print "The selected word is "; word
    Close #1
End Sub
```

43.
```
Sub Command1_Click ()
    Dim entries As Integer, nom As String
    Dim which As Integer, i As Integer, word As String
    Rem Select random name from file with unknown number of names
    Randomize Timer
    Picture1.Cls
    Let entries = 0
    Open "DATA.TXT" For Input As #1
    Do While Not EOF(1)
      Input #1, nom
      Let entries = entries + 1
    Loop
    Close #1
    Let which = Int(entries * Rnd) + 1
    Open "DATA.TXT" For Input As #1
    For i = 1 To which
      Input #1, nom
    Next i
    Picture1.Print "The winner is "; nom
    Close #1
End Sub
```

CHAPTER 7

Exercises 7.1

1. 3 7 0

3. Stuhldreher
Crowley

5. 6 2 9 11 3 4

7. The Dim statement in the (declarations) section of (general) dimensions companies() with subscripts from 1 to 100 and makes companies available to all procedures. Therefore, the ReDim statement in the Form_Load event procedure produces the error message "Array already dimensioned."

9. Array subscript out of range (when k > 4).

11. Improper syntax in Dim statement.

13.

river(1)	river(2)	river(3)	river(4)	river(5)
Thames	Ohio	Amazon	Volga	Nile

river(1)	river(2)	river(3)	river(4)	river(5)
Ohio	Amazon	Volga	Nile	Thames

15. a) 2
b) 7
c) 10
d) 9

17. Replace lines 18 through 24 with
```
Rem Display all names and difference from average
Picture1.Cls
For student = 1 To 8
  Picture1.Print nom(student), score(student) - average
Next student
```

19. ReDim bestPicture(1975 To 1995) As String

21.
```
Dim marx(1 To 4) As String 'In (declarations) section
                                of (general)
Sub Form_Load ()
  Let marx(1) = "Chico"
  Let marx(2) = "Harpo"
  Let marx(3) = "Groucho"
  Let marx(4) = "Zeppo"
End Sub
```

23.
```
Dim i As Integer
Rem Reverse array a() and store in b()
For i = 1 To 4
  Let b(i) = a(5 - i)
Next i
```

25.
```
Dim i As Integer, k As Integer
Rem Display the elements of the array a()
For i = 1 To 26 Step 5
  For k = 0 To 4
    Picture1.Print Tab(10 * k + 1); a(i + k);
  Next k
  Picture1.Print
Next i
```

27.
```
Dim i As Integer, differFlag As Integer
Rem Compare arrays a() and b() for same values
Let differFlag = 0
For i = 1 To 10
  If a(i) <> b(i) Then
      Let differFlag = 1
  End If
Next i
If differFlag = 1 Then
    Picture1.Print "The arrays are not identical."
  Else
    Picture1.Print "The arrays have identical values."
End If
```

29.
```
Dim i As Integer
Rem Curve grades by adding 7
For i = 1 To 12
  Let grades(i) = grades(i) + 7
Next i
```

31.
```
Sub Command1_Click ()
  Dim range As Integer, dataElement As Integer, score As Integer, interval As Integer
  Rem Create and display the frequency of scores
  Picture1.Cls
  ReDim frequency(1 To 5)
  Rem Set array elements to 0
  For range = 1 To 5
    Let frequency(range) = 0
  Next range
  Rem Read scores, count scores in each of five intervals
  Open "DATA.TXT" For Input As #1
  For dataElement = 1 To 30
    Input #1, score
    Let range = Int(score / 10) + 1    'Number in the range of 1-5
    Let frequency(range) = frequency(range) + 1
  Next dataElement
  Close #1
  Rem Display frequency in each interval
  Picture1.Print "Interval"; Tab(12); "Frequency"
  Picture1.Print
  For interval = 1 To 5
    Picture1.Print 10 * (interval - 1); "to"; 10 * interval;
    Picture1.Print Tab(14); frequency(interval)
  Next interval
End Sub
```

33.
```
Sub Command1_Click ()
  Dim i As Integer, total As Single
  Rem Display names, percentage of total stores of top ten pizza chains
  Picture1.Cls
  ReDim nom(1 To 10) As String, stores(1 To 10) As Single
  Rem Read from data file and record names and number of stores
  Rem Compute total stores
  Open "DATA.TXT" For Input As #1
  Let total = 0                    'Total stores
  For i = 1 To 10
    Input #1, nom(i), stores(i)
    Let total = total + stores(i)
  Next i
  Rem Display names and percentage of total stores
  Picture1.Print "Name"; Tab(30); "Percentage of stores"
  For i = 1 To 10
    Picture1.Print nom(i); Tab(30); Format$(stores(i) / total, "Percent")
  Next i
End Sub
```

35.
```
Dim monthNames(1 To 12) 'In (declarations) section of (general)

Sub Form_Load ()
  Let monthNames(1) = "January"
  Let monthNames(2) = "February"
  Let monthNames(3) = "March"
  Let monthNames(4) = "April"
  Let monthNames(5) = "May"
  Let monthNames(6) = "June"
  Let monthNames(7) = "July"
  Let monthNames(8) = "August"
  Let monthNames(9) = "September"
  Let monthNames(10) = "October"
  Let monthNames(11) = "November"
  Let monthNames(12) = "December"
End Sub

Sub Command1_Click ()
  Dim monthNum As Integer
  Rem Display month name
  Picture1.Cls
  Let monthNum = Val(InputBox$("Enter month number:"))
  Picture1.Print "Month name is "; monthNames(monthNum)
End Sub
```

37.
```
Sub Command1_Click ()
  Dim i As Integer, roll As Integer
  Rem Report results of 1000 rolls of a die
  Randomize Timer
  Picture1.Cls
  ReDim results(1 To 6)
  For i = 1 To 1000
    Let roll = Int(6 * Rnd) + 1
    Let results(roll) = results(roll) + 1
  Next i
  For i = 1 to 6
    Picture1.Print i; "came up"; results(i); "times"
  Next i
End Sub
```

Exercises 7.2

1. No.

3. Michigan

5. less than
greater than
equals
less than

7. The total rainfall for the first quarter is 10

9. Inside procedures, arrays must be declared with ReDim, not Dim.

11. n is incremented by 1 even if the user enters 0 to stop and see the product. Move the incrementing inside the If block just before the statement Let num(n) = number.

13.
```
Sub CopyArray (a() As Integer, b() As Integer)
  Dim i As Integer
  Rem Place a's values in b
  For i = 1 to UBound(a)
    Let b(i) = a(i)
  Next i
End Sub
```

15.
```
Sub Descending ()
  Dim order As Integer, i As Integer
  Rem Determine if array is ascending
  Let order = 1
  For i = 1 To Ubound(scores) - 1
    If scores(i) > scores(i + 1) Then
      Let order = 0
    End If
  Next i
  If order = 1 Then
    Picture1.Print "Array is ascending."
  Else
    Picture1.Print "Array is not ascending."
  End If
End Sub
```

17.
```
Sub WhatOrder ()
    Dim ascend As Integer, descend As Integer, i As Integer
    Rem Determine if order is ascending, descending, both, or neither
    Let ascend = 1
    Let descend = 1
    For i = 1 To Ubound(scores) - 1
      If scores(i) > scores(i + 1) Then
        Let ascend = 0
      ElseIf scores(i) < scores(i + 1) Then
        Let descend = 0
      End If
    Next i
    If (ascend = 1) And (descend = 1) Then
        Picture1.Print "Array is both"
      ElseIf (ascend = 0) And (descend = 0) Then
        Picture1.Print "Array is neither ascending nor descending."
      ElseIf (ascend = 1) Then
        Picture1.Print "Array is ascending."
      Else
        Picture1.Print "Array is descending."
    End If
End Sub
```

19.
```
Sub MergeOrderedWithDups ()
    Dim indexA As Integer, indexB As Integer, indexC As Integer
    Dim doneA As Integer, doneB As Integer
    Rem Merge ascending arrays, with duplications
    ReDim c(1 To 40) As Single
    Let indexA = 1
    Let indexB = 1
    Let doneA = 0
    Let doneB = 0
    For indexC = 1 To 40
      If ((a(indexA) <= b(indexB)) And doneA = 0) Or doneB = 1 Then
          Let c(indexC) = a(indexA)
          If indexA < 20 Then
              Let indexA = indexA + 1
            Else
              Let doneA = 1
          End If
        Else
          Let c(indexC) = b(indexB)
          If indexB < 20 Then
              Let indexB = indexB + 1
            Else
              Let doneB = 1
          End If
      End If
    Next indexC
End Sub
```

21.
```
Dim state(1 To 50) As String    'In (declarations) section of (general)
Dim numStates As Integer
Rem Maintain a list of states

Sub Command1_Click ()
  Dim nom As String, i As Integer, j As Integer
  Rem Enter a new state in the correct position
  If numStates = UBound(state) Then
      MsgBox "Fifty states have already been entered."
    Else
      Let nom = Text1.Text
      Let state(numStates + 1) = nom
      Let i = 1
      Do While state(i) < nom
        Let i = i + 1
      Loop
```

```
      If (nom = state(i)) And (i <= numStates) Then
          MsgBox "State already exists"
        Else  'shuffle array, insert state
          For j = numStates To i Step -1
            Let state(j + 1) = state(j)
          Next j
          Let state(i) = nom
          Let numStates = numStates + 1
      End If
  End If
End Sub

Sub Command2_Click ()
  Dim nom As String, i As Integer, k As Integer
  Rem Delete a state from the list
  Let nom = Text1.Text
  Let i = 1
  Do While (i < numStates) And (nom > state(i))
    Let i = i + 1
  Loop
  If (numStates = 0) Or (nom <> state(i)) Then
      MsgBox "State does not exist"
    Else  ' Shuffle rest of array down by 1
      Let numStates = numStates - 1
      For k = i To numStates
        Let state(k) = state(k + 1)
      Next k
  End If
End Sub

Sub Command3_Click ()
  Dim i As Integer
  Rem Display the states in the list
  Picture1.Cls
  For i = 1 To numStates
    Picture1.Print state(i)
  Next i
End Sub
```

23.
```
Dim grades(1 To 100) As Integer  'In (declarations) section of (general)
Dim numScores As Integer
Rem Report the number of students scoring above the class average

Sub Command1_Click ()
  If numScores = 100 Then
      MsgBox "100 scores have been entered. Cannot process more data."
    Else
      Let numScores = numScores + 1
      Let grades(numScores) = Val(Text1.Text)
  End If
End Sub

Sub Command2_Click ()
  Dim average As Single, aboveAverage As Integer
  Picture1.Cls
  Let average = Avg(grades(), numScores)
  Let aboveAverage = AboveAvg(grades(), numScores, Average)
  Picture1.Print aboveAverage; "students scored above the average"
End Sub

Function Avg (scores() As Integer, num As Integer) As Single
  Rem Compute the average and number of students above it
  Let sum = 0
  Let tot = 0
  For i = 1 To num
    Let sum = sum + scores(i)
  Next i
```

```
        If num <> 0 Then
            Avg = sum / num
          Else
            Avg = 0
        End If
    End Function

    Function AboveAvg (scores() As Integer, num As Integer, classAvg As Single) As Integer
        Dim i As Integer, tot As Integer
        Rem Count number of scores above average
        For i = 1 To num
          If scores(i) > classAvg Then
              Let tot = tot + 1
          End If
        Next i
        AboveAvg = tot
    End Function
```

25.
```
    Sub Command1_Click ()
        Rem Choose 50 people from a data file containing 100 names
        ReDim person(1 To 100) As Integer
        Call ClearArray(person())
        Call SelectPeople(person())
        Call ShowPeople(person())
    End Sub

    Sub ClearArray (person() As Integer)
        Dim i As Integer
        Rem Clear all array elements (no one selected yet)
        For i = 1 To 100
          Let person(i) = 0
        Next i
    End Sub

    Sub SelectPeople (person() As Integer)
        Dim i As Integer, num As Integer
        Rem Select fifty people (person i selected when person(i)=1)
        Randomize Timer
        For i = 1 To 50
          Do
            Let num = Int(Rnd * 100) + 1
          Loop Until person(num) = 0
          Let person(num) = 1
        Next i
    End Sub

    Sub ShowPeople (person() As Integer)
        Dim i As Integer, nom As String
        Rem Display selected people
        Picture1.Cls
        Open "DATA.TXT" For Input As #1
        For i = 1 To 100
          Input #1, nom
          If person(i) = 1 Then
              Picture1.Print nom
          End If
        Next i
        Close #1
    End Sub
```

Exercises 7.3

5. The width of text box Text1 is cut in half.

7. The text box will move left or right so that the upper left corner of text box Text1 is equal distance from the top and the left edge of the form.

9. The text box Text1 will extend all the way across the form. If the left edge of the text box is not at the left edge of the form, then part of the text box will extend beyond the right edge of the form but will not be visible.

11.
```
Sub cmdButton_Click (Index As Integer)
  Let cmdButton(Index).Visible = False
End Sub
```

13.
```
Sub cmdButton_Click (Index As Integer)
  Dim otherIndex As Integer
  Let otherIndex = (Index + 1) Mod 2
  Let cmdButton(Index).FontItalic = True
  Let cmdButton(otherIndex).FontItalic = False
End Sub
```

15.
```
Sub cmdButton_Click (Index As Integer)
  Dim othrIdx As Integer
  Let othrIdx = (Index + 1) Mod 2
  Let cmdButton(Index).Left = cmdButton(othrIdx).Left + cmdButton(othrIdx).Width + 100
End Sub
```

17.
```
Sub cmdButton_Click (Index As Integer)
  Let cmdButton(Index).Width = 2 * cmdButton(Index).Width
End Sub
```

19.
```
Load txtBox(1)
Let txtBox(1).Top = txtBox(0).Top + txtBox(0).Height + 100
Let txtBox(1).Visible = True
```

21. The first line of the event procedure should not have (1) in it, but instead should have (Index As Integer) after Click.

23. The index of the For loop should start at 1, not 0, or If i > 0 Then . . . End If should be put around the Load statement and the Let statement that sets the Top property. With a value of zero for *i*, an attempt will be made to load lbl(0) which has already been created at design time and to set the Top property of lbl(0) based on the Top and Height properties of lbl(–1) which cannot be done.

25. Home expenses for winter were $4271.66

27. Summer bills exceeded winter by $67.09

29. The form displays a vertical column of 4 text boxes, separated from each other by one half the height of a text box and labeled on the left with "Row #". The column is headed by "Col 1".

31. The form displays a horizontal row of 4 touching text boxes labeled above by "Col #". The row is label on the left by "Row 1".

33.
```
Sub txtWinter_LostFocus (Index As Integer)
  Rem recompute totals
  Call Retotal
End Sub

Sub txtSpring_LostFocus (Index As Integer)
  Rem recompute totals
  Call Retotal
End Sub

Sub txtSummer_LostFocus (Index As Integer)
  Rem recompute totals
  Call Retotal
End Sub

Sub txtFall_LostFocus (Index As Integer)
  Rem recompute totals
  Call Retotal
End Sub

Sub Retotal ()
  ReDim total(1 To 4) As Single
  Dim i As Integer, cTotal As Single
  Rem recompute totals
  For i = 1 To 4
    Let total(1) = total(1) + Val(txtWinter(i).Text)
    Let total(2) = total(2) + Val(txtSpring(i).Text)
    Let total(3) = total(3) + Val(txtSummer(i).Text)
    Let total(4) = total(4) + Val(txtFall(i).Text)
  Next i
  For i = 1 to 4
    Let lblQuarterTot(i).Caption = Str$(total(i))
  Next i
  For i = 1 to 4
    Let cTotal = 0
    Let cTotal = Val(txtWinter(i).Text) + Val(txtSpring(i).Text)
    Let cTotal = cTotal + Val(txtSummer(i).Text) + Val(txtFall(i).Text)
    Let lblCategTot(i).Caption = Str$(cTotal)
  Next i
End Sub
```

35.
```
Sub Text1_LostFocus (Index As Integer)
    Let Text1(Index).BackColor = &HFFFFFF
    Select Case Index
      Case 0
        Let Text1(1).BackColor = &HFFFF&
      Case 1
        Let Text1(2).BackColor = &HFF&
      Case 2
        Let Text1(0).BackColor = &HFF00&
    End Select
End Sub
```

37.
```
Dim correctNum As Single   'In (declarations) section of (general)

Sub Command1_Click (Index As Integer)
  If Index = correctNum Then
      Call CorrectAnswer
    Else
      Call IncorrectAnswer
  End If
End Sub


Sub CorrectAnswer ()
  Dim response As String
  Let response = InputBox$("Correct. Would you like another question? (Y/N)")
  Let response = Ucase$(Left$(response,1))
  If response = "N" Then
      Close #1
      End
    Else
      If Not EOF(1) Then
          Call GetQuestion
        Else
          MsgBox "There are no more questions.", , ""
          Close #1
          End
      End If
  End If
End Sub


Sub Form_Load ()
  Open "QUIZ.TXT" For Input As #1
  Call GetQuestion
End Sub


Sub GetQuestion ()
  Dim i As Integer, info As String
  For i = 0 to 4
    Input#1, info        'obtain question and 4 possible answers
    Let Label1(i).Caption = info
  Next i
  Input #1, correctNum    'number of the correct answer
End Sub


Sub IncorrectAnswer ()
  MsgBox "Incorrect, Try Again", , ""
End Sub
```

Exercises 7.4

1. 200 100

3. 11 7 Numbers interchanged.

5. Variables being swapped are not of the same type.

7. Sequential

9. 4 swaps

11. $(n-1) + (n-2) + \ldots + 1$

13. 5 swaps

15. 12 comparisons.

17. Go through the list once and count the number of times that each of the four integers occurs and then list the determined number of 1s, followed by the determined number of 2s, etc.

19. 16; 8 1/2; 5

21.
```
Sub TripleSwap (x As Single, y As Single, z As Single)
    Dim temp As Single
    Rem Interchange the values of x, y, and z
    Let temp = x
    Let x = y
    Let y = z
    Let z = temp
End Sub
```

23.
```
Sub Command1_Click ()
    Rem Display exhibits and number of visitors in alphabetical order
    ReDim exhibit(1 To 10) As String, visitors(1 To 10) As Integer
    Call ReadData(exhibit(), visitors())
    Call SortData(exhibit(), visitors())
    Call ShowData(exhibit(), visitors())
End Sub

Sub ReadData (exhibit() As String, visitors() As Integer)
    Dim i As Integer
    Rem Read exhibit names, visitors
    Open "DATA.TXT" For Input As #1
    For i = 1 To 10
        Input #1, exhibit(i), visitors(i)
    Next i
    Close #1
End Sub

Sub ShowData (exhibit() As String, visitors() As Integer)
    Dim i As Integer, temp As String
    Rem Display exhibit names and visitors
    Picture1.Cls
    Picture1.Print "Exhibit"; Tab(30); "Attendance (in thousands)"
    Picture1.Print
    For i = 1 To 10
        Let temp = Format$(visitors(i),"#")
        Picture1.Print exhibit(i); Tab(36); Format$(temp,"@@@@")
    Next i
End Sub

Sub SortData (exhibit() As String, visitors() As Integer)
    Dim elements As Integer, gap As Integer, doneFlag As Integer, index As Integer
    Dim strTemp As String, numTemp As Integer
    Rem Shell sort data by exhibit names
    Let elements = 10
    Let gap = Int(elements / 2)
    Do While gap >= 1
        Do
            Let doneFlag = 1
            For index = 1 To elements - gap
                If exhibit(index) > exhibit(index + gap) Then
                    Let strTemp = exhibit(index)
                    Let exhibit(index) = exhibit(index + gap)
                    Let exhibit(index + gap) = strTemp
                    Let numTemp = visitors(index)
                    Let visitors(index) = visitors(index + gap)
                    Let visitors(index + gap) = numTemp
                    Let doneFlag = 0
                End If
            Next index
        Loop Until doneFlag = 1
        Let gap = Int(gap / 2)
    Loop
End Sub
```

25.
```
Sub Command1_Click ()
    Rem Input list of words, insert additional element
    Picture1.Cls
    ReDim wordList(1 To 11) As String
    Call InputWords(wordList())
    Call InsertWord(wordList())
    Call ShowWords(wordList())
End Sub

Sub InputWords (wordList() As String)
  Dim i As Integer
  Rem Input first ten words
  Picture1.Print "Input ten words, in alphabetical order"
  For i = 1 To 10
    Let wordList(i) = InputBox$("Enter word number " + Format$(i, "#") + ":")
  Next i
End Sub

Sub InsertWord (wordList() As String)
  Dim word As String, i As Integer
  Rem Insert eleventh word in alphabetical order
  Picture1.Print
  Let word = InputBox$("Word to add:")
  Let wordList(11) = word
  Let i = 1
  Do While word > wordList(i)
    Let i = i + 1
  Loop
  Rem word belongs in slot i; move elements i through 10 up one slot
  For k = 10 To i Step -1
    Let wordList(k + 1) = wordList(k)
  Next k
  Let wordList(i) = word
End Sub

Sub ShowWords (wordList() As String)
  Dim i As Integer
  Rem Show list of eleven words
  Picture1.Cls
  For i = 1 To 11
    Picture1.Print wordList(i); " ";
  Next i
End Sub
```

27.
```
Sub Command1_Click ()
    Rem Sort array of 200 numbers
    ReDim nums(1 To 200) As Integer
    ReDim dist(0 To 63) As Integer
    Call FillArray(nums())
    Call GetOccurrences(nums(), dist())
    Call ShowDistribution(dist())
End Sub

Sub FillArray (nums() As Integer)
  Dim i As Integer
  Rem Generate numbers from 0 to 63 and place in array
  Let nums(1) = 5
  For i = 2 To 200
    Let nums(i) = (9 * nums(i - 1) + 7) Mod 64
  Next i
End Sub

Sub GetOccurrences (nums() As Integer, dist() As Integer)
  Dim i As Integer
  Rem Record occurrences for each number
  For i = 1 To 200
    Let dist(nums(i)) = dist(nums(i)) + 1
  Next i
End Sub
```

```
Sub ShowDistribution (dist() As Integer)
   Dim colWid As Integer, col As Integer, colNum As Integer, i As Integer
   Rem Display distribution array
   Picture1.Cls
   Let colWid = 12                    'Width allotted for a column
   For colNum = 0 To 3                'Display headings at top of four column
      Let col = colWid * colNum + 1
      Picture1.Print Tab(col); " # Occur";
   Next colNum
   Picture1.Print
   For i = 1 To 63                    'Display numbers & count of occurrences
      Let colNum = (i - 1) Mod 4
      Let col = colWid * colNum + 1
      Picture1.Print Tab(col); i; Tab(col + 4); dist(i);
      If col = 3 Then
          Picture1.Print
      End If
   Next i
End Sub
```

29.
```
Dim codes() As String   'In (declarations) section of (general)

Sub Form_Load ()
   Dim i As Integer
   ReDim codes(Asc("A") To Asc("Z")) As String
   Open "MORSE.TXT" For Input As #1
   For i = Asc("A") To Asc("Z")
      Input #1, codes(i)
   Next i
   Close #1
End Sub

Sub Command1_Click ()
   Dim word As String
   Rem Encode word in Morse Code
   Let word = UCase$(Text1.Text)
   Call ShowCode(word)
End Sub

Sub ShowCode (word As String)
   Dim index As Integer, letter As String
   Rem Show code for each index in word
   Picture1.Cls
   For index = 1 To Len(word)
      Let letter = Mid$(word, index, 1)
      Picture1.Print codes(Asc(letter)), letter
   Next index
End Sub
```

31.
```
Sub Command1_Click ()
   Dim nom As String
   Rem Compute average of five highest test scores
   ReDim score(1 To 7) As Integer
   Call InputData(nom, score())
   Call SortData(score())
   Call ShowData(nom, score())
End Sub

Sub InputData (nom As String, score() As Integer)
   Dim i As Integer
   Rem Input student's name and seven test scores
   Let nom = InputBox$("Student's name:")
   For i = 1 To 7
      Let score(i) = Val(InputBox$("Test score " + Format$(i, "#") + ":"))
   Next i
End Sub
```

```
Sub ShowData (nom As String, score() As Integer)
  Picture1.Cls
  Let sum = 0
  For passNum = 1 To 5
    Let sum = sum + score(passNum)
  Next passNum
  Picture1.Print nom, sum / 5
End Sub


Sub SortData (score() As Integer)
  Dim passNum As Integer, index As Integer, temp As Integer
  Rem Bubble sort scores in descending order
  For passNum = 1 To 6
    For index = 1 To 7 - passNum
      If score(index) < score(index + 1) Then
          Let temp = score(index)
          Let score(index) = score(index + 1)
          Let score(index + 1) = temp
      End If
    Next index
  Next passNum
End Sub
```

33.
```
Sub Command1_Click ()
    Dim n As Integer
    Rem Input array of measurements and determine their median
    Call InputNumberOfMeasurements(n)
    ReDim nums(1 To n) As Single
    Call InputNums(nums())
    Call DisplayMedian(nums())
End Sub


Sub DisplayMedian (nums() As Single)
  Rem Display the median of the n measurements
  Picture1.Cls
  Picture1.Print "The median is"; Median(nums())
End Sub


Sub InputNumberOfMeasurements (n As Integer)
  Rem Input number of measurements
  Let n = Val(InputBox$("Number of measurements:"))
End Sub


Sub InputNums (nums() As Single)
  Dim i As Integer
  Rem Input list of measurements
  For i = 1 To UBound(nums)
    Let nums(i) = Val(InputBox$("Enter measurement #" + Format$(i, "#") + ":"))
  Next i
End Sub


Function Median (nums() As Single)
  Dim n As Integer
  Call SortNums(nums())
  Let n = UBound(nums)
  If Int(n / 2) = n / 2 Then      'n is even
      Let m = n / 2
      Median = (nums(m) + nums(m + 1)) / 2
  Else                           'n is odd
      Median = nums((n + 1) / 2)
  End If
End Function


Sub SortNums (nums() As Single)
  Dim n As Integer, i As Integer, j As Integer, temp As Single
  Rem Bubble sort list of numbers
  Let n = UBound(nums)
```

```
      For i = 1 To n - 1
        For j = 1 To n - i
          If nums(j) > nums(j + 1) Then
              Let temp = nums(j)
              Let nums(j) = nums(j + 1)
              Let nums(j + 1) = temp
          End If
        Next j
      Next i
    End Sub
```

Exercises 7.5

1. 12

3. Dorothy

5. 4 1 6
      5 8 2

7. 1 3 5

9. The dimension statement should read Dim a(1 To 4, 1 To 3)
As Integer (currently the error is Subscript Out of Range.)

11.
```
Sub FillArray (a() As Single)
  Dim row As Integer, col As Integer
  Rem Fill an array
  For row = 1 To 10
    For col = 1 To 10
      Let a(row, col) = col
    Next col
  Next row
End Sub
```

13.
```
Sub Exchange (a() As Single)
    Dim col As Integer, temp As Single
    Rem Interchange values of 2nd and 3rd row
    For col = 1 To 10
      Let temp = a(2, col)
      Let a(2, col) = a(3, col)
      Let a(3, col) = temp
    Next col
End Sub
```

15.
```
Sub Command1_Click ()
  Rem Program to calculate inventory
  ReDim inv(1 To 2, 1 To 3) As Single, sales(1 To 2, 1 To 3) As Single
  Call ReadArrays(inv(), sales())
  Call ShowInventory(inv(), sales())
End Sub

Sub ReadArrays (inv() As Single, sales() As Single)
  Dim store As Integer, item As Integer
  Rem Read beginning inventory and sales for day
  Rem Beginning inventory is assumed to reside in BEGINV.TXT
  Rem Sales for day is assumed to reside in SALES.TXT
  Open "BEGINV.TXT" For Input As #1
  Open "SALES.TXT" For Input As #2
  For store = 1 To 2
    For item = 1 To 3
      Input #1, inv(store, item)
      Input #2, sales(store, item)
    Next item
  Next store
  Close #1
  Close #2
End Sub

Sub ShowInventory (inv() As Single, sales() As Single)
  Dim total As Single, store As Integer, item As Integer
  Rem Calculate and show inventory at end of the day
  Picture1.Cls
  Let total = 0
  For store = 1 To 2
    For item = 1 To 3
      Let inv(store, item) = inv(store, item) - sales(store, item)
      Picture1.Print inv(store, item),
      Let total = total + inv(store, item)
    Next item
    Picture1.Print
  Next store
  Picture1.Print "Total inventory is now"; total
End Sub
```

17.
```
Sub Command1_Click ()
    Rem Compute course enrollments by campus, no. of students by course
    Picture1.Cls
    ReDim enrollment(1 To 3, 1 To 10) As Single
    Call ReadData(enrollment())
    Call ShowCampusTotals(enrollment())
    Call ShowCourseTotals(enrollment())
End Sub

Sub ReadData (enrollment() As Single)
  Dim campus As Integer, course As Integer
  Rem Read enrollment data
  Rem Course enrollment data is assumed to reside in ENROLL.TXT
  Open "ENROLL.TXT" For Input As #1
  For campus = 1 To 3
    For course = 1 To 10
      Input #1, enrollment(campus, course)
    Next course
  Next campus
  Close #1
End Sub

Sub ShowCampusTotals (enrollment() As Single)
  Dim campus As Integer, total As Single, course As Integer
  Rem Compute and show total enrollments for each campus
  For campus = 1 To 3
    Let total = 0
    For course = 1 To 10
      Let total = total + enrollment(campus, course)
    Next course
    Picture1.Print "The total course enrollments on campus"; campus; "is"; total
  Next campus
End Sub

Sub ShowCourseTotals (enrollment() As Single)
  Dim course As Integer, total As Single, campus As Integer
  Rem Compute total enrollment for each course
  For course = 1 To 10
    Let total = 0
    For campus = 1 To 3
      Let total = total + enrollment(campus, course)
    Next campus
    Picture1.Print "The total enrollment in course"; course; "is"; total
  Next course
End Sub
```

19.
```
Sub Command1_Click ()
    Rem Compute golf statistics
    Picture1.Cls
    ReDim nom(1 To 3) As String, score(1 To 3, 1 To 4) As Integer
    Call ReadData(nom(), score())
    Call ComputeTotalScore(nom(), score())
    Call ComputeAveScore(nom(), score())
End Sub

Sub ComputeAveScore (nom() As String, score() As Integer)
  Dim round As Integer, total As Integer, player As Integer
  Rem Compute average score for each round
  For round = 1 To 4
    Let total = 0
    For player = 1 To 3
      Let total = total + score(player, round)
    Next player
    Picture1.Print "The average for round"; round; "was"; total / 3
  Next round
End Sub
```

```
Sub ComputeTotalScore (nom() As String, score() As Integer)
  Dim player As Integer, total As Integer, round As Integer
  Rem Compute total score for each player
  For player = 1 To 3
    Let total = 0
    For round = 1 To 4
      Let total = total + score(player, round)
    Next round
    Picture1.Print "The total score for "; nom(player); " was"; total
  Next player
  Picture1.Print
End Sub


Sub ReadData (nom() As String, score() As Integer)
  Dim player As Integer, round As Integer
  Rem Results of 1992 PGA Championships assumed to reside in GOLF.TXT
  Rem Read names and scores
  Open "GOLF.TXT" For Input As #1
  For player = 1 To 3
    Input #1, nom(player)
    For round = 1 To 4
      Input #1, score(player, round)
    Next round
  Next player
  Close #1
End Sub
```

21.
```
Rem In the (declarations) section of (general)
Dim prog(1 To 3) As String, univ(1 To 3, 1 To 5) As String


Sub Command1_Click ()
  Dim university As String
  Rem Access information from University Rankings Table
  Let university = Trim(Text1.Text)
  Call ShowRankings(university)
End Sub


Sub Form_Load ()
  Dim dept As Integer, ranking As Integer
  Rem Read university rankings in three departments
  Open "RANKINGS.TXT" For Input As #1
  For dept = 1 To 3
    Input #1, prog(dept)
    For ranking = 1 To 5
      Input #1, univ(dept, ranking)
    Next ranking
  Next dept
  Close #1
End Sub


Sub ShowRankings (university As String)
  Dim foundFlag As Integer, dept As Integer, ranking As Integer
  Rem Show rankings of university
  Picture1.Cls
  Picture1.Print university; " departments ranked in the top 5:"
  Let foundFlag = 0
  For dept = 1 To 3
    For ranking = 1 To 5
      If univ(dept, ranking) = university Then
          Picture1.Print prog(dept), ranking
          Let foundFlag = 1
      End If
    Next ranking
  Next dept
```

```
      If foundFlag = 0 Then
          Picture1.Print "Sorry! No information listed."
      End If
      Text1.Text = ""
      Text1.SetFocus
    End Sub
```

23.
Object	Property	Setting
Label1	Caption	Name of Student #1:
Text1	Text	(blank)
Label2	Caption	Exam Scores:
txtExam	Index	1 to 5
	Text	(blank)
Command1	Caption	Record Student Data
Picture1		

```
Rem In (declarations) section of (general)
Dim nom(1 To 15) As String, score(1 To 15, 1 To 5) As Integer
Dim student As Integer

Sub Command1_Click ()
  Dim exam As Integer
  Rem Record name and five exam score for another student
  Rem Exam scores are entered in a control array of 5 text boxes
  Rem When last student is entered, process data and prevent further data entry
  Let student = student + 1
  Let nom(student) = Text1.Text
  For exam = 1 To 5
    Let score(student, exam) = Val(txtExam(exam).Text)
  Next exam
  If student = UBound(nom) Then
      Call ProcessData
      Let Command1.Visible = False
    Else
      Let Text1.Text = ""
      For exam = 1 To 5
        Let txtExam(exam).Text = ""
      Next exam
      Let Label1.Caption = "Name of student #" + Format$(student, "0") + ":"
      Text1.SetFocus
  End If
End Sub

Sub ProcessData ()
  Rem Analyze exam scores
  Picture1.Cls
  Call ShowAverages(nom(), score())
  Call SortScores(score())
  Call ShowMedians(score())
End Sub

Sub ShowAverages (nom() As String, score() As Integer)
  Dim index As Integer, sum As Integer, exam As Integer
  Rem Compute and show semester score averages
  Picture1.Cls
  Picture1.Print "Name"; Tab(15); "Semester average"
  For index = 1 To UBound(nom)
    Let sum = 0
    For exam = 1 To 5
      Let sum = sum + score(index, exam)
    Next exam
    Picture1.Print nom(index); Tab(20); Format$(sum / 5, "#")
  Next index
End Sub
```

```
Sub ShowMedians (score() As Integer)
  Dim entries As Integer, exam As Integer, middle As Integer
  Rem Show medians for each exam
  Let entries = UBound(nom)
  For exam = 1 To 5
    Picture1.Print "The median on exam"; exam; "was";
    If Int(entries / 2) = entries / 2 Then    'If even number of entries
        Let middle = entries / 2           'First index of the two "middle" entries
        Picture1.Print (score(middle, exam) + score(middle + 1, exam)) / 2
      Else
        Let middle = (entries + 1) / 2
        Picture1.Print score(middle, exam)
    End If
  Next exam
End Sub


Sub SortScores (score() As Integer)
  Dim entries As Integer, exam As Integer, passNum As Integer
  Dim index As Integer, temp As Integer
  Rem Bubble sort scores
  Let entries = UBound(nom)
  For exam = 1 To 5
    For passNum = 1 To entries - 1
      For index = 1 To entries - passNum
        If score(index, exam) > score(index + 1, exam) Then
            Let temp = score(index, exam)
            Let score(index, exam) = score(index + 1, exam)
            Let score(index + 1, exam) = temp
        End If
      Next index
    Next passNum
  Next exam
End Sub
```

25.
```
Sub Command1_Click ()
  Rem Compute total sales for each storeRevenue and for entire company
  ReDim sales(1 To 3, 1 To 5) As Integer, cost(1 To 5) As Single
  Call ReadData(sales(), cost())
  Call ShowRevenues(sales(), cost())
End Sub


Sub ReadData (sales() As Integer, cost() As Single)
  Dim store As Integer, item As Integer
  Rem Read sales and cost
  Open "SALES.TXT" For Input As #1
  For store = 1 To 3
    For item = 1 To 5
      Input #1, sales(store, item)
    Next item
  Next store
  Close #1
  Open "PRICES.TXT" For Input As #1
  For item = 1 To 5
    Input #1, cost(item)
  Next item
  Close #1
End Sub


Sub ShowRevenues (sales() As Integer, cost() As Single)
  Dim totalRevenue As Single, store As Integer, storeRevenue As Single
  Dim item As Integer, totalStr As String
  Rem Compute and show revenues
  Picture1.FontName = "Courier"
  Picture1.Cls
  Picture1.Print "Store";Tab(12);"Total"
  Let totalRevenue = 0
```

```
    For store = 1 To 3
      Let storeRevenue = 0
      For item = 1 To 5
        Let storeRevenue = storeRevenue + sales(store, item) * cost(item)
      Next item
      Let totalRevenue = totalRevenue + storeRevenue
      Let totalStr = Format$(storeRevenue, "Currency")
      Picture1.Print " "; store; Tab(7); Format$(totalStr, "@@@@@@@@@@")
    Next store
    Picture1.Print "Total revenue for the company was "; Format$(totalRevenue, "Currency")
  End Sub
```

CHAPTER 8

Exercises 8.1

1. `Hello`

3. `Hello`
   `Aloha`
   `Bon Jour`

5. Copies Hello and Bon Jour into the file "WELCOME"

7. No quotes surrounding filename

9. Using EOF(1) as the terminating value in a For loop.

11. Illegal file name NEW.GREET.TXT

13.
```
Sub Command1_Click ()
    Rem Create file of names and prices of items bought by cowboys
    Open "COWBOY.TXT" For Output As #1
    Write #1, "Colt Peacemaker", 12.20
    Write #1, "Holster", 2
    Write #1, "Levi Strauss Jeans", 1.35
    Write #1, "Saddle", 40
    Write #1, "Stetson", 10
    Close #1
End Sub
```

15.
```
Sub Command1_Click ()
    Rem Add Winchester rifle to end of file COWBOY
    Open "COWBOY.TXT" For Append As #1
    Write #1, "Winchester rifle", 20.5
    Close #1
End Sub
```

17.
```
Sub Command1_Click ()
    Dim newItem As String, newPrice As Single
    Rem Insert an item into COWBOY file in proper sequence
    Call InputItemData(newItem, newPrice)
    Call AddItemData(newItem, newPrice)
End Sub

Sub AddItemData (newItem As String, newPrice As Single)
    Dim insertedFlag As Integer, item As String, price As Single
    Rem Create second COWBOY file with new inserted item
    Open "COWBOY.TXT" For Input As #1
    Open "COWBOY2.TXT" For Output As #2
    Let insertedFlag = 0      'Tells if item has been inserted
    Do While Not EOF(1)
      Input #1, item, price
      If (insertedFlag = 0) And (item >= newItem) Then
          Write #2, newItem, newPrice
          Let insertedFlag = 1
      End If
      Write #2, item, price
    Loop
    If insertedFlag = 0 Then
        Write #2, newItem, newPrice
    End If
    Close #1
    Close #2
End Sub

Sub InputItemData (newItem As String, newPrice As Single)
    Rem Input new item name and price
    Let newItem = InputBox$("New item to be inserted:")
    Let newPrice = Val(InputBox$("Price of the new item:"))
End Sub
```

19.
```
Sub Command1_Click ()
    Dim item As String, price As Single
    Rem Produce COWBOY4.TXT with Holster removed
    Open "COWBOY.TXT" For Input As #1
    Open "COWBOY4.TXT" For Output As #2
    Do While Not EOF(1)
      Input #1, item, price
      If item <> "Holster" Then
          Write #2, item, price
      End If
    Loop
    Close #1
    Close #2
End Sub
```

21.
```
Sub Command1_Click ()
    Dim search As String, nom As String, yob As Integer
    Rem Search for a name in YOB.TXT
    Picture1.Cls
    Let search = InputBox$("Enter name to search for:")
    Open "YOB.TXT" For Input As #1
    Let nom = ""
    Do While (search > nom) And (Not EOF(1))
      Input #1, nom, yob
    Loop
    If nom = search Then
        Picture1.Print nom; "'s age is"; 1995 - yob
      Else
        Picture1.Print search; " is not in YOB.TXT"
    End If
    Close #1
End Sub
```

23.
```
Sub Command1_Click ()
    Dim searchTitle As String, filename As String, title As String
    Rem Access publisher's inventory files
    Picture1.Cls
    Call InputData(searchTitle, filename)
    Open filename For Input As #1
    Let title$ = ""
    Do While (title <> searchTitle) And (Not EOF(1))
      Input #1, title, copies
    Loop
    If title = searchTitle Then
        Picture1.Print "Number of copies in inventory is"; copies
      Else
        Picture1.Print "Book is not listed."
    End If
    Close #1
End Sub

Sub InputData (searchTitle As String, filename As String)
    Rem Input book name and determine file name
    Let searchTitle = Text1.Text
    Let bookType = Text2.Text
    If UCase$(bookType) = "H" Then
        Let filename = "HARDBACK.INV"
      Else
        Let filename = "PAPERBCK.INV"
    End If
End Sub
```

Exercises 8.2

1.
```
Sub Command1_Click ()
    Rem Add initial batting average record to AVERAGE.TXT
    Write #1, Text1.Text, 0, 0        'Initialize counters
End Sub

Sub Command2_Click ()
    Close #1
End Sub

Sub Form_Load ()
    Open "AVERAGE.TXT" For Output As #1
End Sub
```

3.
```
Sub Command1_Click ()
    Rem Add a player to the end of the file AVERAGE.TXT
    Open "AVERAGE.TXT" For Append As #1
    Write #1, Text1.Text, 0, 0
    Close #1
End Sub
```

5.
```
Sub Command1_Click ()
    Dim nom As String, subscriber As String
    Rem NY Times subscribers on the block
    Open "BLOCK.TXT" For Input As #1
    Open "TIMES.TXT" For Input As #2
    Open "NAMES.TXT" For Output As #3
    Let subscriber = ""
    Do While Not EOF(1)
      Input #1, nom
      Do While (subscriber < nom) And (Not EOF(2))
        Input #2, subscriber
      Loop
      If subscriber = nom Then
          Write #3, subscriber
      End If
    Loop
    Close #1
    Close #2
    Close #3
End Sub
```

7.
```
Sub Command1_Click ()
    Dim max As Single, lastNum As Single, numRepeats As Single, number As Single
    Rem Count maximum number of repeated integers
    Picture1.Cls
    Open "NUMBERS.TXT" For Input As #1
    Let max = 0
    Let lastNum = 0
    Let numRepeats = 0
    Do While Not EOF(1)
      Input #1, number
      If number <> lastNum Then
          If numRepeats > max Then
              Let max = numRepeats
          End If
          Let lastNum = number
          Let numRepeats = 1
        Else
          Let numRepeats = numRepeats + 1
      End If
    Loop
    Picture1.Print "The maximum number of repeats is"; max
    Close #1
End Sub
```

9.
```
Sub Command1_Click ()
    Dim cntrlVar As Integer, gradeTotal As Integer, total As Integer
    Dim grade As Integer, nom As String, nmbTix As Integer
    Rem Display student raffle ticket totals
    Picture1.Cls
    Open "RAFFLE.TXT" For Input As #1
    Let cntrlVar = 0
    Let gradeTotal = 0
    Let total = 0
    Do While Not EOF(1)
      Input #1, grade, nom, nmbTix
      If cntrlVar = 0 Then        'Reset cntrlVar after first grade is read
          Let cntrlVar = grade
      End If
      If (grade <> cntrlVar) Then   'Display gradeTotal if new grade found
          Picture1.Print "Grade"; cntrlVar; "sold"; gradeTotal; "tickets"
          Let total = total + gradeTotal
          Let gradeTotal = 0
          Let cntrlVar = grade
      End If
      Let gradeTotal = gradeTotal + nmbTix
      If EOF(1) Then              'At end-of-file, print last grade's total
          Picture1.Print "Grade"; cntrlVar; "sold"; gradeTotal; "tickets"
          Let total = total + gradeTotal
      End If
    Loop
    Picture1.Print
    Picture1.Print "Total = "; total
    Close #1
End Sub
```

11.
```
Sub Command1_Click ()
    Dim mstName As String, mstNmb As String, nom As String, newNmb As String
    Rem Update phone number master file
    Open "MASTER.TXT" For Input As #1
    Open "MOVED.TXT" For Input As #2
    Open "TEMP.TXT" For Output As #3
    Do While Not EOF(2)
      Input #2, nom, newNmb
      Do
        Input #1, mstName, mstNmb
        If mstName = nom Then
            Write #3, mstName, newNmb
          Else
            Write #3, mstName, mstNmb
        End If
      Loop Until mstName = nom
    Loop
    Do While Not EOF(1)
      Input #1, mstName, mstNmb
      Write #3, mstName, mstNmb
    Loop
    Close #1
    Close #2
    Close #3
    Open "MASTER.TXT" For Output As #1
    Open "TEMP.TXT" For Input As #2
    Do While Not EOF(2)
      Input #2, mstName, mstNmb
      Write #1, mstName, mstNmb
    Loop
    Close #1
    Close #2
    Kill "TEMP.TXT"
End Sub
```

13. Split the file into two or more files which can be stored in arrays, sort these files using arrays, and then merge the sorted files.

CHAPTER 9

Exercises 9.1

1. `Pacific   Mississipp`

3. `heights are same`
`170`
`eye colors are same`

5. The variables used in the Let statements are invalid. They should be astrology.nom and astrology.sign.

7. Reserved word "name" used as field name and no End Type statement.

9. Number is an invalid data type.

11.
```
Type planet
    planetName As String * 20
    distanceFromSun As Single
End Type
```

13.
```
Type car
    make As String * 20
    model As String * 20
    yr As Single
    mileage As Single
End Type
```

15.
```
Command1_Click ()
    Rem Input three words and display them in first three zones
    Picture1.Cls
    Dim name1 As String * 14
    Dim name2 As String * 14
    Dim name3 As String * 14
    Let name1 = Text1.Text
    Let name2 = Text2.Text
    Let name3 = Text3.Text
    Picture1.Print name1; name2; name3
End Sub
```

Exercises 9.2

1. `VA`

3. ```
   TX
   WI
   VA
    3
   ```

5. ```
   Virginia Tech          VA          1872
   Harvard                MA          1636
   ```

7. `Milwaukee Area Tech. Col.   WI          1912`

9. Cannot take length of a variable type. Should be Len(actor).

11. Cannot print record variable.

13. ```
    Type typeNums
       num1 As Single
       num2 As Single
       num3 As Single
    End Type

    Dim numbers As typeNums
    Open "NUMBERS.TXT" For Random As #1 Len = Len(numbers)
    ```

15. ```
    Rem In BAS Module
    Type typePerson
       nom As String * 15
       yob As Integer
    End Type

    Rem in Form Module
    Sub Command1_Click ()
       Dim recNum As Single, nom As String, yob As Integer
       Rem Make random file YOB2.TXT from sequential file YOB.TXT
       Picture1.Cls
       Dim person As typePerson
       Open "YOB.TXT" For Input As #1
       Open "YOB2.TXT" For Random As #2 Len = Len(person)
       Let recNum = 1
       Do While Not EOF(1)
          Input #1, nom, yob
          Let person.nom = nom
          Let person.yob = yob
          Put #2, recNum, person
          Let recNum = recNum + 1
       Loop
       Close #1
       Close #2
    End Sub
    ```

CHAPTER 10

Exercises 10.1

1. `Picture1.Scale (-1, 30)-(7, -5)`

3. ```
   Picture1.Line (-1, 0)-(4, 0)     'x-axis
   Picture1.Line (0, -8)-(0, 40)    'y-axis
   ```

5. ```
   Sub Command1_Click ()
      Rem Draw axes and line
      Picture1.Scale (-2, 240)-(12, -40)
      Picture1.Line (-2, 0)-(12, 0)         'Draw x-axis
      Picture1.Line (0, -40)-(0, 240)       'Draw y-axis
      Picture1.Line (3, 200)-(10, 150)      'Draw line
      Picture1.Circle (3, 200), .05
      Picture1.Circle (10, 150), .05
   End Sub
   ```

7. ```
   Sub Command1_Click ()
      Rem Draw axes and line
      Picture1.Scale (-.2 * 4, 1.2 * .5)-(1.2 * 4, -.2 * .5)
      Picture1.Line (-.2 * 4, 0)-(1.2 * 4, 0)      'Draw x-axis
      Picture1.Line (0, -.2 * .5)-(0, 1.2 * .5)    'Draw y-axis
      Picture1.Line (2, .5)-(4, .3)                'Draw line
      Picture1.Circle (2, .5), .03
      Picture1.Circle (4, .3), .03
   End Sub
   ```

9. ```
   Sub Command1_Click ()
      Rem Draw a circle in the center of the screen
      Picture1.Scale (-10, 10)-(10, -10)
      Picture1.Circle (0, 0), 4
   End Sub
   ```

11. ```
    Sub Command1_Click ()
       Rem Draw a tick mark at 70 on the y-axis
       Picture1.Scale (-10, 100)-(100, -10)
       Picture1.Line (0, -10)-(0, 100)           'y-axis
       Picture1.Line (-1, 70)-(1, 70)
    End Sub
    ```

13. ```
    Sub Command1_Click ()
       Rem Draw points in the 4 corners of the picture box
       Picture1.Scale (0, 10)-(10, 0)
       Picture1.Circle (0, 0), 1
       Picture1.Circle (0, 10), 1
       Picture1.Circle (10, 0), 1
       Picture1.Circle (10, 10), 1
    End Sub
    ```

15. ```
    Sub Command1_Click ()
       Rem Draw a rectangle
       Picture1.Scale (0, 10)-(10, 0)
       Picture1.Line (1, 1)-(1, 6)
       Picture1.Line (1, 6)-(6, 6)
       Picture1.Line (6, 6)-(6, 1)
       Picture1.Line (6, 1)-(1, 1)
    End Sub
    ```

17. ```
    Sub Command1_Click ()
       Dim r As Single
       Rem Draw five concentric circles
       Picture1.Scale (0, 10)-(10, 0)
       For r = .5 To 2.5 Step .5
          Picture1.Circle (5, 5), r
       Next r
    End Sub
    ```

19. ```
    Sub Command1_Click ()
       Rem Draw a circle and tangent line
       Picture1.Scale (0, 10)-(10, 0)
       Picture1.Circle (5, 5), 1
       Picture1.Line (6, 0)-(6, 10)
    End Sub
    ```

21. The circle will be smaller.

23. The circle will be the same size as in Exercise 21.
    ```

25.
```
Sub Command1_Click ()
    Dim maxX As Single, maxY As Single
    Rem Graph the Square Function
    Let maxX = 10
    Let maxY = maxX * maxX
    Picture1.Scale (-.2 * maxX, 1.2 * maxY)-(1.2 * maxX, -.2 * maxY)
    Picture1.Line (-.2 * maxX, 0)-(1.2 * maxX, 0)   'Draw x-axis
    Picture1.Line (0, -.2 * maxY)-(0, 1.2 * maxY)   'Draw y-axis
    For x = 0 To maxX Step .01
      Picture1.PSet (x, x * x)
    Next x
End Sub
```

27.
```
Sub Command1_Click ()
    Dim maxNum As Integer, interval As Single
    Dim i As Integer, xPos As Single, ticLabel As String
    Rem Draw a number line
    Let maxNum = Val(InputBox$("Enter maximum number to be displayed:"))
    Picture1.Cls
    Picture1.Scale (-10, 10)-(110, -10)
    Picture1.Line (0, 0)-(100, 0)        'Draw x-axis
    Let interval = 100 / (maxNum + 1)
    For i = 1 To maxNum
      Let xPos = interval * i
      Picture1.Line (xPos, -.5)-(xPos, .5)
      Let ticLabel = Format$(i, "0")
      Let Picture1.CurrentX = interval * i - Picture1.TextWidth(ticLabel) / 2
      Let Picture1.CurrentY = -1
      Picture1.Print ticLabel;
    Next i
End Sub
```

29.
```
Sub Command1_Click ()
    Dim x As Single, y As Single
    Rem Draw a sheet of graph paper
    Picture1.Scale (0, 50)-(100, 0)
    For x = 0 To 100 Step 5
      Picture1.Line (x, 0)-(x, 50)
    Next x
    For y = 0 To 50 Step 5
      Picture1.Line (0, y)-(100, y)
    Next y
End Sub
```

Exercises 10.2

1. `Picture1.Scale (-1, 1600)-(6, -250)`

Exercises 10.3

1. The variable numYears will have to be increased and the new data added to the data file.

11. `Picture1.Scale (-7.5, 5)-(2.5, -5)`

13. Only procedure DrawData needs to be changed
```
Sub DrawData (male() As Single, female() As Single, numYears As Integer)
    Dim i As Integer
    Rem Draw rectangles
    For i = 1 To numYears
      Picture1.Line (i - .4, male(i))-(i, 0), , BF
      Picture1.Line (i - .2, female(i))-(i + .2, 0), , B
    Next i
End Sub
```

Exercises 10.4

1. Counterclockwise the numbers are 0, .15, .45, .70, .90.

3. Assume that the data .15, .30, .25, .20, .10 have been placed in the file DATA.TXT.

```
Sub Command1_Click ()
  Dim circumf As Single, i As Integer, startAngle As Single, stopAngle As Single, radius As Single
  ReDim percent(1 To 5) As Single, cumPercent(0 To 5) As Single
  Rem Draw circle and radius lines and fill one sector
  Picture1.Scale (-10, 10)-(10, -10)
  Let radius = 5
  Let circumf = 2 * 3.14159
  Let cumPercent(0) = .0000001 'a "zero" that can be made negative
  Open "DATA.TXT" For Input As #1
  For i = 1 To 5
    Input #1, percent(i)
    Let cumPercent(i) = cumPercent(i - 1) + percent(i)
    Let startAngle = cumPercent(i - 1) * circumf
    Let stopAngle = cumPercent(i) * circumf
    If percent(i) = .1 Then
        Let Picture1.FillStyle = 0 'solid fill
      Else
        Let Picture1.FillStyle = 1 'transparent fill
    End If
    Picture1.Circle (0, 0), radius, , -startAngle, -stopAngle
  Next i
  Close #1
End Sub
```

9.
```
Sub Command1_Click ()
  Dim circumf As Single
  Rem Draw Pacman
  Picture1.Scale (-4, 4)-(4, -4)
  Let circumf = 2 * 3.14159
  Picture1.Circle (0, 0), 2, , -(1 / 8) * circumf, -(7 / 8) * circumf
End Sub
```

CHAPTER 11

Exercises 11.1

1. The currently selected item in List1 is displayed in Picture1.

3. The last item in List1 is displayed in Picture1.

5. Brahms is added to the list (after Beethoven) and is displayed in Picture1.

7. The currently selected item in List1 is deleted.

9. All items are removed from List1.

11. Chopin is removed from the list. (Mozart is not removed because the deletion of Chopin changes the index of Mozart from 3 to 2 while the value of n in the next pass through the For...Next loop is 3.)

13. `Picture1.Print Combo1.List(0)`

15. `Picture1.Print Combo1.List(0)`

17. `Combo1.RemoveItem 1`

19. `Combo1.AddItem "Cervantes"  'Will appear first in the list`

21.
```
Sub DeleteMs ()
  Dim i As Integer
  Rem Delete all items beginning with M
  Let i = 0
  Do While i <= Combo1.ListCount - 1
    If Left$(Combo1.List(i), 1) = "M" Then
        Combo1.RemoveItem i
      Else
        Let i = i + 1
    End If
  Loop
End Sub
```

23. `Picture1.Print Combo1.List(Combo1.NewIndex)`

25.
```
Sub Command1_Click ()
  Dim i As Integer, total As Single
  Let total = 0
  For i = 0 to List1.ListCount - 1
    Let total = total + Val(List1.List(i))
  Next i
  Picture1.Print "The average of the numbers is"; total / List1.ListCount
End Sub
```

27.
```
Sub Command1_Click ()
    Dim i As Integer
    For i = 0 to List1.ListCount - 1 Step 2
      Picture1.Print List1.List(i)
    Next i
End Sub
```

29.
```
Sub Command1_Click ()
    Dim i As Integer, largest As Single, smallest As Single
    Let largest = Val(List1.List(0))
    Let smallest = largest
    For i = 1 to List1.ListCount - 1
      If Val(List1.List(i)) < smallest Then
          Let smallest = Val(List1.List(i))
        ElseIf Val(List1.List(i)) > largest Then
          Let largest = Val(List1.List(i))
      End If
    Next i
    Picture1.Print "The spread of the numbers is"; largest - smallest
End Sub
```

31.

Object	Property	Setting
frmStates	Caption	State Facts
lstStates	Sorted	True
picStates		

```
Dim nickName(4) As String, motto(4) As String    'In (declarations) section of (general)


Sub Form_Load ()
    Dim i As Integer, state As String
    Open "STATEINF.TXT" For Input As #1
    For i = 1 To 4
      Input #1, state, nickName(i), motto(i)
      lstStates.AddItem state
      Let lstStates.ItemData(lstStates.NewIndex) = i
    Next i
    Close 1
End Sub


Sub lstStates_DblClick ()
    picStates.Cls
    picStates.Print "Nickname: "; nickName(lstStates.ItemData(lstStates.ListIndex))
    picStates.Print "Motto: "; motto(lstStates.ItemData(lstStates.ListIndex))
End Sub
```

35.

Object	Property	Setting
frmLengths	Caption	Length Converter
lblFrom	Caption	From
lblTo	Caption	To
lstFrom		
lstTo		
lblLength	Caption	Length to be converted
txtLength	Text	(blank)
cmdConvert	Caption	Convert
lblConverted	Caption	Converted Length
lblNewLen	Caption	(blank)

```
Sub Form_Load ()
    lstFrom.AddItem "inch"
    lstFrom.AddItem "feet"
    lstFrom.AddItem "yard"
    lstFrom.AddItem "meter"
    lstFrom.AddItem "mile"
    lstTo.AddItem "inch"
    lstTo.AddItem "feet"
    lstTo.AddItem "yard"
    lstTo.AddItem "meter"
    lstTo.AddItem "mile"
End Sub
```

```
Sub Command1_Click ()
  Dim fromFact As Single, toFact As Single, newDist As Single
  Rem fromFact is # of inches in "from" unit
  Select Case lstFrom.ListIndex
    Case 0
      Let fromFact = 1
    Case 1
      Let fromFact = 12
    Case 2
      Let fromFact = 36
    Case 3
      Let fromFact = 100 / 2.54 '100 centimeters / 2.54 cm per inch
    Case 4
      Let fromFact = 63360        '5280 feet per mile * 12 inches per foot
  End Select
  Rem toFact is # of inches in "to" units
  Select Case lstTo.ListIndex
    Case 0
      Let toFact = 1
    Case 1
      Let toFact = 12
    Case 2
      Let toFact = 36
    Case 3
      Let toFact = 100 / 2.54 '100 centimeters / 2.54 cm per inch
    Case 4
      Let toFact = 63360        '5280 feet per mile * 12 inches per foot
  End Select
  Let newDist = Val(txtLength.Text) * fromFact / toFact
  If newDist >= 1 Then
      Let lblNewLen.Caption = Format$(newDist, "Standard")
    Else
      Let lblNewLen.Caption = Format$(newDist, "0.000000")
  End If
End Sub
```

Exercises 11.2

1. The word "Income" becomes the caption embedded in the top of Frame1.

3. The Check1 check box becomes unchecked.

5. The Option1 option button becomes unselected.

7. The scroll bar thumb will move to its rightmost position.

9. Clicking on the scroll bar between the thumb and an arrow will move the button the same ("large") distance as clicking on the arrow.

11. The Timer1 control is disabled.

13. The Shape1 control becomes an oval.

15. The Shape1 control becomes filled with a cross-hatch pattern.

17. The thickness of the Line1 control doubles.

19. `Let Frame1.Left = Frame1.Left + 100`

21. `Let Option2.Value = False`

23. `Let HScroll.Value = HScroll2.Min + (HScroll2.Max - HScroll2.Min) / 3`

25.
```
Dim flag As Integer 'In (declarations) section of (general)
Sub Form_Load ()
  Let flag = 0
  Let Timer1.Interval = 65000   'One minute and five seconds
  Let Timer1.Enabled = True
End Sub

Sub Timer1_Timer ()
  If flag = 0 Then
      Let flag = 1
    Else
      Let flag = 0
      Call Event  'Event is procedure that is invoked every 2 minutes and 10 seconds
  End If
End Sub
```

27. `Let Shape1.FillStyle = 3`

29. Option2 is selected (True) and Option1 is unselected (False).

31. Check boxes, Combo list boxes, Horizontal scroll bars, List boxes, Option buttons, and Vertical scroll bars can receive the focus.

33. Yes, the option buttons attached to a frame will become invisible if the frame is made invisible.

35.
```
Sub Command1_Click ()
    Dim numChecked As Integer
    Let numChecked = 0
    If Check1.Value = 1 Then
        Let numChecked = numChecked + 1
    End If
    If Check2.Value = 1 Then
        Let numChecked = numChecked + 1
    End If
    If Check3.Value = 1 Then
        Let numChecked = numChecked + 1
    End If
    Picture1.Cls
    Picture1.Print "You have checked"; numChecked; "check box";
    If numChecked <> 1 Then
        Picture1.Print "es"
    End If
End Sub
```

39.

Object	Property	Setting
frmStyle	Caption	FontStyle
fraSize	Caption	Size
fraEffect	Caption	Special Effects
opt8pt	Caption	8.25
opt12pt	Caption	12
opt18pt	Caption	18
chkBold	Caption	&Bold
chkItalic	Caption	&Italic
chkUnderline	Caption	&Underline
txtInfo	Text	(blank)

```
Sub Form_Load ()
    Rem Make sure effects reflect initial check box settings
    Let txtInfo.FontBold = False
    Let txtInfo.FontItalic = False
    Let txtInfo.FontUnderline = False
End Sub


Sub chkBold_Click ()
    If chkBold.Value = 1 Then
        Let txtInfo.FontBold = True
    Else
        Let txtInfo.FontBold = False
    End If
End Sub


Sub chkItalic_Click ()
    If chkItalic.Value = 1 Then
        Let txtInfo.FontItalic = True
    Else
        Let txtInfo.FontItalic = False
    End If
End Sub


Sub chkUnderline_Click ()
    If chkUnderline.Value = 1 Then
        Let txtInfo.FontUnderline = True
    Else
        Let txtInfo.FontUnderline = False
    End If
End Sub


Sub opt8pt_Click ()
    Let txtInfo.FontSize = 8.25
End Sub


Sub opt12pt_Click ()
    Let txtInfo.FontSize = 12
End Sub


Sub opt18pt_Click ()
    Let txtInfo.FontSize = 18
End Sub
```

43.

Object	Property	Setting
frmTemp	Caption	Temperatures
vsbFahren	Min	32
	Max	212
	LargeChange	5
vsbCelsius	Min	0
	Max	100
	LargeChange	5
lblFVal	Caption	32
	Alignment	1 – Right Justify
lblFMax	Caption	212
lblFMin	Caption	32
lblFahren	Caption	Fahrenheit
lblCVal	Caption	0
	Alignment	1 – Right Justify
lblCMax	Caption	100
lblCMin	Caption	0
lblCelsius	Caption	Celsius

```
Sub vsbFahren_Change ()
  Dim c As Integer
  Let lblFVal.Caption = Str$(vsbFahren.Value)
  Let c = (5 / 9) * (vsbFahren.Value - 32)
  If vsbCelsius.Value <> c Then
      Let vsbCelsius.Value = c
  End If
  Let lblCVal.Caption = Str$(vsbCelsius.Value)
End Sub

Sub vsbCelsius_Change ()
  Dim f As Integer
  Let lblCVal.Caption = Str$(vsbCelsius.Value)
  Let f = (9 / 5) * vsbCelsius.Value + 32
  If vsbFahren.Value <> f Then
      Let vsbFahren.Value = f
  End If
  Let lblFVal.Caption = Str$(vsbFahren.Value)
End Sub
```

Exercises 11.3

1. The number of columns in Grid1 will change to 5.

3. The height of row number 3 (the 4th row) in Grid1 will become 400 twips.

5. The first column of Grid1 will become fixed (will not scroll) and cannot receive the focus.

7. The active cell becomes a cell in row number 3 (the 4th row) of Grid1.

9. The string "Income" will be displayed in the active cell of Grid1.

11. Information in each cell in column number 3 (the 4th column) of Grid 1 will be centered.

13. The grid lines will disappear from Grid1.

15. Any scroll bars displayed on Grid1 will disappear.

17. The menu item menuCut is ungrayed and, if selected, will generate a click event.

19. The menu item menuSave appears without a check mark to its left.

21. The contents of the Clipboard are deleted.

23. The text currently selected in Text1, if any, is copied into the Clipboard.

25. Form2 is made visible (but not modal).

27. Form1 becomes hidden.

29. A color dialog box is opened.

31. The common dialog's type list box will give the user a choice of displaying all files or just files with the extension .TXT.

33. `Let Grid1.Rows = 7`

35. `Let Grid1.ColWidth(0) = 3000`

37. `Let Grid1.FixedRows = 2`

39. `Let Grid1.Col = 2`

41. `Picture1.Print Grid1.Text`

43. `Let Grid1.ColAlignment(1) = 1`

45. `Let Grid1.GridLines = True`

47. `Let mnuExit.Enabled = 0`

49. `Let mnuNormal.Checked = True`

51. `Let street = Clipboard.GetText()`

53. `Clipboard.SetText "Happy"`

55. `Let Text2.SelText = Clipboard.GetText()`

57. `Let Text1.SelText = ""`

59. `Form2.Show 1`

61. `Form2.Hide`

63. `Let CMDialog1.Action = 1`

65. The string " 32" is displayed in the cell in 5th row and 6th column of Grid1.

69.

Object	Property	Setting
frmOrder	Caption	Order Form
grdOrder	Cols	3
	Rows	4
	FixedCols	0
cmdTotal	Caption	Compute Total
picTotal		

```
Sub Form_Load ()
  Rem Set column widths and overall grid size
  Let grdOrder.ColWidth(0) = 2000
  Let grdOrder.ColWidth(2) = 1000
  Let grdOrder.Width = 3000 + grdOrder.ColWidth(1) + 75
  Let grdOrder.Height = 4 * grdOrder.RowHeight(0) + 100
  Rem Assign column headings
  Let grdOrder.Col = 0
  Let grdOrder.Row = 0
  Let grdOrder.Text = "Description"
  Let grdOrder.Col = 1
  Let grdOrder.Text = "Qty."
  Let grdOrder.Col = 2
  Let grdOrder.Text = "Price Each"
  Rem Make first description field the active cell
  Let grdOrder.Row = 1
  Let grdOrder.Col = 0
End Sub

Sub cmdTotal_Click ()
  Dim total As Single, i As Integer
  Dim qty As Integer, price As Single
  Let total = 0
  For i = 1 To 3
    Let grdOrder.Row = i
    Let grdOrder.Col = 1
    Let qty = Val(grdOrder.Text)
    Let grdOrder.Col = 2
    Let price = Val(grdOrder.Text)
    Let total = total + qty * price
  Next i
  picTotal.Cls
  picTotal.Print Format$(total, "0.00")
End Sub

Sub grdOrder_Click ()
  Dim info As String
  If grdOrder.Row > 0 Then
      If grdOrder.Col = 0 Then
          Let grdOrder.Text = InputBox$("Enter description:")
        ElseIf grdOrder.Col = 1 Then
          Let grdOrder.Text = InputBox$("Enter quantity:")
        ElseIf grdOrder.Col = 2 Then
          Let info = InputBox$("Enter price each:")
          Let grdOrder.Text = Format$(Val(info), "0.00")
      End If
  End If
End Sub
```

73. The following changes are required to the solution given in Example2:

Revise the procedure ShowTotals as shown below.
Add the procedure TotalCol as shown below.
In the procedure grdSprdSht_Click, change the Dim statement to

```
Dim temp As String, msg As String, adjCol As Integer
```

and replace the statement

```
Call Show Totals
```

with the statements

```
Let adjCol = grdSprdSht.Col
Call TotalCol(grdSprdSht.Col)
```

```
b ShowTotals ()
  Dim colNum As Integer
  Rem Compute and display total of each numeric column
  Let grdSprdSht.Row = numRows - 1
  Let grdSprdSht.Col = 0
  Let grdSprdSht.Text = "Total"
  For colNum = 1 To numCols - 1
    Call TotalCol(colNum)
  Next colNum
End Sub


Sub TotalCol (colNum As Integer)
  Dim total As Single, rowNum As Integer
  Let total = 0
  For rowNum = 1 To numRows - 3
    Let grdSprdSht.Row = rowNum
    Let grdSprdSht.Col = colNum
    Let total = total + Val(grdSprdSht.Text)
  Next rowNum
  Let grdSprdSht.Row = numRows - 2
  Let grdSprdSht.Text = "----------------"
  Let grdSprdSht.Row = numRows - 1
  Let grdSprdSht.Text = Format$(total, "Currency")
End Sub
```

75.

Object	Property	Setting
frmMain	Caption	Number to Dial
cmdShow	Caption	Show Push Buttons
lblNumber	Caption	(blank)

```
Sub cmdShow_Click ()
  frmDialPad.Show 1
End Sub
```

Object	Property	Setting
frmDialPad	Caption	Push Buttons
grdDialPad	Rows	4
	Cols	3
	FixedRows	0
	FixedCols	0
	ScrollBars	0 – none
lblPhone	Caption	(blank)
cmdClear	Caption	Clear
cmdEnter	Caption	Enter

```
Dim charList As String   'In (declarations) section of (general) in frmDialPad


Sub cmdClear_Click ()
  Let lblPhone.Caption = ""
End Sub


Sub cmdEnter_Click ()
  Let frmMain.lblNumber.Caption = lblPhone.Caption
  frmDialPad.Hide
End Sub


Sub Form_Load ()
  Dim i As Integer, j As Integer, place As Integer
  Let grdDialPad.FontName = "Terminal"
  Let grdDialPad.FontSize = 18
  Let charList = "123456789*0#"
  For i = 0 To 3
    Let grdDialPad.RowHeight(i) = 400
  Next i
  For j = 0 To 2
    Let grdDialPad.ColWidth(j) = 400
  Next j
```

```
  For i = 0 To 3
    For j = 0 To 2
      Let grdDialPad.Row = i
      Let grdDialPad.Col = j
      Let place = 3 * i + j + 1
      Let grdDialPad.Text = Mid$(charList, place, 1)
    Next j
  Next i
  Let grdDialPad.Width = 3 * grdDialPad.ColWidth(0) + 88
  Let grdDialPad.Height = 4 * grdDialPad.RowHeight(0) + 108
End Sub


Sub grdDialPad_Click ()
  Dim place As Integer
  If Len(lblPhone.Caption) = 3 Then
      Let lblPhone.Caption = lblPhone.Caption + "-"
  End If
  Let place = 3 * grdDialPad.Row + grdDialPad.Col + 1
  Let lblPhone.Caption = lblPhone.Caption + Mid$(charList, place, 1)
End Sub
```

Exercises 11.4

1.
```
Rem Set the Sorted property of List1 to True at design-time
Sub FillList ()
   List1.Clear
   Data1.RecordSet.MoveFirst
   Do While Not Data1.RecordSet.EOF
     List1.AddItem Data1.RecordSet.Fields("city").Value
     Data1.RecordSet.MoveNext
   Loop
End Sub
```

3.
```
Sub FillList ()
   List1.Clear
   Data1.RecordSet.MoveFirst
   Do While Not Data1.RecordSet.EOF
     If Val(Data1.RecordSet.Fields("density").Value) > 50000 Then
         List1.AddItem Data1.RecordSet.Fields("city").Value
     End If
     Data1.RecordSet.MoveNext
   Loop
End Sub
```

Index

The diskette in this book has two subdirectories—EXAMPLES and VBPRIMER.

EXAMPLES

The subdirectory EXAMPLES contains programs from the examples and case studies of this textbook. Each program has a name of the form *chapter-section-number*.MAK. For instance, the program in Chapter 3, Section 2, Example 4 has the name 3-2-4.MAK. The following steps, open these programs. (Assume that the diskette is in the A drive.)

1. Press Alt/F/O
2. Enter A:\EXAMPLES
3. Press Tab
4. Cursor to the desired program (**Note:** To move quickly to the beginning of the programs from Chapter 3, press 3.)
5. Press the Enter key

VBPRIMER

The files in the VBPRIMER subdirectory are used to install the Primer Edition of Visual Basic 2.0 on the hard drive of a computer on which Windows has been installed. To install Visual Basic, follow the steps in part A on page 549. **Note:** If your computer does not have a standard configuration, you might be asked one or two additional questions during the installation process.